Kingfisher
Children's
Encyclopedia

Kingfisher
Children's Encyclopedia

General Editor: John Paton

KING*f*ISHER

KINGFISHER
Kingfisher Publications Plc
New Penderel House
283–288 High Holborn
London WC1V 7HZ

First published in 10 volumes by Kingfisher Publications Plc 1989
This revised one-volume edition published by Kingfisher Publications Plc 1991
Reprinted 1991, 1992, 1993 (twice), 1995 (with revisions), 1999

TR / 0599 / TIM / NEW(NEW) / 100GP

A CIP catalogue record for this book is available from the British Library.

ISBN 0 86272 696 4

Printed in China

GENERAL EDITOR
John Paton

EDITORIAL DIRECTOR
Jim Miles

EDITOR
Jennifer Justice

EDITORIAL CONSULTANT
Brian Williams

**EDUCATIONAL
CONSULTANTS**
J.M.B. Tritton, Head
Teacher, Star Primary
School, Newham
Nigel Cox, Framlingham
College Junior School,
Woodbridge

CONTRIBUTORS
Jacqui Bailey
Marie Greenwood
Ann Kay
David Lambert
Keith Lye
Christopher Maynard
Isabelle Paton
Jill Thomas

DESIGN
Terry Woodley
Michele Arron

PICTURE RESEARCH
Elaine Willis

PRODUCTION
Lucy Cooper
Sue Latham

FOREWORD

An encyclopedia must be up-to-date if it is to serve the best interests of its readers. This new edition of The Kingfisher Children's Encyclopedia is the result of a process of continuous growth and revision, based on the world-wide success of the first editions of the work. Many people other than those listed on the previous page have helped and continue to help with the edition and production – consultants, reviewers and authenticators. To all of them is due much of the credit for any success that this encyclopedia brings. My special thanks must go to Jennifer Justice for overseeing the updating of this edition.

John Paton
General Editor

THE SUBJECT SYMBOLS

Each entry in this encyclopedia has its own easily-recognized symbol opposite the heading. This symbol tells you at a glance which area of interest the entry falls into – is it animals, history or science? Below are the 16 subject areas we have used. At the back of the work there is a list of all the articles divided into subject areas.

PLANTS AND FOOD From microscopic plants to gigantic trees – what they are, how they grow, the food they provide.

THE ARTS Drawing, painting, sculpture, crafts, ballet, modern dance, drama, theatre, TV, cinema etc., plus the great artists.

PEOPLES AND GOVERNMENT Descriptions of peoples of the world, the things they do and the way they govern their countries.

LANGUAGE AND LITERATURE How language is constructed plus descriptions of great playwrights, novelists, poets etc.

SPORTS AND PASTIMES Competitive sports, great athletes and sporting stars plus descriptions of many hobbies.

ASTRONOMY AND SPACE Birth of the Universe, the solar system, galaxies, space exploration etc.

SCIENCE How science is applied in everyday life, the elements, sources of energy, important scientists etc.

ANIMALS Descriptions of behaviour, homes and individual species: mammals, birds, reptiles, fishes, insects etc.

MACHINES AND MECHANISMS Explanations of everything from simple machines to jet engines plus descriptions of their inventors.

TRAVEL AND TRANSPORT The history and development of aircraft, ships, railways, cars, motorcycles etc.

HUMAN BODY How the body works, the process of birth, ageing, diseases, immunity, genetics etc.

BUILDINGS The history and development of architecture, modern construction and design, famous buildings and architects etc.

OUR EARTH How the Earth was formed, and how it is still changing, its deserts, mountains, oceans, rivers etc.

HISTORY Great events and great figures from ancient civilizations up to the present day.

COUNTRIES AND PLACES Descriptions, flags, maps, essential statistics etc. for all countries plus places of interest.

RELIGION, PHILOSOPHY AND MYTH How these have changed through history and the ones that have survived.

ABOUT *your* ENCYCLOPEDIA

This encyclopedia is very easy to use. All the entries are arranged in alphabetical order. You should find most of the information you want by first looking up the main entry word. If the subject you are looking for does not have its own entry, look in the Index at the back. Usually you will find some information about your subject in another article.

●

Throughout the encyclopedia you will find words printed in small capitals, like this: HEALTH. These words are cross-references. When you see one, you will know that there is a separate entry on the subject in your encyclopedia. That entry may have more information about the subject you are looking up.

●

Subject symbols appear next to each heading. These are helpful when you are browsing through the encyclopedia and want to find entries on Transport ▰, for instance, or History ▰ or Countries and places ▰ – there are 16 symbols in all.

●

Throughout the encyclopedia you will come across 'special feature' entries. These can be used to help you with your school projects, or you can look them up in just the same way as the other entries. You will find them listed at the back of the work.

●

In addition to the main text there are occasional See-it-Yourself panels which show in a practical way how you can find out more about the subject.

●

There are Fact Panels containing at-a-glance information on the biggest, highest, longest etc. And the outside column has a host of fascinating snippets of additional and often surprising information.

●

By using your encyclopedia you will discover a wealth of information about people, ideas, events, and the world around you.

HOW TO GET THE MOST *from your* ENCYCLOPEDIA

The Kingfisher Children's Encyclopedia **contains many features to help you look up things easily or simply to have fun just browsing through. Almost every page has several illustrations and there are fact boxes, See-it-Yourself panels, special feature entries and literally hundreds of cross references to help you find your way around. Some of those features are shown here. We hope you will enjoy exploring the following pages of your encyclopedia.**

- ■ **Subject symbols**
- ■ **See-it-Yourself panels**
- ■ **Fact boxes**
- ■ **Country boxes**
- ■ **'Nuggets'**
- ■ **Special feature entries**
- ■ **Cross references**

SPECIAL FEATURE entries are longer and more detailed than most entries. They will help you with school projects. You will find a list of these special feature entries at the back of the encyclopedia.

THE TEXT is full of information and yet easy to read. Cross-references appear as SMALL CAPITALS. Turn to these entries for more information on the subject you are looking up.

SUBJECT SYMBOLS allow you to find quickly those entries on a similar theme. They will make browsing more interesting.

OVER 2000 ILLUSTRATIONS and photographs have been used, including hundreds of maps and many cutaway diagrams.

SEE-IT-YOURSELF panels show you how to do simple experiments and make things. They will help you understand the subject you are looking up.

AUSTRALIA

Australia is the world's smallest continent. Even so, it is more than 30 times as big as the United Kingdom. The last continent to be discovered and settled by Europeans, its first inhabitants were the Aborigines, who wandered its wilderness, hunting and gathering food.

Much of Australia is dry, flat desert. Most of its people — more than half of all Australians live in cities (Sydney, Melbourne, Brisbane and Adelaide). Farming is an important activity. Cattle are raised on the inland pastures, while the south-east green grassy highlands provide pasture for millions of sheep. Mining and manufacturing are also important.

One of the most spectacular natural wonders is the Great Barrier Reef, the largest coral reef in the world.

Australia's first European settlers came from Britain. Today its population includes people whose families came from many parts of Europe and South-East Asia. The country is in the Commonwealth of Nations and its head of state is the Queen. Each state has its own government, but national affairs are run by the Federal government headed by the prime minister.

BATTERY

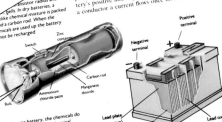

The vampire bat of South America has a very unusual way of feeding. It bites animals with its teeth and drinks their blood. However, vampires do not suck blood, they merely lap it up as it flows.

Most bats are nocturnal—they sleep in the day and fly at night. Scientists have shown in experiments that bats do not need good eyesight for flying. They find their way in the dark by using a 'sonar' system. They make high-pitched shrieks that no human ear can hear, and use the echoes bouncing off objects to tell where they are.

▲ As a bat flies, it utters a series of squeaks that are so high-pitched that a person cannot hear them. The sound waves from these cries bounce off objects and echo back to the bat's ears. From these echoes, the bat can tell where the objects are.

Battery

Batteries make electricity from chemicals stored inside them. Dry batteries like those used in some transistor radios and calculators make electricity for a limited time. Car batteries can be recharged with electricity and used again and again. They contain pairs of lead and lead oxide plates bathed in dilute sulphuric acid. As the battery is used, the chemicals in the plates change until no more electricity is produced. But feeding an electric current into the battery changes the chemicals in the plates back to their original state. When the battery's positive and negative terminals are joined by a conductor a current flows once more.

... properties of electricity ... transistor radios and ... bells. In dry batteries, a pastelike chemical mixture is packed round a carbon rod. When the chemicals are used up the battery cannot be recharged.

Switch
Zinc container
Negative terminal
Positive terminal
Carbon rod
Ammonium chloride paste
Manganese dioxide
Bulb
Lead plate (negative)
Dilute Sulphuric acid
Lead oxide plate (positive)

▶ In a car battery, the chemicals do not get used up as the chemical reaction can be reversed. When the battery has run down it can be recharged by connecting it to an outside electric current.

70

Battles

Some battles have played an important part in the history of the world. Others are only important to the history of the countries that fought them. Some of the important battles that affected many countries are shown on pages 72 and 73.

Bayeux Tapestry

After WILLIAM THE CONQUEROR invaded England in 1066, one of his relations had a tapestry embroidered to record the conquest. This is known as the Bayeux Tapestry. It is a piece of LINEN, 70 metres long. There are 72 colourful scenes on it telling the story of William's victory. Latin words explain what is happening in the pictures.

▼ The picture shows part of the Bayeux Tapestry which is embroidered in different coloured wools on long strips of canvas, joined together. The whole tapestry is kept in a museum at Bayeux in France.

Bean

Beans belong to a family of plants called pulses. They are grown all over the world and have been eaten for thousands of years. There is evidence that beans were being eaten over 10,000 years ago by prehistoric people in Switzerland.

Beans are one of the cheapest and most widely eaten foods of all. They are rich in PROTEINS. Some kinds are used for animal fodder.

There are hundreds of different kinds of beans. A few of the best known varieties are the kidney, French, broad and soybeans. Some, such as SOYBEANS, are used to make vegetable oil. They are also used in making soaps and varnishes.

Government: Democratic, federal
state system
Capital: Canberra
Area: 7,686,849 sq km
Population: 15,400,000
Language: English
Currency: Australian dollar

STATE	CAPITAL
New South Wales	Sydney
Victoria	Melbourne
Queensland	Brisbane
South Aust.	Adelaide
Western Aust.	Perth
Tasmania	Hobart
Aust. Capital Territory	Canberra
Northern Territory	Darwin

Kookaburra

Koala in eucalyptus tree

Wattle—national flower of Australia

▲ One-third of all the wool used in the world comes from Australia. Sheep stations cover thousands and thousands of square kilometres.

◀ Some of the typical emblems of Australia—the koala, the [...] and the wattle [...]

HISTORY OF AUSTRALIA
Prehistoric times Aborigines reach Australia, probably from Pacific islands
1432 Chinese may have landed near Darwin
1600s Dutch are first Europeans to explore Australia's coastline. They name the land New Holland
1642 Abel Tasman (Holland) discovers Tasmania
1688 William Dampier of Britain sails along coast
1770 James Cook sights Australia
1778 First settlers (730 convicts) begin colony at Port Jackson
1790s Bass and Flinders continue British naval exploration of Australia
1817 New Holland becomes Australia
1851 Gold rush in Victoria
1854 First railway in Australia. Eureka Stockade (fighting between gold miners and troops)
1860–61 Burke and Wills cross Australia from south to north but die on the return journey
1880 Capture of notorious outlaw Ned Kelly
1901 Commonwealth of Australia comes into being, uniting the various states
1927 Canberra becomes national capital
1956 Australia hosts Olympic Games
1972 Australian troops leave Vietnam after fighting alongside US soldiers and South Vietnamese in the Vietnam War

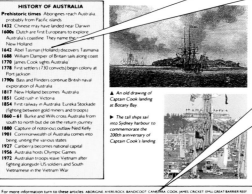

▲ An old drawing of Captain Cook landing at Botany Bay

► The tall ships sail into Sydney harbour to commemorate the 200th anniversary of Captain Cook's landing

For more information turn to these articles: ABORIGINE, AYERS ROCK, BANDICOOT, CANBERRA, COOK, JAMES, CRICKET, EMU, GREAT BARRIER REEF, KANGAROO, KOALA, MARSUPIALS, MELBOURNE, SYDNEY

57

FACT PANELS appear throughout the encyclopedia giving you details on historical dates, facts and figures, highest, longest, biggest etc.

ALL SPECIAL FEATURE entries have a list of other entries you should read for further information.

STRANGE-BUT-TRUE facts and figures appear throughout in 'nuggets'. Many are amusing – all are fascinating.

Alps

The Alps are the greatest mountain range in EUROPE. They are centred in SWITZERLAND, but they stretch from France all the way to Yugoslavia. Mont Blanc, 4807 metres high, is the highest peak in the Alps. There are many lakes in the valleys; the largest is Lake Geneva.

The Alps attract many tourists. They go to ski and climb, and to admire the magnificent scenery.

The Alpine region is known for its life—rare flowers like the white weiss, shown here, and birds such [as the] golden eagle.

Androsace   Edelweiss   Mouflon (wild sheep)   Ring ousel   Golden eagle

Aluminium

There is more aluminium in the Earth's crust than any other metal. But until less than 200 years ago no one had ever seen this silvery metal. When aluminium was first used it was much dearer than gold because it was very difficult to separate the metal from the materials it was mixed up with in the earth.

Most aluminium is now produced from an ore called bauxite. The bauxite is treated with chemicals and placed in a big electric furnace. An electric current is passed through and aluminium falls to the bottom of the furnace.

Aluminium is light—it weighs only a third as much as steel. It and its ALLOYS are especially useful where lightness and strength are important. It is also a good conductor of heat and electricity.

Power cables

Aircraft   Aluminium ('tin') foil

Amazon, River

The Amazon is the mightiest river in South America, and, at a length of 6437 km, is the second longest in the world, after the Nile. It flows from Peru

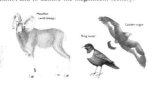

YOURSELF
[...]n or runner bean
[...]ed with blotting
[...]per moist. Soon a
[...]rst from the seed
[...]oot will appear and
[...]furling the first
[...] These start to make
[...]hey reach the light.
[...] seedlings in the
[...]u have watched the
[...]growth.
[...]nis racket

71

26

---

through Brazil to the Atlantic Ocean. Almost the whole of the Amazon basin is dense tropical forest. In the 1540s a Spanish explorer saw female Indian warriors on the Amazon's banks, so the river was named after the Amazons (female warriors) of Greek legends.

America

The word 'America' is often used to mean the United States, but it originally described a much larger area that today is more properly called the Americas. The Americas include North America, Central America and South America, and the islands of the Caribbean.

American Indians

American Indians are the native peoples of the Americas—that is, the first people to live there. They are known as Indians because when Christopher Columbus reached America in 1492 he thought he had arrived in India.

The Indians of the Americas are thought to have crossed to the North American continent from Asia about 20,000 years ago. Very gradually, over the centuries, they spread through North America and down into what is now Central and South America. They developed different ways of life according to where they lived.

The Amazon pours out so much fresh water into the Atlantic that more than 160 km out at sea from the river's mouth the ocean's water is still fresh.

NORTH AMERICA   ATLANTIC OCEAN
PACIFIC OCEAN   SOUTH AMERICA

▼ An early American Indian village. The tepees are made of bison skins. Note the squaw carrying her baby (her papoose) on her back in a sling made of cloth.

A Nigerian man wearing colourful traditional costume (see AFRICA)

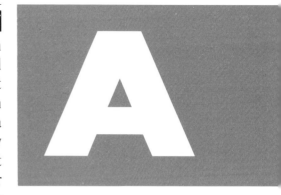

Aardvark

The aardvark is an animal that eats TERMITES. When it has broken open a termites' nest with its powerful claws, it pokes in its long, sticky tongue and pulls it out covered with the insects. The aardvark lives in central and southern Africa. It has large ears like a donkey and is an expert burrower. If caught away from its home it can dig a hole for itself at astonishing speed. The word 'aardvark' is Dutch for 'earth pig'. These shy animals can be 2 metres long and nearly a metre high.

◀ Aardvarks are shy animals that come out mostly during the night.

▼ The abacus here shows what each bead counts when it is pushed toward the centre bar. The top abacus reads 7—two 1 beads pushed to the bar and one 5 bead. If we want to add 171 to the 7, we push one more 1 bead to the bar, add a 50 and two 10s for the 70, and one 100 bead—178.

Abacus

The abacus is a simple counting machine first used by the ancient Greeks and Romans. It consists of rows of beads strung on wires; those on the first wire count as ones, those on the second wire count as tens, on the third wire they count as hundreds, and so on. The abacus is still used in some Eastern countries. The Romans sometimes used small stones as counters. They called these counters *calculi* and it is from this that we get our word 'calculate'.

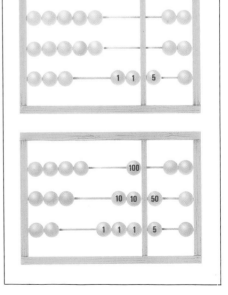

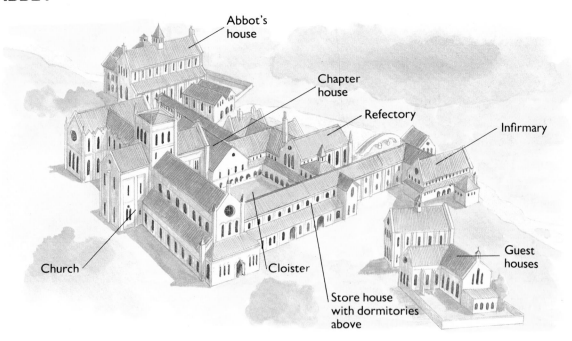

Abbot's house

Chapter house

Refectory

Infirmary

Church

Cloister

Guest houses

Store house with dormitories above

▲ An abbey was a little world on its own. The church was the most important building. The monks made their way from the dormitories to the church long before dawn each morning. While the monks ate their meals in silence in the refectory, a monk would read to them from a special pulpit. In the chapter house, the monks gathered to discuss the business of the abbey. In the cloisters they walked and studied. The abbot had his own house. There were also guest houses and an infirmary.

Abbeys were cold, draughty places. It must have been very hard for the monks to keep warm in winter. Fires were not allowed, except in the infirmary, where the monks went when they were ill, in the kitchen, and in the calefactory or warming room. The monks were allowed to stay in the warming room for only a few minutes at a time.

Abbey

An abbey is a MONASTERY or convent, the home of monks or nuns, headed by an abbot or abbess. During the MIDDLE AGES many abbeys were built all over Europe. Some of them had beautiful churches attached to them. Westminster Abbey in London, for example, is part of an abbey begun by EDWARD the Confessor, though most of the other abbey buildings have been destroyed.

The abbey often included an open space, or great court; cloisters where the monks walked, studied and thought; and a dormitory where they slept. There were also kitchens, stables, storehouses, a guest-house and vegetable gardens within the abbey walls. The monks ate their meals in a refectory, or dining hall.

They did all the work in the abbey, including cleaning, cooking, carpentry, farming and beekeeping. Some abbeys became famous for making wine and spirits. Others were well known for their honey, their medicines and their cheeses. Monks were one of the few groups of educated people then, and their beautiful handwritten and illustrated books were very valuable.

Between 1524 and 1540 all the abbeys in England were closed down by HENRY VIII and their lands and possessions taken away.

Abbreviation

An abbreviation is a shortened form of a word or a group of words. Words and phrases are shortened to save space. Sometimes the first and last letters of a word are used, such as *St* for 'Saint' or *Dr* for 'Doctor'. Sometimes only the beginning of the word is used, as in *Sept.* for 'September'. A full stop may be placed after the abbreviation to show that it is a shortened form.

Aborigine

The word 'aborigine' really means the first people who lived in any country. But it is now used when we talk about the natives of AUSTRALIA. These are slim black people with broad noses and black wavy hair. They came to Australia thousands of years ago from south-eastern Asia. In Australia they had no permanent homes but wandered about the desert hunting or gathering their food. Their weapons were the BOOMERANG and the throwing spear.

The Aborigines were very badly treated by the white men who came to Australia. Today Aborigines have rights as Australian citizens.

In the past, when all writing had to be done laboriously by hand, abbreviations saved time and space. In ancient Greek and Roman manuscripts, abbreviations were carried so far that special training is now needed to decipher them. We still use some of these ancient Roman abbreviations.

Many of the words we use daily began as abbreviations. We seldom stop to think that 'bus' is short for 'omnibus', 'flu' for 'influenza', 'zoo' for 'zoological gardens' and 'cello' for 'violoncello'.

▼ Aborigines like to keep many of their old traditions. Here a group performs a spear dance to the booming music of a didgeridoo.

▼ *When a ball is dropped, it accelerates—goes faster and faster. In the first second it travels 4.9 m, in the next second 14.6 m, and so on. A cricket ball and a tennis ball would fall at the same speed.*

Starting point

After 1 second

After 2 seconds

Acceleration

When a car increases speed, it accelerates. If it is travelling at 40 miles an hour and increases speed to 50 miles an hour after 1 minute, it has accelerated at a rate of 10 miles per hour per minute.

If you drop a ball from the top of a tall building it accelerates—goes faster and faster—as it falls. It reaches a velocity of 9.8 m per second after one second. After two seconds it reaches a velocity of 19.6 m per second. Every second that it falls, it increases its speed by 9.8 m per second. The ball accelerates as it falls because it is being pulled down by the force of GRAVITY. The strange thing is that the force of gravity pulls everything down at the same speed. If there was no air and you dropped a feather and a cricket ball from the top of a building at the same time, they would hit the ground together. Of course, air holds up the feather much more than the ball. The feather's shape makes the difference.

Accounting

Keeping accounts, or accounting, is keeping records of the money and goods that come into and go out of a business. The work of keeping such records is called *bookkeeping*. An *accountant* decides how the records should be set up and studies whether a business is doing well or badly. The business must know how much money it is to be paid by people who owe the business money (*debtors*) and how much it owes to other businesses or people for supplies (*creditors*).

Today, most accounting records are kept on computers, but people still have to feed the right information to the machines.

Acid

An acid is a liquid chemical COMPOUND that is often poisonous. Some acids, such as sulphuric acid, nitric acid and hydrochloric acid, are very strong and can *corrode*, or eat away, even the strongest metals. Other acids are harmless. These include the citric acid that gives lemons and oranges their sharp taste, and the acetic acid in vinegar. Lactic acid is produced when milk goes sour. All acids turn a special sort of paper called *litmus* red.

Some substances are the opposite of acids. They are called *alkalis* or *bases* and turn litmus paper blue. Washing soda is an alkali.

Acid Rain

All rain is very slightly ACID. The weak acid in rainwater can eat away the limestone in buildings and statues. Limestone is an alkali.

Rain can also react with the waste gases sent out by power stations, factories and cars. Such gases can be carried great distances by the wind. Then they fall as weak sulphuric acid and nitric acid, so they are called acid rain. After a time, lakes and streams are slowly poisoned by the acid rain, threatening plants and wildlife. People are trying to reduce the waste gases poured out by industrial nations.

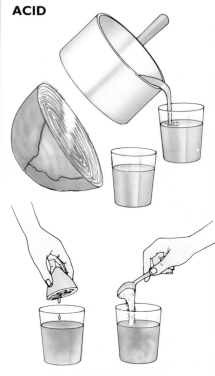

ACID

SEE IT YOURSELF
Cut half a red cabbage into strips. Put the strips into a pan of hot water and let the mixture cool. Strain the liquid and pour into clean glasses. Add a few drops of water. This shows the neutral colour. Now add a few drops of lemon juice to one glass to show its acid colour, and some washing soda to the other glass to show its alkaline colour.

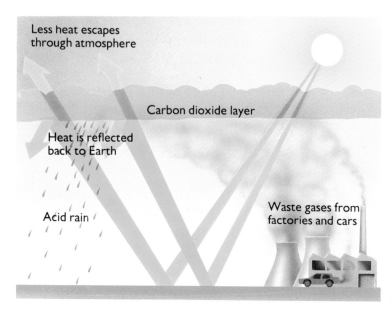

Less heat escapes through atmosphere

Carbon dioxide layer

Heat is reflected back to Earth

Acid rain

Waste gases from factories and cars

▲ *Two of the main threats to our atmosphere are acid rain and the 'greenhouse effect'. They are both caused by gases sent out by power stations, factories and cars. The greenhouse effect is caused by a 'blanket' of carbon dioxide gas in the air which traps the Sun's heat and prevents some of it escaping into space. The Earth can become warmer and warmer over the years.*

▶ *Scientists are not in agreement on how much damage is done by acid rain. The trees in this picture have been damaged severely.*

▲ *A tractor being tested to find out exactly how much sound it gives out. It is in a specially designed room that absorbs all the sound from every part of the vehicle.*

Acoustics

Acoustics is the study of SOUND and how it travels. When an architect designs a concert hall or theatre, he or she must carefully consider the sound quality of the building. Will a full range of sound waves from speech and music reach every seat? Will there be disturbing echoes from the walls and ceiling? Or will the sound from the stage be absorbed too much by soft materials such as curtains, causing sound to be muffled?

Sound waves travel in straight lines, and they can be reflected or absorbed by surfaces that they strike. Various reflectors and baffles can be attached to walls and ceilings to turn the sound waves in the best direction.

Acropolis

'Acropolis' is a Greek word for the high central part of many ancient Greek cities. The most famous acropolis is in ATHENS, the capital of modern Greece. On top of the Acropolis are the ruins of ancient temples built in the 400s BC when Athens

▼ *The Acropolis of Athens as it must have looked about 400 BC. The Propylaea, with its six rows of pillars, was a magnificent entrance gateway. At the highest point stood the Parthenon.*

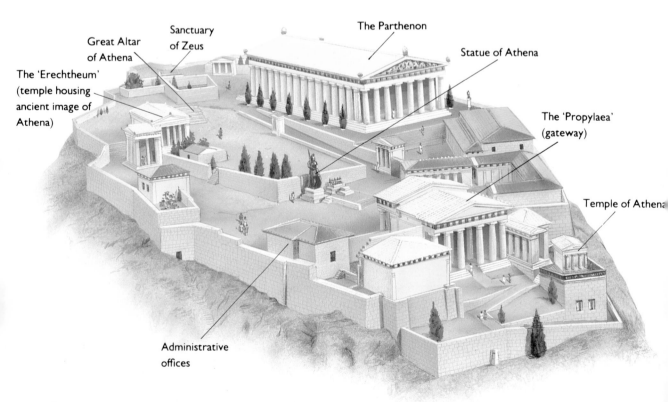

Great Altar of Athena

Sanctuary of Zeus

The Parthenon

Statue of Athena

The 'Erechtheum' (temple housing ancient image of Athena)

The 'Propylaea' (gateway)

Temple of Athena

Administrative offices

was a rich and powerful city. The Parthenon, the largest and most important of these temples, was built to honour Athena, the patron goddess of Athens.

Acting *See* Theatre

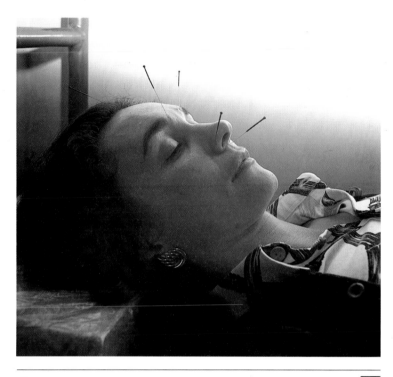

◄ *In acupuncture, the metal needles are usually inserted only a little way into the patient.*

Acupuncture

Acupuncture is an ancient kind of medical treatment in which thin needles are used to puncture various parts of the body. The treatment was developed by the Chinese about 5000 years ago, and it is still used today. Chinese doctors have performed surgery with acupuncture as the only anaesthetic. In recent years, acupuncture has begun to be accepted in the West as a branch of alternative medicine. It is often used in the treatment of such complaints as headache, asthma and arthritis.

Addition

When we collect things together to find out how many there are, we are using addition. It does not matter in which order we add things together. In other words, 4 + 3 is the same as 3 + 4.

The ancient Greeks were very interested in numbers. Over 2000 years ago they discovered some strange numbers that they called 'perfect'. The first perfect number is 6. The numbers 1, 2 and 3 are the only numbers that divide exactly into 6. If you add 1, 2 and 3, what do you get? The next perfect number is 28. Only the numbers 1, 2, 4, 7 and 14 divide exactly into 28. Added together they make 28. The next perfect number is 496. Computers can now find perfect numbers that would fill this page!

For any adhesive to work well, the surfaces to be stuck together must be very clean. Grease, dirt and water prevent the adhesive touching the surfaces as closely as it should. Even the grease of a fingerprint or the moisture of your breath can stop proper adhesion.

Adhesive

Adhesives are substances that are used to stick things together. There are many different kinds of adhesive. For centuries, people have used adhesives made from boiling up animal bones, hide and horn to produce glue. Plants such as corn and potatoes can be made into a starch paste that is good for sticking paper. Natural liquid rubber sticks fast to almost anything.

Modern man-made adhesives are better than natural ones because they are much stronger. Epoxy resins, for example, are very strong.

Adjective

An adjective is any word that describes or modifies a NOUN. 'A grey horse' is more exact than just 'a horse'. We can make it more exact still by writing 'a big, friendly grey horse'. The words *big*, *friendly* and *grey* are adjectives describing the noun *horse*.

Adjectives usually come before the noun, but they can also come after it: 'The pie is *delicious*'. The word *delicious* describes the pie. It is an adjective.

Adolescence

Adolescence is the time when a child is growing up to become an adult. The changes of adolescence usually begin to take place in girls of 10 to 13 and in boys of 11 to 14. The changes go on for several years, and the adolescent's body changes in many ways. A girl's hips become wider and her breasts start to develop. She has her first menstrual period. This is a sign that she can one day have babies. A boy's voice becomes deeper and his beard starts to grow. Both boys and girls develop hair in their pubic areas and under their arms.

During adolescence, young people often feel awkward and have emotional upsets, but these things pass. Soon boys and girls become young men and women and learn to do more and more for themselves, so that they do not depend so much on their parents.

▼ *A Jewish boy prepares for the bar mitzvah ceremony. This ceremony, which takes place on the Sabbath nearest to his thirteenth birthday, marks his passing from adolescence to adulthood.*

Advertising

Advertising is usually a means of telling people about things they can buy and persuading people to buy them. The most popular *media* (means of advertising) are television, radio, newspapers, magazines and posters. Governments use advertisements too. They tell us things like 'Smoking is bad for your health'.

Today, advertising is a huge industry that employs millions of people, including writers, artists, photographers, actors and salesmen. Many of the people who work in advertising are employed by advertising agencies—firms that produce advertisements for clients who have goods or services to sell. Each company uses its own special name for a product. That special name is called the company's *brand name*. No other company can use that name. Advertisers try to make the products they are selling appear as desirable and as good value as possible. Many countries have laws that stop advertisers making false claims about their products.

▼ City centres are favourite places for advertisements because many people see them. Neon signs flash their messages, billboards are all around. Advertising is a multimillion pound industry.

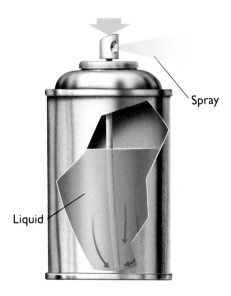

▲ *When you press down the button on an aerosol can, a gas under pressure forces the liquid up a tube to the top and out as a fine spray.*

Aerosol

When scientists talk about an aerosol they mean a cloud of very fine particles floating in air or some other gas. The particles can be liquid, as in a mist, or solid, as in smoke.

When most people speak of an aerosol they mean something that sprays paint, cosmetics or insecticides. It consists of a can containing a liquefied gas under high pressure. The can also contains the paint or other substance to be sprayed. When a button on the cap is pressed, a fine nozzle opens and the gas forces out the paint in the form of a fine spray.

Most scientists are trying to ban the use of harmful chemicals in aerosols. They say that the chemicals in aerosols (chlorofluorocarbons or CFCs) are drifting up in the air and are slowly destroying the OZONE LAYER. The ozone layer is a layer of gas about 20 km above the Earth. It absorbs most of the Sun's dangerous ULTRAVIOLET rays.

Aesop

Aesop (about 620–560 BC) was an ancient Greek storyteller. His stories are today known as *Aesop's Fables*. The characters in his stories are usually animals, but they behave like humans, with virtues and weaknesses. One famous story tells of a race between a tortoise and a hare. The hare is so sure of an easy win that he takes a rest during the race. This allows the slow, plodding tortoise to win.

Some historians believe that Aesop was a slave who was freed because he told his stories so well.

Afghanistan

Afghanistan is a country in ASIA. It is a mountainous land lying between the Soviet Union, Pakistan and Iran. The capital and largest city is Kabul. Nearly all the people are Muslims. In 1978 the government was overthrown by rebels friendly to the USSR, but Muslim bands continued to fight against the new government. In 1979 Russian troops took over the country. This caused world-wide opposition and the Russians had to withdraw their troops in 1988.

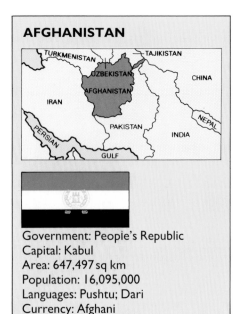

AFGHANISTAN

Government: People's Republic
Capital: Kabul
Area: 647,497 sq km
Population: 16,095,000
Languages: Pushtu; Dari
Currency: Afghani

Africa

Africa is the world's second largest continent. It covers an area of 30,313,000 square km, one-fifth of the world's land. Africa stretches from the Mediterranean Sea in the north to the Cape of Good Hope at its tip in the south. Large parts of Africa are empty wasteland. The scorching SAHARA Desert spreads over much of the northern part of the continent. Near the EQUATOR, which runs through the centre of Africa, are thick rain forests. There the trees grow so close together that their leaves blot out the sunlight.

More than a third of Africa is a high, flat plain, or plateau. Grassland called *savanna* covers much of the plateau region. Great herds of grazing animals roam the savanna. They include zebras, giraffes, wildebeest and impala. Other animals, such as lions, cheetahs and hyenas, prey upon the grazing animals. In the past, many animals were killed by hunters, but today special reserves have been set up to protect them.

Mt Kilimanjaro, the highest mountain in Africa, rises 5895 metres in Tanzania. Africa's largest lake, Lake Victoria, lies between Kenya and Tanzania. The continent's great rivers are the NILE, Zaire (formerly called Congo), Niger and Zambezi.

▲ Africa is a huge continent. It is more than 120 times as big as the British Isles. The great Sahara Desert covers most of northern Africa. It separates the Arab countries along the Mediterranean from the Negro countries of central Africa. Most of the rest of Africa is grassland, or savanna.

▼ Waterholes are very important to the animals of central Africa. Gathered around to drink are zebras, impalas, elands and guinea fowl. An ostrich and a giraffe wait their turn.

Giraffe

Ostrich

Zebra

land

Impala

Guinea fowl

Female impala (hornless)

▲ *This beautifully carved ivory mask was worn as an ornament by the king of the West African kingdom of Benin. Great empires grew up in Africa before the white people came.*

▼ *Africa has many tribal religions. But more and more people are becoming Muslims. Today there are more than 100 million Muslims in Africa. Most of them are in the north of the continent. Here Muslims gather at a mosque in Nairobi, Kenya.*

Many different types of people live in Africa. In North Africa are ARABS and Berbers, who mostly follow the Muslim religion. So-called 'black Africa' lies south of the Sahara Desert. The Negroid peoples who live there make up three-quarters of Africa's population. People with European and Asian ancestors make up the rest of the population.

Most Africans are farmers, growing crops such as cocoa, coffee, cotton, sisal and tea. Africa produces nearly three-quarters of the world's palm oil and palm kernels, which are used to make items like soap and margarine. The continent has valuable mineral resources, too, including gold and diamonds, copper and tin.

The Unexplored Continent

For centuries Africa was called the 'Dark Continent' because Europeans knew little about it or its people. The Phoenicians and Romans had built trading centres along the north coast and they knew of the great early civilization in Egypt. But the lands to the south remained a mystery.

The first Europeans to learn more about this huge unexplored continent were the Portuguese. They were the first to find a sea route to India by sailing around the southern tip of Africa. They hugged the coast, fearing to sail out of sight of land. Soon the African coastline was charted. But it was still a long time before people became interested in exploring inland. From the 1400s, European sailors began to ship slaves from Africa. About 14 million slaves were taken to the Americas between 1500 and the 1800s. Usually these slaves were bought from tribes that lived along the African coast.

By the 1800s the countries of Europe were becoming interested in setting up colonies in Africa. Brave explorers like David LIVINGSTONE, Mungo Park and Henry Stanley travelled into the interior and soon the continent had been carved up between the European powers. The Europeans brought new ways of life to Africa. Missionaries brought the Christian religion and set up schools.

After some years many Africans began to resent being ruled by foreigners. During the 1950s and 1960s most former colonies became independent

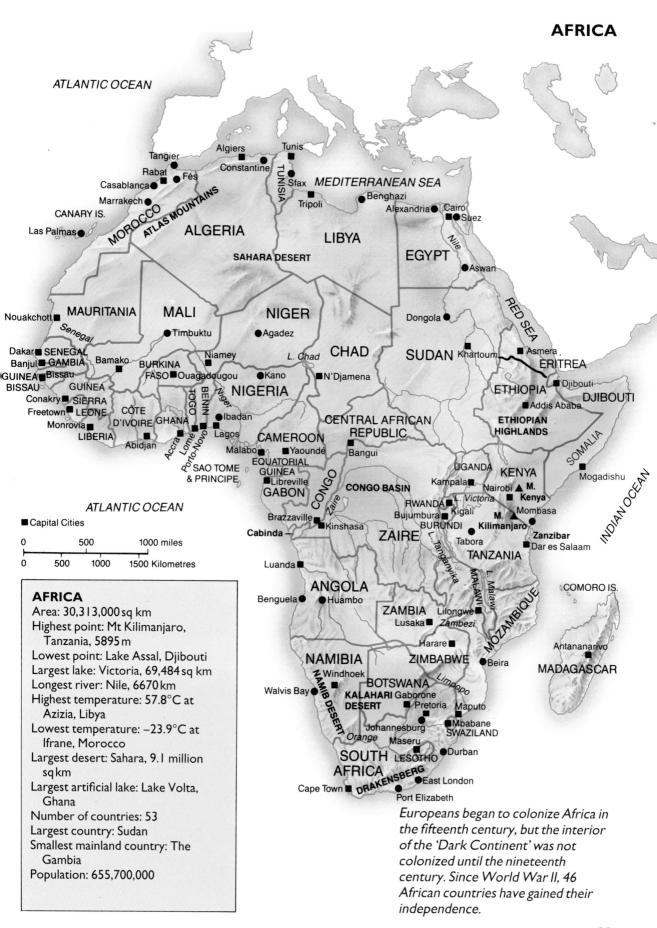

AFRICA

ATLANTIC OCEAN

Tangier
Algiers
Tunis
Constantine
Rabat
Fés
Casablanca
Marrakech
CANARY IS.
Las Palmas

MEDITERRANEAN SEA

TUNISIA
Sfax
Tripoli
Benghazi
Alexandria
Cairo
Suez

MOROCCO
ATLAS MOUNTAINS
ALGERIA
LIBYA
EGYPT
SAHARA DESERT

Nile
Aswan

Nouakchott

MAURITANIA
Senegal
MALI
Timbuktu
NIGER
Agadez
CHAD
L. Chad
SUDAN
Dongola
Khartoum
Asmera
ERITREA

RED SEA

Dakar
SENEGAL
Banjul
GAMBIA
Bamako
Niamey
BURKINA
FASO
Ouagadougou
Kano
N'Djamena
Djibouti
DJIBOUTI
GUINEA
BISSAU
Bissau
GUINEA
NIGERIA
Niger
CENTRAL AFRICAN
REPUBLIC
ETHIOPIA
Addis Ababa
ETHIOPIAN
HIGHLANDS
Conakry
SIERRA
Freetown
LEONE
CÔTE
D'IVOIRE
GHANA
TOGO
BENIN
Ibadan
Lagos
CAMEROON
Bangui
SOMALIA
Monrovia
LIBERIA
Abidjan
Accra
Lomé
Porto-Novo
Malabo
Yaoundé
UGANDA
KENYA
Mogadishu
SAO TOME
& PRINCIPE
EQUATORIAL
GUINEA
Libreville
GABON
CONGO
Zaire
CONGO BASIN
Kampala
L. Victoria
Nairobi
M.
Kenya
RWANDA
Bujumbura
Kigali
M.
Mombasa
Kilimanjaro
Zanzibar
Brazzaville
Kinshasa
BURUNDI
Dar es Salaam
Cabinda
ZAIRE
Tabora
Luanda
L. Tanganyika
TANZANIA
COMORO IS.

ATLANTIC OCEAN

INDIAN OCEAN

■ Capital Cities

0   500   1000 miles

0   500   1000   1500 Kilometres

ANGOLA
Benguela
Huambo
L. Malawi
MALAWI
Lilongwe
MOZAMBIQUE
Antananarivo
ZAMBIA
Lusaka
Zambezi
MADAGASCAR
Harare
NAMIBIA
Windhoek
ZIMBABWE
Beira
Limpopo
Walvis Bay
NAMIB DESERT
BOTSWANA
KALAHARI
DESERT
Gaborone
Maputo
Pretoria
Mbabane
SWAZILAND
Johannesburg
Orange
Maseru
Durban
SOUTH
AFRICA
LESOTHO
DRAKENSBERG
East London
Cape Town
Port Elizabeth

AFRICA

Area: 30,313,000 sq km

Highest point: Mt Kilimanjaro,
Tanzania, 5895 m

Lowest point: Lake Assal, Djibouti

Largest lake: Victoria, 69,484 sq km

Longest river: Nile, 6670 km

Highest temperature: 57.8°C at
Azizia, Libya

Lowest temperature: −23.9°C at
Ifrane, Morocco

Largest desert: Sahara, 9.1 million
sq km

Largest artificial lake: Lake Volta,
Ghana

Number of countries: 53

Largest country: Sudan

Smallest mainland country: The
Gambia

Population: 655,700,000

Europeans began to colonize Africa in the fifteenth century, but the interior of the 'Dark Continent' was not colonized until the nineteenth century. Since World War II, 46 African countries have gained their independence.

Most of Africa is a great plateau or tableland surrounded by a narrow coastal plain. The average height of the African continent is 750 m above sea level—15 times the height of Nelson's Column in London.

African countries. Many were poor and some have had bloody civil wars as different rulers fought for power. But today the countries are working together to help one another and to develop industry and their natural resources. Many of the richer nations of the world are helping them in this task.

Ageing

How old is 'old'? This is a very difficult question to answer. When a mouse is 4 years old it is as old as a dog of 15 or a person of 80. Humans age more slowly than almost any other animal; only some kinds of land tortoise live longer. But our bodies are continually wearing out. As we grow older our eyesight may weaken, our hearing become less clear; our memory may become poor, our skin wrinkle and our limbs become stiff. Doctors are not sure why these changes take place – and why they take place at different ages in different people.

▼ A rabbit aged 4 years is a 'very old' rabbit, but a dog is not 'very old' until it is about 15 years. A human being becomes 'very old' when he or she is about 80. Some tortoises live to be up to 100 years old.

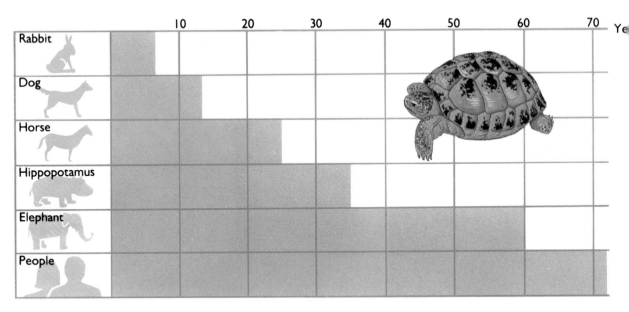

People, on average, live much longer in developed countries than in the underdeveloped world. In Sweden, for example, 22 per cent of the population is over 65. In Zimbabwe only 3 per cent of people reach that age.

Agriculture See Farming

AIDS

AIDS (Acquired Immune Deficiency Syndrome) is caused by a VIRUS named HIV. The AIDS virus attacks white BLOOD cells that fight off viruses and BACTERIA when they enter the body. When these white blood cells are destroyed, the patient can become very ill with a DISEASE that would not be serious to a healthy person. Because the body of a person with AIDS has lost its means of fighting disease, the patient can often die.

AIDS is passed from person to person in three main ways: by intimate sexual contact, by exposure to blood infected with HIV, and by transmission to a baby in an infected mother's womb. One common way for people to catch the disease is by sharing hypodermic needles. People who have been infected with HIV may not become seriously ill until years later. AIDS is a serious world problem.

Air

Air is all around us—it surrounds the Earth in a layer we call the *atmosphere*. We need to breathe air in order to live. Air is colourless and has no smell. Yet it is really a mixture of a number of different gases. We can feel air when the wind blows, and we know air has weight. Air carries sound—without it we would not be able to hear, because sounds cannot travel in a VACUUM.

The chief gas in air is nitrogen, which makes up nearly fourth-fifths of the air. About one-fifth of the air is OXYGEN, the gas we need to keep us alive. Air also holds some water in very fine particles called *vapour*. When we talk about HUMIDITY, it is the amount of water in the air we are measuring.

Air is heavier than you think. The average roomful of air weighs more than 45 kg— about the weight of 20 bags of potatoes! The air we breathe is about 14 times as heavy as the gas hydrogen.

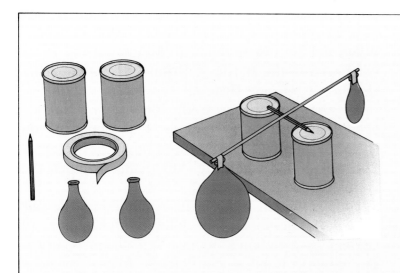

SEE IT YOURSELF
Prove to yourself that air has weight. Make a simple balance using two cans, a pencil and a long stick marked in the centre. Tape two identical balloons to the ends of the stick and see how they balance. Now, remove one of the balloons, blow air into it and fix it back into place. The balloon full of air makes the balance dip down. Air really does have weight.

The air that surrounds the Earth gets thinner the higher you go. All high-flying aircraft have to keep the air in their cabins at ground-level pressure so that passengers can breathe normally. In the same way mountaineers carry their own air supply because the air at the top of high mountains is too thin to breathe properly.

Warm air expands and becomes lighter. The air around a heater becomes lighter and rises. Cool air moves into its place. This too warms and rises, so the entire room is heated.

Aircraft

For thousands of years people dreamed about being able to fly. Myths and legends are filled with tales of supermen who could fly. Yet it was only at the beginning of this century—on December 17, 1903—that the Wright brothers made the first successful powered flight. Seventy years later, *Concorde* was crossing the Atlantic in three hours. (See pages 18 and 19.)

Air Force

AIRCRAFT were first used as fighting machines during WORLD WAR I. By 1939, most countries had an air force. The Germans had built up a strong Luftwaffe (air force) which they used in their successful 'blitzkrieg' attacks at the start of WORLD WAR II. The Germans knew that no land battle could be won without control of the skies above the battle area. When the Luftwaffe failed to knock out the Royal Air Force in the Battle of Britain, Hitler cancelled his plans to invade Britain.

As the war progressed, long-range bombers played an increasing part in the tactics of the British, American, German and Japanese air forces. The war ended when the Americans dropped two atomic bombs on Japanese cities.

Today, guided missiles have cut down the part played by bombers, but piloted planes are still needed as a defence against fast strike bombers. The modern bomber can fly close to the ground at very high speed, slipping under the enemy's radar

▲ *We live under about two hundred kilometres of air. Why are we not squashed flat? We are not squashed because everything inside our bodies is at the same pressure as the air around us. But air pressure changes with height. The higher you go, the less air there is above you. This is why the pilots of high-flying aircraft need to wear special suits and take their own oxygen supply with them. Deep-sea divers also need special suits to prevent their bodies being crushed by the weight of water.*

Sea level

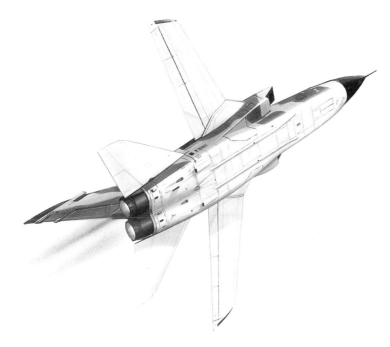

◀ *Some fighter aircraft are designed to do several jobs in air warfare. The* Tornado *can act as a low-level bomber as well as an air defence fighter. Its wings can be swept back for high speed flight or extended to help it travel at lower speeds.*

▼ *At the beginning of World War I the soldiers in the trenches of the Western Front took pot-shots at any aircraft that flew overhead, whether it was friend or foe. So warplanes began to be marked with their national flags. However, as these could often be confusing at a distance, the special symbols of the world's air forces were gradually adopted.*

screen without being spotted.

Transport aircraft can fly troops, complete with tanks and weapons, anywhere in the world in a few hours. The helicopter is now a vital part of any air force. It carries troops and evacuates the wounded. Helicopter 'gunships' can attack ground targets.

Airport

An airport is one of the busiest places in the world, for all day and nearly all night jet airliners take off and land—at peak periods at the rate of one a minute.

Airports have three main jobs: they must handle passengers, mail and freight; they must be sure that all aircraft take off and land safely and on time; and they must provide hangars and workshops so that planes can be checked regularly.

The centre of operations at the airport is the air-traffic control tower, where controllers organize the landing and take-off of each aircraft. With complicated electronic aids, including computers and radar, the ground controller guides the pilot of the aircraft from a height of 6 to 8 km onto a concrete runway about 3 km long and 60 metres wide. The runways are usually parallel and in line with the prevailing wind, so that aircraft can land against the wind, which is always safer. As soon as an aircraft

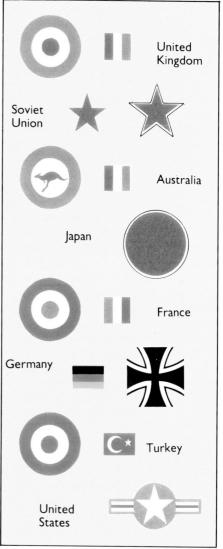

United Kingdom

Soviet Union

Australia

Japan

France

Germany

Turkey

United States

Continued on page 20.

AIRCRAFT

From earliest times people dreamed of being able to fly like the birds. Brave but foolhardy inventors leaped from high towers wearing wings, but all such attempts ended in failure. In the 1500s Leonardo da Vinci drew plans for a helicopter, but such a machine could never have been built in his day.

The conquest of the air by people began with the first balloon flight in 1783. Later, airships, steerable balloons with engines and propellers, took to the sky. Inventors built gliders, proving that flight was also possible using winged aeroplanes that were heavier than air.

It was the development of the petrol engine in the 1880s that made powered aeroplanes a practical possibility. In 1903 the Wright brothers made the first controlled and powered manned flight in their flimsy aeroplane, the *Flyer*.

Since that historic flight progress in aviation has been amazingly rapid. Today we live in a world where people take air travel for granted. Supersonic jet aircraft, such as *Concorde*, can fly the Atlantic Ocean in three hours. Space shuttles can fly into space and return to land on a runway, like an airliner.

▶ *A selection of aircraft throughout the ages, ranging from Leonardo's 16th century helicopter to the popular and highly efficient* Concorde.

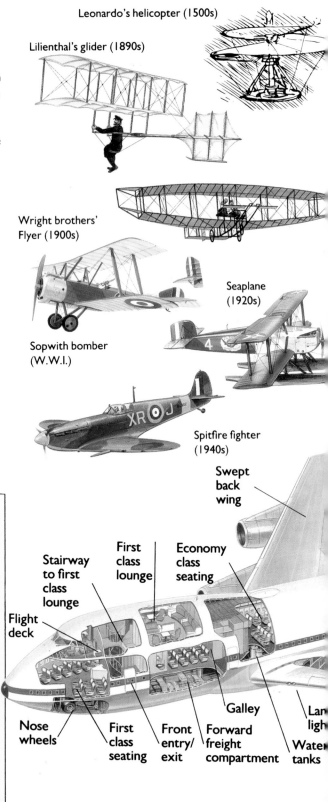

Leonardo's helicopter (1500s)

Lilienthal's glider (1890s)

Wright brothers' Flyer (1900s)

Sopwith bomber (W.W.I.)

Seaplane (1920s)

Spitfire fighter (1940s)

Swept back wing

First class lounge

Economy class seating

Stairway to first class lounge

Flight deck

Nose wheels

First class seating

Front entry/ exit

Forward freight compartment

Galley

Lan light

Water tanks

HOW A PLANE FLIES

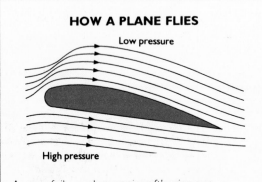

Low pressure

High pressure

An aerofoil—such as an aircraft's wing or a helicopter's rotor blade—is something which creates lift when it moves through the air. It does this by making the air travel further over its curved upper surface than it does under the lower, flat surface. As a result, air pressure is higher beneath than above the aerofoil. This creates a sort of upward suction which makes the wing or rotor rise together with the aircraft. The illustration above shows a cross-section of an aerofoil and also the pattern of the airflow around it.

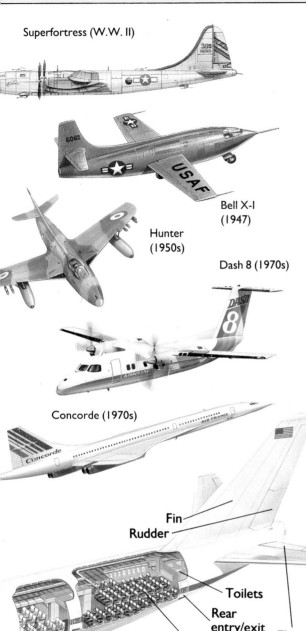

Superfortress (W.W. II)

Bell X-I
(1947)

Hunter
(1950s)

Dash 8 (1970s)

Concorde (1970s)

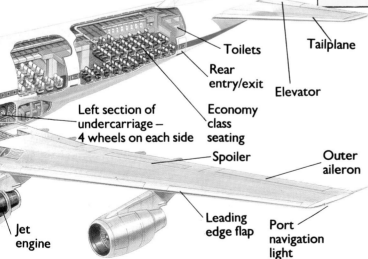

Fin

Rudder

Toilets

Rear
entry/exit

Elevator

Tailplane

Left section of
undercarriage –
4 wheels on each side

Economy
class
seating

Spoiler

Outer
aileron

Jet
engine

Leading
edge flap

Port
navigation
light

◀ The Boeing 747 was the first of the big 'jumbo jets'. This highly successful aircraft carries up to 500 passengers, although it is not usually arranged to take this number. It has a wing span of 60 metres, a length of 70 metres and weighs nearly 320 tonnes. The 747 first flew in February 1969 and entered service in 1970. It can fly at a speed of 900 km/h for a distance of 10,000 km.

For more information turn to these articles: AIR FORCE; AIRPORT; BALLOON AND AIRSHIP; BLERIOT; GLIDING; HELICOPTER; JET ENGINE; LINDBERGH; RADAR and WRIGHT, ORVILLE AND WILBUR.

Runway

Taxiway

Apron

Terminal building

Control tower

Pier

▲ *Some modern airports have just one runway facing the prevailing wind—the direction from which the wind usually blows.*

has landed, it moves along, or *taxis*, to an area called an *apron*. Here trucks are waiting, ready to carry baggage to the terminal. Fuel tankers move in to refill the craft's fuel tanks.

Airship *See* Balloon and Airship

Albania

Albania is a small, rugged country that lies between Yugoslavia and Greece on the eastern shore of the Adriatic Sea. Most Albanians live in small, remote mountain villages. Albanian farmers grow wheat, barley, tobacco and cotton. Beneath the ground there are deposits of chrome, copper, iron, oil and natural gas. Albania was ruled by Turkey for over 400 years. After World War II it became a communist state, but by 1992, a multi-party system and progressive leaders were in place. In 1997 the country was torn apart by armed rebellion.

ALBANIA

BULGARIA

FORMER YUGOSLAVIA

ADRIATIC SEA

ITALY

ALBANIA

GREECE

AEGEAN SEA

Government: Republic
Capital: Tirana
Area: 28,748 sq km
Population: 3,285,000
Language: Albanian
Currency: Lek

Albatross

The albatross is a large seabird that spends most of its time in the air over the oceans. The wandering albatross can have a wingspan of 3·5 metres, the largest span of any bird. Most albatrosses live in regions south of the Equator, where they soar gracefully over the waves. They come ashore only to breed or in stormy weather. Albatrosses will follow ships for hundreds of kilometres, picking up scraps of food thrown overboard.

The albatross can sleep peacefully on the ocean's surface. It drinks so much sea water that it needs special glands in its head to get rid of all the salt it takes in.

▲ For a long time people thought that albatrosses slept on the wing. In fact, they settle on the water to sleep and feed.

Alchemy

The chemistry of the MIDDLE AGES was called alchemy. It was a strange mixture of magic, science and religion. The people who practised alchemy dreamed of producing a magic substance which they called the 'philosopher's stone'. This substance would be able to change cheap metals such as lead into gold; it would also cure diseases and keep people young. Needless to say, the alchemists never found the philosopher's stone, but in their search they learned a great deal about chemistry and invented apparatus that chemists still use today.

▼ An alchemist and his assistant. Alchemists experimented with the impossible task of changing cheap metals into gold.

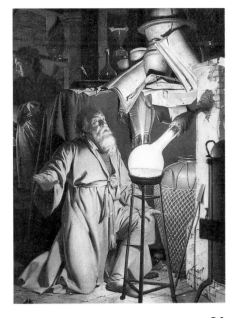

Alcohol

There are many different kinds of alcohol. The kind we know best is the alcohol in wines and spirits such as whisky and gin that can make people intoxicated.

Alcohol is formed by a process called FERMENTATION. In fermentation, YEASTS act on the sugar in

When Alexander was a boy, he tamed the great and spirited Bucephalus, a horse that no one else dared to ride. This famous horse carried Alexander as far as India, where it died. Alexander built a city over its grave and named the city Bucephala. The city has been lost, but people think it is somewhere in modern Pakistan.

grain and fruit to produce alcohol. If strong alcohol is needed, the liquid has to be *distilled*.

Alcohols are found in many things. They are used in the making of perfumes, drugs and antiseptics. They dissolve oils, fats and plastics. The alcohol called glycol is used as an anti-freeze in car radiators because, like all alcohols, it has a very low freezing point.

Alexander the Great

Alexander the Great (356–323 BC) was a ruler of GREECE and one of the greatest generals who ever lived. The son of Philip of Macedon, the young Alexander was taught by Aristotle, the famous Greek philospher. His father taught him to plan and win battles.

Alexander conquered the Greek city-states after he became king when Philip died in 336 BC. He then marched east to conquer Persia, which was at that time the greatest empire in the world. By 327 Alexander's empire stretched from Greece to India. When his armies reached India they were worn out from marching and fighting. Alexander had to turn back. When he reached BABYLON he became ill with a fever and died. He was still only 33. Alexander's body was carried back to Alexandria, the great city he had founded in EGYPT. There it was placed in a magnificent tomb.

▶ As can be seen on this map, most of the cities founded by Alexander were named after himself. The above picture of the great general is part of a mosaic found at Pompeii in Italy.

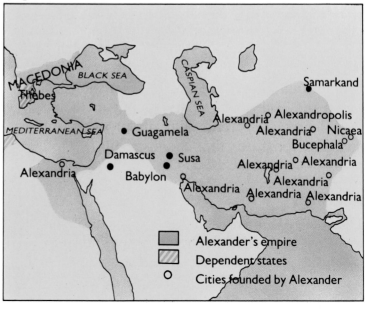

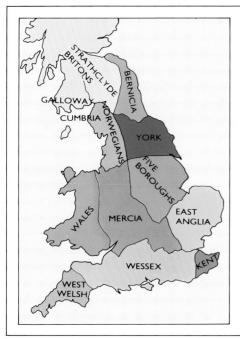

Alfred the Great

Alfred the Great (849–899) was a wise and able ruler who saved England from being conquered by the Danes. He formed an army and a navy to defend his Kingdom of Wessex from the invaders, and drove out the Danes in 896. When peace returned, Alfred did much to bring justice and education to his people. Under his direction the Anglo-Saxon Chronicle was begun. It was a record of the events of each year, and much of our knowledge of King Alfred's time comes from this record.

▲ *In the time of Alfred the Great, England was divided into small kingdoms. Alfred was king of Wessex. By 955, Alfred's successors had pushed out the Danes until almost the whole of England was Anglo-Saxon. The Anglo-Saxons built boats like the one above.*

Algebra

Algebra is a branch of mathematics in which letters stand for numbers. A letter can represent one number at one time and an entirely different number at another time. Algebra also uses signs to represent connections between letters.

An algebraic *equation* is a statement in which

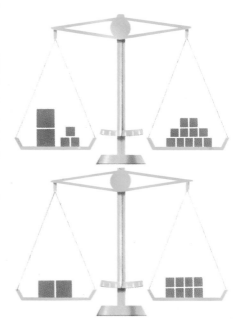

▶ *The two sides of an algebraic equation are like two equal weights. If they are changed in the same way, they remain equal. If we call the large blocks x, the top balance shows how 2x + 3 balances 11. Take away 3 from each side and 2x = 8. Then we can halve both sides of the equation and find that x balances 4 — x = 4.*

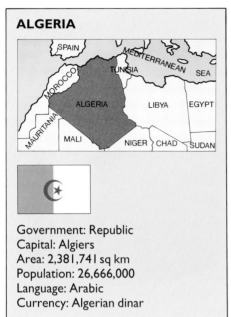

ALGERIA

Government: Republic
Capital: Algiers
Area: 2,381,741 sq km
Population: 26,666,000
Language: Arabic
Currency: Algerian dinar

both sides of the equals sign (=) balance each other out; for example $x+3=9$. Solving an equation means finding the number which makes the statement true. To solve an equation of this kind we take 3 from 9 to give 6 ($x=6$).

Algeria

The large African country of Algeria covers an area nearly ten times the size of the United Kingdom. It is bordered by six countries and the Mediterranean Sea. The great Sahara Desert covers most of Algeria, and few people live there. Most Algerians live in a narrow strip along the Mediterranean. Algiers is the capital and largest city.

Many nations have controlled Algeria. The French captured the country in 1830 and stayed there until the Algerians rebelled in 1954. The country won its independence in 1962 after a war.

Algeria is a republic and most of its wealth comes from oil, natural gas and other minerals.

Alligator and Crocodile

The alligator is a large reptile that belongs to the same family as the crocodile. There are two species: one is the American alligator of the south-eastern USA; the other is the smaller Chinese alligator that

▼ *Crocodiles are sometimes bred for their skins to make shoes, handbags and other articles. This is a crocodile farm in Zimbabwe.*

lives in the YANGTZE RIVER. Alligators look very like crocodiles, but have broader, flatter heads with rounded snouts.

Crocodiles are clumsy on land, but in the water they move swiftly without a sound. They hunt fish, turtles and water mammals. Crocodiles and alligators lay their eggs in nests or holes in the ground.

▲ When the crocodile (top) closes its jaws, the fourth tooth in its lower jaw sticks out. The alligator (centre) has heavier jaws than its relative the gharial (bottom).

Alloy

An alloy is a mixture of two or more METALS. The mixture is usually more useful than each metal on its own. For example, a soft metal such as COPPER can be strengthened by adding ZINC to it to form *brass*, or TIN to form *bronze*, both of which are strong metals.

USEFUL ALLOYS		
Alloy	**Made mostly of**	**Some uses**
Steel	Iron, carbon and other elements	Cars, beams, tools etc.
Brass	Copper and zinc	Gears, propellers, scientific instruments etc.
Bronze	Copper and tin	Scientific instruments, bells etc.
Pewter	Tin, antimony, lead and copper	Household utensils
Dentist's amalgam	Mercury and copper	Teeth fillings
Cupronickel	Nickel and copper	'Silver' coins
Invar	Nickel and iron	Precision instruments, watch balance wheels
Sterling silver	Silver and copper	Tableware

Alphabet

An alphabet is a group of letters, or symbols, used to write down a language. The world 'alphabet' comes from the names of the first two letters in the Greek alphabet: *alpha* and *beta*. The 26 letters in the English alphabet come from the Roman alphabet of 2500 years ago. Other alphabets in common use today include the Greek, Arabic, Hebrew and Russian or *Cyrillic* alphabets. Most contain symbols for vowels (soft sounds like 'a' and 'e') and consonants (hard sounds like 't' and 's'). But the Arabic and Hebrew alphabets have consonants only. Vowels are expressed by marks above and below the consonants.

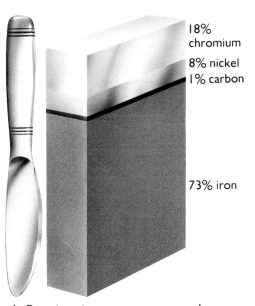

18% chromium

8% nickel

1% carbon

73% iron

▲ Pure iron is not very strong and rusts easily. It is mixed with chromium, nickel and carbon to make stainless steel, the alloy used for cutlery.

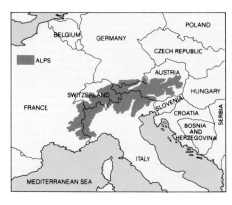

Alps

The Alps are the greatest mountain range in EUROPE. They are centred in SWITZERLAND, but they stretch from France all the way to former Yugoslavia. Mont Blanc, 4807 metres high, is the highest peak in the Alps. There are many lakes in the valleys; the largest is Lake Geneva.

The Alps attract many tourists. They go to ski and climb, and to admire the magnificent scenery.

▼ *The Alpine region is known for its wildlife – rare flowers like the white edelweiss, shown here, and birds such as the golden eagle.*

▼ *Because aluminium is a good conductor of electricity and heat, it is used for electric power cables and cooking ('tin') foil. Its lightness is the reason for its use in aircraft and tennis rackets.*

Aluminium

There is more aluminium in the Earth's crust than any other metal. But until less than 200 years ago no one had ever seen this silvery metal. When aluminium was first used it was much dearer than gold because it was very difficult to separate the metal from the materials it was mixed up with in the earth.

Most aluminium is now produced from an ore called bauxite. The bauxite is treated with chemicals and placed in a big electric furnace. An electric current is passed through and aluminium falls to the bottom of the furnace.

Aluminium is light—it weighs only a third as much as steel. It and its ALLOYS are especially useful where lightness and strength are important. It is also a good conductor of heat and electricity.

Amazon, River

The Amazon is the mightiest river in South America, and, at a length of 6440 km, is the second longest in the world, after the Nile. It flows from Peru

through Brazil to the Atlantic Ocean. Almost the whole of the Amazon basin is dense tropical forest. In the 1540s a Spanish explorer saw female Indian warriors on the Amazon's banks, so the river was named after the Amazons (female warriors) of Greek legends.

> **The Amazon pours out so much fresh water into the Atlantic that more than 160 km out at sea from the river's mouth the ocean's water is still fresh.**

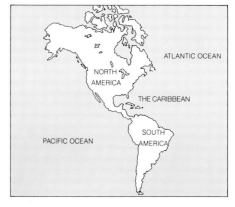

America

The word 'America' is often used to mean the United States, but it originally described a much larger area that today is more properly called the Americas. The Americas include North America, Central America and South America, and the islands of the Caribbean.

American Indians

American Indians are the native peoples of the Americas—that is, the first people to live there. They are known as Indians because when Christopher COLUMBUS reached America in 1492 he thought he had arrived in India.

The Indians of the Americas are thought to have crossed to the North American continent from Asia about 20,000 years ago. Very gradually, over the centuries, they spread through North America and down into what is now Central and South America. They developed different ways of life according to where they lived.

▼ *An early American Indian village. The tepees are made of bison skins. Note the squaw carrying her baby (her papoose) on her back in a sling made of cloth.*

The greatest American Indian contribution to our way of life has been the hundreds of plant species that were unknown in Europe before the time of Columbus. Among the strange plants being grown by the Indians when white people first set foot in America were potatoes, beans, maize (Indian corn), tomatoes, cacao (for chocolate), pineapples and Jerusalem artichokes.

When Europeans began to settle in North America, conflict broke out as they invaded the Indians' hunting grounds. Many Indians were killed or forced to move farther west. By the late 1800s almost all the tribes had been sent to live on special reservations by the US government. Today many Indians are working to gain equal opportunities for themselves as American citizens.

Amphibian

Amphibians are animals such as FROGS, TOADS, salamanders and newts. They can live in water or on land, but most of them start their lives in water. Amphibians are cold-blooded creatures. They do not drink like other animals but absorb water directly through their skins. For this reason they must keep their skins moist. Amphibians were one of the earliest groups of animals on Earth. They crawled out of the water and onto the land about 400 million years ago.

All amphibians have backbones. Nearly all of them lay their eggs in water, in a layer of jelly which protects them. When the young amphibians hatch, they feed on algae (tiny water plants). A young frog at this stage is called a tadpole. It breathes the

▼ Millions of years ago, amphibians such as these developed on earth. They probably crawled out of the water to feed on land. The top two are named Diadactes, the lower one Seymouria.

oxygen dissolved in water through gills. After two or three months the tadpole begins to change into an adult. Its tail gradually disappears, and its gills turn into LUNGS. Hind legs and then front legs appear. The little frog leaves the water and spends the rest of its life as an air-breathing adult. But it must return to the water to mate and lay its eggs.

Amsterdam

Amsterdam is the biggest city in the NETHERLANDS (pop. 1,038,000). It is, with Venice, one of the two most beautiful canal cities in Europe. Amsterdam was one of the world's greatest trading centres in the 1600s. Today it is still an important commercial city.

Amundsen, Roald

Roald Amundsen (1872–1928) was a Norwegian explorer. In 1910 he set out to be the first to reach the North Pole, but was beaten by the American, Robert Peary. Amundsen then decided to go for the South Pole, which he reached on December 14, 1911, the first person ever to do so. He reached the pole a month before the ill-fated expedition led by Captain SCOTT.

Andersen, Hans Christian

Hans Christian Andersen (1805–1875) was a Danish storyteller, whose fairy tales, such as *The Little Mermaid* and *The Ugly Duckling*, are still popular all over the world.

Andes

The Andes mountain range is the longest in the world. It stretches for more than 7000 km down the west side of South America, running the whole length of the continent. Several peaks are more than 6000 m high, and Aconcagua, on the border between Argentina and Chile, is the highest mountain in the Americas at 6960 m. Many of the peaks are active volcanoes. The Andes are rich in minerals such as copper, silver and gold.

▲ *Amphibians such as the toad and newt are creatures that are at home both on dry land and in the water. All amphibians have tails when they are babies. Some kinds, such as toads, lose their tails as they grow, but others, such as newts, keep them all their lives. The toad has stubbier legs than a frog, and its body is usually wider and flatter. It also has a rougher skin than a frog.*

ANDORRA

Government: Co-principality
Capital: Andorra la Vella
Area: 453 sq km
Population: 54,000
Language: Catalan
Currency: French franc and Spanish peseta

Andorra

Andorra is a tiny country on the border between France and Spain. It is so small that you could fit four Andorras into Greater London. Since 1278 the principality of Andorra has been ruled jointly by the bishop of Urgel in Spain and the president of France. The main industry is tourism. The capital is Andorra la Vella, and there are only 54,000 people in the country.

Angle

An angle is formed when two straight lines meet. The size of all angles is measured in degrees. The angle that forms the corner of a square is called a 'right' angle and has 90 degrees. An *acute* angle is less than 90 degrees; an *obtuse* angle is between 90 and 180 degrees.

Anglo-Saxons

Anglo-Saxon is the name given to the group of Germanic tribes who settled in Britain during the AD 400s and 500s. These tribes were the Angles, Saxons and Jutes. They gradually occupied all of England, driving the original Celtic people of Britain into

▶ Life was hard for the Anglo-Saxon peasants. Many of them lived in very simple houses like the ones shown here. Note the 'chimney hole' in the straw roof!

Wales and Cornwall. By the 700s there were seven main Anglo-Saxon kingdoms—Wessex, Sussex, Kent, Essex, East Anglia, Mercia and Northumbria. About half the words in the English language come from Anglo-Saxon.

Angola

The People's Republic of Angola is a large country facing the Atlantic Ocean in south-western Africa. Portugal claimed the region in 1482.

Black Angolans rebelled against the Portuguese in 1960 and fighting broke out. In 1975 Portugal granted the Angolans full independence. A fierce struggle then began between rival Angolan factions, some of them aided by foreign troops. The war ended in 1991 when the government and the rebels agreed to a cease-fire. Fighting broke out again in 1992 and continued into 1994, when a peace treaty was agreed.

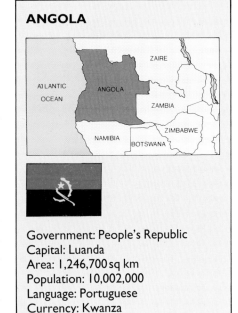

ANGOLA

Government: People's Republic
Capital: Luanda
Area: 1,246,700 sq km
Population: 10,002,000
Language: Portuguese
Currency: Kwanza

Animals

An animal is any living thing that is not a PLANT. No one knows how many different kinds of animals there are on Earth; hundreds of new kinds are discovered every year. The biggest difference between animals and plants is in the way they get their

▼ Some common vertebrates (animals with backbones) and invertebrates (those without). As invertebrates have no internal bones, some of them have an outside shell for protection.

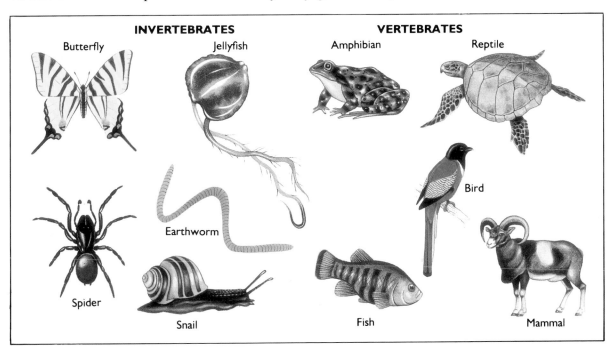

INVERTEBRATES   VERTEBRATES
Butterfly   Jellyfish   Amphibian   Reptile
                                             Bird
          Earthworm
Spider   Mammal
     Snail   Fish

The biggest land animal so far discovered is a dinosaur called Ultrasaurus. The fossil remains of this huge creature were found in 1979 in Colorado, USA. It stood about 8 metres high at the shoulder—four times the height of a tall man—and must have weighed about 130 tonnes. Ultrasaurus was about 30 metres long—the length of 1½ cricket pitches!

food. Animals eat plants or other animals. Plants make their food out of substances taken in through their roots or leaves. Animals can also, unlike plants, move about at some time in their lives.

Some animals such as the tiny amoeba reproduce by just splitting in two. In most other animals the female produces eggs that are fertilized by the male. Creatures such as the cod produce millions of eggs, of which only a very few ever hatch and even fewer reach maturity. These animals never see or care for their young. Other animals such as elephants and human beings develop the fertilized egg inside their bodies, and the mother feeds and cares for her infant for months or years.

Anne, Queen

Anne (1665–1714) succeeded to the throne of Great Britain and Ireland in 1702 after her brother-in-law William III. She was the daughter of James II, and was the last Stuart monarch. Anne was queen when England and Scotland were united in 1707.

Ant

Ants are 'social' insects—they live together in colonies. Some colonies are in heaps of twigs; others are in chambers deep in the ground. Still others are hills of earth or sand. There are three types of ant: males, queens which lay eggs, and workers or females that do not mate or lay eggs.

▼ An ant colony showing the different chambers which the ants use for laying their eggs and bringing up their young.

Worker ants with aphids

Worker ants with larvae

Wood ant

Adult ant emerges from pupae

Queen ant lays eggs

The Legionary or Army ants march across country in a great horde that may have as many as several million ants. They devour anything in their path, even tied-up farm animals.

Antarctic

The Antarctic is the continent that surrounds the SOUTH POLE. It is a vast cold region, with very little animal or plant life on land. Nearly all of the Antarctic is covered by an ice cap, broken only by a few mountain ranges. This ice cap averages 2500 metres in thickness, but is as much as 4700 metres thick in places.

▲ *The Norwegian, Roald Amundsen, was the first person to reach the South Pole in 1911. He was closely followed by Captain Scott.*

▼ *Very few animals can live in the freezing conditions near the South Pole. Those that do often have large amounts of fat or fur to protect them.*

McCormick's skua

Adelie penguins

Emperor penguin and chick

Antarctic cormorant

Weddell Seal

▲ *Anteaters live in the tropical forests and swamps of South America. They are active only at night.*

▼ *A male waterbuck, an antelope native to the area of Africa south of the Sahara.*

Anteater

The anteater of South America is a curious creature with a long, tapering snout. This snout is specially shaped to winkle ants, termites and grubs from their nests. It catches the insects with its long, whip-like tongue. An anteater may measure over 2 metres from the tip of its tail to its snout. It uses its strong front claws to tear open ant and termite nests.

Antelope

Antelopes are grazing animals with horns and hoofs. They look rather like DEER, but are actually related to the goat and the ox. Most antelopes live on the African plains. They are fast runners and often live in large herds, fleeing suddenly at any hint of danger. Some of the best known are the impala, the waterbuck, the hartebeest, the gnu, the eland and the little dik-dik, hardly bigger than a rabbit.

Antibiotics

Antibiotics are substances, produced by living things, that are poisonous to harmful bacteria. For a long time it was thought that any medicine that was able to kill a particular microbe would also kill the patient. Then, early in this century, scientists began to discover drugs that would kill bacteria but do the patient no harm. The most important of these drugs was penicillin, a drug produced by a mould. Penicillin was a 'wonder drug' that saved many lives. It was especially useful against pneumonia. The antibiotic streptomycin has almost got rid of the disease tuberculosis. Scientists have found many more useful antibiotics that can fight diseases such as whooping cough and typhus.

Antibiotics do not work against viruses, organisms that cause the common cold, flu, mumps, measles, AIDS and other diseases.

Antigua and Barbuda

This country is made up of two tiny islands in the Caribbean Sea. Antigua and Barbuda gained independence from Britain in 1981, but Queen

Elizabeth II is still head of state.

Antigua was discovered by Columbus in 1493, and it was colonized by the British in 1663.

Apartheid

The word 'apartheid' was used by the white rulers of SOUTH AFRICA to describe their policy for the separate development of the white and non-white peoples of South Africa. The word is Afrikaans for 'apartness'. Beginning in the later 1940s, the white South African government passed laws that made apartheid the official government policy.

Strict apartheid laws kept whites and non-whites apart, but in 1991 the government repealed major laws separating whites and blacks. In 1994, free elections led to the black African National Congress being the governing party, with NELSON MANDELA as president.

Ape

Apes are our closest animal relatives. We share the same kind of skeleton and have the same kind of blood and catch many similar diseases. Apes have large brains, but even the gorilla's brain is only half the size of a person's. Unlike monkeys, apes have no tails. There are four kinds of ape: the GORILLA and CHIMPANZEE are African; ORANG-UTANS live in Borneo and Sumatra; gibbons live in South-East Asia.

ANTIGUA AND BARBUDA

DOMINICAN REP.
PUERTO RICO
BARBUDA
LESSER ANTILLES
ANTIGUA
ATLANTIC OCEAN
CARIBBEAN SEA
TRINIDAD & TOBAGO
SOUTH AMERICA

Government: Constitutional monarchy
Capital: St John's
Area: 442 sq km
Population: 79,000
Language: English
Currency: East Caribbean dollar

▼ Apes have highly developed hands and fingers and enjoy swinging from branches.

Gibbon

Chimpanzee

Gorilla

Orang-utan

▲ Astronaut James Irwin salutes the American flag beside Apollo 15 after landing on the moon in July 1971.

▼ The Lunar Excursion Module stood 7 metres high and weighed 15,000 kilograms, but only a sixth as much on the Moon, because of our satellite's low gravity.

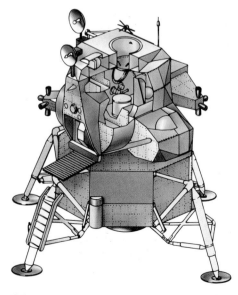

Apollo Space Programme

The American Apollo Space Programme was launched as part of the 'space race' between the USA and the Soviet Union to be first to reach the MOON with a manned spacecraft. For several years the Americans experimented with spacecraft that orbited the Earth; finally in 1968, they launched a manned spacecraft that circled the Moon and returned to Earth. The climax of the programme came on July 20, 1969, when astronaut Neil Armstrong became the first man to step onto the Moon's surface.

Apostles

The Apostles were the twelve followers of JESUS Christ, chosen to spread his teachings throughout the world. Jesus knew he did not have much time on Earth and concentrated on telling them exactly what his message meant. One of the apostles, Judas Iscariot, betrayed Jesus to his enemies, and Jesus was put to death. Later, Judas killed himself. The other apostles, together with followers such as St Paul, went on preaching the message of Jesus. CHRISTIANITY gradually spread through the Roman Empire and eventually through the entire world.

The Bible does not tell us much about the Apostles but we know that some of them were simple and uneducated. They laid the foundations for the success of Christianity.

Aquarium

An aquarium is a place where fish and other water animals are kept and studied. Many large public aquariums have become famous for their expertly trained performing animals, such as DOLPHINS and WHALES. A home aquarium is a small tank for fish and other water life, including plants. It is usually made of glass or has a glass side through which its contents can easily be seen. Many people keep beautiful TROPICAL FISH in aquariums that are specially heated to keep the water warm. These fish need very special care and attention.

In the many pictures that have been painted of the apostles, they are often shown with a special sign or symbol that can be recognized. St Peter, for example, carries keys, St Andrew is seen with a cross like an X, St John with an eagle and St Matthew a winged lion.

SEE IT YOURSELF
You can keep many pond creatures at home in a simple glass or plastic aquarium. Put some clean sand or gravel and a few stones on the bottom of the tank (not a fish bowl), together with a few plants. Stand the tank in the light, but not in the full sun, and fill it with pond water. You can add most of the common pond creatures as well, but avoid dragonfly nymphs and the great diving beetle. Feed with fish food and, as a treat, give water fleas from time to time.

Arabs

Arabs were originally those people who lived in Arabia. But from the AD 600s Arabian Arabs, inspired by their new faith, ISLAM, swept through western Asia and North Africa, conquering and settling a huge area. They taught the inhabitants the Arabic language and their Islamic religion. Today an Arab is anyone whose mother tongue is Arabic.

The Arabic language is spoken by more than 100 million people. Arabic writing (calligraphy) is given a high rank among the arts. In fact, the names of those who excelled in the art of writing far outnumber those of painters and architects.

This includes Arabic-speaking peoples from countries such as Algeria, Syria, Iraq and Libya. Muslims in Iran, India and Pakistan pray in Arabic, but do not use it in everyday speech, so they are not considered Arabs.

The Arabs ruled North Africa and south-west Asia for 900 years, until they were defeated by the Turks in the 1500s. They lived under Turkish rule until World War I. After World War II many Arab countries became extremely rich from the production of huge quantities of valuable OIL. There have been several attempts to unify the Arab nations, but in recent years conflict with Israel has caused a split in the Arab ranks. The oil-producing countries hold great power in the world because of their control of important oil resources.

▲ *The Bedouin are an Arab people who lead a nomadic way of life, moving from place to place with their families and animals. They live in the deserts of the Middle East.*

▼ *Excavations in progress on the Greek island of Kithira. Archaeology began in the Mediterranean area and a lot of work is still being done there.*

Archaeology

Archaeology is the study of history through the things that people have made and built. They may include tools, pottery, houses, temples, or graves. Even a garbage pit can help to reveal how people lived. Archaeologists study all these things, from the greatest of monuments to the tiniest pin. Modern archaeology began during the RENAISSANCE, when people became interested in the culture

of ancient GREECE and ROME. At first archaeological sites were ransacked for the treasures they contained. But by the early 1800s archaeologists had begun to uncover sites carefully, noting all they found and where they found it. Many exciting and important discoveries were made, including the remains of ancient Troy (1871); the early Greek civilization at Mycenae (1876); and the tomb of the pharaoh TUTANKHAMUN in Egypt (1922).

Today, science helps the archaeologist in his work. Radiocarbon dating and *dendrochronology* (dating by tree rings) help tell us when particular objects were made. INFRARED and X-RAY photography can show up designs under the rotted surface of a bronze bowl. Archaeology has even gone under the sea. With modern diving equipment, archaeologists can explore sunken wrecks and other long-lost remains of the past.

Archery

Archery is the use of the bow and arrow, once for hunting and warfare, now mostly for sport. No one knows when bows and arrows were first used, but prehistoric man certainly used them to shoot animals for food and to protect himself. Until the discovery of gunpowder the army with the best archers usually won the battle.

Today, archery is a popular sport. In target shooting the target is 1.2 metres (4 feet) across. The length of the arrow is about 71 cm (28 inches) for men and slightly shorter for women. Bows are usually made of laminated wood or fibreglass.

Archimedes

Archimedes (282–212 BC) was a famous Greek scientist who lived in Sicily. Among many other things, he discovered Archimedes' Principle which tells us that if we weigh an object in the air and then weigh it again submerged in a liquid, it will lose weight equal to the weight of the liquid it displaces. Archimedes is supposed to have discovered this when he stepped into a bath full to the brim, and water spilled onto the floor.

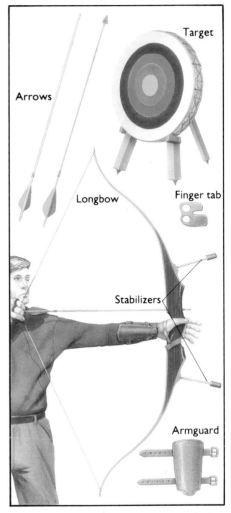

▲ A variety of equipment is needed for the sport of archery. The arm-guard is to protect the arm from the bowstring.

Archimedes is supposed to have played a part in the construction of one of the Seven Wonders of the Ancient World. It was the Pharos of Alexandria, a lighthouse designed by Ptolemy I of Egypt. The lighthouse was about 122 metres high, and at the top fires were kept burning. The fires were reflected by mirrors designed by Archimedes so that they could be seen 50 km away at night.

Ancient Egyptian style (2000–500s BC) – Temple of Amon at Luxor

Ancient Roman style (100s BC – AD 400s) – Pont du Gard aqueduct, Nîmes, France

Ancient Greek style (600s – 100s BC) Temple of Artemis at Ephesus

Byzantine style (AD 400s-1453) – Santa Sophia church, Istanbul, Turkey

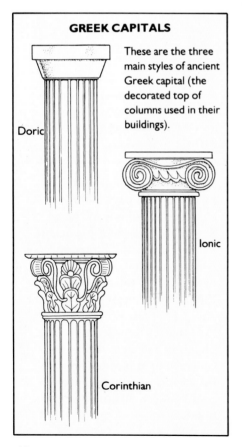

GREEK CAPITALS

These are the three main styles of ancient Greek capital (the decorated top of columns used in their buildings).

Doric

Ionic

Corinthian

Architecture

Architecture is the art of designing buildings. If we look at old buildings still standing we can learn a great deal about the people who built them.

Architecture as we know it began about 7000 years ago in ancient EGYPT. The Egyptians built huge PYRAMIDS as tombs for their kings, and many of these pyramids still stand.

Greek architecture began to take shape about 600 BC and developed into the beautiful styles we can see today on the ACROPOLIS at ATHENS.

When the Romans conquered GREECE they copied Greek architecture. But they soon discovered how to make an arch, so they could build larger, stronger buildings. They also began to make DOMES for the first time.

About AD 800 the Romanesque period of architecture began in Europe. Romanesque architecture at first imitated the style of ancient Rome, but soon took on a style of its own—a style that was strong and heavy. This style was followed by the Gothic. Most of the fine old cathedrals are in the Gothic

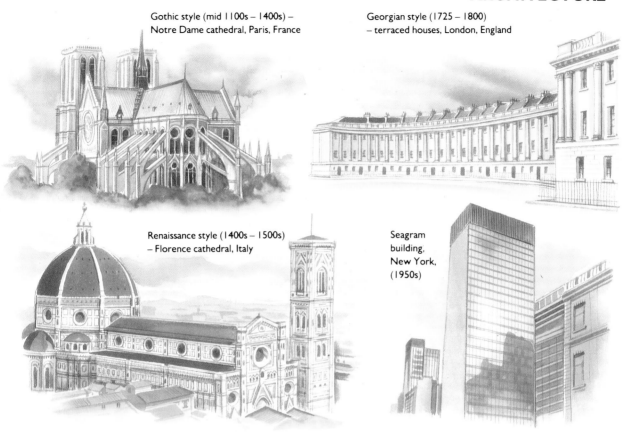

Gothic style (mid 1100s – 1400s) –
Notre Dame cathedral, Paris, France

Georgian style (1725 – 1800)
– terraced houses, London, England

Renaissance style (1400s – 1500s)
– Florence cathedral, Italy

Seagram building, New York, (1950s)

style. They have graceful pointed arches over doors, windows, and often in the roof as well. The roof of a Gothic cathedral is usually made of a series of criss-cross arches which take the weight of the ceiling. Roofs like this are called *vaulted* roofs.

In about 1400 a new style of architecture began in Italy. This was during the RENAISSANCE (the word means re-birth) and it spread all over Europe. Renaissance architects paid almost as much attention to public buildings and people's houses as they did to churches.

Later, many famous architects changed the building styles to fit the times in which they lived. Sir Christopher WREN (1632–1723) designed St Paul's Cathedral and many other London churches.

Today people still build with brick and stone, but they also have new materials which have changed the way in which buildings are constructed. Concrete and steel, glass and plastic are shaping the new world in which we live. Architects are designing offices, factories and sports arenas so as to make the best use of these new materials. They even have the opportunity sometimes to design whole new cities.

▼ *An example of modern architecture. This building is in Munich in Germany.*

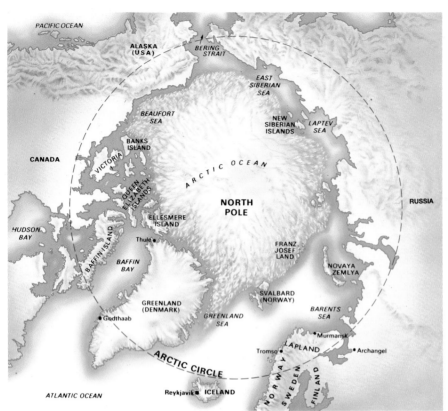

▲ *The Arctic tern is the world's migration champion. It breeds on seacoasts along the Arctic Ocean and in August migrates to the Antarctic at the other end of the world.*

Arctic

The Arctic is the region around the NORTH POLE. At the North Pole itself there is no land, only a huge area of frozen sea. The land in the Arctic region is frozen solid for most of the year. In the short summer the surface soil thaws and some plants can grow, even brightly coloured flowers. There are now more people in the Arctic than there used to be. This is because valuable minerals and oil have been found there. You can find the Arctic Circle at 66½ degrees north on a map.

It is cold near the North Pole because the Sun never rises high in the sky. In winter there are days when it does not rise at all. In summer there are days when it can be seen all day and night.

Argentina

Argentina is the second largest country in SOUTH AMERICA. Most of the country's 32,901,000 people are farmers and ranchers, for much of Argentina's wealth comes from livestock and crops. Argentina is

ARGENTINA

Government: Republic
Capital: Buenos Aires
Area: 2,766,889 sq km
Population: 32,901,000
Language: Spanish
Currency: Peso

one of the world's top producers of beef and veal, fruit, wheat, millet and sorghum, and wool. The chief farming region is on the *pampas*, a Spanish word meaning 'plains'. The pampas lie to the north-west and south of Argentina's capital, Buenos Aires. Here, vast farms raise millions of cattle and sheep which graze on the rich pasture. Northern Argentina is an area of tropical forests, and is little developed. In the far south, near the tip of South America, is Patagonia, a desert waste. The western part of the country is dry, and the land rises to the ANDES MOUNTAINS, including Aconcagua, at 6960 metres the highest peak in South America. Argentina was ruled by Spain from 1535 to 1810. Today most Argentinians are descended from Europeans, though there are still about 20,000 native Indians.

▲ *Gauchos are South American cowboys of the pampas region.*

Aristotle

Aristotle (384–322 BC) was a Greek philosopher and a student of another famous Greek philosopher Plato. At the age of 17 Aristotle went to Athens to become Plato's pupil. He worked there for 20 years and then became tutor to ALEXANDER THE GREAT. Aristotle invented the method of thinking called *logic*. His writings cover many areas, including nature and politics.

Arkwright, Richard

Richard Arkwright (1732–1792) was an English inventor best known for his spinning frame, which made factory production of cotton cloth possible. Arkwright patented his spinning machine in 1769, after which he built his first spinning mill. He became the pioneer of the modern factory system. His great success laid the groundwork for the INDUSTRIAL REVOLUTION.

Armada

Armada is a Spanish word for a great fleet of armed ships. The most famous armada was the Spanish fleet that tried to invade England in 1588. The 130 Spanish ships were large, clumsy and heavily armed.

The Spanish called the Armada the 'Great Enterprise', and indeed it was. Enough food had to be taken on board for six months: 5 million kg of biscuit, 300,000 kg of salt pork, 180,000 litres of olive oil, 14,000 barrels of wine were but a part of the necessities for a force of over 30,000 men. With the great fleet were 6 surgeons, 6 physicians, 180 priests, 19 justices and 50 administrators.

▲ The Spanish Armada suffered one of its greatest defeats at the battle of Gravelines in 1588. Six hundred Spaniards were killed.

The English ships were faster and easier to manoeuvre, and were manned by more skilful seamen. The English sent fire ships towards the Spanish fleet, which retreated out to sea. Later, several Spanish ships were sunk and many damaged in battle. The Armada was forced to flee around the northern tip of Britain. Only 67 of the original 130 ships reached Spain.

▼ The armadillo is able to protect itself by rolling into a tight ball when under threat of attack.

Armadillo

Armadillos are strange animals that live in Central and South America. Their backs are covered with an armour of bony plates. Some kinds of armadillo can roll themselves into a ball when attacked, giving them complete protection. They have strong claws which they use for digging burrows and tearing open termite nests to find food. There are ten different kinds of armadillo, the biggest being about 1.2 metres long.

Armenia

Armenia is a mountainous country, bordering Turkey and Iran. Until 1991, it was a republic of the former Soviet Union. It has mining and chemical industries, and cotton, figs and grain are grown.

In 1988, Armenia was struck by a great earthquake that killed over 55,000 people.

Armour

Armour is covering used to protect the body in battle. It was first worn at least 5000 years ago and was originally made of tough leather. Then men made metal breast-plates, helmets and shields. But the rest of the body was still protected by leather or chain mail, many small iron rings linked together to form a flexible metal coat. In the MIDDLE AGES, knights rode into battle encased from head to toe in plate armour which weighed up to 30kg.

Today, light metals and plastics are used in armoured jackets worn by soldiers and the police.

Army

Most armies today are made up of combat troops, service troops and staff officers. Combat troops include the infantry, armoured troops, artillery and paratroopers.

Service troops are vital to the modern army. They provide the ammunition, food, fuel and other supplies needed by the combat troops. They include medical staff, and engineers who lay mines, build bridges and prepare landing strips for aircraft.

The staff is made up of headquarters officers who plan army operations and control all the combat and service troops. If atomic weapons were ever used, the role of the modern army would have to change.

Art

Since the earliest times people have painted and made sculptured objects. We can still admire cave paintings that were drawn over 20,000 years ago.

ARMENIA

Government: Republic
Capital: Yerevan
Area: 30,000 sq km
Population: 3,415,000
Language: Armenian
Currency: Ruble

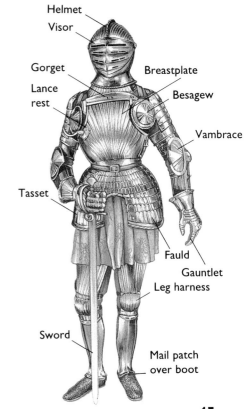

▼ Plate armour such as this was first introduced in the 13th century. By the 16th century, it was not uncommon for a knight and his horse to wear 60 pieces!

Helmet
Visor
Gorget
Lance rest
Tasset
Sword
Breastplate
Besagew
Vambrace
Fauld
Gauntlet
Leg harness
Mail patch over boot

▲ *Giotto's painting shows St Francis driving out the devils. It dates back to the 13th century.*

▲ *This sculpture of Tutankhamun, the boy pharaoh, was found in his tomb.*

▲ *A prehistoric painting of a bison from the caves at Altamira in northern Spain.*

◄ *Michelangelo's* Pietà *(the Virgin Mary cradling Christ's body after the Crucifixion). This was the most important sculpture of the artist's youth – he was 23 at the time. It is now in St Peter's Church in Rome.*

► *Raphael's 16th century fresco* The School of Athens.

The Christian religion has had a great influence on art. During the MIDDLE AGES painters worked on religious scenes, often in a rather stiff way. But when the RENAISSANCE came in the 1400s art began to flower and artists became famous for their work. Painters such as LEONARDO DA VINCI and MICHELANGELO began to make their subjects more life-like. Great Dutch painters such as REMBRANDT painted everyday scenes. In the 1700s and 1800s many artists went back to making their work look something like early Greek and Roman art.

Later, painting became more real looking, but by the 1870s a new style called IMPRESSIONISM was starting. Artists such as Monet (1840–1926) and Renoir (1841–1919) painted with little dabs of colour, making soft, misty outlines. Painting in the 1900s became even freer. Styles included Abstract Art and Cubism, with famous painters such as Cézanne (1839–1906) and PICASSO.

The oldest pieces of sculpture we know were made by STONE AGE artists about 30,000 years ago. The ancient Egyptians made very fine sculptures between 2000 and 4000 years ago. Many of them were huge statues of kings and queens. Some of the world's most beautiful carving was done by the sculptors of ancient Greece and Rome, in what is known as the Classical period. During the Renaissance, especially in Italy, the art of sculpture advanced by leaps and bounds. Michelangelo carved superb statues such as his famous *David*.

Modern sculptors often create sculptures in which the general shape is more important than showing the likeness of a figure.

▲ *Monet's* Spring *in the Fitzwilliam Museum, Cambridge.*

Artery

An artery is a BLOOD vessel that carries blood from the HEART to all parts of the body. VEINS are different from arteries because they carry used blood back to the heart. Arteries have thick and elastic walls. The largest is the *aorta*, which is connected directly to the heart. The word *artery* comes from Greek words meaning 'air carrier'. Because dead bodies have little or no blood in the arteries, the ancient Greek doctors who dissected them thought that they carried air around the body.

Arthur, King

King Arthur was a legendary British ruler of the AD 500s. His kingdom was supposed to have been in the west of England. Many stories grew up around King Arthur's court, and his Knights of the Round Table. These stories were first collected by Sir Thomas Malory in the 1400s.

▲ *Picasso's* Weeping Woman, *a fine example of modern art.*

Asia

Asia is the largest of all the continents. It also has more people (3,202,900,000) than any other continent. Places such as the Ganges-Brahmaputra delta, the river valleys of CHINA and the island of Java are among the most heavily-populated places in the world.

Northern Asia is a cold, desolate tundra region. In contrast, the islands of INDONESIA are in the steamy tropics. The world's highest mountain

▲ *Jackson Pollock's* Yellow, Grey, Black 1948 *was painted by dribbling paint onto the canvas.*

Continued on page 50.

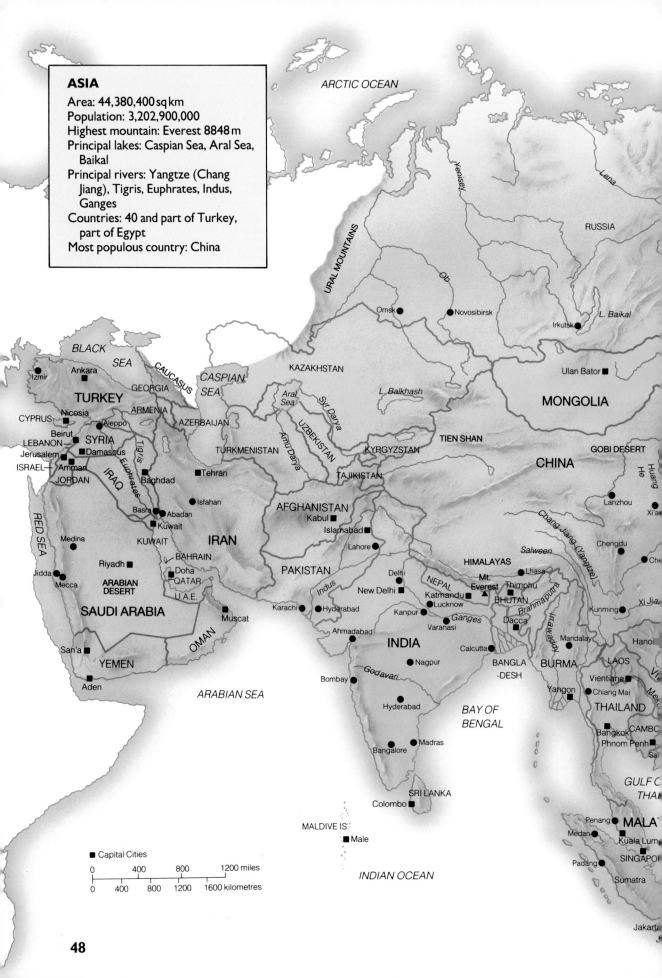

ASIA
Area: 44,380,400 sq km
Population: 3,202,900,000
Highest mountain: Everest 8848 m
Principal lakes: Caspian Sea, Aral Sea, Baikal
Principal rivers: Yangtze (Chang Jiang), Tigris, Euphrates, Indus, Ganges
Countries: 40 and part of Turkey, part of Egypt
Most populous country: China

ARCTIC OCEAN

RUSSIA

Yenisey

Lena

Ob

Omsk ■
Novosibirsk ●
Irkutsk ●
L. Baikal

URAL MOUNTAINS

KAZAKHSTAN

L. Balkhash

Ulan Bator ■

MONGOLIA

BLACK SEA

CAUCASUS

CASPIAN SEA

Izmir ●   Ankara ■
GEORGIA
TURKEY
ARMENIA
CYPRUS ● Nicosia ■
Aleppo ●
AZERBAIJAN
Beirut ●
LEBANON
SYRIA
Jerusalem ■ Damascus ■
ISRAEL
Amman ■
JORDAN
Tigris
IRAQ
Baghdad ■
Basra ●
Abadan ●
Kuwait ■
KUWAIT
Euphrates
Tehran ■
Isfahan ●
IRAN
BAHRAIN
Doha ■
QATAR
U.A.E.

Aral Sea
Syr Darya
UZBEKISTAN
Amu Darya
TURKMENISTAN
KYRGYZSTAN
TAJIKISTAN
TIEN SHAN

GOBI DESERT
CHINA
Lanzhou ●
Xi'a
Huang He
Chengdu ●
Ch
Chang Jiang (Yangtze)
Xi Jia
Kunming ●

RED SEA
Medina ●
Jidda ●
Mecca ●
Riyadh ■
ARABIAN DESERT
SAUDI ARABIA
San'a ■
YEMEN
Aden ●

AFGHANISTAN
Kabul ■
Islamabad ■
Lahore ●
PAKISTAN
Indus
Karachi ●
Hyderabad ●
Ahmadabad ●
Bombay ●

HIMALAYAS
Mt. Everest ▲
NEPAL
Katmandu ■
Lucknow ●
Delhi ●
New Delhi ■
Kanpur ●
Varanasi ●
Ganges
Lhasa ●
Thimphu ■
BHUTAN
Dacca ■
Brahmaputra
Salween
Mandalay ●
Irrawaddy
Hanoi
LAOS
Vi

Muscat ■
OMAN

Nagpur ●
INDIA
Godavari
Hyderabad ●
Bangalore ●
Madras ●

Calcutta ●
BANGLA-DESH
BURMA
Yangon ●
Vientiane ●
Chiang Mai ●
THAILAND
Bangkok ■
CAMBO
Phnom Penh ●
Sai

ARABIAN SEA

BAY OF BENGAL

GULF O THA

SRI LANKA
Colombo ■

MALDIVE IS
■ Male

INDIAN OCEAN

Penang ●
Medan ●
MALA
Kuala Lum
Padang ●
SINGAPO
Sumatra

Jakarta

■ Capital Cities

| 0 | 400 | 800 | 1200 miles |
| 0 | 400 | 800 | 1200 | 1600 kilometres |

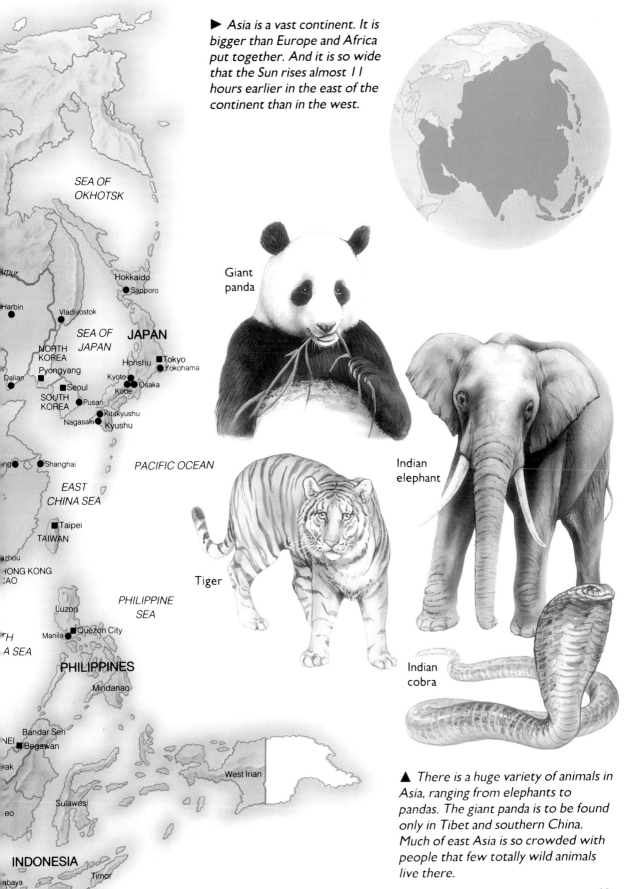

▶ Asia is a vast continent. It is bigger than Europe and Africa put together. And it is so wide that the Sun rises almost 11 hours earlier in the east of the continent than in the west.

SEA OF OKHOTSK

Hokkaido
Sapporo

Harbin

Vladivostok

mur

SEA OF JAPAN

JAPAN

NORTH KOREA

Pyongyang

Dalian

Honshu
Tokyo
Yokohama

Kyoto
Osaka

Seoul
Kobe

SOUTH KOREA

Pusan

Kitakyushu

Nagasaki
Kyushu

PACIFIC OCEAN

ng
Shanghai

EAST CHINA SEA

Taipei
TAIWAN

zhou

HONG KONG
CAO

PHILIPPINE SEA

Luzon

Manila
Quezon City

'H
A SEA

PHILIPPINES

Mindanao

Bandar Seri
Begawan

NEI

'ak

West Irian

Sulawesi

eo

INDONESIA

abaya
Timor

Giant panda

Indian elephant

Tiger

Indian cobra

▲ There is a huge variety of animals in Asia, ranging from elephants to pandas. The giant panda is to be found only in Tibet and southern China. Much of east Asia is so crowded with people that few totally wild animals live there.

▲ Tokyo, the capital of Japan, today resembles many Western cities.

Asia has the deepest lake in the world—Lake Baikal in Siberia, Russia. It has a maximum depth of 1,620m—more than three times the height of the world's tallest building. Lake Baikal also contains more fresh water than any other freshwater lake —a fifth of all the fresh water on the Earth's surface.

range, the HIMALAYAS, is in Asia, and so is the lowest point on land, the shores of the Dead Sea. Asia's people belong to the three main races: Caucasoids live in the south-west and northern INDIA; Mongoloids, including the Chinese and Japanese, live in the east. A few Negroids are found in the south-east. And all the world's great religions began in Asia—JUDAISM, CHRISTIANITY, ISLAM, HINDUISM, BUDDHISM, CONFUCIANISM and SHINTO.

Most Asians are farmers, and many are very poor. The chief food crops are wheat and rice. Other crops are exported: they include tea, cotton, jute, rubber, citrus fruits and tobacco. Many nations such as China are developing their industries, but JAPAN is the only truly industrialized nation.

Asia was the birthplace of civilization, and was the home of many great civilizations, including those of Mesopotamia, BABYLON, China and the Indus Valley in what is now PAKISTAN. Europeans began to visit Asia in the 1400s and trade quickly grew up between the two continents. Later, for several centuries, China and Japan closed their doors to trade with Europe. By the late 1800s most of the rest of Asia was ruled by European powers. But after World War II, during which Japan occupied parts of east Asia, most European-ruled colonies became independent. In 1949 the Chinese Communists took control of mainland China. In 1975 Communists took over VIETNAM, LAOS and CAMBODIA, after a seven-year war for control, fought mainly in Vietnam.

► Asiatic elephants are used in the logging industry in several Asian countries. Elephants are very intelligent and can be trained to carry heavy loads.

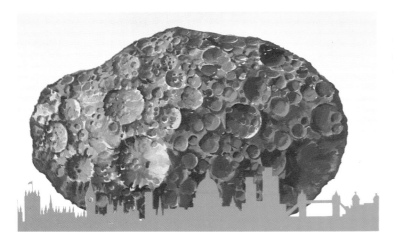

◀ *A very small asteroid, compared in size with part of London. There are probably thousands of bodies of this size in the solar system.*

Asteroid

Asteroids are countless thousands of tiny planets left over from the time when the Sun and planets were being formed. Most of them can be found in the wide gap between the orbits of MARS and JUPITER. Asteroid collisions formed the craters that can be seen on the MOON and MERCURY.

The largest asteroid is Ceres, about 1000 km across, but most of the 30,000 asteroids big enough to be photographed are less than a tenth of this size.

Astrology

Astrology is the art of foretelling the future by observing the movements of the Sun, Moon, planets and stars. Ancient peoples believed that the heavenly bodies influenced people and their affairs. This led to the growth of a priesthood of astrologers, men and women who claimed to be able to read the future in the heavens. Throughout history, kings, generals and other powerful rulers have listened to their advice. Today, some people still follow the predictions of astrologers.

Astronomy

Astronomy is the scientific study of the heavenly bodies, and is the oldest science in existence. Early observations of the heavens enabled people to divide the year into months, weeks, and days, based on the movements of the SUN, EARTH and MOON. The development of the calendar helped early

▼ *Astrology is based on the zodiac, an imaginary circle in the sky in which the Sun, Moon and planets move. Also in this circle are the 12 constellations or groups of stars that look like different shapes. Each shape is a sign of the zodiac and occupies a month in the astrologer's calendar. Some people believe that persons born under each sign have special character traits.*

SIGNS OF THE ZODIAC

♑	CAPRICORN	December 22–January 19
♒	AQUARIUS	January 20–February 18
♓	PISCES	February 19–March 20
♈	ARIES	March 21–April 19
♉	TAURUS	April 20–May 20
♊	GEMINI	May 21–June 20
♋	CANCER	June 21–July 22
♌	LEO	July 23–August 22
♍	VIRGO	August 23–September 22
♎	LIBRA	September 23–October 22
♏	SCORPIO	October 23–November 21
♐	SAGITTARIUS	November 22–December 21

astronomers to forecast the appearance of COMETS and the dates of ECLIPSES. For many centuries people believed that the Earth was the centre of the UNIVERSE, until, in the 1540s, Nicolaus COPERNICUS revived the idea that the Sun was at the centre of the SOLAR SYSTEM. In 1608 Hans Lippershey invented the TELESCOPE, an important new tool for astronomers. Today, big optical telescopes are aided by radio telescopes which collect radio waves sent out by objects in space, such as PULSARS and QUASARS.

▲ During the Middle Ages, the Arabs were very interested in astronomy, studying the planets and stars.

Athens

Athens is the capital of GREECE, but it was once the centre of the world's civilization and learning. It was already an important city when its citizens took a leading part in driving the powerful Persians from Europe in 479 BC. After this, Athens quickly rose to become the most important city in Greece under a leader called Pericles (490–429 BC). Pericles built many magnificent buildings, especially on the hill called the ACROPOLIS. Even after the Romans conquered Greece, Athens remained famous as a centre of culture.

▼ An ancient Greek statue called The Discus Thrower. The Greeks paid great attention to exercising both mind and body.

Athletics

Athletics events have been organized for nearly 3000 years. They were a main part of the old Olympic Games held in Greece from 776 BC.

Today, running, jumping and throwing events, called 'track and field', hold a high position in the world of sport. Sprinting events are run over distances of 100 and 200 metres. The 100 metres is run over a straight course. The 200 metres usually includes a bend, but is run in lanes. Middle distance events are often classified as those between 400 and 1500 metres. Mile races also come into this class.

Races over one mile can be classified as long-distance events. They are usually run over 5000 and 10,000 metres. The marathon starts and finishes on a track but the remainder of the 26 miles 385 yards race is through the surrounding streets. The 3000 metres steeplechase is run over a track with four hurdles and a water jump.

◀ *Thousands of runners enter marathon races like this one every year. Often they are sponsored for charity.*

MAIN ATHLETIC EVENTS

MEN	WOMEN
100 metres	100 metres
200 metres	200 metres
400 metres	400 metres
800 metres	800 metres
1000 metres	1500 metres
1500 metres	Mile
Mile	3000 metres
2000 metres	5000 metres
3000 metres	10,000 metres
Steeplechase	Marathon
5000 metres	100 m hurdles
10,000 metres	400 m hurdles
20,000 metres	High jump
30,000 metres	Long jump
Marathon	Shot put
110 m hurdles	Discus throw
400 m hurdles	Javelin throw
High jump	Heptathlon
Long jump	4 × 100 m relay
Pole vault	4 × 200 m relay
Triple jump	4 × 800 m relay
Shot put	
Discus throw	
Hammer throw	
Javelin throw	
Decathlon	
20-km walk	
30-km walk	
50-km walk	
4 × 100 m relay	
4 × 200 m relay	
4 × 400 m relay	
4 × 800 m relay	
4 × 1500 m relay	

The main hurdles events are the 110 metres high hurdles (the hurdles are 106 cm high) and the 400 metres intermediate hurdles, in which the hurdles are 91 cm high. Women run 100 metres over 84 cm hurdles, and 200 metres over 76 cm hurdles. The most popular relay races are the 4 × 100 metres and the 4 × 400 metres.

Field events include high and long jumping, the triple jump, pole vault, throwing the discus, javelin, shot and hammer. Almost all high jumpers now use the 'flop' method in which the jumper twists the body after take-off and goes over the bar backwards. In pole vaulting, the pole is of flexible glass fibre and about 4.5 metres long.

The discus is thrown from a circle 2.5 metres in diameter, the shot and hammer from a 2.1 metres circle. The standard shot weighs 7.257 kg (16 pounds), the same weight as the hammer and its steel wire. The women's shot weighs 4 kg.

Two of the most testing events are the decathlon and heptathlon. The decathlon (for men) is made up of ten events contested over two days. They are the 100 and 400 metres, high jump, long jump, shot put, 1500 metres, 110-metre hurdles, pole vault, javelin and discus. The heptathlon for women has seven events: 100 metres hurdles, high jump, putting the shot, 200 metres, 800 metres, long jump and javelin.

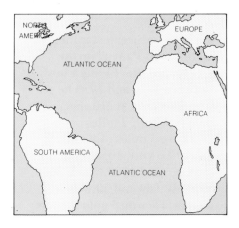

Atlantic Ocean

The Atlantic Ocean is the second largest ocean in the world, after the PACIFIC OCEAN. It lies between Europe and Africa in the east and the Americas in the west. Its average depth is more than 1800 metres. There are a number of strong currents in the Atlantic. The best known is the GULF STREAM which carries warm water towards the coasts of Europe. It is this current which keeps Europe comparatively warm in the winter months.

Atmosphere

The blanket of air and moisture that surrounds our planet is called the atmosphere. It is divided into four bands. The lowest level is the *troposphere*. Most of the air is concentrated here, from sea level to about 18 km high. Then comes the *stratosphere* (to 80 km), where jet aircraft often fly. The third layer is the *ionosphere* (to 500 km), above which is the *exosphere*. This is the fringe of the atmosphere and the start of outer space.

Atom

Everything is made of atoms. Things you can see, like the wood in a table; things you cannot see, like the air, are all made of atoms. You are made of atoms, too. If the atoms in something are packed closely together, that something is a solid. If the atoms in something are not so tightly packed—if they move about more—that something is a liquid, like water. And if the atoms move about a great deal, we have a gas, like air.

It is very difficult to imagine how small an atom is. We cannot see them—they are far too small. Look at the full stop at the end of this sentence. It has in it about 250,000 *million* atoms! But even atoms are

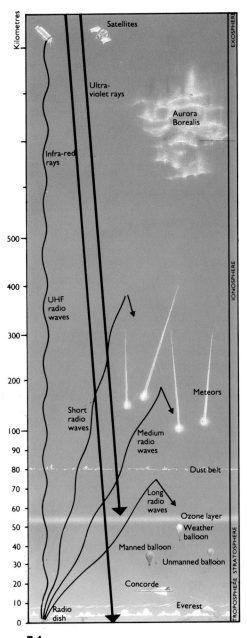

◀ *Air surrounds the Earth like a transparent shell. We could not live without this atmosphere. It gives us oxygen to breathe and keeps the Earth's temperature at just the right level. It also shields us from most of the Sun's dangerous rays. The atmosphere reflects most radio signals back to Earth.*

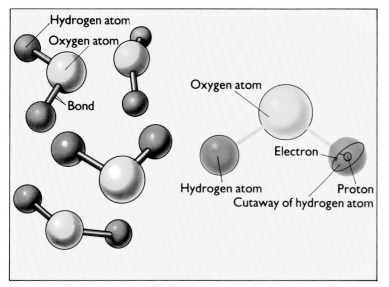

◄ *Water is made up of tiny molecules. Each molecule contains two atoms of hydrogen and one of oxygen. One of the hydrogen atoms in the picture is cut away to show its central proton and the single electron spinning round about it.*

made up of smaller pieces. The simplest atom is that of the light gas HYDROGEN. The centre is a tiny body called a *proton*. Around it spins an even smaller *electron*. Other atoms are much more complicated than the hydrogen atom. The carbon atom, for example, has at its centre 6 protons and 6 other things called *neutrons*. Around these spin 6 electrons. The biggest normal atom is a uranium atom. It has 92 electrons and its nucleus is made up of 92 protons and 146 neutrons.

Atomic Energy *See* Nuclear Energy

Australia

Australia is one of the world's seven CONTINENTS. It is a huge island about three-quarters the size of the whole of Europe, but the population is only about 15 million compared to Europe's 680 million. (See pages 56–57.)

Austria

Today, this small country is hardly much bigger than Ireland. But once it was one of the largest and most powerful nations in Europe.

For almost 700 years, from 1278 to 1918, Austria was ruled by a dynasty of kings and queens called the Hapsburgs. Their lands covered most of Central

AUSTRIA

Government: Parliamentary democracy
Capital: Vienna
Area: 83,849 sq km
Population: 7,867,000
Language: German
Currency: Schilling

Continued on page 58.

AUSTRALIA

Australia is the world's smallest continent. Even so it is a huge landmass, more than 30 times as big as the United Kingdom. Australia was the last continent to be discovered and settled by Europeans. Its first inhabitants were the Aborigines, who wandered its wilderness hunting and gathering food.

Much of Australia is dry, flat desert. Most of its people live along the coasts, and more than half of all Australians live in the four largest cities (Sydney, Melbourne, Brisbane and Perth). Farming is an important activity. Cattle are raised on the inland pastures, and in the east and south-east green grassy highlands provide pasture for vast numbers of sheep. Mining and manufacturing are also important.

One of the most spectacular natural wonders of Australia is the Great Barrier Reef, the largest coral reef in the world.

Australia's first European settlers came from Britain, but today the population includes people whose families came originally from other parts of Europe and South-East Asia. The country is a member of the Commonwealth of Nations and its head of state is Queen Elizabeth. Each state has its own government, but national affairs are looked after by the Federal government headed by the prime minister.

Government: Democratic, federal state system
Capital: Canberra
Area: 7,686,849 sq km
Population: 17,576,000
Language: English
Currency: Australian dollar

STATES and TERRITORIES	CAPITAL
New South Wales	Sydney
Victoria	Melbourne
Queensland	Brisbane
South Aust.	Adelaide
Western Aust.	Perth
Tasmania	Hobart
Aust. Capital Territory	Canberra
Northern Territory	Darwin

Kookaburra

Koala in eucalyptus tree

Wattle—national flower of Australia

▲ One-third of all the wool used in the world comes from Australia. Sheep stations cover thousands and thousands of square kilometres.

◄ Some of the typical emblems of Australia—the koala, the kookaburra bird and the wattle (mimosa) flower.

HISTORY OF AUSTRALIA

Prehistoric times Aborigines reach Australia, probably from Pacific islands
1432 Chinese may have landed near Darwin
1600s Dutch are first Europeans to explore Australia's coastline. They name the new land New Holland
1642 Abel Tasman (Holland) discovers Tasmania
1688 William Dampier of Britain sails along coast
1770 James Cook sights Australia
1788 First settlers (730 convicts) begin colony at Port Jackson
1790s Bass and Flinders continue British naval exploration of Australia
1817 New Holland becomes 'Australia'
1851 Gold rush in Victoria
1854 First railway in Australia. Eureka Stockade (fighting between gold miners and troops)
1860–61 Burke and Wills cross Australia from south to north but die on the return journey
1880 Capture of notorious outlaw Ned Kelly
1901 Commonwealth of Australia comes into being, uniting the various states
1927 Canberra becomes national capital
1956 Australia hosts Olympic Games
1972 Australian troops leave Vietnam after fighting alongside US soldiers and South Vietnamese in the Vietnam War

▲ An old drawing of Captain Cook landing at Botany Bay.

► The tall ships sail into Sydney harbour to commemorate the 200th anniversary of Captain Cook's landing.

For more information turn to these articles: ABORIGINE; AYERS ROCK; BANDICOOT; CANBERRA; COOK, JAMES; CRICKET; EMU; GREAT BARRIER REEF; KANGAROO; KOALA; MARSUPIALS; MELBOURNE; SYDNEY.

AZERBAIJAN

Government: In transition
Capital: Baku
Area: 87,000 sq km
Population: 7,100,000
Languages: Azeria, Turkish, Russian
Currency: Manat

Europe. They included Hungary, Czechoslovakia, large parts of Italy, Yugoslavia, Poland, Germany, Spain and the Netherlands.

The Austrian Empire collapsed after World War I. But there are many relics of the Hapsburg emperors. Vienna, the capital city, is filled with castles, beautiful buildings and churches, statues and parks.

Ayers Rock

Ayers Rock is the world's largest solitary stone. It is 440 km south-west of Alice Springs in Australia. The rock is 335 metres high and 10 km around its base. Caves at the base contain paintings and carvings made by the ancestors of today's ABORIGINES.

Azerbaijan

Azerbaijan, on the edge of the Caspian Sea, became a republic of the former Soviet Union in 1936, and declared independence in 1991. Since 1992, fighting has been going on between Azerbaijan and its neighbour, Armenia.

▼ The Aztecs built great pyramids with broad stairways leading to a temple at the top. They sacrificed many people there, usually by cutting out their heart. The Aztecs were expert craftsmen. They fashioned fine sculptures and masks, like those shown here.

Aztecs

The empire of the Aztecs was a great Indian civilization in Mexico and Central America when Spanish soldiers discovered it. A Spanish commander by the name of Hernando Cortés landed with 600 men on their shores in 1519. Within two years he had smashed the Aztec empire for ever.

Montezuma was the last ruler of the Aztecs. He was captured by Spanish soldiers soon after a small army of them arrived in his capital city. By holding him hostage, they were able to control his subjects even though they were greatly outnumbered.

Babbage, Charles

Charles Babbage (1792–1871) was a British inventor and mathematician who is often called 'the father of the computer'. In 1833 he began working on an 'analytical engine' which was intended to do any arithmetical calculation. Although Babbage's engine worked by using wheels and levers, it contained the main parts of a modern computer – including a memory. Numbers and instructions were to be fed in on punched cards.

But Babbage's invention was never completed, and the partially finished machine can be seen in the Science Museum, London

Babylon

Babylonia was one of the greatest civilizations of the ancient world. It rivalled Egypt in its splendour. Babylonia lay between the fertile valleys of the Tigris and Euphrates rivers in a region that is today called Iraq.

The first signs of civilization appeared about 3000 BC—almost 5000 years ago. At first Babylonia was a collection of small cities, each with its own

▼ A typical Babylonian house, showing how simply the people lived. Note the burial chamber on the left with the mummified figure.

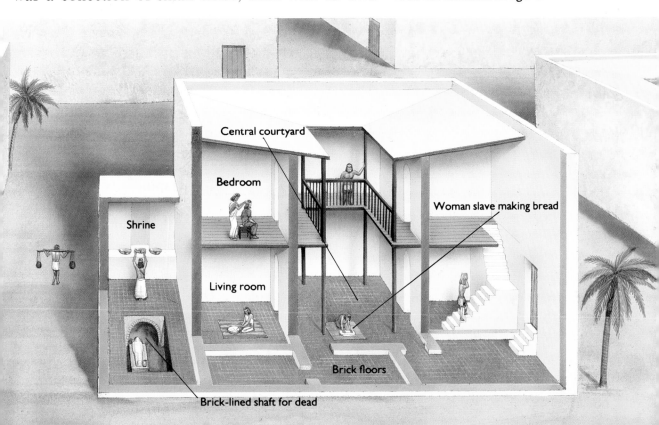

Central courtyard

Bedroom

Shrine

Woman slave making bread

Living room

Brick floors

Brick-lined shaft for dead

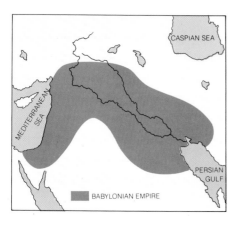

ruler. Then the city of Babylon grew more powerful and began to dominate its neighbours. Under the rule of its great king Hammurabi it became the capital of Babylonia in the 1700s BC. Hammurabi was a scholar and a poet. He drew up fair laws for his people. These set out the rights of women and children as well as many other laws.

When Hammurabi died, other tribes raided and lived in Babylon. A new king called Nebuchadnezzar built magnificent temples and palaces. He also built the Hanging Gardens of Babylon, one of the SEVEN WONDERS of the ancient world.

Bach, Johann Sebastian

Johann Sebastian Bach (1685–1750) was one of the greatest composers of all time. He was born at Eisenach in Germany, and all his family were musical. In fact, there were more than sixty musical Bachs before the family died out in the 1800s. From an early age Bach played the violin and the viola. He studied music passionately, often creeping out of bed to copy music from his brother's collection.

At the age of 38 Bach moved to Leipzig, where he lived for the rest of his life. Here he wrote some of his greatest pieces of music—mostly music for singing and for the organ.

When Bach died, his music was almost at once forgotten. No one even put up a monument to him. Almost a hundred years passed by before people began to realize what a genius Johann Sebastian Bach had been.

▲ *Bach's most famous pieces of music include the* Brandenburg Concertos, *the* Passions *and the* B Minor Mass.

In 1242 Roger Bacon produced a secret formula for gunpowder. He said that it should be made up of 41.2 parts saltpetre, 29.4 parts charcoal and 29.4 parts sulphur. Because he wanted to keep his formula secret he wrote it in the strange form of a Latin anagram that was very difficult to decipher.

Bacon, Roger

Roger Bacon (1214–1294) was a famous scientist of the MIDDLE AGES. He was born in England, but spent some time living and studying in Paris. Bacon taught that it is better to see and try things for yourself than believe everything that other people tell you. He was always experimenting.

His scientific studies were a great success. He invented the magnifying glass, and described how it might be used in both microscopes and telescopes, although neither had yet been invented.

Bacteria

Bacteria are tiny living things—so tiny that they cannot be seen by your naked eye. They are some of the simplest kinds of life.

Bacteria are more like plants than animals. They come in various shapes and sizes. Under a good MICROSCOPE it is possible to see that some are rod-like, some spiralled and others round in shape.

There are thousands of different kinds of bacteria. They are found in huge numbers almost everywhere you care to look. Some live in the SOIL. They help to break down animal and vegetable matter and thus make the soil rich. Bacteria also take the gas nitrogen from the air and turn it into forms that help plants to grow. Some bacteria even live inside our bodies. They help with the digestion of our food.

Although most bacteria are quite harmless, some can cause diseases. These kinds are known as germs. Pimples and boils are caused by bacteria. A few are even deadly once they get inside the human body.

Bacteria multiply very quickly. Some of them can divide into two every 20 minutes. From a single bacterium there can be millions of bacteria in only a few hours.

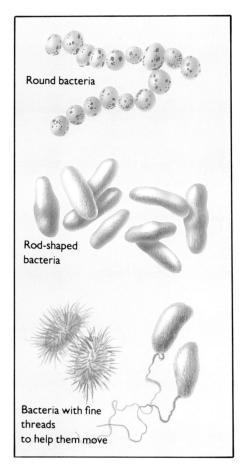

Round bacteria

Rod-shaped bacteria

Bacteria with fine threads to help them move

▲ There are many different kinds of bacteria. A few of them are shown here. There are now drugs, such as penicillin, which destroy bacteria, but because they multiply so quickly, new kinds soon develop which are not affected by the drugs.

◄ This picture of a bacterium was taken through a very powerful microscope. It is about to divide in two.

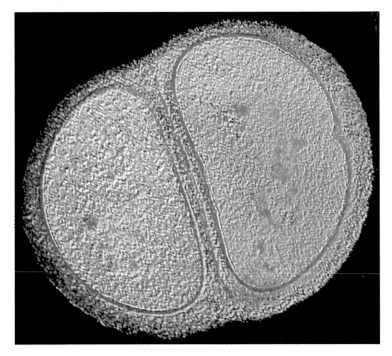

Bacteria are measured in micrometres. A micrometre is one-millionth of a metre or one-thousandth of a millimetre. Some bacteria are only 1 micrometre long. The tip of a sharp pencil would cover at least 1000 of even the largest bacteria.

Bacteria are found everywhere and can live in conditions that would kill any other organism. They have been found in the almost airless upper atmosphere; they have been found 10 km deep in the ocean. They can live in frozen soil and in boiling hot springs. Some bacteria cannot be killed except by boiling in high pressure steam for hours!

▼ Badgers live in holes in the ground called sets. They line them with bracken or other plants for bedding and stay snug inside them during the day, only coming out to eat at night.

We now have drugs which kill bacteria. *Sulphonamides* are chemicals which stop bacteria growing. Antibiotics such as penicillin destroy bacteria. But because bacteria multiply so quickly, they soon develop new kinds that are not affected by the drugs that used to kill them. Then new drugs have to be made to kill the new kinds of bacteria.

The famous French chemist Louis PASTEUR was the first to study bacteria. It was he who found out that it was bacteria that made food go bad. However, we also use bacteria to make pleasant food flavours. Cheeses and some meats are improved by 'ripening'. Harmless bacteria live in them for a while and make, for example, the green or blue parts in certain cheeses. When we put food in a refrigerator, the cold slows down the action of bacteria. The colder it is, the longer we can keep food fresh.

Badger

Badgers are big, weasel-like animals. They are common in Europe, North America and Asia.

Badgers are MAMMALS. They have thickset bodies, long blunt claws used for digging, sharp teeth and powerful jaws. A fully-grown adult badger measures about 75 cm from nose to tail and stands almost 30 cm high.

People rarely see badgers during the day. They are night creatures. After sunset they emerge from their underground dens to begin feeding. They browse on plant roots and hunt mice, rats and voles, insects, frogs and other small animals.

Badgers build elaborate underground burrows which are called *sets*. A set has several entrances, a system of long tunnels and a number of rooms. Here, the badger couple makes its home and raises from two to four young at a time.

▲ *The American badger, shown here, is smaller than the European one and is widespread in North America.*

Bahamas *See* West Indies

Bahrain

Bahrain is an independent country made up of 33 islands in the Persian Gulf. From 1820 to 1971 Bahrain was under British protection. Most of the people are employed in the oil industry, the main source of Bahrain's wealth.

Balboa, Vasco Núñez de

Vasco Núñez de Balboa (1475–1519) was a Spanish soldier and explorer who was the first European to set eyes on the Pacific Ocean in the New World.

Balboa joined a Spanish expedition to South America in 1501, exploring the north coast of the continent. After living in two Spanish colonies there, Balboa led an expedition across the Isthmus of Panama. There, from a mountaintop, he looked down upon the Pacific Ocean.

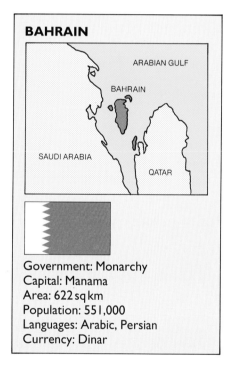

BAHRAIN

ARABIAN GULF

BAHRAIN

SAUDI ARABIA

QATAR

Government: Monarchy
Capital: Manama
Area: 622 sq km
Population: 551,000
Languages: Arabic, Persian
Currency: Dinar

Balkans

The Balkan peninsula is a mountainous region of south-eastern EUROPE. It includes the countries of GREECE, ALBANIA, former YUGOSLAVIA, ROMANIA, BULGARIA and the European part of TURKEY.

The Turks ruled much of this region for 500 years, from the 1300s to the 1800s.

It was in the Balkans that Archduke Ferdinand of Austria was assassinated in 1914. This event triggered off WORLD WAR I.

▲ Swan Lake, *by the Russian composer Tchaikovsky, is a favourite ballet of many people.*

Ballet

Ballet is a precise and beautiful form of dancing that is performed in a theatre. A kind of ballet first appeared in Italy in the 1400s, but ballet as it is danced today began in France. During the reign of King Louis XIV, in the 1600s, it was officially recognized as a form of art. The French Royal Academy of Dance was founded in 1661 to promote ballet.

Traditional, or *classical*, ballet follows strict rules and traditions. There are standard positions for the arms, legs and hands, and special movements that make the dance flow smoothly.

Classical ballet uses orchestras, elaborate scenery and splendid costumes. Many ballets tell a story, but the dancers do not speak any words. They MIME (act out) the story, using their bodies. The person who arranges the dance movements is called the *choreographer*.

Some ballets are very famous. They have been danced for many years. *Giselle*, a story of a tragic young village girl who dies in love-stricken grief, was first performed in 1841. Two other long-time favourites are *Swan Lake* and *Sleeping Beauty*. These two ballets are as famous for their music as for their dancing.

Modern ballets often look very different from classical ones. They include freer, more modern dance steps. Sometimes, instead of telling a story, they dwell on certain moods or themes. Special effects may be produced with lighting, rather than scenery.

▼ *Modern ballet often uses striking costumes and poses like this one to achieve a stunning effect.*

Balloons and Airships

Balloons and airships use lighter-than-air gases to fly. Balloons can only drift in the wind, but airships can be flown and steered.

The first manned balloon was a hot-air craft launched in 1783. It was built by two French brothers, the Montgolfiers. Their balloon was an open-ended bag. A fire was burned under the opening to fill it with hot air and hot air rises.

In the same year, the first gas-filled balloon took to the air. The gas used was HYDROGEN, and it was a simpler craft to fly. To go down, one simply opened a valve and let some gas out.

In the 1800s, manned balloons were used by the military for observations. Today, balloons are used to study the weather. Hot-air ballooning is a popular sport.

Airships

Most airships are bigger than balloons. The simplest sort looks like a cigar-shaped bag under which is slung a cabin and engines. More advanced airships have a rigid skeleton covered with fabric.

The first successful airship flew in 1852. It was

▲ *This brightly coloured balloon, built by the Montgolfier brothers, was the first one to carry passengers.*

▼ *Airships like this one were popular in the 1920s but they were slow, clumsy and often dangerous—many people lost their lives in airship accidents.*

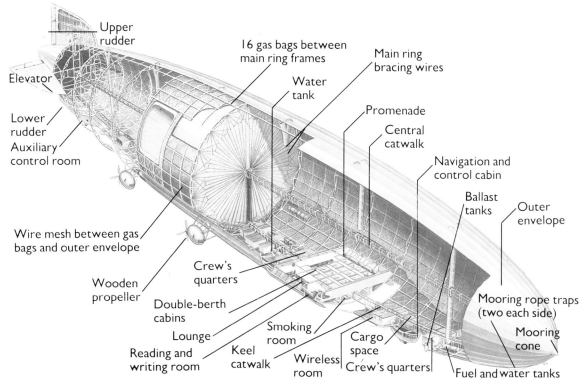

Upper rudder

Elevator

Lower rudder
Auxiliary control room

Wire mesh between gas bags and outer envelope

Wooden propeller

Crew's quarters

Double-berth cabins

Lounge

Reading and writing room

Keel catwalk

Smoking room

Wireless room

16 gas bags between main ring frames

Water tank

Cargo space

Crew's quarters

Main ring bracing wires

Promenade

Central catwalk

Navigation and control cabin

Ballast tanks

Outer envelope

Mooring rope traps (two each side)

Mooring cone

Fuel and water tanks

BALTIC STATES

ESTONIA

Government: Republic
Capital: Tallinn
Area: 45,096 sq km
Population: 1,607,000
Languages: Estonian, Russian

LATVIA

Government: Republic
Capital: Riga
Area: 64,595 sq km
Population: 2,728,000
Languages: Latvian, Russian

LITHUANIA

Government: Republic
Capital: Vilnius
Area: 65,196 sq km
Population: 3,788,000
Languages: Lithuanian, Russian

▼ A baby bandicoot climbing into its mother's pouch.

powered by a steam engine and could manage a speed of 8 km/h. During World War I, airships were used to bomb cities. In 1919, the British-built R34 made the first Atlantic crossing. In 1929 the famous *Graf Zeppelin* of Germany flew round the world. But a series of disasters brought the building of airships to an end. They were simply not safe enough for regular passenger use because they were filled with dangerous hydrogen gas. Today's airships are lifted by helium, a gas that is safer because it does not catch fire. They are used for special purposes such as advertising and filming.

Baltic States

The Baltic States, Estonia, Latvia and Lithuania, are situated north of Poland, on the Baltic Sea. Formerly part of the Russian Empire, they became independent countries in 1918. In 1940 during World War II, they were seized by the SOVIET UNION and became Soviet republics. German troops invaded and controlled the Baltic States until they were driven out by the Soviet army at the end of the war. In 1991 while the Soviet Union was in a state of turmoil, Estonia, Latvia and Lithuania declared their independence. These three States are once more free of Soviet control.

The Baltic States have kept their own languages, literature and traditions. Estonia has textile, shipbuilding and mining equipment industries. Latvia is an important producer of railway passenger coaches and telephone exchanges. Lithuania produces cattle, pigs and electrical appliances.

Bandicoot

Like kangaroos, bandicoots belong to a group of animals called MARSUPIALS. These creatures all have pouches of loose skin in which they carry their young. The bandicoot's pouch opens at the back.

Bandicoots have grey-brown coloured fur and are similar in size and shape to rats, though some can be bigger. They make their nests in underground burrows and feed on insects, worms and roots. Bandicoots live in Australia and New Guinea.

Bangladesh

Bangladesh is an Asian country that came into being in 1971. Before then it was part of PAKISTAN. It is one of the world's most densely populated countries and most of the people are very poor. In the rainy season, branches of the Ganges and Brahmaputra rivers flood the flat land. A cyclone in 1991 killed 125,000 people. Rice, jute, tea and sugarcane are the main crops. After years of military rule, a parliamentary system was adopted in 1991, but political turmoil still exists.

The biggest cities are Dhaka, the capital, and Chittagong, the main port.

Bank

Banks are companies that take people's money for safe keeping. When someone's money is first put in the bank, this is called 'opening an account'. Every time you put more money in, you make a *deposit*. If you wish to take some out, you make a *withdrawal*.

Banks do not only hold money in safety. They also make loans to people and provide other ways of making saving and spending easier.

Barbados *See* West Indies

Bark

The outer layer of WOOD on the trunk and branches of a TREE is the bark. Bark is dead wood. It is tough and waterproof and protects the living wood underneath. In this way it has the same purpose as the outer layers of skin on our bodies.

As trees grow, they form layers, or rings, of new wood and become thicker. When this new wood is formed inside a tree it pushes against the dead bark and makes it crack and peel off.

The most useful bark is probably CORK, which comes from the cork oak, a tree found in southern Europe. The cork is carefully removed from the tree and used for many different purposes. Other types of bark are used for tanning and dyeing.

BANGLADESH

Government: Parliamentary democracy
Capital: Dhaka
Area: 143,998 sq km
Population: 119,000,000
Language: Bengali
Currency: Taka

SEE IT YOURSELF
You can collect bark rubbings of different kinds of trees. You need some large sheets of fairly tough paper and a thick wax crayon. Make sure the paper can't move, then rub the crayon firmly over it. Watch the bark pattern appear. Label your rubbing with the tree's name.

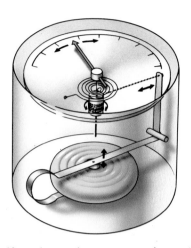

▲ *If you have a barometer at home it is probably an aneroid barometer. If the air pressure rises, it pushes in the sides of the thin metal (yellow) box. This moves the pointer around.*

Barometer

Put simply, high air pressure is a sign of good weather. Low air pressure is a sign of changing and bad weather. The barometer is used to measure such changes.

There are two kinds of barometer, the aneroid and the mercury. The aneroid is more widely used. Inside it is a flat metal box. The air inside the box is at very low pressure. The metal walls of the box are so thin they will bend very easily. They do not collapse because a spring keeps them apart.

As air pressure drops, the spring pushes the sides of the box apart. As it rises, the sides of the box are squeezed together. These movements are picked up by levers and gears that move a pointer around.

▼ *The baseball bat is narrow and round. It is therefore more difficult to hit a ball with it than with a cricket bat. The baseball bat must not be more than 107 cm long.*

Baseball

Baseball is the American national game. It began in 1845 when Alexander Cartwright organized a club in New York. Cartwright's rules said the game would consist of 9 innings, that each team would have 9 players and that the 'diamond' playing area would have four bases 90 feet apart.

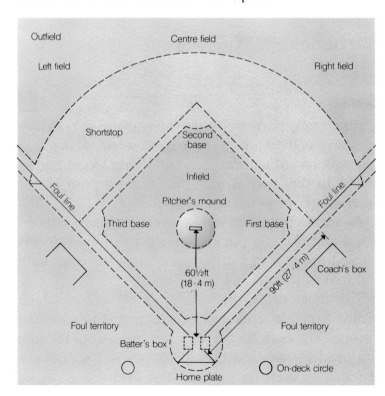

► *Baseball is played on a large field on which is marked a square. The square, known as the 'diamond', has sides 27.4 metres long. At the base of the diamond is the home plate where the batter stands.*

In the game, each batter tries to advance around the bases safely and score a run. A team bats until three players are out. The pitcher throws a *ball* when the batter does not swing and the umpire says the ball does not cross the home plate at a height between the batter's knees and his armpits. A *strike* is a pitch that crosses the plate correctly. When the batter swings at a pitch and misses or if he hits a foul ball, it is a strike. Three strikes and the batter is out. A batter can also be caught out, or he is out if a fielder picks up and throws the ball to a base before the batter reaches it.

Basketball

Basketball is an American game that has won popularity all over the world. It has been an Olympic sport since 1936. Professional basketball is played by two teams of five players each. Each team tries to score points by shooting a ball into a net, or basket. The basket is 10 feet (3 metres) from the floor and 18 inches (46 cm) in diameter at the top. The ball can be advanced by bouncing it along the floor (dribbling) or by passing it to a teammate. A player cannot take more than one step while holding the ball. The opposing players try to block him or her without making physical contact. A field goal counts two points. Free throws count one point.

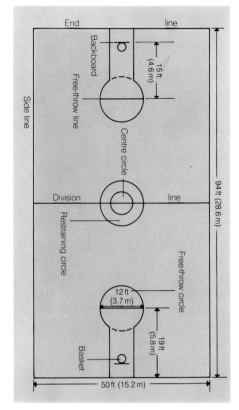

▲ Professional basketball is played on a court measuring 94 ft (28.6 m) long by 50 ft (15.2 m) wide. A match consists of two 20-minute halves, with a ten-minute interval at half time.

Bat

Bats fly like birds, yet in fact they are MAMMALS. They are the only mammals that can truly be said to fly. Their wings do not have feathers, but are made of a thin sheet of skin stretched between the long 'finger' bones. In most bats the wings are also joined to the legs and tail.

There are more than 2000 different kinds of bat. Most live in the tropics and warm parts of the world.

The biggest of all bats are the fruit-eaters or flying foxes. One, the kalong, has a wing-span of 1·5 metres. The insect-eaters are usually smaller. Their wing-span is rarely as much as 30 cm. They live in most parts of the world. Where winters are cold, they HIBERNATE.

▼ The greater horseshoe bat gets its name from the shape of its nose. It is the largest bat in Europe, being about 70 mm long.

▲ *As a bat flies, it utters a series of squeaks that are so high-pitched that few people can hear them. The sound waves from these cries bounce off objects and echo back to the bat's ears. From these echoes, the bat can tell where the objects are.*

▼ *Dry batteries are useful for supplying small quantities of electricity for torches, transistor radios and electric bells. In dry batteries, a pastelike chemical mixture is packed round a carbon rod. When the chemicals are used up the battery cannot be recharged.*

The vampire bat of South America has a very unusual way of feeding. It bites animals with its teeth and drinks their blood. However, vampires do not suck blood, they merely lap it up as it flows.

Most bats are nocturnal—they sleep in the day and fly at night. Scientists have shown in experiments that bats do not need good eyesight for flying. They find their way in the dark by using a 'sonar' system. They make high-pitched shrieks that few human ears can hear, and use the echoes bouncing off objects to tell where they are.

Battery

Batteries make electricity from chemicals stored inside them. Dry batteries such as those used in some transistor radios, torches and calculators make electricity for only a limited time. Car batteries can be recharged with electricity and used again and again. They contain pairs of lead and lead oxide plates bathed in dilute sulphuric acid. As the battery is used, the chemicals in the plates change until no more electricity is produced. But feeding an electric current into the battery changes the chemicals in the plates back to their original state. When the battery's positive and negative terminals are joined by a conductor a current flows once more.

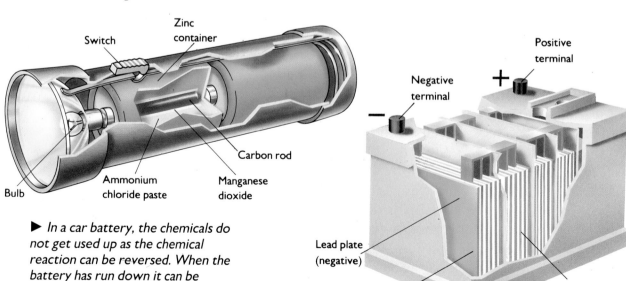

▶ *In a car battery, the chemicals do not get used up as the chemical reaction can be reversed. When the battery has run down it can be recharged by connecting it to an outside electric current.*

Battles

Some battles have played an important part in the history of the world. Others are only important to the countries that fought them. Some of the important battles that affected many countries are shown on pages 72 and 73.

▼ *The pictures in the Bayeux Tapestry were worked in eight different coloured wools on small strips of linen. Then they were sewn together into one long strip. The tapestry is kept under glass in a museum at Bayeux, France.*

Bayeux Tapestry

After WILLIAM THE CONQUEROR invaded England in 1066, one of his relations had a tapestry embroidered to record the conquest. This is known as the Bayeux Tapestry. It is a piece of LINEN 70 metres long. There are 72 colourful scenes on it telling the story of William's victory. Latin words explain what is happening in the pictures.

Bean

Beans belong to a family of plants called pulses. They are grown all over the world and have been eaten for thousands of years. There is evidence that beans were being eaten over 10,000 years ago by prehistoric people in Switzerland.

Beans are one of the cheapest and most widely eaten foods of all. They are rich in PROTEINS. Some kinds are used for animal fodder.

There are hundreds of different kinds of bean. A few of the best known varieties are the kidney, lima, broad and SOYBEANS. Some, such as soybeans, are used to make vegetable oil. They are also used in making soaps and varnishes.

SEE IT YOURSELF
Put some broad bean or runner bean seeds in a jam jar lined with blotting paper. Keep the paper moist. Soon a young root will burst from the seed. Then the young shoot will appear and grow upwards, unfurling the first leaves as it goes. These start to make food as soon as they reach the light. You can plant the seedlings in the garden when you have watched the early stages of growth.

BATTLES

War and battles are as old as mankind. It was in the Middle East more than 3500 years ago that the first effective armies appeared. In the ancient world the warriors of Egypt, Assyria, Greece and Rome were feared by their enemies. Until modern times infantry (foot soldiers) made up the bulk of most armies. The armoured corps of the armies of the past were knights on horseback, protected by metal and leather armour.

The invention of gunpowder and cannon made warfare more destructive. The Chinese used gunpowder rockets before AD 1000; in Europe, cannon were in use on the battlefield by the 1300s. Later, after the Industrial Revolution of the 1800s, came mechanized warfare—battles between war machines. Modern weapons such as missiles, aircraft and tanks have made the battlefield even more terrible than in ancient times when armies met in hand-to-hand combat.

Battles have been fought on land, in the air, and both on and beneath the sea. The most successful military commander is not always the person leading the largest force. Many famous victories have been won against seemingly hopeless odds. Some battles have decided the course of history and the destiny of nations.

◄ The sea battle of Salamis was fought in 480 BC between the Greeks and Persians. The Greeks, with 380 ships, defeated a Persian fleet of up to 1000 oared galleys.

SOME FAMOUS BATTLES

Marathon 490 BC 10,000 Greeks defeated 60,000 Persians
Tours AD 732 Franks defeated Arabs
Hastings 1066 Normans led by William defeated Saxons and conquered England
Agincourt 1415 English led by Henry V defeated much larger French army
Constantinople 1453 Turks overran Byzantine Empire
Armada 1588 English fleet defeated Spanish invasion
Blenheim 1704 During War of Spanish Succession, Marlborough's British-Austrian army defeated French and Bavarians
Yorktown 1781 Americans defeated British to win independence
Trafalgar 1805 Nelson's British fleet defeated combined French-Spanish fleet
Waterloo 1815 Napoleon's final defeat by Allies, led by Wellington
Alamo 1836 Heroic defence by Texans against Mexicans
Balaclava 1854 Battle between Allies (Britain, France and Turkey) and Russia, famous for the Charge of the Light Brigade
Gettysburg 1863 North defeated South in crucial battle of American Civil War
Little Big Horn 1876 Sioux Indians defeated US cavalry
Somme 1916 Bloodiest battle of World War I
Jutland 1916 Only major sea battle between British and Germans during World War I
Alamein 1942 Montgomery's British army drove Rommel's German army out of North Africa: World War II
Stalingrad 1942–43 Germans failed to capture city from Soviets
Leyte Gulf 1944 Largest sea battle of World War II between US and Japanese navies. US broke Japanese sea power
Dien Bien Phu 1954 Vietnamese defeated French

RECORD BATTLES

Longest siege: Leningrad (USSR), 880 days from August 1941 to January 1944
Largest retreat: Dunkirk, May 1940: 338,000 Allied troops evacuated from France
Bloodiest: First battle of the Somme, 1916: more than one million casualties
Longest war: Hundred Years' War, 1346–1453, between England and France
Shortest modern war: Six Day War, 5–10 June 1967, between Israelis and Arabs

▲ The Battle of Gettysburg, fought in 1863 between North and South in the American Civil War, was a turning point in the war.

◄ An American pilot destroys a German observation balloon during the battle of the Marne in World War I.

▼ A modern Swedish self-propelled gun.

...or more information turn to these articles: CIVIL WAR; CRIMEAN WAR; HASTINGS, BATTLE OF; HUNDRED YEARS' WAR; REVOLUTIONARY WAR, ...MERICAN; WORLD WAR I; WORLD WAR II.

▲ The sloth bear, also called the honey bear, lives in the forests of India and Sri Lanka.

▲ The brown bear was once common in Europe and Northern Asia, but is now much rarer.

▲ The polar bear lives in the Arctic. It is one of the biggest bears.

Bear

Bears are found in most parts of the world except for Australia and Africa. They are some of the biggest meat-eaters on Earth.

The largest of all bears are the brown bears of Alaska. These can reach a weight of over 750 kg. Other giants include the polar bear of the Arctic and the grizzly of western North America.

The only bear that lives in South America is the small spectacled bear. Its name comes from the ring-like markings around its eyes.

The smallest bear in the world is the sun bear of the jungles of South-East Asia. It weighs no more than 65kg.

Bears can be slow, lumbering beasts. They have short, powerful limbs and heavy, broad heads with powerful jaws. They also have long, dangerous claws for digging and tearing.

Bears do not have very sharp eyesight, but their sense of smell is very good. Although they look clumsy, all but the biggest bears can climb trees.

Bears eat almost anything. They browse on leaves, roots, berries, fruit and nuts. They enjoy eating honey and ants and often attack beehives and anthills. They also eat other insects, and catch fish and small animals.

Bears are usually shy, but if they are disturbed and cornered they will attack fiercely.

Beaver

Beavers are big RODENTS more than a metre long, including the tail, and weigh more than 25 kg. They live in woods by the side of lakes and rivers and are good swimmers. Beavers are able to stay under water for up to 15 minutes. They have a broad, flat tail covered in scaly skin. This is used for steering when they swim.

Beavers need pools to build their homes in, and often block up, or dam, streams with mud and sticks to make one. They cut down small trees with their sharp teeth and drag them to the pool to strengthen the dam.

They build a home of mud and sticks by the side

◄ *The beaver's hind feet are webbed like a duck's, making it a powerful swimmer. The animal cuts down trees with its strong front teeth and trims off branches to build its island home.*

of the pool. This home, called a lodge, has an underwater entrance and an escape hole. Inside, there is a nest above water for the young beavers.

Beavers eat bark, mainly from alder and willow trees. They store twigs in their homes to feed on during the winter. Beavers have thick fur which keeps them warm. They live in many parts of North America and Europe.

Becket, Thomas à

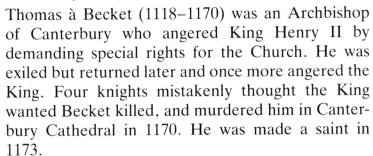

Thomas à Becket (1118–1170) was an Archbishop of Canterbury who angered King Henry II by demanding special rights for the Church. He was exiled but returned later and once more angered the King. Four knights mistakenly thought the King wanted Becket killed, and murdered him in Canterbury Cathedral in 1170. He was made a saint in 1173.

Bee

There are many different kinds of bee, but the best known kind is the honey bee. Honey bees live in hives or colonies of about 50,000 worker bees. Worker bees are female but they do not breed. Each colony also has a queen bee which breeds, and a few hundred stingless drones which are male.

A bee can see the colours green, blue and ultra-violet, the last of which is invisible to us. But pure red is no colour to a bee. It sees red objects as black.

A bee must visit over 4000 flowers in order to make a tablespoon of honey.

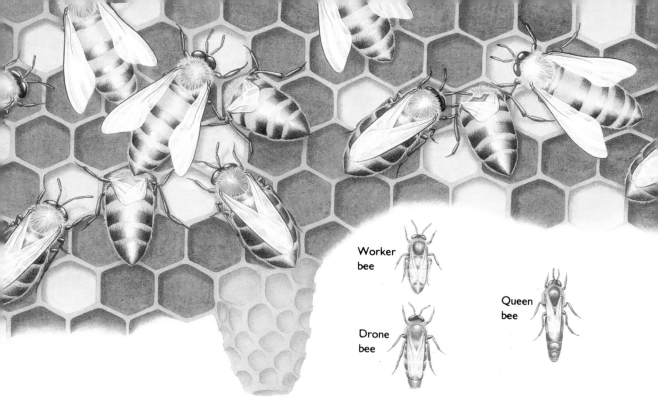

Worker bee

Drone bee

Queen bee

▲ inside the hive of the honey bee are cells made of wax. The queen lays eggs in the cells. Larvae hatch out of the eggs and are fed by the workers. Worker bees collect nectar and pollen from flowers. The nectar is made into honey, which is stored in the hive for food.

The worker bee's life is very short, usually about four weeks, so the queen has to lay many eggs to provide enough bees. She can lay up to 1500 eggs in one day. From time to time a new queen is born. The old queen then leaves the hive with a *swarm* of about half the workers to seek another home.

The workers collect *pollen* and nectar from flowers. The nectar is made into honey. It is stored in the hive to feed the bees in winter. Beekeepers carefully remove the honey from the hive. They give the bees sugar syrup to replace the honey they take.

There are other types of bee which do not live in large colonies. These are called solitary bees. They produce a small family of a few hundred bees which die each winter. The queen hibernates and produces a new family the following year.

▲ When Beethoven was young he studied under Mozart and Haydn.

Beethoven, Ludwig Van

Ludwig van Beethoven (1770–1827) was a German musician who composed some of the greatest music ever known. This included symphonies, concertos, choral and chamber music. When he was young, Beethoven was well-known as a pianist and was admired by many famous people. He began to go deaf at the age of 30 but continued to compose music even when he was totally deaf.

Beetle

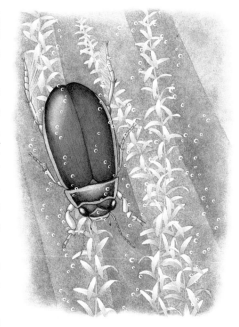

Beetles are INSECTS. There are over 300,000 species of beetle known.

Some beetles are as small as a pinhead. Others are very large. The giant African goliath beetle measures up to 10 cm long and can weigh 100 grams.

In prehistoric times all beetles had two pairs of wings. But over millions of years the front pair changed, or *evolved*, into hard, close-fitting coverings for the second pair underneath. All beetles used to be flying insects but now many of them live on the ground.

Beetles start their lives as eggs which hatch into grubs, or larvae. The larvae then turn into chrysalises, or pupae, before the adult beetles emerge.

Many beetles and their larvae are destructive pests. Woodworms, weevils, wireworms, cockroaches, Colorado and flea beetles do great damage to crops, trees and buildings.

Some beetles can be very useful. Ladybirds are small beetles which eat harmful insects such as greenflies. Dung beetles and burying beetles clear away dung and dead animals.

▲ The great diving beetle catches its prey at the bottom of ponds and streams.

▲ The Colorado beetle is a pest that ruins potato crops.

◀ Burying beetles bury the corpses of small birds and mammals by digging soil from under them. They lay their eggs on the buried animal and the grubs feed on it.

Beijing (Peking)

Beijing, formerly called Peking, is the capital of China. In AD 1267 the Mongol conqueror Kublai Khan made it the capital of his empire. In the centre of the city is the walled Forbidden City containing the palace of the ancient Chinese emperors. Modern Beijing is a centre of industry and learning. Its population is more than 6,000,000.

In 1267 Beijing was called **Khanbalik** ('City of the **Khan'). In 1421 it was given the name Peking** ('Northern **Capital'). In the modern system used for translating Chinese 'Peking' is written 'Beijing'.**

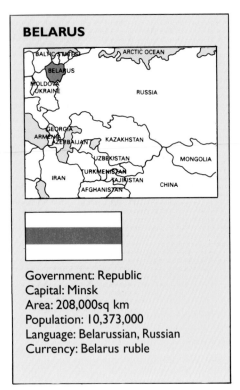

BELARUS

Government: Republic
Capital: Minsk
Area: 208,000sq km
Population: 10,373,000
Language: Belarussian, Russian
Currency: Belarus ruble

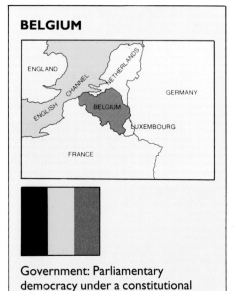

BELGIUM

Government: Parliamentary democracy under a constitutional monarch
Capital: Brussels
Area: 30,513 sq km
Population: 10,016,000
Languages: Flemish; French
Currency: Belgian franc

Belarus

Belarus became independent when the Soviet Union dissolved in 1991. It is in Northern Europe, bordered by Poland, the Baltic States, Ukraine and Russia. Much of the country is forested and timber is a major industry. Food processing industries such as dairy products, canning and bottling are also important.

Belgium

Belgium is a small country sandwiched between France, Germany and Holland. Its capital is Brussels. Belgium's population is made up of two main groups: the Germanic Flemings of the north, and the French-speaking Walloons of the south. Because of its central and strategic position, Belgium has been invaded and fought over throughout the course of European history. Today the headquarters of the EUROPEAN UNION (EU) and NATO are both in Brussels.

Belize

Belize is a small country on the east coast of Central America. It was Great Britain's last American mainland colony, becoming independent in 1981. The capital is Belmopan and the main export is sugar.

Bell, Alexander Graham

Alexander Graham Bell (1847–1922) was the inventor of the TELEPHONE. Through his work with devices to help the deaf, Bell became interested in sending voices over long distances. On March 10, 1876, the first sentence was transmitted by telephone.

Benin

Benin is a small country in West Africa, known from 1960 to 1975 as Dahomey. The climate is mostly hot and humid and the people are poor. Benin's economy depends very largely on one crop: the palm kernel. Benin became independent from France in 1960.

Berlin

Berlin is the largest city in GERMANY and, since re-unification, is the capital of all of Germany. In 1945, when Germany was divided into two countries, East and West, Berlin was divided into four zones between the Americans, British, French and Russians.

In 1948 the Russians quarrelled with the other allies and blockaded the city by cutting its road and rail links with West Germany. But Britain and the USA flew in supplies to keep the city going. After a year the Russians gave up and re-opened the roads and railways. Berlin was largely destroyed by bombing during World War II, but at the end of the war rebuilding was rapid.

Today West and East Berlin are almost completely rebuilt. The Berlin Wall, built by the communists in 1961 to divide the eastern and western parts of the city, was broken down by the East German authorities in 1989.

BELIZE

Government: Parliamentary
Capital: Belmopan
Area: 22,965 sq km
Population: 190,000
Languages: English; Spanish
Currency: Belize dollar

◀ *The Brandenburg Gate is on the dividing line between the former East and West Berlin. This picture was taken when Berlin was a divided city.*

Bernhardt, Sarah

Sarah Bernhardt (1844–1923) was one of the most famous actresses of her time. Her excellent speaking voice won her the admiration of audiences everywhere she went. She acted in many countries, though France was her home. After studying at the

BENIN

Government: Republic
Capital: Porto-Novo
Area: 112,622 sq km
Population: 4,997,000
Language: French
Currency: CFA franc

BHUTAN

Government: Monarchy
Capital: Thimphu
Area: 47,000 sq km
Population: 1,660,000
Language: Dzongkha
Currency: Ngultrum

Paris Conservatory, her acting career began in 1862 at the Comédie-Française. She became best known around the world for her performance in *Camille*, a play by Alexandre Dumas.

Bhutan

Bhutan is a mountainous country lying on the slopes of the Himalayas between Tibet and Assam. The government is under a king, a position handed down from father to son. The country became independent of Britain in 1949 and India now helps Bhutan with foreign relations and money. The capital is Thimphu and the population is about 1,600,000.

Bible

The Bible is the sacred book of the Judaeo-Christian religion. It is in two parts. The first is called the Old Testament and records the history of the Jewish people and the teachings of their prophets before the birth of Jesus. The second part, the New Testament, records the life and sayings of Jesus and his disciples.

▶ *The caves at Qumran, on the shores of the Dead Sea, in which over a hundred scrolls of Old Testament books have been found.*

The Bible has always been the best-selling book. More than 2½ billion copies have been sold since 1816. It has been translated into more than 1500 languages.

Bicycle

The bicycle is a two-wheeled vehicle powered by its rider, who turns two pedals by foot. The earliest bicycles, called 'dandy-horses', were invented in the 1700s. They were simply two wheels joined by a rod, with a seat on top. The rider pushed it along the ground by foot.

The first bicycle with pedals did not appear until 1865. These machines were known as 'bone-shakers' because the seats had no springs. The next important development was the 'penny farthing', which had an enormous front wheel and a tiny rear wheel. The modern style of bicycle appeared in the 1880s. It had a chain-driven rear wheel and air-filled tyres, and this basic style has changed very little since then except for the addition of gears.

▲ *In 1817 Karl von Drais built his 'dandyhorse', or 'draisine'. It had no pedals, and the rider pushed it along by foot.*

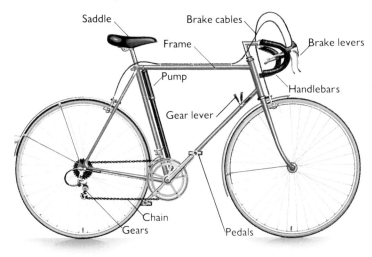

Saddle
Frame
Pump
Gear lever
Chain
Gears
Brake cables
Brake levers
Handlebars
Pedals

▲ *The Matchless ordinary bicycle, produced in 1883, was a 'penny farthing'. It had solid tyres and a step to help the rider get on.*

◀ *A modern bicycle may have as many as 10 or 15 gears.*

Binary System

The binary system is a number system that uses only two numerals—0 and 1. Our everyday *decimal system* uses ten numerals—0 to 9. In the decimal system you multiply a number by 10 by moving it one place to the left—2, 20, 200 etc. In the binary system, when you move a numeral one place to the left you multiply its value by two. A 1 by itself is 1. Move it a place to the left and it becomes 1 times 2, or 2. It is written 10. Move it another place to the left and it becomes 1 times 2 times 2, or 4. It is written 100. The binary for 93 is 1011101—one 1, no 2s, one 4, one 8, one 16, no 32s, and one 64.

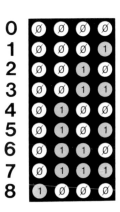

▲ *A diagram of the binary system, in which the numerals 1 and 0 are used to represent all numbers.*

Biochemistry is a vast subject. Some biochemists are busy designing new drugs. Others are searching in the muscles to find molecules that expand and contract like tiny rubber bands. Still others are trying to find out which chemicals existed in the oceans when the Earth was new. They want to find out how life first began.

▼ *Biologists study all living things and how they are related to each other. Green plants store energy in the form of food, which is eaten by animals. Dead leaves are recycled in the soil. The droppings of plant-eating animals are also recycled. Nothing is wasted in the system. Even the lion is recycled when it dies.*

Biochemistry

Biochemistry is the study of the chemical reactions that take place inside tiny cells that make up all living things. Biochemists find out about the food people must eat to be healthy. They help fight disease by making chemicals that kill harmful bacteria. They also help farmers by finding out what foods are needed by plants and animals.

Biochemists also study special molecules in living things called *nucleic acids*. One kind of nucleic acid—DNA (deoxyribonucleic acid)—is found in the nucleus of cells. It carries and passes on the plan of a living thing from one generation to the next. It is the substance that makes each human being different from any other person that has ever lived. Biochemists are finding out more and more about the chemistry that makes us what we are.

Biology

Biology is the study of living things, from the tiniest amoeba, which consists of just one CELL, to a mighty oak tree or a human being. The part of biology that deals with the PLANT world is called BOTANY. The study of ANIMALS is called zoology. One of the earliest biologists was the ancient Greek thinker ARISTOTLE, who was the first to dissect, or cut open, and classify animals.

There was little interest in biology for more than a thousand years, until the RENAISSANCE, when scholars and artists such as LEONARDO DA VINCI tried to discover how living things grew and worked. At first

Energy from the Sun

Energy 'fixers'

Plant food

Plant–eaters

Meat

Meat–eaters

Nutrients

Droppings

Droppings

Decomposers

the study of the human body by dissection was frowned upon by the Church. But this changed after the 1500s, and William HARVEY was able to show how the BLOOD travels around the body, and other people were able to compare the structure of various animals with that of man.

The invention of the MICROSCOPE in the 1600s opened up whole new areas of study for biologists. They were able to learn more about the animal and plant cells that are the building blocks of life. The study of other microscopic organisms, such as BACTERIA, helped people like Louis PASTEUR understand more about disease and how to prevent it.

In the 1800s the English naturalist Charles DARWIN revolutionized biology with his theory of EVOLUTION. Today biology is divided into dozens of separate sciences. Biologists can spend their entire careers studying one tiny part of living matter.

Bird

Birds come in all shapes and sizes, but they all have wings and feathers. Some birds can fly thousands of kilometres. Others, such as the OSTRICH and the PENGUIN, cannot fly at all. The ostrich is the largest

▼ There are many different kinds of bird. Tropical birds, such as the macaw and the bird of paradise, are often brightly coloured. The emperor penguin is a flightless bird but an excellent swimmer. It finds its food under water, as does the flamingo, a wading bird.

Gold and blue macaw

Lesser bird of Paradise

Little owl

Green woodpecker

Robin

Long–tailed tit

Magpie

Hoopoe

Wren

Rosy flamingo

Emperor penguin

BIRD

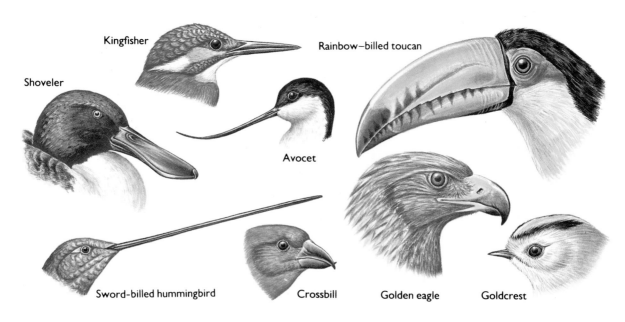

Shoveler

Kingfisher

Rainbow–billed toucan

Avocet

Sword-billed hummingbird

Crossbill

Golden eagle

Goldcrest

▲ *Birds' beaks are well suited to their feeding habits. The hummingbird, for example, probes for nectar, the crossbill cracks seeds and the golden eagle tears flesh with its beak.*

SEE IT YOURSELF
A bird table will attract lots of birds to your garden. Try making one for yourself. The tray should be about two metres from the ground to prevent cats from leaping onto it. Put the table near a window so you can watch it from inside. You can hang up a bit of fresh coconut for blue tits and great tits.

bird. It can weigh more than 150 kg. The smallest bird, a HUMMINGBIRD, weighs less than 2 grams.

Birds developed from scaly REPTILES that lived about 180,000,000 years ago. Their scales changed over millions of years into feathers, and their front legs became wings. Birds have hollow bones for lightness in the air and strong breast muscles for working their wings. Large birds can flap their wings slowly and float, or hover, on air currents. Small birds need to flap their wings fast to stay in the air.

All birds lay EGGS. Most birds are busy parents who work hard to rear their young. Some, like the CUCKOO, lay their eggs in other birds' nests for foster parents to rear. Other birds bury their eggs in warm places and leave them. Most birds are wild but some, such as chickens, pigeons and canaries, have been tamed or *domesticated*. Some birds are bred on farms for their eggs and meat.

Birds' beaks have many different shapes. Sparrow-hawks have hooked beaks for tearing up their prey. Blue tits have short beaks for eating small nuts, seeds and insects. The nuthatch has a powerful, pointed beak for breaking open nuts.

Blackbirds have sharp beaks for digging up worms and slugs. The strange-looking crossbill has a crossed beak for tearing open pine cones to reach the kernels inside. Nightjars have short, wide beaks for snapping up moths and other night-flying insects on the wing.

Wading birds, such as the oyster-catcher, have long, thin beaks for probing in the mud. Many birds have beaks adapted for one kind of food only, but others such as the sparrow and the thrush thrive on a mixed diet.

Birth Control

Birth control is the means by which people can choose the number of children they have. It is sometimes known as 'family planning'. Birth control has been used since ancient times but modern methods did not become widespread until the 1800s and 1900s.

There are many methods of birth control. Some of them work by stopping the seed, or *sperm*, of the male from fertilizing the EGG, or *ovum*, of the female. This is known as *contraception*.

Some people are forbidden by their religion to use certain kinds of birth control. However, birth control is now encouraged in many countries with large populations.

▲ A bird skeleton, with hollow and lightweight bones. The breastbone is deep and large.

Bison

The bison is a large animal of the cattle family. Its head and humped shoulders are covered in long shaggy hair.

There are two kinds of bison, the American and the European. There used to be great herds of bison in North America. The Indians were the first people

▼ Once huge herds of bison roamed the prairies of North America. They were hunted by Plains Indians, who depended upon them for food, clothing and for their 'buffalo-hide' tepees.

It is difficult to imagine just how terrible the effects of the Black Death were. The English population fell from 3¾ million in 1348 to just over 2 million in 1400.

to hunt them. When Europeans went to America they killed great numbers of bison until, by 1889, there were only about 500 left. Today, there are no bison living in the wild in America and Europe. Those that survive all live in parks and zoos.

Black Death

The Black Death was a terrible disease which was at its worst during the MIDDLE AGES. In one outburst in the 1300s, 25 million people died of the disease. About a third of all the people in Europe were killed by it. The Black Death is now known as bubonic PLAGUE. It is carried by the FLEAS on RATS. The fleas suck the blood of a rat with the disease. When the fleas next bite another rat or a person, the disease is passed on. It spreads very quickly.

A black hole turns space inside out. From outside it might appear to be a round black object only a few kilometres across. But if you were inside it, it would seem as big as a universe. You could not see anything outside it.

Black Hole

Stars are made up mostly of hydrogen. It is the turning of this hydrogen into helium that makes stars like our Sun shine and give out heat. When a massive star uses up all its hydrogen fuel, it collapses. This collapse is called a *supernova* explosion. All that is left after such an explosion is a tiny star only a few kilometres across—a *neutron star*. The material in a neutron star is so squashed together— so dense—that a pinhead-sized piece of it would

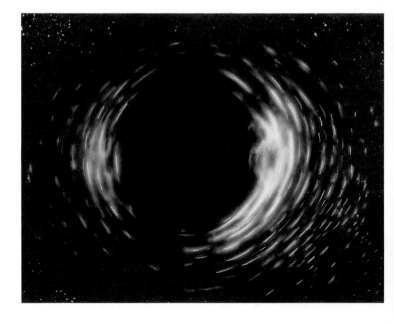

▶ *A close-up view of a black hole might appear like this – a pattern of bright light around its edge. The light, coming from distant stars behind the black hole, has been 'bent' by the extra strong gravitational force around the hole.*

weigh as much as a large building! The GRAVITY of some neutron stars is so great that even light waves find it impossible to escape from them. As the light waves cannot get out, we call them *black holes*. Because these strange objects are entirely black, astronomers have never actually seen one, but they have found stars that could have an invisible black hole nearby. There could be a huge black hole at the centre of our Milky Way Galaxy.

▼ *Louis Blériot made his epic flight across the English Channel in a monoplane which he had designed and built, powered by an Anzani engine.*

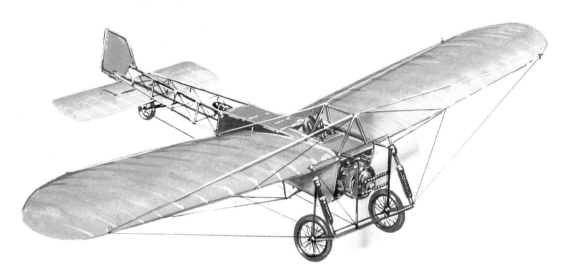

Blériot, Louis

Louis Blériot (1872–1936) was a famous French airman. He was a pioneer of aviation and designed and built a number of early aeroplanes. On July 25, 1909, he took off from Calais in one of his own AIRCRAFT. Twenty-seven minutes later he touched down at Dover, becoming the first man to fly the English Channel. In doing so he won a prize of £1000 offered by the London *Daily Mail* newspaper. Blériot went on to design other aircraft and became the owner of a large aircraft company.

Blood

Blood is the fluid that nourishes our bodies and removes waste products. It takes in food from the digestive system, and OXYGEN from the LUNGS, and carries them to all the CELLS in the body. Each cell takes exactly what it needs from the blood and the blood carries away cell waste, including water and

▼ *Blood is made up of red and white blood cells. Red cells carry oxygen to all parts of the body. White cells fight harmful bacteria. Platelets help blood to clot in a wound, stopping bleeding and sealing the wound against bacteria.*

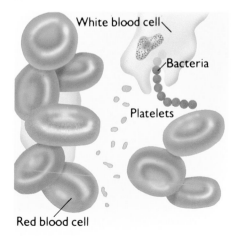

White blood cell

Bacteria

Platelets

Red blood cell

BLOOD

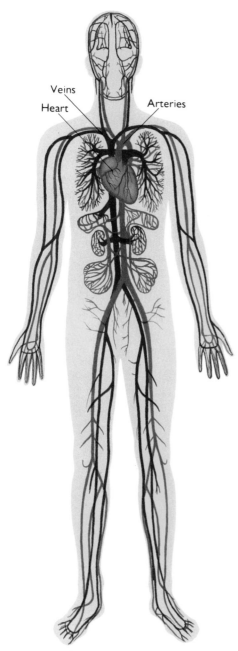

Veins
Heart
Arteries

▲ *The heart pumps blood round the body, through a system of arteries, veins and capillaries.*

carbon dioxide. Blood also carries special body chemicals to where they are needed. And it kills germs and keeps the body at the right temperature.

Blood is made in the marrow of the bones. The adult human body contains about five litres of blood. This blood is made up of a pale liquid called *plasma*, and millions of cells, or *corpuscles*. Corpuscles are tiny red discs that give the blood its colour. The blood also contains white corpuscles. There are about 5 million red corpuscles and between 5000 and 10,000 white corpuscles in every tiny cubic millimetre of blood.

Fighting Disease
White corpuscles attack germs that enter the body by absorbing them. Often many white corpuscles are killed in the fight against disease or infection. Large numbers of dead white corpuscles collect as *pus*. Other blood particles, called *platelets*, help our blood to clot when we bleed. This helps scratches and other wounds to heal more quickly.

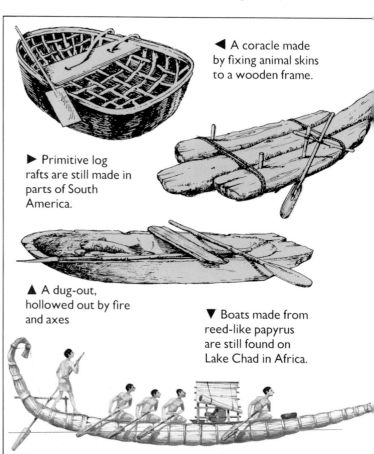

◀ A coracle made by fixing animal skins to a wooden frame.

▶ Primitive log rafts are still made in parts of South America.

▲ A dug-out, hollowed out by fire and axes

▼ Boats made from reed-like papyrus are still found on Lake Chad in Africa.

We can all be classified into blood groups A, B, AB, or O, according to the type of blood we have. Blood groups are important when patients are given blood transfusions. Transfusions are given to replace either diseased blood, or blood that has been lost through an injury. The blood a person is given is generally the same blood type as their own.

Boat

Boats, unlike SHIPS, are usually small, open craft, although the name is sometimes given to larger vessels such as the motor torpedo boat. The first boats date back to prehistoric times, and were simply floating logs or driftwood paddled with the hands. The first real boats appeared later. One was the dug-out canoe, which was a log hollowed out by fire or stone tools. Another was a raft made of logs or bundles of reeds tied together. When there were no logs or reeds, boats were made of skins stretched over a light framework. Small round boats called

Our red blood cells live for about 127 days. About 8000 of them are destroyed and replaced every hour. An adult's body contains about 4.7 litres of blood, running through more than 96,000 kilometres of blood vessels. One cubic centimetre of blood contains as many as 512 billion red cells and about 11 million white cells.

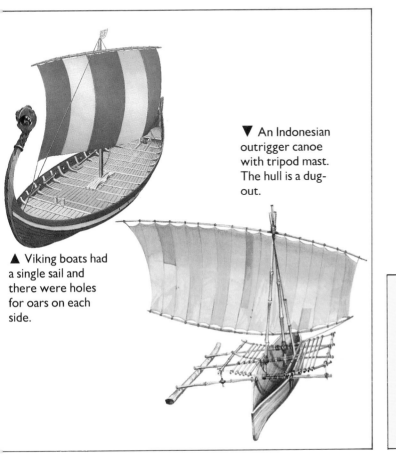

▼ An Indonesian outrigger canoe with tripod mast. The hull is a dug-out.

▲ Viking boats had a single sail and there were holes for oars on each side.

Sailing boats can, given the right conditions, achieve very high speeds. The world sailing record is 66.8 km/h over a 500-metre course, achieved by an outrigger craft in 1980. Even higher speeds have been reached by windsurfers.

▲ *Fishing boats change little over the years. These were pictured at Mevagissey in Cornwall.*

coracles and Eskimo kayaks were made in this way.

After a while the dug-out and the raft were built up with sides of wooden planks to make them drier and sturdier. A keel was added at the bottom to make the boat more seaworthy. Different types and shapes of sails were fitted so as to catch as much wind as possible. Until the 1800s, all boats were driven by sails, oars or poles, but the invention of the STEAM ENGINE made paddle wheels and propellers possible. Today, motor boats, sailing boats, canoes and rowing boats are used by people all over the world.

Every Boy Scout and Girl Guide in the world knows the name Baden-Powell. Robert Baden-Powell was in command of the town of Mafeking during its 217-day siege by the Boers during the Boer War. When the town was freed, Baden-Powell returned to England a hero. In 1910 he retired from the army and devoted the rest of his life to the Scouting movement.

Boer War

The Boer War (1899–1902) was fought in SOUTH AFRICA between the Boers—settlers of Dutch descent—and the British. The slow and badly-led British troops were no match for the fast and lightly-armed Boers in the early days of the war. But in the end Britain's overwhelming strength won. There were about 450,000 soldiers in the British armies during the Boer War, and only about 60,000 Boers.

Bolivia

Bolivia is a land-locked country in central SOUTH AMERICA, west of Brazil. Most of Bolivia is an enormous plain stretching from the Brazilian border to the eastern foothills of the Andes Mountains. High in the Andes lies the great Bolivian plateau, over 4000 metres high. Two-thirds of Bolivia's people live here. The capital is La Paz, the highest capital in the world, and Lake Titicaca, at 3812 metres above sea level, is one of the highest lakes in the world.

Spain ruled Bolivia from 1532 until 1825. It gained freedom from Spain with the help of Simón Bolívar, a Venezuelan general, after whom Bolivia is named. More than half the people are Indians, a third are *mestizos* (people who are part European, part Indian) and the rest are direct descendants of Europeans. Bolivia is the world's second largest producer of tin, and mining is the country's most valuable industry.

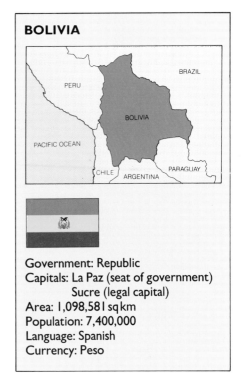

BOLIVIA

Government: Republic
Capitals: La Paz (seat of government)
Sucre (legal capital)
Area: 1,098,581 sq km
Population: 7,400,000
Language: Spanish
Currency: Peso

Bone

Bones make up the hard framework that supports the flesh and organs of all vertebrates (animals with backbones). All bones are made up of the same thing, mostly calcium. Bones are hard on the outside but soft on the inside. Bone *marrow*, in the hollow centre of the bone, is where new red BLOOD cells are made.

The human skeleton has four kinds of bones: long bones, such as arm and leg bones; flat bones such as the skull; short bones, including ankle and wrist bones; and irregular bones, such as those that make up the backbone. If bones are broken they will knit together again if they are rejoined or *set* properly. The cells in the broken ends of the bone produce a substance that helps the ends to grow together again so that the mended bone is as strong as it ever was. But as human beings get older their bones become more brittle and will break more easily. Children's bones, on the other hand, are able to bend a little and are not so easily broken or injured. Adults have about 206 bones in their skeleton.

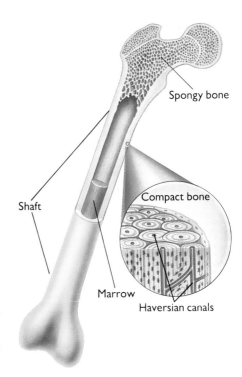

▼ Bones may look lifeless, but they are a mass of living cells. The Haversian canals contain blood vessels.

Spongy bone

Shaft

Compact bone

Marrow

Haversian canals

▼ *A medieval illuminated manuscript. Before the invention of printing, books were copied out and often elaborately decorated by hand.*

Book

Books are used for storing and passing on all kinds of knowledge, ideas and stories. Some of the earliest books were made by the ancient Egyptians. These were written by hand on rolls of paper made from the papyrus plant.

By the time of the Roman Empire many books were handwritten on parchment or *vellum*. This material was made from animal skin. It was cut into sheets which were fastened together to look much the same as a modern book. During the MIDDLE AGES monks made many beautiful books. They were decorated, or *illuminated*, by hand with bright colours and sometimes gold and silver.

In the 1400s PRINTING on paper was introduced to Europe. At first this was very slow because much of the work still had to be done by hand. Then Johannes GUTENBERG invented a machine with movable type which could print books quickly. Today, many millions of books are produced every year, in all the languages of the world.

Boomerang

The boomerang is a wooden throwing stick used mainly by the Australian ABORIGINES. There are two kinds. One is very heavy and is thrown straight at the target. The other is lighter. It is shaped in a special way so that when it is skilfully thrown it is possible to make it return to the thrower.

BOSNIA AND HERZEGOVINA

Government: Republic
Capital: Sarajevo
Area: 51,125 sq km
Population: 4,365,000
Language: Serbo-Croat
Currency: Dinar

Bosnia and Herzegovina

Bosnia and Herzegovina was formerly a republic of YUGOSLAVIA, but became independent in 1992. Its people are Croats, Muslims and Serbs. Fighting broke out between the Bosnians and the Serbian-dominated Yugoslav army as the Serbs attempted to make Bosnia and Herzegovina part of Yugoslavia again. Muslims and Croats were forced out of parts of Bosnia conquered by the Serbs. This was called 'ethnic cleansing'.

A peace agreement was signed in 1995, with NATO troops remaining to police the fragile accord.

Botany

Botany is the study of PLANTS and how they grow. There are more than 300,000 different kinds of plants. They vary from tiny *algae* that can be seen only with a microscope, to giant redwood trees nearly 100 metres high. New kinds of plants are being discovered all the time.

Without plants there would be no animals, because animals depend on plants for all their food. There would be no cattle for us to eat if there was no grass for the cattle to eat. Animals also breathe the gas OXYGEN that plants give out.

By studying the way in which the qualities of one generation of plants are passed on to the next generation, scientists are able to grow bigger and better crops. They can breed varieties that are better at fighting plant disease.

In 1753 Carl von Linné (known as Linnaeus), a Swedish botanist, invented the first real system for naming plants. He gave every plant a name made up of two Latin words.

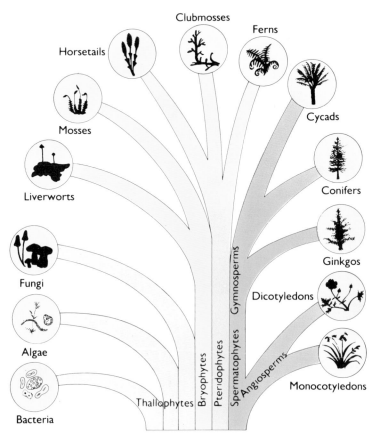

◀ Plants are classified, or grouped, into four main divisions, which are further subdivided. For example, the flowering plants, or angiosperms, are divided into two groups – dicotyledons and monocotyledons – according to the number of seed leaves they have.

BOTSWANA

Government: Republic, parliamentary democracy
Capital: Gaborone
Area: 581,730 sq km
Population: 1,300,000
Languages: English, Setswana
Currency: Pula

▼ *Queen Boudicca led her people into battle against heavily armed Roman forces. Half of Britain joined Boudicca in the rebellion.*

Botswana

Botswana is an African country that lies far from the sea. It is bordered by Zimbabwe, South Africa and Namibia. In 1885, the country, then called Bechuanaland, came under British control. Independence came in 1966. Botswana is a hot, dry country that includes the Kalahari Desert. Cattle raising and mining are the main industries. The capital is Gaborone.

Boudicca

Boudicca – often called Boadicea – was the ruler of the Iceni, a Celtic British tribe, in about AD 60. She became ruler of the Iceni when her husband died. But the Roman rulers in Britain said that the Iceni kingdom should become part of the Roman empire and ordered Boudicca to be whipped. Led by their tall, red-headed queen, the Iceni tribe at once rebelled. They sacked Camulodunum (Colchester), Verulamium (St Albans) and Londinium (London), slaying 70,000 Romans and their allies. A strong Roman army quickly crushed the rebellion and Boudicca poisoned herself.

◄ *Bowling is a popular sport for young and old. It was played in England as early as 700 years ago. The green requires constant attention to keep the turf in top condition.*

Bowling

There are several different kinds of bowling. The most popular kind world-wide is the game played on a bowling green of smooth green turf. The object of the game is to roll the bowl or 'wood' as near as possible to a small white ball called a 'jack'. The jack is first rolled up the green to a point at least 18 metres from the players. The woods are specially made with a bias which makes them roll in a curve. Indoor bowling on an artificial surface is becoming increasingly popular in many countries, especially in the winter months.

In *crown-green* bowling the green has a hump in the middle which makes the game more difficult. This game is played mostly in the north of England.

Tenpin bowling is played indoors on smooth wood alleys about 19 metres long and 106 cm wide. The object is to knock down wooden pins arranged in a triangle, with the point of the triangle toward the player. Tenpin balls weigh up to 7.3 kg and have three holes drilled in them for the player's fingers.

Boxing

People have fought with their fists since ancient times. But boxing as we know it began in 1867 when the Marquess of Queensberry drew up a set of rules. Boxers today are divided into weight categories, from 8-stone (51 kg) flyweights to heavyweights

BOXING WEIGHT LIMITS

Professional
Flyweight: 112 lb (50.8 kg)
Bantamweight: 118 lb (53.5 kg)
Featherweight: 126 lb (57.1 kg)
Lightweight: 135 lb (61.2 kg)
Welterweight: 147 lb (66.7 kg)
Middleweight: 160 lb (72.6 kg)
Light-heavyweight: 175 lb (79.4 kg)
Heavyweight: any weight

Amateur
Light-flyweight: 48 kg
Flyweight: 51 kg
Bantamweight: 54 kg
Featherweight: 57 kg
Lightweight: 60 kg
Light-welterweight: 63.5 kg
Welterweight: 67 kg
Light-middleweight: 71 kg
Middleweight: 75 kg
Light-heavyweight: 81 kg
Heavyweight: no limit

> The size and weight of our brains are in proportion to our body size and weight. Men have slightly heavier brains than women. Tall people have heavier brains than short people, but it has been found that there is very little connection between a large head and intelligence. Doctors have discovered that the average man's brain has increased in weight from 1370 grams in 1860 to 1420 grams today. The average woman's brain has increased from 1245 grams to 1270 grams.

(any weight). Points are awarded after each 3-minute round for skill in attack and defence. Amateur contests usually consist of 3 rounds of 3 minutes each, with 1 minute rests between rounds. Professional contests can be of any number of rounds up to 12 or even 15.

Brain

The brain controls all the other parts of the body. In some tiny insects it is no bigger than a speck of dust. Even in some mighty dinosaurs it was no bigger than a walnut. But MAMMALS have big brains in relation to their size, and a human has the biggest brain of all. The human brain is largely made up of grey and white matter. Grey matter contains NERVE cells, and white matter contains the nerve fibres that carry messages from the nerve cells to the body. These nerve fibres leave the brain in large bundles and reach out to all parts of the body. Messages from the body are travelling back along the fibres to the brain all the time.

Different parts of the brain control different parts of the body. For example, most thinking is done in the front part. Sight, on the other hand, is controlled from the back of the brain.

▶ The brain is the body's control centre. It uses a fifth of all the energy produced in the body. The medulla and hypothalamus control involuntary activities such as breathing and blood pressure. The cerebellum controls muscles and organs of balance. The cortex, the largest area, controls conscious feeling and voluntary movements such as writing and running. The corpus callosum is a band of nerves linking the two halves of the cortex.

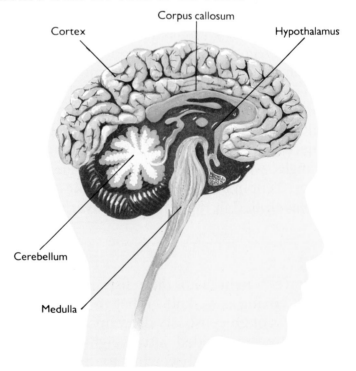

Cortex

Corpus callosum

Hypothalamus

Cerebellum

Medulla

Brazil

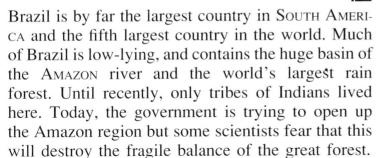

Brazil is by far the largest country in SOUTH AMERICA and the fifth largest country in the world. Much of Brazil is low-lying, and contains the huge basin of the AMAZON river and the world's largest rain forest. Until recently, only tribes of Indians lived here. Today, the government is trying to open up the Amazon region but some scientists fear that this will destroy the fragile balance of the great forest.

Over half of Brazil's people live in cities that include Rio de Janeiro, São Paulo, Belo Horizonte and Recife. Brasilia, a specially built modern city, has been the capital of Brazil since 1960.

Brazil was ruled by Portugal from the early 1500s until 1822, and most people still speak Portuguese. About three-quarters of the people are descended from Europeans; most of the rest are of mixed European, Indian and African ancestry. Most Brazilians work on farms. The country leads the world in producing coffee, and oil is becoming a more important product. Brazil is also one of the biggest producers of beef, cocoa, cotton, maize, sugar cane and tobacco. Most of Brazil's great mineral wealth is still undeveloped.

▲ *Rio de Janeiro is a beautiful city lying among bays, islands and rounded hills.*

BRAZIL

Government: Federal republic
Capital: Brasilia
Area: 8,511,965 sq km
Population: 158,000,000
Language: Portuguese
Currency: Cruzeiro

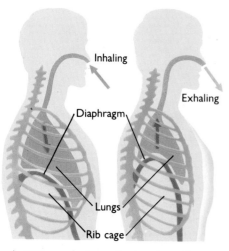

▲ *When you breathe in, your rib cage is pulled upwards and the diaphragm is lowered. Air is sucked into your lungs. These actions happen in reverse when you breathe out.*

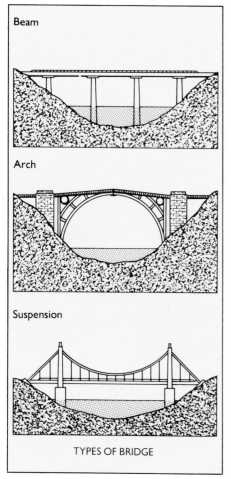

TYPES OF BRIDGE

Bread

Bread is one of our oldest foods, dating back to at least 2000 BC. It may be made from wheat, maize, oats, barley, or rye flour. At first bread was flat, but the Egyptians added YEAST to make the dough rise. Today most bread is baked with yeast.

Breathing

Breathing is something we rarely have to think about. As soon as a baby is born, it starts to breathe, and we go on breathing all our lives. It is the OXYGEN in the air that we need. Like all other animals, we must have oxygen to stay alive. This oxygen is used with the food we eat to give us energy to move about and keep our bodies going.

We draw air into our LUNGS. From there it goes through tiny tubes which allow the oxygen to pass into the BLOOD vessels. So oxygen goes all round our bodies in the blood. We breathe out another type of gas called carbon dioxide. An adult normally breathes in and out about 20 times a minute (children usually breathe faster than this).

Bridge

Bridges are used to take roads, paths and railways over rivers, valleys or other obstacles. People have been building bridges for thousands of years.

The first simple bridges were probably fallen tree trunks placed across a river or small valley. Later, they may have been supported underneath by stones or logs. Another kind of simple bridge is the rope bridge made from long pieces of rope slung across a river.

The Romans were among the first great bridge builders. Some of their stone bridges are still standing today. In the MIDDLE AGES bridges in towns often had shops and houses built on top of them.

Today there is a great variety of bridges. They have to be carefully planned and built. The weight of the bridge must be balanced so that it does not fall down. It must also be strong enough to carry traffic and stand up to the force of the wind.

There are three main kinds of bridge. These are the *beam*, the *arch* and the *suspension* bridge. Some are fixed and others can be moved.

Different kinds of bridge

A modern beam bridge works in the same way as a simple tree trunk bridge. It is made of strong girders, or beams, which stretch from one bank to the other. Sometimes the middle of the bridge rests on pillars. Railway bridges are often girder bridges.

An arch bridge may have one arch or more. In the past, it was usually built from stone, but today some are made of steel, like the Sydney Harbour Bridge in Australia. It has a span (the distance from one side to the other) of 503 metres. Others, such as Waterloo Bridge in London, are made of CONCRETE.

▼ The Firth of Forth Bridge, opened in 1890, had two arches either side of Inchgarvie Island. About 55,000 tonnes of steel were cast in foundries set up on shore to build the bridge.

▲ *The Golden Gate Bridge in San Francisco, California, USA, is one of the world's best known suspension bridges.*

LONGEST BRIDGE SPANS	
Akashi-Kaikyo, Japan (suspension)	1980m
Humber Estuary, England (suspension)	1410m
Verrazano Narrows, USA (suspension)	1298m
Golden Gate, USA (suspension)	1280m
Mackinac Straits, USA (suspension)	1158m
Second Bosporus, Turkey (suspension)	1090m
First Bosporus, Turkey (suspension)	1074m
George Washington, USA (suspension)	1067m
Tagus river, Portugal (suspension)	1013m
Forth Road, Scotland (suspension)	1006m
Severn, England–Wales (suspension)	988m
Tacoma Narrows, USA (suspension)	853m
Kanmon Strait, Japan (suspension)	712m
Transbay, USA (suspension)	704m

Suspension bridges are hung by strong steel cables from tall towers. The towers also have cables fixed to the ground.

Some beam bridges over rivers can be moved to let ships pass through. Tower Bridge in London is a *bascule* bridge. Both sides of the bridge can be lifted up in the middle, like drawbridges. *Swing* bridges are on pivots and can be swung sideways.

Modern bridge building began with IRON bridges in the 1700s. Later, many of these were built for the railways. The first modern suspension bridge was built by Thomas Telford at Menai in North Wales.

By the end of the 1800s steel was being used. Brooklyn Bridge in New York, finished in 1883, was one of the first steel suspension bridges. It has a span of 486 metres. The longest suspension bridge in Britain is the Humber Estuary bridge. It has a span of 1410 metres. The Akashi-Kaikyo bridge in Japan is even longer at 1780 metres.

▲ *Tower Bridge across the river Thames in London has a roadway carried on bascules, or arms, which are pivoted and lift to allow ships to pass beneath it.*

The British Isles are rather rainy. But the west coast has much more rain than the east. The hilly west coast has an average of 2540 mm of rain a year, while low areas in the east have only between 500 and 750 mm. The London area is the driest.

British Isles

The British Isles are made up of two main islands, Britain and IRELAND, and more than 5000 smaller ones. These range from large islands such as the Isle of Man, Shetland, the Orkneys and the Channel Islands, to bare rocks sticking out of the sea.

Britain is divided into ENGLAND, SCOTLAND and WALES. Ireland is divided into Eire (the Republic of Ireland) and Northern Ireland.

The British Isles are part of EUROPE. They are on the European CONTINENTAL SHELF. During the last ICE AGE Britain was joined to Europe by a wide land bridge across what is now the English Channel.

The climate of the British Isles is mild and quite wet. Most of the country is low-lying. There are some mountains and high ground in Scotland, Wales, the north of England and parts of Ireland. Much of the country used to be covered in forests or bog but most of this has been cleared or drained.

> The seas around the British Isles are all quite shallow – evidence that the islands were once part of the continental mainland. If London's Telecom Tower were set down almost anywhere in the Irish Sea, the North Sea or the English Channel, it would stand high above the water.

◄ The discovery of oil in the North Sea brought a new source of wealth to the British Isles. Here, an oil rig temporarily out of service lies offshore of the city of Dundee in Scotland.

Brontë Sisters

Brontë was the name of three English sisters who became famous writers. Charlotte Brontë (1816–1855), Emily Brontë (1818–1848) and Anne Brontë (1820–1849) wrote novels that are among the classics of English literature.

In 1847 all three produced their first novels. *Jane Eyre* by Charlotte was largely based on her own life and it became an immediate success. Emily's *Wuthering Heights* was rather too shocking for its time but is today considered a great book. Anne's novel was entitled *Agnes Grey*. The sisters published these and later works under pen names because few people in the 1800s would buy books written by women.

▲ Charlotte Brontë is best known for her novel Jane Eyre.

In many parts of the world the Bronze Age came after a period sometimes called the Copper Age. This was when people had discovered copper and its uses but had not learned to mix it with tin to make the stronger bronze. Other parts of the world did not have a Bronze Age at all. In certain parts of Africa, for example, people went straight from the use of stone to the use of iron.

▼ Bronze Age people used bronze to make swords and tools. This useful metal could also be cast into shape by heating it until it melted and pouring it into a mould.

Bronze Age

Bronze is the ALLOY of copper and tin. It was first made in the countries at the eastern end of the Mediterranean in about 3000 BC. It took another thousand years to reach Europe.

Bronze changed the lives of the STONE AGE people in Europe. With bronze they could make better tools and weapons much more quickly. Bronze weapons were much stronger and sharper than their old stone or flint axes and knives. Bronze swords were sharp on both sides, so that warriors no longer used the points only.

The Bronze Age people used their new tools to make other objects more quickly. These included pots, shields, helmets and ornaments. As the Stone Age gave way to the Bronze, huts were replaced by towns and people began to build palaces and temples.

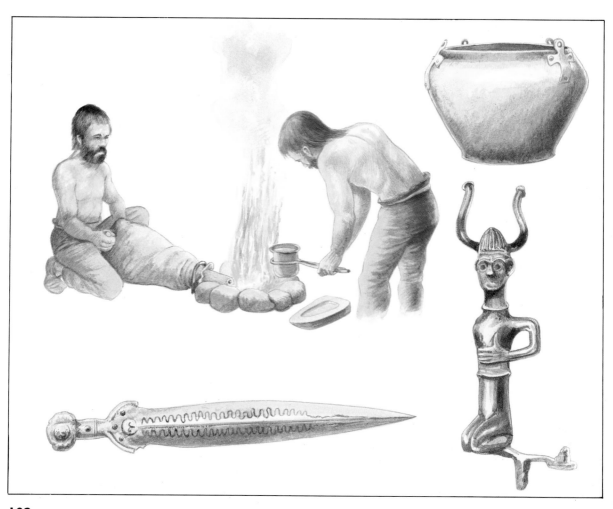

The Bronze Age lasted until about 800 BC. At this time iron started to be used in Europe. Iron became important because it was even more useful than bronze. But bronze was still used in England 400 years later, and for hundreds of years after this in Scotland and Ireland.

Many Bronze Age tools and ornaments are still found today. Some of these are kept in museums and may be seen there.

Statues made of bronze weather to a brown or green coating or *patina* which protects the metal.

Brunei

BRUNEI

Government: Independent sultanate
Capital: Bandar Seri Begawan
Area: 5765 sq km
Population: 369,000
Language: Malay
Currency: Brunei dollar

Brunei is a tiny country on the north-western coast of the island of Borneo. It is only about a quarter of the size of Wales and has a population of about 369,000. The country's chief exports are oil, rubber and hardwood. During the 1800s, Brunei was a stopping place for British ships travelling to China, and the country came under British protection in 1888. Brunei achieved full independence under a sultan in 1984. The capital is Bandar Seri Begawan.

Bud

A bud is an undeveloped shoot of a PLANT. There are two kinds of bud, FLOWER buds and LEAF buds. If the covering of the bud is peeled off, the tightly-packed flowers or leaves can be seen inside. Some buds are eaten as food. These include asparagus, brussels sprouts and globe artichokes.

Buddha

The word Buddha means 'Enlightened One'. This name is given to great teachers of the Buddhist RELIGION.

The first Buddha was Siddhartha Gautama. He was born about 563 BC in northern India. For most of his life he travelled around India teaching people.

▶ *If you cut a few twigs from a horse chestnut in the spring, you can watch the buds grow. Put the twigs in water and soon the sticky bud scales will fold back to reveal the leaves.*

Leaves covering bud

Bud opening as leaves unfold

New leaves

▲ *Buddha in a characteristic pose, with legs folded. His restful expression reflects the Buddhist ideal state of complete happiness and peace.*

Buddha taught his followers that the only way to true happiness was to be peaceful and kind to other people and animals, and to avoid evil.

Like the HINDUS, Buddhists believe that after they die they are born again as an animal or human being. If they are very good, they are not born again but live in a kind of heaven called *Nirvana*.

Buffalo

The buffalo is a large relative of the cow. The Asian buffalo originally came from India where it has been used as a work animal for many centuries. Today the buffalo is used to plough and pull loads all over the Far East and also in Syria, Turkey, Hungary and the Balkans. It is often called the water buffalo because it loves to wallow in the mud by the side of rivers, or at water holes. The water keeps off flies and keeps the animal cool.

Another kind of buffalo lives by the swamps and rivers of central and southern Africa. It is wild and has never been tamed by man. This buffalo can be very dangerous and will charge without warning. The North American BISON is often called a buffalo but it is not a close relative.

▼ *A buffalo draws a plough on a farm in Asia. This strong animal has been a beast of burden for centuries.*

▼ *The great pyramids of ancient Egypt were early engineering feats. Huge blocks of stone were cut and hauled up ramps by hundreds of men.*

▲ *Early shelters were made from the most available materials – in this case animal bones and hide.*

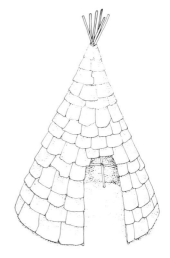

▲ *An early North American Indian tepee made of birch bark laid over a framework of birch poles.*

Building

Early people built with the materials they found around them—stones, branches, mud and turf. In Europe, poor people usually lived in houses made of wattle and daub. Wattle was a wickerwork of branches, and this was plastered over with a 'daub' of wet mud. When this hardened it made quite a strong wall.

Because in some areas certain materials were easily available, buildings look quite different in different places. Where there was plenty of clay, people built with bricks; where there was plenty of limestone or sandstone, people built their houses with those.

Today, houses being built everywhere look very much the same. Large buildings have a framework of steel girders or reinforced *concrete* which takes all the weight of the building. The walls can be light and there can be plenty of windows.

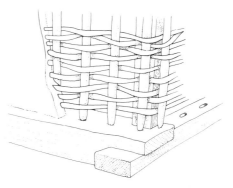

▲ *Early houses in Europe had walls of woven branches, or* wattle, *filled in with hardened lumps of mud, or* daub.

▶ *Modern buildings are constructed using reinforced concrete and prefabricated sections. Towering cranes make the job of moving building materials fast and efficient.*

▲ *The garlic we use in the kitchen is actually the bulb from which the garlic plant grows. Each 'clove' of garlic is one of the bulb's fleshy scales.*

BULGARIA

Government: Multi-party republic
Capital: Sofia
Area: 110,912 sq km
Population: 8,995,000
Language: Bulgarian
Currency: Lev

All buildings, especially high ones, have to be built on firm foundations. If they are not they may collapse or sink into the ground like the Leaning Tower of Pisa in Italy.

Bulb

Many PLANTS, such as tulips, daffodils and ONIONS, grow from bulbs. The bulb is the underground part of the plant where food is stored during the winter months. When the plant has finished flowering, the bulb begins to grow under the ground. Then the leaves above the ground wither away, leaving only the bulb. It is made up of fleshy scales packed tightly together. The scales feed the bud as it grows.

Bulgaria

Bulgaria is a country in Eastern EUROPE. Like several of its European neighbours, it has had a communist government, with restrictions on personal freedom. However, by the early 1990s, non-communists were in control.

Bulgaria has 8,995,000 people and covers 110,912 sq km. Its capital city is Sofia.

In the north are the Balkan Mountains. To the east is the BLACK SEA where many people spend their holidays. In the centre of Bulgaria is a big valley with many farms. The farmers grow fruit, flowers, vegetables, grain and tobacco. There are also many factories and mines in Bulgaria.

Burkina Faso

Burkina Faso is an inland republic in West Africa. It used to be called Upper Volta but the name was changed in 1984. The country was controlled by France from 1896. Full independence came in 1960. Most people are farmers and raise cattle, sheep and goats. Millet, maize and rice are grown. There are valuable deposits of minerals including gold and bauxite, but they have not yet been developed. The capital is Ouagadougou and the population of Burkina Faso is 9,653,000.

Burma (Myanmar)

Burma (Myanmar) is a country in SOUTH-EAST ASIA. It has mountains, forests and rivers. The biggest river is the Irrawaddy which is 2080 km long.

Burma has over 40,000,000 people and covers 676,552 sq km. The capital city is Yangon on the Yangon River. Most of the people are farmers. By 1997 the military government refused to hand over power to a democratically elected party.

BURKINA FASO

Government: Republic
Capital: Ouagadougou
Area: 274,200 sq km
Population: 9,653,000
Language: French
Currency: CFA franc

BURMA (MYANMAR)

Government: Military
Capital: Yangon
Area: 676,552 sq km
Population: 42,642,000
Language: Burmese
Currency: Kyat

◀ *Two fierce lions guard the entrance to a golden-roofed pagoda in Burma. Most Burmese are Buddhists, though in the countryside many still worship the nats – spirits of forests and mountains.*

BURUNDI

Government: Republic
Capital: Bujumbura
Area: 27,834 sq km
Population: 6,022,000
Languages: French, Rundi
Currency: Burundi franc

Burundi

Burundi is a small country in the centre of Africa. It is sandwiched between Zaire, Tanzania and Rwanda. Most of the people are Bantu peasant farmers. Burundi is one of the poorest and most densely populated countries in Africa. The capital is Bujumbura and the population is about 6,000,000.

Butterfly

Butterflies are flying INSECTS. There are about 17,000 kinds of butterfly. They are related to MOTHS, and live in most parts of the world, even as far north as the Arctic circle.

Butterflies have many colours and sizes. One of the smallest, the dwarf blue of South Africa, has a

▲ Butterflies are found in virtually every part of the world apart from the polar regions, and come in a variety of sizes and colours. Some live only a few weeks; others live for nearly a year. Once they emerge from the chrysalis they do not grow.

wing-span of only 14 mm. The largest, the Queen Alexandra birdwing, has a wing-span of 28 cm.

All butterflies begin their lives as CATERPILLARS which hatch from eggs. The caterpillars spend their lives eating the plant they were hatched on. They change their skins several times as they grow. When a caterpillar is fully grown it changes into a chrysalis with a hard skin. Inside this the chrysalis changes into an adult butterfly. When it is ready, the butterfly breaks out and flies away to find a mate and lay eggs of its own.

Some butterflies *migrate*. They fly from one part of the world to another at certain times of the year. One of the most famous migrating butterflies is the monarch butterfly in North America. In the summer it lives all over the United States, Canada and Alaska. In the autumn, the butterflies gather together in groups. They fly south to Mexico, Florida and southern California for the winter. Sometimes thousands of monarchs are seen flying together. In spring, they fly north again.

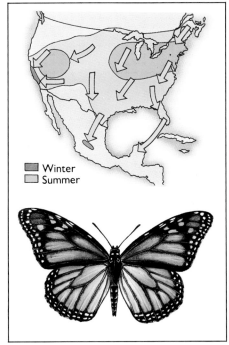

Winter
Summer

▲ *The monarch butterfly of North America travels thousands of miles to winter in Mexico and southern California. Sometimes huge clusters of them are spotted 'resting' in trees en route.*

Byzantine Empire

The Byzantine Empire was founded by the Roman emperor Constantine I in AD 330. It was an eastern division of the Roman Empire. Constantine decided to move the headquarters of the empire to the east. He built a new city as his capital, which he called Constantinople after himself. It is now Istanbul. The Byzantine Empire lasted until 1453, when Constantinople was captured by the Turks.

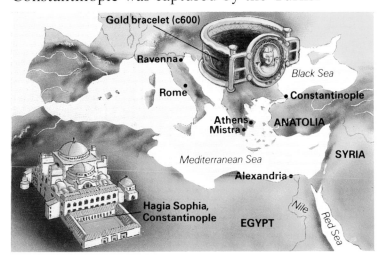

Gold bracelet (c600)

Ravenna

Black Sea

Rome

Constantinople

Athens
Mistra

ANATOLIA

SYRIA

Mediterranean Sea

Alexandria

Hagia Sophia,
Constantinople

EGYPT

Nile

Red Sea

◀ *In the AD 500s, the Byzantine Empire ruled most of the lands around the Mediterranean Sea and the Black Sea.*

CACTUS

▶ Cacti come in all shapes and sizes, from small pincushion-sized specimens to the giant saguaro cactus that may reach 15 metres in height.

▼ Julius Caesar was a military genius. During his nine years campaigning in Gaul, he lost only two of the battles in which he took part.

Cactus

There are hundreds of different cacti, but they all have one thing in common. They are able to grow in hot DESERT climates. Cacti can do this because they store water in their fleshy stems. They are covered with prickly spines instead of leaves. The spines protect the plant's store of water from the desert animals.

Caesar, Julius

Julius Caesar (c. 102–44 BC) was a great leader of the ROMAN EMPIRE. He is most famous for his part in turning the Roman Republic into an empire ruled by one man.

He first became powerful when he commanded an army that conquered what is today France, the Netherlands and Germany. In 55 BC, he crossed the Channel and invaded Britain. He rebelled against the Roman Senate (the government), when he led

his victorious armies into Italy itself. He captured Rome without a struggle, and in 48 BC he defeated Pompey, his main rival for power. Caesar then became the sole ruler of Rome.

Caesar made many enemies who hated what he was doing to the Republic. A group of them plotted to kill him. On the 'Ides of March' (the 15th of the month), 44 BC, they stabbed him to death in the Roman Forum.

Calculator

About 5000 years ago, someone invented the ABACUS. This was the first calculator. Then in 1642 the French scientist Blaise Pascal built the first machine for adding numbers. It worked by turning dials. After this, mechanical adding machines were used for years in offices and shops. They were useful but slow, and could not do difficult calculations.

Everything changed in the 1970s when the SILICON CHIP was invented. Soon everyone could have a small pocket-sized electronic calculator. These calculators can add, subtract and divide as fast as we can press the keys. More advanced calculators can also do more difficult calculations needed in science.

Although they are electronic, not all calculators need batteries. Some are solar-powered – they get their power from light.

Electronic cash registers are very important in shops. They add up the price of goods, print out a bill and calculate your change.

▲ Modern calculators like this one can solve advanced mathematical problems in seconds. Nearly all are installed with a memory, allowing the user to store information for later use. Calculators are useful in engineering, accountancy and business.

◄ Pascal's adding machine of 1642 looks ungainly and primitive next to a modern electronic pocket calculator.

CAMBODIA

Government: Constitutional
  Monarchy
Capital: Phnom Penh
Area: 181,035 sq km
Population 7,249,000
Language: Khmer
Currency: Riel

When a thirsty camel finally gets a chance to drink, it can swallow as much as 80 litres of water at one time.

Cambodia

Cambodia is a country in South-east Asia. It changed its name from Cambodia to Kampuchea in 1976 and back to Cambodia in 1988. Most of Cambodia's people live in small villages and grow rice, fruit and vegetables. The country was formerly part of the French colony of Indochina. It became independent in 1955. Since then Cambodia has seen bitter CIVIL WAR and starvation. In 1993 the country became a constitutional monarchy again.

Camel

With their wide splayed feet, gangly legs, humped body and long thick neck, camels look as if they have been made up from the parts of half a dozen other animals. But if it were not for these beasts of burden, life in some desert regions would have been almost impossible.

The camel is one of the few creatures that can stand up to extreme heat and still do work carrying heavy loads. They are ideally suited for the job of making long journeys across deserts. Their wide padded feet grip well on loose sandy ground. They are powerful and swift and can go for days without eating or drinking, living off the fat stored in their humps. Camels will eat almost anything, including the thorny shrubs and thistles found in the desert.

▶ *The single-humped camel on the right is an Arabian camel. The two-humped one on the left is a Bactrian camel of Asia.*

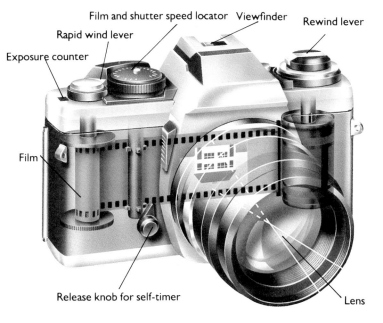

Rapid wind lever
Film and shutter speed locator   Viewfinder   Rewind lever
Exposure counter
Film
Release knob for self-timer
Lens

◄ *To take a picture, the shutter opens and light passes through a lens into a small aperture – the iris. From there it is focused onto the film by a second set of lenses. The image formed is upside down.*

Taking pictures with the early cameras was a slow process. The first real camera, invented by the Frenchman Louis Daguerre at the beginning of the 19th century, needed a very long exposure time. The subject had to sit motionless for as much as ten minutes, usually with his or her head in a clamp to keep it still. Some modern cameras have shutter speeds as fast as one thousandth of a second to take pictures of fast-moving objects.

Camera

Modern cameras work in much the same way as those of a hundred years ago. A shutter opens to let light from the scene being photographed pass through a glass lens to fall on the film. The amount of light that gets through can be varied by adjusting the size of the hole through which the light passes – the 'aperture'. Apertures are measured in 'f-numbers'. A high f-number such as 16 or 22 means a small aperture. With a low f-number such as 2 or 2.8 the aperture is large. The light forms an upside-down image of the scene on the film. The film is then treated with chemicals (developed). The image on the developed film is printed onto a special type of paper. The result is a photograph.

Today, most cameras have a lot of different parts to help us to take photographs in many kinds of light and from close up or from far away.

Cameroon

Cameroon is a republic on the west coast of Africa. It is twice the size of the United Kingdom. Most of the country's people live in scattered tribal villages and are farmers. Cocoa, coffee, peanuts, bananas and cotton are the chief crops. Oil is produced. The capital is Yaoundé.

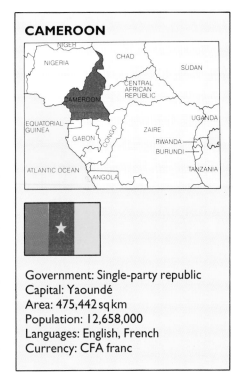

CAMEROON

Government: Single-party republic
Capital: Yaoundé
Area: 475,442 sq km
Population: 12,658,000
Languages: English, French
Currency: CFA franc

CANADA

Government: Confederation with
parliamentary democracy
Capital: Ottawa
Area: 9,976,130 sq km
Population: 27,351,000
Languages: English, French
Currency: Canadian dollar

▼ *Some of the most spectacular scenery in North America can be seen in the Canadian Rockies in Jasper National Park in Alberta.*

Canada

The second biggest country in the world, Canada covers an area of some ten million square km.

In the ARCTIC, Canada reaches almost as far north as Greenland. To the south, it extends to the same LATITUDE as southern France. The distance from the Pacific coast in the west to the Atlantic in the east is further than from North America to Europe. But in spite of its size, two-thirds of the population of Canada lives in a narrow belt of land no more than 200 km from the U.S. border.

In the east are the Great Lakes that lie on the border with the United States. These huge inland seas empty into the St Lawrence River, which links them with the Atlantic Ocean. The centre of government and finance is in Ontario, as are many of Canada's industries.

Britain and France each governed Canada in the past. Today, 18 per cent of Canadians still speak only French.

Canada is often called 'a land of the future'. The country's enormous oil and mineral resources have hardly been touched. Canada is among the ten leading industrial nations of the world.

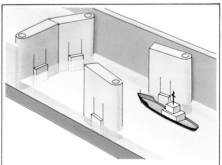

◀ *A ship negotiates one of the three sets of locks on the Panama Canal, whose 80 km length links the Atlantic and Pacific oceans.*

The gates open to allow a ship into the lock before closing again.

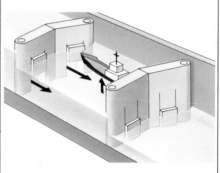

Openings in the upper gates release water into the lock.

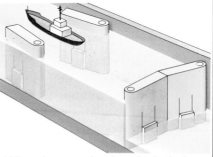

When the water level inside the lock is the same as that above the gates, they are opened to allow the ship to pass through.

Canal

A canal is a man-made waterway built to carry water traffic.

Until the 1500s, canals could be built only across flat country. With the invention of canal locks, however, they could be built across high ground too.

Early canals could only be used by narrow, shallow-bottomed boats. These boats were pulled along by horses that walked on tow paths running alongside the canal. Some canals, like the SUEZ CANAL and the PANAMA Canal, are big enough to let ocean liners pass through them.

Canberra

Canberra is the capital of AUSTRALIA. It is a small city whose main activity is government. The city has little industry.

Canberra was founded in 1908 by an Act of the Australian parliament. At this time, Australia was governed from Melbourne. A site for the new city was chosen in New South Wales, and it was built from nothing soon after World War I. All the major departments of government have their headquarters here. There is also a university.

▲ *How a canal lock works. Before the ship can enter, the level of water in the lock must be the same as that in the lower pool.*

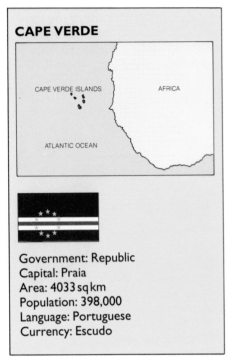

CAPE VERDE

CAPE VERDE ISLANDS · AFRICA

ATLANTIC OCEAN

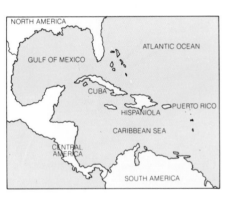

Government: Republic
Capital: Praia
Area: 4033 sq km
Population: 398,000
Language: Portuguese
Currency: Escudo

NORTH AMERICA

ATLANTIC OCEAN

GULF OF MEXICO

CUBA

HISPANIOLA · PUERTO RICO

CARIBBEAN SEA

CENTRAL AMERICA

SOUTH AMERICA

Cats are very efficient carnivores. They are well known for their hunting skills, their stealthy stalking of their prey, their final pounce with deadly teeth and claws. This applies to all the cat family, from lions and tigers to our domestic animals. All cats are very similar inside. For instance, it is almost impossible to tell the difference between the skull of a lion and that of a tiger.

Cape Verde

The 15 islands of the tiny African republic of Cape Verde lie in the Atlantic Ocean about 650 km west of Senegal. The majority of the inhabitants farm and fish. The islands were discovered by the Portuguese in 1456 and Cape Verde became independent in 1975. The capital is Praia.

Carbon

Carbon is an important ELEMENT that is found in every living thing—both plant and animal. Many of the things we use every day have carbon in them, such as sugar and paper. Forms of carbon also exist as COAL, OIL, graphite (the 'lead' in our pencils is graphite) and DIAMONDS.

Caribbean Sea

The Caribbean Sea is bounded by the West Indies, the east coast of Central America and the north coast of South America.

In the 17th century, British and French pirates sailed the Caribbean to attack and plunder Spanish possessions. After the completion of the Panama Canal in 1914 the sea became one of the busiest waterways in the world. It lies on the route between the Atlantic and Pacific oceans.

Carnivore

Carnivores are a group of MAMMALS that feed mainly on the flesh of other animals.

Although carnivores mostly live on meat, they will sometimes eat insects and plants. But what they all have in common is a set of very powerful jaws for chopping up their food, deadly curved claws for tearing, and long sharp teeth for seizing, stabbing and killing their victims.

Carnivores include CATS, DOGS, FOXES, RACCOONS, weasels and HYENAS. All have good eyesight, smell and hearing and are fast, intelligent and skilled at hunting down other animals. Some carnivores, like wild dogs and hyenas, hunt in packs. In this way

they can kill animals much larger than themselves. Other carnivores, like the LEOPARD and the JAGUAR, hunt alone.

 ▲ Foxes, along with badgers, are Britain's largest carnivores. They like eating rabbits and often scatter bones and feathers around their dens.

Carroll, Lewis

Lewis Carroll (1832–1898) is the pen-name of an English writer called Charles Dodgson. Dodgson was a mathematics professor at Oxford University, but he is best known for his children's stories. The most famous is *Alice in Wonderland*. The story was written for the daughter of a fellow professor at the university.

 ▼ To create a cartoon, the original sketch is drawn onto sheets of transparent film, called 'cels', then photographed onto film.

Cartoon

Most people think of short, funny films with talking creatures and plants when they speak of cartoons. But originally, cartoons were rough sketches of the design for a PAINTING or a TAPESTRY. These sketches were drawn to the same size as the finished work. Comic strips in newspapers are called strip cartoons.

Cartoon films are made by joining together a series of drawings. Each drawing is a little different from the one before. When they are shown one after another at a very fast speed it looks as if the scene is moving.

CASTLE

All kinds of tactics and siege machinery were needed in an attack on a heavily fortified medieval castle. From giant siege towers wheeled up to the walls, armed men rushed the ramparts. Powerful catapults hurled stones against the walls or into the castle to spread confusion. Huge bombards mounted on fixed platforms fired heavy stone shot at the outer walls to make a breach. Archers kept up a steady hail of arrows to force the defenders back from the walls while men with scaling ladders swarmed up to the ramparts.

Castle

One of the few places where kings and lords in the MIDDLE AGES could feel safe was behind the thick stone walls of their castles. There, they and their men could fight off attacks by roving bandits and sit out long sieges by invading armies.

As castles developed they became larger and more comfortable. Instead of having all the living quarters crowded into the main keep, small 'villages' of huts and buildings sprang up inside the castle walls.

Castles had high, thick stone walls. A wall-walk ran right around the top, and through each tower.

▲ *This castle in southern Germany, built with tall, rounded towers, is much like the castle of fairy tale and fable.*

> **What do the cat, the camel and the giraffe have in common? Very little, except one surprising fact. Other animals move their front leg on one side at the same time as the back leg on the other side. The cat, the camel and the giraffe move their front and back legs on the same side at the same time, then the front and back legs on the other side.**

Soldiers could run from one point of attack to another without ever showing themselves to their enemies.

Rounded towers could stand up to battering rams and hurled rocks much better than square towers. The towers jutted out from the main wall. This gave the defenders a better chance to fire on the attackers and stop them from reaching the castle walls.

Cat

A cat belongs to the group of MAMMALS called the feline family. Although the cat family ranges in size from domestic breeds to TIGERS, they all have many things in common. Cats have short, rounded heads, long face whiskers, sharp teeth that serve as deadly weapons for grabbing and biting their prey to death, and powerful claws. All cats except the cheetah can pull their claws back into a sheath of skin when they are not in use. Their long tails help them balance and make them superb at jumping and climbing. LIONS and cheetahs live in families. All other cats live mostly alone.

▼ Cats come in all sizes, from the house cat to the powerful lion and tiger. On the front row with the tabby cat are, left to right, a wild cat, a lynx, a black panther and a snow leopard.

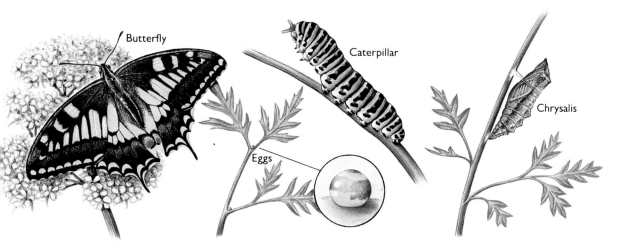

Butterfly

Caterpillar

Chrysalis

Eggs

▲ *From egg to winged beauty – the life cycle of a butterfly. In very cold regions, some species take two or three years to pass from the egg to the butterfly stage.*

Caterpillar

The middle or 'adolescent' stage in the lives of BUTTERFLIES and MOTHS is when they are called caterpillars.

Butterflies and moths usually lay their eggs on plants. After they hatch, small, soft, worm-like creatures—the caterpillars—emerge. Some are smooth-skinned. Others are spiny or hairy.

Caterpillars spend their whole time feeding. Their only purpose in life is to eat and grow and prepare for the change into adulthood. For this reason they have powerful jaws for chewing up plants. Many feed on crops and can cause great damage.

As caterpillars grow, they become too big for their skins. After a while the skin stretches and splits and they emerge with a new one. This happens several times. The last 'skin' is quite different from the others. It forms a hard layer which makes it impossible for the caterpillar to move. In this state it is called a *chrysalis*. Inside the chrysalis, the caterpillar changes into a butterfly. A moth caterpillar will spin a cocoon around itself before turning into a chrysalis. Caterpillars take almost a year to grow to full size.

Cathedral

Cathedrals are CHURCHES—only bigger. They are the grandest and most impressive kinds of Christian churches ever to be built. A cathedral is the home church of a bishop. It is the centre from which he looks after all the other churches under his care.

SEE IT YOURSELF

Caterpillars are easy to rear if you have plenty of the right food plant. A big box like the one below makes a good container. Make some holes. The food plant can be fixed into moist Oasis, or you can put it in a small jar of water. Put fresh food plant in each day. Watch the caterpillars turn into pupae and butterflies.

▶ *Salisbury Cathedral in Wiltshire, built in the 1200s, is a splendid example of Early English Gothic style. Its magnificent 123-metre spire is the tallest in England.*

▼ *How limestone caves are formed. 1. Water seeps through cracks in the rocks. The acid in the water gradually widens the cracks into passageways and caverns. 2. The water forms an underground stream, which further widens the caverns. 3. Over the years, dripping water forms stalactites and stalagmites.*

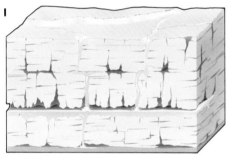

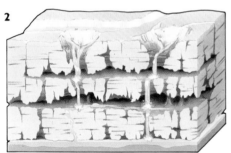

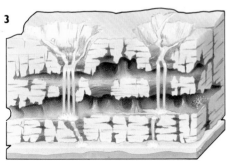

Cathedrals are also places of worship. Most can hold large numbers of people, as well as having room for choirs, organs, chapels, statues, paintings, stained glass windows and other religious items of decoration. Cathedrals were built with great splendour as they were seen as being built in honour of God. There are many styles of cathedral ARCHITECTURE.

Cattle *See* Cow

Cave

A cave is an underground hollow or passage that is formed when slightly ACID waters flow or seep through limestone rocks. The water dissolves the rock, sometimes leaving behind a whole network of caves, like a huge decayed cavity in the Earth.

After a cave has been formed, water may go on dripping through the walls and ceiling. This often results in odd-shaped deposits known as *stalactites* and *stalagmites*.

Cave Dweller

Anybody who lives in a cave could be called a cave dweller. But what we usually mean are people who were the ancestors of modern man. Caves are natural places to shelter from the weather and from wild animals. They were some of the first dwelling places used by human beings.

The mouth of a cave is often dry and it is possible to build a fire inside when the weather is cold. In hot weather, caves give shelter from the sun. Also, with walls all around them, the cave people could fight off dangerous animals from the cave mouth. The remains of ancient cave dwellers have been found in sites all around the world—in China, southern Asia, Europe and Africa. Here, bits and pieces of their tools and weapons have been dug up, along with bones of the animals they hunted. Remains of their fires have also been found. Deep toward the back of the caves, graves of cave people have been unearthed. On the walls of some caves, paintings of animals have been found. From all these things, archaeologists have been able to piece together a great deal about the way of life of these people of long ago.

▼ Many cave dwellers built their shelters in the entrances to caves. The dark interiors were often only used for ceremonies and rituals.

Cell

Cells are the smallest living parts of plants and animals. Single cells can only be seen under a MICROSCOPE. Even a tiny bit of human skin contains millions of them.

Cells are usually round in shape. A few are spiralled and some, like nerve cells, have sprawling tree-like branches.

In 1665, a scientist called Robert Hooke looked at a piece of cork under a microscope and saw that it was made up of tiny compartments. He named them cells and this term has been used ever since.

▼ *Every living thing – plant or animal – is made up of cells. They differ in shape, size and function. The diagrams below are 'typical' cells only in that they show the characteristics of plant and animal cells. The nucleus is the control centre of the cell. Plant cells have a* cell wall *containing cellulose, a stiffening substance. They also have* chloroplasts, *which contain the green substance* chlorophyll *used in photosynthesis.*

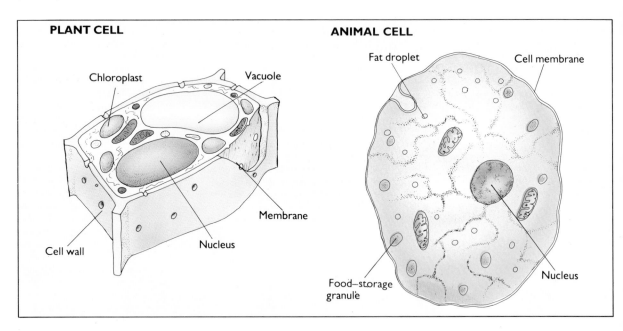

PLANT CELL

Chloroplast

Vacuole

Cell wall

Nucleus

Membrane

ANIMAL CELL

Fat droplet

Cell membrane

Food–storage granule

Nucleus

Celts

The Celts were an ancient people of north-western Europe. At one time, over 2000 years ago, they lived all over Britain, France and parts of Spain and Germany. In about 400 BC they even crossed into Italy and attacked Rome.

The Celts were tall, fair and very warlike. They lived in tribes made up of a chief, nobles, free men and slaves. The tribes often fought each other. They were good metal-workers and liked to decorate their weapons and armour with bright designs and curious creatures. And they were gifted musicians and poets. The Celtic religion was known as Druidism, and their priests were called druids.

The Celtic priests called druids have long been associated with the great standing stones of Stonehenge, near Salisbury. However, it is now known that Stonehenge was built well over a thousand years before the first Celts reached Britain in 550–450 BC.

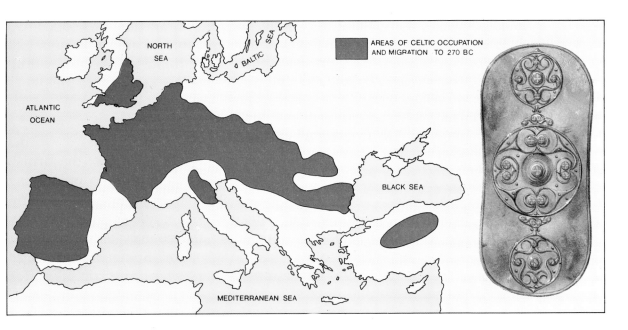

When the armies of the ROMAN EMPIRE spread out, many Celts fled to remote regions. In the lands they had once conquered, the Celtic way of life was soon lost. It was only in the far-off corners of Europe that their language and way of life survived.

Celtic speech was very common in Ireland, Cornwall, Wales, Scotland and Brittany up until a few hundred years ago. Today, although less common, Celtic speech can still be heard. Irish and Scottish Gaelic and Welsh are Celtic languages. The Celtic people of Scotland were known to the Romans as the Picts.

▲ At one time the Celtic occupation of Europe had spread as far as Italy. Typical of the Celtic type of metalwork is this bronze shield, which was found in the river Thames in London.

Census

Nearly all countries of the world regularly count the number of people living in them. This population count is called a census. Most countries take a census every ten years. A census also gives important facts about how much money people earn, what kind of homes they live in, whether they are married or single and how many children they have.

The word 'census' comes from the Latin word *censere*, meaning to tax. In ancient Rome, census takers made lists of people and their property, chiefly for purposes of taxation. When William the Conqueror defeated England in 1066, his officials made a count of the country's land and property. This census was listed in the Domesday Book.

Centipede

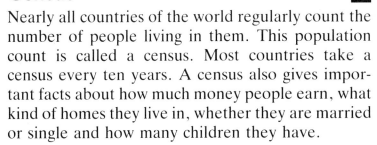

Centipedes are long worm-like creatures. Their bodies are made up of many parts, often up to 100 or more. Each part has a pair of clawed legs. The

The largest known centipede is a 46-legged giant that lives in the forests of South America. It is about 25 cm long and 2.5 cm thick!

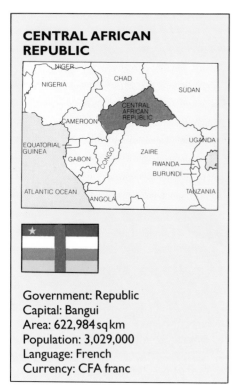

CENTRAL AFRICAN REPUBLIC

Government: Republic
Capital: Bangui
Area: 622,984 sq km
Population: 3,029,000
Language: French
Currency: CFA franc

head has long feelers, powerful jaws and two stinging claws that are able to inject poison into their prey. Centipedes are found all over the world. They feed mainly on worms, insects and snails.

Central African Republic

This African country is twice the size of the British Isles but there are only about 3 million people living there. The Central African Republic has a warm climate. Rain falls nearly every day during the rainy season. At other times the country is hot and dry. Most of the people are poor. Some of them raise cattle. Others are farmers who grow cotton, coffee and grain.

The country was once part of French Equatorial Africa. It became independent in 1960. Bangui is the capital and largest town.

Central America

Central America forms a land bridge between the continents of North and South America. It consists of the independent republics of COSTA RICA, EL SALVADOR, GUATEMALA, HONDURAS, NICARAGUA, PANAMA and BELIZE.

This land bridge was created many millions of

▼ Buildings in Guatemala City reflect the Spanish colonial style. Guatemala, Honduras, El Salvador, Nicaragua and Costa Rica became independent republics in 1838.

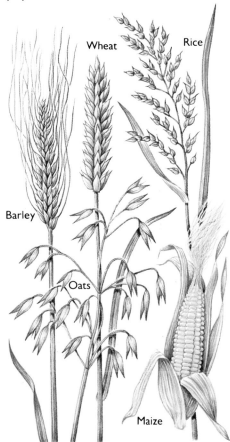

◀ Many people outside the cities in Central America live in primitive one-room huts of adobe and grass, farming small plots on the hillsides around.

▼ Cereals are all members of the grass family that are grown for food. Wheat, rice and rye are grown mainly for people to eat, while barley, oats, maize and millet are more often grown as animal feed. Rice is the major food crop for half the world's population.

Wheat

Rice

Barley

Oats

Maize

years ago by volcanic activity. In the east, Central America has a flat coast covered with jungle. Central America is a hot area. Most of the large cities are in the cooler highlands.

Central America, along with Mexico and the West Indies, is said by many people to be the tropical part of North America. Also, most of this 'tropical' area, along with much of South America, is often called Latin America. This is because the people there speak Spanish or Portuguese, which come from ancient Latin.

Most of the people of Central America are of Indian, Spanish or mixed origin. Spanish is the main language, but many Indians still speak their native language. Central Americans farm tropical crops such as sugar, bananas, cotton and coffee.

Cereal

Cereals are the SEEDS of a group of plants that belong to the GRASS family. Throughout human history they have been the most important of all types of FOOD. In ancient times, cereals were collected from wild plants. Later, when they began to be grown on farms, they became the most important food of early civilizations.

Some cereals such as RICE and maize, are eaten in their natural form. Others, such as WHEAT and rye, are ground into flour before being baked or cooked. Cereals are also used to make alcoholic drinks and to feed farm animals.

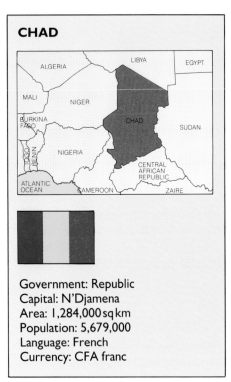

CHAD

Government: Republic
Capital: N'Djamena
Area: 1,284,000 sq km
Population: 5,679,000
Language: French
Currency: CFA franc

Chad

Chad is a large country in the centre of Africa. It is named after Lake Chad, which lies on the western border of the country. This lake can be as large as 26,000 square km during the wet season – larger than Wales. North Chad is part of the great Sahara Desert. The southern part gets plenty of rain and is covered with grass and trees. Chad became a French colony in French Equatorial Africa in 1913 and gained its independence in 1960. The capital is N'Djamena.

Chalk

Chalk is a pure white, soft and crumbly form of limestone. Land that is rich in chalk is found in the south of England, in France and in parts of North America.

Most chalk was formed between 135 and 65 million years ago. It is made up of the crushed shells of countless tiny sea creatures. When these creatures died their shells built up in thick layers at the bottom of warm, shallow seas. As the shape of the Earth's surface changed, these layers were lifted out of the seas to become land.

We usually think of chalk as something that we use to write with, but it is also used in many other ways. Mixed with other things, chalk is used to make paints, medicines, rubber, paper, ink and toothpaste.

▼ *The famed white cliffs of Dover are made of thick layers of chalk formed during the Cretaceous Period, 100 million years ago.*

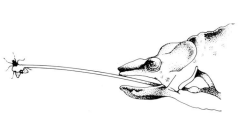

▶ *The chameleon shoots out its long tongue to snare its prey. The sticky, knob-like tip of the tongue swells up to trap the insect.*

Chameleon

Chameleons are a group of LIZARDS found in Africa, Asia and parts of Europe. They have narrow bodies with a crest along the back, and helmeted or horned heads. The most unusual thing about a chameleon is that it can change the colour of its skin.

Chameleons live in trees. They move very slowly and will sit on branches for hours, as still as a statue, waiting until insects come close to them. They catch insects with a long sticky tongue, which shoots out with such speed that the insects seem to vanish without a trace.

Chaplin, Charles

Charlie Chaplin (1889–1977) was one of the most famous comic CINEMA actors of all time. He is best known for his role as the gentle, well-meaning tramp who was always making mistakes and getting into trouble.

Chaplin was born in London, but he spent most of his working life in the United States. He started as an actor on stage, but he became famous for the parts he played in silent films in Hollywood. He also wrote, directed and produced the films that he made in later years.

Charlemagne

Charlemagne (AD 742–814) was a great military leader. In the AD 700s he founded an empire that covered most of western Europe.

In the year 768, Charlemagne became the king of

▼ *Charlie Chaplin, seen below in his famous role as the little tramp, was one of the most versatile people in cinema history. He wrote and directed nearly all his films, and composed the music for all his sound films.*

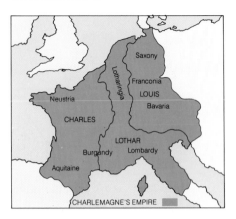

▲ *This map shows the extent of Charlemagne's empire at its height. When he died, his sons fought among themselves. Eventually Charlemagne's empire was divided between his grandsons, Charles, Louis, and Lothar.*

▲ *Charles I defied Parliament and was ultimately convicted of treason and beheaded.*

the Franks, a people who lived in the country we now call France. Through his skill in war he soon took over northern Spain, Italy and Germany. He fought for the Church in Rome, and in return, the POPE crowned him Holy Roman Emperor on Christmas Day in the year AD 800.

Charles I

Charles I (1600–1649) is known in history as the only British king to have caused his people to rebel and execute him. He came to the throne in 1625, but he was such a bad king he made enemies almost everywhere and in 1642 the country was split by CIVIL WAR.

Charles II

As King of Britain, Charles II (1630–1685) was liked as much as his father was disliked. He spent most of his youth in exile in Europe, while CHARLES I fought to save his crown and his life, and lost both.

In 1660, after being ruled by Oliver CROMWELL

for ten years, the English invited Charles II to return and take back the crown. He was a wise ruler and he was very careful in the way in which he treated his people and PARLIAMENT. His court was very lively and gay and his personal charm won him many friends. His subjects called him the 'merry monarch'.

Chaucer, Geoffrey

Geoffrey Chaucer (1345–1400) was a great English poet. He was one of the first people to write in the ENGLISH LANGUAGE rather than in Latin. His best known work is *The Canterbury Tales*. It is a collection of stories told by an imaginary group of pilgrims as they travelled to Canterbury Cathedral.

▲ *After the stark years of Puritan rule under Cromwell, Charles II won the hearts of the people with his great personal charm.*

◄ *A detail from an early illustration from* The Canterbury Tales. *Chaucer wrote the work in Middle English, the form of English used from about 1100 to 1450.*

Cheese

Most cheese is made from cows' MILK but it can be made from the milk of goats, sheep, buffalo and even reindeer. To make cheese, the milk is turned sour so that it will *curdle*.

The solid bits, called the *curds*, are taken away from the liquid, or *whey*, and are pressed into a more solid form and dried. The cheese is then left to ripen.

The greatest cheese-eaters are the French. They eat more than 18kg per person every year. There are over 240 different kinds of French cheese.

▲ *Research into cancer at a biochemistry laboratory in the United States. Growth, genetics and reproduction are all of great interest to biochemists.*

Chemistry

Chemistry is the study of materials—solids, liquids and gases. A chemist finds out what things are made of and how they are joined together. If a piece of wood is burned in a fire, this is a *chemical reaction*. The wood turns to ash and, at the same time, heat and light are given off. It took chemists a long time to find out that burning is the joining together of the wood with the gas oxygen from the air. There are lots and lots of chemical reactions.

The true science of chemistry as we know it began only in the 1600s. Chemists at this time began to find out how chemicals really work. Then they discovered the ELEMENTS, simple substances which make up all the millions of different substances on Earth. There are only about a hundred elements, each of them made up of tiny ATOMS. The atoms of elements often join together to make different substances. The salt you put on your food is made up of atoms of the elements sodium and chlorine.

Our bodies contain many different chemicals. More than half the atoms in the body are hydrogen. Next in abundance comes oxygen. Then there is carbon, making up one-tenth of the body's weight. That is enough carbon, if it were pure, to fill 3000 pencils!

An atom of sodium joins with an atom of chlorine to make a molecule of salt.

Sodium   Chlorine   Sodium chloride (salt)

Chemistry is today a very important science, and chemists are employed in a vast number of industries.

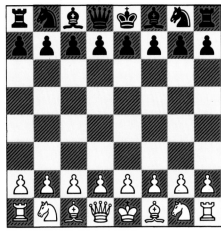

▲ A chess board, showing the opening positions of the pieces. The line-up is always the same, with a white or light-coloured square in the bottom right-hand corner.

Chess

Chess is a game that has been played for hundreds of years. It is played by two people on a board with 64 black and white squares. Each of the two players has 16 pieces which they line up on either side of the board. Every piece can only be moved around the board in a special way. They are used to attack and retreat, to defend each other, and can be captured and taken out of play. The most important piece for each player is the 'king'. The game is won when one player manages to capture the other player's king.

Chess pieces

Pawn   Rook   Knight   Bishop   Queen   King

Chile

Chile is a narrow country that lies along 4265 km of the western coast of South America. Its habitable area is made even narrower by the Andes Mountains, which lie along its eastern border.

Chile has over a quarter of the world's copper resources, as well as other minerals. Its people are Spanish-speaking and are mainly Roman Catholics. In 1973, a military government seized power in Chile, but in 1988 the Chilean people voted for an end to military rule.

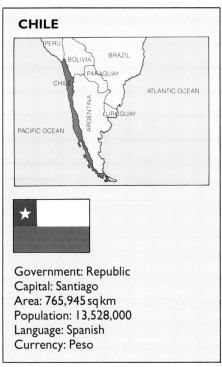

CHILE

Government: Republic
Capital: Santiago
Area: 765,945 sq km
Population: 13,528,000
Language: Spanish
Currency: Peso

CHIMPANZEE

▶ *A chimpanzee infant watches as an adult probes a termite nest with a stick. Chimpanzees are intelligent animals capable of using simple tools.*

Chimpanzees are among the noisiest of all animals. They scream and shriek, drum on trees, slap the ground and keep up an almost constant hooting and muttering. But when a human appears they usually fall silent and disappear into the forest.

SEE IT YOURSELF

Plants need light to make green chlorophyll. You can prove this for yourself by fixing a piece of black paper across part of a leaf. If you leave the plant for a few days you will see a light patch begin to appear under the paper. No light, no chlorophyll.

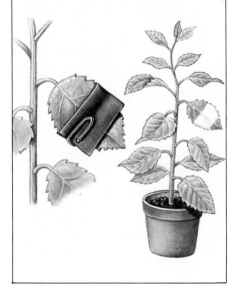

Chimpanzee

Chimpanzees are the most human-looking of all the APES. Fully grown, they are about 1·3 metres tall and are able to walk upright, although they often use their hands to help push themselves along the ground. Chimpanzees come from the jungles of Africa. They live in family groups and are very fond of their young and take good care of them. They are playful and intelligent animals. Tame chimpanzees have been taught to behave like humans in many ways. They can even learn to talk in simple sign language.

China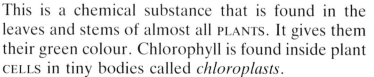

China is the third biggest country in the world, and it has a population larger than that of any other country. A fifth of all the people on Earth are Chinese – over 1000 million. (See pages 136-137.)

Chlorophyll

This is a chemical substance that is found in the leaves and stems of almost all PLANTS. It gives them their green colour. Chlorophyll is found inside plant CELLS in tiny bodies called *chloroplasts*.

Plants need chlorophyll to make their food. Sunlight, falling on the leaves, acts with the

134

chlorophyll to turn carbon dioxide from the air, and water, which the plant's roots suck up from the soil, into food made up of SUGARS and STARCHES. At the same time, the plant's leaves give out OXYGEN. This whole process is called *photosynthesis*. It is a very important part of life on our Earth, as all living things need oxygen in order to breathe.

Plants can only produce chlorophyll when they are grown in the light. Plants kept in darkness often turn white or yellow because they lack chlorophyll.

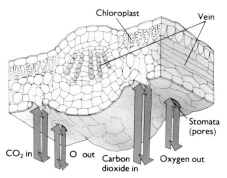

▲ *In most plants, photosynthesis happens in the upper part of the leaf. Water and nutrients are carried to the food-producing cells by a network of veins, while gases such as carbon dioxide (CO_2) pass in and out of the leaf by tiny pores called 'stomata'. The leaf gives out oxygen (O) which we breathe.*

Chocolate

The chocolate we eat is made from the beans of the cacao tree. The beans grow inside pods, which hang from the trunk and the branches of the tree.

To make chocolate, the beans are first roasted, then ground up to give an oily liquid called 'chocolate liquor'. Other things may then be added to the liquor. The milk chocolate we buy in shops, for example, has milk and sugar added to it.

▼ *Cacao trees grow huge pods which are cut off with a large knife. The beans inside are dried to make chocolate and cocoa.*

Christianity

Christianity is one of the world's great RELIGIONS. More than 1000 million people call themselves Christians. These are people who follow the teachings of JESUS, and who believe that he is the son of God who came to Earth in human form.

Christianity is almost 2000 years old. In fact, we date our calendar from the year in which it was thought that Jesus was born. Christians accept the

Continued on page 138

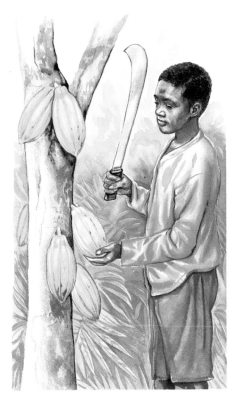

SOME CHRISTIAN GROUPS

Anglo-Catholics	Members of the Church of England who favour some of the ritual of the Catholic faith.
Baptists	Protestants who believe in total immersion of adults during baptism.
Christian Scientists	People who practise spiritual healing.
Church of England	Church that came into being when Henry VIII broke with the pope and became head of the Church.
Methodists	Movement founded by John Wesley in the 1700s.
Roman Catholics	Christians who accept the pope as their spiritual leader on earth.

135

CHINA

China is the third largest country on Earth, and the nation with the greatest population. There are more than 1 billion Chinese – a fifth of the Earth's people. China has the oldest continuous civilization of any country.

Natural barriers, including the Himalaya Mountains and great deserts, cut off China from its neighbours on the Asian mainland. In the east are great plains and rivers, including China's longest river, the Chang Jiang (or Yangtze Kiang) and the slightly shorter Huang Ho or Yellow River. It is here that most of the people live. Many Chinese are city-dwellers, working in factories. Others till the soil, as their forefathers have done for centuries.

For more than 3000 years China was an empire. Chinese inventions included paper, printing, silk, porcelain and gunpowder – all discovered long before such things were known in Europe. Since 1912 the country has been a republic. A bitter civil war between Nationalists and Communists ended in 1949 with the Communists victorious. Under Mao Tse-tung Communist rule was often harsh, and China became isolated from the rest of the world. Later leaders increased contacts with the West, but pro-democracy movements were suppressed.

CHINA

Government: People's republic
Capital: Beijing (Peking)
Area: 9,596,961 sq km
Population: 1,169,619,000
Language: Mandarin Chinese
Currency: Yuan

我妥马上找医生
我这里痛上
请别理得太短

HE CHINESE LANGUAGE

ore people speak Chinese than any
her language. Chinese is written in
ture-signs or characters. A
hinese person can manage
rfectly well using about 5000
aracters. But there are many
ore: a dictionary of 1716 listed
ore than 40,000! To spell the
unds of Chinese in the Western
phabet, the Chinese use a system
own as Pinyin. In Pinyin, the old
me for the capital of China, Peking,
comes Beijing. Another city,
nton, becomes Guangzhou, and
on. Pinyin is based on Mandarin,
e standard form of the language
ght in China.

▶ *The Great Wall of
China stretches for
more than 2400 km
and is the longest
fortification ever
built. It was begun in
approx. 200 BC to
keep out the invading
Tartars.*

▼ *The giant panda, a native of
China, is now a rare and protected
species.*

▶ *China covers such a vast area that
transport is not yet well developed. Its
network of rivers are still important
'highways' for people and goods.*

THE HISTORY OF CHINA

700 to 1000 BC *Shang dynasty*: bronze tools used and
writing developed.

000 to 256 BC *Chou dynasty*: Confucius and
foundation of Chinese civilization.

00 BC Barbarians invade China.

21 to 207 BC *Ch'in dynasty*: China becomes an
empire. The Great Wall is built.

02BC to AD 221 *Han dynasty*: invention of paper.

89 to 618 Sui dynasty.

18 to 906 *T'ang dynasty*: invention of printing. Poetry
and painting flourish.

07 to 960 Period of unrest, with weak rulers.

60 to 1279 *Sung dynasty*: movable printing type
invented. Cities are built, firearms invented.

215 Mongol ruler Genghis Khan conquers China.

275 Marco Polo reaches China.

280 to 1368 *Yuan dynasty*: Kublai Khan is great ruler
and science flourishes. Mongols are driven out.

368 to 1644 *Ming dynasty*: European traders and

missionaries visit China. Splendid temples, palaces and
tombs built, beautiful porcelain and metalwork made.

1644 to 1912 *Ch'ing dynasty*: China gradually becomes
weak and dominated by foreign traders.

1839 to 1860 Opium Wars: Europeans force Chinese to
open their ports to foreign trade, including the harmful
drug opium.

1900 Boxer Rebellion against foreigners.

1912 *End of the dynasties*: China becomes a republic.

1928 Chiang Kai-shek seizes power.

1930s War with Japan and civil war between Chiang Kai-
shek's Nationalists and Communists.

1949 China becomes a Communist republic, led by Mao
Tse-tung.

1966 to 1969 'Cultural Revolution' takes place.

1976 Death of Mao. New rulers restore order and set
about modernization of China.

1989 Army sent to disperse students' pro-democracy
demonstration in Tiananmen Square, Beijing.

r more information about China, turn to the following articles which you will find elsewhere in the encyclopedia: ACUPUNCTURE;
DDHA; COMMUNISM; CONFUCIUS; EVEREST, MOUNT; GENGHIS KHAN; GREAT WALL OF CHINA; HIMALAYAS; MAO TSE-TUNG; MARCO POLO; PANDA.

We know very little about the early part of Christ's life. He grew up in Nazareth, learning to be a carpenter. The only recorded event of Jesus' youth took place when he was 12 years old. We are told he went to the temple in Jerusalem and discussed questions about God with the wise men. When Jesus next appears he is a man of about 30.

BIBLE as their holy book and Sunday is their holy day, when they go to church, pray and observe other religious traditions.

In some ways Christianity grew out of the religion of JUDAISM. But the teachings of Jesus upset the Jewish and Roman leaders of the time, and in AD 29 he was crucified. After his death, the followers of Jesus, the disciples, spread his teachings far and wide. Today, there are many different forms of Christianity.

Christmas

This festival, celebrated by Christians on December 25, marks the birth of JESUS. It is not known if Jesus was actually born on this date. In fact, the first mention of a festival of Christmas comes from a Roman calendar over 300 years after his death. However, there were a number of Roman and pagan festivals that were held on this day, and early Christians may have thought that by celebrating the birthday of Jesus on the same day as the others, it would show that this festival was just as important.

▼ All illustration from a Victorian Christmas card. The sending of cards at Christmas time is a tradition dating back to the 1840s.

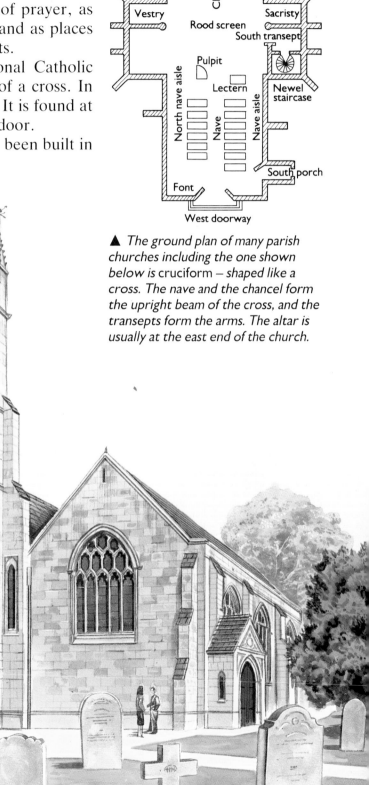

Church

Christian churches are as varied as the countries in which they are found. They come in all shapes and sizes—from tents and tiny wooden huts to towering stone CATHEDRALS. But all churches are used for the same purposes. They serve as places of prayer, as settings for holding religious services and as places that house all kinds of religious objects.

Larger churches, especially traditional Catholic ones, were usually built in the shape of a cross. In most, the altar is built at the east end. It is found at the end furthest away from the main door.

Throughout the ages, churches have been built in

East window

Altar

Buttress

Altar rails

Chancel

Vestry

Sacristy

Rood screen

South transept

Pulpit

Newel staircase

North nave aisle

Lectern

Nave

Nave aisle

South porch

Font

West doorway

▲ The ground plan of many parish churches including the one shown below is cruciform – shaped like a cross. The nave and the chancel form the upright beam of the cross, and the transepts form the arms. The altar is usually at the east end of the church.

▲ *Building a big church in the Middle Ages was an enormous task that went on for many years. In this picture the workmen are building a Gothic abbey.*

▼ *Sir Winston Churchill was Britain's greatest wartime leader. His speeches and courage inspired the country.*

many different styles of ARCHITECTURE, depending on the period of history and which country they were built in. In the 1000s and 1100s, many churches adopted the Romanesque style of architecture. They all had wide, rounded arches and low, round DOMES. In the MIDDLE AGES, in western Europe, a style known as *Gothic* appeared. After the 1000s, cathedrals with pointed spires, narrow, soaring arches, richly stained glass windows and lots of stone carvings became very popular. These churches were cool and dark on the inside. The huge space inside them helped to give churchgoers a sense of awe at being in the presence of God.

Most cathedrals were laid out in the same way on the inside. The worshippers sat in the centre, in a section called the *nave*. They faced towards the altar and the place where the choir sang. On either side were the wings, called *transepts*, which gave the church its cross shape.

Churchill, Winston

Sir Winston Churchill (1874–1965) was a great British prime minister, war leader and writer. Although he was a senior minister in PARLIAMENT before and during World War I, he was not very powerful. But in 1940, when World War II threatened Britain, the country chose him as its prime minister. As a leader during war-time he showed great courage and determination. His rousing speeches helped the people of Britain to fight on when they stood alone against Germany and her allies. He told the people, 'I have nothing to offer but blood, toil, tears and sweat'.

Cinema

The art of making moving pictures came from an invention called the *kinetoscope*, built by an American, Thomas EDISON, in 1891. Soon after Edison's machine became known, two French brothers, Auguste and Louis Lumière, built a similar machine of their own called a *cinématographe*. This machine projected pictures from a piece of film onto a screen. The pictures were shown one after the

▲ Famous stars of the big screen include (top, left to right) Rudolf Valentino, Bette Davis, Meryl Streep, Humphrey Bogart, and (bottom) John Wayne and Marilyn Monroe.

other, so quickly that the images on the screen appeared to move. In 1896, in Paris, the Lumière brothers gave the world's first public film show. Soon, people all over Europe and North America were making films.

These early films did not look much like the ones we are used to seeing today. They were only in black and white, the movements were very jerky and they had no sound. At first, films were made to show news and real events, but by 1902 film-makers began to make up their own stories, using actors to play the parts of imaginary people. These films were very popular in France and the United States, and Hollywood in California became the film-making centre of the world. The first 'talkie', or moving picture with sound, was shown in America in 1927. It was called *The Jazz Singer*.

▲ King Kong *was perhaps the most famous of the early special effects films. At the time, amazed audiences didn't know how he had been brought to life.*

◀ Gone with the Wind, *made in 1939, was an American Civil War epic that became one of the most popular films ever.*

▶ *The thrill-a-minute formula of* Raiders of the Lost Ark *depended heavily on special effects.*

Which story character has been a film hero more often than any other? The answer is Sherlock Holmes, Conan Doyle's famous detective. There have been 187 films about him between 1900 and the present time. And no doubt there will be lots more!

As the industry grew, huge amounts of money were spent on lavish productions. But after World War II, a more realistic type of film became popular. Nearly all films were made in colour.

Today, films are made all over the world, although the United States still produces most of the big feature films, using modern technology to create fantastic visual effects. Television has been a threat to the film industry since the 1960s, and there have been many experiments in recent years to develop new kinds of films.

▼ *Dr Martin Luther King led the movement for racial equality and civil rights in the United States in the 1950s and 60s. He was assassinated in 1968.*

Circus

The Romans first used the word 'circus' to describe a large open-air space where exciting displays of horsemanship, acrobatics, chariot racing and wrestling were held. The modern type of circus began in the 1700s, and circus acts today include jugglers, clowns, acrobats and all sorts of trained animals, even bears and lions.

CIS *See* Soviet Union (former)

Civil Rights

People have always fought for the right to govern themselves. But this does not always mean that people have freedom in their own lives, and sometimes they must fight for this freedom—for their civil rights. The most important of these rights are freedom to follow your own religion, freedom to say what you like in speech and in newspapers, equality in law, and the right to elect and dismiss a government. In the United States, civil rights became an important issue for blacks in the 1950s.

Civil War

Civil war happens when a whole country is divided into two or more groups who fight each other over their different political or religious beliefs. In England, the last civil war lasted from 1642 to 1649 and was fought between the king, CHARLES I, and PARLIAMENT.

By this time it was agreed that although the King ruled the country he could tax money from the people only if Parliament agreed. Charles believed that God had given him the right to do this alone. So in 1629 he got rid of Parliament and ruled without it, taxing the people whenever he needed money.

People became very unwilling to pay their taxes to Charles. In 1640 Charles was forced to recall Parliament because he needed more money. Instead of giving him money, Parliament argued with the King and said he could not rule or tax the people on

In 1959 the United Nations declared that children everywhere have special rights. These rights were listed in 'The Declaration of the Rights of the Child'. Among the things the declaration said were that a child should be able to grow up in a healthy and normal way, free and dignified; have a name and nationality; love and understanding; free schooling and an opportunity to play.

▼ Royalist forces clash with Cromwell's troops at the Battle of Naseby. Cromwell's sweeping victory actually decided the war, though fighting went on for some time in the west of England.

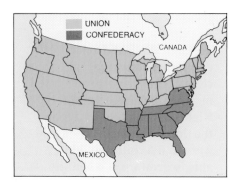

▲ *When the American Civil War broke out, 11 states left the Union to join the Confederacy. The North had much more industry than the South, and that in the end decided the war.*

his own. Charles angrily dismissed Parliament and later tried to arrest some of its leaders.

In 1642 the King called his friends to arm themselves. They were called Royalists. Parliament had its own army. They were called Roundheads because they had short hair. The Roundheads had a great general called Oliver CROMWELL. He was very strict and trained his army carefully.

After several battles the Royalist forces lost the war and the King was captured. Charles was put on trial and in 1649 he was executed. For some years, Parliament ruled without a king, with Cromwell as its leader.

Civil War (American)

The American Civil War took place in the United States from 1861 to 1865. It was fought between the government (Union), backed by the northern states, and the southern states (Confederacy). In 1861 a number of southern states tried to break away from the USA and form their own country. The main quarrel was over SLAVERY. People in the northern states wanted to free the black slaves who

▼ *The American Civil War was one of the first wars to be photographed. This photo of a gun crew was taken at the Battle of Williamsburg in 1862.*

still worked on the big farms, or plantations, in the south. These quarrels led to civil war.

At first the Confederates, under General Lee, won many battles but they were defeated at the Battle of Gettysburg in 1863. The Union army, under General Grant, began to win the war. In April 1865, the Confederate army surrendered to General Grant. The slaves were finally freed.

Clans

A clan is a group of families who claim to share the same ancestor. This ancestor is sometimes real but often is legendary because no one knows whether the ancestor ever really existed. Each clan shares the same surname or family name.

In Scotland the clan name often begins with 'Mac'. This means 'son of', so Macdonald means 'the son of Donald'. In Ireland 'O' also means 'son of', so O'Neill means 'son of Neill'.

Scottish clans often lived in the same valley or glen where they kept cattle. They defended these fiercely against all strangers and enemies. Cattle-stealing raids were common between clans. These sometimes caused quarrels, or feuds, that often lasted for generations.

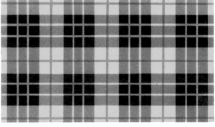

▲ Scottish clans have individual tartan patterns. Shown above are the tartans of clans MacLeod of Lewis (top), MacLeod (centre) and Ross (bottom). Where there are two branches of the same family, different tartans have evolved.

Clay

Clay is rock which has been broken down by millions of years of weathering. It is made of tiny particles that make a thick, sticky paste.

Clay particles are so small and closely packed together that a layer of them is waterproof. When a thick layer of clay lies underground, rain that seeps down through the soil cannot go through it. The water forms an underground pool, or *reservoir*. People can get the water out by digging wells. London lies over a layer of clay like this and still gets some of its water from wells.

Clay is easy to mould and can be baked hard in an oven, or *kiln*. People began making pots from clay in prehistoric times. Today even the finest porcelain is made from clay. Clay is also used to make bricks for houses and other buildings.

▼ Animal figures being fashioned out of clay. Clay that has been fired (baked in a kiln) is called terracotta, which simply means 'baked earth'.

Cleopatra was the name of
seven queens of ancient Egypt.
The famous queen we mention
here was Cleopatra VII.
Historians are not quite sure
as to which kind of snake
Cleopatra allowed herself to
be bitten by. The most likely
snake was the Egyptian cobra.
Its bite causes death quite
quickly.

▼ Although queen of Egypt,
Cleopatra was Greek by blood, one of
the Ptolemy line that Alexander the
Great had set on the throne of Egypt.

Cleopatra

Cleopatra (69–30 BC) was a queen of Egypt. She was
made ruler with her brother at the age of 17, but her
brother's supporters soon drove her from the
throne. When Julius CAESAR visited Egypt he fell in
love with Cleopatra and helped her to become
queen again. Cleopatra followed Caesar back to
Rome and lived in his house until he was murdered
in 44 BC. After this she went back to Egypt.

Three years later Cleopatra met Mark Antony,
who ruled the Roman Empire with Octavian.
Antony also fell in love with Cleopatra and left his
wife, the sister of Octavian, to live with her.
Octavian did not trust Cleopatra or Antony and
started a war with them. He defeated them in a
naval battle at Actium in Greece in 31 BC.

Cleopatra and Antony fled to Alexandria in
Egypt. They were followed there by Octavian and
his army. Cleopatra began to realize that she could
never beat the Romans. She and Antony decided to
kill themselves. Antony stabbed himself first and
died in Cleopatra's arms. Cleopatra then died from
a poisonous snake bite.

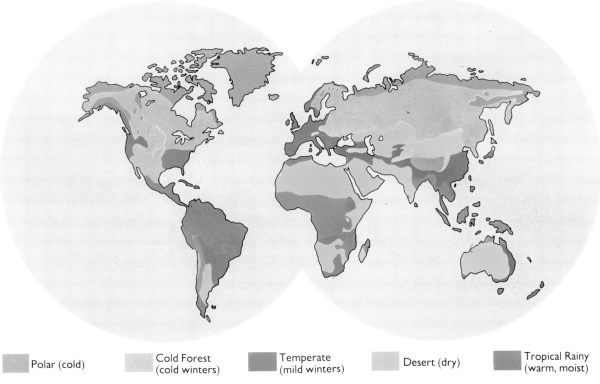

Polar (cold)		Cold Forest (cold winters)		Temperate (mild winters)		Desert (dry)		Tropical Rainy (warm, moist)	

Climate

Climate is the usual WEATHER of a place over a long period of time. The weather can change from day to day but the climate stays the same.

The Sun has the greatest influence on the climate. It heats the land, the seas and the air. Countries near the equator get more of the Sun's rays and usually have a hotter climate than places further north or south. The Sun's rays do not get to the Arctic and the Antarctic easily. They have very cold climates.

When the Sun heats the air it causes winds which can make the climate hotter or colder. The winds may also carry rain or dry air which can make the climate wet or dry.

▲ The Earth can be roughly divided into five climatic zones. Within each zone there are variations because climate is determined by altitude as well as by latitude.

▼ The Poles get less heat than the equator because the Sun's rays have to travel farther through the Earth's atmosphere. The rays also reach the Poles at a slant because the Earth is round.

Clinton, Bill (William Jefferson)

Bill Clinton was elected President of the United States in 1993. Formerly Governor of Arkansas, he is the first Democrat president since Jimmy Carter (1977-81). One of his major aims is to reform America's health care system. His wife, Hillary Rodham Clinton, now heads a commission to plan health care reforms.

147

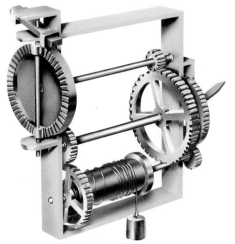

▲ Early mechanical clocks in Europe were driven by a weight on the end of a cord wound round a drum. As the drum rotated, it turned the hands of the clock.

▼ One of the most famous clocks in the world is at the Houses of Parliament in London. It is often mistakenly called Big Ben – this is actually the name of its biggest bell.

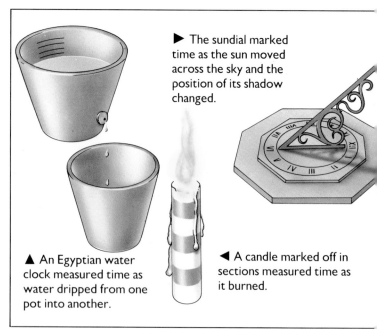

▶ The sundial marked time as the sun moved across the sky and the position of its shadow changed.

▲ An Egyptian water clock measured time as water dripped from one pot into another.

◀ A candle marked off in sections measured time as it burned.

Clock

Long ago people measured TIME by putting a stick in the ground and watching its shadow move with the Sun. Sundials work in the same way. Sun clocks work only when the Sun is shining, so people began to measure time by watching how long it took a candle to burn or a tank of water to empty.

The first mechanical clocks were made in Europe in the 1200s, although the Chinese probably had clocks as early as the 600s. European clocks were first used in churches and abbeys to mark the time of services. A clock in Salisbury Cathedral dates from 1386.

Early clocks like these were bad time-keepers and could lose or gain an hour a day. In 1581 the great astronomer Galileo discovered that the PENDULUM could be used to measure time. This helped people to make much more accurate clocks. From then on improvements were made and ordinary clocks are now accurate to within a few minutes a year.

Today's scientists need very accurate clocks. They invented first the electric and then the quartz crystal clock. The most accurate clock today is at the United States Naval Research Laboratory in Washington, D.C. It is an atomic hydrogen maser clock and is accurate to one second in 1,700,000 years.

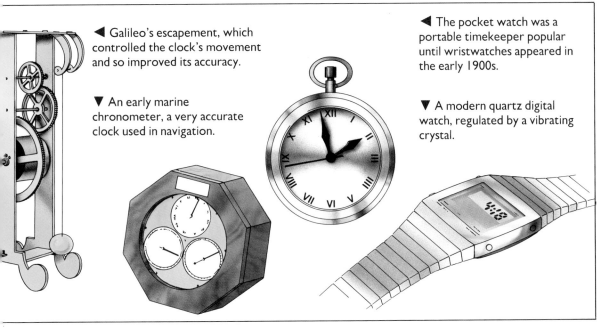

◄ Galileo's escapement, which controlled the clock's movement and so improved its accuracy.

▼ An early marine chronometer, a very accurate clock used in navigation.

◄ The pocket watch was a portable timekeeper popular until wristwatches appeared in the early 1900s.

▼ A modern quartz digital watch, regulated by a vibrating crystal.

Clothing

Most people in the world wear some sort of clothing. What they wear depends on the climate and how they live. Because clothes decorate us as well as protect us, styles of clothing change with fashion.

The earliest clothes were animal skins. In the ancient world people wore loose, draped tunics. By the MIDDLE AGES the dress of poorer people remained simple and crude, but the wealthy dressed in fine silks and damasks from the East. The new

▲ Timekeeping through the ages. Early peoples used sundials and water clocks. For accurate timekeeping today scientists use atomic clocks.

▼ Elizabeth I led the fashion of her day. When she died she is said to have left 3000 dresses in her wardrobe.

▼ Clothing styles from prehistoric to medieval times. The ancient Greeks and Romans wore loosely-draped tunics and togas. Costume became more elaborate after rich silks and muslins were imported from the East.

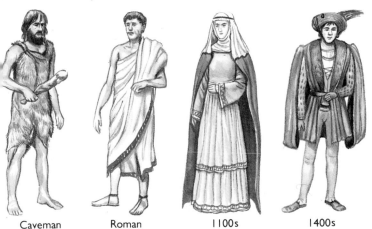

Caveman   Roman   1100s   1400s

Elizabeth I

▶ *Fashion is big business. Every season brings shows where models display the latest top fashion designs.*

1630s 1740s

1850s

1960s

▲ *Popular clothing styles over four centuries. Modern fashion reflects the change in lifestyle in this century – designs are practical and clothes are sewn from man-made fabrics that are easy to care for.*

wealth and interest in art during the RENAISSANCE made rich, colourful fabrics popular. In the 1700s in Europe costume became very grand to match the grand buildings of the period. People wore huge wigs and wide, stiffened skirts, often beautifully embroidered. By the 1900s, fashions had become more practical, especially for women. Today Western dress is worn by many people throughout the world. How styles change from year to year is decided by top fashion designers.

Cloud

Clouds are great clusters of tiny water droplets or ice crystals in the air. A cloud may float more than 10,000 metres up, or drift so low that it touches the ground, when it is known as mist or fog.

There is always a certain amount of water *vapour* in the air. It is made up of tiny specks of water. Warm air that contains water vapour often rises and cools. Since cool air cannot hold as much water as warm air, the vapour particles start to form droplets (condense) around bits of dust, pollen and salt.

As more water vapour condenses, the droplets grow in size and clouds begin to form. At first they are white and gauzy. As they become heavy with water they become thick and grey. Finally the droplets become so heavy that they clump together and fall to the earth. If the temperature is high

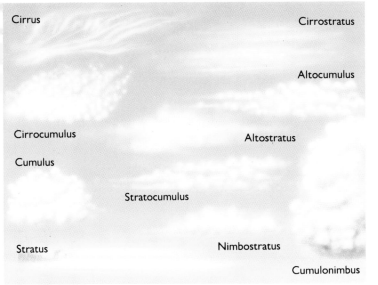

◀ *Different types of cloud bring different weather. The high cirrus clouds are made of ice, and are sometimes called 'mares' tails'. Puffy cumulus clouds often mean fine weather. Low, grey, stratus clouds bring rain and the towering cumulonimbus are thunder clouds.*

enough they come down as rain. Otherwise they land as hail or snow.

Most clouds form along the boundaries between cold and warm air masses. By watching how they build and move it is possible to tell what sort of weather is coming. Different types of clouds tell weather forecasters different things. Clouds are one of the best ways we have of predicting the WEATHER.

Coal

Coal is a FUEL which is found in layers, or *seams*, under the ground. It is known as a FOSSIL fuel because it was made millions of years ago from dead plants. Coal is used for heating and in making electricity, gas and chemicals. It is also made into another fuel called coke.

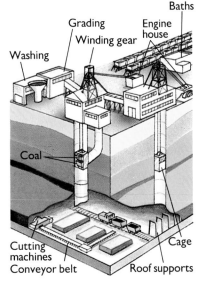

▲ *Most coal is now cut by machines. The workings of a coal mine may stretch for miles underground.*

Coffee

Coffee is a drink made from the beans of the coffee plant. The coffee tree can grow as high as 12 metres, but it is kept trimmed to only 2 or 3 metres so that the fruit can be reached easily. The trees bear red berries which contain two seeds or beans in yellow pulp, surrounded by a tough skin. The skin and pulp are removed and the beans dried and roasted until they are brown. Then they are ground to brew the coffee we drink.

▼ *Coffee comes from beans that are found inside the fruit of the coffee tree. These berries are red when ripe. The beans are roasted to bring out the coffee flavour.*

► Coins are made in different shapes and in different metals. Collecting coins can be a satisfying hobby.

Coin

The first metal coins were minted (made) about 800 BC. Before then, all trade has been done by barter – by exchanging goods. For a long time coins were made of precious metals, particularly gold and silver. Then people realized that any metal would do as long as everybody agreed that each coin was a symbol for a certain value.

COLOMBIA

Government: Republic
Capital: Bogotá
Area: 1,138,914 sq km
Population: 34,296,000
Language: Spanish
Currency: Peso

Colombia

Colombia is a country in north-west South America. The Andes Mountains cover about a third of its area. Most of the people live in the north-west, where the highlands are fertile. Coffee is Colombia's most important crop. Bogotá is the capital, and the population is over 34 million.

The Colombians won their independence from Spain in 1819 under the leadership of Simón Bolívar. The country is a democratic republic but has many social and economic problems.

Although the Colosseum has suffered several earthquakes, much of it still stands. Only a portion of the outer masonry remains, however, because it served as a handy quarry during the Middle Ages. Much of the stone that went to build St Peter's Basilica in Rome was taken from the Colosseum.

Colosseum

The Colosseum of Rome was a giant sports stadium built by the ancient Romans. It could hold more than 50,000 people and was the largest building of its kind in the Roman Empire. It still stands in the centre of Rome but is partly in ruins.

The floor, or *arena*, was used for GLADIATOR combats, battles between men and animals and

◀ The Colosseum, now a ruin, was a great open-air arena where the ancient Romans watched displays and combat.

▼ Coloured light behaves differently from coloured pigments (the substances that give inks and paints their colour). All the colours in light (1) combine to make white light, but mixing coloured pigments (2) results in black.

fights between different kinds of animals. It was also used for showing rare wild creatures. The floor could also be flooded so that sea battles could be fought on it. Underneath the arena were pens in which to keep the wild beasts. When the Colosseum was finished it was opened with a ceremony in which 5000 animals were killed.

Colour

The first man to find out about coloured light was Isaac Newton. He shone sunlight through a piece of glass called a *prism*. The light that came out of the prism was broken up into all the colours of the rainbow—red, orange, yellow, green, blue and violet. Newton had found out that ordinary white light is made up of many colours added together.

When sunlight falls on rain or spray from a garden hose, we sometimes see a rainbow. Rainbows are caused by the drops of water behaving like tiny prisms. They break up the Sun's light into a *spectrum* of colours. The colours are always in the same order, from red to violet.

▶ *Why we see colour: a green plant looks green to us because it absorbs all the colours in light apart from green, which it reflects back to our eyes.*

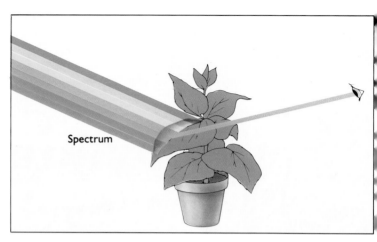

Spectrum

A red flower is red because it takes in all the other colours and throws back only red. A white flower gives back to our eyes all the colours of light. We know that all the colours added together make white.

Columbus, Christopher

Christopher Columbus (1451–1506) was a sailor and explorer. He discovered America for Spain in 1492. Although Columbus returned to America three more times, he died believing that the land he had reached was Asia.

Like many people of his time, Columbus knew that the Earth was not flat but round. Sailors from Europe used to sail east to the 'Indies' (Asia). They brought back rich cargoes of gold, spices and treasure. Columbus thought that if he sailed west instead he could reach the Indies quicker. The Queen and King of Spain gave him ships and money to make this voyage.

In 1492 Columbus sailed west with three small ships, the *Santa Maria*, the *Pinta* and the *Niña*. The ships sailed for three weeks without seeing any land and the crews became afraid. Then, on 12 October, they reached an island in the Americas. Columbus named it San Salvador – an island in the Bahamas. When he returned to Spain, Columbus had a hero's welcome.

Columbus thought he had sailed to the Indies. This is why the people he met in America were called Indians. The islands he first reached are still known as the West Indies.

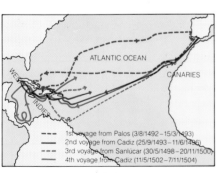

ATLANTIC OCEAN

CANARIES

WEST INDIES

1st voyage from Palos (3/8/1492–15/3/1493)
2nd voyage from Cadiz (25/9/1493–11/6/1496)
3rd voyage from Sanlúcar (30/5/1498–20/11/1500)
4th voyage from Cadiz (11/5/1502–7/11/1504)

▲ *Christopher Columbus made four voyages to the Americas, first landing in San Salvador. His flagship on the first voyage, the 100-tonne caravel* Santa Maria, *ran aground and had to be abandoned.*

Comet

Comets travel round the SOLAR SYSTEM in paths, or ORBITS. Sometimes they pass close to the Sun. At other times they move far beyond the path of Pluto, the outermost planet. A complete orbit by a comet is called its period. Encke's Comet has the shortest period of all. It lasts for three years and four months. Others have periods of centuries or even thousands of years.

Comets are clouds of frozen gases, ice, dust and rock. The biggest are only a few kilometres across, but their bright tails may be millions of kilometres long.

Most of the time comets cannot be seen, even through the biggest telescopes. But whenever their orbits bring them back into the middle of the solar system they flare up and look very bright.

As a comet travels towards the Sun, the Sun's rays knock particles out of the comet and push them away to make a long tail. The tail is made of glowing gas and dust. But the tail is so fine that a rocket passing through it would not be harmed. The Earth has passed through the tails of several comets. One of the most famous comets is named after the astronomer Edmond HALLEY. In 1682 he studied the path of a bright comet and accurately forecast when it would return.

▲ Some of the comets that return regularly to the Sun every few years. Part of the much bigger orbit of Halley's Comet is also shown. Encke's Comet has the smallest period and it passes close to the Sun every three years and four months, although it cannot be seen without a telescope. Comets are usually named after those who discovered them. They were once thought to foretell the coming of evil events, since they appeared so unexpectedly and dramatically.

◀ Comet West, photographed on March 9, 1976, showing its dust tail (white) and its gas tail (blue).

▲ *Commercial artists prepare advertisements for magazines and newspapers. This old advertisement for a German airline is a fine example.*

INDEPENDENT MEMBERS OF THE COMMONWEALTH

Antigua and Barbuda	Namibia
Australia	New Zealand
Bahamas	Nigeria (suspended)
Bangladesh	Pakistan
Barbados	Papua New Guinea
Belize	Western Samoa
Botswana	Seychelles
Brunei	Sierra Leone
Cameroon	Singapore
Canada	Solomon Islands
Cyprus	South Africa
Dominica	Sri Lanka
Gambia	St Kitts-Nevis
Ghana	St Lucia
Grenada	St Vincent and the Grenadines
Guyana	Swaziland
India	Tanzania
Jamaica	Tonga
Kenya	Trinidad and Tobago
Kiribati	Tuvalu
Lesotho	Uganda
Malawi	United Kingdom
Malaysia	Vanuatu
Maldives	Zambia
Malta	Zimbabwe
Mauritius	
Nauru	

Commercial Art

Commercial art is the art that has to do with business – the word 'commerce' means business. Commercial artists are usually trained in an art school, where they learn to design, draw and paint. They learn to 'lay out' books and magazines – that is, to arrange pictures and text on a page. They prepare advertisements for newspapers and magazines, and illustrate books. Fashion designers design clothing; industrial designers design products and appliances. Nearly everything we see around us has been 'designed' in some way or other.

Common Cold

The common cold is the most widespread disease. Many people miss several days of work or school a year because of it. The disease is caused by tiny organisms called viruses. The viruses are carried through the air by coughs and sneezes. Anyone nearby can catch the cold if the viruses enter the nose or mouth. That is why it is very important to cover your nose and mouth when you cough or sneeze.

There are more than a hundred different cold viruses and many more may exist. This is one of the reasons why scientists have not so far found a cure for the common cold.

Commonwealth

A commonwealth is a group of countries or people who are friendly and help each other. The Commonwealth of Nations is made up from most of the countries that were once ruled by Britain. Most of these countries now have their own governments and laws but many of them still have the queen or king of Britain as their monarch.

The Commonwealth came into being at a meeting held in 1926. Commonwealth countries share some of the same beliefs and TRADE with each other. The heads of Commonwealth countries that have their own governments meet together often. They talk about their problems and try to help each other.

Communication

Communication means the transmission of ideas, information or feelings from one person to another. When you answer a question, discuss something or tell someone something you are communicating through speech. This is one of the most important means of communication. But there are many other kinds. (See pages 158–159.)

Communism

Communism is a set of ideas about the way a country should be run. The main idea of communism is that people should share wealth and property. This makes people more equal because nobody is very rich or very poor. In most communist countries the people own the factories and farms but it is usually the government that runs them. The government controls almost everything, and personal freedoms are restricted. However, during the late 1980s, the then USSR and most eastern European countries adopted a freer form of Communism and obtained more democratic government.

Many countries became communist during the course of the twentieth century. They included the Soviet Union, China and Cuba, and some countries in Eastern Europe and the Far East. LENIN and MAO TSE-TUNG were among the great communist leaders of the twentieth century.

Comoros

The Comoro Islands are a cluster of volcanic islands in the Indian Ocean between Madagascar and Africa. Most of the people are poor and live on small farms. France took the islands from the Arabs in 1886, and in 1975 the islands declared their independence. However, one island, Mayotte, voted to remain French. There are about half a million people on the islands, and the capital is Moroni.

Compact Disc *See* Recording

COMOROS

INDIAN OCEAN

COMOROS

AFRICA

MADAGASCAR

Government: Republic
Capital: Moroni
Area: 2171 sq km
Population: 551,000
Language: French
Currency: CFA franc

COMMUNICATION

Communication is the exchange of ideas – through words, pictures, and numbers. We learn by communication with other people. And it is by means of communication that civilization has grown. Imagine a world without any way of storing and recording information (such as a printed book). Each new generation would have to reinvent the wheel, relying on word of mouth and memory alone to pass on wisdom and knowledge.

Communication began with the first human languages, and with the cave paintings of Stone Age people. The first writing, using picture-signs, was invented more than 5000 years ago. But it is in the last 500 years that the communications 'explosion' has taken place. The invention of printing made books available to everyone who could read. Since the Industrial Revolution of the 1800s communications science has changed our lives, bringing amazing new ways of message-sending and message-storing. Inventions such as photography, sound recording, radio, telephones, television and computers have brought about the modern communications revolution.

ADVANCES IN COMMUNICATION

Year	Invention
AD 100	Paper, by the Chinese
950	Arabic numerals reach Europe
1440	Printing with movable type, by Gutenberg
1600s	Newspapers become popular
1829	Braille alphabet for the blind
1837	Telegraph invented by S. B. Morse
1840s	Photography invented by Daguerre and others
1876	Telephone invented by A. G. Bell
1877	Sound recording, by phonograph (Edison)
1899	Sound recording on tape (Poulsen)
1901	First transatlantic radio signal (Marconi)
1929	Television, using electronic system (Zworykin)
1936	BBC begins first public television broadcasts
1940	Invention of the photocopier (Carlson)
1946	Electronic computer (Eckert, Mauchly, Turing and others)
1948	Transistor (Shockley, Bardeen and Brattain)
1956	Videotape recording (Poniatoff)
1962	Telstar, world's first communications satellite
1970s	Desktop computers, video recorders in the home
1980s	Fax machines, compact discs, digital tapes

WRITING AND PRINTING

◀ Before the invention of printing, books were copied out by hand. Printing came to Europe in the 1400s.

▲ With the invention of movable type, printing became faster and more efficient. The pieces of type could be used again and again.

◀ Writing implements, from quill pen to the fountain pen.

▶ Hammond's typewriter of 1880. A hammer hit the back of the paper, pressing it against a letter on a fixed cyclinder.

IMPORTANT INVENTIONS

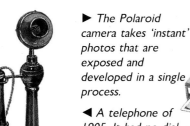

▶ The Polaroid camera takes 'instant' photos that are exposed and developed in a single process.

◀ A telephone of 1905. It had no dial — all calls had to be connected by the operator.

▶ The gramophone, which plays flat discs, was invented by a German, Emile Berliner, in 1887.

◀ Home video recorders allow us to view recorded programmes.

An early Daguerreotype camera.

.-	A	····	H
-···	B	··	I
-·-·	C	·---	J
-··	D	-·-	K
·	E	·-··	L
··-·	F	--	M
--·	G	-·	N

▲ The Morse code was once the main way of sending signals along wires or by radio.

▶ Small portable cassette players make it possible to listen to sound recordings almost anywhere.

THE ELECTRONIC REVOLUTION

The first radio signals were sent across the Atlantic Ocean by Guglielmo Marconi in 1901.

The desktop microcomputer can be a useful educational tool.

▶ Large dish aerials are used to send TV signals up to a satellite, from where they are directed to a dish in the receiving country and transmitted to TV receivers.

For more information turn to these articles: ADVERTISING; BELL, ALEXANDER GRAHAM; BOOK; CINEMA; COMPUTER; EDISON; GUTENBERG; HIEROGLYPHICS; LANGUAGE; MARCONI; NEWSPAPER; PHOTOGRAPHY; PRINTING; RADIO; SATELLITE; TELEPHONE; TELEVISION; TYPEWRITER; WRITING.

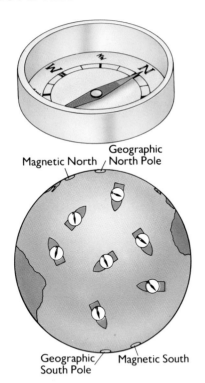

Geographic
Magnetic North / North Pole

Geographic / Magnetic South
South Pole

▲ A compass does not point directly at the North Pole. This is because the Earth's magnetic field does not line up with the geographic Poles. The difference between the geographic and magnetic poles is called the 'magnetic variation'.

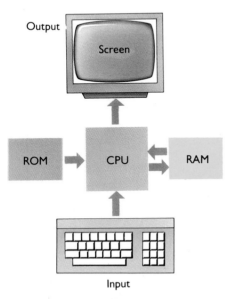

Output

Screen

ROM → CPU → RAM

Input

▲ A computer has four basic parts, the 'input' (keyboard), memory (RAM and ROM), central processing unit (CPU), and the 'output', a screen or printer.

Compass

A compass is an instrument for finding the way. A magnetic compass always points to the Earth's magnetic poles, which are close to the North and South Poles. The magnetic compass has been used for centuries by sailors and explorers to find the right direction.

A magnetic compass works by MAGNETISM. It has a magnetic needle fixed to a pivot so that it is free to swing round. The needle always points north and south when it is at rest. With a compass showing where north and south are, it is easy to travel in a straight line in any direction you wish to go.

The needle always points north and south because the Earth itself is a big magnet. The compass lines up parallel with the Earth's magnetic field.

Compound

Compounds are chemicals that are made up of two or more ELEMENTS. For example, salt is a compound made up of the elements sodium and chlorine.

Compounds are formed when elements come together and make a new substance which is completely different from the elements. Water is a compound of the gas elements hydrogen and oxygen, and it is very different from either of them.

There are millions of compounds in the world. They can be very simple, like water (with three ATOMS in each molecule), or complex like some plastics with hundreds of atoms in their molecules.

Computer

Computers are playing a bigger and bigger part in all our lives. They can play a game of chess with you, guide a spacecraft, check fingerprints and draw a map of Australia. They can do all these things and many more merely because they can add, subtract and compare one number with another. Computers are special because they can do millions of calculations in a second.

Although the computer works with numbers, the information it uses does not have to start off as

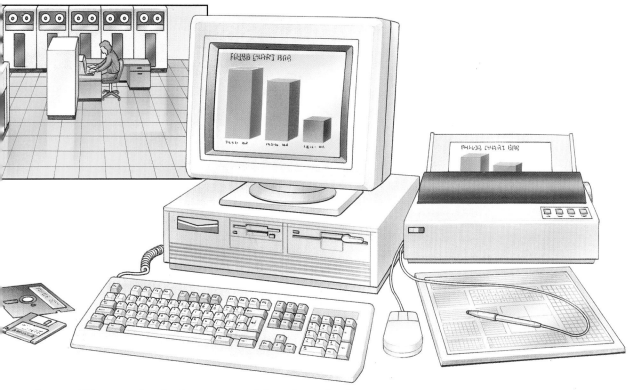

numbers. We can feed almost anything into it, but the first thing the computer does is to turn everything into numbers. But the numbers it uses are not quite the same as ours. We use the numbers 0 to 9. All the computer needs is 0 and 1. In fact, it can only count up to 1! This is called the BINARY SYSTEM. The computer uses the binary system because it has been designed to work with electrical currents. It can recognize the difference between a big current and a small current flow. If there is a big current, it registers 1; if there is a small current, it registers 0. When we type on the keys of a computer keyboard, we are making little electrical currents flow through tiny circuits in microchips. It is these tiny currents that give us the answers we need.

▲ *Computer programs and data can be stored on a cassette or on a floppy disk. Floppy disks are more efficient. They store information in concentric tracks that enable data to be located quickly.*

Concrete

Concrete is a mixture of cement, gravel and sand, together with water. The paste-like concrete sets hard and is used to make buildings, roads, bridges and dams. The cement that is the starting point for concrete is usually made from limestone and clay, but chalk and sand may also be included. These materials are crushed and mixed, then heated in a

One disadvantage of concrete is that it can be very heavy. The ancient Romans knew this, so they mixed cement with lightweight substances to lighten their building materials. The great dome of the Pantheon in Rome, larger than that of St Paul's in London, was made with concrete mixed from pumice stone – lightweight volcanic ash from the slopes of Mount Vesuvius.

▲ *To make concrete, cement is mixed with sand, gravel and water. Too much water will weaken the concrete, and mixing concrete of good quality is a highly skilled job.*

kiln. When cool, the mixture is ground into cement powder. Concrete is often strengthened by placing steel rods in it when it is soft. This *reinforced* concrete is very strong indeed.

Confucius

Confucius (551–479 BC) lived nearly 2500 years ago in China. He was a very famous thinker. He taught people how to live and behave in a good way. The Chinese people followed his teaching for centuries.

The most important rule made by Confucius was that people should think of others, and not do to others anything that they would not like done to themselves.

Congo

The Congo is a country in the west of central AFRICA. It was formerly part of a huge French colony and became independent in 1960. It has an area of 342,000 sq km.

The Congo is a hot, wet country. It has great forests and swamps, and a low grassy plain on the coast. The capital is called Brazzaville. The Congo produces a lot of timber, but it also has diamonds, sugar, oil, cocoa and coffee.

Along the Congo's border with its larger neighbour, Zaire, runs a great river. This river used to be called the Congo, but is now called the Zaire River. It is 4667 km long, one of the longest in the world.

CONGO

Government: Single-party republic
Capital: Brazzaville
Area: 342,000 sq km
Population: 2,376,000
Language: French
Currency: CFA franc

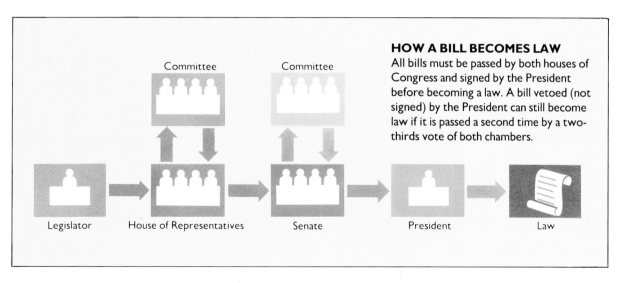

HOW A BILL BECOMES LAW
All bills must be passed by both houses of Congress and signed by the President before becoming a law. A bill vetoed (not signed) by the President can still become law if it is passed a second time by a two-thirds vote of both chambers.

Legislator | House of Representatives | Senate | President | Law

Congress

Congress is the parliament of the United States of America. It is the part of the government which makes laws.

Congress is made up of two chambers: the House of Representatives and the Senate.

To make a new law, a 'bill' is introduced by a member into one of the chambers. It is discussed by groups, or *committees*, and then voted on by the members of the chamber. The bill then goes to the other chamber. When it has been passed by both chambers, the president signs it and it becomes law.

Conifer

Conifers are TREES and shrubs which have cones instead of flowers for making pollen and seeds. Many of them are found in the cool parts of the world. Some even grow north of the Arctic Circle.

Norway spruce

Scots pine

▲ *Conifers include pines, firs, spruces, larches and cedars. Most have needle-like leaves which they do not lose in winter.*

Cedar of Lebanon

▲ Felling trees to meet the world demand for paper and wood has laid bare thousands of acres of forest land. Conservation means careful use of such resources.

▼ When the Turks captured Constantinople in 1453, mosques such as this one, the Blue Mosque, replaced the Christian churches.

Conservation

Human beings use plants, animals, soil, water and minerals for nearly everything they make. Often they waste and destroy those natural resources. Conservation means using these resources wisely and protecting them. It also means preserving areas of natural beauty.

Today the need to conserve wildlife and natural resources is a world problem. It involves the study of ECOLOGY, the branch of BIOLOGY that deals with the relationship between all living things and their surroundings. People must avoid upsetting Nature's balance.

Constantinople

Constantinople is the old name for the city of Istanbul in Turkey. It lies between Asia and Europe.

Constantinople was the most important city in the western world for more than a thousand years. It was named after the Roman emperor Constantine. In AD 330 Constantine founded the city on the site of the ancient Greek town of Byzantium. He divided the Roman Empire into two to make it easier to manage. Constantinople was the capital of the eastern half, which became known as the Byzantine Empire.

After the last Roman emperor was overthrown in AD 476, Constantinople and the Byzantine Empire continued to be powerful. The city was a great centre of Christianity, trade and western learning until it was invaded by the Ottoman Turks in 1453.

The Byzantines built many beautiful buildings. One of these is the famous Cathedral of Saint Sophia which was begun in the reign of Constantine. It was first a Christian church and then a Muslim place of worship, or *mosque*. Today it is a museum containing fine pieces of Byzantine art.

The Orient Express is a famous first-class train that ran between Paris and Constantinople in the last half of the 19th and the first half of the 20th century. For many years, the service on the Orient Express was so luxurious that it was known as the 'king of trains and the train of kings'.

◀ *Some constellations of the Northern Hemisphere*

1 *Equuleus, Colt*
2 *Delphinus, Dolphin*
3 *Pegasus, Flying Horse*
4 *Pisces, Fishes*
5 *Cetus, Sea Monster*
6 *Aries, Ram*
7 *Triangulum, Triangle*
8 *Andromeda, Chained Maiden*
9 *Lacerta, Lizard*
10 *Cygnus, Swan*
11 *Sagitta, Arrow*
12 *Aquila, Eagle*
13 *Lyra, Lyre*
14 *Cepheus, King*
15 *Cassiopeia, Lady in Chair*
16 *Perseus, Champion*
17 *Camelopardus, Giraffe*
18 *Auriga, Charioteer*
19 *Taurus, Bull*
20 *Orion, Hunter*
21 *Lynx, Lynx*
22 *Polaris (Pole Star)*
23 *Ursa Minor, Little Bear*
24 *Draco, Dragon*
25 *Hercules, Kneeling Giant*
26 *Ophiuchus, Serpent-Bearer*
27 *Serpens, Serpent*
28 *Corona Borealis, Northern Crown*
29 *Boötes, Herdsman*
30 *Ursa Major, Great Bear*
31 *Gemini, Twins*
32 *Cancer, Crab*
33 *Canis Minor, Little Dog*
34 *Hydra, Sea Serpent*
35 *Leo, Lion*
36 *Leo Minor, Little Lion*
37 *Canes Venatici, Hunting Dogs*
38 *Coma Berenices, Berenice's Hair*
39 *Virgo, Virgin*

Constellation

Constellations in early times were simply patterns of stars in the sky. They were named after ancient gods, heroes, animals and everyday objects whose shapes people saw in the patterns—Orion the Hunter, Leo the Lion, Lyra the Lyre. There are now 88 constellations over the whole sky. Twelve of them form a wide track where the Sun appears to travel in the course of the year, and where the

▶ *Some constellations of the Southern Hemisphere*

 1 Cetus, Sea Monster
 2 Sculptor, Sculptor
 3 Aquarius, Water-Bearer
 4 Piscis Austrinus, Southern Fish
 5 Capricornus, Sea Goat
 6 Grus, Crane
 7 Phoenix, Phoenix
 8 Fornax, Furnace
 9 Eridanus, River Eridanus
10 Hydrus, Little Snake
11 Tucana, Toucan
12 Indus, Indian
13 Sagittarius, Archer
14 Aquila, Eagle
15 Corona Australis, Southern Crown
16 Pavo, Peacock
17 Octans, Octant
18 Dorado, Swordfish
19 Pictor, Painter's Easel
20 Columba, Dove
21 Lepus, Hare
22 Orion, Hunter
23 Monoceros, Unicorn
24 Canis Major, Great Dog
25 Puppis, Poop
26 Carina, Keel
27 Volans, Flying Fish
28 Chamaeleon, Chameleon
29 Apus, Bird of Paradise
30 Triangulum Australe, Southern Triangle
31 Ara, Altar
32 Scorpio, Scorpion
33 Serpens, Serpent
34 Ophiuchus, Serpent-Bearer
35 Lupus, Wolf
36 Centaurus, Centaur
37 Crux, Southern Cross
38 Musca, Fly
39 Vela, Sails
40 Pyxis, Compass
41 Hydra, Sea Serpent
42 Sextans, Sextant
43 Crater, Cup
44 Corvus, Crow
45 Libra, Scales
46 Virgo, Virgin

planets are usually found. These are the constellations of the Zodiac.

About 45 constellations were first named thousands of years ago. But there is a large group of 'modern' constellations, particularly in the southern sky, which were not charted until the great sea voyages of the 17th and 18th centuries.

Continental Shelf

Continents do not end where their coasts meet the sea. Their true edge lies far out under the sea. Each continent is ringed by a gently sloping shelf of land under the sea called the continental shelf. This shelf sometimes stretches for hundreds of kilometres from the shore. Beyond the continental shelf is the deep ocean floor.

In the past, the sea level was lower and much of the continental shelf was dry land. Rivers flowed through it to the sea and made valleys or canyons. These canyons are still there, but today they are under the sea.

Most sea life is found on the continental shelf. Sunlight shines through the water, helping plants, fish and other animals to grow.

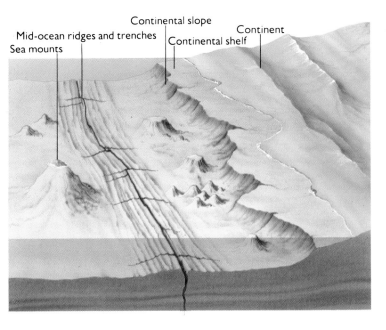

Mid-ocean ridges and trenches
Sea mounts
Continental slope
Continental shelf
Continent

◀ *Most of the continental shelf lies under about 140 metres of water. At its edge, the seabed falls steeply to the deep ocean floor.*

Continent

A continent is a large area of land. The Earth has seven continents: Africa, Antarctica, Asia, Australia, Europe, North America and South America. Some people say that because Europe and Asia are joined, they are one big continent called Eurasia.

The continents are not fixed. They are made of lighter rock than the rock on the ocean floor. The great heat in the centre of the Earth has made the surface rocks break into huge pieces called *plates*.

▼ *Continental drift at various stages in the Earth's history. Over millions of years, the single continent we call Pangaea broke up to produce the pattern of continents we know today.*

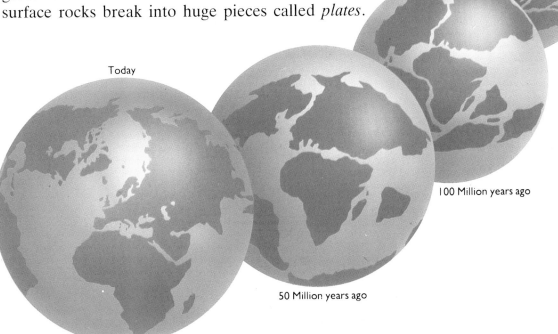

200 Million years ago

Today

100 Million years ago

50 Million years ago

During the Ice Age, the northern and southern parts of the world were covered by great ice-caps. So much water became ice that the sea-level dropped by as much as 150 metres. This meant that vast areas of the shallow continental shelf became dry land. It has been estimated that a total area of about 30 million square km of sea became dry land – an area bigger than the Soviet Union, the biggest country in the world.

In 1934, the cottage in which James Cook lived as a boy at Great Ayton in Yorkshire was presented to the government of Victoria in Australia. It was carefully taken apart and re-erected in Fitzroy Gardens, Melbourne.

When the plates move they move the continents with them. This movement is very slow. A continent moves only a few centimetres in one century.

A few hundred years ago some people saw that the shapes of America, Europe and Africa looked like jigsaw pieces that would fit closely if they were pushed together. This gave them the idea that the continents used to be one big piece of land which broke up. This idea is called continental drift. Continental drift was first suggested in 1912 by Alfred Wegener. He found evidence to show that America was once in contact with Africa. Today, people who study GEOLOGY believe this idea is true.

Geologists think that the movements of the continents pushed up some pieces of land to make mountains such as the Alps and the Himalayas.

Cook, James

James Cook (1728–1779) was a famous British sea captain and explorer. His expeditions took him round the world and all over the Pacific Ocean. Cook's discoveries led to Australia, New Zealand and many South Pacific islands becoming British colonies.

After serving in the Royal Navy for 13 years, Cook was put in command of an expedition to Tahiti in 1768. After Tahiti, Cook carried on to New Zealand. He sailed around both North and South Islands, and then went on to Australia. Cook landed

▶ The routes followed by Captain Cook on his three voyages. On his first voyage in 1768 he was in command of The Endeavour, with a crew of 80 and 3 scientists on board. Many of the places Cook discovered are named after him. His detailed surveys and observations set new standards for the explorers that followed him.

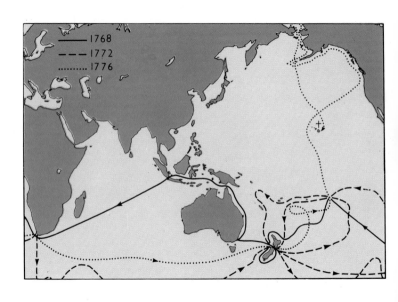

▼ In New Zealand Cook met the warlike Maoris, who paddled elaborately carved war canoes and tattooed their faces. Cook found the strait between North and South Islands and charted nearly 4000 km of coast. He was very popular with his crew and insisted that his men ate sauerkraut (a kind of pickled cabbage), fruit and carrots to prevent the disease scurvy.

in Botany Bay in 1770 to claim the continent for Britain.

On his second voyage (1772–1775), Cook set off to look for the 'southern continent', which many people believed lay south of Australia. He crossed the Antarctic Circle and explored the edges of Antarctica. He also charted many unknown Pacific islands.

Cook's third and last voyage began in 1776. He left England with two ships—the *Resolution* and *Discovery*—to try to find a route around North America. Again he sailed to the Pacific. In early 1778 he discovered the Hawaiian Islands. From there Cook sailed north along the west coast of America. He got as far as the Bering Strait off Alaska before being forced back by ice. Returning to Hawaii, he was killed in a scuffle with natives over a stolen boat. Today Cook is remembered as a skilled navigator and a great explorer.

▲ The Maoris were skilful craftsmen. They often carved clubs and charms from a green stone. Their houses were made of wood, and finely carved.

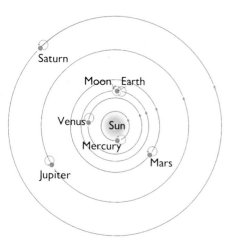

▲ *Copernicus realized that the Earth-centred universe theory was not supported by the actual movements of the planets. He correctly showed that all the planets revolved round the Sun. But he wrongly thought that all the planets move in small circles as well.*

At the beginning of the 19th century Swansea in south Wales was the centre of the world's copper industry. Three-quarters of world production of the metal was smelted in the Swansea valley. There were about 600 furnaces in the valley, chiefly smelting copper, and the 'copper smoke' did great damage to the countryside.

Copernicus, Nicolaus

Nicolaus Copernicus (1473–1543) was a Polish scientist. He is sometimes called the father of modern ASTRONOMY.

Copernicus showed that the Earth is not the centre of the UNIVERSE, as people used to believe. Instead, the Earth and PLANETS revolve round the Sun. Copernicus also showed that the Earth itself moves round, or *rotates*, each day.

Copper

Copper is a reddish-brown METAL. It was probably one of the first metals that people used. About 7000 years ago the ancient Egyptians and people in Iraq began to use copper for their tools and weapons. They also made copper ornaments. At first they used pure copper which they found in the ground. But most copper is found with other metals and minerals in a mixture called ore. People began to heat, or *smelt*, copper ores so that the pure copper melted and flowed out.

Copper is very soft when it is pure. But if it is mixed with other metals it makes ALLOYS such as brass and BRONZE, which are harder and better for making tools. If copper is exposed to the air for a long time it turns green.

▶ *Copper is often mined in large open-cast mines like this one in Cyprus. Copper is the world's second most widely used metal after iron.*

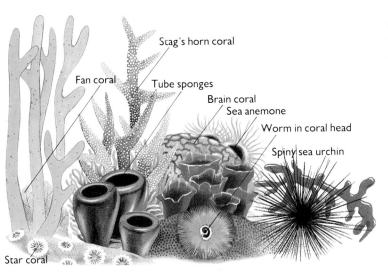

Stag's horn coral
Fan coral
Tube sponges
Brain coral
Sea anemone
Worm in coral head
Spiny sea urchin
Star coral

◀ *Coral reefs provide homes for many sea animals which find shelter in crevices or burrow into the soft coral rock.*

Copper can be beaten into sheets or pulled out into wire. It lets heat and electricity pass through it very easily, so it is often used for making pots and pans and electric wires.

Coral

Coral is a kind of limestone found mostly in warm, shallow seas. It is made by tiny animals, called coral polyps, that build limestone 'shells' around themselves for protection. Most coral polyps live in groups, or colonies. These may take many shapes, from lacy fans to stubby branches, all in beautiful colours. Other colonies form thick underwater walls known as reefs.

Along some reefs waves may throw up bits of sand and coral which gradually build up on top of the reef until it is above water. The reef then becomes an island. One kind of coral island is the atoll, a ringed reef that encloses a central lagoon.

Cork

The cork that is used to make bottle stoppers comes from the smooth bark of the cork oak tree of the Mediterranean. It is a light, spongy material that forms a thick layer about 3 cm deep around the trunk of the tree.

Cork is stripped from cork oaks once every nine or ten years until the trees are about 150 years old.

HOW AN ATOLL IS FORMED

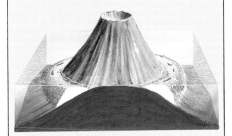

Coral grows in the warm waters surrounding an island; in this illustration an island that has been formed by volcanic action.

Coral continues to grow on the reefs as the island sinks or the sea rises.

Once the island has completely disappeared, the coral reefs remain, forming a typical atoll.

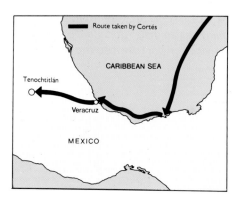

▲ Cortés founded the town of Veracruz on the coast of Mexico. There he dismantled his ships and set out to explore the country, arriving in the Aztec capital, Tenochtitlán, in November 1519.

Cortés, Hernando

Hernando Cortés (1485–1547) was a Spanish soldier and explorer who in 1519 landed on the coast of Mexico. With a force of only 600 men and a handful of horses he conquered the great AZTEC empire. His horses and guns helped convince the Aztecs he was a god. Cortés marched on their capital, captured the Aztec emperor Montezuma, and by 1521 had taken control of Mexico.

Cosmetics

Cosmetics have been used since prehistoric times when cave people decorated their dead with dyes and paints. Lipsticks, eye-shadow, nail paint, rouge and hair dyes were used widely by the ancient Egyptians. The Greeks and Romans bathed with many kinds of scented oil and wore perfumes to make their bodies and clothing smell sweet.

Today, cosmetics are big business. Modern cosmetics are used for cleaning the skin and for colouring and decorating the face and body in countless ways.

The ancient Egyptians used many different kinds of cosmetics. They edged the underside of their eyes with a green paste made from ground malachite rock, and outlined the eyes with a mixture of ground ants' eggs. Rouges, whitening powders and lipsticks were used daily by both men and women.

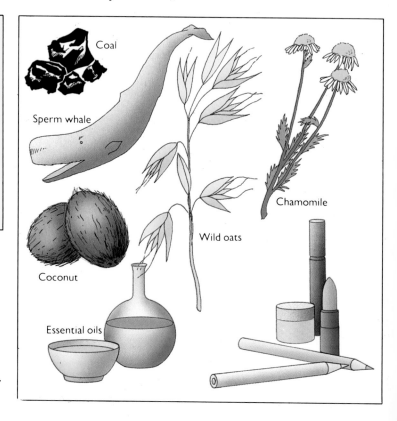

Coal

Sperm whale

Chamomile

Wild oats

Coconut

Essential oils

▶ Most modern cosmetics are made from a base of fats and oils, to which a variety of substances, natural and man-made, are added.

◀ *Grass-roofed huts in a Costa Rican village. In country areas the highlight of the year is the coffee harvest.*

Costa Rica

Costa Rica is a Spanish-speaking country lying between Nicaragua and Panama in Central America. It is largely an agricultural country, the chief crops being coffee, bananas, sugar and cocoa. Costa Rica has an area smaller than Ireland. The capital is San José and the population is about 3,000,000.

Costa Rica was a Spanish colony from 1530 to 1821 and became an independent republic in 1848.

Côte d'Ivoire (Ivory Coast)

A republic in West Africa. It is slightly larger than the British Isles and its capital is Abidjan. The country's major products are cocoa, coffee and timber. Formerly a French territory, Côte d'Ivoire became independent in 1960. The official language is still French and its population is just under 13,500,000.

Cotton

Cotton grows in warm and tropical places all round the world. It is one of the most important plants grown by people; its fibres and seeds are both used. The fibres are made into cloth and the seeds are used for oil and cattle food. The oil is used in soaps, paints and cosmetics.

Cotton has green fruits called bolls. When they

COSTA RICA

Government: Multi-party republic
Capital: San José
Area: 50,700 sq km
Population: 3,187,000
Language: Spanish
Currency: Colón

CÔTE D'IVOIRE

Government: Republic
Capital: Abidjan
Area: 322,463 sq km
Population: 13,497,000
Language: French
Currency: CFA franc

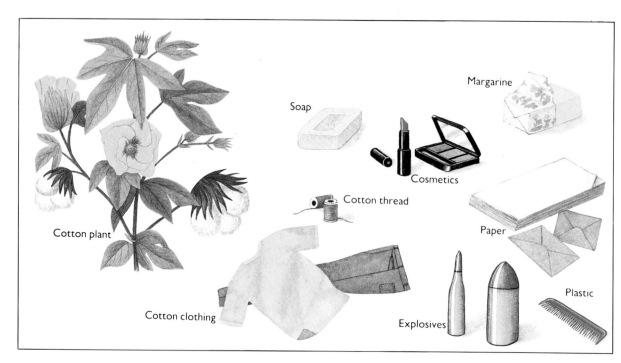

▲ Cottonseed oil goes into cooking oil, margarine, soap and cosmetics. The seed itself is a source of cellulose for making explosives, paper and plastics.

are ripe, the bolls split open. Inside them is a mass of white fibres and seeds. The bolls are harvested and the fibres are separated from the seeds. The fibres are spun into yarn and then woven into cloth.

▲ The Swiss Simmental is bred for both milk and meat.

Cow

The cow that gives us milk is a member of the cattle family. Cattle are large grass-eating animals. Grass is difficult to digest, and all cattle have four stomachs to make it easier. During digestion the food is returned to the mouth to be chewed and

▲ The Jersey is a small cow that produces very rich milk and cream.

▶ The Hereford is a popular beef breed in North America and Australia.

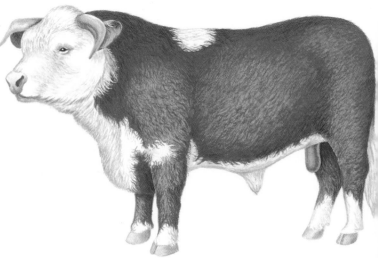

swallowed again. When a cow does this we say it is 'chewing the cud'. The farm cow is descended from an extinct wild cow called an *aurochs*, and has been tamed by people for about 6000 years.

Cowboy

There are still many people in the American West who ride horses and herd cows, but the great days of the cowboys lasted only 40 years, from the 1860s to 1900.

At that time, there were open grasslands stretching from Texas to Canada. Cattle were grazed there and then driven in great herds by cowboys to the railroad stations.

A cowboy's life was simple and hard. Out on the grassland, or *range*, he was his own boss. He often stayed in the wild for many months. There was usually no one to help him except other cowboys, so each cowboy had to know how to do many things.

Because of the roaming life they led, cowboys travelled light. Usually they owned nothing more

▲ Nearly two-thirds of all cows in Britain are Frisians.

▲ The dairy shorthorn, bred for meat, is red, white or roan.

▼ Cowboys Roping a Steer, *an oil painting by Charles M. Russell.*

than their horse, saddle, bed-roll and the clothes they wore. Although many cowboys had guns, they rarely carried pistols when they worked. The pistols were too heavy and got in the way.

▼ The cantilever crane is most often used in shipyards and on building sites. It is used for heavy loads and usually worked by electricity. The shorter side of the cross frame always carries the balancing weight.

Crab

Most people think that crabs live only in the sea, but there are some kinds that live in fresh water (rivers or lakes) and some tropical kinds that make their home on land.

Crabs belong to a group of animals called CRUSTACEANS. They have hard, thick shells that cover their flat bodies. They also have long, spidery legs for walking underwater, swimming and burrowing. The first pair of legs have pincers which are used for attacking and holding prey. Crabs have their eyes on the end of short stalks. These can be pulled into the shell for safety.

Crane

Cranes are long-necked, long-legged birds. They live in marshes or rivers and eat mainly berries, fruits and fish. Cranes have a loud cry that can be heard over a long distance and the big birds fly in large flocks. The whooping crane of North America is in danger of dying out.

Crane

A crane is a piece of machinery that is used for lifting heavy objects. It usually has a long arm, or *jib*. Cranes may be fixed in one place, like the tower cranes erected on building sites. Sometimes they are mounted on special wheels, railway wagons, or the backs of trucks so they can be moved around.

Modern jib-cranes have a powerful motor which winches the hook, raises and lowers the crane's arm, and also moves the driver's cab round.

Some of the biggest cranes are travelling ones. The hook hangs from an overhead arm which can move back and forth along a set of rails. These cranes can lift hundreds of tonnes at a time.

Cricket

Cricket is a very old game. It was probably first played in the 1300s in England. The early bats were curved, and there were no wickets. But by the early 1800s the game was very much as it is now. The pitch is 22 yards (20 metres) from wicket to wicket; the three stumps are 28 inches (71·1 cm) high and 9 inches (22·9 cm) wide. The ball must weigh between 5½ and 5¾ ounces (156 and 163 grams); the bat must not be more than 4¼ inches (10·8 cm) wide.

The Marylebone Cricket Club (M.C.C.), whose ground is at Lords in London, was started in 1787. It has governed the game for many years.

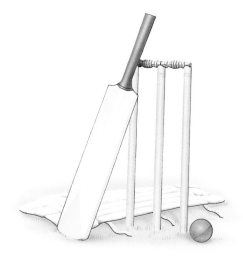

▲ The equipment for cricket: the stumps and bails that make up the wicket, the bat, ball, and pads.

Crimean War

The Crimean War (1854–56) was a struggle between Russia on one side and Turkey, France and Britain on the other. At that time the Turkish Empire was very weak. Russia hoped to make its power greater by taking CONSTANTINOPLE.

The British, French and Turks succeeded in pushing the Russian army back into the Crimean peninsula, where the war was fought. There was much

▼ The British light cavalry rode to their deaths at the battle of Balaclava in the Crimea. The poet Tennyson commemorated the battle in his poem 'The Charge of the Light Brigade'.

CROATIA

Government: Republic
Capital: Zagreb
Area: 56,533 sq km
Population: 4,784,000
Language: Croatian
Currency: Kuna

misery and suffering.

For the first time, newspaper reporters and photographers went to the battle-grounds. They reported the terrible conditions of the soldiers in newspaper articles.

Croatia

Croatia was formerly a republic of Yugoslavia, but it declared its independence in 1991. This was followed by fierce fighting between Croatia and the Serbian-dominated Yugoslav army.

Croatia has a long and beautiful coastline with many islands. Before the fighting, it was a popular tourist destination. Steep mountains sweep down to the sea, separating the coast from the inland part of Croatia. Olives, figs and vines are grown on the coast, while maize, wheat and sugar beet are produced on the inland plains. Croatia's capital, Zagreb, is an industrial city, but it also has many parks and beautiful buildings.

Crocodile *See* Alligator and Crocodile

Cromwell, Oliver

Oliver Cromwell (1599–1658) was the only ruler of Britain never to have been a king or queen. He came to power after the CIVIL WAR of the 1640s. Cromwell was a member of PARLIAMENT. He fought against CHARLES I with the army of Parliament and became its leader.

After Charles I was executed, Cromwell became the head of the country but he never made himself king. From 1653 he was called the 'Lord Protector'. After Cromwell died, CHARLES II became king.

Crown Jewels

The crown jewels belong to the kings and queens of Britain. They show that the queen or king is head of the country. Some of the crown jewels are worn by the monarch when he or she is being crowned.

The crown jewels include crowns, sceptres, staffs,

Only once has anyone tried to steal the crown jewels. In 1671, a Colonel Thomas Blood, disguised as a parson, gained the confidence of the keeper of the jewels. When the keeper showed Blood the jewels he was seized by Blood and his friends and stabbed. They escaped with the crown, sceptre and orb, but were captured on the banks of the Thames. Blood was pardoned by Charles II, who admired his audacity.

spurs, swords and bracelets. They are made of gold and precious stones such as diamonds, rubies, emeralds and sapphires. The Imperial State Crown, made for Queen VICTORIA, has in it a huge ruby, called the Black Prince's Ruby. The jewels are all kept in the Tower of London. Other countries have crown jewels on display. The crown jewels of France can be seen in the Louvre in Paris. The Secular Treasury in Vienna houses the crown jewels of the Holy Roman emperors. The crown jewels worn by Danish monarchs are in Rosenborg Castle, Copenhagen.

▼ To attack the strong walls of cities and castles, the Crusaders used catapults and battering rams. They built tall towers from which they could fire arrows and climb over the walls.

Crusades

The Crusades were wars between Christians and Muslims in the MIDDLE AGES. They took place in Palestine, the Holy Land. In 1071, Turkish Muslims captured the city of Jerusalem in Palestine. The Muslims stopped Christians from visiting the holy places in Palestine.

The Christian rulers in Europe were very angry about this. A few years later, the Byzantine emperor in CONSTANTINOPLE asked the Pope to help him drive the Turks from the Holy Land. The Pope started the first Crusade. He said he would forgive the sins of all the people who went and fought in the Holy Land.

The armies of the first Crusade were successful. They took Jerusalem from the Muslims in 1099. The Crusaders set up Christian kingdoms along the coast of Palestine and Syria and built strong fortresses to defend their new lands.

There were seven more Crusades after the first one. Many of them failed because the Crusaders quarrelled with each other. The Muslims took back much of the Holy Land from the Christians. When the Muslims took Jerusalem in 1187, the third Crusade set off from Europe. When they got to the Holy Land, the Crusaders were defeated by the Muslims who had a new general called Saladin.

Later, the Crusaders forgot that they were fighting for their religion. Many of them went to Palestine hoping to take the land and become rich. By 1291, the Muslims had taken the last remaining Christian city at Acre.

During the Crusades, European people learnt more about the eastern parts of the world. When they returned to Europe they took back with them many new things including foods, spices, silk clothes and paper. They learnt about medicine, mathematics and astronomy from the Arabs of the east, and trade between east and west began to grow.

Crustacean

Crustaceans are a large group of about 10,000 animals. They include sandhoppers, wood-lice, waterfleas, barnacles, crayfish, shrimps, prawns, CRABS and LOBSTERS. All have hard, jointed bodies and jointed legs. Most crustaceans live in the sea.

Crustaceans are *invertebrates* (animals with no backbones). Most have SHELLS around their bodies. This keeps their soft bodies safe. Many have a set of claws, or pincers, on their front legs. They use these to defend themselves and to grab their prey.

Crustaceans began life as EGGS. These hatch into tiny *larvae* which make up much of the floating *plankton* which other sea animals eat. As each larva grows, it sheds its shell and grows a new one which is bigger. This is called *moulting*. When the larva becomes an adult, it continues to grow and moult.

The best-known crustaceans are the large shellfish

The heaviest crustacean is the North Atlantic lobster. Specimens weighing more than 20 kg and over a metre long have been caught. This lobster is also the longest-lived crustacean. Some may be 50 years old.

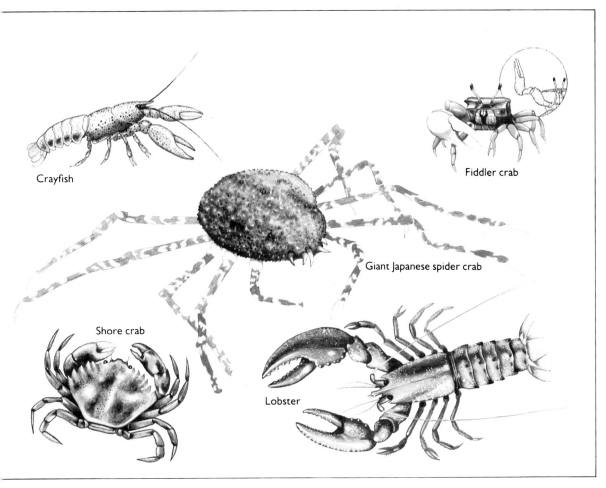

Crayfish

Fiddler crab

Giant Japanese spider crab

Shore crab

Lobster

such as lobsters, shrimps, crabs and crayfish. They all have ten jointed legs, including the pair with pincers. Except for crayfish, they all live in the sea. Many of them are very good to eat.

Barnacles live on rocks, on pieces of wood and often on the bottom of boats. They open their shells and put out long, feathery hairs which trap food floating in the water.

▲ The creatures above are all crustaceans. The male fiddler crab (see inset) uses its large claw to signal aggression.

Crystal

If you look closely at sugar through a magnifying glass, you will see that it is made up of thousands of tiny glassy pieces with flat sides. They are sugar crystals. SNOW is made up of tiny crystals of frozen water. So are the beautiful patterns on a frosty window. Some crystals are so small they can be seen only through a microscope. Others can grow to be as big as a person.

All crystals have a definite shape. They have

▼ Crystals can be many different shapes. Some are combinations of two or more patterns, making complicated designs.

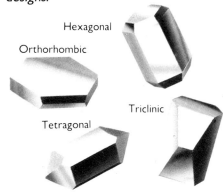

Hexagonal

Orthorhombic

Triclinic

Tetragonal

SEE IT YOURSELF

You can grow crystals yourself, using minerals such as salt or washing soda. Pour hot water into a bowl and add the mineral little by little, stirring all the time. Eventually no more mineral will dissolve. Now let the solution cool. Hang a thread in the solution and crystals will form on the end.

CUBA

USA
ATLANTIC OCEAN
GULF OF MEXICO
BAHAMAS
CUBA
DOMINICAN REPUBLIC
MEXICO
HAITI
BELIZE
JAMAICA
HONDURAS
CARIBBEAN SEA

Government: Communist state
Capital: Havana
Area: 114,524 sq km
Population: 10,846,000
Language: Spanish
Currency: Peso

▶ Modern Havana, the capital of Cuba, has many new buildings but retains some built in the colonial style.

smooth, flat sides that meet in sharp edges. The shape of any one type of crystal never changes, but there are many different crystal shapes. The differences between them are caused by the ATOMS in the crystals arranging themselves in different ways.

For example, the salt you eat is made up of two different kinds of atoms—sodium atoms and chlorine atoms. The tiny sodium and chlorine atoms are arranged in cube patterns. If you look at salt grains through a magnifying glass, you will see that most of them are little CUBES. All salt crystals are built in the same way.

Cuba

Cuba is an island country in the Caribbean Sea. It is part of the WEST INDIES. Cuba has 10,846,000 people and covers an area of 114,524 sq km. The capital city is Havana.

Part of the island is hilly, with high mountains in the south-east. In the centre are large cedar and mahogany forests. Cuba has big sugar cane plantations and tobacco farms.

The climate is warm and pleasant, but Cuba lies in the path of HURRICANES which come blowing through the West Indies every year. Hurricanes are very strong winds which travel fast and often damage buildings and farms.

Cuba was ruled by Spain after Christopher COL-UMBUS went there in 1492. The United States took Cuba from Spain in 1898. In 1902 the island became independent. Cuba became a communist country in 1959 under its leader Fidel Castro.

Cube

A cube is an object with six square sides. All the edges are the same length. Sugar and ice are often made in cubes.

The space a cube fills is called its volume. You can find the volume of a cube by multiplying the length of a side by itself and then by itself again. If the length of a side is 3 cm, the volume of the cube is $3 \times 3 \times 3 = 27$ cubic cm.

Many kinds of CRYSTAL have a cube shape. This is because of the way their ATOMS are arranged.

Cuckoo

Cuckoos are a family of birds. There are many kinds of cuckoo. They are found in a lot of countries, but most live in the warm parts of the world. Cuckoos that live in cool countries fly to warm places for the winter.

The European cuckoo is a large bird about 30 cm long. It is blue-grey in colour with stripes under-

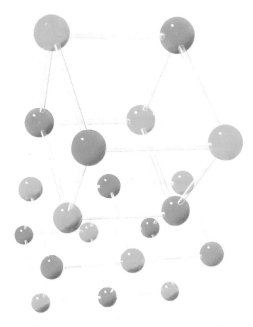

Sodium ion

Chlorine ion

▲ The atoms in a crystal of salt are all arranged in cube patterns. Thousands and thousands of these tiny cubes join together to make one grain of salt, which is also a cube.

▼ Cuckoos from northern Europe fly to Africa for the winter.

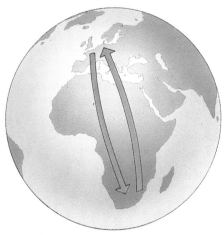

◄ Young cuckoos grow quite large before they leave the nest. This young cuckoo is already much bigger than its foster parent, a willow warbler.

There are many kinds of cuckoo all over the world. But very few of them lay their eggs in other birds' nests as the European cuckoo does. American cuckoos, for example, are shy birds that build their own nests and take good care of their young. They also do not have the cuckoo call of the European birds.

neath. It eats mainly insects. The call of the European cuckoo sounds just like its name. The birds can be heard calling in spring when they return from Africa.

European cuckoos do not build nests. They lay their eggs in the nests of other birds such as warblers and sparrows. The female cuckoo watches while the other birds build their nests and lay their eggs. When they leave the nest to find food the cuckoo pulls one of the eggs out of the nest with her beak. Then she lays her own egg in its place and flies away. When the other birds return they do not notice the strange egg.

After about two weeks the young cuckoo hatches. It pushes the other eggs or baby birds out of the nest. The foster parents feed and take care of the cuckoo until it is ready to fly away. Young cuckoos are greedy and usually grow much bigger than their foster parents.

Curie, Marie and Pierre

Marie Curie (1867–1934) and Pierre Curie (1859–1906) were scientists who worked together. She was Polish, he was French. They studied RADIOACTIVITY and discovered the elements RADIUM and polonium. They married each other in 1895.

For their work on radioactivity and their discovery of radium in 1898, they were given the NOBEL PRIZE for physics in 1903. When Pierre was killed three years later, Marie took over his job as professor at the Sorbonne University in Paris. In 1911 she was given a second Nobel Prize, this time for chemistry.

▲ *Pierre and Marie Curie devoted their lives to their research, spending their money on equipment and often living in conditions of hardship.*

Current, Electric

Electric current is the movement, or flow, of ELECTRICITY. Current must always be flowing before electricity can work. Electricity is usually made in a GENERATOR at a POWER STATION. From there the current travels through wires to your home. Before it reaches your home, a *transformer* reduces its force, or *voltage*, so that it does not burn up the wires and electric equipment in your house.

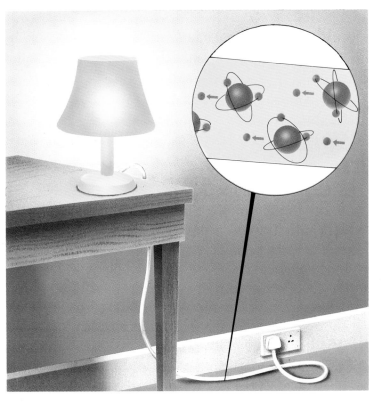

◀ *Electricity flows along a wire when electrons jump from one atom to the next. Electrons are tiny units of negative electricity. The protons in the centre of the atoms are positive.*

The unit of electric current is the amp, short for ampere. The current in one of our nerves to make us raise an arm is about one hundred thousandth of an amp. A 100-watt light bulb carries one amp. A lightning flash can peak at about 20,000 amps. A nuclear power station can deliver 10 million amps.

The current flows out of the plugs in the walls of your house and through the equipment you are using. Then it returns to the generator in the power station through another set of wires.

Electricity in houses flows in one direction and then in the opposite direction. It is called *alternating* current. Each movement back and forth happens very quickly (about 50 times a second). This is too fast for us to notice, for example, that lights flicker.

Electricity from *batteries* flows in only one direction. It is called *direct* current.

Cyclone *See* Hurricane

Cyprus

Cyprus is a large, mountainous island in the eastern Mediterranean. It covers an area of 9251 sq km and has about 700,000 people. The capital city is Nicosia. Cyprus has a warm climate and the farmers grow grapes, lemons, oranges and olives.

Cyprus was ruled by Turkey for 300 years until 1878, when Britain took it over. It gained full

CYPRUS

Government: Republic
Capital: Nicosia
Area: 9,251 sq km
Population: 742,000
Languages: Greek and Turkish
Currency: Pound

CZECH REPUBLIC

CZECH REPUBLIC

Government: Republic
Capital: Prague
Area: 127,869 sq km
Population: 10,400,000

independence in 1960. The people are Greek Cypriots who are Christian, and Turkish Cypriots who are Muslim. These two groups often quarrelled with each other and in the 1960s there was a civil war. Today, Cyprus is split into two parts, one part ruled by Greek Cypriots, the other by Turkish Cypriots.

Czech Republic

The Czech Republic is in eastern Europe. It was part of the country known as CZECHOSLOVAKIA, which split into two nations, the Czech Republic and SLOVAKIA, in 1993.

In the 9th century, the Czech people split from the Great Moravian Empire. Czech land later came under the control of the Austro-Hungarian Empire. With the defeated Austria-Hungary in World War I, the Czechs became independent. In 1918, the Czech and Slovak lands were joined into Czechoslovakia.

In 1938, Germany took control of the Czech region of the country. This ended with the defeat of Germany during World War II, and the Czech and Slovak states were reunited. In 1948, Communists seized control of the government.

Communist rule ended in 1989, and was replaced with a democratic government. However, Slovak people soon called for independence, and in 1993, two separate republics were born.

Czechoslovakia

Czechoslovakia was a country in eastern EUROPE. It was surrounded by Germany, Poland, the Ukraine, Hungary and Austria. The country was about the same size as Louisiana.

Much of the land is covered by hills and mountains. There are also coal and iron and an important steel industry.

Czechoslovakia had been ruled by a communist government, but communism crumbled in eastern Europe in the late 1980s. In late 1989 Czechoslovakia's communist government fell. It was replaced by a democratic government. In 1993 the country split into two separate nations, the CZECH REPUBLIC and SLOVAKIA.

Prague, the capital of the Czech Republic, is one of the most beautiful and historic cities in Europe. When the communist 'Iron Curtain' was lifted in 1989, Western tourists were free to visit for the first time. The city was so crowded that there was hardly a hotel room to be found!

Dam

A dam is a barrier built across a river or stream to control its flow. There are many reasons for building dams. The most common is to make a *reservoir*. A reservoir is a man-made lake in which water is stored and sent across the country in pipes so that people can use it for drinking, washing and cooking.

Another reason for building dams is to store water for irrigating fields in the dry season. People have been doing this in hot countries for hundreds of years.

Whenever water is at a height from which it can fall it can be made to do work. Dams are built to harness this power. In the past, small dams were built to force streams of water into narrow channels. The rushing stream turned water wheels that drove machinery. Today, huge dams build up an enor-

▼ Dams are among the biggest structures built by people. This dam in Morocco is an arch dam. The curved shape makes the water press against the sides of the canyon instead of pushing against the dam wall.

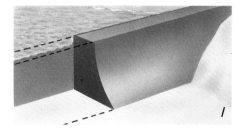

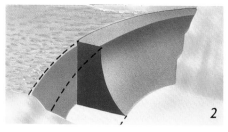

▲ *A gravity dam (1) made of stone or concrete blocks that take the whole weight of the water. An arch dam (2) is curved so that the weight of water pushes against the sides of the canyon instead of against the dam wall. An embankment dam (3) is just a heap of rocks and earth, with an outside layer of concrete.*

HIGHEST AND LARGEST DAMS				
Highest	**Location**	**Type**	**(m)**	**Completed**
Rogunsky	Tajikistan	earthfill	335	*
Nurek	Tajikistan	earthfill	317	1980
Grande Dixence	Switzerland	gravity	284	1962
Inguri	Georgia	arch	272	1980
Vaiont	Italy	multi-arch	262	1961
Mica	Canada	rockfill	242	1973
Mauvoisin	Switzerland	arch	237	1958
Largest	**Location**	**(cub. m)**		**Completed**
Syncrude Tailings	Canada	540,000,000		*
Chapetón	Argentina	296,200,000		*
Pati	Argentina	238,180,000		*
New Cornelia	Arizona, USA	209,506,000		1973
Tarbela	Pakistan	148,000,000		1979
Fort Peck	Montana, USA	96,050,000		1940
Lower Usuma	Nigeria	93,000,000		*
Under construction				

mous pressure of water that falls through big pipes. The rushing water hits the blades of turbines, making them spin and turn generators. From the generators comes ELECTRICITY.

Dance

Dance is probably the oldest of the arts. People have always danced to express their feelings. Today there are many different kinds of dancing. (See pages 190–191.)

Dark Ages

Early scholars gave the name Dark Ages to the period in Europe after the fall of the great Roman Empire in the AD 400s. During this period barbarian Goths, Vandals and Huns swept down on Europe from the north and east. They destroyed many fine buildings and works of art that had existed during Roman times. This is why the time was called the Dark Ages. It lasted for about 500 years.

During the Dark Ages knowledge survived only in monasteries, and there were very few schools. Many of the old arts and crafts were lost.

At this time, however, people were still writing and thinking and making fine works of art in other

One country did not experience the Dark Ages. What for most of Europe was a period of decay was for Ireland a golden age. It was at this time that religious art and learning flourished in Ireland. Beautiful illuminated manuscripts such as the Book of Kells were produced, one of the world's finest examples of Christian art.

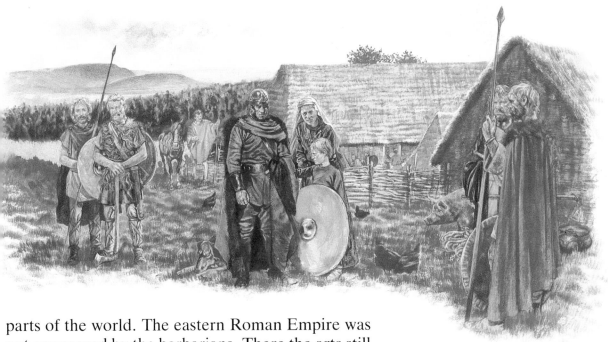

parts of the world. The eastern Roman Empire was not conquered by the barbarians. There the arts still flourished. And in China and India great civilizations grew and spread.

In the AD 1000s Europe began slowly to recover from its artistic darkness. The lost knowledge of the ancient Greeks and Romans was found again. There was a new interest in learning and the richer life of the MIDDLE AGES began.

▲ During the Dark Ages, Viking raiders from Scandinavia threatened much of Europe. They were also settlers and traders, founding colonies from North America to Russia.

Darwin, Charles

Charles Darwin (1809–1882) was an English biologist. In 1859 he published his great book *On the Origin of Species*. Before this, almost everyone believed that the world was created by God exactly as the Bible described. Darwin put forward the theory that all living things *evolved* from earlier forms. They were alive because they had won the struggle to survive.

Within any species of living thing there would be small variations in shape, size or habit. Some of these variations would increase the living thing's chance of survival. For example, a giraffe with a long neck could reach leaves a giraffe with a shorter neck could not. In times of famine, the taller giraffe would survive while the shorter one would die. The

▲ Darwin's theory of evolution stirred up much controversy. Here he is mocked in a cartoon of the time.

Continued on page 192.

DANCE

Dance is one of the most ancient human arts. Thousands of years ago people acted out stories in dance. Dance became part of religion; people danced to bring rain to make crops grow and to guarantee good hunting. Warriors danced war dances to make themselves feel brave before a battle.

People all over the world dance. Dancing is usually done to a rhythmic beat, and some music is written especially for dancing. Every country has its own folk dances, with traditional steps.

Ballet developed in the 1600s from court dancing in Europe. Ballroom dancing became popular in the 1800s, with popular dances such as the waltz and, later, the tango which was borrowed from a South American folk dance. Today, in the theatre, on film and television, and in the disco dance is enjoyed in different styles.

Dancing is excellent exercise. Everyone can enjoy dance; through moving your body in time to music you can express your feelings, and have fun. What's more, in today's disco, you can dance either with a partner, in a group, or on your own.

▲ Dancing figures have been found in the wall paintings of ancient Egypt.

▼ Terpsichore was one of the nine Muses, who represented the arts in ancient Greek mythology. She was the Muse of Dance and Poetry.

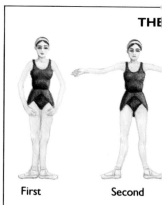

THE

First   Second

SOME WORDS USED DANCE

ballerina female ballet dancer

barre exercise bar used i training

corps de ballet main boc of dancers

entrechat leap in which dancer rapidly crosses a uncrosses feet in the air

jeté leap from one foot to another

pas de deux dance performed by two peop

pirouette spin on one foc

◄ Stars such as Fred Astaire popularized modern dance, including tap dancing, in films.

190

...ET POSITIONS

Third **Fourth** **Fifth**

◀ *The ballet positions from which all movements begin.*

...ances performed by the Cossacks of ...aine require both energy and agility.

...Morris dancing is a form of English folk ...ce, usually performed by men.

▶ *Dancers in a chorus line wear identical costumes and dance the same steps in a well-drilled line.*

▲ *In formation ballroom dancing, a team of couples moves in patterns across the floor.*

SOME FAMOUS DANCERS

Isadora Duncan (1878–1927) An American, she studied ancient Greek dance and performed wearing flowing classical-style costumes. Her dancing helped make new ideas about dance more popular.

Margot Fonteyn (1919–1991) British ballerina, who studied at the Sadler's Wells school and became a star of the British Royal Ballet. Best known for her performances in *Swan Lake* and *The Sleeping Beauty*.

Vaslav Nijinsky (1890–1950) Russian dancer, remarkable for his dramatic performances and amazingly high leaps (elevation). He danced with the famous Ballets Russes run by the impresario Serge Diaghilev.

Rudolf Nureyev (1939–1993) Russian dancer who left the Kirov Ballet in 1961 to dance in the West. He formed a much-admired partnership with Margot Fonteyn.

Anna Pavlova (1882–1931) Russian ballerina, famous for solo performances, especially as the Dying Swan. Trained at the Imperial School of Ballet in St Petersburg she became an international star.

...r more information turn to these articles: AMERICAN INDIANS: BALLET; CINEMA; GYMNASTICS; LOUIS, KINGS; MUSIC; POP MUSIC; ...EHISTORIC PEOPLE; SKATING; THEATRE.

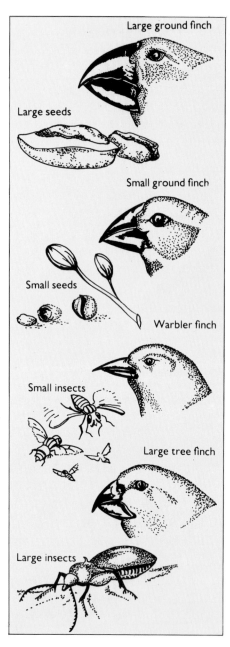

▲ *Darwin discovered a variety of finches on the Galapagos Islands, each species of which had evolved different beaks suited for eating different foods. All had originally come from a South American finch that had reached the islands long before.*

▶ *Day and night happen because the Earth spins like a top as it circles the Sun. Only one half of the Earth faces the Sun at any one time.*

taller giraffe that survived would, in time, replace the variety with the shorter neck.

This theory outraged many people. They thought it was against the teachings of the Bible. But today most people accept Darwin's theory, and many churches have decided that it does not conflict with their teachings or threaten religious beliefs.

Day and Night

The Earth turns on its own axis as it moves around the Sun. So the part of the Earth facing the Sun is light while the part facing away from the Sun is dark. The lighted part is 'day' and the dark part 'night'. Because the Earth turns around, day and night follow each other continually.

Scientists have another way of describing a 'day'. They say it is the time the Earth takes to complete one full turn on its axis. If you measure how long it takes from one sunrise or one sunset to the next you will find that it takes almost exactly 24 hours.

The length of time that any particular part of the Earth is in daylight varies depending on where it is on the globe. This is because the axis of the Earth is tilted at an angle to its path around the Sun. This also means that some parts of the Earth have different amounts of day and night at certain times

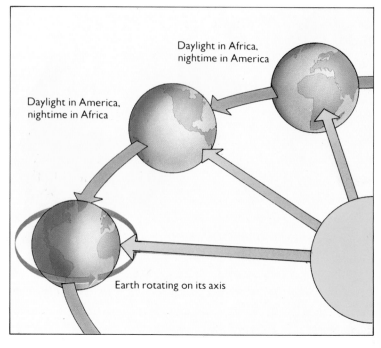

Daylight in Africa, nightime in America

Daylight in America, nightime in Africa

Earth rotating on its axis

SEE IT YOURSELF

If you shine a torch on a globe you will see why we have day and night. The Earth rotates from west to east. As we travel eastwards on the revolving Earth we pass into sunlight. We see the Sun first in the east in the morning. In the evening the Sun disappears (sets) in the west. It takes the Earth 24 hours (a day) to complete one turn on its axis.

of the year. For instance, in June in the Arctic it is always daylight. In the Antarctic, it is always night. In December it is the other way round—dark all the time in the Arctic and light all the time in the Antarctic.

Because the Earth turns all the time it is always day in one place when it is night somewhere else. The world is divided into 'time zones'. There is no single time, such as 'noon', for the whole world. When it is noon in London it is midnight in New Zealand.

To make a clear difference between one day and the next, an imaginary line was drawn from the North to the South Pole. On one side it is one day, and on the other side, the day following. This line, known as the 'dateline', runs through the Pacific Ocean. It has a strange effect: if you cross the dateline going eastwards you gain a day, while those travelling westwards miss a day.

D-Day

D-Day was the day of the Allied landings in Normandy, France, during WORLD WAR II. It took place on June 6, 1944, and led to the defeat of Hitler's Germany. On this famous day, about three million men – British, Americans and their allies – and 11,000 ships and aircraft crossed the English Channel. It was by far the greatest invasion force the world had ever seen. The supreme commander of this force was the American, General Eisenhower. At the same time the Soviets attacked from the east and the Germans had to retreat on all fronts. They surrendered on May 7, 1945.

▼ *Before D-Day, the Germans were led to believe that the Allied landings would take place across the Straits of Dover. Instead, they were on the Normandy coast between Cherbourg and Le Havre.*

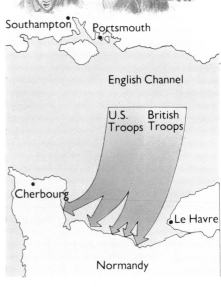

Southampton Portsmouth

English Channel

U.S. Troops British Troops

Cherbourg

Le Havre

Normandy

▲ Electronic aids are used in teaching deaf children today.

Deafness

There are many different kinds of deafness, or hearing loss. We all lose some hearing as we get older – but some people are born deaf, and some go deaf as children or later in life from illness or accident. There are many ways of communicating if you are deaf. Sometimes it is difficult for deaf people to use their voice if they have never heard spoken language, and they may use sign language, speaking mainly with their hands and body rather than with their voice. There are many famous and successful deaf people.

Deep-Sea Life

Most of the animals and plants that live in the sea stay in the top 200 metres. Below this, conditions become less and less suitable for living things. At a depth of a kilometre it is very cold and very dark. No sunlight gets down that far. Plants cannot live there because they need light to make their food. Some animals do, however, live at great depths.

▼ Strange fishes live at the bottom of the ocean, called the bathypelagic zone. Little or no daylight reaches these depths, and many animals, such as the deep sea angler and the lantern fish, give out light of their own.

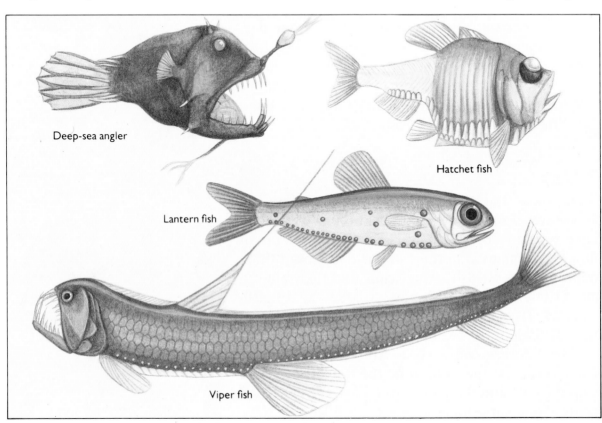

Deep-sea angler

Hatchet fish

Lantern fish

Viper fish

Their bodies are specially designed to withstand the enormous pressure deep down. Most of them are quite small, often with enormous jaws, teeth and eyes. Many deep-sea fishes have light-producing organs. These lights may help them to recognize their own kind in the darkness and may also act as lures for their prey.

Deer

Deer are animals related to cattle and antelopes. They are different from their relatives because they have antlers rather than permanent horns. Male deer grow new antlers every year. Female deer, except for reindeer, do not grow antlers.

Every year in early spring, a lot of blood starts to flow into two bony lumps on the male deer's forehead. The blood carries a bony substance that makes the antlers grow quite rapidly. At first they are covered with a soft, hairy skin known as velvet. In early summer the antlers are fully grown. The blood supply is then cut off and the velvet dies. The male deer rubs off the velvet until his antlers are

Scientists have brought up tiny bacteria from a depth of 11,000 metres – nearly 7 miles. They look very much like the bacteria we have on land, but they cannot live at a pressure of less than a thousand atmospheres! These creatures of the deep live with a pressure of about 1000 kg pressing in on every square centimetre of their bodies!

▼ The moose is the largest of all deer. The reindeer is well adapted to life in northern latitudes, while the fallow deer is often found in parks. The red deer is the most important British species. The little muntjac is about 45 cm high and barks like a dog.

Red Deer

Moose

Muntjac

Fallow Deer

Reindeer

▼ *Deer antlers develop each year from tender stumps covered in a layer of soft, hair-covered skin to fully grown branches. The four stages cover the period from spring to autumn.*

Deer have a common origin with giraffes. They became separated from the giraffes about 20 million years ago. Fossil bones show that prehistoric people often dined on deer meat. Deer hides were used for clothing, and antlers were made into weapons and tools.

hard and shiny. Some antlers can be very big indeed. One red deer's antlers weighed as much as 35 kg. A moose's antlers have measured 2 metres across.

Deer are mainly found in the Northern Hemisphere. But there are some species in South America and Asia.

In autumn, male deer become very aggressive. They fight each other for the right to mate with groups of females which they guard very jealously.

Deer vary enormously in size. The biggest is the Alaskan moose which stands up to 2·3 metres at the shoulder and weighs over 800 kg. The smallest is the Pudu of Chile which can measure as little as 33 cm at the shoulder and weigh as little as 8 kg.

Reindeer can be tamed to pull sledges, and their meat and hides are valued by the Lapp people of Scandinavia. Red deer can be kept on farms, for their meat (called venison). Deer are naturally wild animals but some of them, such as reindeer, have been successfully domesticated.

De Gaulle, Charles

Charles de Gaulle (1890–1970) was a French general and statesman. He went to the Military Academy at St. Cyr. He fought in World War I, and in 1916 was badly wounded. After the war he continued his army career. When World War II broke out in 1939 he was put in command of a tank division. After the Germans occupied France in 1940 De Gaulle went to Britain and formed the Free French Movement which fought very bravely.

In 1944 he returned to France as head of govern-

▲ *Charles de Gaulle dominated the European Community in its early days and in 1963 and 1967 blocked Britain's entry.*

ment. But two years later he resigned when the political parties could not agree. By 1958 France was in desperate political trouble. The French settlers in Algiers and the French army were rebelling. De Gaulle became president of France in 1959 and settled the Algerian problem. He stayed in office until he retired in 1969.

Delta

When a river flows across a flat plain into the sea, it flows very slowly. On its way it deposits soil and sand on the plain. In time this sediment begins to form mudbanks. The river flows through these in many channels, often changing direction. This wide, blocked-up mouth with many channels is called a delta. This is because its shape is often like the Greek letter *delta* Δ.

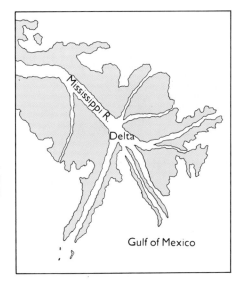

▲ *The Mississippi Delta stretches 320 km into the Gulf of Mexico, and is still growing at the rate of one kilometre every 20 years.*

Democracy

Democracy is a type of government, organized by the people, for the people. In a democracy people elect their own government. Representatives of different political parties stand for election and people vote for the one they prefer. The people can also dismiss their government if they want to. In a democracy people can say and read what they like. They cannot be put into prison without a proper trial.

> **The great American president Abraham Lincoln described democracy as 'government *of* the people, *by* the people and *for* the people'. He meant that in a democracy everyone takes part in making the laws that everyone has to obey.**

◀ *The Statue of Liberty stands at the entrance of New York Harbor as a symbol of freedom under American democracy.*

DENMARK

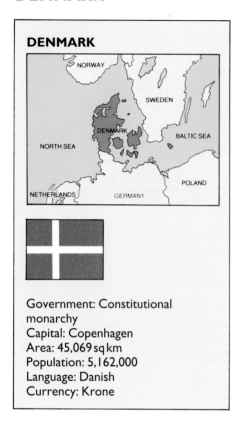

DENMARK

NORWAY

SWEDEN

DENMARK

BALTIC SEA

NORTH SEA

NETHERLANDS

GERMANY

POLAND

Government: Constitutional
monarchy
Capital: Copenhagen
Area: 45,069 sq km
Population: 5,162,000
Language: Danish
Currency: Krone

▼ Wind-sculpted dunes in the Sahara
desert in Morocco. Not all deserts are
sandy; many are stony and barren.

There are many different kinds of democracy. The British form is a monarchy with an elected PARLIAMENT. The American form is a republic with an elected president and an elected CONGRESS. There is no one perfect democracy in the world, but all free nations are trying to work towards a perfect democracy.

Denmark

Denmark is a small Scandinavian country in the north of EUROPE. It consists mainly of a peninsula called Jutland surrounded by 600 islands. In the west is the North Sea, to the east is the Baltic Sea, and to the south is Germany. The capital is Copenhagen. Denmark is a flat country whose soil and climate are ideal for agriculture. Dairy and pig farming are especially important. Denmark is a member of the EUROPEAN COMMUNITY. It exports a great deal of butter and bacon to Britain. The Danes also make and export lager beer. There is little heavy industry. The Danes prefer to concentrate on high-quality goods like china, furniture and textiles. There are just over five million people in Denmark.

▼ There are two types of camel, the Bactrian (two-humped) of the Gobi desert and the Arabian (one-humped).

▲ The Gila monster is a poisonous lizard. Its poison travels along grooves in its teeth while it is biting its victim.

▼ The frilled lizard opens its jaws with a hiss and unfolds its frill to frighten intruders.

▲ Dingoes are wild dogs, descended from dogs brought to Australia by the first people to arrive there.

▼ The sand grouse soaks its feathers in a waterhole and takes the water to its thirsty young.

◄ The peregrine falcon preys on small desert animals. It is one of the fastest flying birds.

Desert

Not all deserts are hot and sandy. Some are cold, and some are rocky. But all are very dry. Some scientists say that a desert is any area where less than 8 cm of rain falls in a year. Other scientists call a place a desert when there is more rain than this but where it evaporates quickly in the sun or sinks rapidly into the ground.

Many big deserts are in the tropics, often inland on large continents where rainbearing winds cannot reach them.

There are three main types of desert. The first is rocky, where any soil is blown away by the wind. The second has large areas of gravel. The third is made up of great sand dunes, burning hot by day and bitterly cold at night.

It is difficult for plants and animals to live in such conditions. Some plants, like the CACTUS, store

▲ Many animals keep cool in the desert by hiding away during the daytime, coming out after the Sun sets. To conserve water, desert animals sweat very little.

LARGEST DESERTS

Sahara	9.1 million sq km
Gt. Australian	1.5 million sq km
Arabian	1.3 million sq km
Gobi	1.3 million sq km
Kalahari	520,000 sq km
Atacama	65,000 sq km
Mohave	39,000 sq km

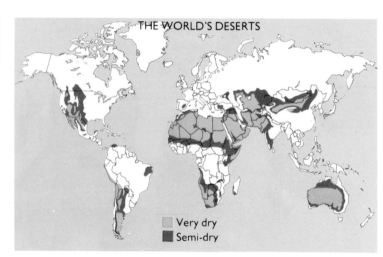

THE WORLD'S DESERTS

Very dry
Semi-dry

The Cullinan diamond, named after its finder, Thomas Cullinan, was the largest ever found. It was discovered in 1905 at Pretoria in South Africa. The great uncut stone was about 13 cm across and weighed nearly three-quarters of a kilogram. In 1908, the diamond was cut by expert diamond cutters in Amsterdam and finished up as 105 separate stones. One big diamond cut from the Cullinan is called the Star of Africa. It is in the royal sceptre. Another is in the State Crown, and others are in jewellery worn by the Queen.

The world's most famous coloured diamond is the large Hope diamond. It is deep blue and came originally from India. The Hope is now in the gem collection of the Smithsonian Institution in Washington, D.C. Although diamonds are usually colourless, they are found in a variety of colours in shades of blue, yellow, pink and champagne.

moisture in their fleshy stems. Others have seeds that lie apparently lifeless in the ground for long periods. When a shower of rain falls they burst into life and can flower and produce new seeds within weeks. Many desert animals shelter from the sun by day and come out only at night. Some never drink, but get all the moisture they need from their food.

The world's largest desert is the SAHARA in Africa. The driest desert is the Atacama in South America, where it may not rain for several years. There are also cold deserts. These include Antarctica and a large part of the Arctic.

Detergent

The word *detergent* means any substance that will clean things. *Soap* is a detergent. But today the word detergent usually means synthetic, or man-made, detergents such as most washing powders. Detergents are similar to soaps, but soaps leave behind filmy deposits, such as the familiar bath-tub ring. Detergents can reach soiled areas better than soaps and do not leave deposits.

Diamond

Diamonds are CRYSTALS. They are harder than anything else in the world. They are formed by great heat and pressure deep beneath the surface of the earth. Diamonds are made of pure CARBON, the same mineral that is found in ordinary coal. They are usually colourless and have to be cut in a special

◀ *A cut and uncut diamond. The finished diamond has usually lost about 50 per cent of its original weight after cutting and polishing.*

way to catch the light and 'sparkle'. A diamond cutter is very skilled and uses tools tipped with diamonds, for only another diamond is hard enough to cut a diamond. Diamonds are used in industry for drilling and cutting.

Dickens, Charles

Charles Dickens (1812–1870) was a great English writer. His books give us a vivid picture of life in Victorian England in the middle 1800s. Several of his stories are about children, especially poor children and orphans. Dickens tried to improve the lives of the poor by making their suffering more widely known through his books. He also created some of the liveliest and best-known characters in English literature. Some of his most famous books are *Oliver Twist, David Copperfield, Great Expectations* and *A Christmas Carol*.

▲ *Charles Dickens wrote all his novels in weekly or monthly instalments for magazines.*

▼ *An illustration from Charles Dickens' novel* Oliver Twist, *which portrayed the harsh conditions suffered by orphans in Britain at the time.*

Dictator

A dictator is the leader of a country who rules with absolute power and authority. In ancient Rome a dictator was a magistrate who was given absolute power to deal with emergencies, when decisions had to be made quickly. Today the term is used to describe a tyrant who takes away people's rights and freedoms and rules by force. Often those who try to oppose a dictator are killed, imprisoned or forced to leave the country until such time as the dictator is overthrown.

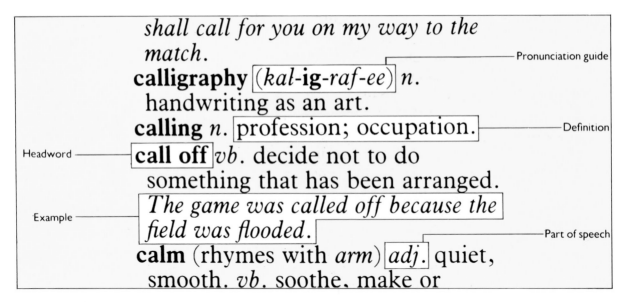

> shall call for you on my way to the match.
>
> **calligraphy** *(kal-**ig**-raf-ee)* *n.* — Pronunciation guide
> handwriting as an art.
>
> **calling** *n.* profession; occupation. — Definition
>
> Headword — **call off** *vb.* decide not to do something that has been arranged.
>
> Example — *The game was called off because the field was flooded.*
>
> **calm** (rhymes with *arm*) *adj.* quiet, — Part of speech
> smooth. *vb.* soothe, make or

▲ A dictionary definition has a number of standard parts, though not every dictionary includes them all. After the word itself, called the headword, *comes a pronunciation guide and the part of speech, usually abbreviated (n., adj.). Next comes the definition, or what the word means. Finally, other forms of the same word may be listed.*

Dictionary

A dictionary is a book that tells us what words mean. The words are arranged in alphabetical order from A to Z. Often the meanings, or definitions, include the history of the words and how they are used and pronounced. Dictionaries may vary in size from many volumes to dictionaries small enough to slip into your pocket. Dr Samuel Johnson (1709–84) made one of the first large dictionaries of English words.

▼ London taxis are driven by diesel engines, which are cheaper to fuel and cause less pollution.

Diesel Engine

Diesel engines are a type of INTERNAL-COMBUSTION ENGINE in which fuel is burned inside the engine. Diesel engines are named after their inventor, Rudolf Diesel, who built his first successful engine in 1897 to replace the steam engine. Diesel engines use a cruder, heavier fuel oil than petrol. They are cheaper to run than petrol engines, but they are heavier and more difficult to start, so until recently they were not widely used in cars. They are used to drive heavy machines such as trains, tractors, ships, buses and trucks. A properly-working diesel causes less pollution than a petrol engine.

A diesel engine is similar to a petrol engine. But instead of using a spark from a sparkplug to ignite the fuel, the diesel engine uses heat that is made by a piston squeezing air inside a cylinder. When air is very tightly compressed, or pushed into a much smaller space than it filled before, it gets very hot. This heat sets fire to the diesel oil, which burns instantly, like a small explosion. The burning oil heats the air and forces it to expand again to push the piston downwards and thus drive the engine.

Many RAILWAYS began using diesel engines after World War II. Railways badly damaged in the war took the opportunity to modernize their engines and replaced the old steam locomotives with diesel engines. Diesel engines were first used regularly on the railroads of the United States in the 1930s. Today, diesel-electric engines are in use all over the world. In these engines the diesel motor is used to make electricity. The electricity then drives the train.

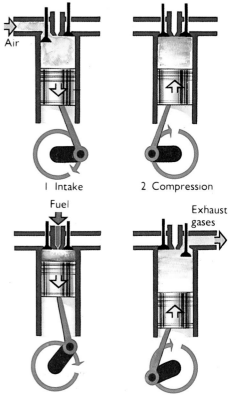

1 Intake   2 Compression

3 Injection and power   4 Exhaust

▲ How a diesel engine works. As the piston goes down (1), air is drawn into the cylinder. When the piston goes up, the air is squeezed and becomes very hot (2). When the piston gets to the top, oil is squirted in and bursts into flame. The hot gases expand and push the piston down (3). When the piston goes up again it pushes the spent gases out through the exhaust valve (4).

Digestion

Digestion is the way in which the food we eat is broken down into substances that can be used by the body. It takes place in the digestive tract, or *alimentary canal*, a long tube that runs from the mouth to the anus. Digestion starts in the mouth, where the teeth and special chemicals in the saliva help to break down the food. The food then passes

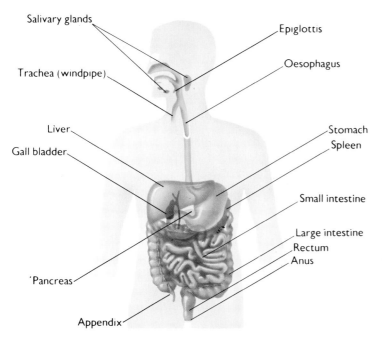

◀ The human digestive tract. The alimentary canal in an adult is eight to ten metres long.

Triceratops

Tyrannosaurus

▲ *Many of the dinosaurs of the late Cretaceous Period could survive an attack from great meat-eaters such as* Tyrannosaurus. *The ostrich dinosaurs such as* Struthiomimus *could run very fast, while the ceratopsian* Triceratops *and the ankylosaur* Ankylosaurus *had strong armour.*

The largest flying creature that we know about was a pterosaur that glided over parts of North America about 70 million years ago. Scientists calculate from its fossil remains that it had a wingspan of about 11 metres – more than half the length of a cricket pitch!

down a tube called the *oesophagus*. Muscles in the oesophagus push and squeeze the food down into the STOMACH. There, acids and more chemicals help to turn the food into a creamy liquid. Then a muscle at the lower end of the stomach opens from time to time to release food into the small intestine.

Inside the small intestine, bile from the LIVER and juice from the pancreas help to break down the food still further. Much of it passes through the thin walls of the intestine into the bloodstream. The remainder goes into the large intestine. There, liquids and salts are absorbed until only solid waste material is left. Bacteria in the large intestine digest any remaining food products. The final waste product is passed out of the body as *faeces*.

Dinosaur

The word *dinosaur* means 'enormous lizard'. These creatures lived between 65 and 225 million years

Ankylosaurus

Struthiomimus

Robinson

ago, long before there were any people on earth. They developed from primitive REPTILES.

There were two main groups of dinosaurs – the *saurischians* and the *ornithischians*. The ornithischian dinosaurs were all plant-eaters and most of them went around on all fours. Some of these, like *Stegosaurus* and *Triceratops*, were large and lumbering but had bony armour to protect them from the teeth and claws of the great meat-eating dinosaurs.

The saurischian group contained both plant-eaters and meat-eaters. The plant-eaters included the largest dinosaurs, the biggest of which scientists are calling '*Ultrasaurus*'. The remains of this creature are incomplete, but they include a huge arm and shoulder girdle which show that it was about 8 metres high at the shoulder – four times the height of a tall man! It probably weighed as much as 130 tonnes, even heavier than the blue whale. But these great beasts were harmless plant-eaters.

During the age of the dinosaurs, 200 million years ago, the continents were all joined together in one great land mass. This is why dinosaurs have been found in every continent except Antarctica. About 300 different species of dinosaurs have been found, but some of these are known only from a single tooth or a small bone fragment.

205

HOW DISEASES ARE SPREAD

Bacteria and viruses are often spread when we cough or sneeze.

Hands should always be washed thoroughly before preparing food.

Flies, cockroaches and mice live in dirty places and can pass on bacteria.

Avoid sharing food or drink. Harmful germs are often found in saliva.

Food left uncovered can encourage bacteria that cause food poisoning.

Perhaps the most famous of the dinosaurs are the great carnivores, or meat-eaters. *Tyrannosaurus*, which was up to 14 metres from snout to tail, stood on its hind legs. Its toes had claws as long as carving knives. Sabre-like teeth – some nearly the length of a man's hand – lined the jaws. No flesh-eating beasts that ever lived on land were larger or more menacing than these monsters.

No one knows why all the dinosaurs, great and small, died out about 65 million years ago.

Discrimination

There are a few harmless forms of discrimination, but most kinds are bad. If you have a photographic club, anyone who is not interested in photography is excluded. That is harmless discrimination. The oldest form of discrimination is in religion. People who did not belong to the popular religion were punished. For example, until 1829 Roman Catholics in Britain could not vote or sit in Parliament.

Other forms of discrimination are being fought today. One kind is *racism* – discriminating against people because of their race. In the United States, blacks were discriminated against for many years. South African APARTHEID was a kind of discrimination.

Another form of discrimination is by sex. In some countries women are still barred from some jobs just because they are women.

Disease

Diseases make us ill. Some are caused by BACTERIA, or germs, that invade our bodies. Others are caused by VIRUSES. Some diseases are passed down from parents to children in the genes they are born with.

The body resists diseases through its *immune system*. Special CELLS, such as white blood cells, fight the invading organisms. The body also produces antibodies to fight disease. Antibodies produced to fight diseases such as measles or chickenpox stay in our systems and usually prevent us from having the same disease again – we are immune.

Doctors have developed many ways of helping us fight diseases with DRUGS and INOCULATIONS.

Disney, Walt

Walt Disney (1901–1967) was an American filmmaker best known for his cartoons and films for children. Disney characters, especially Mickey Mouse and Donald Duck, are famous all over the world. Walt Disney began his work in the 1920s. His cartoon artists, or animators, produced characters and settings that moved realistically. Full-length Disney cartoon features such as *Snow White and the Seven Dwarfs*, *Pinocchio*, and *Bambi* are still popular everywhere.

Distillation

When water boils it turns into steam. When the steam cools it turns back into water again. The steam from a boiling kettle on hitting a cool window *condenses* into drops of water. But the water on the window is not quite the same as the water in the kettle. It is *pure* water. When salt sea water is boiled it is pure fresh water that condenses from the steam. The salt is left behind in the boiler. This boiling and cooling of liquids to make them pure is called distillation. An apparatus used for distilling is called a still. Large stills are used in some places to turn sea water into fresh water.

Distillation is often used to separate liquids that are mixed together. The mixture is heated and the

▲ *A monorail at the Epcot Center at Disney World, a huge amusement park in Florida, USA. Walt Disney opened the first of these parks, Disneyland, in California in 1955. In 1992, EuroDisney opened at Marne-la-Vallée in France.*

▲ *Walt Disney, shown here with his most famous creation, Mickey Mouse, began as a commercial artist and made the first of his short films with sound, Steamboat Willie, in 1928.*

▶ *To distil water in a simple laboratory experiment, the water in the flask is heated. Steam rises into the cold condenser. Cold water circulating around the condenser cools the steam, which turns back into liquid and collects as distilled water in the beaker.*

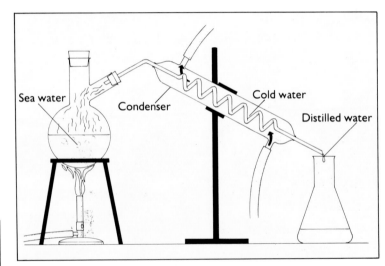

Sea water
Condenser
Cold water
Distilled water

Two thousand years ago, Greek sailors made drinking water from sea water by distillation. They boiled sea water and hung sponges in the steam. Then they squeezed pure distilled water out of the sponges.

liquid that boils at the lowest temperature evaporates first and is separated from the other liquids. Then the liquid with the next lowest boiling point is condensed off, and so on.

This is called *fractional distillation* and it is used to separate the materials in the crude OIL that comes from oil wells. Distilling is also used in making alcoholic drinks such as whisky.

Djibouti

The small republic of Djibouti is in north-east Africa beside the Red Sea. It is about the size of Wales. Much of the country is desert and there are few natural resources. About a third of the people are nomads who rear goats, cattle and camels.

The country's capital is also called Djibouti. It is a port, and handles most of the exports from neighbouring ETHIOPIA. Djibouti was formerly a French colony. It gained independence in 1977. The official language of Djibouti is French, although many speak Arabic, Afar or Somali.

Dodo

About 400 years ago a Dutch ship landed explorers on Mauritius, a lonely island in the Indian Ocean. They found doves, fish and large flocks of birds as big and fat as turkeys. These birds had no proper wings and could not fly. In time people called them dodos, from the Portuguese word *doudo*. This word

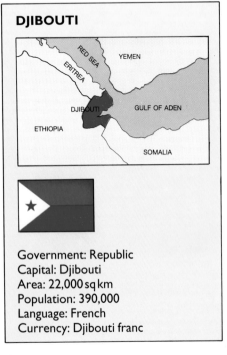

DJIBOUTI

RED SEA
YEMEN
ERITREA
DJIBOUTI
GULF OF ADEN
ETHIOPIA
SOMALIA

Government: Republic
Capital: Djibouti
Area: 22,000 sq km
Population: 390,000
Language: French
Currency: Djibouti franc

means 'simpleton', or a stupid person.

Sailors quickly learnt that dodos were good to eat. Ships that visited Mauritius sailed off with holds full of salted dodo meat. Rats and dogs from the ships started eating dodo eggs and chicks.

By the 1690s all the dodos were dead. Only drawings, bones and one stuffed bird remained.

▲ *The dodo was said to have a cry like a gosling. It laid one white egg on a nest of grass.*

Dog

People have been keeping dogs for perhaps 10,000 years. Most dogs are kept as pets but some do useful work like herding sheep or guarding buildings.

The first dog was probably descended from a WOLF and looked much like a wolf. Today there are

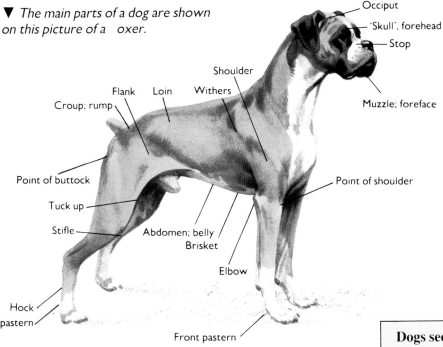

▼ *The main parts of a dog are shown on this picture of a oxer.*

Occiput
'Skull', forehead
Stop
Muzzle; foreface
Shoulder
Withers
Loin
Flank
Croup; rump
Point of buttock
Tuck up
Stifle
Abdomen; belly
Brisket
Point of shoulder
Elbow
Hock
pastern
Front pastern

more than 100 breeds of dog of many colours, shapes, and sizes. The St Bernard is the largest breed. A St Bernard may weigh nearly twice as much as a man. The Yorkshire terrier is one of the smallest dogs. A fully grown Yorkshire terrier may weigh less than a small pot of jam.

Most of the modern breeds of dog were developed to be good at special kinds of work. Airedales and other terriers make fine rat nunters. Labrador retrievers bring back ducks shot by hunters and also make excellent guide dogs.

Dogs see a world that is blurred and has no colour. They are shortsighted and see only shades of grey. But a dog's sense of smell is thousands of times better than ours. Customs officers use specially trained dogs for sniffing out illegal drugs. It is not necessary to open cases or crates – one sniff is enough for a dog, even if the drugs are packed in tins.

▲ *These beautifully-dressed dolls were made in the 1600s and can be seen in the Victoria and Albert Museum in London.*

▼ *Dolphins and porpoises are small whales. The bottle-nosed dolphin has a shorter, more up-turned beak than the common dolphin.*

Collies round up sheep. Dachshunds were once used for hunting badgers. Dobermanns are ferocious guard dogs.

All puppies are born blind and helpless, and at first only feed on their mother's milk. But small dogs are fully grown in a year or so. Most kinds of dog live for about 12 years.

Doll

Children all over the world play with dolls. Dolls may be made of wood, china, plastic or many other substances. The very first doll may have been just a forked twig that looked a bit like a human being. Homemade dolls can cost nothing, but doll collectors will pay a lot of money for rare old dolls.

Dolphin and Porpoise

Dolphins are small whales. Although they never leave the sea, they are mammals. They breathe air and are warm-blooded. They have sharp teeth and their heads end in beaklike mouths. Porpoises, close relatives of the dolphins, have no beak and the front of the head is rounded. Because the dolphin is a friendly creature, it has been well-known since ancient times. Dolphins are intelligent and communicate with each other by means of whistles and clicks. Tame dolphins can learn many tricks.

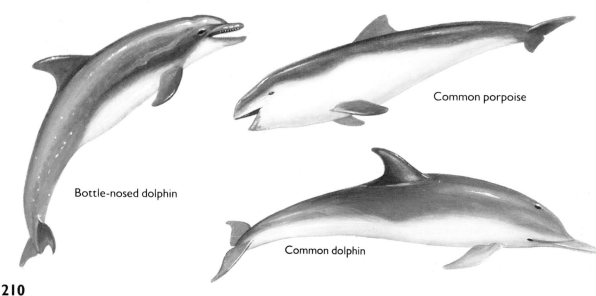

Bottle-nosed dolphin

Common porpoise

Common dolphin

Dome

Domes are roofs like giant upturned pudding bowls. Some domes are made from bricks or stones. Other domes are made of concrete, steel, or plastic. Domed roofs cover famous religious buildings such as St Sophia in Istanbul, St Peter's in Rome and St Paul's Cathedral in London. The world's largest dome is the Louisiana Superdome in the American city of New Orleans. It is as wide as two football pitches end to end.

The Romans were the great dome builders. In AD 112 they built the Pantheon in Rome. Its dome is 43 m in diameter and 43 m high.

▲ *Domes, large and small, decorate the church of Santa Maria della Salute in Venice. The word dome comes from the Latin* domus, *meaning 'house'.*

Domesday Book

Twenty years after the Norman Conquest, William the Conqueror ordered that a great survey of property owners in England should be made. It was called the Domesday Book (or Doomsday) because it spared no one and there was no appeal from it. William wanted to find out how much land people held so that he could be sure that he was getting all the taxes that were due to him. The survey was completed in 1086 and can be seen in the Public Record Office in London.

▼ *The Domesday Book recorded who owned land, how much land they owned, how many people worked the land, how many animals they owned, and how many pastures, mills and fish ponds they had.*

DOMINICA

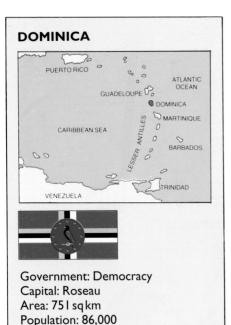

Government: Democracy
Capital: Roseau
Area: 751 sq km
Population: 86,000
Language: English
Currency: East Caribbean dollar

DOMINICAN REPUBLIC

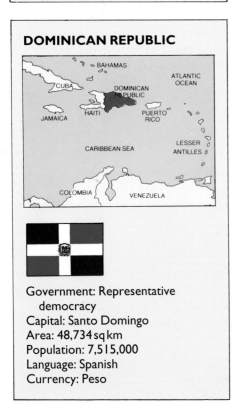

Government: Representative
 democracy
Capital: Santo Domingo
Area: 48,734 sq km
Population: 7,515,000
Language: Spanish
Currency: Peso

► Donkeys can carry very heavy loads
for their size. They are patient and
hard-working, and have been used as
pack animals for centuries.

Dominica

This small island country in the Caribbean Sea was a British colony until it became independent in 1978. The main products are bananas and citrus fruits. The capital is Roseau.

Dominican Republic

The Dominican Republic occupies the larger part of the island of Hispaniola in the Caribbean Sea. The rest of the island is occupied by Haiti. The main crop is sugar. It has an area of 48,734 sq km and the population is over 7,000,000. The capital is Santo Domingo.

Donkey

Donkeys are small and sturdy relatives of the HORSE. They are descended from the wild asses of Africa. A donkey has a large head with long ears. It has a short mane, and its tail ends in a tuft of hair.

Donkeys are sure-footed and can carry heavy loads over rough ground. They have long been used as pack animals and are still at work in southern Europe, North Africa, Asia and Latin America.

 One of the best known legendary dragons was that said to have been slain by St George, the patron saint of England. The story inspired this painting by Paolo Uccello.

Dragon

Dragons are storybook monsters, but once many people believed that they really lived. Artists showed them as huge snakes or lizards with wings of skin and terrifying claws. They were supposed to breathe fire and swallow people and animals whole.

Fighting dragons called for great bravery. Legends tell how Hercules, St George and other heroes killed these evil monsters.

Not everyone thought dragons were wicked. The Chinese looked upon the creatures as gods.

When we read about Sir Francis Drake's exploits, it is hard to imagine how small his ships were. When he set out to pillage Spanish possessions in the West Indies, his two ships weighed just 71 tonnes and 25 tonnes. The *Golden Hind*, in which he sailed around the world, was a large merchant ship of its day – it displaced about 100 tonnes!

Drake, Francis

Sir Francis Drake (about 1540–1596) was a sea captain who helped to make England a great sea power. In the 1570s he led sea raids against Spanish ships and ports in the Caribbean Sea. He also became the first Englishman to sail around the world. In 1588 he helped to destroy the Spanish ARMADA.

Drawing

Drawings are pictures or designs usually made in line with pencil, pen or some similar material other than paint.

Drawing has been a natural human activity since prehistoric times, when people began to express

▲ Sir Francis Drake got his first command as captain of a ship at the age of 24.

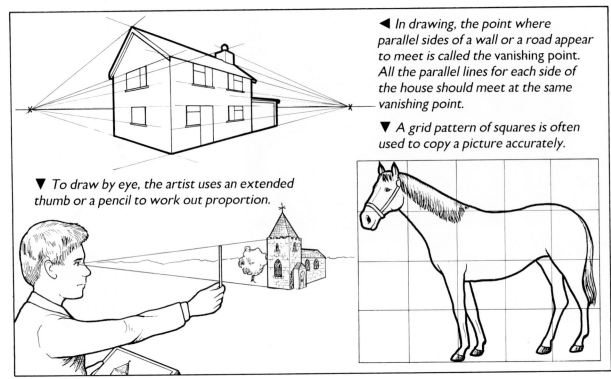

◀ *In drawing, the point where parallel sides of a wall or a road appear to meet is called the vanishing point. All the parallel lines for each side of the house should meet at the same vanishing point.*

▼ *A grid pattern of squares is often used to copy a picture accurately.*

▼ *To draw by eye, the artist uses an extended thumb or a pencil to work out proportion.*

▼ *A profile of an armoured warrior drawn by Leonardo da Vinci in about 1480. Leonardo did numerous sketches and studies from nature.*

their thoughts and ideas on the stone of cave walls. All children draw naturally. Many famous artists have included drawings in their best work. Some drawings are very precise and realistic. Every detail is picked out. In others, a powerful effect is produced by using very few lines and little detail. LEONARDO DA VINCI made scientific drawings and sketches for his paintings. Other painters who were also expert at drawing include Pieter Bruegel (the Elder), Paul Cezanne and Pablo PICASSO.

Dream

Dreams occur when our brains are active while we are asleep. Some dreams are of everyday occurrences. Others may be just a series of jumbled images. On waking, we may or may not remember what we have dreamed. A frightening dream is called a nightmare.

We do not know exactly why people dream. Dreams may be sparked off by indigestion or a similar physical cause, such as a cramped sleeping position. External noises may also cause dreams. Some dreams are very common. These include dreams of falling, or being chased, or of water.

Drug

Drugs are chemicals that affect the way the body works. Doctors give drugs to patients to help them fight disease. Antibiotics attack certain kinds of germs. These drugs help to cure people suffering from pneumonia and other illnesses. Drugs like aspirin help to deaden pain. The strongest pain-killers are called anaesthetics. Some people need drugs containing VITAMINS or other substances their bodies must have.

Certain drugs come from plants or animals. For instance, the foxglove gives us a drug called digitalis. This makes weak hearts beat more strongly. Many other drugs are made from MINERALS.

Some people take drugs such as cocaine, cannabis or alcohol just because these give a pleasant feeling. Some of these drugs can be addictive (habit-forming), cause illness and even death.

▲ Foxgloves are still cultivated for the drug digitalis that is used in the treatment of heart disease.

Drum

Drums are the most important percussion instruments: MUSICAL INSTRUMENTS that are played by being struck. The sound is made by hitting a tightly stretched sheet of skin or plastic called a drumhead. A kettledrum has one drumhead stretched over a metal basin. A bass drum or a side drum has two drumheads, one across each end of a large open 'can'.

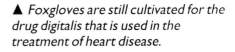

▼ Tribal drums were once used to send messages in a drum code from village to village. Today they are chiefly used for ceremonial occasions.

Duck

These web-footed water birds are related to swans and geese. Ducks look rather like small geese with short necks.

The two main groups of ducks are dabbling ducks and diving ducks. Dabbling ducks feed at the surface of the water. They may put most of their body under the water, but they do not dive. Dabbling ducks include the mallards that swim on pools and rivers in the northern half of the world. (Farmyard ducks were bred from mallards.) Other dabbling ducks include teal and widgeon, and the pretty mandarin and Carolina ducks.

Diving ducks dive completely underwater in their

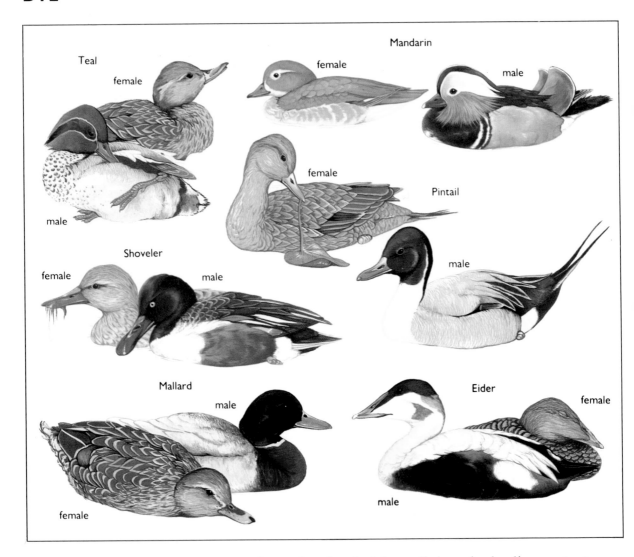

Teal

female

male

Mandarin

female

male

female

Pintail

male

Shoveler

female

male

male

Mallard

male

female

Eider

female

male

▲ *Six kinds of ducks in pairs: the best known of the surface-feeders, or dabbling ducks, is the mallard. The teal is another surface-feeder and is the smallest European species. The shoveler is characterized by its spoon-shaped bill. The male pintail has a long, pointed tail, and the eider duck gives us the soft breast feathers known as eider down. The mandarin was introduced into Britain from China and is now found wild in parts of southern England.*

hunt for food. Most diving ducks live out at sea. These ducks include the eider duck from which we get eiderdown. Sawbills are also diving ducks. Their long, slim beaks have inside edges like the teeth of a saw. Sawbills are good at grasping fish. The long-tailed duck is a diving duck that can fly at 112 km an hour.

Dye

Dyes are substances that people use to colour TEXTILES and other materials. Some dyes come from plants. Cochineal, a red dye, comes from the cochineal insect. Most dyes are now made from chemicals. To dye an object you dip it in water containing dissolved dye. If the dye is *fast* the object will keep its dyed colour however much you wash it.

Eagle

Eagles are large birds of prey. Most hunt small mammals and birds. Some catch fish or reptiles. The harpy eagle and the monkey-eating eagle catch monkeys. Each of these great birds measures more than 2 metres across its outspread wings. These eagles are the largest in the world.

Many eagles soar high above the ground. Others perch on a tree or rock. When an eagle sees its prey it swoops suddenly and pounces. It seizes its prey with its sharp claws and tears off pieces of flesh with its strong, hooked beak.

The short-toed eagle, below and left, has white underparts. The booted eagles, right, show the light and dark forms of the bird. Bonelli's eagle, right below, is usually found in mountains.

Short-toed eagle

Booted eagle

Bonelli's eagle

Ear

Our ears help us to hear and to keep our balance. Each ear has three main parts. These are the outer ear, middle ear and inner ear.

The outer ear is the part we can see, and the tube leading from it into the head. Sounds reach the outer ear as vibrations, or waves, in the air. The cup-like shape of the ear collects these sound waves and sends them into the tube.

Next, the sound waves reach the middle ear.

If you spin round quickly and stop suddenly, the liquid in the hollow loops in your inner ear keeps on spinning for a while. The nerve cells in your ear send confusing messages to your brain, and you feel dizzy. The dizziness ends when the liquid in the loops stops moving.

Here, the waves make the *eardrum* move to and fro. This is a thin 'skin' across the entrance of the middle ear. The moving eardrum sets tiny bones vibrating in the middle ear.

The vibrations travel on into the inner ear. Here they set liquid moving in the *cochlea*. This looks like a snail's shell. The nerves inside it turn vibrations into messages that travel to your brain. The inner ear also has three hollow loops containing liquid. These loops send signals to the brain to help you keep your balance.

Ears are delicate and easily damaged. Hitting or poking into an ear can cause injury and may lead to DEAFNESS.

▶ *This picture shows the main parts of the outer, middle and inner ear. The eustachian tube helps to keep air pressure the same on both sides of the eardrum.*

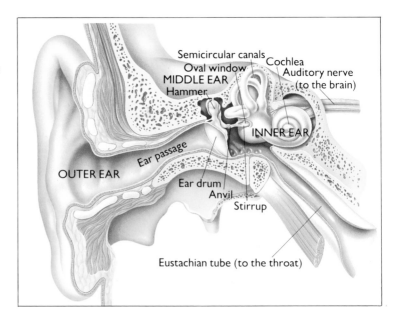

FAMOUS EARTHQUAKES
Shensi Province, China, 1556: Over 800,000 people perished – more than in any other earthquake.
San Francisco, USA, 1906: An earthquake and the fires it caused destroyed the city.
Kwanto Plain, Japan, 1923: Some 570,000 buildings collapsed. This was the costliest earthquake ever as measured by damage to property.
Lebu, Chile, 1977: The strongest earthquake shock ever recorded.
Armenia, USSR, 1988: About 25,000 people died and several towns and villages were buried.

Earth

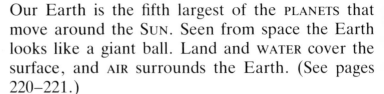

Our Earth is the fifth largest of the PLANETS that move around the SUN. Seen from space the Earth looks like a giant ball. Land and WATER cover the surface, and AIR surrounds the Earth. (See pages 220–221.)

Earthquake

People often use the saying 'safe as houses'. But in certain lands houses sometimes topple over because the ground starts trembling. This trembling is called an earthquake. About half a million earthquakes

◀ *A devastating earthquake in Alaska, USA, in 1964 was followed by a tsunami (tidal wave) that was almost as destructive.*

happen every year. Most are so weak that only special instruments called *seismographs* show that they have happened. Only one earthquake in 500 does any damage. But some earthquakes can cause terrible damage and suffering. Three-quarters of a million people are thought to have died when an earthquake hit the Chinese city of Tangshan in 1976.

Small tremors can happen when VOLCANOES erupt, when there is a landslide, or when the roof of an underground cave falls in. The largest earthquakes occur when one huge piece of the Earth's crust slips suddenly against another piece. This slipping may take place deep underground. But the shock travels up through the crust and sets the surface quaking.

A seabed earthquake may set off a huge ocean wave called a *tsunami*. These can rise higher than a house and travel faster than the fastest train.

▲ *A seismograph shows earth tremors as wriggles in a line traced on a turning drum. A tremor vibrates the weight that holds the tracer.*

Earthworm *See* Worm

Easter

Easter is the day when Christians remember the resurrection of JESUS. Most Christians celebrate Easter on the Sunday following the first full moon after the first day of spring in the northern half of the world.

We have eggs at Easter because they tell us of the new life that returns to nature about this time. People have been exchanging eggs at Easter since ancient times. The Egyptians and Persians dyed eggs and gave them to their friends. The Persians also believed that the Earth had hatched from a giant egg.

EARTH

So far as we know, the Earth is the only planet that supports life. Our world is a medium-sized planet, orbiting a star (the Sun) along with eight other planets. What makes our Earth unique are its atmosphere and its water. Together, these make possible a rich variety of animal and plant life. Seen from space, Earth can look mostly covered by ocean, wreathed in swirling clouds. Land covers only about one quarter of the planet's surface. Beneath the surface is an intensely hot, dense core.

If the Earth was the size of a football, the highest land masses such as the Himalayas would be no higher than a coat of paint on the ball. The deepest ocean trenches would be almost invisible scratches in the paint.

Although the Earth is between 4 and 5 billion years old, no rocks as old as this have ever been found. It is thought that the Earth's original rocks have all been worn away. Rocks found in the USA have been dated at about 3,800,000,000 years old.

EARTH'S VITAL STATISTICS

Age: about 4550 milllion years
Weight: about 6000 million million tonnes
Diameter: from Pole to Pole through the Earth's centre 12,714km; across the Equator through the Earth's centre 12,756km
Circumference: round the Poles 40,000km; round the Equator 40,076km
Area of water: about 362 million sq km – 71 per cent
Area of land: about 148 million sq km – 29 per cent
Volume: 1,084,000 million cubic km
Average height of land: 840 metres above sea level
Average depth of ocean: 3795 metres below sea level

INSIDE THE EARTH

Core Mantle Crust

The Earth's **outer core** lies below the mantle and above the inner core. It 2240 km thick. The outer core is made mainly of metals, under enormous pressure and so hot they are molten (melted). Four-fifths of it may be iron and nickel. The rest is probably silicon.

The **inner core** is a solid ball, about 2440 km across. Like the outer core, may be made mainly of iron and nickel. The core temperature is 3700°C and the pressure there is 3800 tonnes per square centimetre.

The **mantle** lies beneath the crust and above the outer core. Nearly 2900 km thick, the mantle is made up of hot rocks. Temperature and pressure here are lower than in the core. Even so, much of the mantle rock is semi-molten.

The **crust** is the Earth's solid outer layer. It is up to 30 km thick beneath mountains, but only 6 km thick under the oceans. Its rocks float on the denser rocks of the mantle.

◄ The Earth photographed from space. Cloud 'swirls' are depressions – areas of low atmospheric pressure where warm tropical air meets cold polar air. Such views help weather experts to plot the paths of hurricanes and so give warning of dangerous storms. Astronauts see the Earth outlined by a black sky.

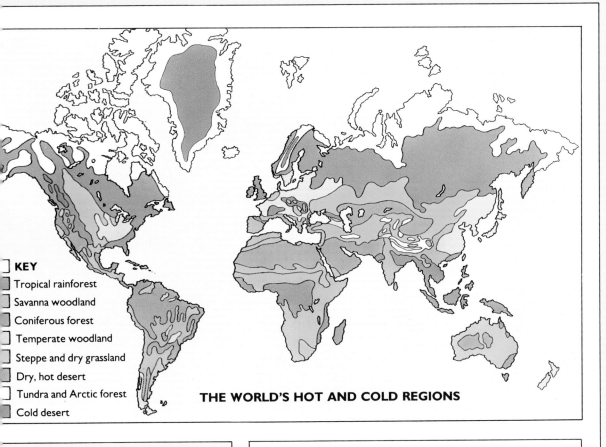

KEY

- Tropical rainforest
- Savanna woodland
- Coniferous forest
- Temperate woodland
- Steppe and dry grassland
- Dry, hot desert
- Tundra and Arctic forest
- Cold desert

THE WORLD'S HOT AND COLD REGIONS

WORLD FACTS AND FIGURES

Highest mountain: Everest (Asia) 8848 m

Longest river: Nile (Africa), 6695 km

Greatest ocean depth: Marianas Trench (Pacific Ocean) 11,034 m

Largest desert: Sahara (Africa) 9,096,000 km

Largest ocean: Pacific 181,000,000 sq km

Highest navigable lake: Titicaca (South America) 3812 m above sea level

Deepest lake: Baikal (USSR) 1940 m

Largest lake: Caspian Sea (Asia) 1,000 sq km

Highest waterfall: Angel Falls (Venezuela, South America) 979 m

Hottest place: Al'Aziziyah in Libya, where 7.7°C (136°F) was recorded in 1922

Coldest place: Vostok, Antarctica, where 89.2°C (−128.6°F) was recorded in 1983

Wettest place: Mt Waialeale, Hawaii, with ,680 mm of rainfall a year

Driest place: Atacama Desert, Chile, with an average rainfall of only 0.76 mm a year

HOW MOUNTAINS ARE FORMED

Fold mountains (below right) are thrown up when huge forces buckle rock layers into giant wrinkles. The Rocky Mountains and the Andes were formed in this way when the Earth's crustal plates collided. Some rocks were folded over onto others, and over millions of years a new mountain range was born. Other kinds of mountains are formed when faults (breaks) in the Earth's crust take place.

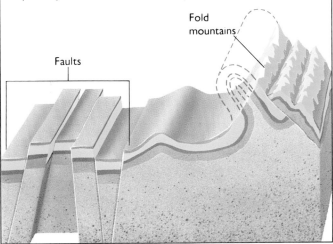

Faults

Fold mountains

For more information turn to these articles: CONTINENTS; DESERT; GEOGRAPHY; GEOLOGY; ISLAND; LAKE; MOUNTAIN; OCEAN; ER; SOLAR SYSTEM; WEATHER.

▲ *When you hear an echo, you hear the sound twice or more. This is because the sound waves that reach your ears also bounce off nearby cliffs or walls. These waves reach your ears a second or two later, and you hear an echo.*

Echo

An echo is a SOUND bounced back from a wall or some other object. Sound travels at a known, fixed speed, so we can use echoes to find how far off some objects are. A ship's SONAR uses echoes to find the depth of the sea. Echoes help BATS to fly in the dark. RADAR depends on echoes from radio signals.

Eclipse

An eclipse happens when the shadow of one planet or moon falls on another. If the shadow hides all of the planet or moon there is a total eclipse. If the shadow hides only a part there is a partial eclipse.

The only eclipses you can easily see without a telescope take place when the Sun, Moon and Earth are in line. When the Earth lies between the Sun and the Moon, the Earth's shadow falls on the Moon. This is an eclipse of the Moon. When the Moon lies between the Earth and the Sun, the Moon's shadow falls on a part of the Earth. An eclipse of the Sun, or solar eclipse, can be seen from that part. Two or three of each kind of eclipse happen every year.

The centre of the shadow of a solar eclipse is called the *umbra*. It is a dark circle only about 270 km across. Inside the umbra, the eclipse is complete – the Moon completely hides the Sun. Around the umbra is a lighter shadow about 3000 km across, in which part of the Sun can be seen.

▼ *A solar eclipse is caused as the Moon's shadow falls on the Earth, and a lunar eclipse as the Earth's shadow falls on the Moon. Only the umbra – the dark middle part of the Moon's shadow – is shown for the solar eclipse.*

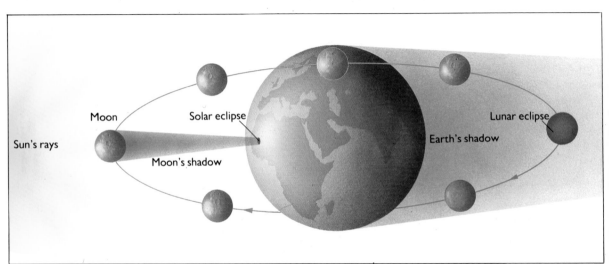

Sun's rays

Moon

Solar eclipse

Moon's shadow

Earth's shadow

Lunar eclipse

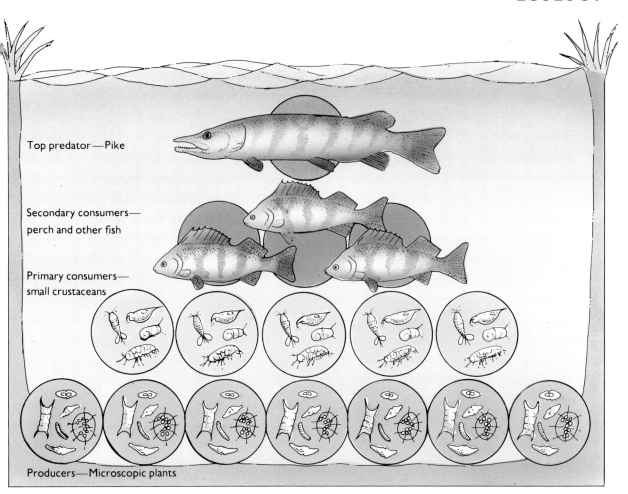

Top predator—Pike

Secondary consumers—
perch and other fish

Primary consumers—
small crustaceans

Producers—Microscopic plants

Ecology

Ecology is the study of living things and their surroundings. Scientists called ecologists try to find out how living things and their surroundings affect each other. Ecology shows us that most plants and animals can live only in a special set of surroundings such as a pond, field, forest or desert. Within each place live plants that are suited to a certain soil, temperature, and so on. All the animals living there eat the plants or one another. So the plants and animals are linked in what ecologists call a food web. If some kinds die out, those that eat them lose their food and may die too.

Everything in the world changes. Human inventions and discoveries are causing rapid changes. Sometimes the air is being filled with poisons; waterways are being polluted. Ecologists can help us to use the inventions and discoveries without making the world sick.

▲ *The food pyramid above gives some idea of just how much food it takes to keep the creatures in a pond alive and healthy. About 1000 kilograms of plant life is needed to feed the animals that feed the fish that in turn feed just 1 kilogram of pike.*

The introduction of animals from foreign lands can have harmful effects on the balanced ecology of a place. In 1850, three pairs of European rabbits were turned loose in Australia. With no natural enemies, the rabbits multiplied so quickly that they became a plague to farmers. Only the introduction of a disease that was fatal to rabbits halted the plague.

▲ *Business as usual on the Tokyo stock exchange. The buying and selling of shares is a basic part of the capitalist economic system, in which land, resources and industries are owned by private individuals and companies rather than by governments.*

ECUADOR

Government: Republic
Capital: Quito
Area: 283,561 sq km
Population: 10,933,000
Language: Spanish
Currency: Sucre

▶ *A woman sells leeks and plantains in a market in Ecuador. Indians and mestizos (of mixed Indian and European ancestry) make up about 80 per cent of the population.*

Economics

Economics is the study of people's needs, such as food, clothes and housing, and the ways in which people fill these needs. Economists study the ways in which a community's needs can be met. No country has enough resources to supply all the things that its people want. It has to decide the best way of using the resources that it has. Many economists believe that deciding how to economize is the most important decision nations must make.

Ecuador

Ecuador is a country slightly bigger than the British Isles, but only about 11 million people live there. It is in north-west South America and lies on the equator. Its name is Spanish for *equator*. More than half of the people live in the high mountain valleys where sheep and llamas graze. The chief products are bananas, oil, coffee, rice and sugar. The Galapagos Islands, 960 km off the Pacific coast of South America, belong to Ecuador.

Ecuador has been torn by many rebellions in its history and has been ruled by civilian and military dictatorships. Since 1979 the country has been governed by a democratic civilian government. The capital is Quito.

Edison, Thomas

Thomas Alva Edison (1847–1931) was an American inventor. As a boy he spent only three months at school, and his teacher thought him stupid. But he went on to produce over 100 inventions. The most famous were the electric light and the phonograph for RECORDING and playing back sounds.

▲ In 1877 Edison produced a hand operated 'phonogram' that played recordings made on tin foil cylinders.

◄ Edward VIII and Mrs Simpson, the American divorcee for whom he abdicated (gave up the throne).

Edward (Kings)

Nine kings of England were called Edward. Edward 'The Confessor' (about 1002–1066) founded Westminster Abbey. Edward I (1239–1307) brought Wales under English rule. Edward II (1284–1327) was the first English Prince of Wales. Edward III (1312–1337) began the Hundred Years' War. Edward IV (1442–1483) took the crown from Henry VI in the Wars of the Roses. Edward V (1470–1483) was murdered in the Tower of London. Edward VI (1537–1553) reigned as a boy king for only six years. Edward VII (1841–1910) was Prince of Wales for 60 years. Edward VIII (1894–1972) gave up the throne to marry Mrs Simpson, a divorced American.

Eel

Eels are long, slim fish with fins like narrow ribbons. Some eels have tiny scales. Some are covered with slime. European and American freshwater eels swim thousands of kilometres and spawn far out in

▲ Two English kings called Edward: Edward the Confessor (top) ruled from 1042–1066, before the Norman conquest. Edward VII was the eldest son of Queen Victoria.

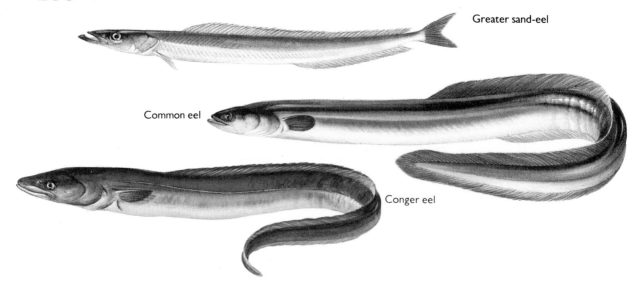

Greater sand-eel

Common eel

Conger eel

▲ *Eels look like snakes, but are actually fishes. The common eel lives in lakes and rivers but returns to the sea to breed. The conger eel and the greater sand-eel both live in the sea.*

the Atlantic Ocean. Then they die. The tiny, transparent young that hatch look nothing like their parents. These babies find their way all the way back to their parents' homes in America and Europe. There, they travel up rivers and streams. The young eels grow up in fresh water and stay there until they are ready for their long journey back across the Atlantic.

Egg

An egg is a female CELL that will grow into a new young plant or animal. Most eggs only grow if they are joined with, or fertilized by, male cells. In most MAMMALS the fertilized eggs grow inside the mother's body, but birds and most reptiles and fish lay eggs that contain enough food to help the developing young grow inside the egg.

Egypt

Modern Egypt dates from AD 642 when Egypt was conquered by Muslim soldiers from Arabia. Egypt is now a Muslim, mainly Arab, country. It has over 50 million people, more than any other nation in Africa. No other African city is as large as Cairo, Egypt's capital. But Egyptians still depend upon the waters of the river NILE that made Egypt great.

In 1979 Egypt signed a peace treaty with ISRAEL. This agreement was disliked by other Arab states, leaving Egypt isolated from its Arab neighbours.

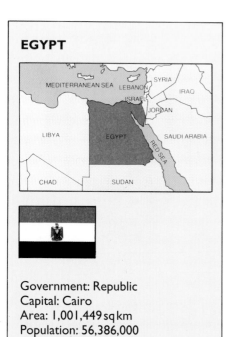

EGYPT

MEDITERRANEAN SEA LEBANON SYRIA IRAQ ISRAEL JORDAN LIBYA EGYPT SAUDI ARABIA RED SEA CHAD SUDAN

Government: Republic
Capital: Cairo
Area: 1,001,449 sq km
Population: 56,386,000
Language: Arabic
Currency: Egyptian pound

Egypt, Ancient

About 5000 years ago the ancient Egyptians began to build one of the world's first great civilizations. For the next 2500 years, ancient Egypt was one of the strongest, richest nations on Earth.

The people who made Egypt great were short, slim, dark-skinned men and women with black hair. They probably numbered no more than six million. Scarcely any of them lived in the hot sand and rock deserts that cover most of Egypt. Almost all the people settled by the river NILE that runs from south to north across the land.

Each year the river overflowed and left rich mud on nearby fields. Farmers learnt to dig and plough the fields. They could grow two crops a year in the

▼ A scene showing how the ancient Egyptians farmed by the Nile. They grew flax to make linen, and corn for food. They also caught birds and fish, raised chickens and grew produce in their gardens. In the picture, men are threshing corn. In the foreground women are winnowing. Part of all produce was paid in taxes to the government.

EGYPT, ANCIENT

▲ The sphinx is an imaginary creature found in the folk tales of many ancient peoples. Egyptian sphinxes combined the body of a beast – usually a lion – with the head of the ruling pharaoh. The most famous sphinx is the one shown above. It guards the great pyramid of Khafre at Giza, 10 km from Cairo. It is 73 metres long and about 20 metres high. Unfortunately, the sphinx's nose is missing. It was used by soldiers for target practice.

Several times during the Twentieth Egyptian Dynasty the workmen building a tomb for the pharaoh were not paid their food and other goods on time. The men went on strike. They marched to the temple where supplies were kept, and sat down outside calling for bread. They soon got what they wanted because it was unthinkable that the pharaoh's tomb should not be finished on time.

warm, fertile soil. The farmers grew more than enough grain, fruit and vegetables to feed themselves. The rest of the food helped to feed Egyptian craftsmen, miners, merchants, priests, noble families, and the PHARAOHS who ruled over the entire land.

Most Egyptians were poor and lived in mud-brick huts with palm-leaf roofs. Rich Egyptians lived in large, well-furnished houses and had meat and cakes to eat. They wore fine clothes and jewels.

The most splendid buildings in the land were tombs and temples. Thousands of workers toiled for years to build the mighty PYRAMIDS. In each such tomb, Egyptians would place the mummy (preserved body) of a pharaoh. They believed the dead went on living, so they buried food and furniture beside each mummy. Thieves later emptied almost all the tombs. But the boy pharaoh TUTANKHAMUN's tomb shows us what royal burials were like.

The dry Egyptian air has preserved HIERO-GLYPHICS written on fragile paper made from the papyrus plant. Paintings and hieroglyphics tell us a great deal about how the ancient Egyptians lived. The ancient Egyptians also left many fine statues.

In time, foreign armies using iron weapons defeated the Egyptians. Their land fell under foreign rule after 525 BC.

Einstein, Albert

Albert Einstein (1879–1955) was a great scientist who was born in Germany. His theory of relativity was a new way of looking at time, space, matter and ENERGY. Einstein showed that a small amount of matter could be changed into a vast amount of energy. This made it possible for people to use NUCLEAR ENERGY.

Elasticity

When you pull a rubber band it stretches. When you let it go, it springs back to its original size. It is elastic – it has elasticity. If you drop a rubber ball, the part of the ball that hits the ground is flattened. Then the ball springs back into its original round shape. As this happens, the ball pushes on the ground and it jumps up – it bounces. The ball has elasticity.

Elasticity happens because the molecules that make up the elastic material like to stay at a certain distance from each other. If they are squeezed more tightly together they immediately push apart. If they are pulled apart, they want to get together again. All solids and liquids have some elasticity. Even a steel ball bounces a little when it hits a concrete floor.

Election

Most countries and local areas hold elections from time to time. Elections give people the chance to elect, or choose, a new government or council. They do this by voting. In Britain each voter goes to a certain building on election, or polling, day. He or she is given a paper, or ballot, printed with the names of several candidates. The voter marks a cross against the name of the person he wants to represent him in PARLIAMENT or on the local council. Each area has its own candidates. Those who win the most votes are elected.

In some countries anyone may be a candidate. In others the government chooses candidates. Teams and clubs also hold elections to choose leaders.

▲ Albert Einstein helped to develop the first atomic bomb, but he was also passionately concerned about the control of nuclear weapons after World War II.

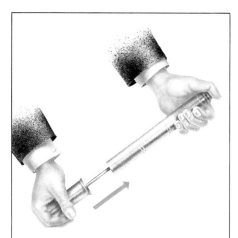

SEE IT YOURSELF
Air has elasticity too. It can be squeezed into a container and the energy stored in it can be used to drive machines such as pneumatic drills and hammers. You can feel the elasticity of air by putting your thumb over the end of a bicycle pump and pushing the pump handle.

In 1752, the American scientist and statesman Benjamin Franklin wondered whether lightning and thunder were caused by electricity. During a thunderstorm he flew a kite with a metal tip joined to a silk string. He attached a key to the string at a point near the ground. In a few seconds Franklin had the answer to his question. When he touched the key there was a spark. He could *feel* the electricity. But don't try this; it is very dangerous.

▼ Electricity travels from a power station through a network of high-voltage power lines. It passes through transformers and substations, where the current is changed to the lower voltage used in homes and factories.

Electricity

Electricity is the kind of ENERGY that powers electric trains, vacuum cleaners, radios, television sets and many more devices.

The electricity that we use flows through wires as electric CURRENT. Current flows when tiny particles called electrons jump between the ATOMS that make up the metal in the wire. Current can flow only if a wire makes a complete loop called a circuit. If a gap is made in the circuit, the current stops flowing. Switches are simply devices that open and close gaps in circuits.

BATTERIES produce electric current that can be used to start cars, light torch bulbs and work radios. But most of the electricity we use is produced in POWER STATIONS. In a power station GENERATOR, coils of wire are made to rotate between powerful magnets. This makes electric current flow through the coils in wire. This current then flows through other long wires to our homes.

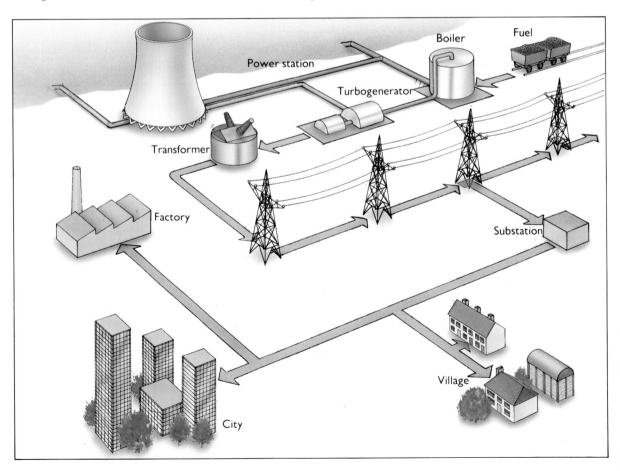

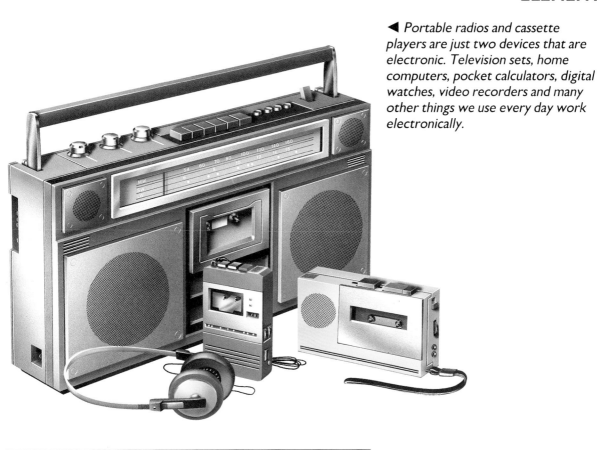

◄ *Portable radios and cassette players are just two devices that are electronic. Television sets, home computers, pocket calculators, digital watches, video recorders and many other things we use every day work electronically.*

Electronics

Electronics is an important part of the study of ELECTRICITY. It deals with the way in which tiny particles called electrons flow through certain CRYSTALS, GASES or a VACUUM. Electronic devices like TRANSISTORS and SILICON CHIPS are used in such things as COMPUTERS, RADAR, television sets and radios. Electronics helps us to see the smallest living things, to guide planes, and to do difficult sums instantly. Without electronics, space travel would be impossible.

▼ *This pellet of the element plutonium shines from the glow of its own radioactivity. Plutonium (Pu) does not occur in nature except in tiny quantities from the decay of Uranium-238.*

Element

Your own body and everything you see around you is composed (made up) of chemical ingredients called elements. In each element all the ATOMS are of the same kind. You can join different elements to make more complicated substances called COMPOUNDS, but you cannot break an element into a simpler kind of substance.

Chemists have found more than 100 different

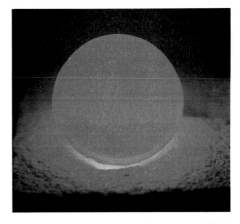

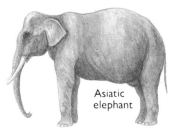

Asiatic
elephant

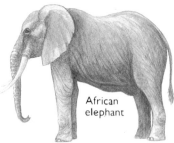

African
elephant

▲ *The African elephant has larger ears and tusks than the Indian, or Asiatic, elephant. It also has a different-shaped back.*

▼ *The African elephant protects the herd with an aggressive display – ears forward and trunk raised.*

elements. Ninety-two of these occur naturally. Scientists have produced other elements in laboratories. At ordinary temperatures, some elements are GASES, some are LIQUIDS, and some are solids.

OXYGEN is the most plentiful element on Earth. Half of the Earth's crust and most of your body is made of oxygen.

Elephant

Elephants are the largest living land animals. A big bull (male) elephant may stand twice as high as a man and weigh as much as seven family cars. An elephant has larger ears, thicker legs, a longer nose and longer teeth than any other creature. Its skin is nearly as thick as the heel of a man's shoe.

Baby elephants stand no taller than big dogs. Elephants are fully grown after 20 years. They live almost as long as people.

Indian elephants can be trained to move heavy loads. African elephants are harder to tame. Many thousands have been killed just for the IVORY of their tusks. Today, most are protected by law.

Elizabeth I

Elizabeth I (1533–1603) was a famous English queen. She never married, but she reigned for 45 years with the help of wise advisers. She worked for peace between quarrelling religious groups but had her rival MARY QUEEN OF SCOTS put to death. Elizabeth's seamen crushed the Spanish ARMADA and made England powerful at sea. Great English playwrights, poets and scholars lived in her reign. People often call it 'the Elizabethan Age'.

Elizabeth II

Elizabeth II (1926–) is Queen of the United Kingdom of Great Britain and Northern Ireland and head of the COMMONWEALTH. Her husband is the Duke of Edinburgh. Her eldest son, and heir to the throne, is Charles, Prince of Wales.

▲ *Elizabeth I reviews her troops at Tilbury before the arrival of the Spanish Armada. With the defeat of the Armada, England gained wealth and confidence.*

Queen Elizabeth I was vain of her good looks, especially her long hands. She wore extravagant clothes and ornate wigs. It is also said that she wore makeup so thick that sometimes she found it difficult to smile.

▶ *Despite their political troubles, the people of El Salvador still enjoy their festivals.*

▼ *Embroidery is an ancient craft. This colourful figure was embroidered by Peruvian Indians living in pre-Inca times.*

El Salvador

El Salvador is Central America's smallest country, but it has more people per square kilometre than any other country in Central America. Most of the 5½ million people are *mestizos* (of mixed Indian and European descent). Their main occupation is farming. Leading crops are coffee, cotton, maize and sugar. The capital is San Salvador.

El Salvador has had several clashes with its neighbour Honduras. A 12-year civil war between government forces and left-wing guerrillas ended in 1992.

Embroidery

Embroidery is a decoration stitched onto cloth with a needle and thread. People usually make embroideries on such materials as canvas, cotton, wool, or silk. They often embroider with coloured threads of cotton, linen, silk, or wool. People can even stitch patterns made up of beads, pearls, or jewels.

The oldest embroidery was made over 2300 years ago. One of the longest embroideries is the BAYEUX TAPESTRY.

Emu

Only the ostrich is larger than this big Australian bird. An emu is as tall as a man but not as heavy. Emu feathers are thick and dark. Its wings are small and an emu cannot fly, but it can run as fast as a horse on its long, strong legs.

Emus eat leaves and insects. Big herds of emus sometimes attack farm crops.

Each female lays up to 10 green eggs in a nest on the ground. The male sits on the eggs and later guards the chicks.

▲ *Emus are now rare in their native Australia, though they are being bred successfully in captivity.*

Energy

Having energy means being able to do work. MUSCLES and machines have mechanical energy – they can move loads. Energy exists in several forms. There are two main kinds – *potential energy* and *kinetic energy*. Potential energy is the energy of position – stored energy. For example, the water in a high dam has potential energy. Then, when the water falls through pipes and works turbines to make electricity, it has kinetic energy – energy of movement. Other forms of energy are electrical, heat, chemical, sound, radiant and nuclear. These forms can be changed into each other. For example, the chemical energy of petrol is turned into kinetic energy as it moves a car's pistons; to electrical energy in the car's generator, to light in the head-

▼ *When an archer draws back a bow, he or she gives it a store of potential energy. As the arrow is released the potential energy is turned into kinetic (moving) energy.*

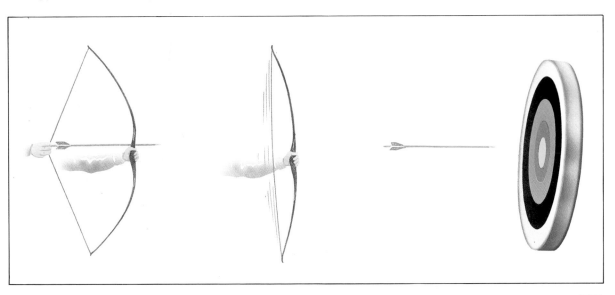

DIFFERENT KINDS OF ENERGY

Potential

Kinetic

Electric

Chemical

Radiant

Magnetic

Nuclear

Heat

▲ *Energy can exist in many forms. All forms of energy can do work.*

▼ The Rocket, *built by George Stephenson in 1829, was the first locomotive to use steam power successfully as a means of fast travel.*

lamps; to sound in the car's horn, and so on. At every stage some energy is turned into heat.

Radiant energy from the Sun gives us most of our energy on Earth. Coal, oil and natural gas – the fossil fuels – were formed from plants and animals that depended for their life on the Sun's light and warmth.

Engine

Engines are devices that change potential (stored) energy into useful energy that does work. People have used simple engines such as windmills and waterwheels for hundreds of years.

In the 1700s the STEAM ENGINE took over to drive everything from ships, trains and cars to all kinds of factory machinery. Steam still drives many machines – such as the steam turbines in nuclear power stations.

INTERNAL COMBUSTION ENGINES – petrol engines and DIESEL ENGINES – are easier to handle than steam engines and light enough to be fitted in aircraft. After them came JET and ROCKET engines.

Engineering

Engineers do a great many different types of jobs. Mining engineers find useful MINERALS and take them from the ground. Metallurgical engineers separate METALS from unwanted substances and make them usable. Chemical engineers use chemicals to make such things as explosives, paint, plastics, and soap. Civil engineers build bridges, tunnels, roads, railways, ports, airports and so on. Mechanical engineers make and use machines. They design JET ENGINES and factory machinery. Electrical engineers work with devices that produce and use electricity. Some specialize in building a particular type of GENERATOR. Others, such as those who design and build computers, are known as electronic engineers. Electronic engineers form the newest branch of electrical engineering. Power engineers maintain machinery in power stations. Most kinds of engineering fall into one or other of these groups.

The ancient Egyptians were the first real engineers. When the pyramids were being built about 2500 BC, Egyptian workmen were already using tools such as the lathe. They smelted and cast metals. Their quarrying and stoneworking techniques were so advanced that they could fit blocks of stone 12 metres long so closely together that a hair couldn't be passed between them.

▼ Engineers design big machines such as this excavator to save time, labour and cost. One such machine can do more work in an hour than a hundred men using hand tools could do in a day.

▲ *As an island nation, the English have had a long association with the sea. This small village in Yorkshire was once a thriving fishing community, but the fishing declined as long ago as the early 1900s.*

England

England is the largest country in the UNITED KINGDOM of Great Britain and Northern Ireland. If Great Britain were divided into five equal parts, England would fill three of them. England's neighbours are Scotland and Wales, but most of England is surrounded by sea. Green fields spread over the plains and low hills that cover most of the country. In the north and west there are mountains with moors and forests. Most English people live and work in big cities like London, Birmingham, Liverpool and Manchester.

England gets its name from the Angles, a group of the ANGLO-SAXONS who sailed to this island and settled down here about 1500 years ago.

English Language

More people speak English than any other language except Chinese. English is the main language spoken in the United Kingdom, Ireland, Australia, New Zealand, Canada, the United States and some other countries. Altogether more than 450 million people speak English as their everyday language. Another 100 million or more speak at least some English. Most English words come from old ANGLO-SAXON, French, or Latin words.

ENGLAND

Area 130,439 sq km
Population: 47,536,000
Highest point: Scafell Pike 977 m
Greatest width: 515 km
North to south: 570 km
Longest rivers: Thames 346 km
                Severn 338 km
Largest lake: Windermere

Equator

The equator is an imaginary line around the world, halfway between the NORTH and SOUTH POLES. The word 'equator' comes from an old Latin word meaning 'equalizer'. The equator divides the world into two equal halves, the Northern Hemisphere and the Southern Hemisphere. Distances north and south of the equator are measured in degrees of LATITUDE. The equator itself has a latitude of 0 degrees. A journey round the equator covers 40,076 km.

Equatorial Guinea

Equatorial Guinea is a small country on the west African coast. The largest territory is on the mainland, and there are several offshore islands. The largest island is Bioko, which has the country's capital. Most of the people speak Spanish, for the country was a Spanish possession until 1968.

Eritrea

Since 1962 the people of Eritrea have been seeking independence from Ethiopia. They achieved this in 1993, after years of destructive fighting. Eritrea lies between the Sudan and the Red Sea, and is one of the hottest and driest places in Africa. Eighty per cent of the people work in agriculture. The chief products are sesame seeds and lentils. Eritrea has been plagued by famine for over twenty years.

EQUATORIAL GUINEA

Government: Republic
Capital: Malabo
Area: 28,055 sq km
Population: 388,000
Language: Spanish
Currency: Ekuele

ERITREA

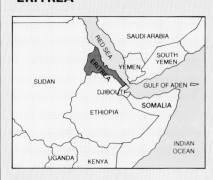

Government: Republic
Capital: Asmara
Area: 117,600 sq km
Population: 3,318,000
Language: Arabic
Currency: Ethiopian birr

◄ Only five per cent of land is cultivated in Eritrea, so most people live as nomads. These families are constantly on the move, herding sheep, cattle and goats.

ESTONIA

Government: Republic
Capital: Tallinn
Area: 45,096 sq km
Population: 1,607,000
Languages: Estonian, Russian
Currency: Kroon

ETHIOPIA

Government: Interim coalition
Capital: Addis Ababa
Area: 1,221,900 sq km
Population: 51,070,000
Language: Amharic
Currency: Ethiopian dollar

Eskimo

Eskimos are hardy people who live in the cold, ARCTIC lands of Greenland, North America and north-east Asia. Nowadays they like to be known as Inuits.

Eskimos once wore only fur clothes. Some lived in tents in summer and built snow homes called igloos for the winter. They made bows and arrows and harpoons, and hunted in skin BOATS and canoes called kayaks. Dogs pulled their sledges.

Many Eskimos no longer lead this kind of life. They now live and work in towns.

Estonia

Estonia is a country bordering the Baltic Sea in northern Europe. It is low-lying land of plains, forests and swamps. From 1940 until 1991 Estonia was a republic of the former Soviet Union. Until 1940 it was mainly a farming country, but during the years of Soviet control many factories were built. Through the centuries, Estonia has been occupied by many nations, including Denmark, Germany, Poland and Sweden. However the Estonians have kept their own language, which is related to Finnish, and culture.

Ethiopia

Ethiopia covers a huge area of the north eastern part of AFRICA. It was formerly called Abyssinia. Much of Ethiopia consists of high, cool tablelands. Here, Ethiopian farmers grow grain and coffee. The RED SEA coast in the north is one of the hottest places on Earth.

For years Ethiopia has suffered from CIVIL WAR and drought. Famine is wide-spread and there has been a world-wide campaign to raise money for relief. In 1991 rebel armies took possession of the capital. A coalition government was formed. On 4 June 1994, Ethiopians voted for a new federal constitution. For the first time ever, power was shared between fourteen regional governments.

Europe

Europe is a peninsula sticking out from the western end of Asia. Other small peninsulas jut from the main one and there are many offshore islands. Australia is the only continent smaller than Europe, but Europe holds more people than any continent except Asia.

European people have settled in the Americas, Australia, New Zealand, South Africa, and Siberia. European ideas and inventions helped shape the way of life of many people all around the world.

Mountains cross the countries of southern Europe. From west to east there are the Pyrenees, Alps, Apennines, Balkans, Carpathians, Caucasus and other ranges. The Caucasus has Mount Elbrus, Europe's highest peak.

In northern Europe low mountains cover much of Iceland, Ireland, Scotland, Wales, Norway, and Sweden. Between the mountains of the north and south lies a great plain. Here flow Europe's longest rivers. The Volga in the former Soviet Union is the longest of them all.

All Europe lies north of the hot tropics and most of it lies south of the cold Arctic. So most of Europe does not have extremes of temperature. But Mediterranean lands have hot summers and countries in the north and east have long, cold winters.

Shrubs and flowering plants grow in the far north. Next come the great northern forests of CONIFERS. Farther south lie most of Europe's farms and cities.

▲ Europe has more advantages for people than any other continent. It has scarcely any desert and a greater proportion of the land can be farmed than in any other continent. It is rich in coal and iron, essential for industry. Its climate is seldom either too hot or too cold.

▼ Like much of Mediterranean Europe, Italy's coast has wide bays and rocky headlands. Behind lie volcanic mountains and hills cut into terraces for vineyards and olive groves.

EUROPE

ARCTIC OCEAN

Murmansk

Narvik

NORWEGIAN SEA

Arkhangelsk

FAROE IS.

SWEDEN   FINLAND   L. Onega

ICELAND   Trondheim   Tampere   Vyborg

Reykjavik   SHETLAND IS.   NORWAY   Sundsvall   Helsinki   L. Ladoga

ORKNEY IS.   Bergen   Oslo   Stockholm   St. Petersburg

Aberdeen   NORTH SEA   Stavanger   Vänern   ESTONIA   Novgorod   RUSSIA   Yaroslavl

Glasgow   Edinburgh   Vättern   Gothenburg   LATVIA   Riga   Moscow

Belfast   UNITED   DENMARK   BALTIC SEA   Smolensk

IRELAND   KINGDOM   Copenhagen   Malmö   LITHUANIA   Kaliningrad   Minsk

Dublin   Manchester   Hamburg   Gdańsk   Warsaw   BELORUSSIA

Cork   Birmingham   NETHER-   Elbe   Poznań   Kharkov

Cardiff   London   -LANDS   Berlin   POLAND   Kiev

English Channel   Amster-   Rhine   GERMANY   Dnepr

Brussels   -dam   Bonn   Frankfurt   Kraków   UKRAINE   Dnepropetrovsk

Brest   Le Havre   BELGIUM   Prague   Dnestr   Odessa

Paris   LUX-   CZECH REP   Vienna   CARPATHIANS   Prut   MOLDAVIA

Nantes   Loire   Seine   EMBOURG   Stuttgart   SLOVAKIA   BLACK SEA

La Coruña   Bordeaux   ALPS   Munich   AUSTRIA   Budapest   ROMANIA

Santander   FRANCE   Bern   Zurich   HUNGARY   Bucharest

Oporto   Valladolid   Bilbao   Geneva   SWITZ-   LIECHTENSTEIN   Zagreb   Danube

Lisbon   PYRENEES   Lyon   ERLAND   Turin   Milan   Venice   Trieste   Belgrade   BULGARIA

PORTUGAL   Madrid   ANDORRA   MONACO   Po   SAN MARINO   FORMER   Sofia   Istanbul

Tagus   Marseille   Nice   Florence   ADRIATIC SEA   YUGOSLAVIA   Dubrovnik   TURKEY

Seville   SPAIN   Barcelona   Corsica   ITALY   ALBANIA   Thessaloniki

Cádiz   Málaga   BALEARIC IS.   Ajaccio   Rome   Naples   Bari   Tirana   GREECE

GIBRALTAR   Sardinia   Cagliari   Taranto   Athens

Palermo   Messina

Sicily   Crete

MALTA

MEDITERRANEAN SEA

ATLANTIC OCEAN

Valencia

Toulouse

Douro   Ebro

Guadiana

Guadalajara

■ Capital Cities

```
0    100   200   300   400 miles
|----|-----|-----|-----|
0      200     400     600 Kilometres
```

Much of Europe's wealth comes from its factories, farms and mines. Europe's richest nations include Germany and Switzerland. The largest European country is Russia. The smallest European country is Vatican City in Rome.

▲ *This valley along the river Moselle in the Rhineland in Germany is one of the chief wine-producing regions in Europe. Vineyards can be seen on the hillside in the foreground.*

European Union

This is a group of western European nations that work together to help goods, people, and money travel between countries in the Union. Its members are Austria, Belgium, Denmark, Finland, France, Ireland, Italy, United Kingdom, Greece, Luxembourg, the Netherlands, Portugal, Spain, Sweden and Germany. Several other European countries have applied to join the 15 nations, who in recent years have been working towards a closer economic and political union.

Everest, Mount

Mount Everest is the world's highest peak. It rises 8848 metres above sea level. The mountain stands in the HIMALAYAS on the borders of Nepal and Tibet. Gales and falling masses of rock and snow sweep the steep, cold slopes. Many climbers tried to reach the top before two finally succeeded in 1953. They were the New Zealander Edmund Hillary and Tenzing Norgay, a Nepalese Sherpa tribesman.

EUROPE

Area: 10,534,600 sq km, 7 per cent of the world's land area

Population: 696,000,000 (9.3 per cent of world total)

Highest point: Mount Elbrus, 5633 m

Lowest point: Caspian Sea, 28 m below sea level

Longest river: Volga, 3531 km long

Biggest lake: Lake Ladoga in Russia, 18,388 sq km

Northernmost point: North Cape, Norway

Southernmost point: Cape Tarifa, Spain

Westernmost point: Dunmore Head, Ireland

Easternmost point: Ural Mountains

▲ *The modern horse evolved from an animal no bigger than a dog, with four toes on its front feet and three on its hind feet.*

Evolution

The theory of evolution states that today's plants and animals are descended from other forms that lived long ago. This slow process of change has been going on for millions and millions of years—ever since life first appeared on earth—and is still happening. Much of the evidence for evolution comes from FOSSILS. Rocks contain the remains of extinct plants and animals and so help to build up a family tree for species now living.

The theory of evolution says that plants and animals must adapt to their surroundings if they are to survive. Those which adapt best are most likely to survive.

Charles DARWIN, an English naturalist, first put forward the theory of evolution in 1859, in a book entitled *On the Origin of Species*.

Exercise

Exercise usually means activities that strengthen the muscles and improve health. Nearly all sports are good ways to exercise, but it is better to take regular mild exercise than to take strenuous exercise only once in a while. Brisk walking is one of the best exercises.

Exercise helps the blood to circulate through our bodies, cleaning out waste and supplying plenty of oxygen. When people want to lose weight they should take exercise as well as dieting.

▲ *Jogging is a good form of exercise. It keeps the heart and lungs fit.*

Explorer

Explorers are people who travel to find out about unknown places. There have always been explorers. The Stone Age men and women who wandered across continents were in a way explorers. Phoenician seamen sailed the Mediterranean about 2600 years ago. Alexander the Great, in the 300s BC, explored and conquered all of the Middle East as far as India. In the Middle Ages, MARCO POLO reached China from Europe.

But the great age of exploration began in the 1400s. Sailors like Vasco da GAMA, Christopher

On April 30, 1978, Neomi Uemura, a Japanese explorer, became the first person to reach the North Pole alone. During his 54-day dogsled trek over the ice, Uemura survived several attacks by a polar bear.

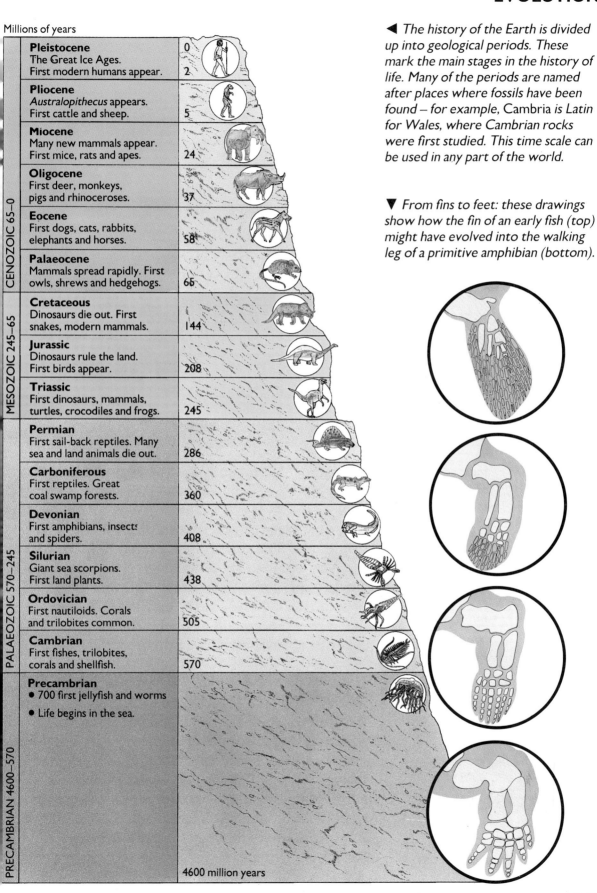

Millions of years

Pleistocene The Great Ice Ages. First modern humans appear.	0 / 2	
Pliocene *Australopithecus* appears. First cattle and sheep.	5	
Miocene Many new mammals appear. First mice, rats and apes.	24	
Oligocene First deer, monkeys, pigs and rhinoceroses.	37	
Eocene First dogs, cats, rabbits, elephants and horses.	58	
Palaeocene Mammals spread rapidly. First owls, shrews and hedgehogs.	65	
Cretaceous Dinosaurs die out. First snakes, modern mammals.	144	
Jurassic Dinosaurs rule the land. First birds appear.	208	
Triassic First dinosaurs, mammals, turtles, crocodiles and frogs.	245	
Permian First sail-back reptiles. Many sea and land animals die out.	286	
Carboniferous First reptiles. Great coal swamp forests.	360	
Devonian First amphibians, insects and spiders.	408	
Silurian Giant sea scorpions. First land plants.	438	
Ordovician First nautiloids. Corals and trilobites common.	505	
Cambrian First fishes, trilobites, corals and shellfish.	570	
Precambrian • 700 first jellyfish and worms • Life begins in the sea.		

CENOZOIC 65–0

MESOZOIC 245–65

PALAEOZOIC 570–245

PRECAMBRIAN 4600–570

4600 million years

◄ *The history of the Earth is divided up into geological periods. These mark the main stages in the history of life. Many of the periods are named after places where fossils have been found – for example, Cambria is Latin for Wales, where Cambrian rocks were first studied. This time scale can be used in any part of the world.*

▼ *From fins to feet: these drawings show how the fin of an early fish (top) might have evolved into the walking leg of a primitive amphibian (bottom).*

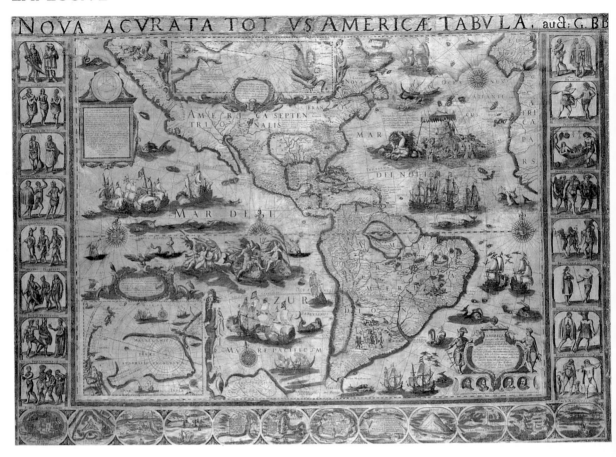

▲ *This Dutch map of newly-explored America was originally drawn in 1608 and updated in 1655.*

▲ *Robert Peary, the American naval officer who reached the North Pole in 1909.*

COLUMBUS, Ferdinand MAGELLAN and James COOK discovered the shape, size and position of continents and oceans. Later, David LIVINGSTONE, Roald AMUNDSEN and others explored wild, untamed continents. The world's highest peak, Mount Everest, was climbed by Edmund Hillary and Tenzing Norgay in 1953. SPACE EXPLORATION now takes people beyond the Earth, and the explorations of the next century will probably make all past discoveries seem minor by comparison.

Explosive

Explosions happen when people heat or strike certain solid or liquid substances. These suddenly turn into hot GASES. The gases fill more space than the solids or liquids, so they rush violently outward. High explosives like dynamite explode faster and do more damage than low explosives like gunpowder. Engineers use explosives to break up rocks and old buildings. Armies use explosives to destroy vehicles and cities.

Eye

Our eyes show us the size, shape and colour of objects in the world around us. Our eyes can see something as small and near as a tiny insect crawling on this page, or as far off and large as the Moon or stars.

A human eye is much larger than the part you can see. The eye is a ball bigger than a marble. It works much like a camera. Both bend LIGHT rays to form a picture of the object that the rays are reflected from.

Light rays enter the eye through a layer of transparent skin called the *conjunctiva*. The rays pass through a hard, transparent layer called the *cornea*. This bends the rays. The LENS brings them into focus on the *retina* at the back of the eye. But you do not 'see' the picture formed here until light-sensitive nerve endings on the retina send the brain a message along the *optic nerve*.

To see properly, all the parts of the eye have to work correctly. For example, the *iris* (the eye's coloured part) can open and close to let more or less light through the *pupil*.

Human eyes have a better sense of colour than those of any other animal. We can distinguish 250 different pure colours, from red to violet, and about 17,000 mixed colours. We are also able to distinguish about 300 shades of grey between black and white.

The animal with the largest eye is the giant squid. One big specimen has eyes nearly 40 cm in diameter. The biggest whales have eyes about 10 cm across.

▼ Inside the eye the image on the retina is upside down, but the brain turns it over so that we see things the right way up.

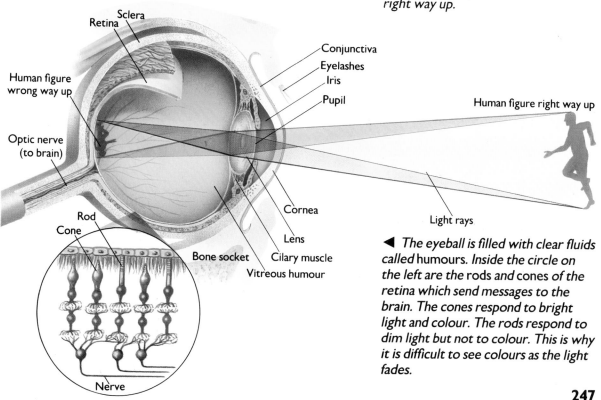

Sclera
Retina
Conjunctiva
Eyelashes
Iris
Pupil
Human figure wrong way up
Human figure right way up
Optic nerve (to brain)
Cornea
Light rays
Rod
Cone
Lens
Bone socket   Cilary muscle
Vitreous humour
Nerve

◄ The eyeball is filled with clear fluids called humours. Inside the circle on the left are the rods and cones of the retina which send messages to the brain. The cones respond to bright light and colour. The rods respond to dim light but not to colour. This is why it is difficult to see colours as the light fades.

Fable

Fables are short tales in which the main characters are usually animals that can speak and act like human beings. Fables always teach a lesson. Some of the most famous are those of AESOP, an ancient Greek storyteller. His fables of the fox and the crow, and of the grasshopper and the ant, are told to this day.

▲ *The merlin is one of the smallest of the falcons. It flies low and fast as it chases smaller birds.*

Falcon

Falcons are a group of birds of prey that are found all over the world. They can be recognized by the dark markings around their eyes and by their pointed wings. Falcons use their large, hooked beaks for tearing flesh, but they kill their prey with their sharp claws. Falcons swoop down on their victims from above, hitting them with their claws. This act is called 'stooping'. It is used to kill smaller birds in mid-flight and also to take RODENTS and other small animals on the ground.

The biggest of all falcons is the gyrfalcon of the Arctic. It may reach over 60 cm in size. The smallest is the pygmy falcon of southern Asia. It is less than 15 cm long and feeds mainly on insects.

The peregrine falcon is one of the fastest flyers in the world. In a fast dive, it can reach 280 km/hr.

Falkland Islands

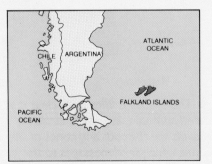

FALKLAND ISLANDS

Area: 12,000 sq km
Capital: Stanley
Population: 2000
Average temperature: 6°C

These are a group of cold, windy islands that form a British colony in the stormy South Atlantic Ocean. They lie about 770 km north-east of the tip of South America. Sheep farming is the main industry.

Argentina claims the islands although 97 percent of the inhabitants are of British origin. In 1982 Argentina invaded the Falklands, but the Argentine troops were defeated by British forces.

Famine Relief

Sometimes a country does not have enough food to feed the people who live there. People may even starve to death. This is famine. Many of the

▲ Ethiopian children receive food during one of the terrible droughts of the 1980s, when thousands of people died of starvation and disease.

developing countries of Africa and Asia are subject to famine, often because there has not been enough rain to grow enough food for an increasing population. This is when famine relief is needed. Richer countries organize a supply of food for the starving people, but getting the food to the places where it is most needed is seldom easy. There are usually transport difficulties and in some cases civil war. To prevent future famines, help with irrigation and farming methods is needed.

Faraday, Michael

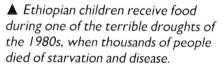

Michael Faraday (1791–1867) was a brilliant English scientist. His studies of chemistry and physics made him world famous. Faraday is best known for his experiments with ELECTRICITY. He showed that it could be made to flow in a wire when the wire was passed between the poles of a magnet. Today this is how most electricity is produced in big generators.

Farming

Farming is the world's most important human activity. More people work at it than at any other job. (See pages 250–251.)

▲ For many years Michael Faraday gave science lectures for children. One of the best-known lectures is called 'The Chemical History of a Candle'.

FARMING

Farming began somewhere in the Middle East around 9000 years ago. Today about half the world's people are farmers. Many are *subsistence* farmers, growing just enough to feed themselves. Others grow *cash crops*, to sell.

Farming has become more and more scientific. In the 1600s turnips and clover were introduced to winter-feed farm animals, which had always been killed as winter approached. Now breeders could keep good stock longer, and so develop larger, fatter breeds of cattle, sheep and pigs. New plants, such as potatoes and tomatoes, came from the New World. In the 1800s came steam engines and motor tractors to replace horses and oxen.

Today, most farms in developed countries are mechanized. Few people are needed to work on them. Poultry and calves are often reared indoors, as if in a factory. The rich countries produce more food than they need. But despite the success of the 'green revolution' which has brought new crops and new farm methods to the Third World, many people in the poor countries still starve. In Africa, Asia and South America most farms are small and the work is done mostly by hand.

STRIP FARMING

In Saxon times people shared fields. They each had a narrow strip. The strips were ploughed up and down the slope of the field, seldom across. Thus the strips of one group ran in one direction, those of a neighbouring group in another.

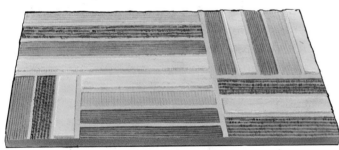

CROP ROTATION

In the 17th century it was found that fodder crops put goodness back into the soil. In the four-course method of farming, cereals such as wheat and barley alternate with clover and root crops such as turnips.

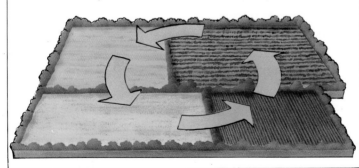

THE HISTORY OF FARMING

7000 BC Farming begins when people discover how to grow grain and rear domestic animals.

4000 BC Irrigation of crops in Mesopotan and Egypt.

500 BC Iron tools and heavy ox-drawn ploughs in use.

AD 600 Open-field system common in northern Europe. Peasants share fields, growing crops in narrow strips.

1400s Enclosure (fencing or hedging) of open fields. Sheep-rearing important.

1500s New plants brought to Europe fron America.

1600s Improved breeds of farm animals a developed in Europe.

1700s New machinery, such as Eli Whitne cotton gin (1793).

1800s Steam power, threshing and reapin machines, new fertilizers; North Ameri and Australia become important farmin regions.

1900s Wide use of chemicals as fertilizers and pest-killers; new strains of plants ab to resist disease; factory farming and th 'green revolution' improve food production.

IMPORTANT FARM CROPS

Bananas grow in the tropics. Plantains (cooking bananas) are eaten in Asia, Af and America.

Barley is an important cereal grown in temperate climates.

Cassava is a tropical root crop.

Maize (corn) grows well in warm, moist conditions.

Oats are grown in North America and Europe.

Potatoes, originally from America, are a important crop in Europe.

Rice is the main food of half the world's people. It grows best in warm, wet are

Sorghum is grown for food by people in Asia and Africa.

Sugar comes either from sugar beet, gro in cool climates, or from sugar cane grown in the tropics.

Vegetable oils come from coconuts, cotton seed, groundnuts, sunflowers, soybeans, olives and maize.

Wheat is a cereal grown worldwide, in ar with moist, mild winters and warm, dr summers.

Ploughing with oxen

Winnowing rice

tea

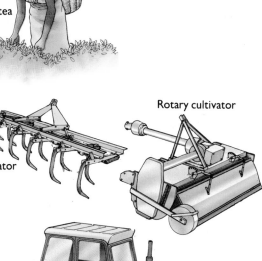
Rotary cultivator

...ator

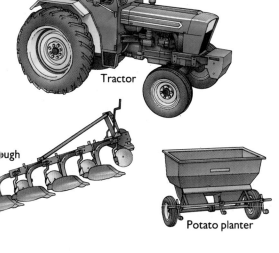
Tractor

...ugh

Potato planter

▲ In battery farming, poultry are reared so as to produce more eggs in less time and at a low cost.

▲ Combine harvesters at work on a prairie wheatfield in North America.

...some parts of the world old farming methods are still ...Modern machinery is slowly taking over.

...more information turn to these articles: BEAN; COFFEE; COTTON; COW; FERTILIZER; FOOD; GOAT; HORSE; IRRIGATION; OLIVE; OX; PIG; ...ATO; POULTRY; RICE; SHEEP; SUGAR; TEA; VEGETABLE; WHEAT.

▶ *The Fascist followers of the Italian dictator Mussolini adopted black shirts as an official uniform.*

The *fasces*, an ancient Roman symbol of authority, became the Fascists' symbol.

SOURCES AND USES OF FATS

Animal fats

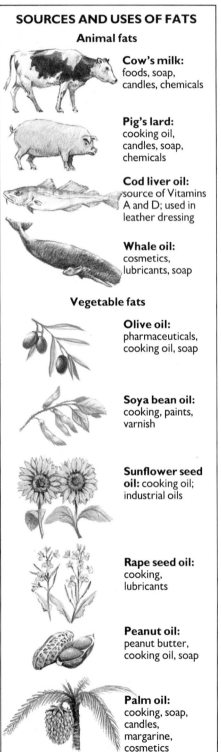

Cow's milk: foods, soap, candles, chemicals

Pig's lard: cooking oil, candles, soap, chemicals

Cod liver oil: source of Vitamins A and D; used in leather dressing

Whale oil: cosmetics, lubricants, soap

Vegetable fats

Olive oil: pharmaceuticals, cooking oil, soap

Soya bean oil: cooking, paints, varnish

Sunflower seed oil: cooking oil; industrial oils

Rape seed oil: cooking, lubricants

Peanut oil: peanut butter, cooking oil, soap

Palm oil: cooking, soap, candles, margarine, cosmetics

Fascism

Fascism is a political belief. It was founded in Italy in the 1920s by Benito MUSSOLINI. Mussolini seized power in 1922 as DICTATOR of Italy and head of the Italian Fascist Party. Fascism takes its name from the Roman *fasces*, the bundle of rods and the axe that were the symbol of authority in ancient Rome.

Fascist political ideas include the belief that the government of a country should be all-powerful. Its citizens must work hard and obey the government for the good of the nation. Fascists believe in strict discipline and training for all people, including children, and in the wearing of military-style uniforms.

Anybody opposed to a Fascist government is made an outlaw. In Fascist Italy, many people were jailed, exiled or put to death because they did not agree with the Fascists. All the other political parties were made illegal.

Fat

Fat is an important food for both animals and plants. The tissue of these living things contain fat. Fat in a pure state can take the form of a liquid, such as vegetable oil, or a solid such as butter or lard.

Fat is a store of ENERGY. A unit of fat contains twice as much energy as the same amount of PROTEIN

or STARCH. Fats play an important part in our diet. We get most vegetable fat from the seeds and fruits of plants, where it is stored. In animals and human beings fat is stored in tiny 'droplets' in a layer under the skin and in the CELLS of the body. Pigs and cattle are our main sources of animal fats. Fats are also important in making SOAPS, PERFUMES and polishes.

Fawkes, Guy

Guy Fawkes (1570–1606) and his group of ROMAN CATHOLIC plotters sought to kill King JAMES I of England by blowing up the House of Lords with gunpowder. They were protesting against laws which tried to control the rights of Roman Catholics. The plot failed. Fawkes was arrested on 5 November 1605 in the cellars of the House of Lords and, with the other conspirators, was executed.

▲ *A close-up of part of a feather, showing the thread-like barbs which are 'glued' together by smaller hooked fibres called barbules.*

▲ *Guy Fawkes and the other conspirators who plotted to blow up the king and members of Parliament in 1605. He was to be responsible for setting up and triggering the explosion.*

Feather

The only animals with an outer layer of feathers are BIRDS. Feathers protect birds and keep them warm. They give their bodies a smooth, streamlined shape. Feathers also form the broad surface area of the wings that allows birds to fly.

Feathers are replaced once or twice a year. This process is called moulting. Old feathers that are worn and broken fall out. New ones grow in their place.

SEE IT YOURSELF
Collect feathers in the woods and look at them with a magnifying glass to see how they are made. 'Unzip' part of the flat vane to see the tiny hooked branches that fit neatly together to form it. Fix your feathers in a notebook and label them with the birds' names if you know them.

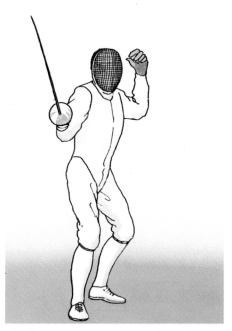

▲ *Fencers wear wire mesh masks, thick jackets and a glove for the weapon hand.*

Fencing

Fencing can be described as the sport of 'friendly duelling'. Fencers wear a special glove, jacket and a face mask. They fight with blunted swords. The winner is the one who scores the most points by touching his opponent with his sword.

Today, fencing is a popular sport and an OLYMPIC GAMES event, but in the past it was a form of sword practice for real duels.

Fermentation

Milk goes sour, bread dough rises, grape juice turns into wine. All these are examples of fermentation. Fermentation is caused by the work of very tiny living BACTERIA, YEASTS and MOULDS These tiny things break up substances into simpler forms. People have been using fermentation since the earliest times to make bread, beer, wine and cheese. But it was not until the 1800s that the French scientist Louis PASTEUR found out how fermentation really works.

Fermi, Enrico

Enrico Fermi (1901–1954) was a great Italian scientist. His studies of the ATOM were rewarded by the NOBEL PRIZE in 1938.

In 1942, during World War II, Fermi built the first atomic reactor. He constructed it in an empty squash court under a football stadium in Chicago, USA. Here he set off the first man-made nuclear chain reaction. Later, Fermi helped to develop the atom bomb.

▼ *The common polypody grows on rocks and walls in damp woodlands. The small adder's tongue looks more like a leaf than a fern. Its spores develop on the slender spike.*

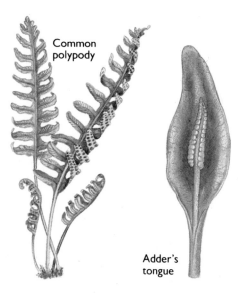

Common polypody

Adder's tongue

Fern

The primitive ferns were some of the earliest land plants. Today their delicate, feathery leaves look much the same as they did millions of years ago.

About 10,000 different kinds of ferns live on the Earth today. They are found all over the world, usually in damp, shady places. In the tropics, giant tree-ferns grow to over 15 metres high.

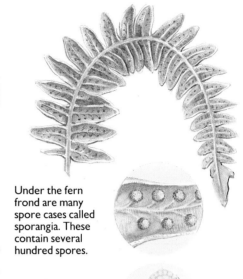

Ferns do not have FLOWERS or SEEDS. Instead they form spores from which new ferns develop.

Fertilizer

Fertilizers are chemicals. They are dug into the SOIL to nourish it. In this way fertilizers help plants to grow bigger and healthier by giving them the chemical nutrients, or 'foods', they need to grow. The most important fertilizers are calcium, phosphorus, potassium and SULPHUR.

Fertilizers are usually added to soils that do not contain enough natural nutrients. This can happen if the same crops have been planted in the soil year after year, or if the rain has washed out all the nutrients.

Under the fern frond are many spore cases called sporangia. These contain several hundred spores.

The sporangia burst, and the spores are carried by the wind. When they settle on damp ground, each spore grows into a prothallus, producing both male and female organs.

Fibre Optics

An optical fibre is a flexible glass strand thinner than a human hair. Along this fine fibre a beam of light can travel very easily. The light can be used to carry telephone conversations and television pictures or to allow doctors to see inside our bodies. The fibres are made of specially pure glass designed to reflect the light in towards the centre of the strand. Using LASER light, signals can be sent for more than 50 km

The young fern develops from these organs, feeding on the prothallus. The leaves unroll as the plant grows.

▲ Ferns reproduce themselves from spores rather than seeds. It can take several years before a fern is able to produce spores.

◀ A bundle of optical fibres. Each has a thickness of about 10 to 150 millionths of a metre.

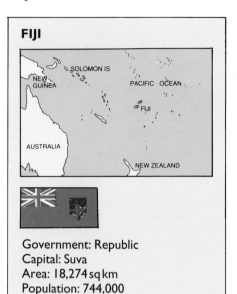

FIJI

Government: Republic
Capital: Suva
Area: 18,274 sq km
Population: 744,000
Languages: English and Fijian
Currency: Fiji dollar

before they have to be amplified. This means that optical fibres are much more efficient than copper cables and much thinner and lighter. A pair of fibres can carry hundreds of telephone conversations at the same time.

Fiji

Fiji is a country made up of hundreds of islands in the Pacific Ocean. The biggest island is Viti Levu. Fiji became a British possession in 1874, but gained its independence in 1970. The main product of the islands is sugar. In 1879, Indians were brought to the islands to work on the sugar plantations. The offspring of these Indians now outnumber the original Fijians and tension between the two groups led to an army takeover in 1987. A civilian government was later restored.

► Ceremonial dancers on the little island of Taveuni, now a Fijiian national park.

Films  *See* Cinema

Fingerprint

Fingerprints are marks we leave behind whenever we touch something. You can see them by pressing your fingertips into an ink pad and then onto a sheet of white paper. Everybody has patterns of lines and swirls on their fingers. But each person's fingerprints are different from everybody else's. Because of this, police officers use fingerprints to help identify criminals. They keep files of thousands of different prints. By comparing those on file with

In many hospitals the footprints of babies are taken shortly after birth. Footprints, like fingerprints, never change, so the baby will always be known by these prints. The owners of valuable dogs sometimes have nose prints made of their animals in case they should stray.

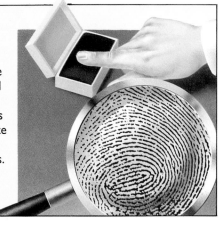

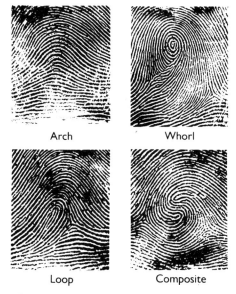

Arch | Whorl

Loop | Composite

those found at the scene of a crime they can often trace the guilty person. Computers can now hold details of the fingerprints of half a million people. In a few seconds the computer will match any of these prints with those of a suspect.

▲ All fingerprints can be divided into four main types – the arch, the whorl, the loop and the composite.

Finland

Finland is a country in northern EUROPE tucked between Scandinavia and Russia. Northern Finland stretches north of the Arctic Circle.

The thousands of lakes and rivers that dot the Finnish landscape form a great inland waterway. About 75 percent of the land is covered by thick forests of spruce, pine and larch trees. The main industries of Finland are logging and the making of wood products, such as paper.

Five million people live in Finland. The capital, Helsinki, has a population of about 490,000.

FINLAND

Government: Constitutional republic
Capital: Helsinki
Area: 337,032 sq km
Population: 5,004,000
Languages: Finnish and Swedish
Currency: Markka

◀ The Lapps of northern Finland raise herds of reindeer for use as draught animals and as a supply of skins and meat.

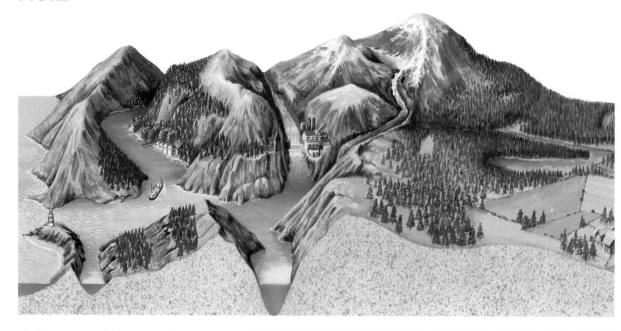

▲ The coast of Norway is broken by hundreds of fiords, some with steep, rocky sides several hundred metres high.

Fiord

Along the coasts of NORWAY and GREENLAND are a series of steep-sided valleys called fiords. Here the sea has invaded the land. Narrow tongues of water wind inland in narrow mountain gorges.

Fiords were formed when the great glaciers of the ICE AGES gouged out valleys as they flowed to the sea. When the ice melted, the sea flooded the valleys. Fiords are very deep and make perfect shelters for large ocean-going ships.

Fire

The ability to make and use fire is one of the great advantages people have over animals. Primitive people found fire frightening, just as animals do. But once they learned to make and control fire, it became a necessary part of life. It kept out the cold, lit up the dark, cooked food, kept people warm, and scared away animals. But even today fires that get out of control cause terrible damage and suffering.

▼ In ancient times people found that two flints struck sharply together produced a spark. Later, a flint was struck against a piece of steel to make a spark which could be used to light an easily-burnt material called tinder.

Fireworks

Fireworks are devices that produce spectacular displays of lights, colours, smoke and noise in the night sky. They were invented in China centuries ago, but only became known in Europe in the 1300s.

Fireworks are often launched in ROCKETS. They are shot in the air and made to explode by a black powder called *gunpowder*. The brilliant colours of fireworks come from burning different chemicals.

Fir Tree *See* Conifer

Fish

There are more fish than all the other backboned animals put together. The fish shown on pages 260–261 are just a few of more than 30,000 different kinds.

Fishing

Fishing is one of the world's most important activities. In one year, about 60 million tonnes of fish are taken from the seas, rivers and lakes.

Although fish are a good source of food, much of the catch ends up as animal feed or FERTILIZER. Oil

Continued on page 262

In 1749, George Frideric Handel wrote his *Fireworks Music* for a display in London's Green Park. A report written at the time says: 'Although Signor Servandoni's display of fireworks was not a complete success, Mr Handel's music was enthusiastically received.'

▼ *Some of the ways in which fish are caught. From left to right: fish such as cod and haddock are caught by their gills in gill nets; in long-line fishing, a series of baited hooks are attached to a long main line; in purse seine fishing, a net is drawn around a shoal of fish; lobsters are caught in traps; the otter trawl net has boards or buoys which keep the net open as it is dragged over the seabed, trapping bottom fish. The diagram also shows some important food fish.*

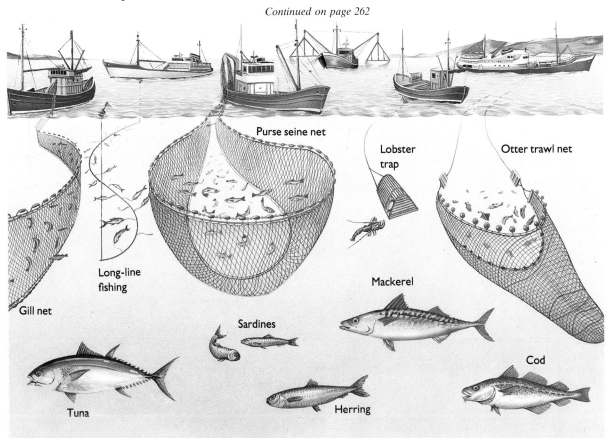

Purse seine net

Lobster trap

Otter trawl net

Long-line fishing

Gill net

Mackerel

Sardines

Tuna

Herring

Cod

FISH

Fish were the first animals with backbones (vertebrates) to develop on Earth. They are the animals best adapted to life in water. They breathe by means of gills, and they swim by using their fins and tails. Fish are found in salt and fresh water, from the cold polar seas to the warm tropics.

Scientists divide fish into three groups. The *cartilaginous* fish have gristly, rather than bony, skeletons, and leathery skins, not scales. They include the sharks and rays. The *bony* fish make up the next and largest group. All these fish have bony scales covering their body. The third and smallest group are the *lungfishes*, which are unusual in being able to come out on land and breathe air.

People have eaten fish since earliest times. Today the world's fishing fleets catch millions of tonnes of fish every year.

▲ A catch is sorted on a Scottish trawler. British trawlers in waters as far away as Greenland and the Arctic Ocean. Some stay out for weeks at a time, storing their catches in deep freezers on board.

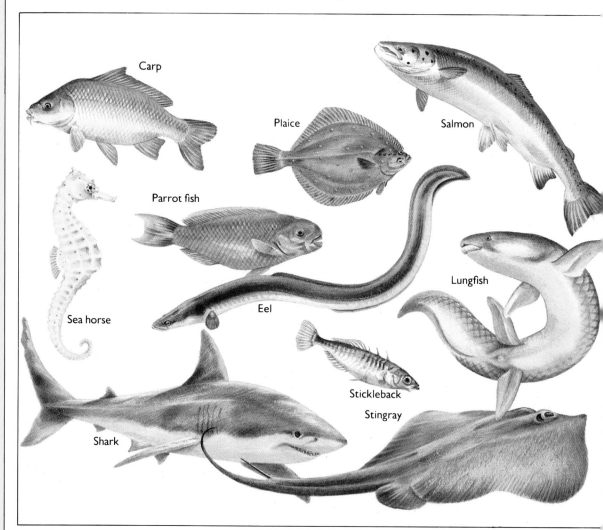

Carp

Plaice

Salmon

Parrot fish

Sea horse

Eel

Lungfish

Stickleback

Stingray

Shark

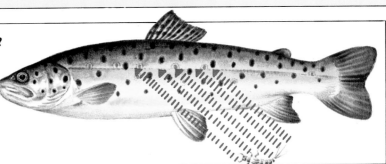

WHAT IS A FISH'S SIXTH SENSE?

Fish have an organ called the lateral line, found in no other animal. It detects vibrations in the water through sensors beneath the fish's scales. Using this sixth sense, a fish can detect another fish before it comes into view.

HOW DOES A FISH BREATHE?

A fish breathes by means of gills either side of its head. It takes in water through its mouth and, as the water passes over the gills, the gills extract oxygen from the water. The oxygen enters the fish's bloodstream. Fish are cold-blooded.

HOW DOES A FISH SWIM?

Most fish swim by beating their tails from side to side. They use their fins for steering and balance.

WHY CAN'T SEA FISH LIVE IN FRESH WATER?

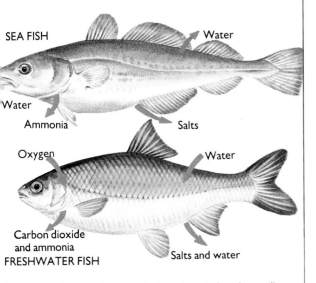

SEA FISH

Water

Water

Ammonia

Salts

Oxygen

Water

Carbon dioxide and ammonia
FRESHWATER FISH

Salts and water

Sea fish need the sea's salt and other chemicals to keep alive. Because sea water is saltier than their own body fluids, sea fish lose water through their skins by *osmosis*. They drink sea water to prevent their bodies drying out.

SOME INTERESTING AND UNUSUAL FISHES

Archer Fish This river fish catches insects by squirting water at them.

Catfish, like other bottom-dwelling fish, have feelers or 'barbels' to help them find food.

Cleaner fish remove parasites and food scraps from the jaws of fierce barracuda.

Eels have an amazing life cycle, migrating from Europe and America to the Sargasso Sea to breed.

Flatfish A baby plaice swims upright. But as it grows, one eye travels across its head and its body twists until the fish is lying on its side.

Flying Fish glide using their long stiffened fins as wings. They take to the air to escape pursuing enemies.

Mudskippers use their leg-like fins to crawl over the mud to find food.

Pilot Fish often swim with sharks. They feed on the sharks' leftovers.

Porcupine Fish have prickly skins and blow themselves up, like balloons, to baffle a hungry enemy.

Salmon swim upriver to breed, often returning to the spot where they were born.

Scorpion Fish This fish is one to keep away from, for it has poisonous spines.

Sea Horse This curious-looking fish carries its young in a pouch.

For more information turn to these articles: EEL; FISHING; GOLDFISH; LAKE; OCEAN; RIVER; SALMON; TROPICAL FISH; TUNA.

The United States flag, or 'Stars and Stripes', has had the same basic design since 1777, during the War of Independence. It has 13 horizontal stripes which represent the original 13 colonies that rebelled against British rule. Fifty white five-pointed stars, representing the 50 states of the Union, appear on a dark blue field in the *canton*, the rectangular area in the top corner near the staff.

▼ *International signal flags used by ships at sea include a flag for each letter of the alphabet as well as for the numerals one to ten, shown below. On the right are shown the basic patterns in flag design. The* canton *design is seen in the United States flag above. The* quarterly *is used for the flag of Panama; the* triangle *is seen in the flags of Guyana and Jordan. The* serration *appears in Qatar's flag, the* border *in Grenada's.*

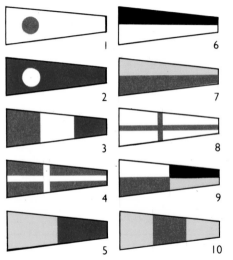

from fish is used to make SOAPS or for tanning—turning animal skins into leather.

Often the catch is made far from the home port. The fish must be preserved or they will quickly spoil. In the past fish were often dried, smoked or salted, because there were no refrigerators. Today they are packed in ice or frozen. Some fishing fleets include large factory ships. These take fresh fish straight from the other ships, and can them or package them on the spot.

The best places to fish at sea are where the sloping sea bottom is no more than 180 metres deep. Here, fish can be found feeding in huge numbers. The Grand Banks off the coast of Newfoundland is one such region. It has been fished for hundreds of years.

Flag

Flags are pieces of coloured cloth, often decorated with bold markings. They have special fastenings so that they can be flown from masts and poles. Flags are used by countries, armies and groups such as marching bands and sports teams.

Flags have been used as emblems since the time of the ancient Egyptians. Their flags were flown on long poles as battle standards, held by 'standard-bearers'. Flying high in the air, flags helped soldiers to find their companions as they plunged into battle.

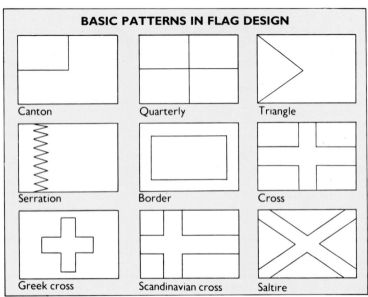

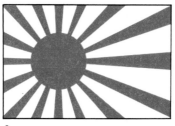

1   2   3   4

And they showed which soldiers belonged to which king or general.

Today, national flags are flown as a symbol of a country's history, its power and its importance, or *prestige*. They are also a symbol of people's loyalty to one nation and one government.

Flags are also used for signalling. Since 1857 there has been an international code for flag signals. It is used by ships. A yellow flag, for example, means that a ship is in quarantine because of illness on board. For thousands of years flags have been important as a way of identifying ships at sea.

Other well known signals are a white flag—a sign of truce—and a flag raised to half-mast—a sign that people are mourning someone's death.

▲ *The World Scout flag (1) and the flag of the Red Cross (4) both represent organizations. The Japanese naval ensign (2), flown from the stern of a ship, is a recognized flag of nationality. The personal standard of Queen Elizabeth (3) is just one of the royal standards.*

▼ *Flamingoes are timid birds and usually live together in large colonies on the edges of lakes and marshes.*

Flame

When something is heated enough to make it burn, it will also often burst into flames. These flames are gases that are given off during burning. Bright flames that give off plenty of light, such as those of candles, wood or coal, have tiny CARBON particles in them that glow brightly. Flames are not all equally hot. Wood fires burn at about 1000°C. The flames of acetylene WELDING torches are about 3000°C.

Flamingo

Flamingos are tropical birds found in huge flocks in many parts of the world. The bright colour of their feathers ranges from pale to deep pink. Flamingos live in marshes and shallow lakes, wading on their stilt-like legs. A flock of thousands of these splendid birds is a wonderful sight.

The flamingo's body is not much bigger than that of a goose, but its long legs and neck can make it up

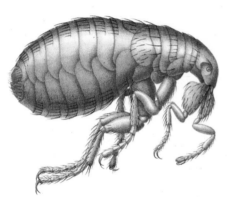

▲ *This greatly magnified body of a flea shows the large abdomen where blood is stored.*

▲ *Sir Alexander Fleming, the British bacteriologist who discovered penicillin.*

▼ *A pointed flint tool and a tool for scraping, both made by Neanderthal people about 50,000 years ago.*

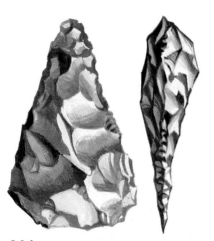

to 1.8 metres tall. These elegant birds feed on tiny plants and animals that are found in shallow waters. When feeding, they tuck their heads right under the water and use their broad, hooked beaks like sieves to filter food from the water and mud.

Flea

Fleas are tiny wingless insects less than 3 mm long. They live on the bodies of birds, animals and human beings. Fleas are PARASITES, and feed on their hosts by biting through the skin and sucking the blood. Fleas carry germs from one host to another. Rat fleas, for example, can give bubonic plague to people.

Fleming, Alexander

Sir Alexander Fleming (1881–1955) was a British doctor who discovered the antibiotic drug penicillin. It is one of the most important drugs known. Penicillin fights infections caused by many kinds of GERMS and BACTERIA. Although the drug fights the infection it does not usually harm the body. Penicillin has saved thousands of lives.

Fleming discovered the drug by accident in 1928. He found an unknown kind of MOULD growing in his laboratory. From this he was able to make penicillin. For his work, Fleming shared the 1945 Nobel Prize in medicine with Howard W. Florey and Ernst B. Chain, the doctors who found a way to produce penicillin in large quantities.

Flint

Flint is a glassy MINERAL that is a form of QUARTZ. It is found in beds of chalk and limestone. A lump of flint is dull white on the outside and shiny grey to black on the inside.

Flint is very hard, but it can be easily chipped into sharp-edged flakes. Stone Age people made tools and weapons out of flint. Because it will give off a spark when struck against iron, it can be used for starting a FIRE. A spark from a flint also ignited the powder in a flintlock GUN.

Flood

There are two main kinds of floods: those caused by rivers overflowing their banks, and ocean floods caused by high tides and strong winds blowing from the ocean towards the land. Rivers usually flood in the spring when spring rains add to water produced by melting snow and ice. The water overflows, causing much destruction in the area of the river.

Throughout history, three great rivers have flooded regularly – the Nile in Egypt, the Yellow River in China, and the Mississippi in the United States. Before its waters were controlled by the Aswan Dam, the annual Nile floods made a strip of fertile land in the middle of a great desert.

The best known flood story is that in the Book of Genesis. The event on which this Old Testament story is based may have occurred about 3000 BC, when the river Euphrates flooded a vast area, including Ur in southern Mesopotamia. According to the Bible, the flood was caused by 40 days of continual rain, producing high water that lasted for 150 days and flood depths of 7.5 metres.

◀ Unexpected floods can cause great damage. They often destroy entire communities.

▼ The parts of a flowering plant.

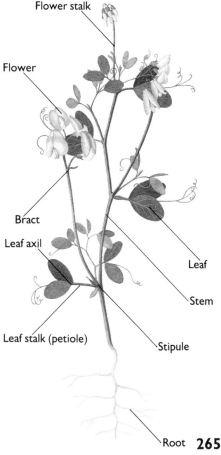

Flower stalk

Flower

Bract

Leaf axil

Leaf

Stem

Leaf stalk (petiole)

Stipule

Root

Flower

There are about 250,000 different kinds of flowering plants in the world. Their flowers come in a dazzling array of colours, sizes and shapes. Some grow singly. Some grow in tight clusters. Many have showy colours, a strong scent and produce a sweet nectar. Others are quite drab and unscented.

Whatever they look like, flowers all have the same part to play in the life of the plant. Flowers help plants to reproduce themselves. Inside a flower are male parts, called *stamens* made up of *anthers*

► A flower cut away to show its parts. Fertilization occurs when pollen from the anther unites with an ovule in the ovary. The ovule becomes a seed from which a new plant will eventually grow.

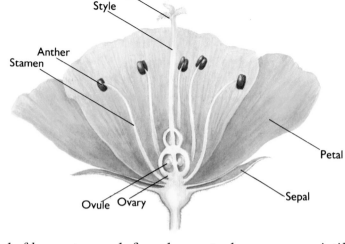

Stigma
Style
Anther
Stamen
Petal
Ovule Ovary
Sepal

One of the slowest-growing flowering plants is the saguaro cactus of Arizona. In its first ten years it grows only about three centimetres. It lives for about 200 years and by that time it can be 15 metres tall. Most of the inside of the plant is water – a large plant can hold eight tonnes of it – but during the dry season the water is used up and the plant shrinks. In a single rainstorm each cactus plant can take in as much as a tonne of water.

and *filaments*, and female parts known as *pistils* made up of *stigmas*, *styles* and *ovaries*. The stamens contain hundreds of powdery grains of pollen. These fertilize the pistil. Then a FRUIT begins to form and grow. Inside the fruit are the SEEDS for a new generation of plants. The seeds are scattered in different ways. They may be blown by the wind, or carried off by birds and animals.

Fly

Flies are winged insects. They are one of the largest groups of insects in the world. They have two pairs of wings, one pair for flying and a smaller set behind the main pair to help them to balance in flight. Many flies are dangerous. They spread deadly diseases such as cholera and dysentery. They pick up germs from manure and rotting food and carry

▼ Houseflies lay their eggs in decaying matter. The life cycle can be complete in a week in warm weather. The sponge-like mouth is drawn in the circle.

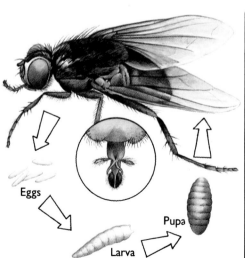

Eggs
Larva
Pupa

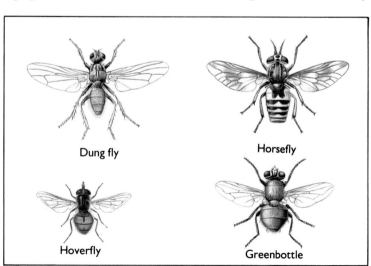

Dung fly

Horsefly

Hoverfly

Greenbottle

them into homes where they leave them on our fresh food.

Some flies bite and feed on the blood of animals. Horseflies and gadflies attack cattle and horses in great swarms. Tsetse flies, which live in the tropics, spread sleeping sickness among humans. Blowflies lay their eggs in open wounds on the skin of animals. The maggots that hatch from the eggs eat into the flesh and cause great harm.

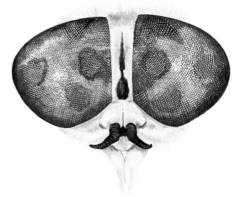

▲ A fly has two huge compound eyes made up of thousands of six-sided lenses.

Fog

What we call fog is simply a low-lying bank of CLOUD. Fog forms when warm, moist air comes into contact with cold ground. As the air cools, the moisture it contains forms the tiny droplets that make up any cloud.

Fog may form when warm air currents blow across chilled water or land. This kind is common around the coast. Another kind occurs on still, clear winter nights when the cold ground chills the air above it and there is no wind to blow the resulting fog away.

> The famous London fogs of Sherlock Holmes's day are now a thing of the past. They were not really fogs, but smogs. Smog is caused by drops of water condensing on smoke particles. About 4000 people are believed to have died as a result of the severe London smog of 1952.

Food

Anything that people eat can be called food. But it makes more sense to talk of it as being only those plant and animal products people enjoy eating.

Primitive and ancient peoples often ate insects and animals raw, or only very roughly cooked.

Monday				
Tuesday				
Wednesday				
Thursday				
Friday				
Saturday				
Sunday				

SEE IT YOURSELF
You can find out whether you are eating enough healthy foods by making a chart like the one on the left. Draw pictures at the top to show the four main food groups – fruit, meat or fish, bread or rice, and vegetables. Every day, put a tick in the box under each group when you have eaten something in that group. After a few days, check to see how you have done. If you have at least one tick in each box every day you are probably eating a healthy diet.

FOOD CHAIN

Today, food may be very skilfully prepared, decorated and cooked before being eaten. Much of our food is prepared in factories. It is bottled, canned, frozen or dried before it is sold to us.

Food is essential for life. It gives us the energy to move about and stay warm, and keeps our bodies healthy. A 'balanced diet' is necessary for good health. The three main kinds of food are carbohydrates, PROTEINS and FATS. We also need certain MINERALS and VITAMINS.

Food Chain

When you eat a piece of fish, such as cod, you are taking part in a food chain that began somewhere in the sea. There the tiny floating plants and animals called plankton were eaten by tiny fish. The tiny fish were eaten by bigger fish, and these bigger fish were eaten by even bigger fish such as your cod.

▶ In this diagram, arrows show how food energy is passed along a typical food chain. Here there are two possible chains – one from plants to crustaceans to perch to pike, and the other taking a different route – plants to crustaceans to stickleback to pike. There are many other possible food chains.

At each stage in any food chain, energy is lost. This is why food chains seldom extend beyond four or five links. In overpopulated countries, people often increase the total food supply by cutting out a step in the food chain. Instead of eating cows that eat plants, the people themselves eat the plants. Because the food chain is made shorter, the total amount of energy available to the people is increased.

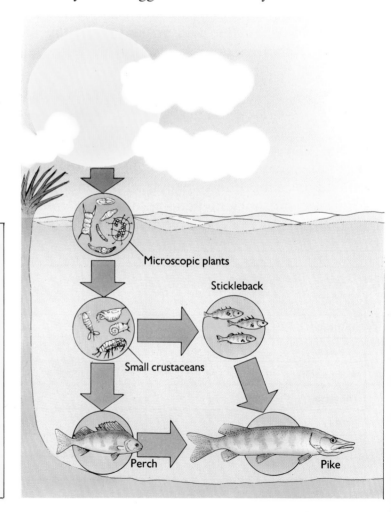

Microscopic plants

Stickleback

Small crustaceans

Perch

Pike

Every living thing has its place in one or many food chains. The chain begins with green plants. They make their own food from water, chemicals in the soil and air, and sunlight. Animals cannot make their own food as plants can. Instead, they eat plants or other animals. When animals or plants die, tiny BACTERIA that live in the soil break down the animal or plant tissues. The chemicals that make up the animals or plants are released into the soil. These chemicals act as FERTILIZERS to enrich the soil and help the green plants to grow. And so the food chain begins all over again.

▲ In American football, the players carry or throw the ball much more than they kick it.

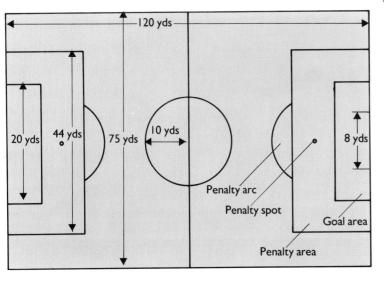

◄ The dimensions of a football pitch.

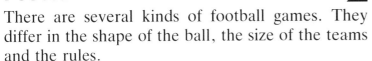

▼ Soccer is called football in most countries of the world. In this game the ball must not be handled, and the players rely on agility and speed.

Football

There are several kinds of football games. They differ in the shape of the ball, the size of the teams and the rules.

Soccer is played all over the world. The ball is round, the field, or 'pitch', can be from 90 to 118 metres long, and each team has 11 players. Teams score by kicking the ball into the goal at the opposite end of the field. The ball may not be touched by the hand or arm, except by the goalkeeper within his goal area.

American football uses an oval ball. The game consists mostly of tackling, passing and running, with very little kicking. The players—11 on each side—are protected by helmets and pads. This type of football is sometimes very violent.

▲ *The Ford family of motor cars spans nearly a century from the production of the first Model T to the cars of today.*

▼ *Acres of forest can be laid waste through the careless use of fire by people.*

RUGBY football is played in Britain, the Commonwealth and parts of Europe. The ball may be kicked or carried. Australian Rules football has 18 players to a side. All players can kick and catch the ball.

Ford, Henry

Henry Ford (1863–1947) was a pioneer MOTOR CAR maker in the United States. He was the first to use assembly lines. By building his cars out of standard parts he was able to turn out hundreds a day. His cars were so cheap that many people could afford to buy them. Ford's biggest success was the Model T. His Detroit factories turned out 15 million Model Ts during the 19 years it was in production.

Forest

Forests are large areas of tree-covered land. Tropical rain forests are found near the EQUATOR. In this hot and steamy climate many kinds of trees and plants grow very quickly. In some places the trees grow so closely together that the sunlight cannot reach the dark, bare forest floor.

Coniferous forests are nearly always found in cold

northern lands. These forests are mostly made up of one kind of tree, such as spruce, fir or pine. Few other plants grow there. In temperate lands like Europe and the cooler parts of Africa, there are deciduous forests with trees like oak and beech, which shed their leaves. Most Australian forest trees are eucalyptus.

Fossil

Fossils are the hardened remains or impressions of animals and plants that lived a very long time ago. A fossil may be a shell, a bone, a tooth, a leaf, a skeleton, or even sometimes an entire animal.

Most fossils have been found in areas that were once in or near the sea. When the plant or creature died its body sank to the seabed. The soft parts rotted away but the hard skeleton became buried in the mud. Over millions of years more and more mud settled on top of the skeleton. Eventually these layers of mud hardened into rock, and the skeleton became part of that rock. Water seeping through the rock slowly dissolved away the original skeleton. It was replaced by stony MINERALS which formed exactly the same shape.

These fossils lay buried until movements in the Earth's crust pushed up the seabed and it became dry land. In time, water, ice and wind wear away the rock and the fossil is exposed. The oldest known fossil is over three billion years old.

▼ *Five layers can be seen in a tropical forest. At ground level fungi, mosses and ferns grow in the rich leaf litter. Then comes a layer of tree ferns, shrubs and lianas. Above this is a layer of young tree crowns and then the thick canopy, the crowns of mature trees. The topmost layer consists of the few trees that stand above the canopy.*

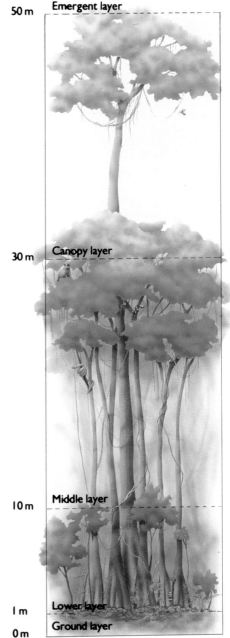

50 m — Emergent layer

30 m — Canopy layer

10 m — Middle layer

1 m — Lower layer

0 m — Ground layer

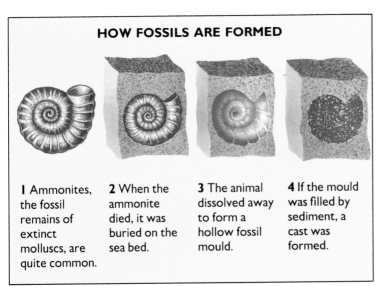

HOW FOSSILS ARE FORMED

1 Ammonites, the fossil remains of extinct molluscs, are quite common.

2 When the ammonite died, it was buried on the sea bed.

3 The animal dissolved away to form a hollow fossil mould.

4 If the mould was filled by sediment, a cast was formed.

▼ The red fox is about a metre long from its nose to the tip of its tail. It stands about 30 to 40 centimetres high. Its back is reddish brown and the underside white.

▼ The fennec fox (below) is the smallest of the foxes. The bat-eared fox (bottom) looks more like a jackal than a fox. Both these animals have very large ears because they live in open desert country and their ears help to get rid of excess heat from their bodies. Their big ears also give them acute hearing.

Fox

Foxes belong to the same animal family as dogs. The most common kind is the red fox, which is found in Europe, North Africa, North America and parts of Asia. It eats small birds, animals and insects, and occasionally poultry or lambs.

Foxes live in holes called 'earths' which they either dig themselves or take over from rabbits or badgers. Recently, more and more foxes have been found in cities. They live under the floors of buildings or in any hidden place they can find. They eat scraps from dustbins.

Foxes are very cunning animals. Sometimes they catch rabbits and other prey by chasing their own tails very fast. This fascinates the rabbit who watches without realizing that the fox is gradually getting nearer and nearer. When the fox gets close enough it suddenly straightens out and grabs its dinner.

Fraction

If you cut a cake into equal parts, each part is a fraction of the whole cake. We can write this as a number, too. If the cake is cut into two, each half can be written like this: ½. If the cake is cut into four, each quarter is written ¼. The number above the dividing line in a fraction is called the *numerator*. The number below is called the *denominator*.

Until fractions were invented, people had to manage with just *whole* numbers. It was not possible to express a length or weight between two whole numbers.

Fractions help us to divide things. They can be used to mean a part of one: a half of one is a half ($\frac{1}{2} \times 1 = \frac{1}{2}$). They can also be used to divide numbers greater than one. A box of eggs has 12 eggs in it. Half the box has 6 eggs ($\frac{1}{2} \times 12 = 6$).

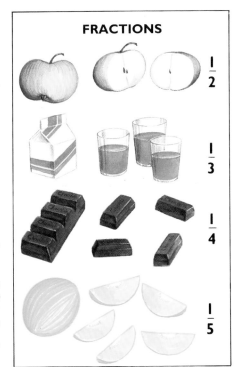

FRACTIONS

$\frac{1}{2}$

$\frac{1}{3}$

$\frac{1}{4}$

$\frac{1}{5}$

France

France is the largest country in western EUROPE. It has a population of 57,287,000. In ancient times France was inhabited by CELTS, but Julius CAESAR conquered it and for 500 years it was part of the Roman Empire. The Franks, from whom the country got its name, invaded in the AD 400s. France was once divided into hundreds of small parts. There was no standard language until the founding of the French Academy in the 1630s.

France is a very varied and beautiful country. It has a temperate climate and is very fertile. Farmland covers about half the country and many of the people are employed in farming, fishing or forestry. France produces a lot of grain, fruit, and vegetables, and it is famous for its WINES.

The history of France is long and turbulent. For centuries the French and English were enemies and fought many wars. The French people suffered under the rule of greedy kings and nobles. Then in 1789 the people started the FRENCH REVOLUTION. They overthrew their king and made France a republic.

But the country was soon taken over by NAPO-

FRANCE

Government: Republic
Capital: Paris
Area: 547,026 sq km
Population: 57,287,000
Language: French
Currency: French franc

▶ *The Tour de France, an annual bicycle race around France, is an internationally popular event.*

▼ *Three well-known French monuments – from top to bottom, the Eiffel Tower, Sacré Coeur and the Arc de Triomphe. The Arc de Triomphe, in Paris, was built by Napoleon. The white-domed church of Sacré Coeur is a landmark on Montmartre, the tallest hill in Paris. The Eiffel Tower was erected for the Paris Exhibition of 1889.*

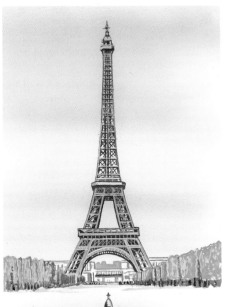

LEON, who made himself Emperor. He went to war and conquered most of Europe before he was finally defeated at Waterloo in 1815. Later, France became a republic once again.

Today France is one of the wealthiest nations in Europe. It was one of the first members of the EUROPEAN COMMUNITY. The capital city is PARIS on the river Seine.

Francis of Assisi

St Francis (1182–1226) was born in Assisi in central Italy. When he was 22 he suffered a severe illness. Afterwards he decided to devote his life to the service of God. He lived in poverty and gathered around him a band of monks who became known as the Franciscans. St Francis was very fond of birds and animals whom he called his brothers and sisters.

Franklin, Benjamin

Benjamin Franklin (1706–1790) was a gifted American politician and scientist. He was born in Boston, the youngest of 17 children. Franklin became a printer and then went on to publish a yearly almanac which made him his fortune.

He became involved in the REVOLUTIONARY WAR, which brought America freedom from British rule. He was one of the men who signed the Declaration of Independence and helped draw up the peace treaty at the end of the war.

His scientific inventions include bifocal eyeglasses, and the lightning conductor, a rod that protects buildings from lightning.

French Revolution

In the 1700s the poor people of FRANCE suffered under the rule of their kings and nobles. Rich people built themselves lavish palaces and mansions while many others starved in misery. French kings forced the peasants and shopkeepers to pay taxes to support their extravagant way of life, and to finance the wars they were always fighting.

There was no parliament to stop the king from treating his subjects badly, and eventually, in 1789, the French people's anger exploded into revolution. King LOUIS XVI was imprisoned but tried to escape. Violent leaders like Danton, Robespierre and Marat directed the Revolution, and the king and queen and many nobles were beheaded.

Then followed the 'Reign of Terror', when the

▲ *By flying a kite in a thunderstorm, Benjamin Franklin proved that lightning was electricity.*

▼ *On July 14, 1789, a Paris mob stormed the Bastille, a prison, and sparked off the French Revolution.*

▲ *Sigmund Freud, whose theories did much to advance the study of nervous diseases.*

Revolutionary leaders began to quarrel among themselves, and many of them were beheaded too. The people tired of bloodshed and in 1795 they set up a government called 'The Directory'. But it ruled the country badly, and in 1799 it was overthrown by NAPOLEON.

Freud, Sigmund

Sigmund Freud (1856–1939) was an Austrian doctor who made a great contribution to our understanding of the human mind.

Freud received a degree in medicine from the University of Vienna in 1881 and began to devote himself to the study of mental illness. He taught that the *subconscious*—the thoughts and memories we are not aware of—held the key to a person's mental state. To open up the subconscious he developed the system of *psychoanalysis*, a kind of clinical examination of the mind. Freud published several books on this and other subjects.

Friction

When two things rub together it causes friction. Friction makes it hard to move something across a surface. Smooth objects cause much less friction than rough objects, so when things need to go fast we try to reduce friction. This is why the wheels of a train and the rails of the track are smooth. When we want things to slow down we add friction; for example, putting on the brakes in our cars. If two

Without friction the world would be a strange place. We could not walk because our shoes would not grip the ground. Cars would stand still no matter how fast their wheels turned. Nails and screws would not hold.

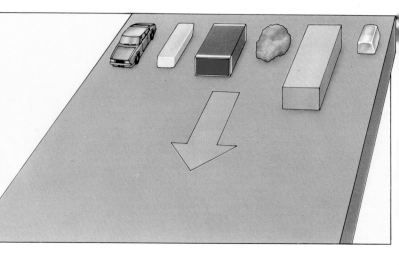

SEE IT YOURSELF
Investigate friction by sliding various objects of roughly the same size, but with different surfaces, down a sloping board or metal tray. Wheels move down very easily, others need a greater slope before they begin to move. It all depends on the amount of friction between their surface and the surface of the slope.

things rub together at great speed the friction produces HEAT. If you rub your hand very fast against your leg you can feel the heat made by the friction.

Frog and Toad

Frogs and toads are AMPHIBIANS. This means that they can live both on land and in water. Frogs and toads are found all over the world except in very cold lands that are always frozen. There are hundreds of different kinds. The biggest is the Goliath frog of Central Africa. This frog can be over 30 cm long and weigh over 3 kg. The smallest is a tree frog from the United States, which is less than 2 cm long.

Frogs and toads breathe through their skins as well as their LUNGS. It is important that they keep their skins wet, because if the skin became too dry they could not breathe and would die. This is why you will never find a frog very far away from water.

Common frogs feed on insects, grubs and slugs. They catch their food with a long sticky tongue

The poison of the arrow-poison frog of South America is so powerful that one millionth of a gram is enough to kill a person.

▼ These are just a few of the world's 2500 different species of frogs and toads. The brightly-coloured arrow-poison frogs of South America are among the most poisonous of all. Indians of the Amazon basin use their poison to tip hunting arrows. Tree frogs have pads on their fingers and toes which help them to climb trees. Gliding frogs have webs on their feet which they use as 'wings'. The male midwife toad carries the eggs laid by the female on his legs and back. After three weeks he takes them into the water and the baby tadpoles hatch out.

Green tree frog
(North America)

Midwife toad
(Europe)

Gliding frog
(Malaysia)

Common toad
(Europe)

Arrow-poison frog
(South America)

Spadefoot toad
(North America)

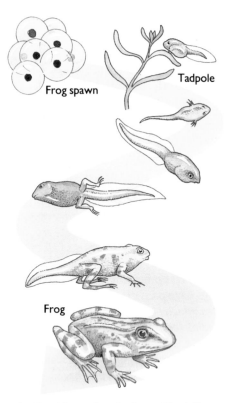

Frog spawn

Tadpole

Frog

▲ The life cycle of a frog: The jelly-like eggs, or spawn, are laid in a pond and hatch into tadpoles. The tadpoles gradually develop legs and their tails shrink. They develop lungs instead of gills. They become adult frogs in about 3 years.

▼ In many plants the seeds are enclosed in fleshy fruits. Many fruits are good to eat. As the fruits develop from the flowers, the sepals and petals wither and finally drop off.

which is attached to the front of the mouth. A frog can flick its tongue in and out in a fraction of a second. Really big frogs eat snakes, small animals and other frogs, as well as insects.

Toads' skins are rough, dry and lumpy. They can live in drier places than can frogs.

Frost

Frost is a covering of tiny CRYSTALS of ice that form on cold surfaces. There are three kinds of frost. Hoarfrost forms when tiny drops of water in the air freeze, as they touch cold objects. Hoarfrost makes lacy patterns on windowpanes. Glazed frost forms when rain falls on a cold road and covers the surface with a glassy coat. Rime frost is white ice that forms when cold fog or drizzle freezes on surfaces such as cold aircraft wings.

Fruit

To most of us 'fruit' means juicy foods which grow on certain plants and trees. Apples, oranges and pears are three examples. These fruits taste good and are important in our diet. They give us mineral salts, sugar and VITAMINS. The water, skins and seeds of fruit help our DIGESTION.

To scientists who study plants, fruits are the ripe SEED cases of any flowering plant. The fruits protect the seeds as they develop and help spread them when they are ripe. Some fruits scatter seeds. Others are eaten by birds and animals that spread the seeds.

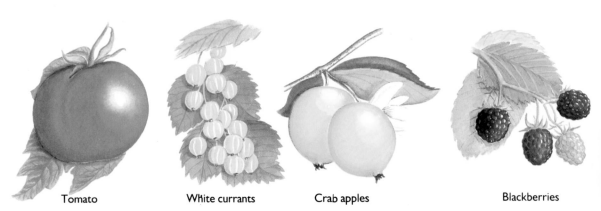

Tomato   White currants   Crab apples   Blackberries

◄ *Coal is a solid fuel. Like other fuels, it is a combination of three chemical elements – carbon, hydrogen and oxygen.*

Fuel

Fuels are substances that give off heat when they burn. Fuels provide our world with the ENERGY we use for heating, cooking, powering ships, planes, cars and machines, and producing electricity.

The most important fuels are COAL, OIL and NATURAL GAS. These were formed underground from the remains of prehistoric plants or animals. People often call them fossil fuels.

Some fuels give out more heat than others. A kilogram of coal gives nearly three times as much heat as a kilogram of wood. Oil gives nearly four times as much, and HYDROGEN gas ten times as much. But URANIUM can give more than half a million times as much heat as hydrogen.

As fossil fuels are used up we shall have to make more use of NUCLEAR ENERGY, SOLAR ENERGY, and wind and water power.

Fuel Cell

A fuel cell is a special kind of electric battery that keeps on making electricity as long as fuel is fed into it. The main use for the fuel cell is in spacecraft. Fuel cells supplied electricity in the Apollo spacecraft that flew to the Moon in 1969–72. These cells used oxygen and hydrogen as fuel. Inside the cells, the oxygen and hydrogen combined together to produce electricity and water. The astronauts drank the water.

FUELS

Natural gas is a fuel that is widely used for cooking and heating. It is found deep underground close to oil pools.

Coal is still used to produce most of our electricity. For a century and a half it has been the most important fuel for producing heat to make steam.

Oil, or petroleum, comes from oil wells sunk deep into the Earth. Petrol, kerosene and diesel oil are all separated from petroleum.

Nuclear fuel is usually uranium. It is put into nuclear reactors and produces great amounts of energy. Nuclear reactors generate electricity.

Solar energy – energy from the Sun – is radiant energy, energy that travels in waves. It gives us light and heat, and is the source of most of the energy on Earth.

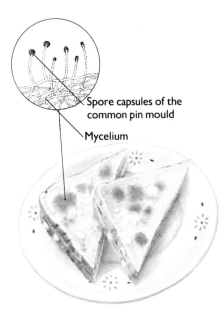

▲ *The fungus family includes moulds. Uncovered food offers a perfect place for moulds to grow. The tiny, thread-like growths (inset) spread quickly.*

Spore capsules of the common pin mould

Mycelium

Fungus

A fungus is a simple PLANT with no true roots, stems, or leaves. Fungi do not have the chlorophyll that helps green plants to make food. So fungi have to find a ready-made supply of food. Some feed as parasites on living plants or animals. Others feed on animal and plant remains.

There are more than 50,000 kinds of fungus. Some have only one CELL. Other fungi are chains of cells. These produce tiny, thread-like growths that spread through the substance they feed on. Many fungi grow a large fruiting body that sheds spores to produce new fungus plants. The MUSHROOMS we eat are the fruiting bodies of a fungus. Some fungi are useful. Penicillin, the ANTIBIOTIC drug, and YEAST are both fungi.

Furniture

Furniture is used for resting things on and for storing things in. Beds, chairs and tables all support some kind of load. Chests and cupboards hold such things as sheets and china.

The first pieces of furniture were simple slabs of stone and chunks of wood. In time, people tried to make furniture that was beautiful as well as useful.

Wealthy Egyptians had carved and painted beds,

▼ *Throughout history furniture has often been beautiful as well as useful. Below are some very individual designs for everyday furniture from 4000 years ago to the 20th century.*

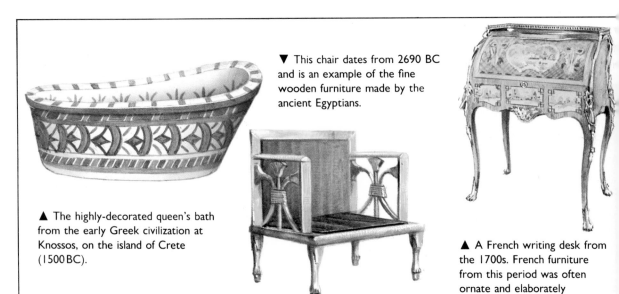

▼ This chair dates from 2690 BC and is an example of the fine wooden furniture made by the ancient Egyptians.

▲ The highly-decorated queen's bath from the early Greek civilization at Knossos, on the island of Crete (1500 BC).

▲ A French writing desk from the 1700s. French furniture from this period was often ornate and elaborately decorated.

chairs and tables 4000 years ago. The Romans used bronze and marble, and made tables with legs carved in animal shapes. From the end of the MIDDLE AGES onwards many different styles of furniture have been made.

More recently, people have tried using new materials and machines to make furniture with clean, simple shapes. Today you can buy metal or plastic furniture, as well as copies of older styles.

Fuse

This word has two meanings. One kind of fuse is a safety device in an electric circuit. Fuse wire is made so that it will melt at a low temperature. If too much ELECTRICITY flows through the circuit the wire 'fuses', or melts. This breaks the circuit.

In this way, an electric fuse stops the wire in the circuit from becoming too hot and possibly setting fire to nearby objects. Electric current must pass through fuse wire to get from the main power line to the electric wiring in a house. Inside the house, each electric plug also has a fuse.

The other kind of fuse is a device that sets off EXPLOSIVES. A safety fuse burns slowly until the flame reaches the explosive. A detonating fuse explodes itself and this explosion sets off a much larger amount of dynamite or other explosive.

Furniture was so scarce in Europe during the Middle Ages that it was quite common for a visitor to bring along his or her bed and other pieces of furniture.

In England until the 17th century, the three-legged stool was still widely used. People thought that a proper chair should only be used by the lord of the manor.

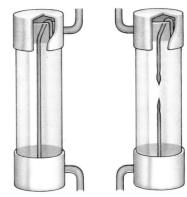

▲ A cartridge fuse (left) is fitted inside ordinary household plugs. Too large a current will cause the wire inside it to melt, thus breaking the circuit (right).

The sturdy Welsh dresser is a fine example of good country furniture of the 1800s.

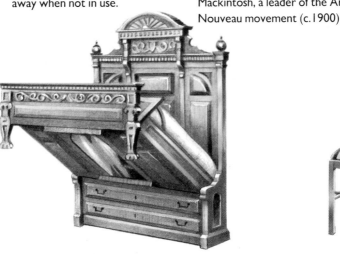

▼ An American parlour bed, dating from 1891, which folded away when not in use.

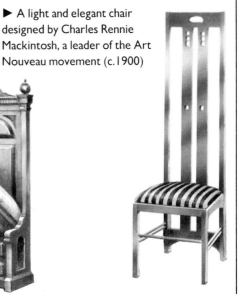

▶ A light and elegant chair designed by Charles Rennie Mackintosh, a leader of the Art Nouveau movement (c.1900)

Gabon

Gabon is a country about twice the size of England on the west coast of Africa. It lies on the equator, so it is hot and rainy there. Gabon is a land of high plateaus, mountains and dense tropical forests. The country is rich in mineral resources, and trees are cut down for export. The capital is Libreville, and the population is about a million.

Gagarin, Yuri

Yuri Gagarin (1934–1968) was the first human being to travel into space. The Soviet cosmonaut was rocketed upward in *Vostok I* on April 12, 1961. He circled the Earth once in 108 minutes and landed by parachute within 10 km of the planned spot. After his famous flight, Gagarin continued to train as a cosmonaut, but he was killed in a plane crash in March 1968.

Galaxy

Someone once called galaxies 'star islands' in space. A galaxy is made up of a huge group of STARS. Our SUN is just one star of about 100,000 million stars that belong to the Milky Way galaxy. A beam of light would take about 100,000 years to shine from one side of the Milky Way to the other. Yet the Milky Way is only a middle-sized galaxy.

Beyond our galaxy there may be as many as 10,000 million more. The nearest large galaxy is

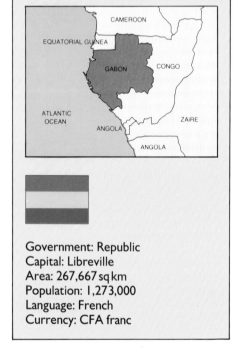

GABON

Government: Republic
Capital: Libreville
Area: 267,667 sq km
Population: 1,273,000
Language: French
Currency: CFA franc

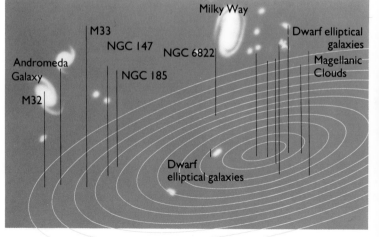

▶ Our galaxy belongs to what we call the Local Group – a collection of about 30 galaxies. This diagram of the Local Group shows the galaxies so far discovered at their correct distances apart, although their sizes are not to scale.

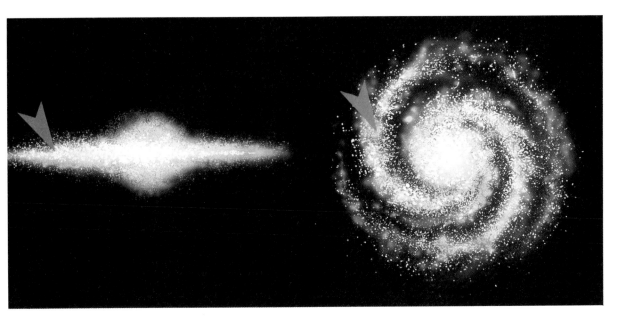

called Andromeda. The light we see it by took more than two million years to reach us.

Some galaxies have no special shape. Others have spiral arms made up of many millions of stars. The Milky Way and Andromeda galaxies both look like this. There are also galaxies that look like saucers or balls. Astronomers used to think that these changed into galaxies with spiral arms. Now some astronomers believe instead that the spiral galaxies shrink into the other kind.

RADIO ASTRONOMY has shown that radio waves are sent out from many galaxies. Strong radio waves also come from strange starlike objects known as QUASARS. Quasars are very powerful energy sources. Some people think that a quasar may be the beginning of a new galaxy. Scientists think that galaxies may form where GRAVITY pulls huge clouds of gas together.

▲ Edge on, our Milky Way galaxy looks like a flat disc with a swollen middle – the nucleus. From above, it looks like a whirlpool of stars. The position of our solar system is marked by the red arrows.

Galileo

Galileo Galilei (1564–1642) was an Italian mathematics teacher and one of the first true scientists. Instead of believing old ideas about the way the world worked, Galileo made careful experiments to find out for himself. He learnt that a PENDULUM took the same time to make a long swing as it did to make a short one. He showed that light objects fell as fast as heavy ones when pulled

▲ Galileo was a mathematician, astronomer and physicist, and one of the first true scientists.

283

towards the Earth by what we know as GRAVITY. He built a TELESCOPE and became the first man to use this tool for studying the Moon and PLANETS. What he saw made Galileo believe COPERNICUS's idea that the Earth was not the centre of the UNIVERSE. The Church punished him for his belief in this idea. But later scientists like Isaac NEWTON built new knowledge on Galileo's discoveries.

Galleon

This kind of heavy, wooden sailing ship was used for carrying fighting men and cargoes over oceans in the 1500s. A galleon was four times as long as it was wide. It had a special deck to carry cannons. There were square sails on its two front masts and three-cornered *lateen* sails on its one or two rear masts. Lateen sails helped galleons to sail against the wind. Galleons were faster and easier to manage than some other ships, but some Spanish galleons were clumsy and top heavy.

▲ *A galleon sets sail. A gang of seamen unfurl the mainsail, and others in the main top adjust the running rigging.*

INSIDE A GALLEON

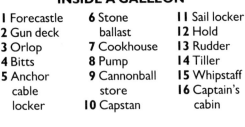

1 Forecastle	6 Stone	11 Sail locker
2 Gun deck	ballast	12 Hold
3 Orlop	7 Cookhouse	13 Rudder
4 Bitts	8 Pump	14 Tiller
5 Anchor	9 Cannonball	15 Whipstaff
cable	store	16 Captain's
locker	10 Capstan	cabin

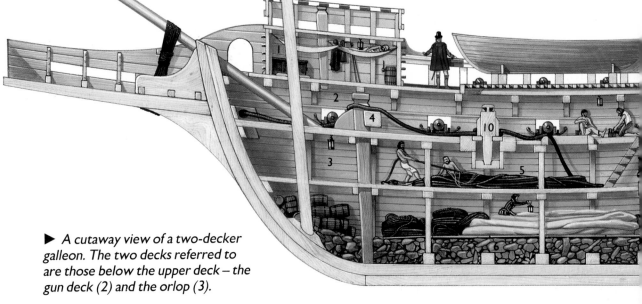

▶ *A cutaway view of a two-decker galleon. The two decks referred to are those below the upper deck – the gun deck (2) and the orlop (3).*

Gama, Vasco da

Vasco da Gama (about 1469–1524) discovered how to sail by sea from Europe to India by way of southern Africa. This Portuguese navigator left Lisbon with four ships in July, 1497. In East Africa he found a guide who showed him how to sail across the Indian Ocean. Da Gama reached Calicut in southern India in May, 1498. But Arab traders who were jealous of the Portuguese tried to stop him from trading with the Indians. On the journey home, 30 of his 90 crewmen died of scurvy, and only two of the four ships got back to Lisbon.

But da Gama had found a way to reach the spice-rich lands of the East.

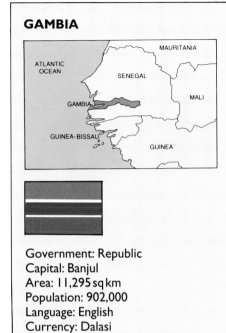

GAMBIA

Government: Republic
Capital: Banjul
Area: 11,295 sq km
Population: 902,000
Language: English
Currency: Dalasi

Gambia

Gambia is mainland Africa's smallest country. It is on the west coast and is about half the size of Wales. Most Gambians earn their living by farming. Peanuts are the main crop. In recent years tourism has increased. Once a British colony, Gambia became independent in 1965.

▲ *Gandhi was called the* Mahatma *by his followers, which means 'Great Soul'.*

▼ *The Ganges rises in the Himalayas and flows south-east through India and Bangladesh.*

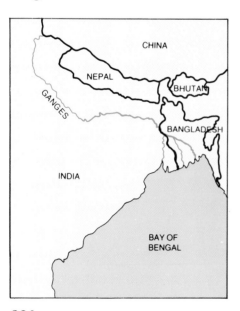

Gandhi

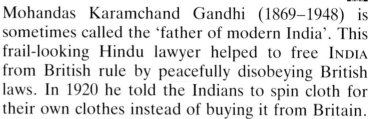

Mohandas Karamchand Gandhi (1869–1948) is sometimes called the 'father of modern India'. This frail-looking Hindu lawyer helped to free INDIA from British rule by peacefully disobeying British laws. In 1920 he told the Indians to spin cloth for their own clothes instead of buying it from Britain.

People admired Gandhi's beliefs, his kindness, and his simple way of life. He was called the Mahatma, meaning 'Great Soul'. In 1947 Britain gave India independence. Soon after, one of his fellow HINDUS shot Gandhi for preaching peace between Hindus and Muslims (followers of ISLAM).

Gandhi, Indira

Indira Gandhi (1917–1984) was prime minister of India from 1966 until 1977 and from 1980 until her death. Her father, Jawaharlal Nehru, supported GANDHI and became India's first prime minister after independence. In 1942, Indira married a lawyer, Feroze Gandhi. For years she helped her father, then went into politics herself. When in power, Mrs Gandhi fought for economic progress, social reforms and national unity. In 1984 she was killed by two Sikhs, members of an Indian religious group. Her son Rajiv succeeded her as prime minister but was assassinated in 1991.

Ganges, River

The Ganges is the greatest river in INDIA. It flows for about 2500 km and drains an area three times the size of Spain. The river rises in the HIMALAYAS and winds across northern India and BANGLADESH, then through a DELTA to the Bay of Bengal. Rich farmlands and great cities line its banks. HINDUS believe the river is sacred.

Garden

Gardens are pieces of land kept especially for growing lawns, flowering plants, fruits, vegetables, or attractive shrubs and trees. There were gardens

in Egypt 4500 years ago. BABYLON was later famous for its hanging gardens. RENAISSANCE Italy had gardens with fountains, pools, terraces and steps.

In the 1700s English landscape gardeners placed natural-looking lawns and trees around big houses. In the 1800s cities laid out gardens where anyone might walk. Today, many houses have some sort of garden.

▲ Grand houses were adorned with grand gardens. The Pond Garden at Hampton Court Palace, near London, was laid out to a strict formal pattern.

Garibaldi, Giuseppe

Giuseppe Garibaldi (1807–1882) was an Italian patriot who helped to turn Italy from a collection of small states into a united and independent country. After two periods of exile in the United States of America, Garibaldi led his followers, known as Redshirts, against the Austrians, who then controlled Italy. In 1860 he gained control of Sicily and southern Italy. Then he invaded mainland Italy and captured the important city of Naples. This victory helped make possible the uniting of Italy under King Victor Emmanuel. Garibaldi is remembered as one of Italy's greatest heroes.

▲ Giuseppe Garibaldi, who helped to create the modern state of Italy, began his career as cabin boy on a ship.

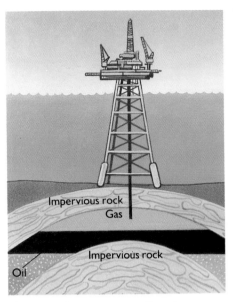

▲ *Oil and natural gas collect in porous rocks (rocks that allow liquids to soak through). They are trapped between impervious rocks (which will not allow liquids to pass through).*

▼ *Gear wheels turn at different speeds in proportion to the number of teeth they possess. The small wheel turns twice as fast as the large one if it has half the number of teeth.*

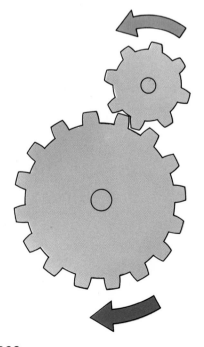

Gas

Gases are substances with no special shape or size. They take up the size and shape of any container that holds them. This can happen because a gas is made of ATOMS moving freely in space. When a gas becomes cold enough it turns into a liquid. Liquids have a fixed size but no fixed shape. If that liquid becomes much colder still it turns into a solid. Solids have a fixed shape and size.

The gas we use to cook with and heat our homes is called NATURAL GAS. This gas is found beneath the Earth's surface in many parts of the world.

Gear

A gear is a wheel with teeth along its rim. These teeth can fit into the teeth of other gear wheels. Metal rods, or *axles*, are fitted into the centre of each gear. If one axle is turned, its gear turns and makes the second gear turn. This makes the second axle turn too.

Gears are used to increase or decrease the *speed* at which wheels turn. They are also used to increase or decrease the *turning power* of wheels.

In the picture on the left, the large gear wheel has twice as many teeth as the small wheel. If the small wheel is turned by an engine, the big wheel will turn at only half the speed of the small wheel, and the big wheel will turn in the opposite direction to the small wheel. But the big wheel will have twice the turning power of the small wheel. When a motor car is in low gear, this is what happens. The car goes quite slowly, but it has plenty of power for starting or going up steep hills.

Gem

Some rocks hold hard CRYSTALS that can be cut to show clear, brilliant colours. These gems are often used in making JEWELLERY. DIAMONDS are among the rarest, finest gems but red rubies, blue sapphires, and green emeralds are also much sought after. Pearls are gems produced by oysters. Today, artificial gems are made from glass and plastic.

Inside an AC generator a coil of wire is turned between the poles of a magnet. Halfway through each turn, the coil becomes positioned for an instant at right angles to the magnet. This causes the direction of the current to change.

ALTERNATING CURRENT

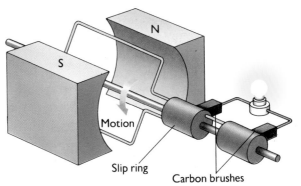

Motion

Slip ring

Carbon brushes

DIRECT CURRENT

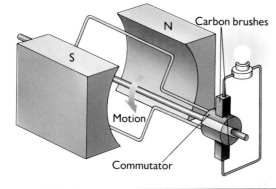

Carbon brushes

N

S

Motion

Commutator

Direct current, similar to that from a battery, can be obtained from a generator by using a device called a commutator. This makes the current flow continuously in the same direction.

Generator

Generators produce electric CURRENT. Huge generators in POWER STATIONS provide ELECTRICITY for homes and factories. The largest generators can light 20 million 100-watt electric lamps. But there are tiny generators too. A bicycle dynamo is a generator you can hold in one hand.

If a loop of wire is turned between the ends of a horseshoe-shaped magnet, an electric current flows in the wire. Generators work much like this. They change the ENERGY of motion into electrical energy. The energy to work a generator's moving parts can come from wind, flowing water, or steam produced by heat from FUELS such as oil or coal. Big generators have thousands of coils of wire which are made to turn very quickly between powerful magnets.

Genetics

Each animal or plant passes on certain characteristics to its offspring. For example, we say that someone has 'his father's eyes' or 'her mother's hair'. The science of genetics explains why living things look and behave as they do.

Heredity works in an amazing way. Each individ-

▲ *An AC and a DC generator. Each has a wire coil held between the poles of a magnet.*

▼ *Albino animals such as this hedgehog are born white, with no colouring matter in their skin or hair. They have pink eyes. Albinos inherit their colourless condition from their ancestors' genes. An albino parent may produce normal young, and the young may later produce albinos.*

The chances of a baby being a girl or a boy are about the same. But one in 16 families with four children is likely to have four boys, while another such family will have four girls. Much longer strings of boys or girls have been recorded. One French family had nothing but girls – 72 of them – in three generations.

ual produces sex cells. If a male and a female cell join, the female cell grows into a new individual. Inside every cell there are tiny chromosomes, largely made of a chemical called DNA. Different parts of each chromosome carry different coded messages. Each of these parts is called a *gene*. The genes carry all the information needed to make a new plant or animal look and behave as it does. They decide its sex and also every other characteristic it inherits from its parents.

► *Each of us has two genes for a characteristic such as eye colour, one from each parent. If the two genes are different, one may have a stronger influence than the other. It is called the* dominant *gene. If someone inherits one brown eye gene and one blue eye gene, they will have brown eyes because the brown eye gene is dominant. The blue eye gene is called the* recessive *gene. If someone inherits two blue eye genes, one from each parent, he or she can only have blue eyes.*

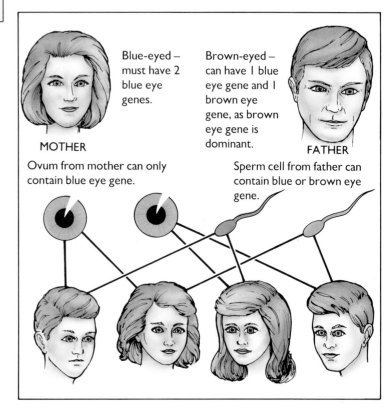

Blue-eyed – must have 2 blue eye genes.

Brown-eyed – can have 1 blue eye gene and 1 brown eye gene, as brown eye gene is dominant.

MOTHER

FATHER

Ovum from mother can only contain blue eye gene.

Sperm cell from father can contain blue or brown eye gene.

▼ *At its height, the Mongol empire under Genghis Khan stretched from China in the east right across Asia.*

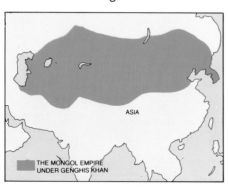

ASIA

THE MONGOL EMPIRE UNDER GENGHIS KHAN

Genghis Khan

Genghis Khan (1167–1227) was a Mongol chief who cruelly attacked many Asian peoples and won a mighty empire. His real name was Temujin ('iron-smith').

At 13 he took his dead father's place as chief of a small Mongol tribe of NOMADS. He soon won power over nearby tribes as well. In 1206 he became known as Genghis Khan, 'Very Mighty King'. Genghis Khan formed a huge army of tough, hard-riding nomads on the great grasslands of central Asia. Then he set off to conquer the lands around

him. His troops pushed south-east to Beijing in China, and south into Tibet and what are now Pakistan and Afghanistan. In the south-west they invaded Persia (Iran) and southern Russia.

After he died, other Mongol rulers won more land and made the empire even larger.

Geography

Geography is the subject we study when we want to learn about the surface of the Earth. Geographers study everything on the Earth—the land, sea, air, plants, animals and people. They explain where different things are found, how they got there, and how they affect one another.

There are many different areas, or branches, of geography. For instance, physical geography describes things like mountains, valleys, lakes and rivers. Meteorology describes weather. Economic geography deals with farming, mining, manufacturing and trade. Human geography divides the peoples of the world into *cultures*.

MAPS AND CHARTS are the geographer's most useful tools.

▲ *Genghis Khan put together a huge, organized army. Each man had five ponies, ridden in turn so that they would not get tired. When the Mongols besieged a city, most of the inhabitants were killed and the land around was laid waste.*

Ptolemy of Alexandria was the most famous ancient geographer—he lived about AD 150. Ptolemy drew a map of the then-known world that is remarkably accurate, considering what was known about the Earth in those days. His eight-volume *Guide to Geography* consisted of a list of all known places, each with its latitude and longitude, a system Ptolemy devised.

GEOLOGY

▶ *Geologists study rocks, which tell them about the Earth's structure. There are three kinds of rock:* igneous, *formed when molten rock is pushed up from deep inside the Earth;* sedimentary, *which is hardened layers of sediment; and* metamorphic, *which is igneous or sedimentary rock that has been changed by heat and pressure inside the Earth. Of the rocks shown here, obsidian (1) and granite (2) are igneous rocks, marble (3) and slate (4) are metamorphic rocks, and coal (5), limestone (6) and sandstone (7) are sedimentary rocks. Conglomerate (8) is made up of stone stuck together in a sedimentary 'concrete'.*

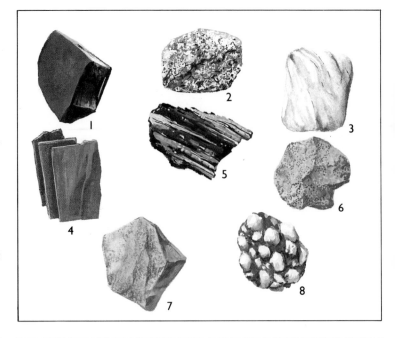

For a long time, people have tried to work out the age of the Earth. In the 1600s, an Irish archbishop named Ussher decided from reading the Scriptures that the world was created in 4004 BC. It was not long, however, before geologists realized by examining the rocks that this date was very wrong. We now know that the Earth was formed about 4500 million years ago.

In geometry we learn that the three angles of any triangle add up to 180 degrees – a straight line. You can prove this by cutting out a triangle from a piece of paper. Tear off the three angles and rearrange them so that the sides, angles and corners are together. They make a straight angle of 180°.

Geology

Geology is the study of the Earth itself. Geologists discover what things the Earth is made of, where they are found, and how they got there. Geologists study the chemicals in ROCKS and MINERALS. They also try to find out how rocks are formed, and how they are changed by movements beneath the surface of the Earth. VOLCANOES and EARTHQUAKES give us useful clues about movements deep down underground.

Geologists also study the history of the Earth. They have found rocks 3800 million years old, and FOSSILS showing that EVOLUTION began over 3400 million years ago.

Geologists help engineers to choose where to build a road or tunnel. They help miners to find coal, oil or gas beneath the ground. By studying rocks brought back by astronauts they were able to tell us what the Moon is made of.

Geometry

Geometry is a branch of MATHEMATICS. It can help you to find out the shape, size and position of an object, or how much a container holds. People draw lines and measure ANGLES to help them solve geometric problems.

George (Kings)

Six British kings were called George.

George I (1660–1727) was a German ruler who inherited the British throne.

George II (1683–1760) reigned when Britain was winning Canada and India.

George III (1738–1820) lost what became the UNITED STATES. In old age he went mad.

George IV (1762–1830) was a spendthrift who loved to be in fashion. As Prince Regent he took his mad father's place from 1811.

George V (1865–1936) was a naval officer before he was king. He reigned during WORLD WAR I.

George VI (1895–1952) reigned during WORLD WAR II. He was the father of ELIZABETH II.

▲ *George II was the last British ruler to lead troops on the battlefield.*

Georgia

Georgia, until 1991 a republic of the former Soviet Union, is a country that borders the BLACK SEA. The landscape varies from high mountains to a narrow coastal plain. Agriculture is important, and many different crops are grown, including tea, citrus fruits and grapes. Mining is the most important industry. Since independence, there has been considerable civil unrest in the country.

Germ *See* Bacteria; Virus

Germany

Until the late 1800's, Germany was a country of separate states and cities, each with their own ruler. They were united by Otto von Bismarck, the prime minister of Prussia, one of the most powerful of these states. The united Germany became a great nation, but after WORLD WAR II, the land was divided into two countries: West Germany and East Germany. East Germany was a Communist country, closely allied to the Soviet Union. The two Germanys remained separate until 1990, when they were finally reunited under a federal government.

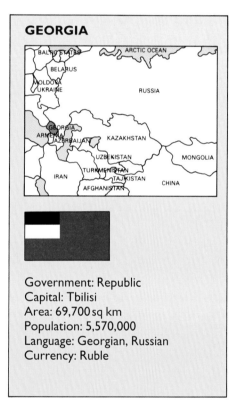

GEORGIA

Government: Republic
Capital: Tbilisi
Area: 69,700 sq km
Population: 5,570,000
Language: Georgian, Russian
Currency: Ruble

▶ *The modern city of Dresden was almost totally rebuilt after being heavily bombed in World War II.*

GERMANY

Government: Federal republic
Capital: Berlin
Area: 356,755 sq km
Population: 80,387,000
Language: German
Currency: Mark

Germany lies in the middle of Europe and has the largest population of any western European nation. Farms and cities stand on a low, flat plain to the north; the south is a region of wooded mountains. In the far south the tall peaks of the Alps rise thousands of metres above sea level. Germany's major rivers are the Rhine, the Elbe and the Oder. They flow north towards the North Sea and the Baltic Sea.

Before reunification, West Germany was the richest nation in Europe. Its mines and factories produced more coal, steel, cars and television sets than any other western European nation. East Germany, less than half the size of West Germany, had mines and factories, too, but much of its industry was old-fashioned and unproductive.

Once the rich West and the poorer East were united, there were problems to be faced. In East Germany, prices rose and many people lost their jobs as inefficient businesses closed. Taxes were raised to pay for the costs of unification. However, Germany is still a very prosperous nation and the German people are working together to overcome any remaining difficulties.

We get our word geyser from the *Geysir* ('gusher') near Mount Hekla in Iceland. It is no longer active, but used to spurt to a height of 50 metres. The Waimangu geyser in New Zealand erupted to a height of 450 metres in 1904.

Geyser

Geysers are hot springs that now and then squirt out steam and scalding water. They work like this. Water fills a deep crack in the ground, often near VOLCANOES. Hot rock heats the water deep underground, but the weight of the water above it stops the hot water from boiling until it is much hotter still. Then it turns to steam that forces the water upward, emptying the crack. The next eruption happens when the crack is full again.

There are many geysers in some parts of Iceland, the United States and New Zealand. The tallest geyser ever known was the Waimangu geyser in New Zealand. In 1904 this squirted steam and water nearly 460 metres into the sky.

Ghana

Ghana is a nation in West AFRICA. It is a bit smaller than the United Kingdom. The country is hot, with plenty of rain in the south where Ghana meets the Atlantic Ocean. The land here is low, with tropical forests and farms. The north is drier and grassy.

Most of Ghana's people are farmers. They grow cocoa and mine diamonds and gold. Lake Volta provides water power to make electricity. This man-made lake covers a greater area than any other man-made lake in the world.

▼ Women sell pineapples in a market in Ghana. Two-thirds of Ghana's people live in the southern third of the country.

▲ A geyser seems to work in a similar way to a pressure cooker. The higher the pressure, the hotter the water has to be to boil. The super-heated steam and water is pushed out as a powerful jet. When enough water has seeped back and heated up, the process starts again.

GHANA

Government: Military
Capital: Accra
Area: 238,537 sq km
Population: 16,185,000
Language: English
Currency: Cedi

GIBRALTAR

Government: Administered by a
governor appointed by the British
Crown
Area: 6 sq km
Highest point: 426 m
Population: 30,000

Gibraltar

This small British colony is a rocky peninsula that juts out from southern Spain. Most of Gibraltar is a mountain called the Rock. Britain won Gibraltar from Spain in 1704. Gibraltar guards the western end of the MEDITERRANEAN SEA.

Giraffe

Giraffes are the tallest animals. An adult male may stand three times taller than a tall man. They have long legs and a long neck. Yet this neck has only seven bones, the same as any other MAMMAL. Giraffes live in the hot grasslands of Africa and feed on leaves from shrubs and trees.

▼ A giraffe's long neck and legs enable it to eat the leaves from branches that are far above the reach of other browsing animals.

Glacier

Glaciers are rivers of ice. Most form high up in mountains where snow falls and never melts. As snow piles up, the lower layers are crushed and turn to ice. This begins to flow very slowly downhill through valleys. Most glaciers take a year to flow as far as you can walk in five minutes. The rocks they

▼ Glaciers move faster at the centre than at the sides. This creates huge gaps, or crevasses.

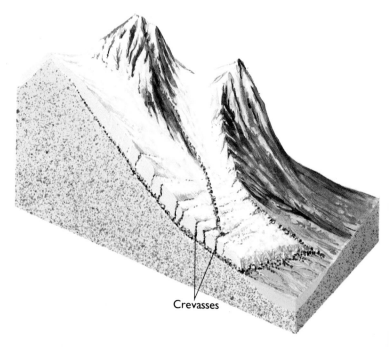

Crevasses

carry grind against the sides and floor of each valley until they make it deep and wide.

During ICE AGES, glaciers spread beyond the mountains. When the weather warms up they melt, leaving a valley behind. Many valleys in the ALPS and ROCKY MOUNTAINS once held glaciers.

Gladiator

Gladiators were men trained to fight to the death in shows to entertain crowds in ancient Rome. Many gladiators were criminals, prisoners of war or slaves. Some fought with a sword and shield. Others had a three-pronged spear and a net. Most fights ended when one gladiator killed the other.

▲ *Successful gladiators became famous in Rome. They were carefully fed and received medical care.*

Gland

Glands are organs that produce special substances needed by the body. There are two kinds—*endocrine* and *exocrine* glands. Endocrine glands send their substances, called *hormones*, directly into the bloodstream. One main endocrine gland is the *thyroid*. Its hormone controls the rate at which the body uses energy.

Exocrine glands release their substances through tubes, either into the intestines or onto the skin. Sweat, tears and saliva come from exocrine glands.

▼ *Endocrine glands produce hormones that control such things as growth and reproduction.*

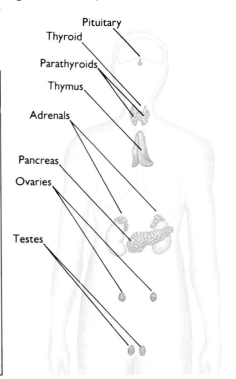

THE ENDOCRINE GLANDS	
Pituitary gland	The small 'master gland' that produces at least nine hormones, including those that control growth and reproduction
Thyroid gland	Controls the rate at which food is converted into energy. The tiny **parathyroids** regulate the amount of calcium in your bones and blood
Thymus	Helps in the immune process
Ovaries	Produce oestrogen and progesterone, which control female characteristics. Also produce egg cells
Testes	Produce testosterone, which controls the production of sperm cells and male characteristics
Pancreas	Produces insulin, which controls the level of glucose, a source of energy
Adrenal glands	Produce adrenaline, the 'emergency' hormone that speeds up heartbeat and breathing rate when danger threatens

▲ *Hang gliding is a popular sport. The glider's design was the result of NASA research into spacecraft re-entry as part of the U.S. space programme.*

Glass

People use glass in windows, eyeglasses, mirrors, tumblers, bottles, electric light bulbs and many other objects. (See pages 300–301.)

Gliding

Gliding is flying without using engine power. Gliding AIRCRAFT called sailplanes have long narrow wings. This gives them extra *lift*. The glider is launched by a winch or a towing aircraft. Once aloft, it loses height very gradually, kept up by rising air currents. If the air is rising as fast as the craft is falling, the glider may stay at the same level above the ground. If the air is rising at a faster rate, the aircraft can climb.

In 1853 the first glider to carry a man flew just across a valley. Modern sailplanes can do much more than that. In 1986 one sailplane reached a height of 11,500 metres over California.

Hang gliding is a sport in which the pilot is suspended from the glider by a harness and a trapeze-like bar. The wing is light – usually 22 to 44 kg in weight – so that it can be carried and launched by one person. Take-off is from a hill, cliff or

Gliding experts aim for the 'diamond badge'. To achieve this honour they must achieve a 4000-metre gain in height, fly 500 km or more cross-country, and also fly 300 km or more to a specified goal.

mountain steep enough to achieve flight. While in the air, pilots use their body weight to control the glider.

Goat

Goats are taller, thinner and more agile animals than their close relatives, the SHEEP. Goats have hooves and hollow horns; the male has a beard.

Wild goats, found in the mountains of central Asia and the Middle East, live in herds and eat grass and leaves. Domestic goats are kept in many lands. They provide milk, meat, hair and skins. Two kinds, Angora and Cashmere goats, are famous for their silky wool which is woven into fine cloth.

Gold

This is a lovely yellow metal that never goes rusty. It is so soft that you can beat it into thin sheets, or pull it out into a wire.

People find thin veins of gold in cracks in certain rocks. It was formed long ago by hot gases and liquids rising from deep underground. If water washes out the gold, lumps called nuggets may

Continued on page 302

Alpine ibex

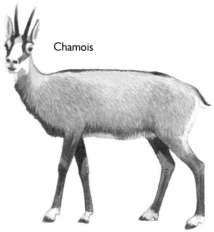

Chamois

▲ *The Alpine ibex is a wild goat that lives above the treeline in Alpine meadows and hillsides. It was hunted almost to extinction and is now protected by law. The chamois is a small mountain goat known for its leaps. Its soft hide is used for polishing.*

◀ *These gold bars in a Swiss bank are checked for purity with a machine that can 'look' inside them by using sound.*

> **The biggest gold nugget ever found weighed about 214 kg. It was discovered in New South Wales, Australia, in 1872. When refined, it yielded about 85 kg of pure gold.**

GLASS

Glass is one of our most useful materials. It is easy to shape and cheap to make. It is also transparent, so you can see through it. Glass can be made as flat sheets, thick castings, or delicate wafers. It can be made into curved lenses for cameras, microscopes and other optical instruments. It can be blown into bottles, or drawn out into tubes, wires and very thin fibres.

Glass is made from mixing and heating sand, limestone and soda ash. When these ingredients melt, they become glass. Special ingredients can be added to make glass that is heat-proof, extra-tough or coloured. Although glass looks like a solid, it is really a 'supercooled' liquid. Glass is a good electrical insulator as it does not conduct current easily. It also resists common chemicals and nuclear radiation.

METHODS OF MAKING GLASS

Blowing   Once done only by hand, glass-blowing is now also done by machines, to make bottles and light bulbs for example.

Pressing   This is done by pushing partly melted glass into a mould, then cooling it. Ovenware and insulators are made by this method.

Drawing   To pull out glass into tubes or wires, molten glass is drawn over a series of pulleys while air is blown through or around it. Drawn glass makes fluorescent tubes and pipes.

Casting   This is done by pouring hot, molten glass into moulds. The big optical telescopes used by astronomers have cast-glass discs.

Rolling   A series of rollers squeeze molten glass into flat sheets (like rolling out pastry).

Floating   This is a method of making sheet glass by floating the molten glass across a bath of molten tin.

▼ *Sparkling crystal glassware has been made in England and Ireland since th*[?] *1700s. Lead is used instead of limestone to give crystal its shine.*

STAINED GLASS

Some of the most magnificent decorative stained glass was made in Europe during the Middle Ages. You can see examples in many churches and cathedrals, especially in Britain, France, Germany and Italy.

The art of making stained glass flourished from the 1100s. By this time glassmakers were able to make glass in many colours, and windows could be made much larger than previously. Artists fitted pieces of coloured glass together with lead, to make beautiful designs for windows. Often medieval stained glass illustrates a Bible story, illuminated by the light streaming through the glass. Modern stained glass artists continue the craft, using similar techniques.

BOTTLE GLASS PRODUCTION

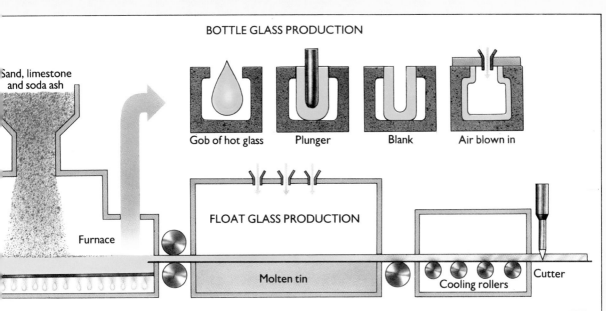

Sand, limestone and soda ash

Furnace

Gob of hot glass

Plunger

Blank

Air blown in

FLOAT GLASS PRODUCTION

Molten tin

Cooling rollers

Cutter

'n glass manufacture, sand, soda ash and limestone are loaded into the
ace, along with 'cullet' – old bits of glass. Molten glass from the furnace
either be moulded and blown into hollow shapes (above), or shaped
flat sheets by the 'float glass' method (below). In the float glass
cess, molten glass is floated on a 'bath' of molten tin and then cooled
cut into lengths.

The edges of float glass are automatically trimmed as it moves over
ers. Glass-blowing (inset) is the traditional way of making glass objects.
bs' of molten glass are placed on the end of a long tube. Blowing down
tube produces a bubble that can be shaped before it cools.

For more information turn to these articles: ARCHITECTURE; BUILDING; CATHEDRAL; LENS; LIGHT; TELESCOPE. Materials used to make glass
also have entries: LEAD; SAND.

GLASS FIBRE

Glass can be drawn out into long threads by
pouring red-hot molten glass through the
bottom of a furnace. One important use for
this thread is in fibre glass. For this, it is
combined with plastic to give an easily
moulded, light and strong substance ideal
for making boat hulls and car bodies.

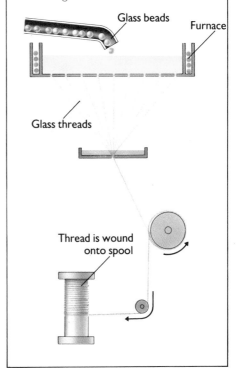

Glass beads

Furnace

Glass threads

Thread is wound
onto spool

▶ *The common aquarium goldfish may be red, gold, yellow or white. The comet is one of the fancy varieties of goldfish.*

▼ *Under Mikhail Gorbachev's leadership the USSR became a more open society.*

collect in the beds of streams and rivers. Half of the world's gold is mined in just one part of South Africa.

Because gold is beautiful and scarce, it is also very valuable. Most of the world's gold is kept in brick-shaped bars (called ingots) in BANKS. People make jewellery from gold mixed with other substances to make it harder. But gold is useful, too. Dentists sometimes put gold fillings in people's teeth.

Goldfish

Goldfish are a type of carp that are usually gold, gold and black, or gold and white in colour. They are easy to keep as pets in tanks or ponds. Goldfish came originally from China. They can grow up to 30 cm long, and may live for 20 years or more.

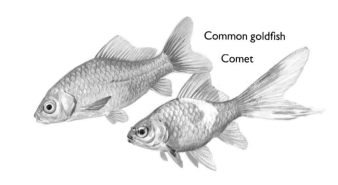

Common goldfish

Comet

Golf

Golf is an old Scottish game that dates from well before the fifteenth century. It is today one of the most popular sports worldwide. The golfer's aim is to hit the small ball from the starting point, or tee, into a small hole in the least number of strokes. A complete game has 18 holes.

Gorbachev, Mikhail

Mikhail Gorbachev became general secretary of the Soviet Communist Party and leader of the SOVIET UNION in March 1985. As leader he tried to reform the Soviet economy and promoted a more open society. He became the first President of the USSR in 1989. Later, he faced growing opposition to his policies and resigned at the end of 1991.

Gorilla

Gorillas are the largest of the APES. A big male may be as tall as a man. Gorillas live in family groups in the warm forests of central Africa. They eat fruit, roots, tree bark and leaves. Every night they make beds of twigs in the low branches of trees.

Government

When people live and work together they need some kind of government. Governments are needed to make laws, control trade and finance, and look after relations with other countries. Most governments fall under two headings: *democratic* forms of government and *totalitarian* forms of government. DEMOCRACY is a system in which the people vote for their leaders and remove them from power if they think the leaders have failed. Totalitarianism is a system in which one person or group has complete control over the people and can't be voted out of office. If one person controls a country, that country is a dictatorship. Hitler and Mussolini were dictators.

There are different kinds of democracies. Great Britain is a monarchy with a king or queen as head of state. The country is, however, governed by

▲ Gorillas live in family groups. The leading male defends the group if danger threatens and takes charge of nest building.

Gorillas in zoos are normally heavier than those in their natural surroundings. It is not unusual for male gorillas in captivity to weigh as much as 260 kg, four times the weight of a man. They can reach a height of 1.8 m. Females are shorter and weigh about half as much as the males.

▲ *The Palace of Westminster in London is the seat of government where both houses of the parliament of the United Kingdom meet.*

FORMS OF GOVERNMENT

System	Ruled by
Anarchy	No rule of law
Aristocracy	Privileged people
Autocracy	One person, absolutely
Bureaucracy	Officials
Democracy	The people
Matriarchy	A mother, or mothers
Meritocracy	The most able
Monarchy	A hereditary king or queen
Patriarchy	A male head of family
Plutocracy	The wealthy

PARLIAMENT. The United States is a republic with a president as head of state. The U.S. government is divided into three branches. Congress makes the laws. The executive, with the president in charge, proposes and enforces the laws. The judicial branch decides which laws are constitutional (agree with the Constitution of the United States).

Grammar

Words must be arranged in special ways to make sentences that are understood. Grammar is the study of the ways in which words are formed and arranged to make sentences.

Words are usually classified as *parts of speech*, according to what they do in a sentence. There are four main kinds of words: VERBS (action words), NOUNS and pronouns (naming words), ADJECTIVES (describing words for nouns or pronouns) and adverbs (describing words for verbs and adjectives). Words can change from one part of speech to another. 'Clean' can be a verb or an adjective. 'Tin' can be a noun or an adjective.

If someone says 'I see the cat', he or she is speaking of something happening now. If they say 'I saw the cat', it happened in the past. The word 'see' changes to 'saw'. Changes like this are called *inflexions*.

The order of words in a sentence is very important. 'The dog bites the girl' means something quite different from 'The girl bites the dog', but exactly the same words are used. It is usual in English for the subject of a sentence – 'dog' in the first example, 'girl' in the second – to come before the verb – 'bites'. Exceptions to this rule are called *idioms* – 'There goes the boy.'

▶ *Every sentence can be broken down into its parts of speech. To be a sentence, it must have a subject (noun) and a verb.*

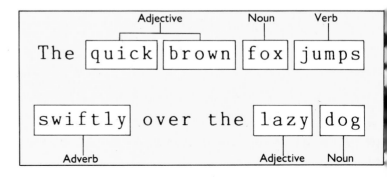

Grand Canyon

The Colorado River carved this deep gash in the Earth's surface. The canyon crosses a desert in Arizona, a state in the west of the United States. The canyon is about 350 km long. It is up to 20 km across, and as much as 2 km deep. This is the deepest gorge anywhere on land.

▲ The layers of rock in the Grand Canyon show the Earth's history over millions of years.

▼ Granite quarried in Scotland was used to build this castle near Fort William. Large blocks of granite for building are often blasted with gunpowder rather than dynamite, as it causes less of an explosion.

Granite

Granite is a hard rock made largely of CRYSTALS of QUARTZ and feldspar. Quartz is transparent, like glass. Feldspar is pink, white or grey. Granite also has specks of dark MINERALS in it.

Granite was once a mass of hot, melted rock underground. As the rock cooled it hardened. Then movements of the Earth's crust forced it up to the surface. The weather very slowly breaks down granite into sand and clay.

Builders use granite when they need a hard, strong stone. People also use granite to make polished stone monuments because they last longer than those made of limestone.

Common reed False oat Meadow foxtail

▲ *Three of the more than 10,000 species of grass. The flowers, and later the grains, are contained in scaly spikelets (inset).*

▼ *A small body, such as this cannonball, orbiting a large one balances its speed against the gravitational pull. The speed in this path is too low, and it falls to the ground (1). When it is fired at a greater speed it is attracted towards the surface at the same rate as the surface curves away, and will go into orbit (2). If its speed is too fast gravity cannot hold it, and it escapes into space (3).*

Grass

Grasses are flowering plants with long, thin, leaves growing from hollow stems. Bamboo is as tall as a tree but most grasses are short. Sheep and cattle eat grass. We eat the seeds of cultivated CEREAL grasses like WHEAT and RICE.

Grasshopper

These insects have feelers, wings, and long back legs. A grasshopper can jump 20 times its own length. Grasshoppers eat leaves, and those called LOCUSTS damage crops. Many males 'sing' by rubbing their back legs on their wings.

Gravity

Gravity is the pull that tries to tug everything towards the middle of the EARTH. It is gravity that makes objects tend to fall, stops us flying off into space, and keeps the MOON circling the Earth. When we weigh something, we are measuring the force with which gravity pulls that object down. The more closely packed the substances in an object are, the heavier it seems.

Not just the Earth, but all PLANETS and STARS exert a pulling force. Scientists call this gravitation. The larger and denser a star or a planet is and the nearer it is to other objects, the more strongly it pulls them towards it. The SUN is far from the planets, but it is so huge that its gravitation keeps

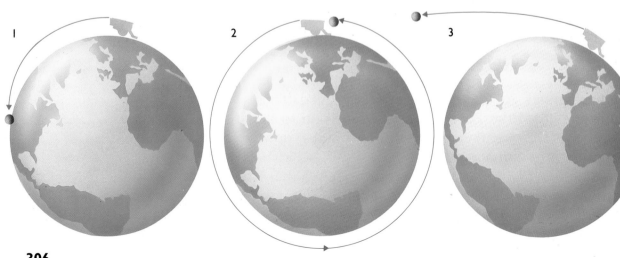

1

2

3

the planets circling around it. The Moon is small and its gravitation is weak. An astronaut on the Moon weighs far less than he weighs on Earth, although his *mass* stays the same.

Great Barrier Reef

This is the longest CORAL reef in the world. It measures about 2000 km from end to end. The reef stands in the sea off the north-east coast of Australia. Most of the top of the reef lies just under water and is a danger to ships. But there are gaps where ships can sail safely through the reef.

The Great Barrier Reef is built of hard limy stone. Most of it was produced by millions of tiny, soft-bodied creatures called coral polyps, related to the SEA ANEMONE. In the 1960s, part of the reef was destroyed by crown-of-thorns starfish. These feed on the little reef builders.

▲ *The Great Barrier Reef is made up of many different kinds of coral and provides protection for a variety of fish.*

Great Britain *See* United Kingdom

Great Lakes

This is the world's largest group of freshwater lakes. They are larger than the whole of Great Britain. Lake Michigan lies in the UNITED STATES. Lakes Superior, Erie, Huron and Ontario are shared by the United States and CANADA. The largest lake of all is Superior. The lakes were formed when a huge sheet of ice melted 18,000 years ago.

Eight states of the United States touch the Great Lakes. These eight states make more than half of the country's manufactured goods. Two-thirds of Canada's population and most of its factories lie on the Great Lakes or on the St Lawrence River. A ship can go from the Atlantic up the St Lawrence River and through the lakes to the western end of Lake Superior, halfway across the continent of North America.

◀ *Lakes Erie and Ontario are at two different levels, linked by the 50-metre Niagara Falls and the Niagara River. Ships avoid this route by using the Welland Canal.*

307

▲ *The sun-baked buildings of this town on the Greek island of Santorini, also known as Thera, perch on the remains of an exploded volcano.*

Rivers and canals connect the lakes to each other and to the Atlantic Ocean. Ships can reach the sea from lake ports that lie 1600 km inland. Lots of factories are built around the lakes. Most of the goods that the factories produce are taken to other parts of the country by boat.

Great Wall of China

More than 2000 years ago the first emperor of CHINA, Shih Huang Ti, built this wall to keep out China's enemies from the north. The Great Wall is the longest wall in the world. It stretches for 2400 km from western China to the Yellow Sea.

The wall is made from earth and stone. Watchtowers were built every 200 metres along it. Chinese sentries sent warning signals from the towers if anyone attacked the wall. The signal was smoke by day and a fire at night.

Greece

Greece is a country that lies in south-east EUROPE. Mountains cover most of the land, and peninsulas poke out into the sea like giant fingers. Greece includes the island of Crete and many smaller islands in the Aegean and Ionian seas. Greek summers are hot and dry. Winters are mild and wet.

About ten million people live in Greece. Many work in the capital city, ATHENS. Greek farmers produce crops of lemons, grapes, wheat and olives. Millions of tourists visit Greece every year.

Greece, Ancient

The first great people in Greece were the Minoans and the Mycenaeans. The Minoans lived in Crete. They had rich cities and farms and led a peaceful life. The Mycenaeans lived on the mainland of Greece. They were warriors and sailors. The heroes of HOMER's poems were probably Mycenaean. Both these civilizations ended in about 1200 BC.

Around this time, new groups of people began to move into Greece. They came from the north, but spoke Greek. Instead of making Greece one king-

GREECE

Government: Presidential parliamentary republic
Capital: Athens
Area: 131,944 sq km
Population: 10,141,000
Language: Greek
Currency: Drachma

dom, they built separate cities. They often fought wars with each other. Sometimes they joined together to fight enemies, such as the Persians. Two of the strongest cities were Athens and Sparta. In the 400s BC Athens was ruled by a *democracy*. It became very powerful.

The Greeks loved the theatre, art and poetry. They had many great thinkers, or *philosophers*, including ARISTOTLE, PLATO and Socrates. Greek cities had many graceful buildings. They were decorated with beautiful SCULPTURE. The Greeks also started the first OLYMPIC GAMES. In 339 BC Greece was conquered by Philip, the father of ALEXANDER THE GREAT.

▲ The marketplace, or agora, of a Greek town was an open area surrounded by temples and public buildings. Storage jars such as the one at the top of the picture were often decorated with figures or scenes.

GREEK GODS	
God	*Title*
Apollo	God of the Sun
Artemis	Goddess of the Moon and Hunting
Athena	Goddess of Wisdom
Demeter	Goddess of Agriculture
Dionysus	God of Wine
Eros	God of Love
Hades, Pluto	God of the Underworld
Hera	Goddess of Marriage
Hermes	Messenger of the Gods
Hestia	Goddess of the Hearth
Hephaestus	God of Fire
Poseidon	God of the Sea and Waters
Zeus	Leader of the Gods

Greek Mythology

The ancient Greeks, like all peoples who lived thousands of years ago, invented gods and goddesses to explain the world around them. Stories about these *deities* are called *myths*. In Greek mythology, many of the gods lived on Mount Olympus. There they ate a special food called *ambrosia* and drank *nectar* to make them immortal. The greatest god was Zeus. When he was angry he made thunder. Zeus had many children. One, Athena, was the goddess of wisdom. The city of Athens is named after her. Another, Apollo, was the sun god. He drove the sun's chariot across the sky each day.

▶ *Fishing boats lie at anchor in the coastal town of Jakobshavn in Greenland. Fishing and processing fish are Greenland's chief activities.*

GREENLAND

Government: Part of Denmark, but with home rule
Capital: Godthaab (Nuuk)
Area: 2,175,600 sq km
Average ice depth: 1500 m
Highest point: Gunnbjornsfjaeld, 3700 m
Official name of Greenland: Kalaallit Nunaat
Population: 56,000

Greenland

Greenland is the world's largest island. VIKINGS discovered it nearly 1000 years ago. It lies north-east of Canada, but belongs to DENMARK, a small European country. Since 1979 Greenland has enjoyed home rule. It is 50 times the size of Denmark, but it holds no more people than a large town. This is because Greenland is so cold. Most of it lies in the ARCTIC. Thick ice covers seven-eighths of the island. Bare mountains make up much of the rest. The capital is Godthaab.

Most Greenlanders live in villages of wooden houses near the coast. Some are Danes, many are ESKIMOS. A few Eskimos hunt seals, but many Greenlanders are fishermen.

Grenada

Grenada is one of the smallest nations in the western hemisphere. It is a group of small islands in the south Caribbean Sea with a total area of 344 square km. Grenada was a British colony until 1958 and gained full independence within the Commonwealth in 1974. The capital is St George's.

Guam

Guam is the largest of the Marianas Islands in the Pacific Ocean. It has a tropical climate with heavy seasonal rainfall. The country depends largely on income from U.S. military installations. Guam became United States territory after the Spanish-American War. The people have U.S. citizenship but are self-governing.

Guatemala

More people live in Guatemala than in any other Central American country. Nearly half of them are Indians, descendants of the MAYAS. Guatemala is a land of dense jungles, volcanoes, dry deserts and sparkling lakes. It is about half the size of the

GRENADA

Government: Constitutional monarchy
Capital: St George's
Area: 344 sq km
Population: 98,000
Language: English
Currency: East Caribbean dollar

GUAM

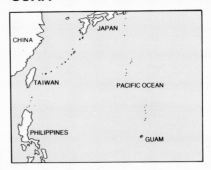

Government: Self-governing US territory
Capital: Agana
Area: 541 sq km
Population: 119,000
Language: English
Currency: Dollar

◀ *This magnificent temple at Tikal in Guatemala was once part of the Mayan Empire, a civilization dating back to the AD 100s.*

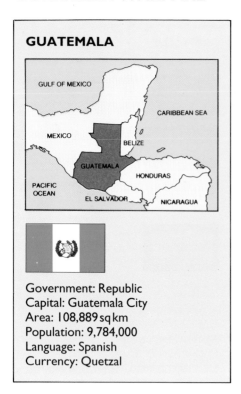

GUATEMALA

Government: Republic
Capital: Guatemala City
Area: 108,889 sq km
Population: 9,784,000
Language: Spanish
Currency: Quetzal

United Kingdom. Most of the people earn their living by farming – coffee, cotton and bananas being the main products. The country was conquered by the Spanish in 1524, declared its independence in 1821 and became a republic in 1839. The capital is Guatemala City.

Guerrilla Warfare

Guerrillas are 'hit and run' fighters. Often they do not wear regular uniforms and live in the country-side, relying on help from friendly local people. The word 'guerrilla' is Spanish for 'little war'. Guerrilla tactics are most often used by small groups of people who are fighting against a larger and more organized force. Guerrillas usually live in places where they can easily hide, such as forests or mountains. Urban guerrillas operate in cities and towns.

Guided Missile

A guided missile is usually a rocket-powered missile armed with an explosive warhead. The missile is guided to its target by radio or radar commands from Earth or by a device inside the missile. A *ballistic missile* follows a path that is partly outside

▼ *A radar system may track both the missile and its target. A computer reads the radar signals and controls the missile's guidance system to guide it to the target by radio.*

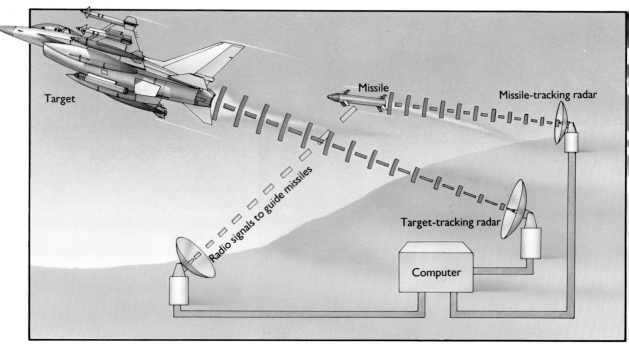

the Earth's atmosphere. It is guided as it goes up, but when its rocket engine burns out, it returns to Earth in an unguided path. The only defence against a ballistic missile is to fire another missile at the incoming missile so as to destroy it before it hits its target. Such defensive missiles are called *anti-ballistic missiles*. However, modern missiles are armed with warheads that split up into several separate nuclear warheads as they descend. This makes defence much more difficult.

Guinea

Guinea is a country on the western coast of Africa. It is the same size as the United Kingdom and has just under six million people. Some of the world's largest deposits of bauxite are in Guinea. Bauxite is the ore from which aluminium is made. The capital is Conakry.

Guinea-Bissau

The small country of Guinea-Bissau is on the west coast of Africa. The 1,000,000 people who live there earn their living by farming. The main crops are peanuts, coconuts and rice. Guinea-Bissau gained its independence from the Portuguese in 1974. The capital is Bissau.

Guinea Pig and Hamster

The guinea pig is a RODENT, not a pig, and it comes from Peru, not Guinea. It is also called a cavy. Guinea pigs are up to 29 cm long, and have no tail. They may be brown, white, black, grey or a mixture. Some have long, silky hair, or hair that

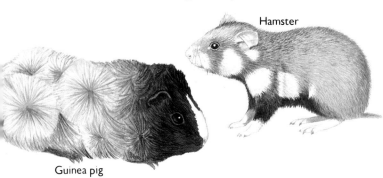

Hamster

Guinea pig

GUINEA

Government: Republic
Capital: Conakry
Area: 245,857 sq km
Population: 7,783,000
Language: French
Currency: Syli

GUINEA-BISSAU

Government: Republic
Capital: Bissau
Area: 36,125 sq km
Population: 1,074,000
Language: Portuguese
Currency: Escudo

◄ *The tame guinea pig is descended from the grizzled brown cavy of the Andes. Hamsters' nearest relatives are gerbils and voles.*

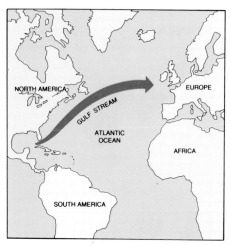

▲ East of Newfoundland the Gulf Stream is more correctly known as the North Atlantic Drift.

▼ Despite its name, the common gull is not the most numerous gull. The herring gull and the black-headed gull are often seen inland, but the larger glaucous gull is found only on coasts and in harbours.

forms rosettes. Scientists use guinea pigs in experiments and many people keep guinea pigs as pets. They eat grass and hay and need a dry cage with clean bedding on the floor.

Hamsters are smaller than guinea pigs and have short tails. They have big pouches in their cheeks where they store food. Most hamsters are light brown on top and white or black underneath.

Gulf Stream

This ocean current is like a giant river flowing through the sea. It carries warm water from the Gulf of Mexico northwards along the eastern coast of the United States. The Gulf Stream is up to 60 km wide and 600 metres deep. The current divides. One branch crosses the ATLANTIC OCEAN and brings warm water to north-western Europe. If it were not for the Gulf Stream, winters in countries from France and Britain to Norway would be much more severe.

Gull

Few birds are more graceful than gulls gliding and soaring over the sea. They have webbed feet and swim well, but most do not stray far from land. They can catch fish, but also eat food scraps washed up on the shore.

Gulls breed in noisy crowds called colonies. Their nests are built on the ground. Many gull colonies live on islands. This helps to keep their eggs safe from rats and foxes.

Herring gull

Glaucous gull

Common gull

Black-headed gull

This breech-loading cannon of the 1400s fired solid balls which could knock down the thickest castle walls.

▼ The Gatling gun was the first successful machine gun. Invented in 1861 and used during the American Civil War, it had up to 10 barrels rotated by a hand crank.

Gun

Guns are weapons that fire bullets or other missiles from a tube open at one end.

Guns were probably invented in the 1200s. By the 1300s guns were firing missiles that could pierce armour and break down castle walls.

Early guns were large weapons, far too heavy for one man to carry. The first gun was a big bucket with a small hole in the bottom. Soldiers put gunpowder into the bucket. Then they piled stones on top. They lit the gunpowder through the hole. When the gunpowder exploded, the stones flew out. The large, long guns called cannons were first used about 1350. Cannons fired big metal cannonballs. In the 1800s came guns which fired pointed shells that exploded when they hit their target. A spiral groove cut in the gun barrel made the shells spin as they flew through the air. Soldiers could fire such shells farther and hit their targets more often than with cannonballs.

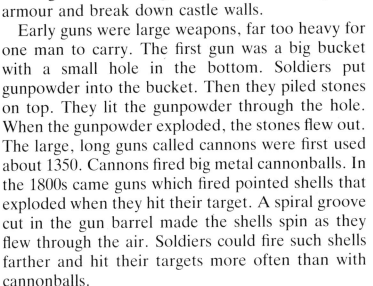

Foresight   Return spring   Firing pin Rear sight

Hammer

Barrel   9-mm cartridge

Trigger guard

Trigger

Butt

Magazine

▲ This modern anti-aircraft gun can destroy attacking aircraft from the ground.

◄ This cutaway view of a Browning self-loading pistol of 1968 shows the pistol when loaded.

▲ *Johannes Gutenberg inspects a printed sheet that has just come off his new press. Despite the importance of his achievement, he never made much money from it.*

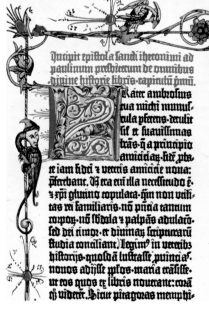

▲ *One of Gutenberg's first books was a Bible printed in Latin in 1455.*

Troops first used small arms in the 1300s. Small arms are guns that one man can carry. Inventors developed short-barrelled pistols and revolvers for firing at nearby targets. They developed muskets, rifles and machine guns for long-distance shooting. In modern guns a hammer sets off an explosion that drives a shell or bullet from the barrel.

Gutenberg, Johannes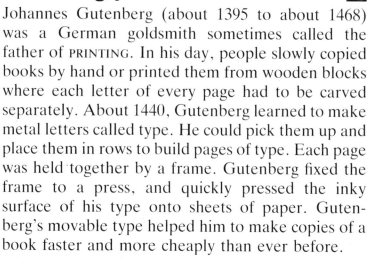

Johannes Gutenberg (about 1395 to about 1468) was a German goldsmith sometimes called the father of PRINTING. In his day, people slowly copied books by hand or printed them from wooden blocks where each letter of every page had to be carved separately. About 1440, Gutenberg learned to make metal letters called type. He could pick them up and place them in rows to build pages of type. Each page was held together by a frame. Gutenberg fixed the frame to a press, and quickly pressed the inky surface of his type onto sheets of paper. Gutenberg's movable type helped him to make copies of a book faster and more cheaply than ever before.

Guyana

Guyana is a hot, rainy country on the north-eastern coast of South America. Most of the people live along the coast in a narrow strip of flat land about 20 km wide. Sugar cane and rice are grown here. Valuable minerals, including gold and diamonds, are found in the hilly region inland. Guyana produces bauxite to make aluminium.

Guyana was once a British colony. It is the only country in South America that has English as its official language. The colony became independent in 1966 and a republic in 1970. The capital is Georgetown.

GUYANA

Government: Republic within the
Commonwealth
Capital: Georgetown
Area: 214,969 sq km
Population: 754,000
Language: English
Currency: Guyanese dollar

Gymnastics

Gymnastics are exercises that help to make and keep the body fit. The OLYMPIC GAMES have separate gymnastic exercises for men and women. Women perform graceful steps, runs, jumps, turns and somersaults on a narrow wooden beam. They hang from a high bar and swing to and fro between

▼ *Modern competitive gymnastics developed from German and Swedish systems of exercise.*

Asymmetrical bars

Rings

Parallel bars

Beam

Pommel horse

Floor

Vault

Modern gymnastics grew considerably in popularity because of the performance of tiny Olga Korbut of the Soviet Union in the 1972 Olympics. The widespread television coverage of her dramatic performance increased interest in the sport almost overnight.

it and a lower one. They leap over a vaulting horse. Women also perform floor exercises to music.

Men hang from a high bar and from rings, swinging up and down, to and fro, and over and over in giant circles. Using two parallel bars, they swing, vault, and do handstands. They grip hoops that jut up from a leather-covered pommel 'horse', and swing their legs and body. They leap over a vaulting horse. Simpler exercises are done by children and adults in gymnastics classes.

▶ *The traditional, brightly-painted gypsy caravan is now a rarity. Most travelling gypsies live in modern caravans.*

▼ *This spinning toy gyroscope is tilted, yet it balances on the tip of a pencil. It seems to defy gravity. As it slows down it will wobble and fall.*

Gypsy

Gypsies are a group of people found all over the world. Some speak a language called Romany, although nowadays most gypsies fit into the culture of the people around them. Some live in houses, others travel all the time and live in caravans. Gypsies like to earn an independent living, perhaps by trading goods or selling arts and crafts.

The name 'gypsy' comes from the word Egyptian. It was once thought gypsies came from Egypt, but they probably came from India 600 years ago.

Gyroscope

A gyroscope is a wheel that spins in a special frame. No matter how the frame tilts, the wheel's axle points in the same direction. Even GRAVITY and the Earth's MAGNETISM do not affect the axle.

On a ship or aircraft, a COMPASS made from a gyroscope always points north. Gyroscopes can also keep an aircraft on course without the pilot steering.

Hail *See* Rain and Snow

Hair

Hair grows like living threads from the skins of MAMMALS. It has the same ingredients that make nails, claws, hooves, feathers, and reptiles' scales. Hair helps to keep the body warm, and protects the skin. There are several kinds of hair. Cats have plenty of soft, thick fur. Porcupines are protected by sharp, stiff hairs called quills.

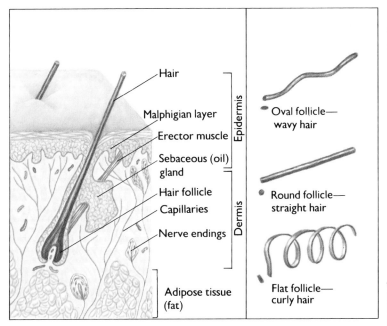

◄ Each hair root is enclosed in its own follicle, which has a blood supply, a tiny erector muscle and a gland. The type of hair you have depends partly on the shape of your hair follicles.

Haiti

Haiti is a small country in the western part of the island of Hispaniola in the West Indies. Much of the country is covered by rugged mountains, but there are fertile valleys and coastal plains where coffee and other crops are grown. Nine-tenths of the people are descended from African slaves.

A French colony from 1677, Haiti became independent in 1804, following a rebellion. Dr François Duvalier became president in 1957. Upon his death in 1971 he was succeeded by his son Jean-Claude. This family dictatorship came to an end in 1986 when Jean-Claude was forced to flee the country. Political unrest continues.

HAITI

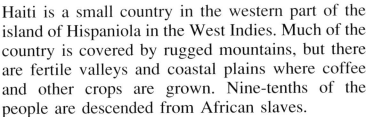

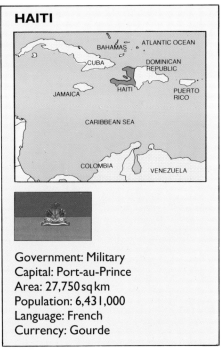

Government: Military
Capital: Port-au-Prince
Area: 27,750 sq km
Population: 6,431,000
Language: French
Currency: Gourde

▶ *When Halley's Comet passed near the Earth in 1985, its nucleus was discovered to be a peanut-shaped mixture of rock, dust and ice about 2 km long. Each return to the Sun leaves the nucleus with a smaller store of ice and dust, and eventually the comet will 'die'.*

Edmond Halley was a friend of Isaac Newton, the great scientist. He encouraged Newton and helped him with money to publish his most famous work, *Mathematical Principles of Natural Philosophy*.

Halley, Edmond

Edmond Halley (1657–1742) was an English astronomer who is best known for his study of comets. In 1676, at the age of 20, he went to the island of St Helena to catalogue the stars of the Southern Hemisphere, something that had never been done before. He became interested in comets and noticed that the path followed by a comet he had seen in 1682 was very much like those reported in 1607 and 1531. He decided that these sightings must be of the same comet and predicted that it would return in 1758. On Christmas Day, 1758, it did, and Halley's Comet reappears regularly every 76 years.

Handel, George Frideric

George Frideric Handel (1685–1759) was a German-born British composer, famous for the oratorio *Messiah* and the orchestral *Fireworks Music* and *Water Music*. He wrote about 21 oratorios and a number of operas.

Hannibal

Hannibal (247–183 BC) was a Carthaginian general who invaded Italy. In 218 BC he left Spain and marched an army over the Alps into Italy. The army included many elephants, brought along to carry equipment. Hannibal won a number of battles. But though he fought the Romans for 15 years he never managed to conquer them. In the end he killed himself.

▲ *Handel was born in Germany but made England his home. He became a British subject in 1726.*

Hapsburgs

Many of Europe's kings and emperors belonged to this royal family. Its name comes from a Swiss castle called *Habichtsburg* ('hawk's castle'). This was built in 1020 by a German bishop. The owners of the castle became the counts of Hapsburg.

In 1273 Count Rudolf was chosen to be the Holy Roman Emperor. In name he ruled Germany and other lands. Rudolf seized Austria. Later, most Holy Roman Emperors were Hapsburgs. Hapsburgs married foreign princesses and so increased their power by gaining countries their wives inherited. By the 1500s the Hapsburgs ruled much of Europe, from Spain to Hungary. Then they began losing power by wars and revolts. NAPOLEON ended the Holy Roman Empire in 1806, and WORLD WAR I finally smashed the Hapsburgs' Austro-Hungarian Empire.

Hare

Hares look like large RABBITS with very long ears and long legs. They live in wide open fields and do not burrow. By day they just crouch in a dip in the ground. At night they come out to eat grass and other plants.

Keen eyes and ears warn hares if danger comes near. But they keep still until they are seen. Then they bound away at up to 70 km an hour.

Unlike rabbits, young hares are born with fur and eyes that can open. They are called leverets.

▲ *Philip II of Spain was the Hapsburg king who sent the armada to attack England in 1588.*

▼ *Brown hares live in fields and meadows and are known for their leaping, chasing and boxing. The mountain hare has a brown summer coat that turns white in winter.*

Brown hare

summer coat

Mountain hare

winter coat

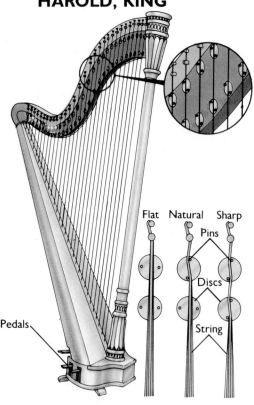

Flat Natural Sharp

Pins

Discs

String

Pedals

▲ *To change the pitch of a string on the harp, pedals turn small discs with pins that grip the string, thus shortening or lengthening them to produce flat or sharp notes.*

Harold, King

Harold II (about 1022–1066) was the last of the ANGLO-SAXONS to rule England. In 1053 he became Earl of Wessex. In 1064 he was shipwrecked off France and caught by his cousin William of Normandy (WILLIAM THE CONQUEROR). Harold was freed when he promised to help William become king of England. But the English nobles chose Harold as king. He died at the Battle of HASTINGS, where William's Norman invaders defeated the English.

Harp

The harp is the oldest of all stringed instruments. The early harp was little more than a bow with strings of different lengths stretched across it. Harps have been played in Wales and Ireland for many centuries. The modern harp has a wooden frame with strings attached between the hollow sounding board and the top of the instrument. There are seven foot pedals that can change the pitch of the strings. The harpist sits with the sounding board between his or her legs and plucks the strings with fingers and thumbs.

In the late 1920s, an archaeologist in Iraq dug down into royal graves 4500 years old. His finds included two mysterious holes in the ground. He poured liquid plaster into the holes, let it set, and then removed the soil. His plaster cast was of one of the oldest known harps. Its wooden frame had rotted away, but its fine gold fittings still survived.

▶ *Harpsichords make a rich sound, but it cannot be made loud or soft as easily as the sound from a piano. So when pianos were invented, harpsichords were forgotten for more than a century.*

Harpsichord

A harpsichord looks rather like a HARP laid on its side and put in a box on legs. The first successful ones date from the 1500s. A harpsichord player plays a keyboard like a PIANO's. Each key lifts a piece of wood called a jack. A quill or a bit of leather fixed to the jack plucks a string.

Harvey, William

William Harvey (1578–1657) was an English doctor who showed that BLOOD flows around the body in an endless stream. Harvey proved that a beating heart squeezes blood through arteries and flaps in the heart, and that blood returns to the heart through veins. He worked out that the amount of blood pumped by a heart in an hour weighs three times more than a man.

Much of what we know about William the Conqueror's invasion and the Battle of Hastings comes from the Bayeux Tapestry. It is this tapestry that seems to show Harold being killed in the battle when an arrow pierces his eye. Many historians now think that the soldier with the arrow in his eye is not Harold. A French account of the battle written in 1068 says that Harold was attacked by four French knights. One of them pierced Harold with his lance, while another 'hacked off his leg and hurled it far away'!

Hastings, Battle of

In 1066 this battle made Norman invaders the masters of England.

WILLIAM THE CONQUEROR sailed with 7000 Norman troops and some war horses from France to

▼ The English, armed with spears, slings and battle axes, fought fiercely against the heavily armoured Norman cavalry, but the Normans eventually wore them down.

▲ The red-shouldered hawk is common in the south-east of the United States. It hunts for rodents, insects and small birds.

▼ The goshawk is widely used in falconry as it is strong enough to catch game birds and rabbits.

England in about 450 open boats. Meanwhile, the English (ANGLO-SAXONS) under King HAROLD were defeating Norse invaders in northern England.

Harold quickly marched south. He fought William at Senlac near Hastings. The Anglo-Saxons defended a hilltop with axes, spears, swords and shields. The Normans attacked with arrows, lances, spiked clubs and swords. The battle lasted all day. Then the Normans pretended to run away. When some Anglo-Saxons followed, Norman cavalry cut them down. Then the Normans showered arrows on the rest and attacked once more. By evening, Harold was dead and his army was beaten.

By 1071, William the Conqueror had subdued all of England. Since then, no foreign army has landed and won a battle on English soil.

Hawk

Hawks are birds of prey in the same family as the VULTURES and all EAGLE species. Hawks are not as large as these relatives. Many look rather like FALCONS but have broader wings with more rounded ends. Broad wings and a long tail help a hawk to fly fast and nimbly through trees. Hawks hunt birds and small mammals.

They live all over the world except on Pacific islands and in and near Australia.

Haydn, Franz Joseph

Franz Joseph Haydn (1732–1809) was an Austrian composer known as the 'father of the symphony'. He wrote 104 symphonies. Many of them used the ORCHESTRA in a powerful new way. He also wrote fine pieces for the piano and quartets for four stringed instruments. MOZART and BEETHOVEN both studied Haydn's music. Later, this helped them compose some of their most splendid music.

Health

Good health is one of the most important things in life. It is something that allows a person to lead a happy, useful and successful life. There are certain rules which help us to stay healthy.

We should eat a balanced diet of the right kinds of FOOD, and drink plenty of water. All foods are fattening if we eat too much of them, but this applies especially to starchy foods, fats and sweets.

We should take regular EXERCISE, if possible in the open air, and get enough sleep. The number of hours' sleep we need depends on our age. Young babies sleep from 20 to 22 hours each day; older people only need between 6 and 7 hours.

We should keep ourselves clean. Regular washing is important, especially the hands after we have

▲ Haydn visited England and his music was played at many important concerts. In 1791 he received the degree of Honorary Doctor of Music at Oxford University.

▼ Plenty of exercise and eating a balanced diet are essential to make a healthy body, while getting enough sleep and maintaining good standards of cleanliness will ensure that you stay strong and well.

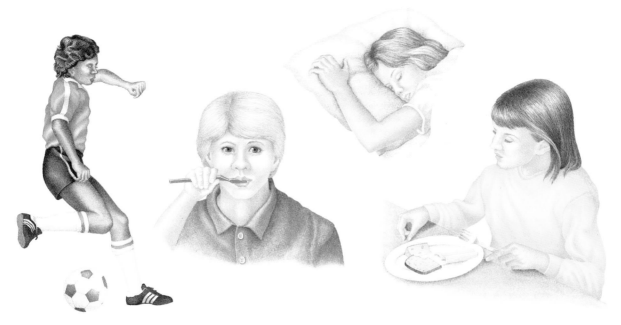

VIBRATIONS PER SECOND

10,000   Frog

20,000   Man

35,000   Dog

100,000   Bat

▲ *The range of vibrations that can be heard varies in different animals. In humans the range is from about 20 to 20,000 cycles per second. A bat and a dog can hear high-frequency sounds that the human ear cannot detect. The frog cannot hear high-pitched sounds.*

▶ *Your heart is about the same size as your clenched fist and is made of strong cardiac muscle. It constantly pumps blood around your body, so that each cell gets the food and oxygen it needs. The areas shown in red in the illustration indicate where oxygen-rich blood travels. The areas shown in blue show where blood low in oxygen travels back to the lungs. The atria (plural of atrium) collect the blood flowing into the heart. The ventricles are strong muscles that pump blood into the arteries.*

been to the lavatory. Teeth, of course, should be brushed night and morning.

Good health is a priceless treasure. It is worth trying to keep it.

Hearing

Hearing is the sense that allows us to pick up SOUND. The sense organ making this possible is the EAR. Some people cannot hear; they are *deaf*. Either they were born without hearing or, at some time, their ears became damaged by an illness or accident. Deaf people can 'talk' by using a special sign language.

Like people, all animals with backbones have hearing organs. Some can hear much better than people. CATS and DOGS, for example, pick up more sounds than we can. BATS hunt by sound, listening for echoes bounced back off flying insects.

Heart

The heart is a muscle in the body. It pumps BLOOD around the body through VEINS and ARTERIES. In an adult person, the heart goes on working at between

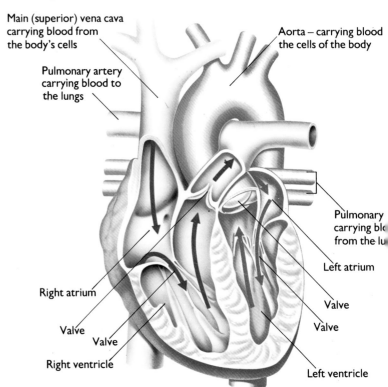

Main (superior) vena cava carrying blood from the body's cells

Aorta – carrying blood the cells of the body

Pulmonary artery carrying blood to the lungs

Pulmonary carrying bl from the lu

Left atrium

Right atrium

Valve

Valve

Valve

Valve

Right ventricle

Left ventricle

70 and 80 beats a minute until death. It was the English doctor William HARVEY (1578–1657) who discovered how the heart works.

The blood carries OXYGEN from the LUNGS and energy from the food we eat. Arteries carry this rich red blood to feed the body. Veins carry away waste products and return the dark 'tired' blood to the heart to be 'recharged' with oxygen from the lungs.

When the heart stops beating, the body is starved of oxygen and quickly dies. But doctors can sometimes massage a stopped heart back to life. People with diseased hearts can be given 'spare parts' to repair them and even a new heart, transplanted from someone who has just died.

Heat

Heat is a form of ENERGY. We can feel it but we cannot see it. We feel heat from the SUN, or when we sit in front of a fire. When something burns, heat is produced. The Sun gives out enormous amounts of heat, which is produced by atoms joining together or 'fusing' inside the Sun. This same kind of energy can be released by a hydrogen bomb on Earth. It is because we get just the right amount of

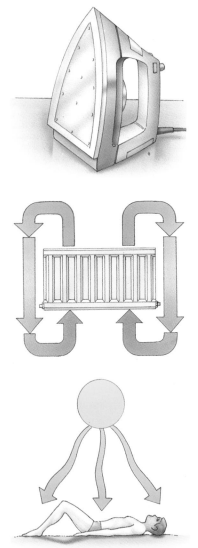

▲ Heat travels in three ways – by conduction, convection and radiation. A conductor, such as a metal iron, allows heat to pass through it. When heat is carried from a radiator by convection, molecules in the air move, taking the heat with them. Heat from the Sun travels by radiation in the form of electromagnetic waves.

◀ The energy in heat can be used in many different ways. This picture shows a solar-powered car which converts the Sun's energy and uses it to drive along.

We need fuel to keep our body warm. This fuel is the food we eat. The human body contains a surprising amount of heat. It gives out about 100 calories of heat an hour. This is about the same as a 120-watt electric bulb. You can see, therefore, why it can become quite hot if a lot of people are gathered in a room!

heat from the Sun that our Earth and ourselves are what they are. A few degrees less heat from the Sun and our world would be a lifeless waste. A few degrees more heat and life could not exist.

Most of the heat we use comes from burning fuels. But heat can also be made by FRICTION, or rubbing. Heat is also produced when electricity travels through a coil of wire. This is what makes the coils inside a toaster glow red.

We can measure how hot a thing is by finding its temperature. This is done with a THERMOMETER. When a substance gets hot, the molecules, or tiny particles, of which it is made move around more quickly. Often the substance expands (gets bigger) as this happens. Metals expand the most when they are heated.

Hebrews

In the early days of their history, the Jewish people were known as the Hebrews or Israelites. There were 12 tribes, descended from Abraham. The greatest Hebrew leader was Moses, who led his people out of slavery in Egypt to the Promised Land of Canaan. Hebrew is the national language of modern Israel.

Hedgehog

Like the PORCUPINE, the hedgehog has a coat of spines to protect it. When frightened, it curls up into a prickly ball.

▼ Hedgehogs need to fatten themselves up if they are to survive their period of hibernation in the winter. You can help by leaving a little dog or cat food out for them in autumn. Also, check inside any winter bonfires before you light them – hedgehogs often choose them as a place to sleep.

Hedgehogs amble along ditches and hedgerows, snuffling for snails, slugs, worms and insects to eat. They will often visit gardens, and drink milk if it is left out for them. During the winter hedgehogs HIBERNATE.

Helen of Troy

Helen of Troy was said by the ancient Greeks to be the most beautiful woman in the world. She was the wife of Menelaus, King of Sparta, but ran away with Paris, Prince of Troy. Menelaus followed with a great army, and so began the TROJAN WAR. The story is told by the poet HOMER.

▲ King Menelaus of Sparta with his wife, Helen of Troy. The war that started because of her went on for ten years, according to the story told by Homer.

Helicopter

The helicopter is an unusual and useful aircraft. It was invented in the 1930s and today is used for all kinds of jobs, especially sea- and mountain- rescue. This is because helicopters can take off and land vertically and can therefore work in areas too small for ordinary aircraft. Helicopters can fly in any direction and hover in mid-air. Instead of fixed wings they have a moving wing called a rotor which acts as a wing and a propeller. The pilot controls the craft by changing the angle, or 'pitch', at which the blades of the rotor go through the air. A smaller rotor on the tail keeps the helicopter from spinning around. Helicopters are also used for carrying passengers over short distances and for transporting troops to remote areas.

▼ The UH-1 Iroquois was used by the United States army in the Vietnam war. A similar type is still being made today. The Ka-26 Kamov Hoodlum is mainly used for farming purposes, although it is also used as an air ambulance. It has two sets of main rotors rotating in opposite directions.

Ka-26 Hoodlum

UH-1 Iroquois

▲ Henry VIII came to the throne in 1509, when he was only 17 years old. When young he was handsome, slim and athletic.

▼ Henry VI was a quiet and religious king, very different from his strong-willed wife, Margaret of Anjou. The Wars of the Roses were fought during his reign.

Henry (kings)

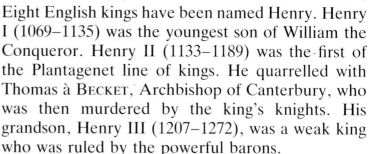

Eight English kings have been named Henry. Henry I (1069–1135) was the youngest son of William the Conqueror. Henry II (1133–1189) was the first of the Plantagenet line of kings. He quarrelled with Thomas à BECKET, Archbishop of Canterbury, who was then murdered by the king's knights. His grandson, Henry III (1207–1272), was a weak king who was ruled by the powerful barons.

During the Wars of the Roses, the families of York and Lancaster fought for the English throne. Three Lancastrian kings were called Henry: Henry IV, or Henry Bolingbroke (1367–1413), Henry V (1387–1422), and Henry VI (1421–1471). Henry V was a brilliant soldier. He is famous for leading his army to victory against the French at the battle of Agincourt.

The first Tudor king was Henry VII (1457–1509), who restored peace. His son, Henry VIII (1491–1547), was clever and popular, but also ruthless. He was married six times and broke away from the Roman Catholic Church to divorce his first wife, Catherine of Aragon. Three of his children reigned after him: EDWARD VI, MARY I and ELIZABETH I.

◀ *These simple designs found on old heraldic shields are called* charges *or* ordinaries. *The designs of many modern flags are based on these shapes.*

Heraldry

In the MIDDLE AGES, a knight in full ARMOUR was hard to recognize, for his face was hidden by his helmet. So knights began to use special designs worn on their surcoats and shields. These designs became special family emblems which no-one else could wear. They were called coats-of-arms.

Heralds were officials who kept records of coats-of-arms and awarded new ones. The College of Heralds in London still does this. There are special names for the colours and patterns used in heraldry.

Herb

Herbs are plants with soft, rather than woody, stems. But the name herbs is also given to certain plants which are added to food during cooking. They are valued for their scent and flavour. A common herb is mint, which is made into mint sauce and served with roast lamb.

Other herbs used in cooking include sage, thyme, parsley, garlic, chervil, rosemary, basil, fennel and

SEE IT YOURSELF

You can preserve herbs by drying them. Spread them out in an airing cupboard for 3 to 5 days. Place them in a sieve over a sheet of clean paper and rub the herbs through the sieve with the flat of your hand. Throw away the stalks and tip the rubbed herbs back into the sieve. Do this until there are no more stalks. Store your dried herbs out of direct light in sealed glass jars.

▼ *These herbs are easy to grow and make attractive garden plants as well as being useful in cooking.*

Tarragon

Rosemary

Sweet marjoram

▲ Slaying the Hydra was the second of the twelve labours of Hercules. As soon as Hercules cut off one of its heads, two more grew in its place.

chives. Most can be grown quite easily, although they came originally from the warm, sunny lands of the Mediterranean region.

Herbs can be used fresh from the garden or they can be cut and dried for storage. People have grown and used herbs for hundreds of years. In the days before modern medicine, herbs were used to treat many illnesses. Even today some herbs are still used in this way.

Hercules

Hercules was a famous hero of ancient stories told by the Greeks and Romans. He was the son of the god Jupiter and a mortal princess. He was amazingly strong. As a baby he strangled two snakes, sent by Jupiter's jealous wife to kill him.

Later, Hercules went mad and killed his wife and children. To make amends, he had to perform twelve tasks, or labours. These included killing the Nemean lion and the many-headed Hydra; and washing clean the stables of King Augeas, where 3000 oxen lived. In the end, Hercules was killed when he put on a poisoned shirt.

Heredity *See* Genetics

Hibernation

When an animal hibernates, it goes to sleep for the winter. It does this because in winter food is scarce. Going to sleep during the cold weather saves certain animals from starving to death.

Before hibernating, animals eat as much food as they can find. The dormouse, for example, stuffs itself until it is fat and round. As autumn approaches, it makes a snug nest, curls into a ball, and falls into a sound sleep. In fact, its heart beats so slowly, the dormouse looks dead. Its body uses hardly any energy while in hibernation, in order to make its store of fat last as long as possible. In spring, a thin and hungry dormouse wakes up and comes out of its nest to look for food.

In cold countries many animals hibernate. Not all

A hibernating marmot may slow down its breathing from 16 to 2 breaths a minute, and its heartbeats from 88 to 15 per minute. In a test, the temperature of a hibernating ground squirrel fell to almost freezing. The creature later woke up unharmed.

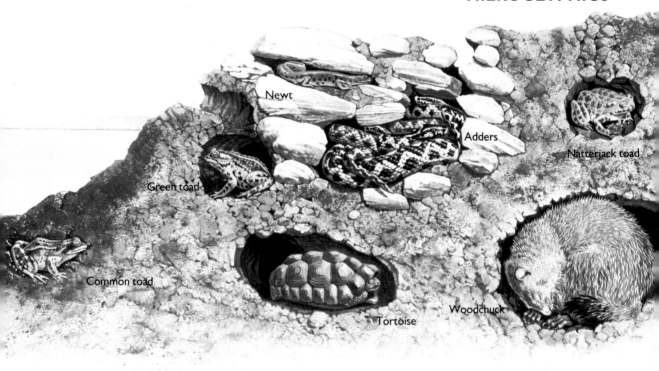

Newt

Adders

Natterjack toad

Green toad

Common toad

Tortoise

Woodchuck

sleep right through the winter. Squirrels wake up on mild days and eat food they had hidden away in the summer. But all hibernating animals find a warm, dry place to sleep, where they are safe from hungry enemies.

▲ *Hibernating animals have to find a warm, safe place to spend the winter. They need to reserve their energy until the weather warms up.*

Hieroglyphics

Hieroglyphics were an ancient form of writing. Our alphabet has 26 letters. However 5000 years ago the ancient Egyptians used picture-signs instead of letters. Later these signs became hieroglyphics—marks which stood for things, people, and ideas. Egyptian hieroglyphics were sometimes written from right to left, and sometimes from left to right.

Hieroglyphic writing was very difficult and only a few people could do it. When the Egyptian empire died out, the secret of reading it was lost. No one could understand the hieroglyphics carved on stones and written on papyrus scrolls. Then, in 1799, a Frenchman found the Rosetta Stone, which is now in the British Museum in London. On it was something written in two known languages, and also in hieroglyphics. By comparing the known languages with the hieroglyphics, experts were at last able to understand and translate the signs.

▲ *Many examples of hieroglyphic writing carved in stone have survived over thousands of years, and can now be understood.*

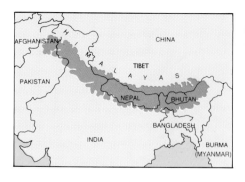

► The Himalayas form a great natural barrier between India and the large plateau of Tibet. The passes that run through the Himalayas are among the highest in the world. Few are lower than 5000 metres.

▼ Hindus believe in many gods, all with different characters. Four-armed Shiva is often shown dancing. Kali is the wife of Shiva. Ganesh, Shiva's son, has the head of an elephant and is believed to bring success if prayed to.

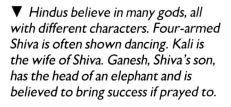

Kali

Shiva

Ganesh

Himalayas

The highest range of mountains in the world is the mighty Himalayas. The name means 'land of snow'. The Himalayas form a great barrier range across Asia, dividing India in the south from TIBET (part of China) in the north. Many of Asia's greatest rivers rise among the Himalayas, fed by the melting snows.

Until aircraft were invented few outsiders had ever been into the Himalayas. There are no roads or railways. The only way to travel is on foot, over steep mountain tracks. Horses, yaks, goats, and even sheep are used to carry heavy loads.

The highest mountain in the world lies in the Himalayas. This is Mount EVEREST, 8,848 metres high.

Hinduism

Hinduism is one of the world's great religions. Most Hindus live in Asia, and particularly in INDIA. Their religion has grown over a period of 4000 years.

Hindus believe that God is present in all things. Only priests (Brahmins) can worship the supreme God. Ordinary people worship other gods, such as Vishnu, God of Life. The most important holy books of the Hindus are the *Vedas*. Hindus believe that certain animals, such as the cobra and the cow, are sacred and must never be killed or eaten.

Hippopotamus

The name hippopotamus means 'river horse', but in fact the hippo is related to the pig, not the horse. It is a huge, heavy animal and lives in Africa. Of all land animals, only the elephant is bigger.

Hippopotamuses live near rivers and lakes. They spend most of their time in the water and are good swimmers. In spite of their fearsome-looking jaws, hippopotamuses eat only plant food. They browse on water weeds and grasses, and at night often come ashore to feed.

These animals are not usually dangerous if left alone, but they can inflict serious wounds with slashes from the tusks in their lower jaws.

▲ Hippopotamuses have eyes on the tops of their heads so they can stand under water and peep out without being seen. They can stay submerged for almost ten minutes without coming up for breath.

History

History is the story of the past. The people who write down the history are called historians. They usually write about important events such as wars, revolutions and governments, because these affect nations. However, historians are also interested in the lives of ordinary people and in what they did and thought about.

Nowadays, we think of history as being written down in history books. But in earlier times, before books and printing, history was passed on by word of mouth. People told stories about their kings, their wars, their adventures, and also about their

▼ The history of ancient civilizations has to be pieced together from clues that have come to us over the years. This bronze head is of a king who lived almost 4500 years ago.

Continued on page 338

335

HISTORY

AFRICA

BC
3,000,000 Australopithecus is early ancestor of modern man
30,000 Human hunters in Africa
5000 Stone Age craftworkers in Nile Valley
4500 Metal-working in Egypt
2780 First pyramid in Egypt
1400 Golden age of Egypt's power
500 Kushite kingdom in Africa
146 Romans destroy power of Carthage, a great North African city-state

AD
500 Kingdom of Ghana
850 Building of citadel at Great Zimbabwe
980 Arabs begin to settle on east coast
1000 Muslims control all of North Africa; Ife bronze art at its peak in West Africa
1307 Empire of Mali in central Africa reaches its height under Munsa Mali
1498 Vasco da Gama begins Portuguese trade along east coast
1500 Empire of Gao
1591 Fall of Songhai empire (which had succeeded Mali)
1652 Europeans led by Jan van Riebeeck settle at Cape of Good Hope
1713 Height of slave trade between West Africa and the New World
1818 Chaka founds the Zulu empire
1821 Liberia (West Africa) founded as free state for ex-slaves from USA
1835–37 Great Trek by Boers to found Transvaal
1869 Opening of Suez Canal creates shorter sea route from Europe to Asia.
1884 Berlin Conference allows European powers to divide Africa between them
1899–1902 Boer War; Britain defeats Boers
1936 Italy conquers Ethiopia, Africa's oldest independent African nation
1949 South Africa adopts policy of apartheid (separation of the races)
1956 President Nasser of Egypt nationalizes the Suez Canal.
1960 Civil war in Congo
1960s Many former European-ruled states become self-governing
1967 Civil war in Nigeria
1980 Zimbabwe (Rhodesia) becomes independent
1980s Civil war in parts of the continent; drought and famine are serious problems
1990 South Africa frees African National Congress leader, Nelson Mandela
1994 Free elections in South Africa. Nelson Mandela elected President. Apartheid ends

ASIA

BC
9000 Beginnings of agriculture in 'fertile crescen
7000 Jericho is world's first town
3500 Copper working in Thailand
3100 Earliest known writing, cuneiform script from Sumer
2300 Mohenjo-daro civilization in the Indus Riv valley (modern Pakistan)
2100 Abraham migrates from Ur
1500 Chinese master the skills of bronze-working
1230 Peak of Assyrian power
565 Birth of Buddha
551 Birth of Confucius
221–210 Reign of Chinese emperor Shihuangdi, builder of the Great Wall: China is the world's largest empire

AD
4? Birth of Jesus Christ
570 Birth of Muhammad
1000 Perfection of gunpowder in China
1100 Temples of Angkor Wat in Cambodia
1190 Genghis Khan begins to conquer an empi for the Mongols
1275 Marco Polo at the court of Kublai Khan
1405–33 Chinese fleets led by Cheng Ho make voyages of exploration in Pacific and India oceans
1498 Vasco da Gama sails from Portugal to Ind
1520s Mogul empire in India
1600 Shogun Ieyasu becomes ruler of Japan
1760 French and British fight for power in India
1854 Japan forced to sign trade treaty with USA
1857 Indian Mutiny
1868 Meiji government begins to 'westernize' Japan
1900 Boxer Rebellion in China
1905 Japan defeats Russians in war
1912 Sun Yat-sen leads new Chinese republic
1930s Rise of Japan as a military power
1939–45 World War II: first atomic bombs droppe on Japan
1947 India gains independence from British rule
1948 Creation of the state of Israel
1949 Communist rule established in China
1954 French pull out of Indochina; beginnings o Vietnam War
1976 Vietnam War ends
1979 Shah of Iran overthrown; Iran becomes ar Islamic republic
1980s Civil war in Lebanon; war between Iran and Iraq (ends 1988); China becomes mo open but suppresses democratic students
1990 Iraq invades Kuwait
1991 UN force drives Iraqis out of Kuwait
1994 Israelis and Palestinians sign peace treaty

EUROPE

00	Planting crops and animal husbandry reaches Europe from Asia
00	Minoan bronze age civilization of Crete
93	City of Troy destroyed by Greeks
9	Foundation of the Roman republic
1	Alexander the Great leads Greeks to victory over the Persian Empire
0	Romans invade Britain
3	Christian religion tolerated throughout Roman Empire
0	Roman emperor Constantine founds Constantinople
6	Roman Empire collapses
2	Charles Martel leads Franks to victory over Moors
0	Charlemagne is crowned first Holy Roman Emperor
1	Alfred becomes king of Wessex in England
66	William of Normandy conquers England
96	First of six crusades against the Islamic rulers of the Holy Land (Palestine)
15	English barons draw up Magna Carta
00s	The Renaissance in arts and sciences begins
48	The Black Death kills millions
53	Constantinople is captured by the Turks
17	Martin Luther's protest begins the Reformation
22	First circumnavigation of the globe by Europeans (Magellan's fleet)
88	English defeat the Spanish Armada
42	Civil War in England
00s	Revolutions in agriculture and industry; beginning of the Age of Machines
89	French Revolution
54–56	Crimean War
70–71	Franco-Prussian War: Prussia defeats France
14–18	World War I: Germany and its allies are defeated by Britain, France, USA, Russia and others. Over 10 million soldiers killed
17	Communist revolution in Russia
33	Hitler becomes ruler of Germany
36–39	Civil war in Spain
39–45	World War II: Allies defeat Germany and Italy in Europe
57	Treaty of Rome establishes European Community (EC)
80s	EC moves towards free market (1992); Gorbachev government brings new ideas in USSR; Eastern bloc countries move towards democracy
90	Reunification of Germany
91	Serbs and Croats fight in Yugoslavia; Soviet Union breaks up into independent states

AMERICAS AND AUSTRALASIA

BC

100,000?	Ancestors of Aborigines reach Australia
40,000	Ancestors of North American Indians migrate across 'land bridge' from Asia
20,000	Indians complete settlement of South America
8400	First domesticated dog (Idaho)
3372	Earliest date in Mayan calendar (Mexico)

AD

1100	Maoris sail to New Zealand from Pacific islands
1400	Inca empire in Peru
1492	Columbus 'discovers' America
1500	Cabral claims Brazil for Portugal
1518	Cortés begins conquest of Mexico, defeating Aztecs
1533	Pizarro conquers Inca empire for Spain
1584	Raleigh founds English colony in Virginia
1620	Voyage of the Pilgrim ship *Mayflower*
1626	Dutch found New Amsterdam (New York)
1642	Abel Tasman discovers Tasmania; French found Montreal in Canada
1763	Britain gains control of Canada, after defeating France
1770	Cook explores coast of Australia and New Zealand
1776	American Declaration of Independence
1783	End of American War of Independence
1788	First British settlement in Australia
1789	George Washington first US President
1824	South American republics break free from Spanish rule
1840	New Zealand becomes British colony
1861–65	American Civil War; Northern states defeat the South
1867	Canada becomes self-governing dominion
1901	Australia and New Zealand are independent
1917	USA enters World War I
1930s	Depression and unemployment in USA
1941	Japanese attack on Pearl Harbor brings USA into World War II
1959	Fidel Castro leads Communist revolution in Cuba
1963	President John F Kennedy of the USA is assassinated
1965	US troops fighting in Vietnam
1969	US lands astronauts on the Moon
1975	Last US forces leave Vietnam
1982	Britain sends forces to regain Falklands from Argentine occupation
1980s	Civil war in Nicaragua; Australia and New Zealand make new trade partners in Asia
1990	US troops overthrow President Noriega of Panama

HISTORY

▶ *Today photography and news reports capture historic moments like this one, where US President Bill Clinton saw Middle Eastern leaders Yitzhak Rabin and Yasir Arafat meet in peace for the first time.*

▲ *We know a great deal about the history of Europe, even in the Middle Ages. This type of ship, called a caravel, was used in the 15th century for voyages of discovery.*

It is sometimes said, 'Those who fail to learn the lessons of history are destined to repeat them.' One of the best-known and most incorrect statements about history came from the famous American car manufacturer Henry Ford. He said: 'History is bunk'. But Ford was in the habit of doing silly things. He sent a peace ship to Europe in 1915, hoping to persuade Germany and the Allies to stop World War I! He also for years financed anti-Jewish propaganda.

own families. It was in this way that the stories of ancient Greece were collected by the poet HOMER to form the *Iliad* and the *Odyssey*. Some early stories such as these were made up in verse, and sung to music. This made it easier for people to remember the stories correctly.

In ancient Egypt, scholars recorded the reigns of the PHARAOHS, and listed the victories they won in battle. Often these accounts were written in HIERO-GLYPHICS on stone tablets. The Chinese, Greeks and Romans were also very interested in history. It was they who first took the writing of history seriously, and they wrote of how their civilizations rose to power. During the MIDDLE AGES in Europe, many people could not read or write, and printing had not been invented. It was the priests and monks who preserved ancient books and kept the official records and documents. These records include the *Domesday Book* (1086), which tells us much of what we know about Norman England. History became an important branch of study in the 1700s and 1800s. Famous historians were Edward Gibbon (1737–1794) and Lord Macaulay (1800–1859).

Historians get their information from hidden remains such as things found buried in old graves, as well as from old books. The study of hidden remains is called ARCHAEOLOGY. But history is not just concerned with the long distant past. After all, history is *our* story. What is news today will be history tomorrow. So modern historians are also interested in recording the present. They talk to old people about the things they remember, and they keep records on film and tape, often made for television news programmes, of the events of today.

Hitler, Adolf

Adolf Hitler (1889–1945) was the 'Fuhrer', or leader, of GERMANY during WORLD WAR II. An ex-soldier, born in Austria, he became leader of the Nazi Party which took over Germany in 1933.

Germany was still weak after its defeat in WORLD WAR I. The Nazis promised to avenge this defeat and create a new German empire. In 1939 Hitler led Germany into World War II and conquered most of Europe. Millions of people were killed in Nazi death camps. But by 1945 Germany had lost the war. Hitler killed himself in the ruins of Berlin to avoid capture.

▲ Hitler used to organize rallies, attended by thousands of people, to spread his ideas.

Hobby

People today have more and more leisure time. Most people work fewer hours and have longer holidays than people did in the past. They retire at an earlier age and live longer. Housework takes less time because of modern household appliances. All this means that people have more free time for their

SEE IT YOURSELF

The hobby of paper-folding is called *origami*, a Japanese word. To make a paper penguin, follow the steps below: 1 and 2. Fold and crease a square along the dotted lines so C meets D. 3 Fold point B up. 4. Fold point B down along dotted line. 5. Fold and crease so that point F meets point E. 6. Fold point F along dotted line to make penguin's foot. 7. Turn over and fold point E to match other foot. 8. Fold point A down along dotted line to make head. 9. Unfold so head points up again. Separate folds of head and push inwards along central crease. Cut to separate tail. Fold tail pieces back so penguin will stand. 10. Draw eyes.

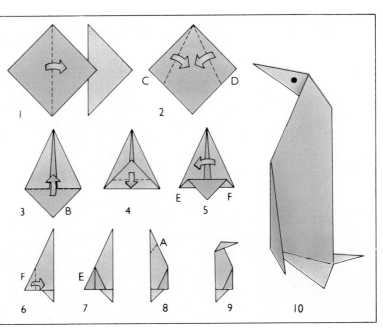

HOLOGRAPHY

Most famous people have hobbies. George Washington collected different kinds of tea. Winston Churchill loved bricklaying. There is a long wall in the grounds of his former home built by the great man himself.

▶ Holograms look so realistic because they are three-dimensional images. You can walk past a hologram and view it from different angles. Unfortunately we cannot print a picture of a hologram in three dimensions.

One of the amazing things about a hologram plate is that it can be cut into pieces and each piece will give, not a part of the picture, but the whole picture.

hobbies. Any activity that is enjoyed during your spare time is a hobby. It can be collecting things such as stamps, butterflies, bottles or rocks. It can be a creative hobby such as weaving, knitting, drawing, painting or photography. Or it can be a playing hobby such as tennis, swimming, fishing, sailing or chess. Part of the fun of any hobby is sharing it. The friendships that people gain from their hobbies are an important part of their interest.

Holography

Holography is a way of making very realistic three-dimensional pictures called *holograms*. It does this by using LASER light instead of a camera.

To make a hologram, a laser beam is split into two; one beam hits the object and is reflected onto a photographic plate; the other beam, angled by mirrors, strikes the plate directly. The photographic plate is developed and a black-and-white pattern, the hologram, appears. When the hologram is lit up by a laser beam and viewed from the other side, it produces a three-dimensional image of the original object. The image seems real, with width, depth and height, but it is not in the object's original colour. Instead, it takes its colour from the laser beam.

Holography was first discovered 40 years ago. But it was not developed until the 1960s when lasers were introduced. Scientists are now looking at practical uses for holography. Holograms could be useful in medicine, to probe the human body; in land surveys, to decipher aerial photographs; and in scientific work, to make very precise measurements.

Holy Roman Empire

For many years, a large part of Europe was loosely united as the Holy Roman Empire. At different times it included Italy, Germany, Austria, and parts of France, the Netherlands and Switzerland.

On Christmas Day in the year 800, Pope Leo III crowned CHARLEMAGNE as the first 'Emperor of the Romans'. The word 'holy' was not added to the emperor's title until years later. After a while, the popes began to have more trouble than help from the emperors, and by the end of the thirteenth century the emperor always came from the HAPSBURG family, the rulers of powerful Austria.

As some German states grew bigger in the 1500s, so the emperors began to lose power. By the 1800s the emperor was really only Emperor of Austria and Hungary.

▲ The double-headed eagle was the emblem of the Holy Roman Empire, first used in the 13th century. The eagle symbolizes power.

▼ Homer's stories are full of excitement. In the Odyssey, Odysseus and his men encountered many dangerous monsters, including the Sirens, three women whose beautiful voices lured sailors to their doom on the rocky shores. Odysseus had himself tied to the mast and his men plugged their ears so they would not be tempted.

Homer

Homer was a Greek poet and storyteller. He probably lived around 700 BC but we know nothing else about him. All we have are two great poems said to be by Homer: the *Iliad* and the *Odyssey*.

HONDURAS

Government: Democratic
constitutional republic
Capital: Tegucigalpa
Area: 112,088 sq km
Population: 4,949,000
Language: Spanish
Currency: Lempira

HONG KONG

Government: Crown colony
Capital: Victoria
Area: Island 75 sq km
     New Territories etc. 971 sq km
Population: 5,841,000
Highest point: Tai Mo Shan 957 m
Climate: Tropical monsoon
Rainfall average: 2160 mm

These poems tell us much of what we know about ancient Greek history and legend. The *Iliad* tells the story of the TROJAN WAR. The *Odyssey* tells of the adventures of Odysseus, a Greek hero, as he made his long journey home after the war.

Honduras

Honduras is a mountainous country in Central America. It has a long coastline with the Caribbean Sea and a short one with the Pacific. Most of the people are farmers. They live mostly in small villages in the west of the country and in the large banana plantations on the north coast. Columbus discovered Honduras in 1502. The country won its independence from Spain in 1821 and became a republic in 1838. The capital is Tegucigalpa.

Hong Kong

Hong Kong is a tiny area off the coast of China. Part of it is a small island, and the rest is a narrow strip of land called the New Territories, which is actually part of mainland China. Hong Kong has been governed by Britain since 1842. It was handed over to Chinese rule in 1997.

    Hong Kong has a fine harbour surrounded by

▶ *The name Hong Kong means 'fragrant harbour'. It is a crowded, busy place and the famous Tiger Balm Gardens are a popular retreat.*

mountains. The capital is Victoria, and another busy city is Kowloon. Hong Kong is a fascinating mixture of East and West. The people live by trade, fishing, and farming. Tall apartment buildings have been built to house them, but there is still little room for the millions of people who crowd this small island.

Hoof

A hoof is the hard covering of HORN which protects the feet of many animals. Animals with hooves are divided into two main groups, those with an even number of toes and those with an odd number. The animals with an even number of toes include DEER, GOATS, CAMELS and SHEEP. All these animals have either two or four toes. Animals with only one toe include HORSES and ZEBRAS. Tame horses have their hooves cut and trimmed, and wear horseshoes.

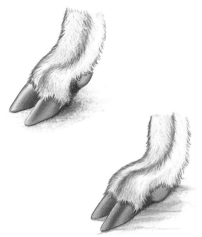

▲ The ibex is a kind of wild goat. It has dual claws that can be brought down to give extra grip when scrambling up smooth rock faces.

Hormone

Hormones are chemical messengers found in all animals and plants. In many animals, hormones are produced in organs called GLANDS. Glands are found in several parts of the body. From these glands, the different hormones are carried in the blood to other parts of the body. There they make the parts do certain jobs.

The pituitary gland in the centre of the head produces several hormones. These 'master' hormones control the hormone secretion of several other glands. The thyroid gland in the neck, for example, is stimulated by the pituitary gland to make a hormone that controls how fast food is used up by the body. Too little of this hormone makes people overweight. The hormone adrenaline is controlled by nerve messages. When it flows, the heart beats faster, the blood pressure rises and the body prepares itself for strenuous physical exertion.

Many hormones can now be made in the laboratory and used to help people suffering from diseases caused by lack of certain hormones. Insulin is a hormone used in the treatment of diabetes, a disease in which too much sugar stays in the blood.

▼ Hormones can affect how much – or how little – people grow. Jockey Willie Carson, shown here with a trainer, is exceptionally small.

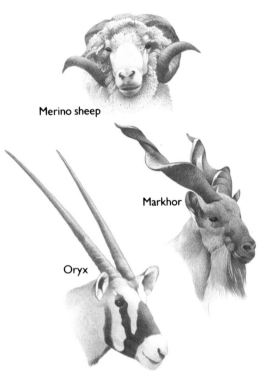

Merino sheep

Markhor

Oryx

▲ *The horns of some animals are very distinctive and decorative. Horns have sometimes been used by man to make drinking cups or musical instruments.*

Horn

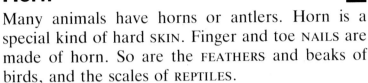

Many animals have horns or antlers. Horn is a special kind of hard SKIN. Finger and toe NAILS are made of horn. So are the FEATHERS and beaks of birds, and the scales of REPTILES.

Cattle, sheep, goats and most ANTELOPES have curved horns. These are bony growths covered with a layer of horn, and they are fixed to the animal's skull. DEER have branched antlers, made of bone covered with skin. Every year the antlers fall off and the deer grows a new set.

Horned animals use their horns to defend themselves against enemies and as weapons for fighting during the mating season.

Horse

The horse was one of the first wild animals to be tamed. Today there are very few wild horses left. Many so-called 'wild' horses are actually descended from domestic horses which have run wild.

The horse is valued for its speed and strength. But the first horse was a small, rather dog-like creature,

▼ *The different parts of a horse are called its points. The most common points are shown here.*

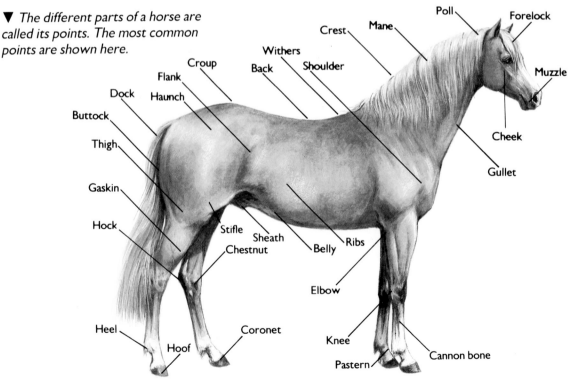

with a way of life quite unlike that of modern horses. Called *Eohippus*, or 'dawn horse', it lived millions of years ago. It had four toes on its front feet and three toes on its back feet, and it probably hid from its enemies in the undergrowth.

Later, horses came out to live on the wide grassy plains. There was no undergrowth to hide in, so they escaped from enemies by running away. Gradually, their legs grew longer, and they lost all their toes except one. Finally, after millions of years of EVOLUTION, the modern horse appeared. It, too, has only one toe, and actually runs on tiptoe. Its toe has become a tough nail or hoof.

Early man hunted wild horses for food. No one knows when horses were first tamed, but horses were being used for riding and for pulling chariots and carts in Egypt more than 5000 years ago. Until the 1800s the horse was the fastest form of transport and our strongest helpmate. Horses did all kinds of jobs, in towns and in the country, until the railway, the motor car and new, modern farm machinery replaced them. Though horses do not work for us as they once did, they are still very much a part of the world of horse races and shows, as well as valued pets.

Hospital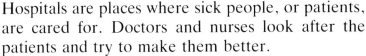

Hospitals are places where sick people, or patients, are cared for. Doctors and nurses look after the patients and try to make them better.

There are two types of hospital. One, the general hospital, deals with everything from accident injuries to contagious diseases. The other type of hospital specializes in certain conditions. For example, there are *psychiatric* hospitals for people who are mentally ill; *maternity* hospitals where women have their babies; and *geriatric* hospitals for the elderly. In hospitals attached to medical schools, student doctors can gain experience through treating real patients.

In the ancient world, temples dedicated to the gods of healing used to have a hospital area. Sick people came there to pray and be treated. Later, in the Middle Ages, hospitals were attached to monas-

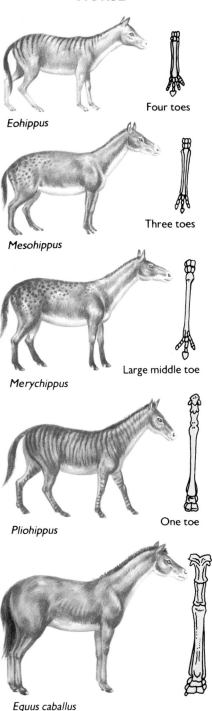

ANCESTORS OF THE HORSE

Eohippus

Four toes

Mesohippus

Three toes

Merychippus

Large middle toe

Pliohippus

One toe

Equus caballus

▲ The horse we know today developed over millions of years from a creature the size of a fox, with short legs and four-toed feet.

▶ *Before entering the hospital operating theatre, doctors and nurses have to 'scrub up'. This means they make themselves as clean and sterile as possible, so no germs are brought near the patient. Before the operation an anaesthetist puts the patient to sleep so that they cannot feel any pain. The surgeon then opens the skin, using special instruments. Various electronic equipment monitors the patient's breathing during the whole process.*

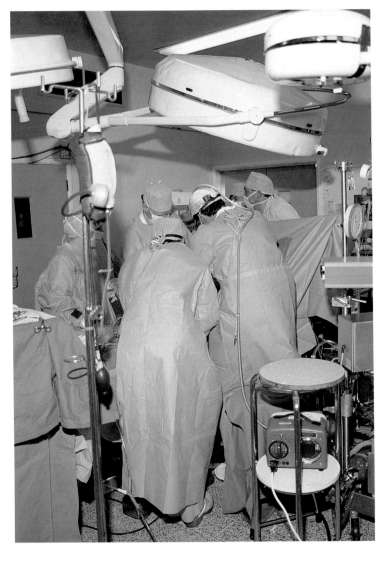

▲ *Lasers help doctors to perform delicate microsurgery, such as this eye operation.*

teries and run by monks and nuns. But in the last 200 years, non-religious hospitals have become the most common. In some countries, hospitals organized by the state provide inexpensive or free medical treatment for all people. In other countries, there are privately-run, as well as government-run, hospitals. Modern hospitals have a wide range of technical equipment, such as X-RAY machines, heart-lung machines, and LASERS. Casualty departments deal with emergencies.

Hotel

Hotels are places where travellers or people on holiday can stay. Before 1800 there were no hotels as we know them. Travellers spent the night at taverns or inns. Wherever people travelled, there were inns that gave food and shelter to the traveller and his horse.

Today, large hotels are like small towns. They provide people who are on business trips or are travelling for pleasure with all the comforts—swimming pools, television, restaurants, shops, travel agencies and hairdressers.

Another kind of hotel is the 'motel'. This gives overnight housing for people who are travelling by car. Motels are found along major roads. Guests can usually drive their car right up to the door of their room.

House

Houses date back to prehistoric times. Some of the first were built in the Middle East. They were simple little boxes with flat roofs. Often doors and windows were simply open spaces in the walls. (See pages 348–349.)

Houses of Parliament *See* Parliament

Hovercraft

Depending on how you look at one, a hovercraft is either a plane with no wings or a ship that rides out of the water.

Hovercraft ride on a cushion of air, blown down-

Continued on page 350

▲ *Hotel kitchens are usually run with great efficiency and discipline. In large hotels the work is very specialized, with one person in charge of making sauces, for example, while someone else will only make desserts, and so on.*

▼ *The cushion of air produced by powerful fans inside a hovercraft makes for a fast ride across water or land.*

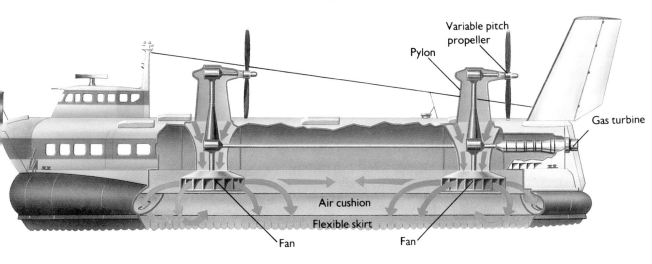

Variable pitch propeller

Pylon

Gas turbine

Air cushion

Flexible skirt

Fan

Fan

HOUSE

Prehistoric people lived in caves. The first houses were rough shelters, made of mud, branches and leaves. Later, people learned how to make bricks by drying wet clay in the sun. Brick, wood and stone were for thousands of years the materials from which almost all houses were built.

The modern house is built to keep out the cold and wet, and to keep in warmth. Double glazing of windows and insulation in the roof and walls help to do this. Many homes have central heating and, in hot climates, air conditioning.

In most countries a house is lived in by either a single family or a family group. A number of houses joined together form a terrace. Two houses joined side by side are 'semi-detached'. A number of homes built on top of one another form a block of flats or apartments. In many big cities, there are not enough houses to provide homes for everybody. In some countries, poor people have to live in slums and shanty towns.

HOUSES AROUND THE WORLD

▶ *Although houses in cities around the world now look very much the same, there are still lots of differences in the way houses are built. Houses in North Africa and Arabia, for example, have thick mud-brick or cement walls and small windows. This helps to keep them cool. In South-east Asia, many people live in houses built on stilts over the water. In Borneo, a whole village may live in one big dwelling called a long-house. In Canada, the USA and Scandinavia many houses are built of wood, whereas in parts of Britain you will see houses made of local stone, perhaps with a roof of thatch (reeds).*

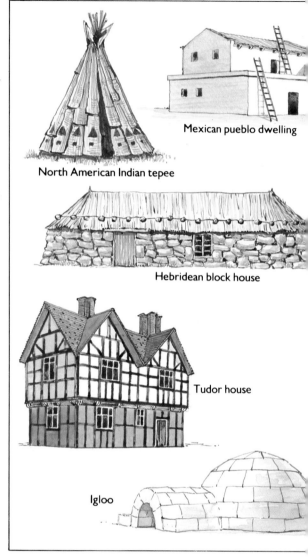

North American Indian tepee

Mexican pueblo dwelling

Hebridean block house

Tudor house

Igloo

HOW HOUSES AND FLATS ARE BUILT

A house is built in a different way from a block of flats. Both must have foundations, with pipes for water and sewage, and cables for electricity laid on. A house often has walls of brick, covered on the inside with plaster. The floors are made of concrete or wood. The roof is usually sloped, so that rain runs off easily, and is covered with rows of slates or tiles. A block of flats has a framework of steel girders to give extra strength. The walls may be factory-made panels, lifted into place by a crane. It will have a lift, as well as stairs, and it may well have a flat roof.

▲ *Traditional building techniques using timber, bricks and tiles are still widely used, particularly for housing.*

▲ *Large-scale building projects often rely on advanced techniques and materials.*

Indonesian stilt house

Sudanese mud huts

Modern block of flats

Thatched cottage

American suburban house

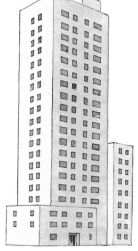

HISTORY OF THE HOUSEHOLD

100 AD Wealthy Romans lived in houses with running water and underfloor heating.

1200s Only rich people could afford glass in their windows.

1500s The water closet was invented, but few people had proper lavatories until the 1900s.

1830 Edwin Budding invents lawnmower.

1840s Gas lighting replaced oil lamps and candles.

1858 Ferdinand Carré invents the refrigerator, allowing people to keep food fresh for later use.

1879 Electric light bulb invented.

1880s Gas cookers introduced, to replace the old kitchen range or stove.

1901 Invention of the vacuum cleaner makes housework easier.

1910 First electric washing machine.

1930s Electric cookers become popular.

1950s First dishwasher invented.

1953 Microwaves appear in the US. They cook food much faster than normal methods.

2000 The home run by a computer?

▼ *The Xanadu experimental house, in Florida, USA, could be the shape of things to come. Built for maximum energy efficiency, it combines convenience with concern for the environment.*

BUYING AND RENTING HOUSES

People wanting to buy a house usually need to borrow most of the money, because houses are expensive. In Britain, house buyers can borrow money from a bank or from a building society. This is called taking out a mortgage. They have to repay the loan over a number of years. They will probably visit an estate agent to see what houses are for sale.

Not all houses are owned by the people who live in them. Many people live in rented flats or houses. They pay rent to the owner.

For information about how houses are built, see ARCHITECTURE; BUILDING. For interesting and unusual houses, turn to AMERICAN INDIANS; CAVE DWELLER; ESKIMO; GYPSY; NOMAD. For the insides of houses, see FURNITURE; TAPESTRY.

HOVERCRAFT

A well-known use of the hovercraft principle is the 'hovering' rotary lawnmower. The engine, besides rotating the grass-cutting blade, creates a cushion of air that raises the machine to the right height above the ground.

wards by fans, and held in by a skirt or side wall around the hovercraft. They work best over flat surfaces like water but can also cross beaches and flat land. The only danger is that rough ground may snag their bottoms.

Hovercraft are much faster than ships. Since they do not have to push against any water but simply skim smoothly through the air, they can easily manage speeds of 120 km/h. Their advantage over planes is the size of the load they can carry. A large craft can load dozens of cars and up to 400 passengers. And of course they do not need harbours or runways to land. They simply climb up the beach to settle on a simple concrete landing pad.

The hovercraft was invented in 1955 by the British engineer Christopher Cockerell. The first working model appeared four years later and had soon crossed the Channel from England to France. Today, fleets of hovercraft shuttle back and forth every day carrying hundreds of cars and passengers.

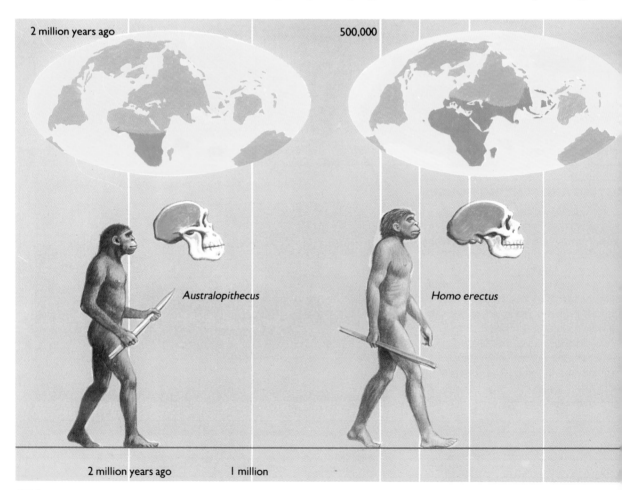

2 million years ago

500,000

Australopithecus

Homo erectus

2 million years ago   1 million

Human Beings

Human beings are mammals, but rather clever ones. They are very like their relatives, the apes. They have the same kind of bones, muscles and other parts inside their bodies. But the main difference between people and any other animal is the size of their brain. The human brain is enormous, compared to body size. People use their brain to think things out, and when they have found an answer to a problem, they can talk about it with other people. This is why the human being is the most successful animal.

Scientists now agree that our ancestors were ape-like creatures who slowly, over millions of years, evolved (changed) into people. People something like ourselves have probably lived on Earth for about 500,000 years.

Today, all people belong to the same *species* (kind of creature). This creature is classified as

▼ *Our ancestors of two million years ago were very different from us, but the world, too, was very different. A series of ice ages meant that huge glaciers covered much of the northern half of the Earth. One of the most important events in the development of people took place about one million years ago, when our ancestors started to make tools. By about 10,000 BC people were beginning to understand how to grow and harvest crops. The brown areas show where humans lived at different times.*

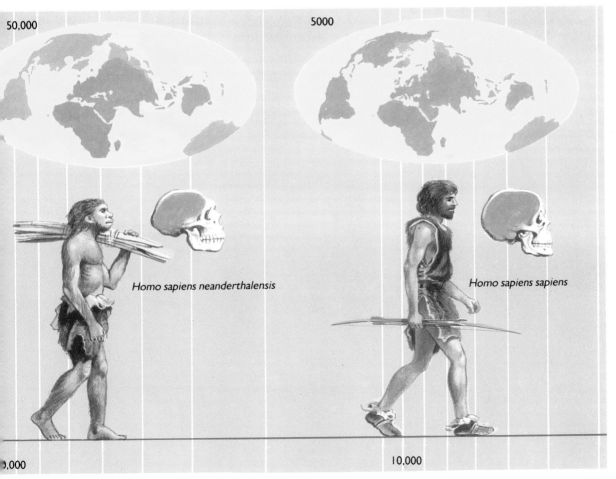

50,000

5000

Homo sapiens neanderthalensis

Homo sapiens sapiens

),000

10,000

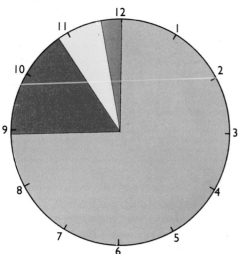

▲ If the history of the Earth to the present day were condensed into twelve hours, the earliest life in the sea would have begun just before nine o'clock. Life moved onto land at a quarter to eleven, and mammals appeared at twenty to twelve. Humans would have arrived just before the stroke of twelve.

▼ The body works through a series of interconnected systems that function all the time to keep us going.

Homo sapiens ('thinking man'). All people, in every country on Earth, whether black, white, brown or yellow, are *Homo sapiens*.

Scientists divide human beings into three main *races*. The *Caucasoid* people are fair-skinned like the people of Europe and America or dark-skinned like the people of India, and others. The *Mongoloid* group takes in most of the yellow-skinned peoples of Asia, plus the American Indians. The *Negroid* group consists of the dark-skinned peoples of Africa and other regions.

Human Body

Your body is a wonderful machine with many parts. Each part has a special job and all the parts work together to keep you alive and healthy. Like all machines, your body needs fuel – food. The oxygen you breathe in from the air helps turn the food you eat into energy. This energy allows you to play, work, think and grow.

Your body is made up of millions of tiny cells – many different kinds of cells. A group of cells that work together is called a *tissue*. For example, cells that allow you to lift things are called muscle tissue. Tissues that work together make up an *organ*. The heart is an organ that pumps blood. Other organs are the LIVER, the LUNGS, the STOMACH and the SKIN.

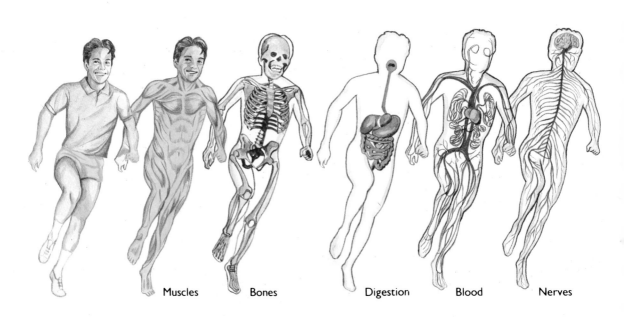

Muscles   Bones   Digestion   Blood   Nerves

Organs that work together are called *systems*. You have a *digestive system* (mouth, stomach and intestines), a *circulatory system* (heart, arteries and veins), and a *nervous system* (brain and nerves). The study of the body is called *anatomy*.

Humidity

All air has some water in it, although we cannot see it. Humidity is the amount of water in the air. If the air contains only a little water vapour, the humidity is low. When air holds a lot of moisture, we say the humidity is high. The warmer the air the more moisture it can hold. Humidity affects the way we feel. When the humidity is high we feel 'sweaty' and uncomfortable. This is because the sweat does not evaporate easily from our skin. But too low a humidity is not very good for us. Some people use *humidifiers* in their homes to put more moisture into the air.

Hummingbird

These birds are among the smallest in the world. They are found only in the New World, from Canada to the tip of South America. The tiniest of the 320 kinds lives in Cuba. It is less than 5 cm— hardly bigger than a large bumblebee.

SEE IT YOURSELF

Scientists calculate the humidity with the help of an instrument called a hygrometer. You can make one by taping two identical outdoor thermometers to a brick. Cut a narrow strip about 20 cm long from an old towel and wrap it around the bulb of one thermometer. Fill a pan with water and put the other end of the strip in it. After a while, take the difference between the temperatures shown on the two thermometers in the shade outdoors. The less the difference, the higher the humidity. Keep a record of the humidity in your area.

▲ *The tiny hummingbird has a specially developed beak and tongue that let it feed from deep inside flowers.*

▲ *The eldest son of Edward III was called the Black Prince. He was a cruel and ruthless soldier.*

▼ *At the Battle of Agincourt, the skill of the English archers led to the defeat of the French, even though the English army was greatly outnumbered.*

The feathers of hummingbirds are coloured in brilliant metallic hues of blue, green, red and yellow. The colours flashing in the sun make hummingbirds look like glittering jewels on the wing.

Hummingbirds can beat their wings up to 70 times a second. This is what causes their distinctive humming sound. It also lets them hover in mid-air and fly backwards and sideways like a helicopter. In this way, they dart from flower to flower and feed while flying. They take nectar and tiny insects from deep within the cups of flowers.

Hundred Years' War

England and France were at war, almost without a break, from 1337 to 1453. This is called the Hundred Years' War. The war was started by the English king EDWARD III. He thought he was the rightful heir to the French crown. Edward landed an army in France in 1346. His foot soldiers and archers routed the French at Crécy in 1346 and Poitiers in 1356. A treaty was signed in 1360.

The war started again in 1369. HENRY V of England decided to try again for the French crown. At the Battle of Agincourt in 1415, the English bowmen mowed down the French cavalry. Another treaty was signed in 1422. Henry married the French king's daughter and was named heir to the French

throne. But the two kings died and war broke out again. This time, the French were led by a young peasant girl, JOAN OF ARC. By 1453, the English were driven from all their lands in France, except Calais. The long war was at an end.

Hungary

This is a small, central European country that covers an area of some 93,000 sq km, not much bigger than Scotland.

Hungary has no coastline. The mighty Danube river flows across the country on its way to the Black Sea, dividing it almost in two. Ships can sail up-river as far as Budapest, the capital and biggest city.

Hungary is low-lying and fairly flat. To the east it becomes a vast grassy plain. Here herds of sheep, cattle and horses are grazed. The climate is hot and dry in summer, and bitterly cold in winter. Agriculture is important, but more Hungarians work in industry than on farms. There are also rich sources of coal, oil and bauxite for making aluminium.

After WORLD WAR I and the collapse of the Austro-Hungarian Empire, Hungary became an independent republic. After WORLD WAR II it was a communist country, but in 1989 the people achieved a more democratic government. In 1991 the last Soviet troops left Hungary.

The main reason for the English victories at the battles of Crécy, Poitiers and Agincourt was the skill of the English archers with the longbow. This weapon was 1.5 to nearly 2 metres long, with a range of as much as 300 metres. The archers needed muscular strength and long training before they could shoot six aimed shots a minute.

HUNGARY

Government: Multi-party system
Capital: Budapest
Area: 93,030 sq km
Population: 10,563,000
Language: Hungarian
Currency: Forint

◀ *The capital of Hungary is actually made up of two cities – Buda and Pest, separated by the river Danube.*

When Attila, the great leader of the Huns, died in 453, his body was taken out into the plains and buried with much of his treasure. All those who had been at Attila's burial were afterwards put to death so that his grave might never be discovered.

Huns

These were a group of fierce wandering warriors who swept into Europe around AD 400 from the plains of Central Asia. They conquered large parts of Germany and France. Their famous general, Attila, attacked Rome and nearly destroyed the Roman Empire. However, the Huns' power grew less after his death in AD 453.

Hunting

In prehistoric times, hunting was the main way by which people lived. Nowadays most hunting is for sport or to keep down pests.

Big game hunting is the sport of tracking, stalking and killing large wild animals. This kind of hunting is dying out since people now want to preserve animals, not kill them. Another kind of hunting is with packs of hounds. The hunters may follow on foot or on horseback as the dogs chase deer, foxes or hares through the countryside. Foxhunting is the most popular kind of hunting in the British Isles. In America, most hunting is done with guns.

Hurdling *See* Athletics

▼ *Hunting on horseback was a popular sport in Ancient China. Cheetahs, dogs and falcons were used in the chase.*

Hurricane

A hurricane is a severe storm. To be called a hurricane, a storm must have wind speeds of at least 120 km/h. People who live around the Pacific Ocean call hurricanes *typhoons*. People who live on the Indian Ocean call them *cyclones*. Hurricane winds whirl around in a great circle and sometimes reach speeds of over 320 km/h. The largest hurricanes have measured 1600 km across. Hurricanes form over oceans near the Equator, where the air is very moist. At the centre of the hurricane is a narrow-column of air that spins very slowly. This is the 'eye' of the hurricane.

▲ *Satellite pictures can help to predict the route a hurricane will take. Hurricane Allen is shown here over the Gulf of Mexico. You can clearly see the 'eye' in the centre of the storm.*

Hydroelectric Power

More than a fifth of the world's electricity is produced by using the energy of fast flowing water. This is called hydroelectric power. Most hydroelectric plants are found below dams, but some are powered by waterfalls.

Water is heavy. When it falls down through large pipes from a high dam it can be made to turn TURBINES with paddle-shaped blades. Shafts connected to the blades turn electric generators, as in ordinary coal- or oil-fired POWER STATIONS.

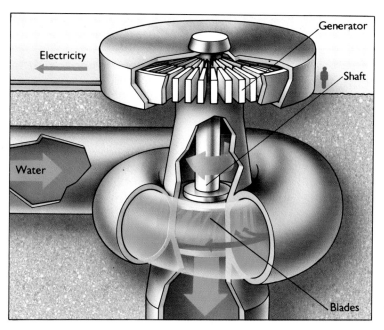

◀ *The huge turbine blades in a hydroelectric power station are turned by water as it flows down from a dam. They in turn rotate a shaft connected to generators which produce electricity in the same way as in ordinary power stations.*

▲ *At rest, a hydrofoil lies in the water like a normal ship, but once it starts moving, the hull rises up and the vessel is supported on its underwater struts.*

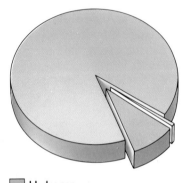

■ Hydrogen
□ Other gases
■ Helium

▲ *This pie chart shows the proportions of the gases that make up our Sun. Hydrogen is the main component by a long way.*

▼ *A pack of hyenas can drive away most hunting animals from their kill, which the hyenas then finish off.*

Hydrofoil

Much of a ship's engine power goes into overcoming the drag of the water around the ship's hull. A hydrofoil solves this problem by lifting the ship right out of the water. It does this with a set of underwater struts attached to the hull of the craft at the bow and stern. These 'water wings' lift the hull as the ship gathers speed. As the water's drag grows less, the craft shoots ahead, travelling far faster than an ordinary vessel can.

Hydrogen

Hydrogen is a gas. It is thought to be the most abundant ELEMENT in the whole universe. It is the single most important material from which stars, including our SUN, are made.

Hydrogen is the lightest of all elements. It is more than 14 times as light as air. It is colourless, has no smell and no taste. Hydrogen burns very easily. Great masses of hydrogen are always being burned in the Sun. It is this fierce burning that gives us light and heat from the Sun.

Coal, oil and natural gas all contain hydrogen. It is also a very important part of all plant and animal bodies.

Hyena

Hyenas are a small group of flesh-eating MAMMALS. Although they look a lot like dogs, they are more closely related to the cat family.

Hyenas feed on dead flesh, or carrion. They scavenge their meals from the kills of other animals such as lions. They have very powerful teeth and jaws for crushing the bones and making the most of their source of left-over food. Hyenas hunt in packs. They feed at night. By day they sleep in holes and caves.

The spotted hyena lives in southern Africa. It is famous for its wild laughing cry and is sometimes known as the laughing hyena. The striped hyena lives in India, south-west Asia and north-east Africa.

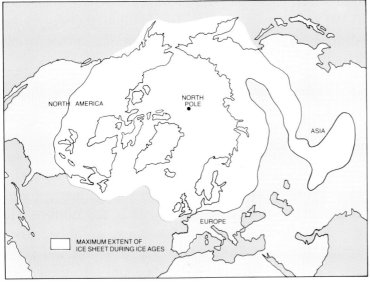

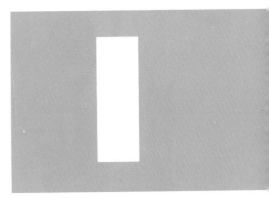

◄ *The glaciers that spread over large parts of the Earth during the Ice Ages carried huge rocks and boulders with them as they went. Geologists can trace the path of the glaciers by studying these rocks and working out where they came from.*

Ice Ages

The Ice Ages were times when vast sheets of ice covered parts of the Earth. Each period lasted for thousands of years. In between were warmer periods. The last Ice Age ended about 20,000 years ago but the ice might return again.

During the Ice Ages the weather was very cold. Endless snow fell and GLACIERS grew and spread. At times the glaciers covered much of North America and Asia, and Europe as far south as London. In some places the ice piled up more than a thousand metres high. This made the sea level lower than it is today. A land bridge was formed between Asia and North America. The first people in America came across this land bridge from Asia.

▼ *Huge icebergs float in the sea because when water freezes it expands, so ice is less dense than water.*

Iceberg

Icebergs are part of GLACIERS and ice shelves that have broken away and float in the sea. They are found in the waters of the ARCTIC and the ANTARCTIC.

Icebergs can be very big. Some weigh millions of tonnes. Most of an iceberg is hidden under the surface of the sea. Some icebergs may be 145 km long. They can be 120 metres high above water. An iceberg this high would be about another 960 metres deep under water.

Icebergs are dangerous to ships. Some icebergs

▲ *Ice hockey players, and particularly the goal keeper, have to wear special padded clothing to protect them against injury.*

float south from the Arctic into the Atlantic Ocean. In 1912, a ship called the *Titanic* hit an iceberg in the Atlantic. It sank and 1500 people on it were drowned.

Ice Hockey

Ice hockey is a team game played on ice. The players, six in a team, wear ice skates. They play on a *rink* that is 60 metres long and 26 metres wide, with a goal at either end. Each player has a long-handled stick with a curved blade at the bottom. He or she uses this to drive the *puck*, a rubber disc, around the rink. Both teams try to shoot the puck past the opposing team's defence and into their goal nets. A game is divided into three periods; each period lasts 20 minutes.

Iceland

Iceland is a small, mountainous island, about 100,000 sq km in size. It was first discovered by VIKINGS in AD 874. The island lies just south of the Arctic in the north Atlantic, between Greenland and Norway. Warm waters from the GULF STREAM keep most of the harbours free of ice all the year round.

Iceland has many VOLCANOES. About 25 of its volcanoes have erupted. There are many hot water springs too. Some are used to heat homes. The

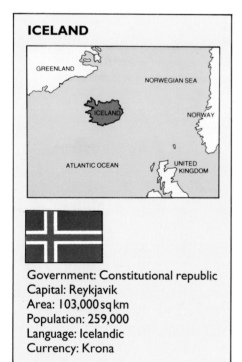

ICELAND

Government: Constitutional republic
Capital: Reykjavik
Area: 103,000 sq km
Population: 259,000
Language: Icelandic
Currency: Krona

▶ *These two volcanic hills rising out of the landscape are typical Icelandic features.*

north of Iceland is covered by GLACIERS and a desert of stone and lava (cooled volcanic matter).

There are about 259,000 people in Iceland. Most live in the south and east where the land is lower. They live by farming and fishing. The capital city is Reykjavik.

Iceland became an independent country in 1944 after breaking its ties with Denmark.

Immunity

You have probably been vaccinated against the disease called polio. The substance the doctor or nurse put into your body contained polio germs, but these germs had been made harmless so you only caught a very mild case of polio. Your body did not know that the polio germs had been weakened, and it got to work fighting them. Your body produced *antibodies*—substances that attack certain disease-causing germs. The important thing is that these antibodies stay in your body to stop more of the same kind of germs from invading your body again. This kind of long-term protection against diseases is called immunity.

People also have *acquired* immunity to disease. This happens when they have a disease and produce antibodies to fight it off. After that, the antibodies are waiting to ward off these germs should they appear again. If you have had measles, you are unlikely to get measles again.

However, some diseases are very difficult or impossible to vaccinate against. Your body stops making antibodies against the common cold almost as soon as you are over it. The VIRUS that causes AIDS damages the body's immune system so that it stops making antibodies against diseases.

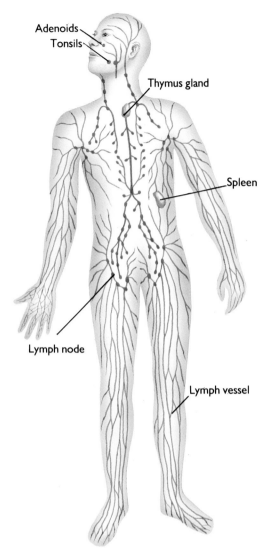

Adenoids
Tonsils
Thymus gland
Spleen
Lymph node
Lymph vessel

▲ *The body protects itself against illness in various ways. The immune, or lymph, system fights diseases that attack the body.*

▼ *The presence of bacteria in the body stimulates the white blood cells which are always present to move in to attack them.*

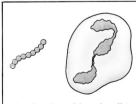

1. A white blood cell is moving to attack a bacterium.

2. It surrounds the bacterium and takes it in.

3. The bacterium is killed by chemicals inside the cell.

4. The bacterium is expelled in the form of pus.

The Impressionists were so interested in light that they never used black. Black is the absence of light. If you look at an Impressionist painting, some things seem to be black, but look closely and you will see that they are dark brown, green or blue.

▶ *Some of Monet's most famous paintings are of his garden at Giverny.*

▼ *The Inca empire, when the Spaniards first encountered it, stretched for about 3200 kilometres north to south on the west coast of South America.*

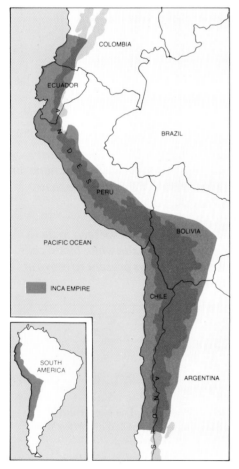

Impressionism

In the 1860s in France, some young artists began to paint in a new way. Most artists worked indoors, but these young men began to paint outdoors. They painted scenes from nature and tried to catch the ever-changing light.

In 1874, the group held an exhibition in Paris. Their work was laughed at, and one newspaper poked fun at a painting called *Impression: Sunrise* by Claude Monet. It called the group 'Impressionists', and the name stuck.

Now, people recognize the Impressionists as being among the greatest artists of all time. In addition to Monet, the most important Impressionists were Edouard Manet, Camille Pissarro, Edgar Degas, Alfred Sisley and Pierre Auguste Renoir.

Incas

The Incas were people who lived in SOUTH AMERICA. They ruled a great empire from the 1200s until the 1500s. The centre of their empire was in PERU. In the 1400s the empire grew. It stretched thousands of kilometres, from present-day Chile to Ecuador.

The Inca king and his nobles ruled over the people in the empire. They were very strict and told

◀ The Incas worshipped the Sun and other nature gods in elaborate ceremonies, at which their priests would offer sacrifices of animals.

the farmers and craftsmen what to grow and make. The Incas built many roads through the empire.

In the 1500s, Spanish soldiers led by Francisco Pizarro reached America. They captured the Inca king Atahualpa and said they would free him in return for gold. Incas brought their treasure to free the king, but the Spanish still killed him. By 1569 the Spaniards had conquered the whole Inca empire.

India

India has a population of over 800 million. It has more people than any other country except China. India is part of ASIA.

INDIA

Government: Federal republic
Capital: New Delhi
Area: 3,287,590 sq km
Population: 886,362,000
Languages: Hindi, English
Currency: Rupee

◀ The river Ganges is sacred to Hindus because, in legend, it flows from the head of the god Shiva.

Monsoon winds bring heavy rains to many parts of India. The Shillong Plateau in eastern India is one of the wettest places in the world with an average of 1087 cm of rain each year.

To the north of India are the HIMALAYAS. Many people live in the fertile northern plains, which are crossed by the great Ganges and Brahmaputra rivers. The south is high, flat land, with mountains called the Ghats along the coast.

India is very hot and dry in summer. Parts of the country are almost DESERT. But winds called *monsoons* bring heavy rain to the north-east every year.

Most Indians are farmers. They live in small villages and grow rice, wheat, tea, cotton and jute. India is also a fast-growing industrial country. Cities such as Calcutta and Bombay are among the world's biggest. The capital is New Delhi.

Hindi and English are the two main languages, but there are hundreds of others. Most Indians practise HINDUISM, but many follow the religion of ISLAM. There are also many other religions in India, including Buddhism and Christianity.

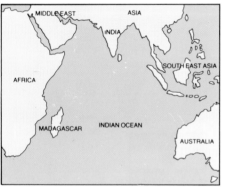

Indian, American *See* American Indians

Indian Ocean

The Indian Ocean is the third largest ocean, with an area of 73,500,000 square km. Two very large islands lie in the ocean—Madagascar, off southern Africa, and Sri Lanka, off the southern tip of India.

Strong winds from the ocean, called *monsoons*, bring moisture to South-east Asia each summer.

Indonesia

Indonesia is a country in South-east ASIA. It is a chain of over 3000 islands around the EQUATOR. The islands stretch over a distance of 4800 km.

Indonesia has over 190 million people. More than half of them live in Java, one of the biggest islands. The capital city, Jakarta, is in Java. Most Indonesians are farmers. They grow many things, including rice, tea, rubber and tobacco. Indonesia also produces minerals, including petroleum, and timber from its forests. Once ruled by the Dutch, Indonesia fought for and won independence in 1949.

INDONESIA

Government: Independent republic
Capital: Jakarta
Area: 1,904,000 sq km
Population: 195,000,000
Language: Bahasa Indonesian (Malay)
Currency: Rupiah

Industrial Revolution

The Industrial Revolution was a great change which took place in Europe in the 1700s and 1800s. People began to make things on machines in factories, instead of by hand at home. The new machines were run by STEAM ENGINES. They made things much faster than people could by hand. Mining and metal-working became more important and the RAILWAYS began. Many people moved from the countryside and began to work in factories in the towns.

▼ *Arkwright's water frame was one of many machines invented during the industrial revolution. It altered work methods that had not changed for hundreds of years.*

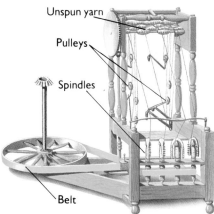

Unspun yarn
Pulleys
Spindles
Belt

◀ *Enormous social changes took place in the 18th century in Europe. Improved farming methods replaced traditional ways and many peasant farmers had to move to towns where the conditions were crowded and unhealthy.*

Some countries have experienced 'hyperinflation', when prices increased by more then 50 per cent *every month*. This means an inflation rate of more than 13,000 per cent a year. A bar of chocolate that cost 10p on January 1 would cost £13 by December 31!

Inflation

Inflation is a word used to mean rapidly rising prices. Every time prices go up, MONEY is worth less because people need more money to buy the same things. In turn, people ask for higher wages. If wages rise, then the cost of making things in factories goes up. This often makes prices rise again. Because prices and wages affect each other like this, inflation is hard to stop. There are many reasons why inflation starts. If inflation becomes very bad, money can become worthless.

Infrared Rays

When you feel the heat from a fire or the Sun you are feeling infrared rays. They are also called *heat rays*. Although you cannot see infrared rays, they behave in the same way as light rays. They can be *reflected* and *refracted*. Photographers use film that is sensitive to infrared rays to take pictures in total darkness. They are called infrared because they lie just beyond the red end of the light SPECTRUM.

Inoculation

Inoculation is a way of protecting people from diseases. It is also called *vaccination*.

Inoculation works by giving people a very weak dose of a disease. The body learns to fight the germs that cause the disease. In this way, the body

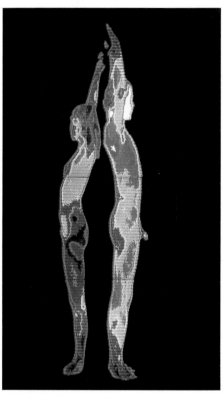

▲ Infrared sensitive film can be used to take pictures in which areas of heat and cold show up as different colours. White areas are the hottest and blue are coolest.

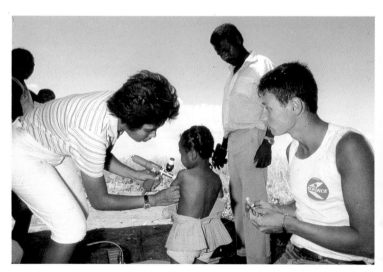

► Inoculation programmes are vital in Third World countries, where diseases can be prevented and thousands of lives saved.

becomes protected, or *immune,* from the disease.

IMMUNITY from a disease may last from a few months to many years, depending on the kind of disease and vaccine. There are many kinds of inoculation. They are used against diseases such as typhoid, cholera, measles and polio. Many people used to fall ill and die from these diseases. Now more people are saved every year through inoculation. A pioneer of inoculation was Edward JENNER.

Insect

There are millions of different kinds of insects in the world. Every year, thousands of new kinds are found. They live everywhere except in the sea. (See pages 368–369.)

Instinct

People have to learn to read and write, but bees do not learn how to sting. They are born knowing how to sting when there is danger. This kind of behaviour is called instinct. Parents pass on instincts to their young through HEREDITY.

Animals do many things by instinct. Birds build nests this way. Simple animals, such as insects, do almost everything by instinct. They have set ways of finding food, attacking enemies or escaping. Animals that act entirely by instinct do not have enough INTELLIGENCE to learn new ways of doing things, and cannot easily change their behaviour.

▼ *Instinctive behaviour is seen in humans and animals alike. Three examples are shown below. Bees sting as an instinctive reaction to danger; a new-born baby will grasp tightly enough with its hands to support its own weight; and a weaver bird makes an elaborate hanging nest out of grasses.*

INSECTS

Insects live all over the world. They are by far the most numerous of all animal species. More than 850,000 different kinds of insects are known. Roughly eight out of ten of all the Earth's animals are insects!

Insects range in size from tiny fleas which can be seen only through a microscope to beetles as big as your hand. Many have interesting life stories, or cycles. Some insects, such as the desert locust of Africa, are destructive pests. But many others are helpful. Without bees and other flying insects, flowering plants would not be pollinated and fruit trees would not bear fruit.

Among the most fascinating insects are the social insects, which live in highly organized communities or colonies. These include ants, bees and termites. Many insects make regular journeys. Some butterflies, beetles and dragonflies migrate at certain times every year.

▼ *These are just a few of the hundreds of thousands of different kinds of insects alive on Earth. Their success as living species is due to the fact that they are small, they can adapt to many environments, and they reproduce rapidly.*

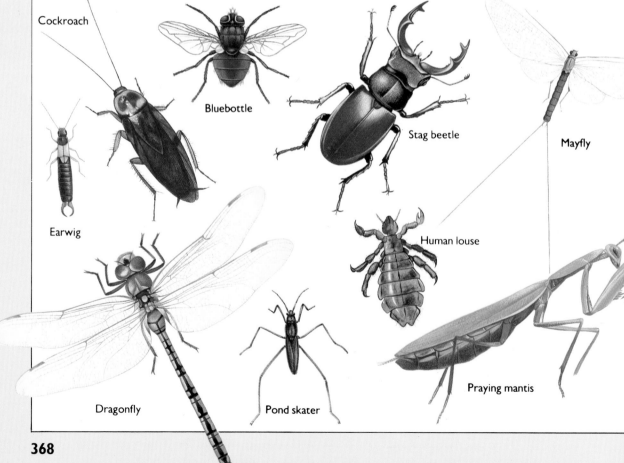

Cockroach

Bluebottle

Stag beetle

Mayfly

Earwig

Human louse

Dragonfly

Pond skater

Praying mantis

INSECT HELPERS

...ful insects include bees, which pollinate flowering ...ts and also give us honey. The silkworm (the larva ...he silk moth) is reared for the silk it spins when ...ing into a pupa. Ladybirds are the gardener's ...nds because they prey on the aphids which attack ...es and other plants. Insects such as the ichneumon ...p prey on other insects, controlling pests. ...venging insects, such as burying beetles, feed on ...d matter and help to make the soil fertile.

The seven-spot ladybird feeds on aphids, *...ts in our gardens.*

INSECT PESTS

...mful insects are those that carry disease and ...troy food grown by farmers. The mosquito (which ...ies malaria) and the tsetse fly (which spreads ...ase in people and cattle) are pests. Flies, lice, fleas ...cockroaches live close to people, often inside ...ses, damaging food and spreading disease. The ...orado beetle destroys potato crops. Locusts are ...ed by farmers in Africa because they swarm in such ...t numbers that they blacken the skies. The locusts ...every plant in their path.

The locust travels long distances in *...tructive swarms.*

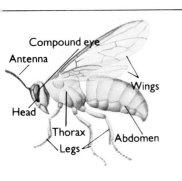

THE BODY OF AN INSECT

All insects have a similar body plan. An insect's body is in three parts: a head, thorax and abdomen. The head has eyes, jaws and feelers (antennae). The middle part, or thorax, carries three pairs of jointed legs and sometimes wings. The abdomen contains the stomach, reproductive organs, and breathing tubes called spiracles.

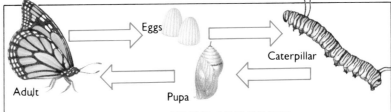

THE LIFE CYCLE OF INSECTS

All insects start life as eggs. In the most advanced insects, there are four stages in the life cycle. The egg hatches into a larva or grub. This larva grows by shedding its skin and finally turns into a pupa or chrysalis. The pupa looks lifeless, but inside many changes are taking place. The pupa finally splits apart and a fully-formed adult insect emerges.

Some insects, such as grasshoppers, hatch from eggs not as larvae, but as nymphs. Grasshopper nymphs do not yet have wings, but otherwise look much like their parents. Nymphs grow by moulting their skins. The most primitive insects, such as silverfish, hatch from the egg looking exactly like adults, only much smaller, and shed their skins many times as they grow.

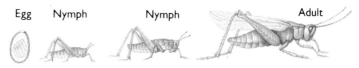

For more information turn to these articles: ANT; BEE; BEETLE; BUTTERFLY; FLEA; FLY; GRASSHOPPER; LOCUST; PARASITE; TERMITE.

The most famous insurance organization in the world is Lloyd's of London. It is said that anything that cannot be insured at Lloyd's cannot be insured at all. Lloyd's takes its name from a 17th-century coffee house in London where ship insurers met to do business. Hanging in Lloyd's headquarters is the famous Lutine Bell which was salvaged in 1837 from a shipwreck. It is rung once for good news and twice for bad news.

Insulin

Insulin is a HORMONE that controls the body's use of sugar. It is produced in a part of the pancreas GLAND. When not enough insulin is produced, the body cannot use or store sugar properly. This condition is called *diabetes*. Many people with diabetes have to be given insulin daily.

Insurance

Insurance is a way of safeguarding against loss or damage. A person with an insurance *policy* pays a little money to an insurance company every year. If they lose or damage something they have insured, the company gives them money to replace it or to pay for its repair.

▼ *An example of a test for measuring intelligence. The idea of this reasoning problem is to spot the 'odd-one-out' in each group. Answers on page 372.*

Intelligence

When someone uses experience and knowledge to solve a new kind of problem, he or she shows intelligence. Intelligence depends on being able to learn. Creatures that act only by INSTINCT lack intelligence. People, apes and whales are the most intelligent creatures.

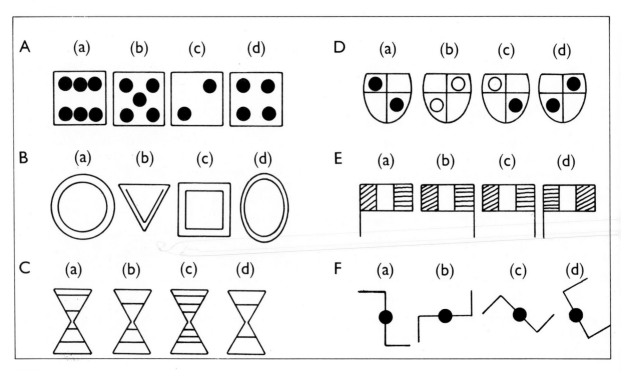

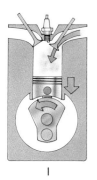 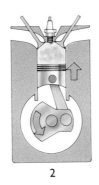  

1　　2　　3　　4

THE FOUR-STROKE ENGINE

In a four-stroke engine, the inlet valve opens (1) and the fuel mixture is drawn into the cylinder by the downward movement of the piston. Then both valves close and the mixture is compressed (2) by the rising piston. The spark plug ignites the mixture (3), forcing the piston down. Finally, the exhaust valve opens and the rising piston expels the burnt gases (4).

Internal Combustion Engine

In internal combustion engines, FUEL burns inside the engines. The most common internal combustion engines are petrol engines and DIESEL ENGINES. In the petrol engine, fuel mixes with air inside a cylinder. A spark sets the mixture alight and it explodes. This happens over and over again. Hot gases from the explosions push a piston to and fro inside the cylinder. Most engines have several cylinders. The pistons work very quickly in turn. They move the crankshaft. This movement turns WHEELS or propellers.

Petrol and diesel engines are used in MOTOR CARS and lorries, and in ships and some planes.

Invention

An invention may be the creation of something completely new or an improvement of something that someone else has produced. Many important inventions have come from the work of one person; others have been created by many people working as a team. We will never know who thought of many of the very early inventions such as the wheel and the plough.

GREAT INVENTIONS

AD 105 Paper (from pulp) (Chinese)
1100 Magnetic compass (Chinese)
1440 Printing press Johannes Gutenberg (Ger.)
1608 Telescope Hans Lippershey (Neth.)
1765 Condensing steam engine James Watt (Scot.)
1816 Camera Nicéphore Niépce (Fr.)
1831 Dynamo Michael Faraday (Eng.)
1837 Telegraph Samuel F. B. Morse (U.S.)
1876 Telephone Alexander Graham Bell (Scot.)
1877 Phonograph Thomas Edison (U.S.)
1895 Radio Guglielmo Marconi (It.)
1903 Aeroplane Wright Brothers (U.S.)
1925 Television John Logie Baird (Scot.)
1948 Transistor John Bardeen, Walter Brattain & William Shockley (U.S.)
1960 Laser Theodore Maiman (U.S.)
1961 Silicon Chip Texas Instruments (U.S.)
1971 Microprocessor Intel Corp (U.S.)

IRAN

Government: Islamic republic
Capital: Tehran
Area: 1,648,000 sq km
Population: 61,183,000
Language: Farsi (Persian)
Currency: Rial

Answers to Intelligence Test on p.370:
A (b); B (b); C (b); D (c); E (a); F (d).

IRAQ

Government: One-party republic
Capital: Baghdad
Area: 434,924 sq km
Population: 18,445,000
Language: Arabic
Currency: Dinar

Invertebrate

Invertebrates are animals that have no spine, or backbone. There are more than a million different invertebrates. They include all the WORMS, SHELLFISH, OCTOPUSES, INSECTS, SPIDERS, CRABS, STARFISH and many others.

Iran

Iran is a country in ASIA. It lies between the Caspian Sea in the north and the Persian Gulf in the south. The country is nearly seven times larger than Great Britain but it has fewer people. Deserts, snowy mountains and green valleys cover most of the land. Much of the country has hot, dry summers and cold winters.

Iranians speak Persian. (Persia is the old name for Iran.) Their religion is ISLAM. Tehran is the capital city.

Many Iranians are NOMADS who travel around with flocks of sheep or goats. Each time they camp, the women set up simple looms and weave beautiful rugs by hand. Iran's most important product is oil.

Iran has a long history. In about 550 BC the Persians had a leader called Cyrus. Cyrus and his army made an empire that stretched from Greece and Egypt to India. The Persian empire was then the largest in the world.

ALEXANDER THE GREAT conquered Persia about 330 BC. Later, the country was ruled by ARABS and MONGOLS. During this century Iran was ruled by emperors, or *shahs*. In 1979 the government of Iran changed and the shah left the country. Religious leaders now rule this Islamic Republic.

From 1980 to 1988 Iran fought a long and bitter war with Iraq.

Iraq

Iraq is an ARAB country in south-west ASIA. Much of Iraq is a dry, sandy and stony plain. It is cool in winter and very hot in summer. The Tigris and Euphrates rivers flow through the plain to the Persian Gulf. Their water helps the farmers to grow rice, cotton, wheat and dates. Iraq is also one of the biggest oil producers in the world. Pipelines carry the oil from the north of the country across the desert to ports in Syria and the Lebanon.

Many Iraqis are NOMADS. They live in the deserts with their sheep and goats. But nearly 4 million people work in the capital city of Baghdad.

Some of the first cities in the world were built near Iraq's big rivers. Ur was one of the earliest cities. Later, the Babylonians built their famous city, BABYLON, in Iraq. Modern Iraq is a republic, with Saddam Hussein as its virtual dictator. It was involved in a war with Iran from 1980 to 1988. In 1990 Iraq invaded Kuwait but was forced to leave after the Gulf War in 1991.

Ireland

Ireland is the second largest island of the BRITISH ISLES. It is shaped like a saucer. Mountains form the rim. The middle is a low plain. Through this flows the Shannon, the longest river in the British Isles. Irish weather is often mild and rainy. Meadows and moors cover much of the land. Northern Ireland is part of the United Kingdom of GREAT BRITAIN and Northern Ireland. Its capital city is Belfast. Southern Ireland is the Republic of Ireland, or Eire. The capital city of Eire is Dublin.

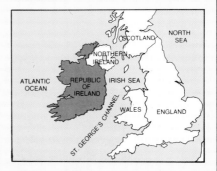

IRELAND

Government: Parliamentary republic
Capital: Dublin
Area: 70,284 sq km
Population: 3,521,000
Languages: English, Irish (Gaelic)
Currency: Irish pound (punt)

▼ A fishing village in County Cork on the south coast of Ireland. Much of the economy of the Republic of Ireland is based on farming and fishing.

IRON AND STEEL

▼ *To produce iron from iron ore, the ore is mixed with coke and limestone, then heated at a very high temperature. A poor quality iron, called pig iron, is made first and this can be made into steel or steel alloys, which are much stronger.*
Most steel (bottom) is made by the 'Linz-Donawitz' method. I. The furnace is filled with scrap iron and molten iron. 2. Oxygen blown into the furnace produces enough heat to burn out impurities. 3. Molten steel is poured from the furnace into ingots.

Iron and Steel

Iron is the cheapest and most useful of all metals. Much of our food, clothes, homes and cars are made with machines and tools made from iron.

Iron is mined, or *quarried*, as iron ore, or MINERALS. The ore is melted down, or *smelted*, in a blast furnace. The iron is then made into cast iron, wrought iron, or mixed with a small amount of CARBON to form steel.

Cast iron is hard but not as strong as steel. Molten cast iron is poured into moulds to make such things as engine blocks. Wrought iron is soft but tough. It is used for chains and gates. Steel is hard and strong. Steel ALLOYS containing metals such as tungsten and chromium are used to make many different things, from bridges to nails.

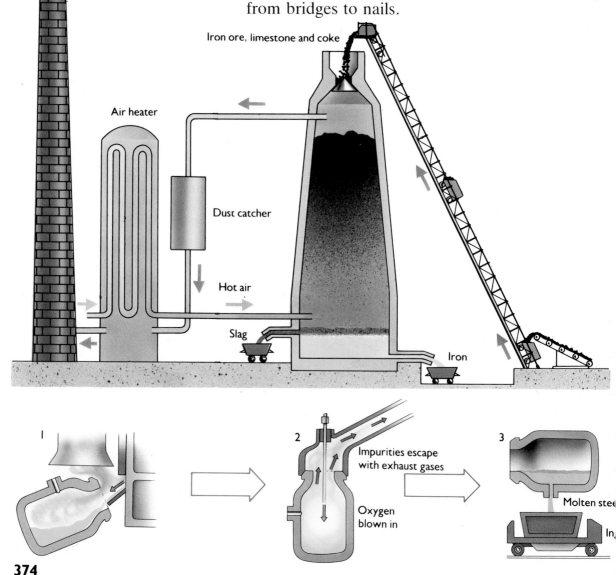

Iron ore, limestone and coke

Air heater

Dust catcher

Hot air

Slag

Iron

1

2   Impurities escape with exhaust gases

Oxygen blown in

3

Molten steel

In

Shaduf

The shaduf was used for irrigation, as long ago as 5000 BC.

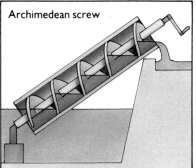

Archimedean screw

The Archimedean screw uses a rotating spiral to raise water.

King Sennacherib's canals

King Sennacherib of Ancient Assyria built canals for irrigation.

Irrigation

Farmers and gardeners who water plants are irrigating them. Irrigation makes it possible to grow crops and flowers in dry soils, even in a DESERT. Farmers in China, Egypt and Iraq have been irrigating large areas of land for thousands of years.

Many countries store water in lakes made by building DAMS across rivers. CANALS take water from the lakes to farms. One irrigation canal in Russia is 850 km long. Ditches or pipes carry water from each canal to the fields. In each field the water flows between the rows of plants. Sometimes it spurts up from holes in the pipes. It sprinkles the plants like a shower of rain.

▲ *Irrigation is as old as farming itself, and many ancient societies have developed their own methods for keeping their crops watered. Some of these are still used today.*

▼ *Islamic styles of building are very graceful, and well suited to hot climates. Mosques, the Islamic places of worship, often have a high tower from which a priest calls the people to prayer.*

Islam

Islam is a religion started in AD 622 by MUHAMMAD. It has more followers than any other religion except Christianity. Islam means 'submission'. Its followers are called Muslims. Muslim means 'submissive one'. Muslims believe they must submit, or give in, to God's will. They believe in one God and in Muhammad as his prophet. Muslims pray five times a day and give gifts to the poor. For one month a year they go without food until sunset and they try to visit Mecca, Muhammad's birthplace, before they die. They also try to obey the rules for good living set out in the KORAN, the holy book of Islam.

Islam began in Arabia. Today it is the main religion in North Africa and most of south-west Asia.

ISLAND

► *This small coral island is typical of the South Pacific.*

ISRAEL

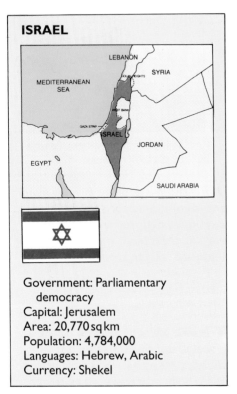

Government: Parliamentary democracy
Capital: Jerusalem
Area: 20,770 sq km
Population: 4,784,000
Languages: Hebrew, Arabic
Currency: Shekel

▼ *The Leaning Tower of Pisa is one of the most famous tourist sights in Italy.*

Island

An island is a piece of land surrounded by water. Some islands are chunks of land that became separated from CONTINENTS. Other islands are VOLCANOES that have poked up above the sea. Yet others lie inland, in lakes and rivers.

Israel

Israel is a country in south-west ASIA, on the shores of the Mediterranean Sea. The state of Israel was only created in 1948 as a homeland for Jewish people from around the world.

Farmers grow oranges, cotton and grain on fertile plains. More than half the land is dry mountain or desert. Summers are hot and winters are mild.

The Israelis have had to fight wars against their Arab neighbours. In 1994 agreement was signed between Israel and the Palestine Liberation Organization for limited Palestinion self-rule.

Italy

Italy is a country in southern EUROPE. It is shaped like a boot stuck out in the Mediterranean Sea to kick Sicily. Sicily and Sardinia are Italian islands.

Much of Italy is mountainous. The sharp, snowy peaks of the ALPS cross northern Italy. The Apennines run like a backbone down the middle. Between the Alps and Apennines lies the plain of

◀ *Venice was a wealthy trading city in the 16th and 17th centuries. It is full of art treasures.*

ITALY

Government: Republic
Capital: Rome
Area: 301,225 sq km
Population: 57,904,000
Language: Italian
Currency: Lira

Lombardy. Italy is famous for its hot, sunny summers. Rain falls mostly in winter.

Crops grow on almost half the land. Italy produces more pears and olives than any other country. The farmers also grow a lot of grapes, lemons, wheat, rice and oranges. Big factories in northern Italy make cars, chemicals and machines.

The capital is ROME. Many tourists visit Rome to see the VATICAN and ruins of the ROMAN EMPIRE.

Ivan the Terrible

Ivan IV, the Terrible (1530–1584), was the first emperor, or *tsar*, of RUSSIA. He was a cruel man who killed his own son. But he helped to make Russia great. In his reign MOSCOW became the Russian capital.

Ivory

Ivory comes from the long teeth, or *tusks*, of some animals. Walrus and narwhal tusks and hippopotamus teeth are made of ivory. Larger pieces of ivory come from ELEPHANT and MAMMOTH tusks.

Elephant ivory was used to make ornaments, piano keys and jewellery. Today, even though elephants are protected, poachers still kill them for their tusks.

Ivory Coast *See* Côte d'Ivoire

▼ *This delicate carving of a woman's head was made from mammoth ivory, perhaps as early as 22,000 BC.*

Jackal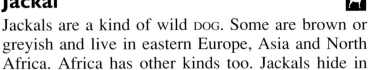

Jackals are a kind of wild DOG. Some are brown or greyish and live in eastern Europe, Asia and North Africa. Africa has other kinds too. Jackals hide in bushes by day. At night they hunt small animals and find food in rubbish heaps.

Jaguar

No other American wild CAT is as heavy or perhaps as dangerous as the jaguar. From nose to tail a jaguar is longer than a man, and may be nearly twice his weight. The jaguar is yellow with black spots. The LEOPARD also has spots, but many of the jaguar's spots are in rings. Jaguars live in the hot, wet forests of Central and South America. They leap from trees onto wild pigs and deer. They also catch turtles, fish and alligators.

▲ Jackals are members of the dog family.

▶ Jaguars look rather like the leopards of Asia and Africa but they are heavier.

JAMAICA

Government: Constitutional monarchy
Capital: Kingston
Area: 10,991 sq km
Population: 2,506,000
Language: English
Currency: Jamaican dollar

Jamaica

Jamaica is a tropical island in the Caribbean Sea. The name Jamaica means 'island of springs'. It is a beautiful island, with hundreds of streams flowing from springs on the sides of its green mountains.

There are more than two million people in Jamaica. Most of them are of African ancestry. Many work on farms that grow bananas, coconuts, coffee, oranges and sugar cane. Jamaica also mines bauxite. Kingston is Jamaica's capital city and an important Caribbean seaport.

James (kings)

James was the name of two kings of Great Britain. James I (1566–1625) was the son of MARY, QUEEN OF SCOTS and a cousin of ELIZABETH I. He became King James VI of Scotland when he was one year old. Queen Elizabeth died without any children in 1603. James VI (who was a descendant of King Henry VII of England) was next in line, and was crowned James I of England. In this way England and Scotland were joined under one ruler.

James II (1633–1701) was the grandson of James I. He tried to restore the ROMAN CATHOLIC CHURCH in England, but Parliament would not let him. In 1688 he was made to leave the country. He was replaced on the throne by his daughter Mary and her Dutch husband WILLIAM OF ORANGE. James's followers were called Jacobites. (Jacobus is Latin for James.) In the 1700s Jacobites twice began rebellions in Scotland. But they did not win the throne back for the STUARTS.

▲ James I was king in 1605 when the Gunpowder Plot, in which Guy Fawkes and his friends planned to blow up parliament, was discovered.

Japan

Japan is a long, narrow string of islands off the mainland coast of Asia. Altogether they make a country slightly larger than the British Isles.

▼ There is very little space in Tokyo, so overhead railways are an ideal way of coping with commuter travel.

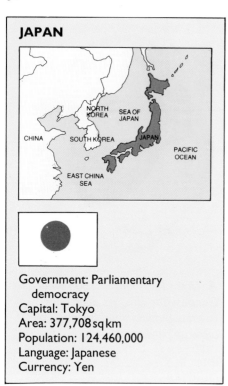

JAPAN

Government: Parliamentary democracy
Capital: Tokyo
Area: 377,708 sq km
Population: 124,460,000
Language: Japanese
Currency: Yen

Mountains cover most of Japan. The highest is a beautiful volcano called Fujiyama, or Mount Fuji. Parts of Japan have forests, waterfalls and lakes. Northern Japan has cool summers and cold winters.

Japan is a crowded country. It has more than 123 million people. To feed them, farmers grow huge amounts of rice and fruits. The Japanese eat a lot of fish and seaweed.

Japan does not have many minerals, so the Japanese buy most of their minerals such as iron ore from other countries. But no other country makes as many ships, television sets, radios, videos and cameras as Japan does. The Japanese also make a lot of cars.

Jazz

Jazz is a kind of music. The players use unexpected rhythms. They can play any notes they like, but they must fit the music made by the rest of the band. In this way, jazz musicians often *improvise*, or make up music as they go along. Jazz began in the United States in the 1800s.

Jenner, Edward

Edward Jenner (1749–1823) was a British doctor who discovered how INOCULATION works. He inoculated a boy with cowpox germs. Cowpox is a disease like smallpox, but it is less dangerous. Jenner then injected the boy with smallpox germs. Because the cowpox germs protected the boy, he did not develop smallpox. Today, millions of people are inoculated against many diseases.

▼ *Louis Armstrong was one of the most famous and influential figures in jazz.*

Jerusalem

Jerusalem is the capital of ISRAEL. It is a holy city of the Jews, Christians and Muslims. David, Jesus and other famous people in the Bible lived or died here.

Jerusalem stands high up in hilly country. It has many old religious buildings. Huge walls surround the city's oldest part. In 1948 Jerusalem was divided between Israel and Jordan, but Israel took the whole city during a war in 1967.

Jesus

Jesus was a Jew. He started CHRISTIANITY. The New Testament of the BIBLE says that Jesus was God's Son.

Jesus was born in Bethlehem. His mother was called Mary. When he grew up he travelled around, teaching and healing sick people. Some Jewish priests were jealous of Jesus. They told their Roman rulers that he was making trouble. The Romans killed Jesus on a cross, but the New Testament says that he came to life again and rose to heaven. Followers of Jesus spread his teachings worldwide.

Jet Engine

A swimmer swims forwards by pushing water backwards. A jet engine works in a similar way. It drives an AIRCRAFT forwards by pushing gases backwards. Engines that work like this are called *reaction* engines. ROCKETS are also reaction engines. The main difference between jets and rockets is that jets take in oxygen from the air to burn their fuel, but rockets have a supply of oxygen in their fuel.

▲ The Baptism of Christ *was painted by the Italian Renaissance artist Piero della Francesca in the 1400s. Many masterpieces of western art have had the life of Jesus as their inspiration.*

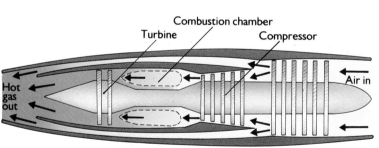

Turbine

Combustion chamber

Compressor

Air in

Hot gas out

◀ *Jet engines provide a powerful thrust to drive both passenger and military planes.*

There are four main kinds of jet engine. These are turbojets, turboprops, turbofans and ramjets.

Jet engines have replaced propeller-driven piston engines in many kinds of plane. There are many reasons for this. Jet engines weigh less than piston engines. They also go wrong less often. Their moving parts spin instead of moving to and fro. This stops the plane from shaking about. Jet engines burn cheap paraffin (kerosene) instead of costly petrol. Jet engines can also carry planes faster and higher than piston engines can. Some jet fighters can travel at 3400 km/hr.

Long ago, in the first century AD, a Greek mathematician named Hero made the first jet engine. He suspended a hollow metal ball containing water. When he boiled the water, the steam escaped through a nozzle on either side of the ball. As the nozzles pointed in opposite directions, the ball began to spin.

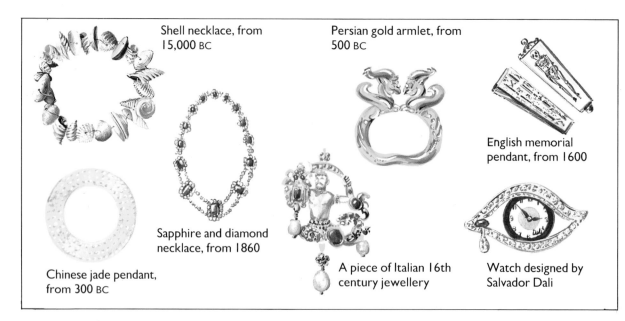

Shell necklace, from 15,000 BC

Persian gold armlet, from 500 BC

English memorial pendant, from 1600

Chinese jade pendant, from 300 BC

Sapphire and diamond necklace, from 1860

A piece of Italian 16th century jewellery

Watch designed by Salvador Dali

▲ *Jewellery has been found dating from the earliest history of mankind, so decorating the body seems to be a basic need.*

Jewellery

Objects worn to decorate the body are called jewellery. People wear different kinds of jewellery on different parts of the body. The kinds you see most often are earrings, necklaces, brooches, bracelets and rings. Expensive jewellery is often made of gold or silver and set with DIAMONDS or other GEMS.

Cheap jewellery is called costume jewellery. It is often made of glass and plastics.

▼ *Joan of Arc successfully took on the role of soldier to lead the French into battle against the English.*

Joan of Arc

Joan of Arc (1412–1431) was a French girl who believed that God told her to free France from its English invaders. At 17 she left the farm where she worked, and persuaded France's King Charles VII to let her lead his army. She won five battles. Then she was captured and burnt as a witch. But she had saved France. In 1920 the Pope made her a SAINT.

John, King

John (about 1167–1216) was a cruel but clever English king. He murdered his nephew, and lost his lands in France, but he ruled strongly in England. His nobles made him sign the MAGNA CARTA. Then some of them started a war against John. He died before it ended.

Johnson, Samuel

Samuel Johnson (1709–1784) was an English writer. He is still famous for the clever things he used to say. Johnson also wrote probably the first good English DICTIONARY. Many of the things we know about him come from a book written by his friend, James Boswell.

Jordan

Jordan is a small Arab country in the north-west corner of the Arabian Peninsula. Most of the country lies on a plateau 1000 metres above sea level. The Jordan River and the salty Dead Sea lie west of the plateau. The Jordanians and the Israelis have for many years been unfriendly neighbours. In 1967 Israel captured Jordanian land west of the Jordan River. This land is known as the West Bank. Jordan's capital is Amman.

JORDAN

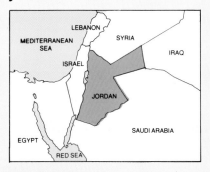

Government: Constitutional monarchy
Capital: Amman
Area: 97,740 sq km
Population: 4,009,000
Language: Arabic
Currency: Jordanian dinar

Judaism

Judaism is a religion that believes in one God and has as its holy book the Bible. The Hebrew Bible consists of the first five books of Moses (the Torah), historical accounts of the tribes of Israel, and books written by prophets and kings. (Christians include

The total number of Jews in the world is estimated to be 16,000,000. Nearly half of that number, 7.3 million, are in North America. There are 2 million Jews in the New York area alone. In Israel there are nearly 3.5 million, while the British Jewish population is nearly 400,000.

◀ Many Jewish religious traditions, such as those involved in this wedding, are very ancient.

all this material in their Bible, calling it the Old Testament.) Judaism's followers are called Jews. They observe the Ten Commandments. They believe God gave the Law to Moses on top of Mount Sinai after Moses led their ancestors out of Egypt, where they had been slaves. The commemoration of this Exodus from Egypt is one of Judaism's most important festivals and is called Passover. Today Jews live all over the world, but regard Israel as their spiritual and historical home.

Jupiter

Jupiter is the largest of the PLANETS in our SOLAR SYSTEM. It is twice the size of all the other planets put together. You could fit 1300 planets the size of the Earth into the space filled by Jupiter. Jupiter's force of GRAVITY is great. Anyone on Jupiter would weigh twice as much as on the Earth. Astronomers believe that most of Jupiter is hot, liquid HYDROGEN. Jupiter is so hot that it would be a glowing star if it were ten times larger. It has 16 moons.

Jupiter spins so fast that a day and night last less than ten Earth-hours. But a YEAR on Jupiter is 12 times longer than one of ours. This is because Jupiter is farther from the SUN than we are.

JUPITER FACTS

Average distance from Sun:
  778 million km
Nearest distance from Earth:
  630 million km
Average temperature: −150°C
Diameter across equator: 142,800 km
Atmosphere: Hydrogen, helium
Number of moons: 17
Length of day: 9 hours 50 minutes
Length of year: 11.9 Earth years

If an astronaut managed to 'land' on Jupiter, he or she would find that there are no seasons. The faint Sun, so distant as to be just a flickering star, would rise and set every nine and three-quarter hours. Jupiter's biggest moon, Ganymede, is bigger than the planet Mercury.

► *The planet Jupiter appears to have light and dark belts around it in its atmosphere.*

Kangaroo

Kangaroos are MARSUPIALS that live in New Guinea and Australia. Most of them live on grassy plains and most of them feed on plants. They move about in troops, springing along on their big, powerful hind legs. Their long tails help them to balance.

There are more than 50 kinds of kangaroo. Red and grey kangaroos are the largest. A red kangaroo may be taller and heavier than a man. Grey kangaroos can bounce along at 40km/h if chased. Wallabies are smaller kinds of kangaroo.

Kazakhstan

Kazakhstan is a large country that until 1991 was a republic of the former SOVIET UNION. It stretches from the shores of the CASPIAN SEA to China. Much of country is dry steppe and desert. There are rich mineral deposits, including lead, copper, zinc, iron, coal and oil.

For centuries the people of Kazakhstan lived a nomadic life, herding livestock from place to place. This lifestyle changed after Russia conquered the country in 1800, advancing industry and farming.

KAZAKHSTAN

Government: Republic
Capital: Alma-Ata
Area: 2,717,000 sq km
Population: 17,101,000
Language: Kazakh, Russian, German
Currency: Ruble

◀ *Kangaroos are considered to be a pest in Australia, and to keep their numbers down, they are sometimes hunted.*

KENYA

▶ *Sisal, used to make rope, is made from the agave plant which is widely grown in Kenya.*

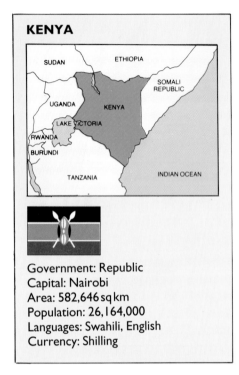

KENYA

Government: Republic
Capital: Nairobi
Area: 582,646 sq km
Population: 26,164,000
Languages: Swahili, English
Currency: Shilling

▼ *The kidneys are part of a vital system for cleaning the blood of impurities and excess liquid. These are drained off through the ureters into the bladder, and leave the body as urine.*

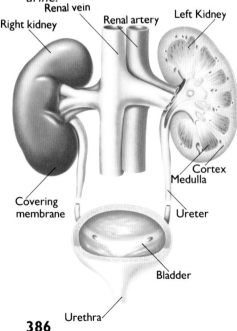

Renal vein
Right kidney
Renal artery
Left Kidney
Cortex
Medulla
Covering membrane
Ureter
Bladder
Urethra

Kenya

Kenya is a country in east AFRICA. It is just a bit larger than France. The south-west border touches Lake Victoria. The Indian Ocean is on the south-east. The EQUATOR goes across the middle of the country. Much of the land is covered by mountains and flat-topped hills. The rest looks like a huge open park. It is hot, dry country.

Kenya is a member of the COMMONWEALTH. Most of the people in Kenya are African. They belong to a number of different tribes. Some tribes, like the Masai, keep cattle. Kenyan farmers grow maize, tea and coffee. Kenya sells a lot of tea and coffee abroad. Many tourists visit Kenya to see the wild animals roaming the huge nature reserves. The capital is Nairobi.

Kidney

All VERTEBRATES (animals with a backbone) have two kidneys. Kidneys look like large reddish-brown beans. Human kidneys are about the size of a person's fist. They lie on each side of the backbone, at just about waist level.

Kidneys clean the BLOOD. They filter out waste matter and strain off any water that the body does not need. Blood pumped from the HEART flows into each kidney through an artery. Each kidney contains tubes that act as filters. Blood cells, tiny food particles, and other useful items stay in the blood to be used by the body. Filtered blood flows out of the kidney through a vein. All the waste matter and extra water mix together to make urine. This drips slowly into the bladder.

King, Martin Luther

Martin Luther King (1929–1968) was an American civil rights leader who worked for racial justice through peaceful means. He was born in Atlanta, Georgia, and became a Baptist minister like his father. It was in Montgomery, Alabama, where he was pastor, that he began his CIVIL RIGHTS crusade. One of King's first actions was to organize a boycott of buses in Montgomery in 1956 as a protest against unfair treatment of black passengers. During the next ten years, he led many peaceful demonstrations and meetings all over the country. Success came when Congress passed CIVIL RIGHTS laws in 1964 and 1965.

In 1964 King won the Nobel Peace Prize for his campaigns of non-violence. In 1968, at the age of 39, he was assassinated in Memphis, Tennessee.

Kipling, Rudyard

Rudyard Kipling (1865–1936) was an English writer of adventure stories and poems. Many were about India and the British Empire. His best-remembered tales were stories for children. *Kim* is a story of an

Martin Luther King made a famous speech in 1963. He was speaking to a crowd of 200,000 people who had come to Washington D.C. to march for civil rights for all people. In his speech he said: 'I have a dream that one day this nation will rise up and live out the true meaning of its creed: "We hold these truths to be self-evident, that all men are created equal."'

Rudyard Kipling was born in India and had a very unhappy childhood. His parents sent him to England when he was only six, and he spent five years in a foster home at Southsea. He later described the horrors of this place in the story *Baa, Baa, Black Sheep*. Kipling was then sent to a boarding school in Devon. He tells about such a school in *Stalky & Co.*

◄ In The Jungle Book, *published in 1894, Kipling gave free rein to his love and understanding of India and its wildlife in his stories of a boy brought up by animals.*

orphan boy's secret service adventures in India. *The Jungle Book* is about Mowgli, a boy brought up by wolves and taught by a bear, a python and a panther. *The Just So Stories* are all about animals.

Kiribati

Kiribati is one of the smallest countries in the Commonwealth. It is a string of islands in the Pacific Ocean, north-east of Australia. The islands were a British protectorate from 1892 until 1979, when they became independent. The people live simply, fishing and growing coconuts.

Kiwi

This strange bird from New Zealand gets its name from the shrill cries made by the male. The kiwi is a stocky brown bird as big as a chicken. It has tiny wings but cannot fly. Instead it runs on short, thick strong legs. Kiwi feathers look very much like hair.

Kiwis are shy birds that live in forests. By day they sleep in burrows. At night, they hunt for worms and grubs. Kiwis can hardly see. They smell out their food with the help of nostrils at the tip of their long, thin beaks. The females lay very large eggs but it is the male who sits on them and waits for them to hatch.

Knight

In the MIDDLE AGES, knights were soldiers on horseback who fought for a king or a prince. In peacetime they served their master in his household.

▼ The armour and weapons used by knights in the Crusades were heavy. Both they and the horses they rode had to be strong.

At first, anybody could become a knight. Then horses and ARMOUR became so expensive that only the rich could buy them. Knighthood became an honour usually given to the rich. Boys trained for it from the age of seven.

Knights lost their usefulness in war when GUNS changed fighting methods. The British monarch still makes people knights as a reward for special service to the country.

When gunpowder first appeared on the battlefield, knights did not immediately stop wearing armour. They had thicker armour made, which became so heavy that if they fell off their horses, they were unable to get up again.

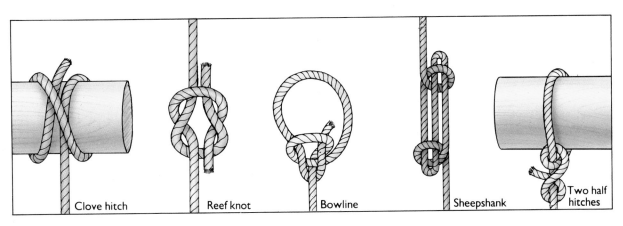

Clove hitch   Reef knot   Bowline   Sheepshank   Two half hitches

Knot

Knots are a way of fastening rope, cord or thread. They are especially important for sailors and climbers. But everyone needs to tie a knot at some time.

Knots are used to make a noose, tie up a bundle, or join the ends of small cords. There are also *bends* and *hitches*. A bend is used to tie the ends of rope together; a hitch is used to attach a rope to a ring or post. Common knots are the reef knot and bowline, both true knots; the clove hitch, half hitch, and sheet bend. Rope ends can also be joined by weaving them together. This is called a *splice* and is not a true knot.

▲ There are many different types of knot for various purposes. Choosing the right knot is half the skill of knot-tying.

▼ Young koalas hold tightly to their mothers' backs as they climb through the trees that form their habitat.

Koala

Koalas are MARSUPIALS that look like small, chubby bears. Koalas live in east and south-east Australia. They live much like SLOTHS. Koalas climb slowly among the branches of trees and hardly ever touch the ground. Their only food is eucalyptus leaves. Forest fires and hunting nearly made them extinct, but many koalas now live safely on reserves.

NORTH KOREA

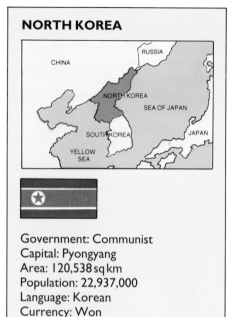

Government: Communist
Capital: Pyongyang
Area: 120,538 sq km
Population: 22,937,000
Language: Korean
Currency: Won

SOUTH KOREA

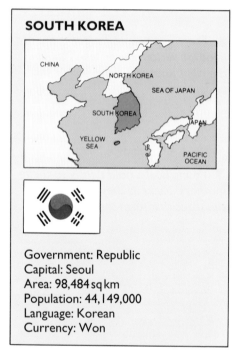

Government: Republic
Capital: Seoul
Area: 98,484 sq km
Population: 44,149,000
Language: Korean
Currency: Won

Koran

The Koran is the sacred book of ISLAM. Its name means 'a recitation'. It has 114 chapters of Arabic verse, and teaches that there is one God whose prophets (messengers) included Abraham, JESUS and MUHAMMAD. The book teaches Muslims to be humble, generous and just. It is said that the Koran was revealed to Muhammad through the angel Gabriel. The way it is written has influenced Arab literature.

Korea

Korea is a peninsula in ASIA which juts out from CHINA into the Sea of Japan. The land has many mountains and small valleys. Forests cover most of the country. Korean farms produce much rice and silk. Korean factories make steel and other products.

Korea was divided into two separate nations in 1945. They are now known as North Korea and South Korea.

War between North and South Korea broke out in 1950, with Soviet and Chinese forces supporting the North and United Nations (mostly American) forces helping the South. There is now an uneasy peace between the two countries.

▶ *The Olympic Stadium in Seoul was the location of the 1988 games. Superbly equipped, it saw many record-breaking achievements.*

KUWAIT

Government: Constitutional
  monarchy
Capital: Kuwait
Area: 17,818 sq km
Population: 1,318,000
Language: Arabic
Currency: Dinar

Kremlin

This is the oldest part of MOSCOW. Some of its buildings date from the 1100s. The Kremlin was once the fortress home of Russia's *tsars*. For most of its history the Kremlin has been the seat of the Russian government.

Kublai Khan

Kublai Khan (1216–1294) was the grandson of GENGHIS KHAN. Kublai became Great-Khan in 1259. Under his rule the Mongol empire reached its peak of power. He conquered CHINA and set up his capital at Cambulac, modern Beijing. It was the first time that China had been completely overcome by outside forces. Neighbouring countries in Southeast Asia were forced to recognize Kublai as their ruler.

KYRGYZSTAN

Government: Republic
Capital: Bishkek
Area: 198,000 sq km
Population: 4,567,000
Language: Kirghiz
Currency: Som

Kuwait

The tiny nation of Kuwait is one of the richest in the world because it is an important supplier of oil. Apart from the capital city, Kuwait, the country is almost all desert. IRAQ invaded Kuwait in 1990 but was forced to leave after the Gulf War in 1991.

Kyrgyzstan

Kyrgyzstan is a country in central ASIA. It became independent in 1991, when the former Soviet Union dissolved. Kyrgyzstan is a remote and mountainous region where travel is difficult.

Lake

Lakes are large areas of water surrounded by land. The world's largest lake is the salty Caspian Sea. It lies between Europe and Asia, east of the Caucasus Mountains. The largest freshwater lake is Lake Superior, one of the GREAT LAKES.

Many lakes were formed in the ICE AGES. They began in valleys made by glaciers. When the glaciers melted they left behind mud and stones that formed DAMS. The melted water from the glaciers piled up behind the dams.

Language

Language is what we use to talk to, or communicate with, one another. Many animals have ways of communicating. These may include special body movements and sounds. But the speaking of words is something that so far only humans can do. Spoken language came first; later people invented a way of writing it down. This is known as written language. Language is always changing as some words are forgotten and others are added.

Today there are about 3000 languages in the world. They can be grouped into a number of language families. Some of the most widely spoken languages are English, French, German, Russian, Chinese, Hindi, Arabic and Spanish.

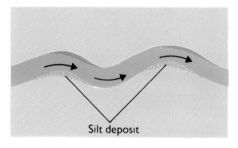

Silt deposit

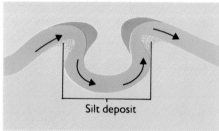

Silt deposit

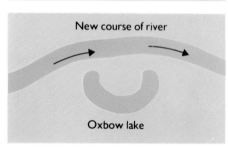

New course of river

Oxbow lake

▲ Rivers can gradually form bends by erosion of one bank and a build-up of material on the other. After a time the river cuts a straight channel through the neck of the bend. The loop of water left over is called an oxbow lake.

► This bewildering array of newspapers from countries all over the world gives an indication of how difficult international relations can be when people are divided by alphabet, language and culture.

Laos

Laos is a country in South-east Asia. It is slightly smaller than the United Kingdom. The country's capital and largest city is Vientiane on the Mekong River. Most of Laos is covered with forests and mountains. Nearly all the people earn their living by farming – especially rice growing. Laos became a French protectorate in 1893 but gained its independence in 1949.

Lapland

Lapland is a region in the ARCTIC. It lies in the far north of Sweden, Norway, Finland and Russia.

Some Lapps are nomads. They travel the land with herds of reindeer. They sleep in tents and eat reindeer meat. Other Lapps are fishermen or farmers. They live in small huts in villages. Lapps speak a language related to Finnish. They keep warm by wearing clothes made from wool and reindeer skins. Their clothes are brightly coloured.

Laser

A laser is a device that strengthens light and makes it shine in a very narrow beam. Many lasers have a ruby CRYSTAL or gas inside them. Bright light, radio waves or electricity are fed into the laser. This makes the ATOMS of the crystal or gas jump around very quickly. The atoms give off strong light.

LAOS

Government: People's Republic
Capital: Vientiane
Area: 236,800 sq km
Population: 4,440,000
Language: Lao
Currency: New kip

▼ In this Los Angeles studio, experiments are being carried out into the use of lasers in games for the future.

Laser light is being used more and more to carry telephone conversations. A narrow cable containing 144 hairlike glass fibres can carry 40,000 telephone conversations at the same time.

The light of lasers can be used for many things. Doctors use small laser beams to burn away tiny areas of disease in the body. They also repair damaged eyes with laser beams. Dentists can use lasers to drill holes in teeth. Some lasers are so strong they can cut through DIAMONDS. Lasers are used in factories to cut metal and join tiny metal parts together.

Lasers can also be used to measure distance. The laser beam is aimed at objects far away. The distance is measured by counting the time it takes for the light to get there and back. Laser beams can also carry radio and television signals. One laser beam can send many television programmes and telephone calls at once without mixing them up.

Latitude and Longitude

Every place on Earth has a latitude and a longitude. Lines of latitude and longitude are drawn on MAPS Lines, or *parallels*, of latitude show how far north or south of the *equator* a place is. They are measured in degrees (written as °). The equator is at 0° latitude. The North Pole has a latitude of 90° north, and the South Pole is 90° south.

Lines, or *meridians*, of longitude show how far east or west a place is.

▼ Some of the lines of latitude and longitude are marked on globes or atlases. They form a kind of network that can be used to pinpoint specific places. They are also measured in degrees. Greenwich, in London, is at 0° longitude. A place halfway around the world from Greenwich is at 180° longitude.

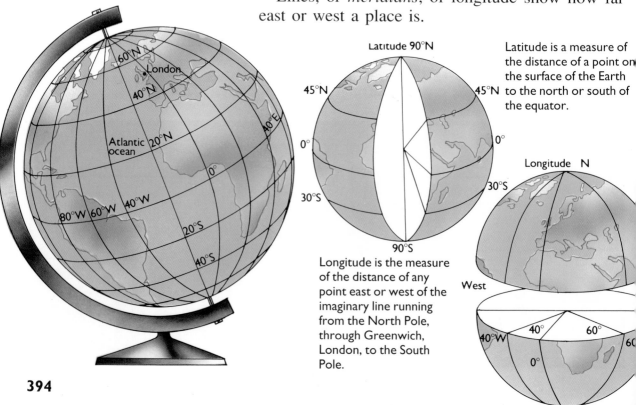

Latitude is a measure of the distance of a point on the surface of the Earth to the north or south of the equator.

Longitude is the measure of the distance of any point east or west of the imaginary line running from the North Pole, through Greenwich, London, to the South Pole.

Latvia

Latvia is one of the three Baltic republics – the others are Estonia and Lithuania – that gained their independence from the former Soviet Union in 1991. The people of Latvia, called Letts, are related to the Lithuanians. Their language is one of the oldest in Europe. Latvia is on the east coast of the Baltic Sea. It is a country of lakes and low hills with many forests.

Law

Laws are rules made by a country's leaders. Laws are made to help people live together in peace. They control many of the things people do. The laws of each country are often different. Some countries have very strict laws about things which other countries do not worry about. Every country has judges and POLICE.

The people of BABYLON had written laws over 3000 years ago. In Europe, many important laws were made by kings and the Church. Today, laws are made by PARLIAMENT.

Lead

Lead is a soft, heavy, blue-grey metal. It does not RUST. Lead is used for many things, but its greatest single use is in car batteries. Lead shields protect ATOMIC ENERGY workers from dangerous radiation. Lead is mixed with TIN to make pewter or *solder*. Solder is used for joining pieces of metal. Many items are now made without lead because lead can be poisonous.

Leaf

Leaves are the food factories of green PLANTS. To make food, leaves need light, carbon dioxide and water. Light comes from the Sun. Carbon dioxide comes from the air. Air enters a leaf through little holes called *stomata*. Water is drawn up from the ground by the plant's roots. It flows up the stem and into the leaf through tiny tubes called veins. Inside

LATVIA

Government: Republic
Capital: Riga
Area: 64,595 sq km
Population: 2,728,000
Languages: Latvian, Russian
Currency: Lat

▼ *Lead was often used to make toys and, in particular, model soldiers, but for reasons of safety it is no longer used.*

LEATHER

▶ *Leaves come in many shapes, sizes and even colours. You can identify a tree by looking at one of its leaves, once you learn a bit about them.*

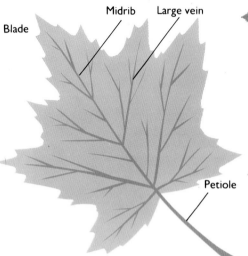

Blade
Midrib
Large vein
Petiole

▲ *Most leaves have the same basic parts. Of great importance are the veins that carry water and food to all parts of the plant.*

Horse chestnut
Black poplar
Wych elm
Whitebeam
Tree of Heaven
Field maple
Common oak
Seville orange

SEE IT YOURSELF

Make a leaf print by rubbing the back of a leaf lightly with shoe polish or paint. Lay the leaf, painted side down, on a clean sheet of paper and cover it with another sheet. Rub over the whole area of the leaf and you will have a clear picture of the veins. To make a leaf rubbing, lay a clean sheet of paper over a leaf and rub firmly all over with a crayon or soft pencil. The leaf pattern will gradually appear.

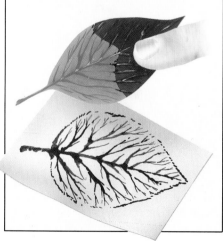

the leaf is a green colouring called chlorophyll. The chlorophyll uses light, water and carbon dioxide to make SUGAR. The way it does this is known as *photosynthesis*. The sugar then passes through tubes to the other parts of the plant.

In the autumn many trees lose their leaves. First they shut off the water supply to the leaves. This destroys the green colour and gives the leaves yellow, red and orange tints.

Leather

Leather is made from the skin, or hide, of animals. The skins are treated to make them strong and waterproof (for the soles of shoes) or flexible (for furniture and luggage). The process of treating them is called *tanning*. Before tanning, the skins are *cured* by being soaked in salt water. Then the remaining hair and meat is taken off. Next the skins are treated with a chemical called *tannin*, which comes from tree bark. Then the leather is oiled to soften it and dyed different colours. It is now ready to be cut, shaped and stitched or glued into the final product.

Lebanon

Lebanon is a Middle Eastern country bordering on the Mediterranean Sea. It is sandwiched between Syria and Israel. Lebanon's coast is flat, but most of the country inland is mountainous.

Lebanon has been a trading centre for centuries. Ancient Lebanon was part of the Phoenician empire. The Phoenicians were great traders all over the Mediterranean. Later, Lebanon became part of the Byzantine empire, ruled from Constantinople. It was famous for the fine cedar wood that came from its forests.

In recent years the country has become a battleground for a number of religious and political opponents.

LEBANON

Government: Parliamentary republic
Capital: Beirut
Area: 10,400 sq km
Population: 3,439,000
Language: Arabic
Currency: Lebanese pound

◀ *Lebanon has a rich and exciting history. This fortress at Sidon was built during the Crusades.*

Legend

Legends are stories that are told as true, but cannot be proved. They may have some truth in them, and may be about a real person or place. But they are usually made-up stories. The adventures of Robin Hood and King Arthur are legends.

Lenin, Vladimir

Vladimir Ilyich Lenin (1870–1924) helped to make Russia the first communist country in the world. Before his time, Russia was ruled by emperors, or

▲ *Lenin's revolutionary ideas united the group of communists called Bolsheviks, who overthrew the Russian government in 1917.*

SHORT SIGHTEDNESS

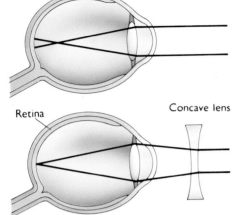

Retina

Concave lens

LONG SIGHTEDNESS

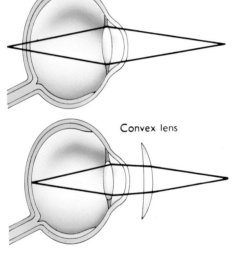

Convex lens

▲ *In people with short sight, light from a distant object is focused by the lens of the eye before it reaches the back of the eye, or retina. This means the object looks blurred. In people with long sight, light from nearby objects is focused at a point beyond the retina, so they appear blurred. Corrective lenses in glasses make the images focus on the retina, so they look sharp and clear.*

▶ *Light rays passing through a convex lens bend outwards, making the virtual image appear larger than it really is. The virtual image is what we see. A concave lens bends the rays inwards and the image looks smaller.*

tsars. Like Karl MARX, Lenin believed in COMMUNISM. He wanted every country run by the workers and no longer split into rich and poor groups. For many years Lenin lived outside Russia. He wrote books, and articles for communist newspapers. In 1917 he went back to Russia. He became the leader of a group of communists called Bolsheviks, who overthrew the government. Lenin then ruled Russia until he died.

Lens

Lenses are used to make things look bigger or smaller. They are usually made of glass or plastic. The lens inside your EYE is made of PROTEIN. Sometimes eye lenses do not work properly. Then people cannot see clearly. The lenses in spectacles make people's eyesight better. The lenses in MICROSCOPES, binoculars and TELESCOPES make faraway things or small things seem much larger.

Each lens has two smooth sides. Both sides may be curved, or one may be curved and the other flat. There are two main kinds of lens. Lenses where the edges are thicker than the middle are called *concave* lenses. Concave means 'hollowed out'. When LIGHT rays pass through a concave lens, they spread out. If you look at something through a concave lens, it looks smaller than it really is.

Lenses where the middle is thicker than the edges

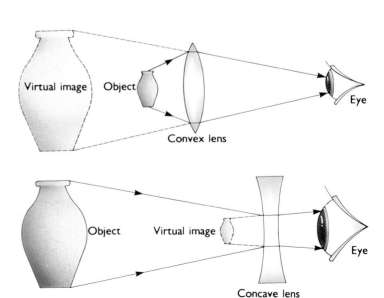

Virtual image | Object | Convex lens | Eye

Object | Virtual image | Concave lens | Eye

are called *convex* lenses. Convex means 'rounded'. When light rays pass through a convex lens, they come together. If you look at things through a convex lens, they seem larger.

Craftspeople who make lenses know exactly how to shape them for various uses. They may fit different lenses together or shape each side of a lens differently. Short-sighted people use spectacles that have concave lenses. People with long sight have spectacles with convex lenses.

Leonardo da Vinci

Leonardo da Vinci (1452–1519) was an Italian artist and inventor. He lived during the RENAISSANCE. One of his most famous paintings is the *Mona Lisa*. It is a picture of a woman who is smiling mysteriously. Many people have wondered what she was smiling at. Leonardo made thousands of drawings of

The 'burning glass' for producing fire from the Sun's rays has been known since ancient times. The magnifying property of a simple lens was recorded by Roger Bacon in the 13th century. Spectacle lenses were first used in the 14th century, and by the 16th century spectacles were commonly used. Benjamin Franklin invented the bifocal lens in 1760.

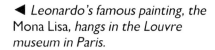
◄ Leonardo's famous painting, the Mona Lisa, *hangs in the Louvre museum in Paris.*

▼ Leonardo's self-portrait, drawn in about 1512, is the only known authentic likeness of the artist.

Leonardo often smoothed in the paint with his fingers to get a special effect. The result is that several of the great artist's paintings have clearly visible fingerprints somewhere on their surface. These fingerprints have been used to prove without doubt that certain paintings are the work of Leonardo.

Leonardo wrote in a strange way. He wrote his lines from right to left, and each letter was reversed. This is called 'mirror writing' because viewed in a mirror it looks quite normal.

human bodies, water, plants and animals. He kept notes of his observations in secret back-to-front 'mirror' writing.

Leonardo worked as an engineer for Italian nobles and for the French king. He designed forts and canals. The canals had locks so that boats could travel up and down hills. Leonardo also drew ideas for things long before they were invented. His drawings include a helicopter, a flying machine and a machine gun.

Leonardo was interested in many other things, including music and architecture. He was also a good musician and singer.

Leopard

Leopards are large, wild cats just a bit smaller than LIONS. They live in Africa and southern Asia. Most leopards are spotted like jaguars, but some are nearly black. These are called panthers.

Leopards are very fierce, strong and agile hunters. They catch and eat antelopes, goats, dogs and sometimes people. They often hunt from trees, lying in wait on a branch. If they cannot eat all their catch at once, they may haul the carcass high up into a tree. This is to stop lazier hunters such as lions or hyenas from stealing it.

▼ Like other members of the cat family, leopards have very flexible spines, enabling them to stretch and bend easily.

Lesotho

The kingdom of Lesotho is a small country completely surrounded by South Africa. Most of the people farm maize, wheat and sorghum, or raise sheep, goats and cattle. Nearly half of Lesotho's adults work in South Africa's mines, industries and farms. Lesotho, once called Basutoland, became a British protectorate in 1868. It gained its independence in 1966. The capital is Maseru.

Liberia

Liberia is one of the oldest independent African countries. It has never been controlled by a European country. Liberia was founded in 1822 as a home for freed slaves from the United States. It is on the west coast and is less than half the size of the United Kingdom. It is easy to register ships in Liberia, so many countries do so. Iron ore is the chief export. More than half the country's people became refugees as the result of a civil war that began in 1989 and has still not been settled.

Libya

Libya is a large country in North AFRICA. It is more than three times the size of France, but very few people live there. This is because most of Libya lies in the SAHARA desert.

LESOTHO

Government: Parliamentary democracy and monarchy
Capital: Maseru
Area: 30,355 sq km
Population: 1,848,000
Languages: Sesotho and English
Currency: Loti

LIBERIA

Government: Military
Capital: Monrovia
Area: 111,369 sq km
Population: 2,607,000
Language: English
Currency: Liberian dollar

◀ The Libyan port of Tripoli, on the Mediterranean, used to be called Medina. Its long history as a trading city dates back to biblical times.

401

LICHEN

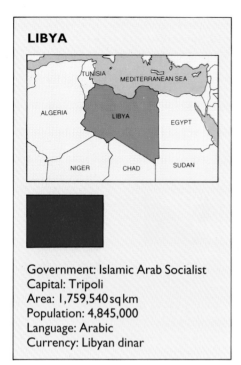

LIBYA

Government: Islamic Arab Socialist
Capital: Tripoli
Area: 1,759,540 sq km
Population: 4,845,000
Language: Arabic
Currency: Libyan dinar

► *A lichen is actually made up of two plants – a fungus and an alga – growing together. Reindeer moss, though called a moss, is actually a lichen.*

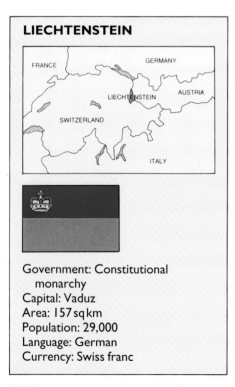

LIECHTENSTEIN

Government: Constitutional
   monarchy
Capital: Vaduz
Area: 157 sq km
Population: 29,000
Language: German
Currency: Swiss franc

Most Libyans are ARABS who farm the land. Libya is also rich in oil. The country became part of the Turkish Ottoman Empire in the 1500s, and was a colony of Italy from 1912 to the end of World War II. It became an independent monarchy in 1952 as the United Kingdom of Libya. In 1969 army officers overthrew the king and took control, and Colonel Muammar al-Qaddafi became head of the government. Since that time Qaddafi has led a revolution in Libyan life and many nations have accused him of interfering in other countries' affairs.

Lichen

A lichen is a simple PLANT. It has no roots, leaves or flowers. Some lichens grow as crusty patches on rocks, trees or walls. They grow very slowly. A patch no larger than your hand may be hundreds of years old. Other lichens grow as shrubby tufts. Lichens can live in places that are too bare, dry, cold or hot for any other plant.

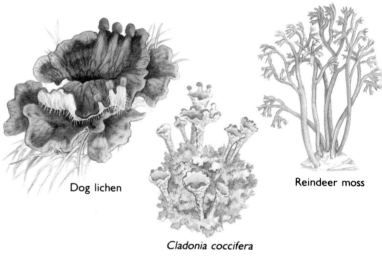

Dog lichen

Reindeer moss

Cladonia coccifera

Liechtenstein

Liechtenstein is one of the smallest countries in the world. It lies between Switzerland and Austria in the Alps. Liechtenstein is a prosperous country. Many international companies have their headquarters there. Tourism brings money into Liechtenstein. Switzerland runs the postal and telephone systems and the two countries use the same money. Liechtenstein is ruled by a prince.

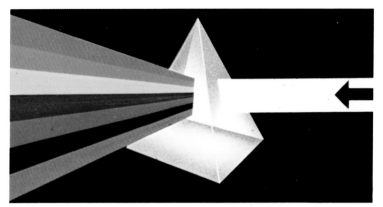

◀ A prism splits white light into a spectrum of colours. When the sun shines through rain, the raindrops act as a prism to make a rainbow.

Light

Light is a kind of ENERGY that we can see. Some objects—stars, lamps, certain chemicals—produce light. Most things do not produce light. We can see them only because they reflect light. For example, we can see the Moon and planets such as Venus and Jupiter in the sky only because they reflect light from the Sun.

Sunlight is the brightest light we normally see. Summer sunlight can be as bright as 10,000 candles burning close enough to touch. Bright sunlight seems white, but it is really made up of the colours of the RAINBOW. Isaac NEWTON showed this. He made a sunbeam shine through a specially shaped chunk of glass called a prism. Red, orange, yellow, green, blue, indigo and violet rays of light came out of the prism.

The prism had split the sunbeam into separate beams, each with its own *wavelength*. This is easy to understand if you think of light travelling in waves. The distance between the tops of the waves is the wavelength. We see each wavelength as a different colour. Long waves are red, short waves are violet, and wavelengths in between show up as all the other colours in the rainbow.

Light travels very fast, more than 300,000 km each second. Even so, it takes eight minutes for the light from the Sun to reach Earth, a distance of 150 million kilometres. A light year is the total distance a beam of light travels in one year— 9,470,000,000,000 kilometres. Scientists use light years to measure how far away STARS are. Some are millions of light years away.

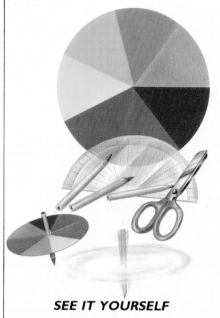

SEE IT YOURSELF

Here is a way to show that white light is made up of the seven colours of the rainbow. Cut a disc from card and divide it into seven equal sections. Colour each section as shown. Make a small hole in the middle of the disc and push a sharp pencil or stick through. Spin the disc quickly. What do you see?

▼ When light rays travel through different substances, in this case air and water, they are bent so the image looks distorted.

► *Lightning is caused by a build-up of static electricity in the atmosphere. When it discharges it causes a flash and the bang we know as thunder.*

▼ *Lincoln was the 16th president of the United States. He was shot just five days after the Civil War ended by John Wilkes Booth, an actor who supported the defeated South.*

▼ *Lindbergh's historic flight across the Atlantic inspired many other pioneering aviators.*

Lightning

Lightning is ELECTRICITY that you can see. It is a sudden flow of electric current between two clouds, between a cloud and the ground, or between two parts of the cloud. There are three types of lightning. Streak lightning flashes in a single line from cloud to earth. Forked lightning happens when the lightning divides to find the quickest way to earth. Sheet lightning happens inside a cloud and lights up the sky, like the flashbulb on a camera.

Lincoln, Abraham

Abraham Lincoln (1809–1865) was president of the United States from 1861 to 1865. He had little schooling, but studied law on his own.

In 1854 a law was passed allowing people in new western territories to own slaves. In 1856 Lincoln joined the new, anti-slavery Republican Party and was elected president in 1860. Abraham Lincoln started a second term of office in 1865, just as he was trying to unite the nation at the end of the CIVIL WAR. But on April 14, 1865, on a visit to Ford's Theater in Washington, D.C., he was shot dead by John Wilkes Booth, an actor.

Lindbergh, Charles

Charles Augustus Lindbergh (1902–1974) was an American pilot who became the first man to fly the Atlantic Ocean alone. His single-engine aircraft,

Spirit of St. Louis, left New York on May 20, 1927. He landed on May 21 in Paris, 33½ hours later, after flying about 5600 km non-stop. Lindbergh's flight made him an international hero. Later he helped to plan air tours to South America and over the Atlantic Ocean.

Lion

Lions are large, tawny-coloured wild CATS. An adult male weighs about 180 kg and measures about 2.7 metres from nose to tail. Females (lionesses) are slightly smaller and have no mane.

Lions usually live in groups called prides. A pride has one male, several females and all their cubs. Lions often hunt as a team. No other big cats seem to do this. They hunt mainly antelope and zebra. Lionesses do most of the hunting.

Many lions today lead protected lives on nature reserves where they are safe from humans.

▲ *When lions are not hunting, they spend long periods resting to conserve their energy. Lions used to roam wild over southern Europe, India and Africa. Now they live only in South and East Africa and a tiny part of India.*

▼ *The elastic 'skin' on the surface of pond water is strong enough to prevent pond skaters from sinking. The 'skin' is caused by the force called 'surface tension'.*

Liquid

A liquid can flow and change its shape. Liquids include water, milk, mercury and oil. When liquid is poured into a container, it takes the shape of the container but its volume remains the same. As a liquid gets hotter, the atoms or molecules in it move faster. They begin to leave the liquid. A GAS is formed. At the boiling point, the liquid boils and in time all of it turns into gas.

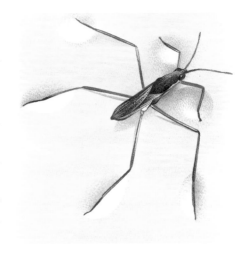

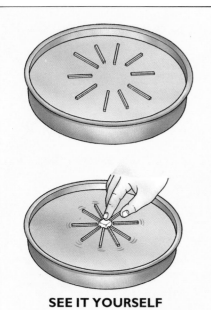

SEE IT YOURSELF

The surface of water is held together by a force called 'surface tension' which makes water appear to have a thin, elastic 'skin' all over it. To show that sugar breaks this 'skin', lay some matches carefully on the surface of a bowl of water as shown. Now dip a lump of sugar in the middle. The sugar absorbs some of the water and a small current of water flows towards the sugar, pulling the matches with it.

LITHUANIA

Government: Republic
Capital: Vilnius
Area: 65,196 sq km
Population: 3,788,000
Languages: Lithuanian, Russian
Currency: Lit

When a liquid gets colder, the atoms or molecules in it slow down. At the freezing point, they settle into rows and the liquid becomes a solid.

Different liquids have different freezing and boiling points. Some solid substances turn into liquids when they are heated, and some gases can be turned into liquids when cooled.

Lister, Joseph

Joseph Lister (1827–1912) was an English surgeon who found a way to stop his patients from dying of infection after operations. He used antiseptics to kill germs on surgeons' hands and instruments.

Lithuania

Lithuania is a low-lying country on the east coast of the Baltic Sea. It has many lakes and rivers, with sandy beaches beside the Baltic.

Until 1991, Lithuania had been a republic of the former Soviet Union for more than fifty years. Earlier, it was ruled by Russia from 1795 to 1918, but the Lithuanian people have always kept their own language and customs alive. Most Lithuanians are Roman Catholics.

Liver

Your liver is a flat, triangular organ tucked under your right ribs. It is larger than your stomach. The liver is a kind of chemical factory and storage cupboard. It produces the digestive juice that burns up the fat you eat. It makes the PROTEINS used in blood. It gets rid of any poisonous substances in the blood or changes them so that they are harmless. Minerals and VITAMINS are stored in the liver.

Livingstone, David

David Livingstone (1813–1873) was a Scottish doctor and missionary who explored much of southern and central AFRICA. He travelled to spread CHRISTIANITY and to help stop traders selling Africans into SLAVERY.

Livingstone made three great journeys between 1841 and 1873. He crossed Africa, discovered the Victoria Falls and searched for the source of the river NILE.

In 1869, people feared that he had got lost or was dead. In 1871, a newspaper reporter, Henry Morton Stanley, found him at Lake Tanganyika. Both men continued their explorations, but Livingstone fell ill and died as he travelled.

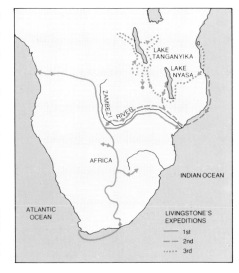

▲ When Livingstone first went to Africa, it was largely uncharted. During his 32 years there, he became one of the greatest African explorers.

Lizard

Lizards are REPTILES with dry, scaly skins and long tails. Most have four legs but some have none. These look like snakes. Some lizards are born live like MAMMALS, but most of them hatch from eggs.

There are about 3000 kinds of lizard. Most live in hot countries. Lizards that live in cooler places spend the winter in HIBERNATION. Lizards mainly eat insects.

Most lizards are only a few centimetres long, but the Komodo dragon of Indonesia is longer and heavier than a man.

▼ Three different lizards. The Australian thorny devil has strong spines which have replaced the scaly skin found on other lizards. Komodo dragons can grow up to 3m long and eat wild pigs, young buffaloes and small deer. The European slow worm is not a worm at all, but a lizard. It has smooth, slippery scales and no limbs.

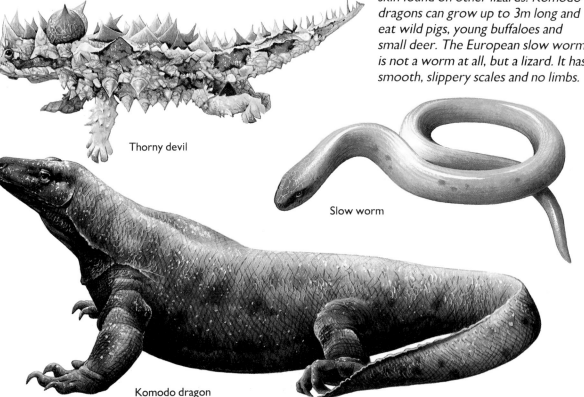

Thorny devil

Slow worm

Komodo dragon

▲ *Llamas are hardy animals, well-adapted to the harsh conditions of the Andes mountains.*

▲ *Norway lobsters are more familiar to us as scampi or Dublin Bay prawns.*

The earliest locks and keys were large wooden instruments. One can get some idea of the size of the keys from an Old Testament reference in Isaiah: 'And I will place on his shoulder the key of the house of David.' This probably shows how people carried their keys.

Llama

The llama belongs to the camel family, but has no hump. It stands about 1·5 metres high at the shoulder and may weigh twice as much as a man. Long, thick hair keeps it warm on the cold slopes of the Andes Mountains in South America, where it lives.

All llamas come from wild ancestors who were tamed at least 4500 years ago by the INCAS. Today, South American Indians still use llamas to carry heavy loads. They make clothes and ropes from the llama's wool and candles from its fat.

Lobster

Lobsters are CRUSTACEANS. They are related to shrimps and CRABS. One kind of lobster can weigh up to 20 kg. The lobster's body has a hard SHELL. It has four pairs of legs for walking and a pair of huge claws for grabbing food. When a lobster is afraid it tucks its tail under its body. This drives water forwards and pushes the lobster backwards to escape.

Lobsters hide among rocks on the sea bed. They feed on live and dead animals. A female lobster can lay thousands of eggs.

Lock and Key

There are two main kinds of lock. In the simplest kind, when the key is turned a piece of metal, called a bolt, moves out and fits into a slot. The key has a few notches that have to fit with similar notches in the lock. The Yale lock was invented in 1860. In it the key can turn a cylinder when all the little pins in the lock are pushed to the right height by the notches on the key.

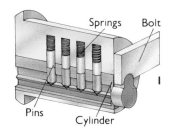

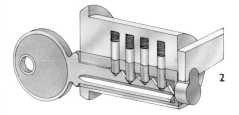

Locust

Locusts are GRASSHOPPERS that sometimes breed in huge numbers. They fly far across land and sea to find new feeding places. A big swarm may have hundreds of thousands of locusts. When they land, the locusts eat everything green. Swarms of locusts have destroyed many farms in warm lands.

Locusts swarm and fly away only when they become too numerous and crowded. Farmers try to kill the young locusts before they are able to fly.

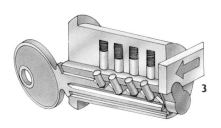

London

London is the capital of the UNITED KINGDOM. It has about seven million people. The river THAMES runs through London.

People from all over the world visit London to see Buckingham Palace, the Houses of PARLIAMENT, Westminster Abbey and the Tower of London. There are many museums, theatres and parks in London, as well as offices and factories.

▲ In a Yale lock there are many combinations possible for the heights of the pins. Before the key is inserted, all the pins are level and held in place by springs (1). The key slides into the lock and its jagged edge pushes the pins to different heights (2). When the right key is used, the pins are pushed to the heights that will allow the cylinder to be turned, opening the lock (3).

◄ The Tower of London has been the site of a fortification since Roman days, and has seen some of the most turbulent moments of British history.

409

London is very slowly sinking into its foundations and the level of the river Thames is slowly rising. As a result, extra-high tides could flood a large part of London. To prevent this happening, a great barrier has been built across the Thames at Woolwich. If very high tides happen, the barrier can be raised and London will be safe.

London began as a Roman settlement called *Londinium*. The PLAGUE came to London in the 1600s, followed by the Great Fire of 1666. The city was badly bombed in WORLD WAR II.

Los Angeles

Los Angeles is the second-largest city in the UNITED STATES. More than 14 million people live in the Los Angeles area. The city lies in the sunny countryside of California. On one side of Los Angeles is the Pacific Ocean. Behind it are the San Gabriel Mountains.

There are thousands of factories and a big port in Los Angeles. Visitors go to see Disneyland and Hollywood. Los Angeles makes more cinema and television films than any other city in the world.

▶ *The air pollution in Los Angeles is so severe it can actually be seen. The smog forms a thick haze over the city, particularly in hot, dry weather.*

▼ *When sound is recorded it is turned into electrical signals. The loudspeaker turns these signals back into sound waves that we can hear. The signals are fed to a coil that is attached to a plastic cone and positioned between the poles of a circular magnet. The signals cause the coil to vibrate, which vibrates the plastic cone. The cone produces sound.*

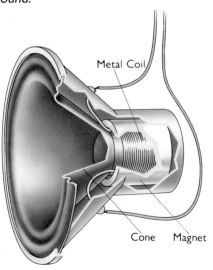

Metal Coil

Cone   Magnet

Loudspeaker

A loudspeaker turns electric signals into SOUND waves. The sounds that we hear on RADIO, TELEVISION, record players and tape recorders all come from loudspeakers.

A moving coil loudspeaker has a cone fixed to a wire coil. Inside the coil is a magnet. Electric signals flow through the coil. The signals make the coil move to and fro. The tiny movements of the coil make the cone shake, or vibrate. Air around the cone also starts to vibrate. These air vibrations reach our ears and we hear sounds.

Louis (French kings)

Eighteen French kings were called Louis.

The first was Louis I (778–840). Louis IX (1214–1270) led two CRUSADES. Louis XI (1423–1483) won power and land from his nobles. Louis XIII (1601–1643) made the French kings very powerful. Louis XIV (1638–1715) ruled for 72 years. He built a great palace at VERSAILLES. All the French nobles had to live in his palace. Louis XVI (1754–1793) was beheaded after the FRENCH REVOLUTION.

Lung

Lungs are organs for BREATHING. People have lungs, and so do many animals. Lungs bring OXYGEN to the body from the AIR. They also remove waste carbon dioxide from the BLOOD.

Your lungs are two large, sponge-like masses in your chest. They fill with air and empty as you breathe in and out.

You breathe in air through the nose. The air flows down the windpipe, or *trachea*. Where the lungs begin, the trachea divides into two hollow branches called bronchial tubes, or *bronchi*. Each divides into smaller tubes called *bronchioles*. These end in cups called air sacs, or *alveoli*. This is where the lungs give oxygen to the blood and take away carbon dioxide.

Lungs need clean air. Smokers and people who live in smoky towns, or work in some kinds of dusty air, may get lung diseases.

◀ Louis XVI was king of France at the time of the French Revolution. He was executed on 21st January 1793, after a two-month trial.

▲ Louis XIV was called the Sun King because of the splendour of his court. His palace at Versailles was more like a small city than a home.

▼ The soft, fragile lungs are well protected inside the rib cage, which expands and contracts to allow for the movements of breathing.

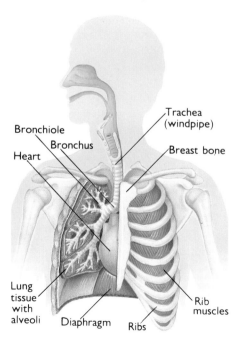

Bronchiole
Bronchus
Heart
Trachea (windpipe)
Breast bone
Lung tissue with alveoli
Diaphragm
Ribs
Rib muscles

▲ *Luther made a list of 95 arguments against the Church's practice of selling pardons, and nailed them to a church door in Wittenburg.*

Luther, Martin

Martin Luther (1483–1546) was a German priest who quarrelled with the ROMAN CATHOLIC CHURCH. He started the Protestant REFORMATION.

Luther did not like the way priests forgave people's sins in return for money. He also believed that God's teachings lay in the BIBLE. The Bible was more important to Luther than what the POPES said.

Under Luther's leadership, a large number of Christians split away from the Roman Catholic Church.

Luxembourg

Luxembourg is one of the smallest countries in EUROPE. Around it are Belgium, France and Germany. Luxembourg has low mountains with large forests. There are farms in the hills. There are also iron mines and towns that make steel. The capital city has the same name as the country. The European PARLIAMENT has offices in the capital.

Luxembourg has less than half a million people. Their own language is Letzeburgesch, but many speak French or German. Luxembourg is in the EUROPEAN COMMUNITY.

LUXEMBOURG

Government: Constitutional monarchy
Capital: Luxembourg
Area: 2586 sq km
Population: 392,000
Languages: French and Letzeburgesch
Currency: Luxembourg franc

Macedonia

Macedonia is a small country in the Balkan Peninsula of south-east Europe. Formerly a republic of Yugoslavia, it became independent in 1991. It is a land-locked country of forested mountains and hills.

Machine (Simple)

All the machines we see working around us are related to one or other of six simple machines. A machine is stronger than a person. It uses a greater *force*. When a force is used to move something, we can say that *work* is done. The *wedge*, for example, helps us to split things. A wedge hammered into a small crack in a tree trunk will split the trunk in two. Chisels, knives, nails and axes are all different forms of wedges.

The SCREW can pull things together or push them apart. With a screw jack, a man can quite easily lift a car weighing far more than himself. There are many kinds of *levers*. The simplest is a long pole, pivoted or balanced on a log and used to lift a heavy rock.

The *inclined plane* makes it easier to raise heavy loads to higher levels. It is easier to pull a load up a slope than to lift it straight up. A simple PULLEY is used in the winding mechanism that raises water from a well.

Probably the most important of all simple machines is the *wheel and axle*. This is used not only for moving loads, but also in all sorts of machines – such as clocks.

MACEDONIA

Government: Republic
Capital: Skopje
Area: 25,713 sq km
Population: 2,141,000
Language: Macedonian
Currency: Denar

▼ *When we operate machines, we do a little work over a long distance so that the machine can do a lot of work over a short distance.*

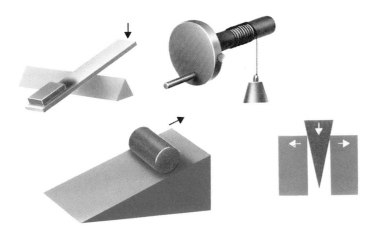

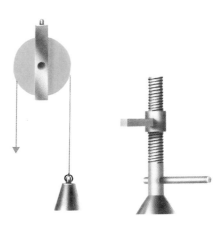

MADAGASCAR

Government: Republic
Capital: Antananarivo
Area: 587,041 sq km
Population: 12,596,000
Languages: Malagasy and French
Currency: Malagasy franc

Madagascar

Madagascar is the fourth largest island in the world. It is in the Indian Ocean, off the east coast of Africa. The country of Madagascar has fertile coastal plains, a rugged central plateau and a warm, tropical climate. Coffee, rice, sugar and vanilla are among the leading crops.

Between the 800s and 1300s, Arab colonies were set up in Madagascar. In the 1800s the island came under French control. It gained independence from France in 1960.

Madrid

Madrid is the capital city of SPAIN. It was chosen by King Philip II (1527–1598) as his capital because it was in the middle of the country. Madrid is a dry, windy city; cold in winter and hot in summer. It is the centre of Spanish life, and the seat of the country's parliament. It has many fine buildings, including the Prado, which has one of the finest collections of paintings in the world. More than 3,000,000 people live in Madrid, which is the centre of Spain's road and railway network.

Magellan set sail from Seville, Spain, on September 20, 1519. His expedition consisted of five ships and about 270 men of many nationalities. When the expedition reached Spain again on September 6, 1522 after its round-the-world voyage, only one ship was left. It had a crew of 17 Europeans and 4 East Indians picked up on the voyage.

Magellan, Ferdinand

Ferdinand Magellan (1480–1521) was a Portuguese sailor and explorer. In 1519 he sailed west from Spain, round Cape Horn and into the Pacific Ocean. Magellan was killed by natives in the Philippines. But one of his five ships returned safely to Spain, having completed the first voyage around the world.

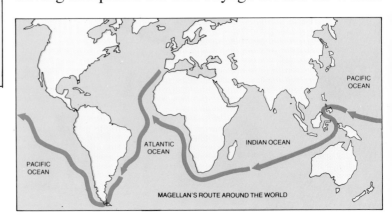

MAGELLAN'S ROUTE AROUND THE WORLD

▶ *Magellan set out to find a new sea route to Asia, heading west and rounding the tip of South America.*

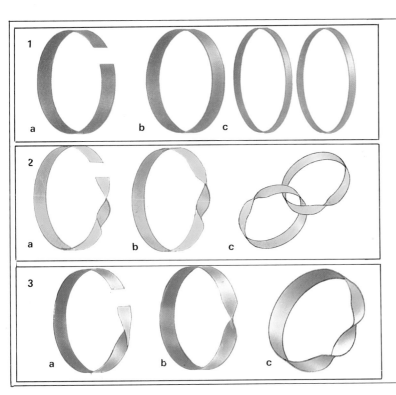

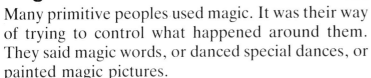

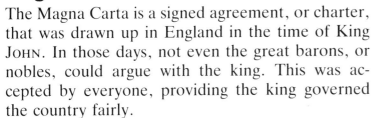

Magic

Many primitive peoples used magic. It was their way of trying to control what happened around them. They said magic words, or danced special dances, or painted magic pictures.

All through history people have believed that certain things (such as talismans or charms) or people (such as witches and sorcerers), have magical powers. Magic is often closely tied up with religion. But most people today think of magic as the conjuring tricks performed by magicians on television, in the theatre or at parties.

Magna Carta

The Magna Carta is a signed agreement, or charter, that was drawn up in England in the time of King JOHN. In those days, not even the great barons, or nobles, could argue with the king. This was accepted by everyone, providing the king governed the country fairly.

But King John was not a good ruler. He demanded extra taxes from the people and quarrelled with the barons. In 1215 the barons met and

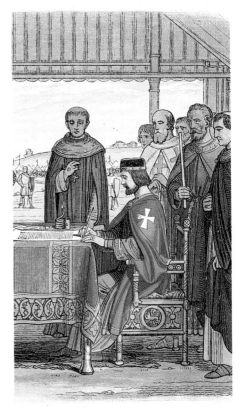

▼ King John was forced to sign the Magna Carta by the rebel barons at Runnymede.

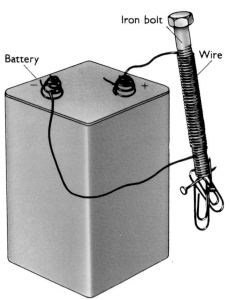

Iron bolt

Battery

Wire

▲ *In an electromagnet, a metal that is not normally magnetic, such as an iron bolt, can be made so by passing an electric current through a coil of wire wrapped around it. As soon as the current is broken, the magnetic field ceases to exist.*

demanded that John sign the Magna Carta, or 'great charter'. This document marked the beginning of a new system of government in which the king had to rule according to the law.

Magnetism

A magnet attracts metals, particularly iron and steel. The Earth is a huge natural magnet. Invisible lines of magnetic force spread out round the planet, joining the North and South magnetic poles. We call this the Earth's *magnetic field*.

The needle in a COMPASS is a magnet. It always turns to face magnetic North. In ancient times people noticed that a kind of iron ore called a lodestone suspended from a string would always swing to point in the same direction. A lodestone is a natural magnet. Another name for it is magnetite.

An electromagnet is made by coiling wire round a metal core and passing electricity through the coil. Electromagnets can be made more powerful than ordinary magnets.

SEE IT YOURSELF

If you have two bar magnets you can show the shapes of force-fields around the magnets. Put one of the magnets under a piece of plain paper and sprinkle some iron filings on top (1). The filings show the lines of force running between the north and south poles of the magnet. Now do the same thing using the two magnets. You will see why a north pole attracts a south pole (2), and why two north poles or two south poles push each other apart (3).

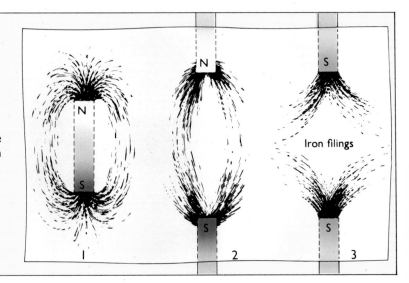

Iron filings

The word 'malaria' means 'bad air' in Italian. It was first called this because people thought that the disease was caused by gases from the swampy regions where many cases occur.

Malaria

Malaria is a common and deadly tropical disease. It is carried by the female *Anopheles* MOSQUITO, which can infect the humans it bites. Drugs are used to treat malaria. Scientists try to destroy the mosquitoes and the swamps in which the insects breed.

◄ In Malawi, traditional methods of farming and the village way of life still exist.

Malawi

Malawi is a long, narrow country in eastern Africa. It is half the size of the United Kingdom. Most of Malawi's people live in small villages and grow their own food. Tobacco, tea and sugar are grown.

The explorer, David LIVINGSTONE, was the first European to come to the region of Malawi, in 1859. In 1891, Britain took over the territory and set up the Protectorate of Nyasaland. Independence was granted in 1964. The name was changed to Malawi, the name of the people who once lived there.

MALAWI

Government: Multi-party Republic
Capital: Lilongwe
Area: 118,484 sq km
Population: 9,605,000
Languages: English and Chichewa
Currency: Kwacha

Malaysia

Malaysia is a country in SOUTH-EAST ASIA. It is in two parts, West Malaysia on the Malay Peninsula, and East Malaysia, which is part of the island of Borneo. The capital, Kuala Lumpur, is in West Malaysia.

Malaysia has over 18,000,000 people, mostly Malays and Chinese. Its main exports are rubber, timber and tin.

Malaysia is a member of the Commonwealth. It is ruled by a sultan, who is head of state, and a prime minister, who is head of government.

Maldives

The Republic of Maldives is a chain of islands south-west of India in the Indian Ocean. Although there are about 2000 islands, the total area is much less

MALAYSIA

Government: Constitutional
  monarchy
Capital: Kuala Lumpur
Area: 329,749 sq km
Population: 18,410,000
Languages: Malay, English and Chinese
Currency: Ringgit

MALDIVES

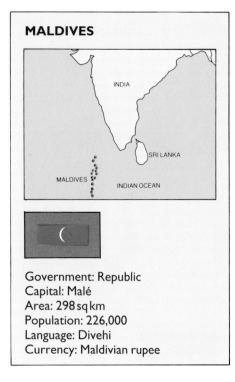

Government: Republic
Capital: Malé
Area: 298 sq km
Population: 226,000
Language: Divehi
Currency: Maldivian rupee

MALI

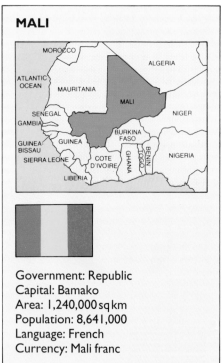

Government: Republic
Capital: Bamako
Area: 1,240,000 sq km
Population: 8,641,000
Language: French
Currency: Mali franc

▶ Fishing boats at anchor in a harbour in Gozo. The Republic of Malta includes the island of Malta and its neighbouring island, Gozo.

than that of London. The climate is damp and hot, with heavy rainfall. Most of the people make their living by fishing.

The islands became a British protectorate in 1887 and gained complete independence in 1965. The Maldives is one of the world's poorest countries.

Mali

The country of Mali is in north-west Africa. It is five times the size of the United Kingdom but has only an eighth of its population. A large part of the country is in the Sahara Desert.

In the 1800s Mali was occupied by the French, and achieved independence in 1960. Famine and drought have plagued the country.

Malta

Malta is an island in the MEDITERRANEAN SEA. It lies south of Sicily. Since ancient times it has been a vital naval base, for it guards the Mediterranean trade routes to the East. For centuries Malta was ruled by the Knights of St John, but in 1813 it became British. During World War II, Malta survived heavy bombing raids and the whole island was awarded the George Cross medal.

Since 1962 Malta has been self-governing. Today, it is a republic. The capital is Valletta, with its splendid Grand Harbour.

Mammal

Mammals are not the largest group of animals on Earth. But they are the most intelligent and show a greater variety of forms than any other group of animals.

All mammals have warm blood and a bony skeleton. Many have hair or fur on their bodies to keep them warm. Female mammals give birth to live young, which they feed on milk from special glands in their bodies. Some mammals (such as mice) are born naked, blind and helpless. Others (such as deer) can run within hours of being born.

Mammals were the last great animal group to appear on Earth. They came long after fish, amphibians, reptiles and insects. When DINOSAURS ruled the Earth, millions of years ago, the only mammals were tiny creatures which looked like SHREWS. But after the dinosaurs died out, the mammals took over. During EVOLUTION, the mammals multiplied into many different forms which spread all over the world.

Scientists divide the mammals into three families.

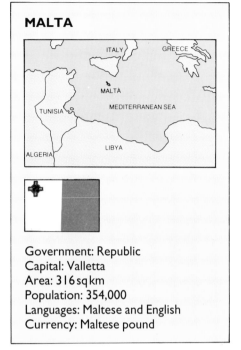

MALTA

Government: Republic
Capital: Valletta
Area: 316 sq km
Population: 354,000
Languages: Maltese and English
Currency: Maltese pound

▼ The age of the mammals began in the Cenozoic era. These mammals of the early Cenozoic include the glider Planetotherium (far left), the plant-eater Barylambda (centre), the long-tailed Plesiadapis (top right) and Taeniolabis (bottom right). At bottom left is an early shrew.

EGG-LAYING MAMMALS

Echidna

Platypus

MARSUPIALS

Koala

Tasmanian devil

PLACENTAL MAMMALS

Elephant

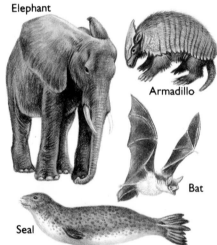

Armadillo

Bat

Seal

▲ *There are three families of mammals: egg-laying mammals, marsupials and placental mammals. The placental mammals are the most advanced group.*

▶ *Woolly mammoths developed from a more primitive creature called the Mastodon, which was also the ancestor of the modern elephant.*

The most primitive mammals still lay eggs, like the reptiles and birds. There are only two left in this family, the echidna and the PLATYPUS. Then come the MARSUPIALS. These mammals give birth to tiny, half-developed young which have to be carried in their mother's pouch until they are big enough to look after themselves. The best known marsupial is the KANGAROO. Almost all the marsupials live in Australia.

The 'placental' mammals, the highest group of all, give birth to fully developed young. There are many different kinds, including flying mammals (BATS); gnawing animals or RODENTS; sea mammals (WHALES and DOLPHINS); and burrowing mammals (for example, MOLES). There are insect-eaters, plant-eaters and flesh-eaters. The flesh-eaters, or CARNIVORES, include the powerful CATS, WOLVES and BEARS. The most intelligent of all the mammals are the primates. This family includes MONKEYS, APES and HUMAN BEINGS.

Mammoth

During the ICE AGES, woolly mammoths roamed the plains of Europe and North America. They looked like shaggy-haired elephants, with long curling tusks. But they lived in much colder climates than the elephants of today.

Mammoths lived together in herds, feeding on plants, grass and leaves. Their enemies included the fierce sabre-toothed tiger, wolves and also CAVE DWELLERS, who hunted mammoths for food. Sometimes a group of hunters drove a mammoth into a pit, where it could be killed with spears.

The frozen bodies of mammoths have been dug up by scientists in the icy tundra of Siberia. Mammoth remains have also been found in tar pits in California. The last mammoths died out about 30,000 years ago.

Mandela, Nelson

Nelson Mandela is one of Africa's most important political leaders. He was born in the Transkei territory of South Africa and became a lawyer. His father was a tribal chief. After World War II, the white South African government introduced a policy of *apartheid* – separate development for blacks and whites. Mandela and others formed the African National Congress (ANC) in 1944 and began a campaign of non-violent opposition to the government. In 1962, Mandela was arrested and put in prison. He was freed in 1990. In 1991, President de Klerk ended apartheid, and in 1994 free elections were easily won by the ANC, with Nelson Mandela as president of South Africa.

▲ *After 28 years in prison, Nelson Mandela was seen as an emblem of the black struggle for equality in South Africa.*

Maoris

The Maoris are the native people of NEW ZEALAND. These well-built, brown-skinned people came in canoes from Pacific islands to New Zealand in the 1300s. The Maoris were fierce warriors who fought with clubs made of bone or greenstone (a kind of jade). They fought many battles against the white people who first came to New Zealand. This war did not end until 1865, and there were some outbreaks of fighting for years afterwards.

The Maoris were very skilful at weaving, dancing, and, above all, carving. Maori carving is full of decoration. Every inch of the surface of their work is covered with curves, scrolls and spirals. Their tools were made from greenstone, and they carved

▲ *Tikis are an important part of Maori art and culture. This tiki, carved from jade, was worn for protection against the ghosts of still-born children.*

▲ *Mao was chairman of the Communist Party in China for 27 years, and brought about many radical changes in culture and economics.*

▼ *Early maps and globes show what a mysterious place the world once was. A lot of guess-work went into mapmaking in years gone by.*

greenstone, a kind of jade, to make little figure ornaments called *tikis*. Tattooing was also an important part of Maori art.

Today, Maoris play an important part in the life of New Zealand. Their population is increasing at a faster rate than that of non-Maoris.

Mao Tse-tung (Mao Zedong)

Mao Tse-tung (1893–1976) was a great Chinese leader. He was the son of a farmer and trained to be a teacher. In 1921 he helped to form the Chinese Communist Party and fought against the Chinese Nationalists under Chiang Kai-shek. In 1934 he led 90,000 Communists on a 368-day march through China to escape Nationalist forces. This feat was called the Long March. When Mao Tse-tung and the Communist armies beat the Nationalists he became head of the Chinese government in 1949. He wanted China to become as rich as America, but many of his plans for his country did not work. He resigned from his job as head of government in 1959 but carried on as head of the Chinese Communists. He had many arguments with the Russian Communists. Mao also wrote books about guerrilla warfare, and poetry.

After Mao's death, China's new leaders criticized his rule and gradually increased contacts with the West.

Map and Chart

We need maps and charts to help us find our way about. There are different kinds of maps. Some show countries, towns, roads and railways. These are *political* maps. *Physical* maps show natural features such as mountains, plains, rivers and lakes. The shape of features such as mountains is shown by colours or by contour lines.

Maps are drawn to different *scales*. The scale of some maps is so big that you might be able to find your house on one. The scale of other maps is very small so that we can even squeeze the whole world onto one page of an atlas. On a small-scale map, 2 cm on the map might represent 200 km, or

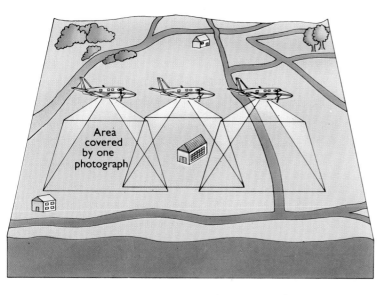

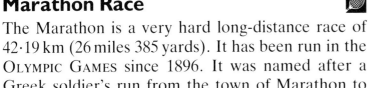

200,000 m, for example, on the ground.

Charts are maps of the sea. They tell sailors about lighthouses, rocks, channels and the depth of water in various places.

Marathon Race

The Marathon is a very hard long-distance race of 42·19 km (26 miles 385 yards). It has been run in the OLYMPIC GAMES since 1896. It was named after a Greek soldier's run from the town of Marathon to Athens in 490 BC to bring news of a Greek victory over the Persians. In 1908 there was a famous finish to the Olympic Marathon. At the end of the race a small Italian, Dorando Pietri, staggered into the stadium in the lead. He collapsed twice in the last 100 metres and had to be helped over the finishing line. He was disqualified because of this, but everyone remembers this as Dorando's Marathon.

Marble

Marble is a rock that is formed when limestone is squeezed and made very hot inside the Earth. Pure marble is white, but most of the rock has other substances in it which give it lots of colours. If a piece of marble is broken, the broken faces sparkle like fine sugar. (The word marble means 'sparkling'.)

Marble has long been used for making statues as

▲ *Pheidippides was the soldier who ran with the news of Greek victory after the battle of Marathon.*

The official distance for the marathon is 26 miles 385 yards. The reason for this strange distance is that the British Olympic committee decided in 1908 to start the race from the royal castle at Windsor and finish in front of the royal box in the stadium in London. This was measured at 26 miles 385 yards, a distance that has remained standard ever since.

▲ Marble cut from a quarry (right) can be used to make beautiful patterns in a floor (left). The many different colours of marble are caused by impurities present when the rock was formed.

well as for building. It is easy to shape and takes a high polish. The most famous marble for sculpture comes from quarries at Carrara in Italy. It is very white and has a very fine grain.

Marconi, Guglielmo

Guglielmo Marconi (1874–1937) was the man who, most people say, invented RADIO. His father was Italian and his mother Irish. When he was only 20 he managed to make an electric bell ring in one corner of a room, set off by radio waves sent out from the other corner. Soon he was sending radio signals over longer and longer distances. In 1901 he sent the first message across the Atlantic. In 1924 he sent signals across the world to Australia.

Marconi shared the Nobel Prize for physics in 1909 and was honoured throughout the world.

Marco Polo *See* Polo, Marco

▲ Marconi left Italy to continue his experiments in England because he did not get enough encouragement from the Italian government.

Margarine

This is a food like butter. It is made from vegetable FATS and OILS. VITAMINS are usually added to make it nearly as nourishing as butter. Margarine was invented in 1867 by a French chemist called Mège-Mouries. He won a prize offered by the French

---

government for finding a cheap substitute for butter. Many people now eat margarine and similar spreads because they are low in unhealthy fats.

Marie Antoinette

Marie Antoinette (1755–1793) was the Austrian-born wife of LOUIS XVI of France. A beautiful and vivacious young woman, she found her husband dull and boring, and hated her duties as queen. Instead she spent money lavishly and cared little for the world outside the royal palace at Versailles. She became a symbol to the poor people of France of all they hated about the royal court. When the FRENCH REVOLUTION broke out in 1789, the king and queen were taken to Paris by force. They were executed on the guillotine in 1793.

Mars (God)

Mars was one of the oldest and most important of the Roman gods. He was the son of Jupiter and Juno and became the god of war. His son, Romulus, was supposed to have been the founder of ROME. The temples and festivals of Mars were important to the Romans. The month of March was named after him. It was the first month in the Roman year.

Mars (Planet)

The planet Mars is only about half the size of the Earth. It takes about two years to travel around the Sun. The surface of Mars has huge volcanoes and great gorges, far bigger than those on Earth. Most of Mars is covered with loose rocks, scattered over a dusty red surface. This is why Mars is called the 'Red Planet'. It has a North Pole and a South Pole, both covered with snow or frost.

Seen through a telescope, the red surface of Mars is criss-crossed by thin grey lines. Some early astronomers thought that these lines were canals which had been dug by intelligent beings. They said these canals had been dug to irrigate the soil, since Mars has very little water. But space probes to Mars in 1965, 1969 and 1976 found no trace of the canals.

▲ *Through her unthinkingly lavish spending, Marie Antoinette made the poor people of France hate her. She showed great courage at her trial, but was condemned to death and executed in October 1793.*

MARS FACTS
Average distance from Sun: 228 million km
Nearest distance from Earth: 78 million km
Temperature on sunlit side: −30 degrees C
Temperature on dark side: −100 degrees C
Diameter across equator: 6794 km
Atmosphere: Carbon dioxide
Number of moons: 2
Length of day: 24 hours 37 minutes
Length of year: 687 Earth days

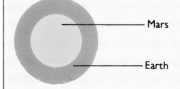

Mars
Earth

▶ *The dusty, red surface of Mars shows no trace of life. Viking space probes to the planet appear finally to have put an end to any ideas that there could be alien beings living there.*

The American Viking spacecraft landed on Mars and took samples of the planet's soil, but it was unable to find any kind of life on Mars.

The planet has two tiny moons – Phobos and Deimos. Phobos, the larger of the two, is only about 24 km across.

Because Mars has a smaller mass than the Earth, things on its surface weigh only about 40 per cent of what they would weigh on Earth. A day on Mars is about the same length as an Earth day.

Marshall Islands

The Marshall Islands are a chain of coral islands in the central Pacific. They were administered by the United States from the end of World War II until 1991, when they became independent.

Marsupial

Marsupials are MAMMALS with pouches – animals such as KANGAROOS, WALLABIES, BANDICOOTS, KOALAS and OPOSSUMS. They all live in Australia, except the American opossum.

A newly-born marsupial is very tiny. It crawls into its mother's pouch and stays there, feeding on her milk, until it can look after itself. There are about 250 species of marsupial.

MARSHALL ISLANDS

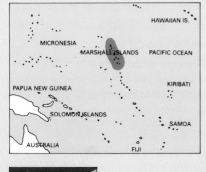

Government: Republic
Capital: Majuro
Area: 180 sq km
Population: 50,000
Languages: English, Marshallese, Japanese
Currency: US Dollar

Martial Arts

The martial arts are various kinds of combat that come from the Far East. They include judo, karate and aikido, all from Japan; and kung-fu, from China.

Judo, meaning 'easy way', is probably the most popular. It originally came from jujitsu, a violent practice that could maim or kill. Today judo is a safe sport practised by men, women and children, and has been an Olympic sport since 1964. It is used in many parts of the world for self-defence. A trained student of judo can quickly unbalance an opponent and throw him or her to the ground.

Marx, Karl

Karl Marx (1818–1883) was a political thinker and writer whose ideas brought about great social and political changes. Marx was born in Germany and his ideas were the starting point of COMMUNISM. He believed that people who own property, the capitalist class, keep those who work for them down so the owners can become richer. He also thought that the workers would one day rise against the capitalists and take control. Marx's ideas later inspired communist revolutions all over the world, notably the Russian Revolution.

▲ Although the martial arts were developed as methods of combat, they are now widely enjoyed as sport. Kendo, judo and karate are all safe if practised with proper supervision.

◀ Karl Marx (right), with Lenin (left) and Engels, heroes of communism. Between them Marx and Engels developed the ideas that inspired Lenin to found the communist state in Russia.

▲ Mary I's attempts to make England a Roman Catholic country were foiled by Elizabeth I when she succeeded as queen.

▼ Mary, Queen of Scots' determination to become Queen of England led to her execution in February 1587.

Mary I, Queen

Mary I (1516–1558) was the daughter of King HENRY VIII and his first wife, Catherine of Aragon. Mary became queen after Edward VI died in 1553. Her marriage to Philip II of Spain involved England in European wars. Mary's attempts to restore Roman Catholicism led to the execution of many Protestants. This is why she was given the nickname, 'Bloody Mary'. She was succeeded by her half-sister, ELIZABETH I.

Mary, Queen of Scots

Mary, Queen of Scots (1542–1587) was the last Roman Catholic ruler of SCOTLAND. The daughter of James V of Scotland, she was educated in France, and did not return to Scotland until she was 19. By that time she thought of herself as more French and Catholic than Scottish and Protestant.

Mary was the heir to the English throne after her Protestant cousin ELIZABETH I. In 1567 Mary was forced to give up the Scottish throne. Later she was imprisoned for 20 years in England. People said she was plotting against Queen Elizabeth. She was executed on the queen's orders in 1587.

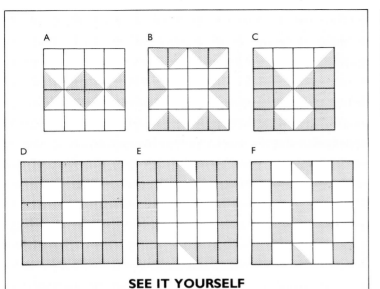

A B C

D E F

SEE IT YOURSELF

You can work out fractions by counting squares and half squares. What fraction of each grid has been coloured? The answers are at the bottom of the page.

Mathematics

We all use mathematics every day. We add up the coins in our pockets to find out how much money we have. We look at a clock and work out how much time we have left before going somewhere. In every business people are constantly using some kind of mathematics; often, nowadays, with the help of calculators and computers. The branch of mathematics that deals with numbers is called arithmetic. ALGEBRA uses symbols such as x and y instead of numbers. GEOMETRY deals with lines, angles and shapes such as triangles and squares.

Matter

Everything you can see and touch is matter – and so are some things you can't. Matter is anything that has *volume* – that takes up space. Scientists say that matter has *mass*, the amount of matter in something. The mass of something always remains the same. The pull of gravity gives you weight, but your weight can change. If you go to the Moon you will weigh only a sixth as much as you do on Earth. But your mass will still be the same.

Matter can be grouped into three main forms –

Some numbers are magic! Take the quite ordinary-looking number 142857, for example. Try multiplying it by 2. You get 285714. The same digits in the same order, but moved along. Now try multiplying our magic number by 3, by 4, by 5 and by 6. (A calculator will make it easier.) See what happens! And there's more. Try dividing it by 2 and by 5.

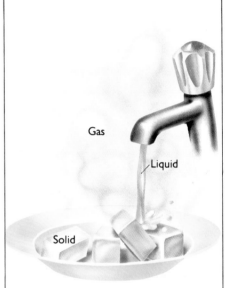

Gas

Liquid

Solid

SEE IT YOURSELF

Every substance is either a solid, a liquid or a gas at room temperature. But if the temperature changes, the substance can change its state. The picture shows the three states of water. Hot water in its normal liquid state is being poured onto ice cubes, which are water in its frozen solid state. Rising above the melting ice is steam, which is water in its gaseous state.

A = 1/4; B = 3/8; C = 5/8; D = 4/5; E = 3/5; F = 2/5.

429

MAURITANIA

Government: Republic
Capital: Nouakchott
Area: 1,030,700 sq km
Population: 2,059,000
Languages: French and Arabic
Currency: Ouguiya

MAURITIUS

Government: Constitutional
  monarchy
Capital: Port Louis
Area: 2085 sq km
Population: 1,081,900
Languages: English and French
Currency: Rupee

▶ *A view of the Rempart Mountains on the island of Mauritius, which has many volcanic hills.*

solid, liquid and gas. This book is solid, the water that comes from the tap is liquid, and the air that we breathe is a gas. The solid, liquid and gas forms are called the three 'states' of matter.

But nearly all matter can exist in all three forms. If air is made cold enough it becomes a liquid. A gas can be turned into a solid by cooling it. Solids such as iron can be turned into liquids by heating them. In the Sun, iron and other kinds of matter exist as gases because it is so hot.

Mauritania

Mauritania is an Islamic republic on the west coast of Africa. It is a very large country, but much of it is desert, where nomads keep cattle, sheep and goats. The valley of the Senegal River and the southern coastal areas are the only fertile regions.

Mauritania became a French protectorate in 1903 and became independent in 1960. There is often a threat of famine.

Mauritius

Mauritius is a small island country in the Indian Ocean. Most of the island is surrounded by coral reefs. The island is thought to be the peak of an ancient volcano. Mauritius is one of the most densely populated places in the world. There are about 500 people for every square kilometre of the island. The chief crops are sugar cane and tea. Tourism is a growing industry.

◀ *Mayan temples are huge and imposing buildings, showing skill in architecture and engineering.*

▼ *A Mayan carving in serpentine, a kind of rock, showing the god Tlaloc.*

Maya

The Maya Indians first lived in Central America in the AD 400s. They grew maize and sweet potatoes and kept pet dogs. Later they built cities of stone, with richly decorated palaces, temples, pyramids and observatories. Even today, many of these wonderful buildings are still standing, hidden in the jungle. The Maya were also skilled in astronomy and mathematics, and they had an advanced kind of writing.

The Maya people did not have any metals until very late in their history. They built with only stone tools, and had no knowledge of the wheel. Their lives were controlled by religion. They worshipped a sun god, rain gods, soil gods and a moon goddess who looked after women.

Measure *See* Weights and Measures

Mecca

Mecca is the Holy City of the Muslims, and MUHAMMAD's birthplace. It is in Saudi Arabia. In the centre of Mecca is the Great Mosque, and in the mosque's courtyard is the Ka'aba, which houses the sacred 'Black Stone'. Muslims believe it was given to Abraham by the archangel Gabriel. This stone is kissed by pilgrims to Mecca.

▼ *An old painting showing Abdul-Muttalib, Muhammad's grandfather, opening the Ka'aba door.*

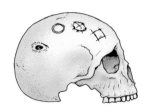

▲ Prehistoric men removed pieces from the skull to release evil spirits.

▲ In Indian medicine, a steam pipe, called a Nadi-Svedi, was used from about 400BC to help wounds heal quickly.

▶ The irong lung was invented in 1876 to keep patients alive when their lungs failed to work.

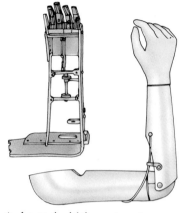

▲ An early 16th century iron hand (left) and a modern arm and hand (right).

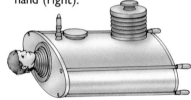

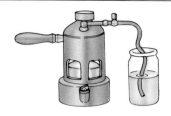

▲ Joseph Lister's carbolic acid sprayer was used to sterilize operating theatres.

▼ This kidney machine helps patients with kidney failure.

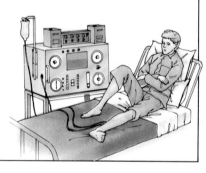

▲ Medicine has made huge advances from superstition and magic to the high-tech hospitals of today.

ADVANCES IN MEDICINE

1590	**Microscope** – Zacharias Janssen
1593	**Thermometer** – Galileo
1628	**Blood circulation** – William Harvey
1796	**Vaccination** – Edward Jenner
1846	**Anaesthetic** – William Morton
1865	**Antiseptic surgery** – Joseph Lister
1865	**Germs cause disease** – Louis Pasteur
1895	**X-rays** – William Roentgen
1898	**Radium** – Pierre and Marie Curie
1922	**Insulin for diabetes** – Frederick Banting and Charles Best
1928	**Penicillin** – Alexander Fleming
1954	**Polio vaccine** – Jonas Salk
1967	**Heart transplant** – Christiaan Barnard

Medicine

When we first think of the word 'medicine' perhaps we think about all the tablets, powders, pills and liquids people take when they are not feeling well. But medicine also means the science of healing. It has taken a long time for medicine to become truly scientific.

In the early days doctors relied mostly on magic cures, prayers and charms. But in the last few hundred years medicine has advanced faster than in all of human history. The development of anaesthetics in the last century was a vital step forward in progress in surgery. And in this century progress has been fastest of all. Scientists have found out about VITAMINS; they have made all kinds of wonder drugs like penicillin; they have almost wiped out DISEASES such as tuberculosis and smallpox; they are finding out more and more about mental illness; and they can now give people spare parts for many parts of their bodies when these organs go wrong. But perhaps the most important area of a doctor's job is still *diagnosis*, finding out what is wrong with a patient by studying the symptoms.

Mediterranean Sea

The Mediterranean is a large sea surrounded by three continents – Africa, Europe and Asia. It flows out into the Atlantic Ocean through the narrow Strait of GIBRALTAR. It is also joined to the Black Sea by a narrow strait, or passage.

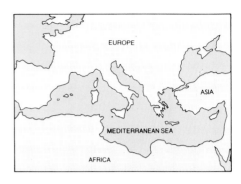

In ancient times the Mediterranean was more important than it is now. In fact, it was the centre of the Western world for a long time. The Phoenicians were a seafaring people who travelled around the Mediterranean from about 2500 BC. Then the Greeks and Romans sailed the sea. The Romans were in control of the whole Mediterranean for nearly 500 years. They even called it *Mare Nostrum*, Latin for 'our sea'.

The SUEZ CANAL was opened in 1869. It cuts across Egypt, joining the Mediterranean to the RED SEA. The canal was very useful because it shortened the distance by sea between Europe and the East. It is still used by cargo ships.

▼ *A 16th century map of the port of Genoa, in Italy. The Mediterranean has long been of vital importance to trade and commerce, and thriving towns grew up around its natural ports.*

Mendel's important findings were not believed at first. It was some years before his laws were generally accepted.

Melbourne

Melbourne is the capital of the state of Victoria and the second largest city in AUSTRALIA. It has nearly three million people. This fine city lies at the mouth of the Yarra River on Port Phillip Bay. Melbourne's port is one of the biggest in Australia. It handles both overseas shipping and shipping to other states. Melbourne was the capital of Australia from 1901 to 1927, when Canberra became the capital.

Mendel, Gregor

Gregor Mendel (1822–1884) was an Austrian priest who became famous for his work on heredity. Heredity is the passing on of things such as eye colour, skin colour and mental ability from parents to their children.

Mendel grew up on a farm, where he became interested in plants. When he entered a monastery he began growing peas. He noticed that when he planted the seeds of tall pea plants, only tall pea plants grew. Then he tried crossing tall peas with short peas by taking pollen from one and putting it in the other. He found that again he had only tall plants. But when he crossed these new mixed tall plants with each other, three-quarters of the new plants were tall and one quarter were short. Mendel had found out that things like the tallness or shortness are controlled by tiny *genes*, passed on from each parent. Mendel also showed that some genes are stronger than other genes.

▼ The god Mercury was supposed to look after writers, athletes, merchants, travellers, and thieves and vagabonds. As well as being the messenger of the gods, he was a bringer of good luck and a protector of flocks and shepherds.

Mercury (God)

Mercury was a Roman god who was the same as the Greek god Hermes. He was the messenger of the gods and is usually shown as a young man with winged sandals and wearing a winged hat.

Mercury (Metal)

Mercury, or quicksilver, is the only metal that is a liquid at ordinary temperatures. When mercury is poured onto a table it forms little bead-like drops.

Most metals dissolve in mercury to make *amalgams*, used as fillings for teeth. Mercury is also used in THERMOMETERS and BAROMETERS.

Mercury (Planet)

The planet Mercury is one of the smallest planets in the SOLAR SYSTEM, and the closest to the Sun. A day on Mercury lasts 59 of our days. During the long daylight hours it is so hot that lead would melt. During the long night it grows unbelievably cold. Little was known about Mercury's surface until the space probe Mariner 10 passed within 800 km of the planet. It showed Mercury to have a thin atmosphere and big craters like those on the Moon.

Mercury travels very fast through space – at between 37 and 56 km per second. This great speed and its nearness to the Sun give it the shortest year of all the planets (a year is the time it takes a planet to go once round the Sun). Mercury's year lasts only 88 of our Earth days.

▲ Drops of mercury look like little round beads. This is because of the attraction between mercury's molecules.

MERCURY FACTS

Average distance from Sun: 58 million km
Nearest distance from Earth: 45 million km
Temperature on sunlit side: 450 degrees C
Temperature on dark side: −170 degrees C
Diameter across equator: 4878 km
Atmosphere: Almost none
Number of moons: 0
Length of day: 59 Earth days
Length of year: 88 Earth days

Mercury

Earth

◀ The Mariner 10 space probe passed Mercury three times in 1974 and 1975. It discovered that Mercury has a huge iron core, probably about three-quarters of the size of the planet.

▲ *In legends, mermaids often lured ships onto the rocks. Seeing a mermaid was a sign of disaster to come.*

▼ *This map shows known metal deposits throughout the world, but there must be many more deposits waiting to be discovered.*

Mermaid

Mermaids are creatures of legend. There are many old stories about mermaids. They have long hair and the head and body of a woman. Their lower half is a long, scaly fish tail. They live in the sea.

In stories, mermaids sat on rocks or shores. They often sang sweetly. Sailors passing by in ships heard their lovely songs. They tried to follow the mermaids and wrecked their ships on the rocks.

Metal

There are more than a hundred ELEMENTS on the Earth. About two-thirds of these are metals. The most important metals are IRON (for making steel), COPPER and ALUMINIUM.

People have used metals since early times. Copper, TIN and IRON were the first metals to be used. They were made into tools and weapons. GOLD and SILVER were also known very early on. They are often made into jewellery.

Most metals are shiny. They all let heat and electricity pass through them. Copper and silver are the best for this. Nearly all metals are solid unless they are heated.

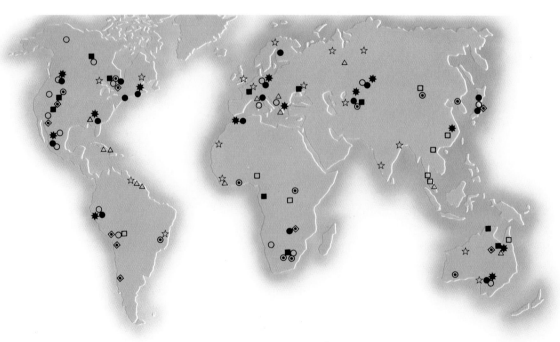

○ Silver　⊙ Gold　☐ Tin　■ Uranium　◇ Copper　△ Bauxite　● Zinc　✳ Lead　☆ Iron

Some metals are soft. They are easy to beat into shapes, and they can be pulled into thin wires. Other metals are *brittle*. This means they break easily. Some metals are very hard. It is difficult to work with them.

Metals can be mixed together to form ALLOYS. Alloys are different from their parent metals. Tin and copper are both soft. When mixed together, they form bronze. Bronze is a strong alloy. It is hard enough for swords and spears.

Metals are found in the ground. Some are found pure. They are not mixed with other things. Many metals are mixed up with other elements in MINERALS. The minerals must be treated to get the pure metal out.

▲ *Metals in the form of ore, such as this lump of iron, are quite unrecognizable except to an expert. The photo of polished titanium (left) was taken through a very powerful microscope.*

Metals vary so much that it is difficult to say exactly what a metal is. The metal lithium is so light it floats easily on water – it is only half the weight of the same volume of water. Osmium is 22 times as heavy as water – twice as heavy as lead. Pure gold is so soft that 20 grams of it can be drawn out into an unbroken wire 50 km long.

Meteor

A meteor is a tiny piece of metal or stone. It travels through space at great speed. Millions of meteors fall on the Earth every day. Most of them burn up before they reach the ground. On clear nights you can sometimes see shooting stars. They are meteors burning up. Sometimes a large meteor reaches the ground. Then it is called a meteorite. Meteorites sometimes make large holes called craters.

▼ *As a meteor enters the Earth's atmosphere, friction heats it and makes it glow.*

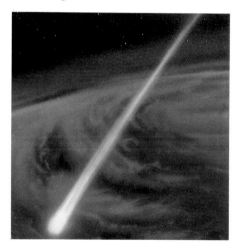

Metric System

The metric system is used for measuring weight, length and volume. It is based on units of ten, or decimals. It was first used in France in the late 1700s. Now it is used in most parts of the world.

MEXICO

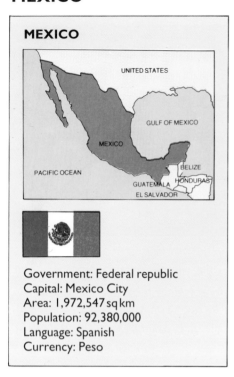

Government: Federal republic
Capital: Mexico City
Area: 1,972,547 sq km
Population: 92,380,000
Language: Spanish
Currency: Peso

▶ *Many Mexicans are Roman Catholics and they celebrate their religious festivals with processions and street parties.*

MICRONESIA

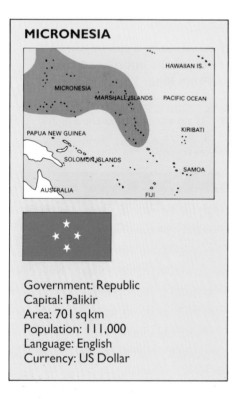

Government: Republic
Capital: Palikir
Area: 701 sq km
Population: 111,000
Language: English
Currency: US Dollar

Mexico

Mexico is a country in NORTH AMERICA. It lies between the United States in the north and Central America in the south. Much of the country is hilly, with fertile uplands. The highest mountains reach over 5700 metres. In the south-east, the low Yucatan Peninsula sticks out far into the Gulf of Mexico. The first people in Mexico were Indians, such as the AZTECS.

Michelangelo

Michelangelo Buonarroti (1475–1564) was a painter and sculptor. He lived in Italy at the time of the RENAISSANCE. Michelangelo is famous for the wonderful statues and paintings he made of people. He spent four and a half years painting pictures in the Sistine Chapel in the VATICAN CITY. Many of his statues are large and very lifelike. His statue of David is 4 metres high. Michelangelo was the chief architect of St Peter's in Rome.

Micronesia

Micronesia was formerly known as the Caroline Islands. It consists of 607 islands in the western Pacific. The islanders grow coconuts, fruits and vegetables. Micronesia became independent in 1991. Before this, it was ruled by the United States.

Microphone

A microphone picks up SOUND waves and turns them into electric signals. The signals can be made into a RECORDING or sent out as RADIO waves. They can also be fed through an amplifier and loudspeakers. These make the sound louder. The mouthpiece of a TELEPHONE has a microphone in it that turns your voice into electric signals.

Microscope

A microscope is an instrument used for looking at tiny objects. It *magnifies* things, or makes them look bigger. Things that are invisible to the naked eye are called *microscopic*. Many microscopic plants and animals, including BACTERIA, can be seen if you look at them through a microscope.

Microscopes work by using lenses. The simplest microscope is a magnifying glass. It has only one LENS. The lenses in many microscopes work by bending light rays. Small microscopes can magnify 100 times. Big microscopes used by scientists may magnify up to 1600 times. The electron microscope is much more powerful. It can magnify up to 2,000,000 times. Instead of bending light rays, it bends beams of electrons. Electrons are parts of ATOMS.

Anton van Leeuwenhoek, a Dutchman who lived

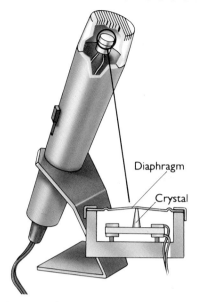

▲ *In this microphone, sound waves hit the flexible diaphragm and make it vibrate. These vibrations are picked up by a crystal and turned into electric signals.*

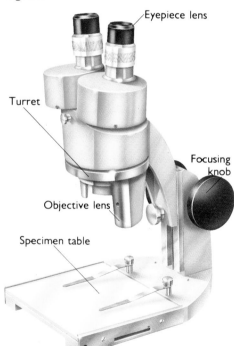

▲ *In an optical microscope, the image can be seen by looking down through the eyepiece and tube, containing a series of magnifying lenses.*

◄ *This electron microscope image shows a dust mite, flakes of skin, soil particles, cat fur and fibres, all taken from a vacuum cleaner.*

The world's most powerful electron microscopes can magnify objects up to about two million times. Measurements as small as one ten-billionth of a metre can be observed.

in the 1600s, made one of the first microscopes. Using his microscope, he showed that fleas hatch from tiny eggs. Before this, people thought fleas came from sand or mud. They could not see the eggs.

Middle Ages

The Middle Ages was a period of history in Europe which lasted for a thousand years. The Middle Ages began when the ROMAN EMPIRE collapsed in the 400s. They ended when the RENAISSANCE began in the 1400s. (See pages 442-443.)

Migration

Many animals make long journeys to breed or find food. Most make the journey every year. Some make the journey only twice in their life. These journeys are called migrations. Animals migrate by INSTINCT. They do not have to plan their journey.

Birds are the greatest migrants. Swallows leave Europe and North America every autumn. They fly south to spend winter in Africa or South America.

▲ Monarch butterflies migrate from Canada and the USA to Mexico in huge numbers each year.

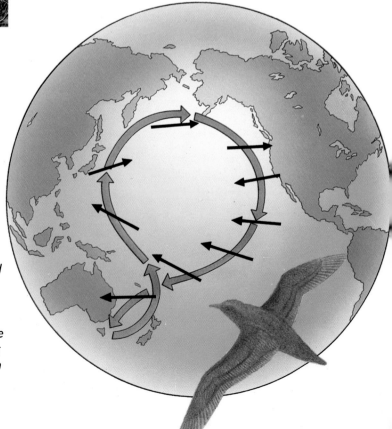

► Each year, the short-tailed shearwater travels from Tasmania and Australia towards the Pacific. Following the wind, the bird flies all the way to Arctic regions via the Asian coast before returning along the North American coast to its breeding ground. It is a round trip of 32,000 km and takes the bird seven months.

These places are warm and the swallows find plenty of food there. The trip may be 10,000 km long. In spring, the swallows fly north again to breed.

But birds are not the only animals that make long trips. Butterflies, fish and mammals migrate too. Whales and fish make long journeys through the sea to find food and breed. The EELS of Europe's lakes and rivers swim thousands of kilometres across the Atlantic Ocean to breed. After breeding they die. The young eels take years to swim back to Europe. Monarch butterflies of North America fly south in great numbers for the winter.

Milk

Milk is a food that all baby MAMMALS live on. It comes from the breasts, or mammaries, of the baby's mother. The baby sucks the milk from its mother's teat or nipple.

At first, the milk is pale and watery. It protects the baby from diseases and infections. Later, the milk is much richer and creamier. It contains all the food the baby needs. Milk is full of FAT, SUGAR, STARCHES, PROTEIN, VITAMINS and MINERALS. After a while the baby starts to eat other kinds of food.

People use milk from many animals. These include cows, sheep, goats, camels, and even reindeer. The animals are kept in herds. Sometimes

Continued on page 444

The white beluga whale lives in the Arctic and migrates south in the summer and north again in the winter. Scientists are not sure why the whale follows this strange 'upside-down' path of migration.

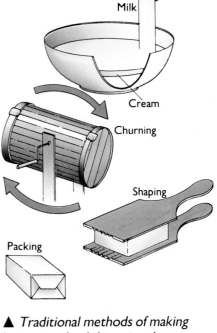

▲ Traditional methods of making butter involved skimming the cream off milk and 'churning' it by agitating it in a butter churn. This made the fat particles come together to form a thick yellow solid. It was patted into shape with wooden paddles, then wrapped and sold.

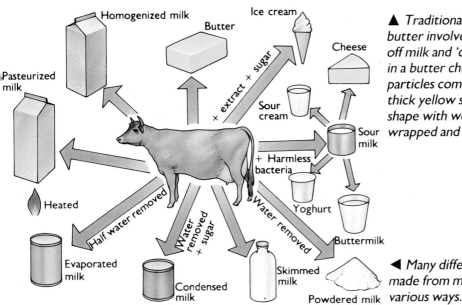

◀ Many different products can be made from milk by treating it in various ways.

MIDDLE AGES

The Middle Ages in Europe began with the collapse of the Roman Empire in the AD 400s and lasted for about 1000 years. The 'Roman peace' ended, and much of Europe suffered wars and invasions. The learning of ancient times was almost forgotten, surviving only in the monasteries. Kings and nobles struggled for power, while the mass of the people dwelt in poverty.

However, the Middle Ages also gave much to later generations. Great cathedrals were built. Universities were started. Painting and literature developed. With the 1400s came a rebirth of learning, the Renaissance, and the voyages of discovery to new lands. The Middle Ages were over.

THE CRUSADES

The Crusades were a series of wars between the Christian armies of Europe and the Muslims who had conquered the Holy Land of Palestine. The First Crusade was in 1096, and there were six Crusades in all. The Crusaders captured Jerusalem in 1099, but lost it again in 1187. They were finally defeated by the Muslims in 1303.

Many knights went to the Holy Land, some seeking honour and glory, others riches and lands. Many died before they ever reached Palestine. An important result of these wars was that Europeans learned about Eastern medicine and science, and new trade routes were opened to Asia.

THE MONK

Monks lived in religious communities, or monasteries. They copied out books by hand, and spent much time in prayer. They also tended their farms, gardens and fishponds.

THE KNIGHT

A knight was trained for war. He wore armour and rode a horse. Knights practised fighting at mock-battles called jousts. They were supposed to obey a code of knightly honour, known as chivalry.

THE PEASANT

Peasants worked on the land, and lived in rough huts which they often shared with their animals. They slept on straw mattresses on the floor. They ploughed the fields with ploughs pulled by oxen.

IMPORTANT EVENTS OF THE MIDDLE AGES

476	Fall of Roman Empire
570	Birth of Muhammad, prophet of the Muslim religion, followed by Muslim conquests
732	Charles Martel defeats Muslims and prevents them conquering Europe
800	Charlemagne is crowned first Holy Roman Emperor
896	Alfred, King of England, defeats Danish invaders
988	Christianity reaches Russia
1066	William of Normandy conquers England
1096	First Crusade to the Holy Land
1206	Genghis Khan founds Mongol Empire
1337	Start of Hundred Years' War between France and England
1347–51	Black Death (plague) in Europe

DID YOU KNOW ...?

* In the Middle Ages, Latin was the language used by scholars throughout Europe
* People did not have potatoes or sugar to eat, or tea and coffee to drink
* The Black Death was spread by rats and killed 25 million people throughout Europe

◄ In the feudal system, *society was organized in a sort of pyramid, with the clergy and nobles at the top and a great many peasants at the bottom. In the middle were the scientists, merchants, craftsmen and yeoman farmers.*

THE SCIENTIST

Most medieval scientists practised the mysteries of alchemy (trying to turn lead into gold). A few, such as Roger Bacon (1214–1294), studied the stars and realized that the Earth was round. Bacon also experimented with gunpowder.

THE MERCHANT

Merchants bought and sold goods such as furs and wool. Some became very wealthy and started the first banks. Merchants and craftsmen formed powerful associations called guilds. They sold their goods at fairs, at which people gathered to trade and have fun.

For more information turn to these articles: ALCHEMY; ARMOUR; BACON, ROGER; BLACK DEATH; CASTLE; CATHEDRAL; CHAUCER, GEOFFREY; HUNDRED YEARS' WAR; KNIGHT; MONASTERY.

It is impossible to imagine the size of the Milky Way. It takes light from the Sun eight minutes to reach us (the Sun is 149,600,000 km away and light travels at a speed of 300,000 km per second). Light from the centre of the Milky Way takes about 30,000 *years* to reach the Earth. From where we are in the solar system it takes about 200 million years for the Earth to make just one trip around the Milky Way.

they live on farms. Reindeer do not live on farms but wander about in the wild.

Milk is used to make many other foods. Cream, butter, yoghurt, cheese and some ice cream are all made from milk.

Milky Way

When you look at the sky on a clear, moonless night you can see a pale cloud of light. It stretches across the heavens. If you look at it through binoculars or a telescope, you can see that the cloud is really millions of stars. All these stars, and most of the other stars we see, are part of our GALAXY. It is called the Milky Way.

Astronomers think that the Milky Way has about 100,000 million stars like our Sun. The Milky Way stretches over a distance of about 100,000 light-years. A light-year is the distance light travels in one year at a speed of 300,000 km a second. Our own SOLAR SYSTEM is 30,000 light-years from the centre of the Milky Way.

The Milky Way has a spiral shape. Its trailing arms turn slowly around the centre. They take 200 million years to make a full circle. From Earth, we see the Milky Way through the arms of the spiral. The cloud of stars in the picture is what we might see from a great distance above the galaxy.

▼ *The view below shows how the Milky Way might appear from a few hundred light-years above the galaxy.*

The Milky Way is not a special galaxy. There are thousands of other galaxies with the same shape. There may be millions and millions of other galaxies in the UNIVERSE.

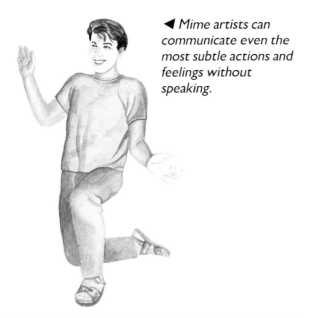

◄ Mime artists can communicate even the most subtle actions and feelings without speaking.

▼ A scale of hardness of minerals was devised by an Austrian, Friedrich Mohs, with the softest at the top and the hardest at the bottom. They are classed from 1 to 10. The hardness of other common things is shown alongside. Each mineral can scratch those above it on the scale, but not below.

A fingernail has a hardness of about 2½

A copper coin has a hardness of about 3½

Minerals of 6 or more will scratch glass

A penknife (5½) will scratch apatite but not orthoclase

A special steel file will scratch quartz

1. Talc

2. Gypsum

3. Calcite

 4. Fluorite

 5. Apatite

 6. Orthoclase

 7. Quartz

8. Topaz

9. Corundum

 10. Diamond

Mime

Mime is the art of acting in silence. A mime artist does not speak. Instead, his or her movements tell the story. The face, hands and body are used to show how the artist feels. Mime artists are like dancers. They must control every movement with great care so that the audience can follow the story.

Mime was popular in ancient Greece and Rome. Then it was noisy and included a lot of acrobatics and juggling. The actors wore masks. Mime was also popular in the Middle Ages. Later, entire plays were mimed without words. Mime is used a lot in dancing, especially ballet.

Mineral

The rocks of the Earth are made up of materials called minerals. There are many different kinds of mineral. Some, such as GOLD or platinum, are made up of only one ELEMENT. Others, such as QUARTZ and SALT, consist of two or more elements. Some minerals are metals, such as COPPER or SILVER. Other minerals are non-metallic, like SULPHUR.

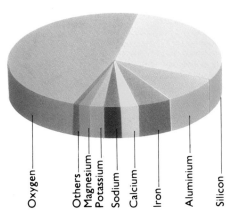

▲ This chart shows the various elements, including minerals, found in the Earth's crust. They are shown in the proportions in which they occur.

Pure minerals are made up of ATOMS arranged in regular patterns, known as CRYSTALS. Minerals form crystals when they cool from hot GASES and LIQUIDS deep inside the Earth. Crystals can grow very large if they cool slowly. But large or small, crystals of the same mineral nearly always have the same shape.

Altogether there are over 2000 minerals. Yet most of the Earth's rocks are made up of only 30 minerals. The most common mineral of all is quartz. Most grains of sand are quartz. Pure quartz is made up of large, well-shaped crystals and has a milky colour.

Mining

Mining means digging MINERALS out of the Earth. It is one of the world's most important industries. When minerals lie in one place in large quantities they are known as ores. People mine minerals such as GOLD, SILVER and TIN. They also mine COAL.

Mines can be open pits or underground tunnels. When the ore is close to the surface the soil that lies on top of it is simply lifted away. Giant diggers then scoop up the rock that contains the minerals. Underground mines can be as deep as 3 km below the surface. Another form of mining is dredging. Here minerals are scooped up from the beds of rivers and lakes.

The 'Big Hole', at Kimberley, South Africa, is an old disused diamond mine that was dug out last century by thousands of miners working with picks and shovels. They dug out more than 25 million tonnes of rock to make a hole 500 m across and nearly 400 m deep.

▶ The Kennecott open-pit copper mine in Utah is the largest in the USA.

◄ *This solar furnace in France uses a huge curved mirror to focus the Sun's rays and produce temperatures as high as 3000°C.*

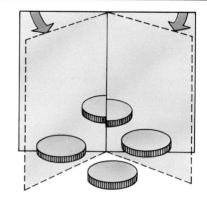

SEE IT YOURSELF

It is possible to see a reflection of a reflection. Lay a coin on a table. Take two mirrors and hold them next to each other with the edges touching as shown above. Now move the outer edges of the mirrors forward, while keeping the inner edges together. How many coins can you see?

Mirror

Mirrors are made from sheets of GLASS which have a thin layer of silver or aluminium sprayed on the back. This is then painted to protect the metal surface from scratches. This method of making mirrors was first used in the 1500s in Venice.

Before then mirrors were usually made of polished metal such as silver or bronze. Some mirrors from ancient Egypt are almost 5000 years old. LIGHT is reflected from (bounces off) a smooth surface. The reflection, called an image, is what we see when we look into a mirror, but the image is reversed. If you raise your left hand, the image raises its right hand.

A plane mirror has a flat surface. A convex mirror curves outwards like the back of a spoon. A concave mirror curves inwards like a hollow bowl.

Mississippi River

The Mississippi River is the longest river in the UNITED STATES. It rises in Minnesota in the north and flows 3779 km southwards to the Gulf of Mexico. It has over 250 tributaries, small rivers that flow into it. The waters of the Mississippi carry a lot of mud. As a result its DELTA, where most of the mud is dumped, is growing out to sea at a rate of a kilometre every 10 years.

MOLDOVA

Government: Republic
Capital: Kishinev
Area: 34,000 sq km
Population: 4,458,000
Languages: Romanian, Ukrainian
Currency: Ruble

Models

Models may be small copies of larger objects. Model planes, cars and trains are all examples of this type of model. Another kind of model is of something that does not yet exist, such as an architect's model of a new building or a design for a new aircraft. Models are used to test products, in teaching, and for special effects in film-making. Today there are many kits available for making all kinds of models at home.

Moldova

Moldova is a small country between Romania and Ukraine. Until 1991 it was part of the former Soviet Union. The climate is relatively mild and there are many vineyards and orchards.

Mole

Moles are small burrowing animals, found all over the world. They have narrow snouts and large clawed feet for tunnelling quickly through the soil.

Moles spend most of their lives underground. Their eyes are almost useless but they have good hearing and very sensitive noses for finding food. Moles feed mainly on worms and grubs.

▼ *Moles use different chambers in their tunnels for sleeping, storing food and bringing up their young.*

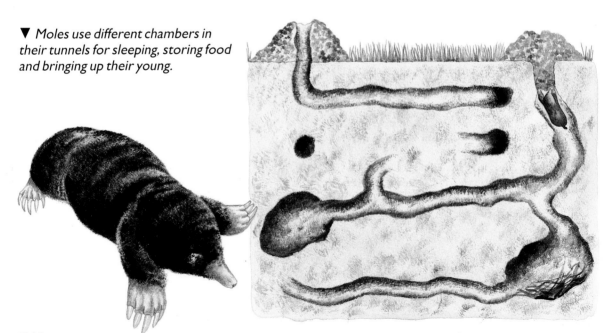

▲ *A great variety of molluscs are found in the sea, and some of them are good to eat.*

Mollusc

Molluscs are a large group of animals. There are about 70,000 different kinds. After insects they are the most numerous of all animals. They are found everywhere from deserts and mountains to the depths of the sea.

Most molluscs grow shells to protect themselves; some have shells inside parts of their bodies; some have no shells at all. But all molluscs have soft bodies and no bones. And all molluscs have to stay moist to live.

Some shells are only a few millimetres wide. Others, such as that of the giant clam, are over a metre wide. As a mollusc grows, its shell grows with it. The shell is made of a hard limy material formed from the food the mollusc eats. Shells have many strange shapes and patterns and some of them are very beautiful.

The largest mollusc is the giant squid. This can grow to as much as 12 metres.

Monaco

The tiny country of Monaco lies on the French coast of the Mediterranean Sea. It has an area of less than two square km. It is called a principality because it is ruled by a prince. Monaco's main industry is tour-

MONACO

Government: Constitutional
    monarchy
Capital: Monaco-Ville
Area: 1.9 sq km
Population: 29,000
Language: French
Currency: French franc

With a population of 29,000 in an area of 1.9 square kilometres, Monaco has a greater population density than any other country in the world – 14,000 people per square kilometre. The United Kingdom's density is 377 per square kilometre.

ism. More than half of the people of Monaco are French.

Monaco has been ruled by the Grimaldi family since the 1200s.

Monastery

Monasteries are places where monks live in a community, or group. They lead a religious life and obey strict rules. Monasteries are especially important in the BUDDHIST and CHRISTIAN religions.

Christian monasteries began in Egypt around AD 300. Hermits were religious men who lived alone. A group of hermits came together and made rules for their way of life. Soon after, communities of monks began to grow up. The monks worked as farmers, labourers and teachers, and helped the poor.

One of the most famous monks was St Benedict. He founded the Benedictine order. Many groups of monks followed his rules for running a monastery. St Benedict divided the day into periods of prayer, religious study and work.

The world's most famous monastery is that at Monte Cassino in central Italy. It was founded in AD 529 by St Benedict, and it was there that he gathered round him the first group of Benedictine monks. The monastery has led a troubled life. It was stormed by the Lombards in 589, the Saracens in 884 and by the Normans in 1030. Each time it was refounded on the same site and became a great centre of the arts and learning. During World War II it was the scene of heavy fighting as the German army retreated before the Allied advance. Then, on February 15, 1944, the monastery was almost completely demolished by Allied bombers. Most of its valuable art collection was destroyed but many treasured manuscripts were saved. The monastery has been rebuilt.

▶ In monasteries, a great deal of time is devoted to prayer, with regular services and ceremonies every day.

THE DEVELOPMENT OF MONEY

The earliest form of trade was bartering, when goods would simply be exchanged.

Money has been made in all shapes and sizes, but it must be easy to use and store.

American Indians used beads and shells, often made into decorative patterns, as money.

Money

We use money every day to pay for things we buy. We pay with either COINS or paper notes. This sort of money is known as cash. There is also another kind of money. It includes cheques, credit cards and travellers' cheques.

Almost anything can be used as money. In the past people have used shells, beads, cocoa beans, salt, grain and even cattle. But coins are much easier to use than say, cattle. They are easy to store and to carry around.

Coins were first used in China. They were also used by ancient Greeks as early as 600 BC. They were valuable because they were made of either gold or silver. They were stamped with the mark of the government or the ruler of the country for which they were made. The stamp also showed how much each coin was worth.

Later, people began to use coins made of cheaper metals. The metal itself had no value, but the coins were still worth the amount stamped on them. They also started to use paper money. It no longer mattered that the money itself had no real value. It was backed by the government and BANKS. This is the kind of money we use today.

Coins have remained popular for centuries. They are easy to produce and last a long time.

Bank notes are a kind of promise, because they represent a sum of money.

Credit cards and cheques are useful because they can be used instead of cash.

Mongolia

Mongolia is a republic in the heart of ASIA. It lies between Russia and China. The country has a population of about 2,000,000.

MONGOLIA

RUSSIA

MONGOLIA

NORTH
KOREA

SOUTH
KOREA

CHINA

Government: Multi-party republic
Capital: Ulan Bator
Area: 1,565,000 sq km
Population: 2,305,000
Language: Mongolian
Currency: Tugrik

Mongolia is a high, flat country. It is mostly desert or rolling grassland, with mountain ranges in the west. The Gobi Desert covers a large part of the land.

The people of Mongolia are descended from the MONGOLS. Until recently a Communist state, Mongolia now has a multi-party system.

Mongols

Mongols were NOMADS who lived on the great plains of central Asia. They herded huge flocks of sheep, goats, cattle and horses, which they grazed on the vast grasslands of the region. They lived in tent villages that they could quickly pack up and take with them when they moved on to find new pastures.

The Mongols were superb horsemen and highly trained warriors. In the 1200s they formed a mighty army under the great GENGHIS KHAN. Swift-riding hordes of Mongols swept through China, India, Persia and as far west as Hungary.

Under Genghis Khan, and later his grandson, Kublai Khan, the Mongols conquered half the known world. But they were unable to hold their empire together. In less than 100 years the Mongol empire had been taken over by the Chinese.

▼ Mongols were wanderers and expert horsemen. Their temporary shelters, known as yurts, were made of wood and hides.

◄ *In a story by Rudyard Kipling, a mongoose called Rikki-Tikki-Tavi bravely kills a snake.*

Woolly monkey

Colobus monkey

Spider monkey

Mandrill

Mongoose

The mongoose is a small MAMMAL that lives in Africa and southern Asia. It is a relative of the weasel. It has a long body, a bushy tail and short legs. An adult mongoose is about half a metre long.

Mongooses live in burrows and feed on small birds, poultry, mice and rats. Their fierceness and speed also helps them to kill dangerous snakes like the cobra.

Monkey

Monkeys are MAMMALS that belong to the same group of animals as APES and HUMAN BEINGS. Most monkeys have long tails and thick fur all over their body. Monkeys are usually smaller than apes. Their hands and feet are used for grasping and are very similar to those of humans.

There are about 400 different kinds of monkey. Most live in the tropics, especially in forests, in Africa, Asia and South America. South American monkeys have long tails that they use like an extra arm or leg when swinging through the branches of trees.

On the ground monkeys usually move about on all four limbs. But when they are using their hands to hold something they can stand or sit up on two legs.

Monkeys live in family groups known as troops. They spend a lot of time chattering, playing, fighting and grooming each other. Each troop of monkeys has its own territory where it lives and feeds. It will fight fiercely to defend this area against other invading groups.

▲ *The colobus and mandrill are both Old World monkeys living in Africa. The colobus has no thumb and the mandrill is one of the largest monkeys. New World monkeys, including the spider and woolly monkeys, live in the forests of South America. They have long prehensile tails that can be used as an extra 'hand'.*

Since ancient times, sailors have used the seasonal turn around of the monsoon winds on their voyages. Sailing ships in the Arabian Sea sail westwards from India to Africa when the monsoon blows towards the south-west. In summer, the monsoon blows from the south-west and the trading vessels return to India.

▲ *This bronze sculpture by Henry Moore is typical of his simple, uncluttered style of work.*

MOROCCO

Government: Constitutional monarchy
Capital: Rabat
Area: 458,730 sq km
Population: 26,708,000
Language: Arabic
Currency: Dirham

Monsoon

Monsoons are winds that blow from land to sea during winter, and from sea to land during summer. They occur mainly in southern Asia. The summer monsoon carries moisture from the sea, and rain falls over the land. Summer monsoons bring the rainy season. In India, about 1700 mm of rain fall between June and September, and only another 100 mm in all the rest of the year.

Moon

The Moon is our nearest neighbour in space. It loops around the EARTH, never coming closer than 356,400 km. It travels at about 3660 km/h and takes 27⅓ days to complete the circuit. (See pages 456–457.)

Moore, Henry

Henry Moore (1898–1986) was a famous British sculptor who worked in wood, stone and metal. His carvings are usually large and are easily recognized by their round, curving shapes and smooth lines.

Moore is also well known for his drawings. His pictures of people sheltering underground during the air raids of World War II are especially famous.

Mormon

Mormons belong to a religious group founded by Joseph Smith in 1830. The name comes from the *Book of Mormon*, which Mormons believe is a sacred history of ancient American peoples. The Mormons began in New York, but were persecuted for their beliefs and driven out. They finally settled in Salt Lake Valley, Utah.

Morocco

Morocco is a country right at the top of north-west AFRICA. It is nearly twice the size of Great Britain and has two coastlines. On the west is the Atlantic Ocean and to the north is the Mediterranean Sea.

Most of Morocco's 25 million people are farmers. They grow wheat, maize, fruit, olives and nuts. Some keep sheep, goats and cattle. Most of the people are Muslims. Casablanca is the largest city and main seaport. The country is ruled by a king.

Morse Code

Morse code is a simple way of sending messages. It is an alphabet of dots and dashes. Each letter has its own dot and dash pattern. The code was invented by Samuel Morse, an American artist, to send messages along a telegraph wire. The telegraph operator presses a key at one end to send a signal along the wire to a sounder at the other end. A short signal is a dot and a long signal is a dash. The first official telegraph message was sent in 1844.

Mosaic

A mosaic is a picture made from small pieces of coloured stone or glass set into cement. The pieces are arranged to make a design or a portrait or to show a scene.

Mosaic making is a very ancient art. The Sumerians made mosaics nearly 5000 years ago. Mosaics are a very practical way of decorating floors and walls, as they can be washed without being spoiled. In ancient Rome, every villa and palace had its

Continued on page 458

INTERNATIONAL MORSE CODE	
A ·—	P ·——·
B —···	Q ——·—
C —·—·	R ·—·
D —··	S ···
E ·	T —
F ··—·	U ··—
G ——·	V ···—
H ····	W ·——
I ··	X —··—
J ·———	Y —·——
K —·—	Z ——··
L ·—··	Full stop (.) ·—·—·—
M ——	Comma (,) ——··——
N —·	Query (?) ··——··
O ———	Error ········

The world's largest mosaic adorns four walls in the National University, Mexico City. It shows historical scenes. The two largest mosaic-covered walls are each 1200 square metres in area.

◀ *Roman mosaics like this one in St Albans have been found in many parts of Britain.*

MOON

People have worshipped the Moon, made wishes on the Moon (because of superstition) and even walked on the Moon. The Moon is our nearest neighbour in space. It is the Earth's only natural satellite, and was probably formed at the same time as our planet. But the rocks on the Moon's surface are older than those on the Earth's surface because the Moon has not changed in over 4000 million years.

The Moon is a dry, lifeless world, without air. Gravity on the Moon is just one-sixth of gravity on Earth, yet the Moon's gravitational pull affects us every day. It is the Moon's pull that causes the rise and fall of the ocean tides. Astronauts landed to explore the Moon in 1969. One day in the future permanent bases may be built there.

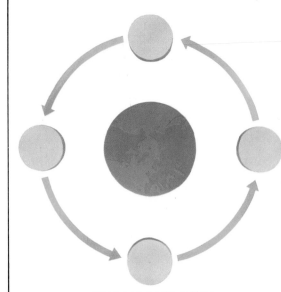

THE MOON'S FACE

When the Moon was newly-formed it was made of molten rock, spinning around once in a few hours. As it cooled, a hard skin or crust formed on the outside. The Earth's gravity, pulling at this crust, slowed the spin down and raised a 'bulge' a few kilometres high on one side. Now this bulge is always turned inwards, and the Moon keeps the same face towards the Earth.

◀ *The Moon has no wind; in fact, no erosion of any kind. This footprint in the Moon-dust, left by an Apollo astronaut, will remain undisturbed for ever.*

THE PHASES OF THE MOON

The Moon takes just over 27 days to travel around the Earth. It also spins on its own axis, and it always presents the same face to us. The Moon has no light of its own; we see it because it reflects light from the Sun.

When the Moon is between the Earth and the Sun we cannot see it, because the dark side is facing us. Gradually a thin crescent Moon appears – the New Moon. The New Moon waxes (gets larger) and at Full Moon (halfway through its cycle) we see the whole face lit by sunlight. Then the Moon wanes (gets smaller). The interval between one New Moon and the next is 29½ days (longer than the time the Moon takes to orbit the Earth). This is because the Earth itself is moving in space, as it travels around the Sun.

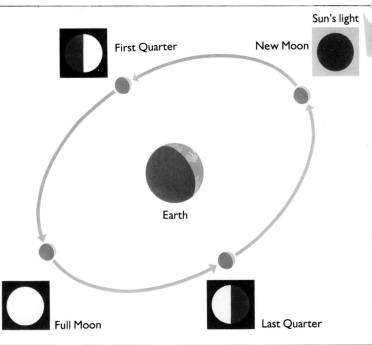

EXPLORING THE MOON

9 Galileo studies the Moon through the newly invented telescope.

7 Johannes Hevelius maps the Moon.

0s First photographs of the Moon.

9 Russian Luna 2 crash-lands on lunar surface. Luna 3 flies around far side.

6 US Orbiter craft photograph Moon in detail to find best landing sites.

8 US Apollo 8 astronauts fly around the Moon.

9 Apollo 11 astronauts land on Moon.

2 Last Apollo Moon-landing.

▲ *The Apollo astronauts explored the Moon on foot and with the aid of battery-powered 'Moon-buggies'.*

▲ *The maria, or plains, look dark in photographs. The Moon's craters and mountains cast long shadows.*

MOON FACTS

- The Moon is 384,000 kilometres from the Earth.
- The Earth weighs 81 times as much as the Moon.
- The diameter (distance across) of the Moon is 3476 kilometres.
- The oldest Moon rock is 4600 million years old.
- The Moon has no seas. Its flat plains are called maria, because early astronomers mistook them for oceans and named them after the Latin *mare*, meaning 'sea'.
- The Moon's surface is pitted with craters. Almost all these holes were made by meteorites crashing into the Moon.
- The Latin word for the Moon is *luna*. From this we get our word 'lunar', meaning 'of the Moon'.
- The Moon once had active volcanoes, but almost all of its volcanoes are now dead.
- No one on Earth had seen the far side of the Moon until a spacecraft photographed it in 1959.

r more information turn to these articles: ECLIPSE; GALILEO; ORBIT; SATELLITE; SPACE EXPLORATION and TIDES.

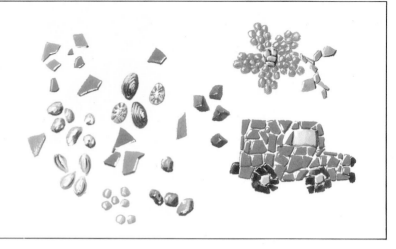

dazzling mosaics showing scenes from everyday life.

Mosaics were also used to make pictures of saints, angels and JESUS in churches all over Greece, Italy and Turkey.

▲ *St Basil's Cathedral is in one of the most historic parts of Moscow, near Red Square and the Kremlin.*

Moscow

Moscow is the capital of Russia. It is also the biggest city in the country. More than eight million people live there. Moscow lies on a plain across the river Moskva. It is the largest industrial and business centre in the country. Everything is made in Moscow, from cars to clothes. It is also the political and cultural centre of the country.

Moscow was first made the capital of Muscovy in 1547, during the reign of IVAN the Terrible, the first *tsar* (emperor) of Russia. It grew up around the KREMLIN, an ancient fort from which the Muscovy princes used to defend their country. Moscow remained the capital of the tsars until 1712 when Peter the Great moved the capital to St Petersburg. The city remained very important, even after it was nearly all burnt down during NAPOLEON's occupation of 1812. After the Revolution of 1917, Moscow became the seat of the Soviet government. In 1992 it became the capital of Russia again.

Some scholars believe that malaria carried by the mosquito sapped the strength of the people and led to the downfall of the Greek and Roman civilizations.

Mosquito

Mosquitoes are a small kind of FLY. They have slender, tube-shaped bodies, three pairs of long legs and two narrow wings. There are about 1400 different kinds. They live all over the world from the tropics to the Arctic, but must be able to get to water to lay their eggs.

Only female mosquitoes bite and suck blood. They have special piercing mouths. Males live on the juices of plants. When the female bites, she injects a substance into her victim to make the blood flow more easily. This makes mosquito bites itch.

Some kinds of mosquito spread serious diseases. Malaria and yellow fever are two diseases passed on by mosquitoes.

Moss

This is a very common kind of PLANT that grows in low, closely packed clusters. There are more than 12,000 different kinds. They are very hardy plants and flourish everywhere, except in deserts, even as far north as the Arctic. Most mosses grow in damp places. They spread in carpets on the ground in shady forests, or over rocks and the trunks of trees.

Mosses are very simple kinds of plants, like LICHENS. They were among the first plants to make their home on land. They have slender creeping stems that are covered with tiny leaves. Instead of proper roots that reach down into the soil, mosses simply have a mass of tiny hairs that soak up moisture and food. Mosses do not have flowers. They reproduce by spores, just like FERNS. One kind, called sphagnum moss, grows in bogs and is the plant that makes peat.

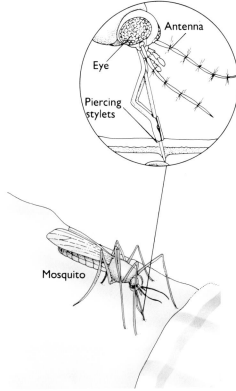

▲ The female mosquito uses its stylets to pierce tiny blood vessels in its victims.

▼ When mosses are ready to reproduce they produce capsules containing tiny spores. They soak up moisture and nutrients through tiny root-hairs called rhizoids.

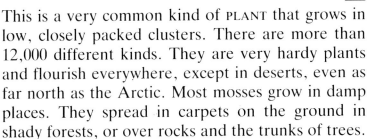

Common hair moss

Silky wall feather moss

Bryum capillare

Capsule

Stalk

Simple leaves

Rhizoids

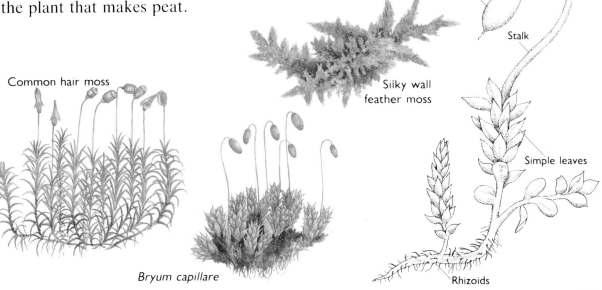

Moth

Clothes moths do not really eat clothes. But they lay an enormous number of eggs from which larvae hatch. It is these that devour our clothes and carpets.

It can be hard to tell moths and BUTTERFLIES apart. These are the signs to look out for. Moths usually fly in the evening and at night, while butterflies can be seen in the daytime. Moths have plumper bodies than butterflies. Moths' antennae are like tiny combs, or have feathery hairs on them. Butterfly antennae end in tiny knobs. When butterflies rest on a plant, they hold their wings upright. Moths spread their wings out flat.

Moths belong to one of the biggest insect groups. There are over 100,000 kinds of moth and they are found all over the world. The smallest scarcely measure 3 mm across. The largest may be bigger than a person's hand. Some moths have very striking colours that warn their enemies that they are poisonous or bad tasting. Moths have a very good sense of smell. They find their food by 'sniffing' their way from plant to plant. A male moth can follow the scent of a female 3 km away.

Moths hatch from eggs, usually in the spring. They hatch into CATERPILLARS. The caterpillar feeds on leaves until it is fully grown. Then it spins itself a silk cocoon. This protects the caterpillar while its body changes into a moth. A few kinds of moth do not spin cocoons, but bury their eggs in the ground or in piles of leaves until they grow into moths.

▼ There is great variety in the appearance of moths and their caterpillars.

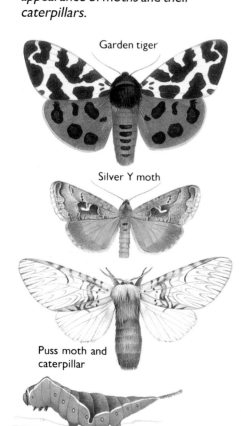

Garden tiger

Silver Y moth

Puss moth and caterpillar

Death's head hawkmoth

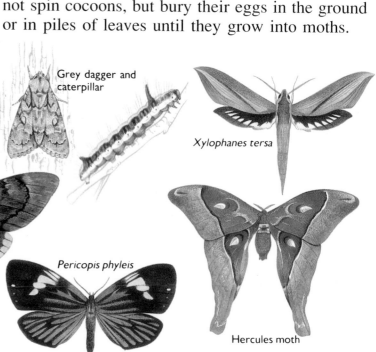

Grey dagger and caterpillar

Xylophanes tersa

Pericopis phyleis

Hercules moth

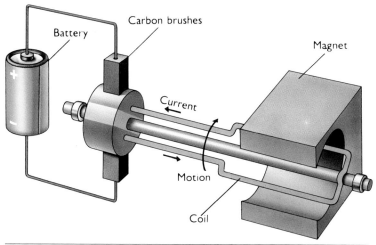

◄ Simple motors change electric current into mechanical energy. A coil is held between the poles of a permanent magnet. When current flows from the battery, it turns the coil into an electromagnet. The poles of the permanent magnet repel and attract those of the electromagnet, making it spin around. Motors such as these are clean and do not produce fumes.

Motor, Electric

There are electric motors all around us. Refrigerators, washing machines, electric clocks, vacuum cleaners, hair-dryers and electric mixers are all driven by electric motors. So are some trains and ships.

Electric motors work because the like poles of a magnet repel (push each other apart), and unlike poles attract each other. A simple motor is made up of a coil of wire held between the poles of a magnet. When an electric current flows through the coil, the coil becomes a magnet with a north pole and a south pole. Since like poles repel and unlike poles attract, the coil swings round between the poles of the magnet until its north pole is facing the south pole of the magnet and its south pole is facing the magnet's north pole. The direction of the current in the coil is then reversed so that the coil's poles are also reversed. The coil then has to swing round again to line up its poles with those of the magnet. So the electric motor keeps on turning because it keeps getting a series of magnetic pushes.

▼ Many household appliances are run by electric motors.

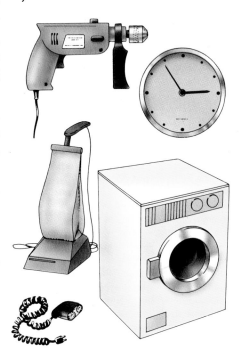

Motor Car

In about a hundred years the motor car has changed the world. The car itself has changed too. The clumsy 'horseless carriage' has become the fast, comfortable and reliable car of today.

Most cars have petrol engines. If petrol is mixed with air and a spark takes place in the mixture, it explodes. The power from this explosion, repeated

The world speed record is held by Richard Noble of Britain. On October 4, 1983 he drove his jet-engined *Thrust 2* at 1019.4 km/h (633.4 mph) on Black Rock Desert, Nevada, USA.

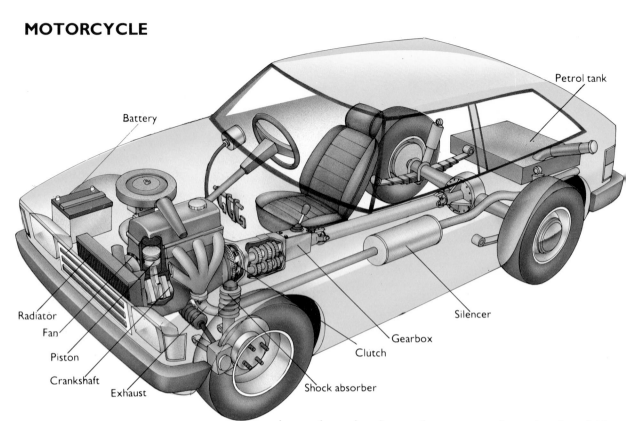

Petrol tank

Battery

Radiator

Fan

Piston

Crankshaft

Exhaust

Silencer

Gearbox

Clutch

Shock absorber

▲ *A cutaway of a modern motor car showing the main parts. Power produced by the engine is transmitted to the driving wheels. For most cars these are the rear wheels, although some cars use the front or all four as driving wheels.*

▼ *Early motorcycles, such as this Daimler of 1885, were very simple, slow and uncomfortable to ride.*

again and again, is made to turn the wheels of the car. (You can read more about this in the article on the INTERNAL COMBUSTION ENGINE.) The driver can make the car go faster by pressing the *accelerator* pedal. This makes more petrol go into the engine.

Cars are pushed along by either their front or back wheels. The engine is usually at the front. As the engine's *pistons* go up and down, they turn the *crankshaft*. The crankshaft is joined to the *clutch* and the *gearbox*, as you can see in the picture. The clutch cuts off the engine from the gearbox. When the driver presses the clutch pedal, the crankshaft is separated from the GEARS. Then the driver can safely change into another gear. If the driver wants maximum power he or she uses a low gear – first gear. The car needs plenty of power for starting or going up a steep hill. When the driver travels along a clear road at speed he or she uses top gear.

Motorcycle

The first motorcycle was built in 1885 by the German Gottlieb Daimler. He fitted one of his petrol engines to a wooden bicycle frame. Today's motorcycles are more complicated machines. The engine is similar to that of a car, but smaller. (See

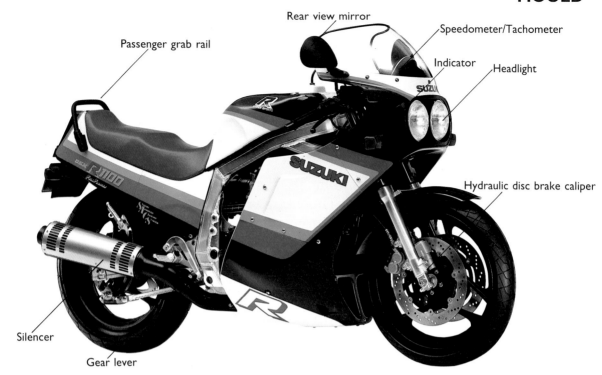

Rear view mirror

Passenger grab rail

Speedometer/Tachometer

Indicator

Headlight

SUZUKI

Hydraulic disc brake caliper

Silencer

Gear lever

INTERNAL COMBUSTION ENGINE.) It is either a two-stroke or a four-stroke engine, and it may have from one to four cylinders. The engine can be cooled by either air or water. It is started with an ignition button on the handlebars. This turns the engine and starts it firing. The speed is controlled by a twist-grip on the handlebars. The clutch works from a hand lever. The gears are changed by a foot lever. Another foot pedal works the brake on the back wheel. A chain or drive shaft connects the engine to the back wheel and drives it round.

▲ *This Suzuki GSXR1100 has a maximum speed of 240 km/h and is designed for high-speed road use. Its engine is as big as that in many small family cars.*

Mould

Moulds are tiny plants that belong to the same group as the MUSHROOM. Unlike green plants, they cannot make their own food. They live on food made by other plants or animals. Moulds grow from a tiny particle called a *spore*. If a spore comes to rest on a piece of damp bread, it grows fine threads and starts to spread. Mouldy food should be thrown away. But some moulds are useful. Certain cheeses such as Stilton, Camembert and Roquefort get their flavour from the moulds that grow in them. The mould *penicillium* is used for making the powerful germ-killing drug penicillin.

▼ *Some cheeses are treated with a penicillium mould to give them their special flavour and appearance.*

WORLD'S HIGHEST MOUNTAINS		
Peak	**Range**	**Metres**
Everest	Himalayas	8848
Godwin Austen	Karakoram	8611
Kanchenjunga	Himalayas	8597
Lhotse	Himalayas	8510
Makalu	Himalayas	8480
Dhaulagiri I	Himalayas	8169
Manaslu	Himalayas	8156
Cho Oyu	Himalayas	8153
Nanga Parbat	Himalayas	8126
Annapurna I	Himalayas	8078
Gasherbrum I	Karakoram	8068
Broad Peak	Karakoram	8047
Gasherbrum II	Karakoram	8033
Gosainthan	Himalayas	8013
Gasherbrum III	Karakoram	7952
Annapurna II	Himalayas	7937
Gasherbrum IV	Karakoram	7925
Kangbachen	Himalayas	7902
Gyachung Kang	Himalayas	7897
Himal Chuli	Himalayas	7893
Disteghil Sar	Karakoram	7885
Kunyang Kish	Karakoram	7852
Dakum (Peak 29)	Himalayas	7852
Nuptse	Himalayas	7841

▼ Different plants grow at different altitudes in mountain areas. This is because the air gets thinner and colder the higher you go.

Mountain

A large part of the Earth's surface is covered by mountains. The greatest mountain ranges are the ALPS of Europe, the ROCKIES and the ANDES of America and the HIMALAYAS of Asia. The Himalayas are the greatest of them all. They have many of the world's highest peaks, including the biggest, Mount EVEREST.

There are mountains under the sea, too. And sometimes the peaks of under-sea mountains stick up above the sea's surface as islands. One mountain called Mauna Loa which rises from the floor of the Pacific Ocean is very much higher than Everest.

Mountains are formed by movements in the Earth's crust. Some mountains are formed when two great land masses move toward each other and squeeze up the land in between. The Alps were made in this way. Other mountains are VOLCANOES, great heaps of ash and lava that poured out when the volcano erupted.

But even the greatest mountains do not last for ever. The hardest rock gets worn away in time by rain, wind, sun and frost. RIVERS cut valleys, GLACIERS grind their way down, wearing away the mountains after untold centuries into gentle hills.

When the height of a mountain is given, it means the height above sea level. This can be a lot more than the height from the base.

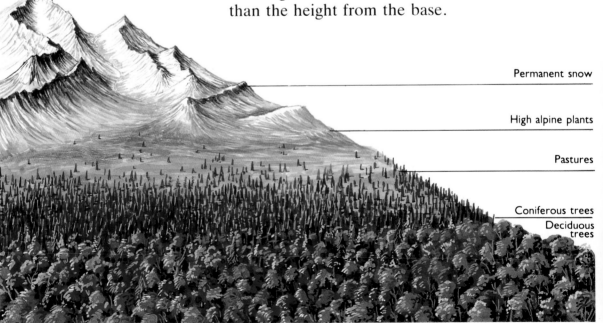

Permanent snow

High alpine plants

Pastures

Coniferous trees

Deciduous trees

Rock mouse

Forest dormouse

Yellow-necked field mouse

Striped field mouse

Mouse

A mouse is a RODENT, like its relative the RAT. And, like the rat, the house mouse is a pest to human beings. It can do a great deal of damage to stores of food, usually at night. One mouse can have 40 babies a year, and when the young are 12 weeks old they can themselves breed. People have used cats to catch mice for thousands of years. The wood mouse, field mouse, harvest mouse, and dormouse are mice that live in the countryside. White mice can be kept as pets.

▲ *Mice are adaptable creatures and live in a variety of habitats.*

Mozambique

Mozambique is a republic in East Africa. It was ruled by Portugal but became independent in 1975. Farming is the most important industry in this hot, tropical country. Mozambique's ports of Maputo and Beira are important for importing and exporting goods to the African interior.

Most of the people of Mozambique are black Africans who speak one of several Bantu languages. There are also some Portuguese and Asians.

In the 1980s, severe droughts and civil war caused hardship in the country.

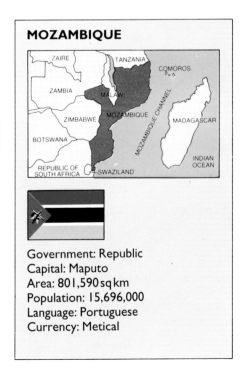

MOZAMBIQUE

Government: Republic
Capital: Maputo
Area: 801,590 sq km
Population: 15,696,000
Language: Portuguese
Currency: Metical

▲ *From a very early age, Mozart was taken on concert tours by his father Leopold, also a musician.*

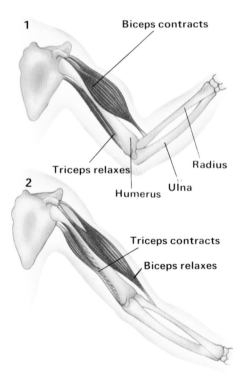

▲ *Muscles often work in pairs, with one contracting as the other relaxes. They are said to be* antagonistic, *or working against each other. This is how the arm muscles work.*

Labels on figure:
1
Biceps contracts
Triceps relaxes
Radius
Humerus
Ulna
2
Triceps contracts
Biceps relaxes

Mozart, Wolfgang Amadeus

Wolfgang Amadeus Mozart (1756–1791) was an Austrian and one of the greatest composers of music that the world has known. He began writing music at the age of five. Two years later he was playing at concerts all over Europe. Mozart wrote over 600 pieces of music, including many beautiful operas and symphonies. But he earned little money from his hard work. He died at the age of 35.

Muhammad

Muhammad (AD 570–632) was the founder and leader of the RELIGION known as ISLAM. He was born in MECCA in what is now Saudi Arabia. At the age of 40 he believed that God had asked him to preach to the ARABS. He taught that there was only one God, called Allah.

In 622 he was forced out of Mecca, and this is the year from which the Muslim calendar dates. After his death his teachings spread rapidly across the world.

Muscle

Muscles are the things that make the parts of our bodies move. When you pick up this book or kick a ball you are using muscles. There are two different kinds of muscles. Some work when your brain tells them to. When you pick up a chair, your brain sends signals to muscles in your arms, in your body and in your legs. All these muscles work together at the right time, and you pick up the chair. Other kinds of muscles work even when you are asleep. Your stomach muscles go on churning the food you have eaten. Your heart muscles go on pumping blood. The human body has more than 500 muscles.

Mushroom and Toadstool

Mushrooms and toadstools are both forms of fungi (see FUNGUS). They grow in woods, fields and on people's lawns – almost anywhere, in fact, where it is warm enough and damp enough. Some mushrooms are very good to eat. Others are so poisonous that people die from eating them. Mushrooms and toadstools have no green colouring matter (CHLORO-PHYLL); instead they feed on decayed matter in the soil or on other plants.

Music

People have been making some kind of music all through history. The very earliest people probably made singing noises and beat time with pieces of wood. We know that the ancient Egyptians enjoyed their music. Paintings in the tombs of the PHARAOHS show musicians playing pipes, harps and other stringed instruments. The ancient Greeks also liked stringed instruments such as the lyre. But we have no idea what this early music sounded like, because there was no way of writing it down.

By the MIDDLE AGES, composers were writing music for groups of instruments. But it was not until the 1600s that the ORCHESTRA as we know it was born. The first orchestras were brought together by Italian composers to accompany their OPERAS. It was at this time that VIOLINS, violas and cellos were first used.

As instruments improved, new ones were added to the orchestra. BACH and HANDEL, who were both born in 1685, used orchestras with mostly stringed instruments like the violin. But they also had flutes, oboes, trumpets and horns. Joseph HAYDN was the first composer to use the orchestra as a whole. He invented the *symphony*. In this, all the instruments

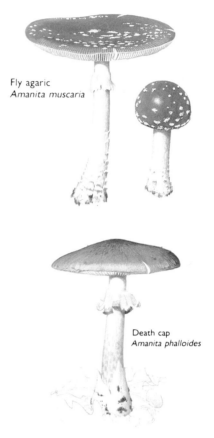

Fly agaric
Amanita muscaria

Death cap
Amanita phalloides

▲ *Poisonous toadstools like these sometimes look dangerous, but even some harmless-looking ones can kill.*

▼ *In music some notes have two names. C sharp, for instance, is the same note as D flat. A ♯ by a note means that it is raised by a semi-tone, a ♭ by a note means it is lowered a semi-tone.*

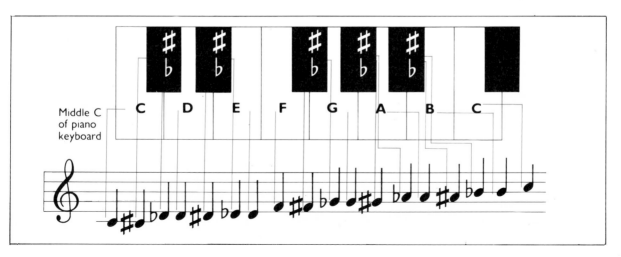

▶ *The layout of a modern symphony orchestra has been developed over many years.*

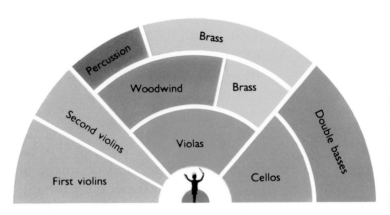

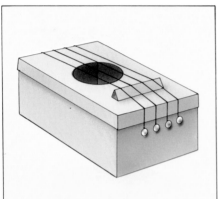

SEE IT YOURSELF

You can make a simple guitar from a cardboard box and some elastic bands. Cut a hole in the lid of the box and tack lengths of elastic of varying thickness tightly across it. Fit a wedge of wood beneath the elastic bands as shown. The bands will give out different notes when they are plucked.

blended together so that none was more important than the others.

A new kind of music began with the great German composer BEETHOVEN. He began writing music in which some of the notes clashed. This sounded rather shocking to people who listened to his music in his day. Later musicians tried all kinds of mixtures of instruments. In the 1900s new kinds of music were made by composers such as Igor Stravinsky and Arnold Schoenberg. Others since then have used tape recorders and electronic systems to produce new sounds which are often rather strange to our ears.

But much music still has three things: *melody*, *harmony* and *rhythm*. The melody is the tune. Harmony is the agreeable sound made when certain notes are played together. Often these notes form a *chord*, an arrangement of notes within a particular musical key. Rhythm is the regular 'beat' of the music. The simplest kind of music is just beating out a rhythm on a drum.

What is probably the oldest kind of musical instrument has been found by archaeologists in Stone Age sites. It is a bull-roarer, consisting of a small oval-shaped piece of bone with a hole in one end in which a cord is tied. It is whirled around by the player and produces a buzzing sound – the faster it is whirled, the higher the buzz.

Musical Instrument

There are four kinds of musical instrument. In wind instruments, air is made to vibrate inside a tube. This vibrating air makes a musical note.

All *woodwind* instruments such as clarinets, bassoons, flutes, piccolos and recorders have holes that are covered by the fingers or by pads worked by the fingers. These holes change the length of the vibrating column of air inside the instrument. The shorter the column the higher the note. In *brass* wind instruments, the vibration of the player's lips makes the air in the instrument vibrate. By changing the pressure of the lips, the player can make different notes. Most brass instruments also have valves and pistons to change the length of the vibrating column of air, and so make different notes.

Stringed instruments work in one of two ways. The strings of the instrument are either made to vibrate by a bow, as in the violin, viola, cello and double bass; or the strings are plucked, as in the guitar, harp or banjo.

In *percussion* instruments, a tight piece of skin or a piece of wood or metal is struck to make a note. There are lots of percussion instruments – drums, cymbals, gongs, tambourines, triangles and chimes.

Electronic instruments such as the electric organ and the synthesizer make music using sounds produced by electronic circuits.

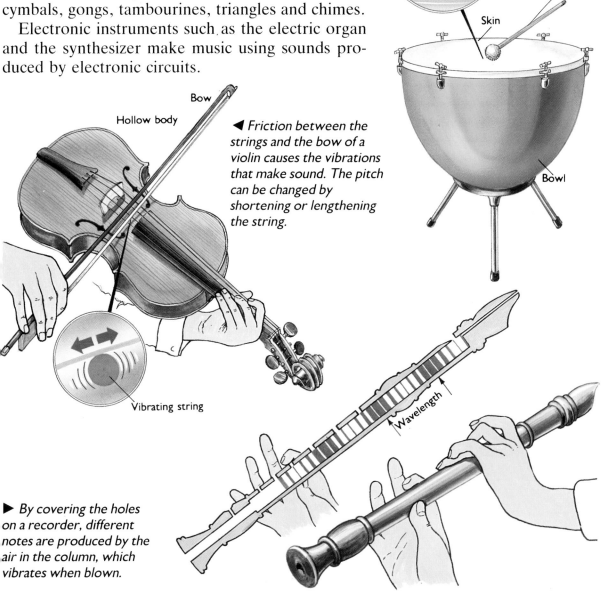

▼ *Percussion instruments are played by striking them. The note made by the timpani can be changed by tightening or loosening the skin.*

Vibrating skin

Mallet

Skin

Bowl

Bow

Hollow body

◀ *Friction between the strings and the bow of a violin causes the vibrations that make sound. The pitch can be changed by shortening or lengthening the string.*

Vibrating string

Wavelength

▶ *By covering the holes on a recorder, different notes are produced by the air in the column, which vibrates when blown.*

Mussolini, Benito

Mussolini (1883-1945) was a DICTATOR and leader of Italy's FASCISTS. In 1922 he bluffed the king of Italy into making him prime minister. Soon he made himself dictator. He wanted to make Italy great; he built many new buildings and created new jobs. But he also wanted military glory and led Italy into World War II on the side of HITLER. His armies were defeated by the Allies and Mussolini was finally captured and shot by his own people.

▲ *Mussolini was known in his native Italy as* Il Duce, *which means 'the leader'.*

Myth

In ancient times, people believed that the world was inhabited by many different gods and spirits. There were gods of war and thunder, the sea, wine and hunting. The Sun and the Moon were gods too. Stories that tell of the gods are called myths. The study of myths is called mythology.

Some myths tell of extraordinary human beings called *heroes* who performed great deeds. Others tell of the tricks the gods played on ordinary mortals. There are myths from all countries, but those of Greece and Rome have become the most familiar. Many of the Greek myths were adopted by the Romans. They even adopted some of the Greek gods.

Mythology teaches us much about the way people of long ago thought and lived.

▼ *The ancient Egyptians believed in many gods. Some were represented with the heads of animals considered sacred by the Egyptians. Osiris, god of the afterlife, was married to Isis, goddess of female fertility, and Horus was their son. Anubis escorted the dead to the afterworld, and Re was the Sun god.*

Horus

Anubis

Isis

Osiris

Re

Nail and Claw

Nails and claws are made of hard skin, like animals' horns. They grow at the end of toes and fingers. When they are broad and flat they are called nails, but if they are sharp and pointed they are claws. Human nails are of little use. But BIRDS, MAMMALS and REPTILES use their claws to attack and to defend themselves.

A close look at an animal's claws will tell you about its way of life. CATS and birds of prey have very sharp claws. They are hooked for holding onto and tearing prey. ANTEATERS have long, strong, curved claws for tearing apart termites' nests.

◄ The claws of birds, reptiles and mammals are all vital to their survival. The claw design of members of the cat family is particularly interesting. The claws can be retracted (pulled back) into the paws at will.

Namibia

Namibia is in the south-west part of Africa. On some maps the country is called South West Africa. Most of the country is a plateau more than 1000 metres high. In the east is a part of the Kalahari Desert. There is not much good farmland. The main industry is mining.

In 1915, the country became a South African territory under the League of Nations. In 1946, the United Nations said that South Africa had no rights over Namibia, but South Africa disputed this. In 1989 it was finally agreed that South Africa would hand over power to the black majority. Independence was achieved in 1990.

NAMIBIA

ANGOLA ZAMBIA
ZIMBABWE
NAMIBIA
BOTSWANA
ATLANTIC OCEAN
REPUBLIC OF SOUTH AFRICA

Government: Republic
Capital: Windhoek
Area: 824,292 sq km
Population: 1,574,000
Languages: Afrikaans, English
Currency: Rand

Napoleon Bonaparte

In 1789 the people of France rebelled against the unjust rule of their king and his nobles. The FRENCH REVOLUTION was supported by a young man born on the island of Corsica 20 years before. His name was Napoleon Bonaparte (1769–1821).

▶ *Napoleon set out to conquer the whole of Europe. Shown here is the extent of his empire at the height of his power.*

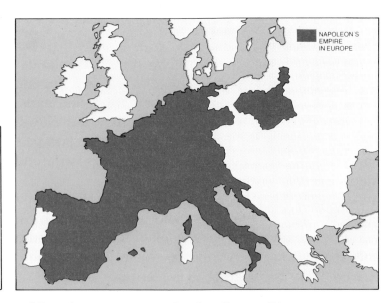

NAPOLEON'S EMPIRE IN EUROPE

As the pope prepared to crown Napoleon emperor in Notre Dame cathedral, Napoleon seized the crown from his hands and placed it on his own head, to show that he, Napoleon, had personally gained the right to wear it.

Napoleon went to the leading military school in Paris, and by 1792 he was a captain of artillery. Three years later he saved France by crushing a royalist rebellion in Paris. Soon Napoleon was head of the French army and won great victories in Italy, Belgium and Austria. In 1804 he crowned himself emperor of France in the presence of the Pope. Then he crowned his wife, Josephine.

But Napoleon could not defeat Britain at sea. He tried to stop all countries from trading with Britain, but Russia would not cooperate. So Napoleon led a great army into Russia in the winter of 1812. This campaign ended in disaster. His troops were defeated by the bitter weather. Then he met his final defeat at the battle of WATERLOO in 1815. There he was beaten by the British under WELLINGTON and the Prussians under Blücher. He was made prisoner by the British on the lonely Atlantic island of St Helena, where he died in 1821.

Napoleon was a small man. His soldiers adored him and called him 'the little corporal'. Napoleon drew up a new French code of law. Many of his laws are still in force today.

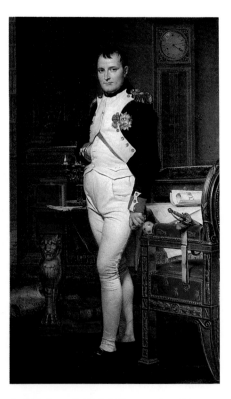

▲ *With political skills equal to his skills as a general, Napoleon reorganized the government of France.*

NATO (North Atlantic Treaty Organization)

NATO is a defensive alliance set up after World War II. In 1949, 12 countries signed a treaty in which they agreed that an attack on one member should be considered an attack on them all. The 12 were Belgium, Canada, Denmark, France, Iceland, Italy, Luxembourg, the Netherlands, Norway, Portugal, the United Kingdom and the United States. Greece and Turkey joined in 1951, West Germany in 1954, and Spain in 1982. The original NATO headquarters were in Paris.

The purpose of the alliance is to unify and strengthen the military defences of the nations of Western Europe. Each member nation contributes soldiers and supplies to NATO forces. But the members of NATO also cooperate on political and economic issues.

In the 1960s some NATO members felt that the United States had too much power in the alliance. France withdrew her NATO forces in 1966. France is still a NATO member, but the headquarters have been moved from Paris to Brussels. With the collapse of many of the Communist governments of Eastern Europe in 1990, NATO is looking closely at its role for the future. In 1991 NATO forces were restructured as the Cold War came to an end. United States forces in Europe are being cut back.

> In 1966, Charles de Gaulle announced France's withdrawal from NATO, though not from the Atlantic Alliance.

Natural Gas

Natural gas is a type of GAS which occurs naturally underground and does not have to be manufactured. It is usually found in OIL fields, but is sometimes found on its own. When there is only a little natural gas in an oil field, it is burned off. If there is plenty, it is piped away and used for cooking, heating and producing ELECTRICITY.

It is found in large quantities in Russia, in Texas and Louisiana in the United States, and in the NORTH SEA oil fields. Half the world's supply of natural gas is used by the United States.

Nauru

Nauru is a tiny island country in the Pacific Ocean. The only industry is mining for phosphate, but by the mid 1990s there will be no phosphate left on the island. Nauru became independent in 1968 and is a member of the Commonwealth.

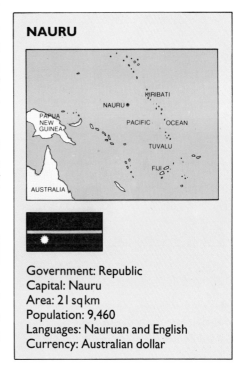

NAURU

Government: Republic
Capital: Nauru
Area: 21 sq km
Population: 9,460
Languages: Nauruan and English
Currency: Australian dollar

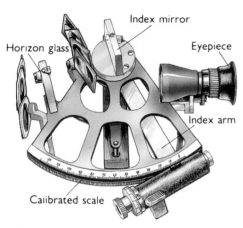

Index mirror

Horizon glass

Eyepiece

Index arm

Calibrated scale

▲ *A sextant can be used to work out a ship's position by measuring the angle between a star or the Sun and the horizon (see below right).*

▶ *Once the angle has been measured, the star's position at that particular time can be looked up in a very accurate table. This allows the position of the ship to be calculated. By taking a series of sextant readings the ship can be kept on the right course.*

▲ *Nelson once ignored an order to stop an attack by pretending he couldn't see the signal – he held his telescope to his blind eye.*

Navigation

Navigation means finding the way, usually in a ship or an aircraft. For hundreds of years, navigators at sea used the changing positions of the Sun and stars to work out their LATITUDE. Knowing the difference between the time on the ship and the time set at 0° longitude at Greenwich helped them to work out their position more precisely.

Today, many navigational instruments are electronic and are very accurate. Radio beacons and SATELLITES send out signals from which a ship can find its position. Then the navigator uses a COMPASS to keep the ship on the right course. COMPUTERS help ships, aircraft and spacecraft navigate so exactly that their position is known precisely.

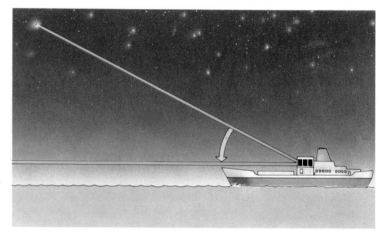

Nelson, Horatio

Horatio Nelson (1758–1805) was a famous British admiral at the time when Britain was at war with the French, led by NAPOLEON BONAPARTE.

Nelson was born in Norfolk, the son of a country clergyman. He joined the navy when he was 12 and was captain of a frigate by the time he was 20. He was made a rear-admiral in 1797. By then he had already lost an eye in battle. Soon he lost an arm too.

In 1798 he led his ships to victory against the French at Alexandria in Egypt. While he was in the Mediterranean he met and fell in love with Lady Hamilton, the wife of the British ambassador to Naples. Nelson loved Lady Hamilton all his life.

Many people thought this was shocking as they were both married to other people.

Nelson's most famous battle was his last. It was fought against a French fleet led by Admiral Villeneuve. For nearly 10 months in 1805, Nelson's ships chased Villeneuve's across the Atlantic and back. Then, on October 21, they met off the Cape of Trafalgar in southern Spain. Nelson defeated the French in the battle that followed but was killed on board his ship, the *Victory*.

Before the battle Nelson sent a famous message to all the ships in his fleet: 'England expects that every man will do his duty.'

Nepal

NEPAL

Government: Constitutional monarchy
Capital: Katmandu
Area: 140,797 sq km
Population: 20,086,000
Language: Nepali
Currency: Rupee

A country smaller than England and Wales, Nepal lies between India and Tibet and is very mountainous. The Himalaya Mountains lie in northern Nepal. Most of the people live in the fertile central valley. The country was almost completely closed to the rest of the world for centuries. Now there are roads and an air service to India and Pakistan.

Neptune (Planet)

The PLANET Neptune is named after the Roman god of water and the sea. It is a large planet far out in the SOLAR SYSTEM. It is about 4500 million km from the SUN. Only PLUTO is farther away. It takes Neptune 164.8 years to circle the Sun. (The Earth takes 365 days.)

▼ If we could observe Neptune from its large moon, Triton, it would probably look like this. The light from the Sun would be no brighter than that of a star.

NEPTUNE FACTS

Average distance from Sun: 4497 million km
Nearest distance from Earth: 4350 million km
Average temperature (clouds): –210 degrees C
Diameter across equator: 48,400 km
Atmosphere: Hydrogen, helium?
Number of moons: 8
Length of day: 18 hours
Length of year: 164.8 Earth years

— Earth
— Neptune

▼ *If the size of the various parts of your body corresponded to the number of nerve cells in them, you would look rather like this.*

▶ *Various receptors in the skin deal with different sensations. They transmit these sensations to the brain with the help of nerve cells.*

Being so far from the Sun, Neptune is a very cold place. Scientists think its atmosphere is rather like JUPITER's, which is mostly made up of the gas HYDROGEN. Neptune has eight moons, and scientists have recently discovered a system of thin rings around the planet.

Early astronomers were unable to see Neptune, but they knew it had to be there. They could tell there was something affecting the ORBIT of the nearby planet URANUS. In 1845 two astronomers, Adams in England and Leverrier in France, used mathematics to work out where Neptune should be. Astronomers used this information the next year, and spotted Neptune.

Nerve

Nerves are tiny fibres made up of CELLS. They reach all through the body. When a part of the body touches something, the nerves send a message through the spinal column to the BRAIN. If we feel PAIN, a message is sent back to make us move away from whatever is hurting. Nerves also carry the senses of sight, hearing and taste. The sense organs have special nerve endings that respond to heat, light, cold and other stimuli around us.

▼ *A motor nerve, with its many dendrites and long axon, carries messages from the brain or spinal cord to the muscles.*

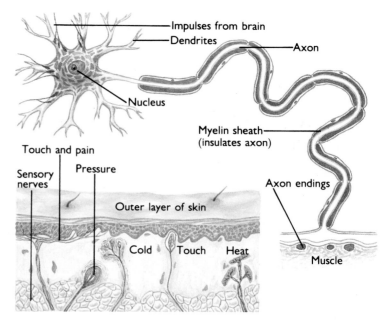

Impulses from brain
Dendrites
Axon
Nucleus
Myelin sheath (insulates axon)
Axon endings
Touch and pain
Sensory nerves
Pressure
Outer layer of skin
Cold   Touch   Heat
Muscle

Nest

A nest is a home built by an animal, where it has its young and looks after them. BIRDS build nests when they are ready to lay EGGS. Sometimes the female builds the nest, sometimes the male will give her some help. Some nests are very complicated, and may be lined with wool, hair or feathers. Others are simple or rather untidy.

A few MAMMALS such as MICE and SQUIRRELS make nests for their young, but these are not as complicated as birds' nests.

Some INSECTS make the most complicated nests of all. These are not at all like birds' nests. They are often built for a whole group, or colony, of insects. There will be one queen, who lays eggs, and hundreds or even thousands of workers to look after them. Most BEES and wasps make this sort of nest. Some wasps build their nests out of paper. TERMITES make huge mud nests.

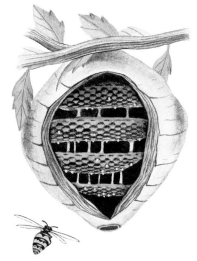

▲ The complex pattern of cells in the hornet's papery nest makes a safe home for the young.

▲ Coots live on open stretches of water, but build their nests on piles of stones or sticks raised above the water.

Netherlands

The Netherlands, or Holland, as it is also known, is a low-lying country in western EUROPE. The sea often floods the flat land near the coast, so sea walls have been built for protection against storms. Living so near the sea, the people of the Netherlands (who call themselves the Dutch) have a long and successful history of seafaring, trade and exploring.

▲ The South American oven bird builds a nest shaped like an old fashioned oven, from mud and bits of grass or straw.

◄ A lot of the inhabited land in the Netherlands was reclaimed from under the sea, and drained using networks of canals.

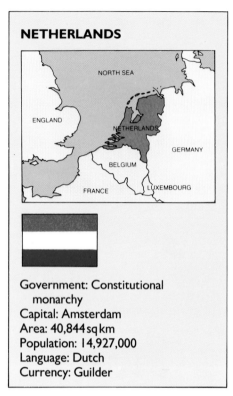

NETHERLANDS

Government: Constitutional
  monarchy
Capital: Amsterdam
Area: 40,844 sq km
Population: 14,927,000
Language: Dutch
Currency: Guilder

▼ *There are many stages and many workers involved in producing a newspaper.*

The Netherlands is a land of canals, windmills farms and bulb fields which burst into colour in spring. It was once part of a group of countries called the Low Countries, but it became self-governing in 1579. Important cities are Amsterdam, the capital, and Rotterdam, which is the busiest port in Europe. The Netherlands is a prosperous country and one of the first members of the EUROPEAN COMMUNITY. It has a queen, but is governed by a democratic parliament.

New Guinea

New Guinea is one of the world's largest islands. It lies to the north of Australia. Its people are dark-skinned with curly hair.

The island is divided into two parts. The west is called Irian Jaya, and belongs to INDONESIA. The east is called PAPUA NEW GUINEA. About three million people live there. It used to belong to Australia but became independent in 1975. The capital is Port Moresby. Most of the people live in the central highlands.

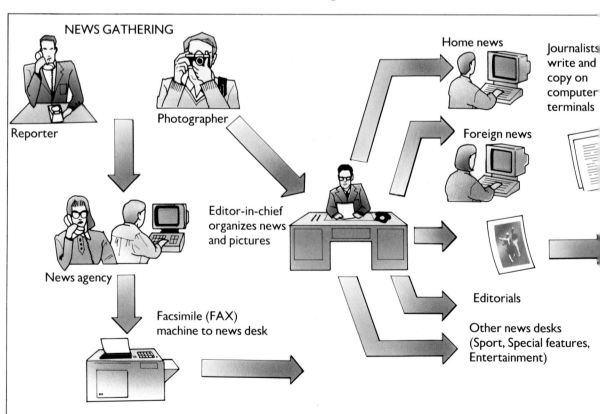

NEWS GATHERING

Reporter

Photographer

News agency

Facsimile (FAX)
machine to news desk

Editor-in-chief
organizes news
and pictures

Home news

Foreign news

Journalists
write and
copy on
computer
terminals

Editorials

Other news desks
(Sport, Special features,
Entertainment)

New Guinea's main exports are tea, cocoa, copra (coconut), copper and gold. The official language is English but some 700 different languages are spoken.

Newspaper

Newspapers are just what their name says they are – papers that print news. They first appeared in the 1400s, just after PRINTING began. Printers produced pamphlets telling people what was happening in the country and what they thought about it.

Modern newspapers first appeared in the 1700s. Today, there are newspapers in almost every country in the world, in many different languages. Some are printed every day, some every week.

One of the oldest newspapers is *The Times* which is printed in London. It began in 1785 when it was called the *Universal Daily Register*. It changed its name to *The Times* in 1788. Other famous newspapers are the *New York Times* and the *Washington Post* in the United States, *Pravda* in Russia, and *Le Monde* in France.

▲ *Some New Guinea tribespeople decorate their faces with brightly coloured pigments during important festivals.*

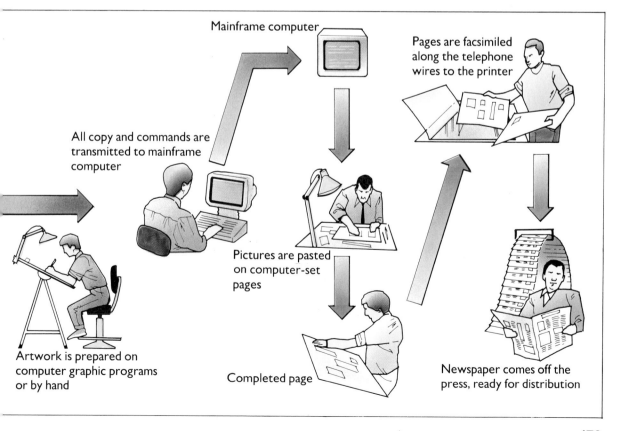

Mainframe computer

All copy and commands are transmitted to mainframe computer

Pages are facsimiled along the telephone wires to the printer

Pictures are pasted on computer-set pages

Artwork is prepared on computer graphic programs or by hand

Completed page

Newspaper comes off the press, ready for distribution

▲ *Newton determined the laws of motion that are still used in physics today.*

New York probably has the most mixed population of any city in the world. Its black community is the largest in the United States. The world's largest Jewish population lives in the New York area. The city has a Little Italy and a Chinatown.

▼ *New York is home to six of the ten tallest buildings in the world, including the World Trade Center and the Empire State Building.*

Newton, Isaac

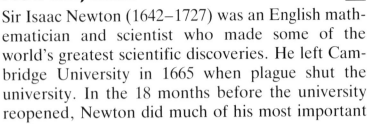

Sir Isaac Newton (1642–1727) was an English mathematician and scientist who made some of the world's greatest scientific discoveries. He left Cambridge University in 1665 when plague shut the university. In the 18 months before the university reopened, Newton did much of his most important work.

Newton's experiments showed that white LIGHT is a mixture of all the colours of the rainbow (the spectrum). By studying the spectrum of light from a star or other glowing object, scientists can now find out what that object is made of. Newton's studies of light also led him to build the first reflecting TELESCOPE.

Newton also discovered GRAVITY. He realized that the same kind of force that makes apples fall from trees also gives objects weight and keeps PLANETS going round the SUN.

New York

New York City is the largest city in the UNITED STATES. More than 11 million people live in New York and its suburbs.

The city stands mainly on three islands that lie at the mouth of the Hudson River. The island of Manhattan holds the heart of New York, and many of its most famous sights. Some of the world's tallest SKYSCRAPERS tower above its streets. Fifth Avenue is a famous shopping street, and Broadway is known for its theatres. Perhaps New York's best-known

sight is the Statue of Liberty, one of the largest statues on Earth. It stands on an island in New York Harbor.

Ships from every continent dock at New York's port, which is the largest anywhere. New York is one of the world's great business centres. Its factories produce more goods than those of any other city in the United States.

New Zealand

New Zealand is a remote island nation in the Pacific Ocean, south-east of Australia.

New Zealand is actually two main islands. North Island is famous for its hot springs and volcanoes. South Island has a range of mountains called the Southern Alps, and many lakes and waterfalls.

The country also has plains and valleys. Here, the

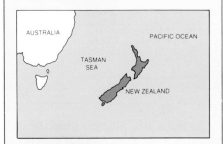

NEW ZEALAND

Government: Parliamentary
Capital: Wellington
Area: 268,676 sq km
Population: 3,390,000
Languages: English, Maori
Currency: Dollar

◀ The Pohutu geyser, in the North Island of New Zealand, erupts because of the natural heat and pressure of underground springs.

▲ The kiwi lives in the forests of New Zealand. Since it cannot fly, it does not need the strong, stiff feathers most birds have. Its feathers look more like shaggy fur.

mild climate helps farmers to grow grains, vegetables and apples. They also raise millions of sheep and cattle. New Zealand is the world's third largest producer of sheep and wool.

There are over three million New Zealanders. Two in three people live in a city or town. Auckland is the largest city, but the capital is Wellington. Both are in North Island.

New Zealand is a member of the COMMONWEALTH. Many of its people are descended from British settlers. Others are MAORIS, descended from Pacific islanders, who lived in New Zealand before the British came.

When the first European settlers arrived in New Zealand, the only animals there were dogs and rats. The ancestors of the country's cattle, sheep, pigs, deer, rabbits and goats were brought in by Europeans.

NIAGARA FALLS

▶ *The sheer size of Niagara Falls has challenged people's courage and ingenuity for many years – Charles Blondin walked across the top of the falls on a tightrope on June 30, 1859.*

As the water plunges over the edge of Niagara Falls, it slowly erodes (wears away) the rock. In this way, the position of the falls is gradually changed. The falls are about 11 km farther north than they were when the water first flowed over them thousands of years ago. In several thousand more years, Niagara Falls as we know them will have disappeared.

Niagara Falls

The Niagara Falls are WATERFALLS on the Niagara River in North America. Water from most of the GREAT LAKES flows through this river. Each minute about 450,000 tonnes of water plunge about 50 metres from a cliff into a gorge.

The falls stand on the border between Canada and the United States. The water pours down on each side of an island. Most of it plunges down the Horseshoe Falls in Canada. The rest plunges down the American Falls in the United States.

People can gaze down on the falls from observation towers, or take a boat that sails up to the wild waters below.

Nicaragua

Nicaragua is a country that stretches across CENTRAL AMERICA from the Pacific Ocean to the Caribbean Sea. Most of the people live on the western coast, where the land is flat and good for farming. A line of high mountains runs down the centre of Nicaragua. Farming is the main occupation, with cotton, coffee, fruit and sugar as the main products.

In 1938, Nicaragua became an independent republic dominated by the Somoza family. In 1979, Sandinista guerrillas took over the country, later opposed by the US-backed 'contras'. In free elections held in 1990 the Sandinista government was defeated.

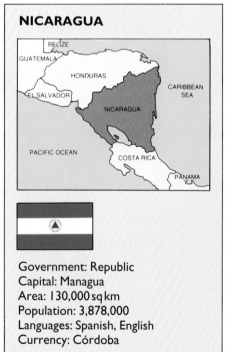

NICARAGUA

Government: Republic
Capital: Managua
Area: 130,000 sq km
Population: 3,878,000
Languages: Spanish, English
Currency: Córdoba

Niger

Niger is a West African country with no seacoast. The north of the country is part of the SAHARA DESERT. The south, through which flows the Niger River, is the agricultural region. The climate is hot and dry. The people are mostly herdsmen and farmers who grow peanuts and cotton. The mining of uranium is important.

Niger was a French colony that became independent in 1960. Severe droughts in the 1970s and 1980s led to great losses of crops and livestock. There has been much political unrest.

Nigeria

This nation in West AFRICA is named after the Niger River that flows through it to the Atlantic Ocean. Nigeria has nearly 120 million people, more than any other nation in Africa. The capital is Abuja.

Nigeria is hot. Dry grass and scrubby trees are scattered across the country. There are a great number of different tribes.

Half the people follow the religion of ISLAM. Most of the people grow cocoa, maize, yams or other food crops. In 1995 international sanctions were declared against Nigeria and the country was suspended from the Commonwealth because of the execution of nine government opponents.

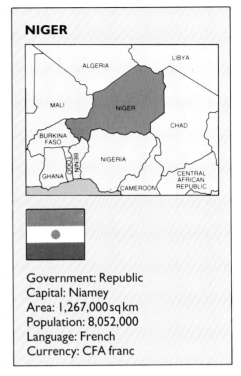

NIGER

Government: Republic
Capital: Niamey
Area: 1,267,000 sq km
Population: 8,052,000
Language: French
Currency: CFA franc

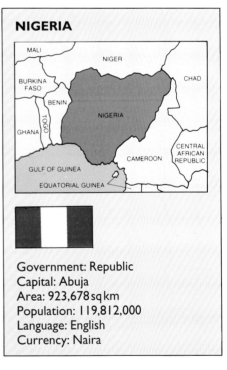

NIGERIA

Government: Republic
Capital: Abuja
Area: 923,678 sq km
Population: 119,812,000
Language: English
Currency: Naira

◄ *There are various types of national dress in Nigeria. From left to right: the* bubu *and skirt made from Guinea brocade, the* babariga *worn by northerners, and the wrapper and blouse worn mostly by Ibo and Benin women.*

▲ Florence Nightingale was known as 'the lady with the lamp' by the soldiers she tended in the Crimea.

Nightingale, Florence

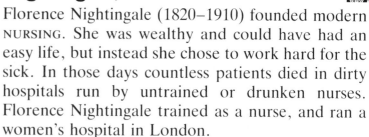

Florence Nightingale (1820–1910) founded modern NURSING. She was wealthy and could have had an easy life, but instead she chose to work hard for the sick. In those days countless patients died in dirty hospitals run by untrained or drunken nurses. Florence Nightingale trained as a nurse, and ran a women's hospital in London.

In 1854 she took 38 nurses to Turkey to tend British soldiers wounded in the CRIMEAN WAR. Her hospital was a dirty barracks that lacked food, medicines and bedding. She cleaned it up, found supplies, and gave the wounded every care she could. Her work saved many hundreds of lives.

Nile

The Nile River in Africa is generally thought to be the longest river on Earth. (Some people think that the AMAZON is longer.) The Nile has been measured

▼ A ship unloads at the quay in an Ancient Egyptian city. The civilization that grew up in Ancient Egypt depended on the Nile for transport, so most large cities were built beside this great river.

at 6690 km. It rises in Burundi in central Africa and flows north through Egypt into the Mediterranean Sea. It is very important to farmers, who rely on it for irrigation.

Nobel Prize

These money prizes are given each year to people who have helped mankind in different ways. Three prizes are for inventions or discoveries in physics, chemistry, and physiology and medicine. The fourth is for literature. The fifth prize is for work to make or keep peace between peoples and the sixth is for economics. Money for the prizes was left by the Swedish chemist Alfred Nobel, who invented the explosive dynamite.

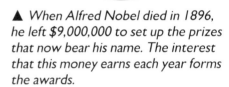

▲ When Alfred Nobel died in 1896, he left $9,000,000 to set up the prizes that now bear his name. The interest that this money earns each year forms the awards.

Nomad

People without a settled home are nomads. Many nomads live in lands too dry to farm. Such people keep herds of animals and travel to find fresh pasture for them. They live in portable homes, such as tents. Many nomads still live in or near the great deserts of Africa and Asia.

▼ Some of the days of our week are named after the Norse gods: Tuesday after Tyr, god of war, Thursday after Thor, god of thunder, and Friday after Frigga, goddess of marriage. Odin was king of the gods. His brother Loki was god of fire, and Freya, Odin's first wife, was goddess of love.

Norse Myth

Norse MYTHS are old north European tales about gods and heroes of long ago.

One story tells how the world was made from the body of the first giant, who was killed by three of

Loki

Thor

Tyr

Frigga

Freya

Odin

Asgarth, the home of the Norse gods, had many gold and silver palaces, the most splendid of which was Valhalla, the home of Odin, ruler of the universe. The myths said that Asgarth would be destroyed at the Twilight of the Gods, the final battle in which the giants and demons would overcome the gods.

▲ *Three-quarters of North America is occupied by just two countries – Canada and the United States.*

NORTH AMERICA

Area: 23,497,000 sq km – 15.7 per cent of world's land area
Population: 432,000,000 – 8 per cent of world population
Coastline: 148,330 km
Highest mountain: Mount McKinley, Alaska, 6194 m
Lowest point: Death Valley, California, 86 m below sea level
Principal rivers: Mackenzie, Mississippi, Missouri, St Lawrence, Rio Grande, Yukon, Arkansas, Colorado
Principal lakes: Superior, Huron, Michigan, Great Bear, Great Slave, Erie, Winnipeg, Ontario
Largest city: Mexico City, 18,748,000
Busiest port: New Orleans

the first god's grandsons. Another story tells how the god Odin and two other gods made the first man from an ash tree and the first woman from an elm. A third tale tells how the jealous god Loki killed Odin's son, Balder the beautiful. In this tale, Balder stands for summer and his death represents the start of winter.

Norse myths said that the gods lived in Asgarth, a home in the sky, but they travelled down a rainbow to visit the Earth.

North America

The continent of North America stretches north from tropical Panama to the cold Arctic Ocean, and east from the Pacific Ocean to the Atlantic Ocean. Only Asia is larger.

North America has the world's largest island (GREENLAND), and the largest freshwater lake (Lake Superior). It contains the second largest country (CANADA), the second longest mountain range (the ROCKY MOUNTAINS), and the third longest river (the MISSISSIPPI RIVER). North America's natural wonders include NIAGARA FALLS and the GRAND CANYON (the largest gorge on land).

The cold north has long, dark, frozen winters. No trees grow here. Farther south stand huge evergreen forests. Grasslands covered most of the plains in the middle of the continent until farmers ploughed them up. Cactuses thrive in the deserts of the southwest. Tropical trees grow quickly in the hot, wet forests of the south.

Peoples from all over the world have made their homes in North America. First, from Asia, came the ancestors of the AMERICAN INDIANS and ES-KIMOS. Later came Europeans, who brought black slaves from Africa. Most North Americans speak English, French or Spanish, and are Protestant or Roman Catholic Christians. They live in more than 30 nations. The UNITED STATES and Canada are large, powerful and rich. But many of the nations of CENTRAL AMERICA and the WEST INDIES are small and poor.

Only one person in every 20 people in the world lives in North America. Yet North Americans make

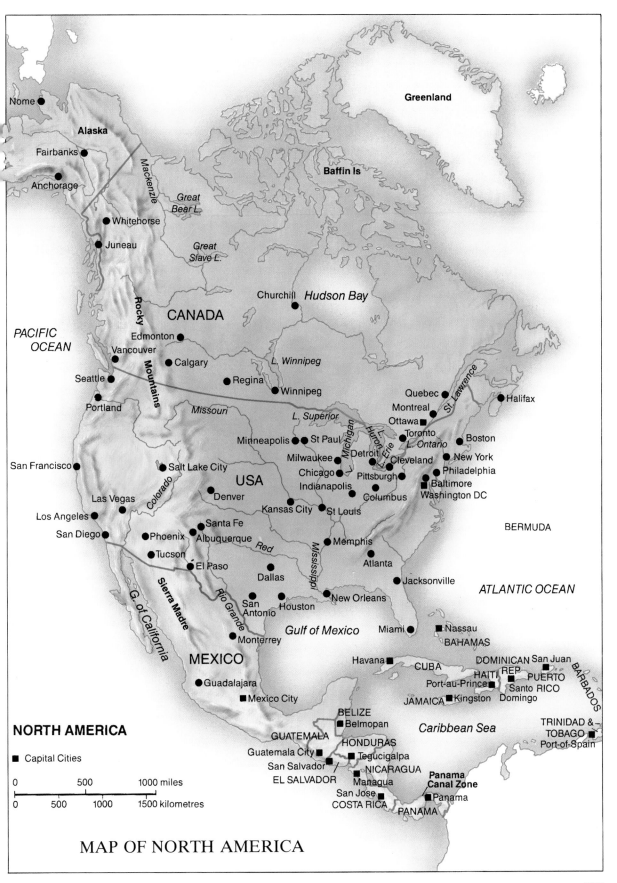

Greenland

Nome

Alaska

Fairbanks

Anchorage

Great Bear L.

Baffin Is

Whitehorse

Juneau

Great Slave L.

Churchill   *Hudson Bay*

CANADA

Rocky

PACIFIC OCEAN

Edmonton

Vancouver

Calgary

Mountains

Seattle

Regina

Portland

Winnipeg

L. Winnipeg

Quebec

St. Lawrence

Halifax

Montreal

Ottawa

Missouri

L. Superior

Toronto

Minneapolis   St Paul

Boston

L. Ontario

San Francisco

Salt Lake City

Milwaukee   Detroit   Cleveland   New York

USA

Chicago   Pittsburgh   Philadelphia

Las Vegas

Indianapolis   Baltimore

Denver

Columbus   Washington DC

Los Angeles

Colorado

Kansas City   St Louis

BERMUDA

San Diego

Santa Fe

Phoenix   Albuquerque   *Red*

Memphis

Tucson

Mississippi

Atlanta

El Paso

Dallas

Jacksonville

ATLANTIC OCEAN

Sierra Madre

Rio Grande

San Antonio   Houston

New Orleans

G. of California

Monterrey

Gulf of Mexico   Miami

Nassau

BAHAMAS

MEXICO

Havana

CUBA

DOMINICAN   San Juan

Guadalajara

HAITI   REP   PUERTO

Port-au-Prince   Santo   RICO

Mexico City

JAMAICA   Kingston   Domingo

BELIZE

Belmopan

Caribbean Sea

TRINIDAD &

TOBAGO

NORTH AMERICA

GUATEMALA

HONDURAS

Port-of-Spain

Guatemala City   Tegucigalpa

■ Capital Cities

San Salvador   NICARAGUA   **Panama Canal Zone**

EL SALVADOR   Managua

| 0 | | 500 | | 1000 miles |

San Jose   Panama

| 0 | 500 | 1000 | 1500 kilometres |

COSTA RICA   PANAMA

Michigan   Huron   Erie

L. Ontario

BARBADOS

MAP OF NORTH AMERICA

▲ *The peaceful countryside around the Mountains of Mourne shows a more tranquil side of life in Northern Ireland than we usually hear about.*

half the world's manufactured goods. This is because North America produces huge amounts of food and raw materials to feed the workers and supply factory machines.

Northern Ireland

Northern Ireland consists of six counties in the north-east corner of the island of Ireland. Northern Ireland was separated from the rest of Ireland in 1921, when the Republic of Ireland (Eire) won independence from Great Britain.

The leading industries are the manufacture of textiles and clothing, shipbuilding and agriculture.

Political problems in Northern Ireland date back to the 1600s, when many English and Scottish Protestants settled there. From the 1960s, protests by the minority Catholics (outnumbered by Protestants in Northern Ireland) against unfair treatment led to civil disorder. Bombings, shootings and other TERRORIST acts have led to great loss of life, though the British and Irish governments are trying to settle Northern Ireland's future peacefully.

NORTHERN IRELAND

ATLANTIC OCEAN
SCOTLAND
NORTHERN IRELAND
ISLE OF MAN
REPUBLIC OF IRELAND
IRISH SEA
ENGLAND
WALES

Area: 14,121 sq km – 17 per cent of the island of Ireland
Population: 1,578,000
Capital and largest city: Belfast (300,000)
Chief industries: Textiles, shipbuilding
Religions: Protestant, 68 per cent of population; 32 per cent Roman Catholic, mostly in Fermanagh and Tyrone

North Pole

The North Pole is the place farthest north on EARTH. Its LATITUDE is 90° north. The North Pole is the northern end of the Earth's axis. This is an

▶ *The tents used by this survey party on Spitsbergen, the Norwegian island in the Arctic Ocean, are specially designed to withstand the extreme cold of the polar region.*

imaginary line around which the Earth spins, like a wheel spinning around its axle.

The North Pole lies in the middle of the Arctic Ocean. Here, the surface of the sea is always frozen. The Sun does not rise in winter or set in summer for some weeks.

The first person to reach the North Pole was the American Robert E. Peary. He arrived in 1909 with sledges pulled by dogs.

The first ship to reach the North Pole was the US nuclear submarine *Nautilus*. It travelled under the ice-covered pole on August 3, 1958.

North Sea

This part of the ATLANTIC OCEAN separates Great Britain from Scandinavia and other northern parts of mainland Europe. The North Sea is quite shallow. If you lowered St Paul's Cathedral in London into the middle of the North Sea, the top would show above the waves. Winter storms often make this sea very dangerous for ships.

The North Sea is an important waterway. Some of the world's largest and busiest ports stand on its shores. Its waters are rich in fish, and the seabed holds oil and natural gas.

▼ *Despite the often stormy conditions in the North Sea, oil production goes on all year round.*

▲ *The huge oil tanker* Manhattan *was the first commercial ship to break a channel through the North-west Passage.*

North-west Passage

This was a longed-for sea route from Europe to Asia round the top of America. Explorers took nearly 400 years to find it. Ice continually hindered ships trying to sail through the ARCTIC Ocean north of Canada.

In 1576 Sir Martin Frobisher began 300 years of English exploration. But it was Roald AMUNDSEN of Norway whose ship first sailed the North-west Passage in 1906. In 1969 an oil tanker broke a path through the ice. But the ice is so thick that ships may never regularly use this sea route.

Norway

Norway is EUROPE's sixth largest country. This long, northern kingdom is wide in the south but narrow in the centre and the north. Mountains with forests, bare rocks and snow cover much of Norway. Steep inlets called FIORDS pierce its rocky coast.

Summers in Norway are cool and the winters long. It is very cold in the ARCTIC north, but the rainy west coast is kept fairly mild by the GULF STREAM.

More than four million people live in Norway. Their capital is Oslo. Norwegians catch more fish than any other Europeans, and their North Sea oil wells are among Europe's richest.

NORWAY

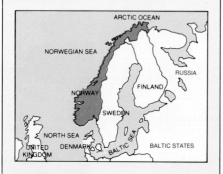

Government: Constitutional
 monarchy
Capital: Oslo
Area: 324,219 sq km
Population: 4,294,000
Language: Norwegian
Currency: Krone

Noun

A noun is a word that names. The name of everything is a noun, whether it is a person (John); a place (China); a thing (book); a quality (kindness) or anything else. The *subject* of a sentence – what a sentence is about – is always a noun or a *pronoun*. A pronoun is a word that is used in place of a noun. The most common pronouns are *I*, *we*, *you*, *he*, *she*, *it* and *they*.

Novel

Novels are long written stories. There are many kinds. For instance, some are adventure tales, like *Treasure Island* by Robert Louis STEVENSON. There are horror novels like Mary Shelley's *Frankenstein*,

▼ *An extract from* The Adventures of Tom Sawyer, *a famous novel by the American writer Mark Twain.*

Now the master began to draw a map of America on the blackboard ... But he made a sad business of it and a smothered titter rippled over the house ... The tittering continued; it even manifestly increased. And well it might. There was a garret above, pierced with a scuttle over his head; down this scuttle came a cat suspended around the haunches by a string; she had a rag tied about her head and jaws to keep her from mewing; she slowly descended. The tittering rose higher and higher, the cat was within six inches of the absorbed teacher's head; down, down a little lower, and she grabbed his wig with her desperate claws, clung to it, and was snatched up into the garret in an instant.

The Adventures of Tom Sawyer

science fiction novels, humorous novels like *Tom Sawyer* by Mark TWAIN, and satirical novels like Jonathan SWIFT's *Gulliver's Travels*, where Swift slyly pokes fun at mankind. Authors such as Sir Walter Scott wrote historical novels: novels set in the past.

Novels can be about people at any place or time. They are all meant to entertain us. But the best novels give us a new way of looking at life. Writers such as Charles DICKENS showed up the harsh lives of poor people in England in the middle 1800s.

Novels grew out of short stories written in Italy in the 1300s. One of the first famous novels was *Don Quixote*, by the Spanish writer Cervantes. Some of the first English novels with believable stories were written by Daniel Defoe.

▲ The 'mushroom cloud' formed by the huge release of destructive energy from a nuclear explosion.

▶ Bombarding an atom of uranium-235 with a neutron can start a chain reaction. As the nucleus of the atom splits, more neutrons are given out to split more atoms, and great amounts of energy are released.

Nuclear Energy

The tiny nucleus at the centre of the atom contains the most powerful force ever discovered. This force gives us nuclear energy – sometimes called atomic energy. The most complicated ELEMENT that occurs in nature is URANIUM. The nuclear fuel used in nuclear power stations is a rare form of uranium called uranium-235.

When the nucleus of a uranium-235 atom is struck by a neutron (see ATOM), it breaks apart and more neutrons shoot out. These new neutrons strike other uranium nuclei, causing them to split and give out still more neutrons. In this way, more and more nuclei split and many atoms give up their energy at once. If the action is not controlled, a tremendous explosion takes place – the atomic explosion that powers nuclear weapons.

Nuclear energy can be controlled to provide us

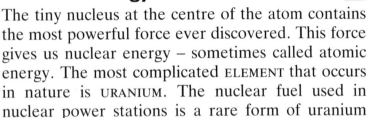

Neutron   Uranium atom

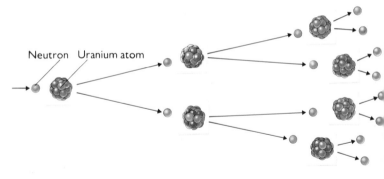

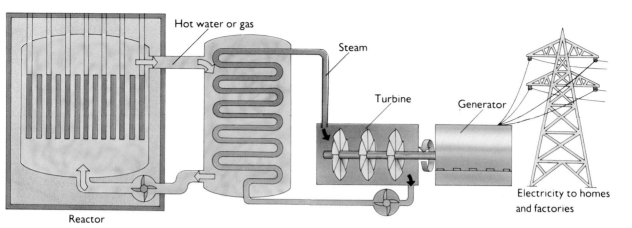

Hot water or gas | Steam | Turbine | Generator

Electricity to homes and factories

Reactor

with power. In a nuclear power station, control rods are lowered into the reactor to keep the reaction in check. But the uranium still gets very hot and so a coolant – a liquid or a gas – moves through the reactor. When the hot coolant leaves the reactor it goes to a boiler to make steam. It is this steam that powers generators to make electricity for our homes and factories.

▲ *In a nuclear power station the energy, in the form of heat, from the controlled nuclear reaction is used to make steam. The steam drives turbines which generate electricity in the same way as in any other type of power station.*

Number

In STONE AGE times people showed a number like 20 or 30 by making 20 or 30 separate marks. In certain caves you can still see the marks that they made.

In time people invented special signs or groups of signs to show different numbers. Such signs are called *numerals*. For centuries many people used Roman numerals. But these are rather clumsy. For instance, the Roman numerals for 38 are XXXVIII. Our simpler system uses Arabic numerals that were first used in India. The most important numeral in our system is the 0. If we write 207 we mean TWO hundreds, NO tens and SEVEN ones. Without the 0 we would not be able to write 207.

There are many very large numbers. The population of the world is very large. The number of blades of grass, and of leaves on the trees must be enormously large. The famous Greek scientist Archimedes estimated the number of grains of sand it would take to fill the universe. He did not know the number exactly, but he said it was *finite*. He also knew that some numbers are *infinite*. If we go on counting 1, 2, 3, 4, 5, . . . and so on, we will never come to the end. This set of numbers is infinite.

1	2	3	4	5	6	7	8	9	10	
1	2	3	4	5	6	7	8	9	10	Arabic
▼	▼▼	▼▼▼	▼▼▼▼	▼▼▼▼▼	▼▼▼▼▼▼	▼▼▼▼▼▼▼	▼▼▼▼▼▼▼▼	▼▼▼▼▼▼▼▼▼	◄	Babylonian
Α	Β	Γ	Δ	Ε	Ζ	Η	Θ	Ι	Κ	Greek
I	II	III	IV	V	VI	VII	VIII	IX	X	Roman
一	二	三	四	五	六	七	八	九	十	Chinese
•	••	•••	••••	—	•̱	••̱	•••̱	••••̱	⬭	Mayan
?	?	?	?	?	?	?	?	?	?°	Indian

◄ *The earliest known written numbers were those used by the Babylonians about 5000 years ago. All the great civilizations have had their own way of writing and using numbers.*

The word 'nursing' comes from the Latin word *nutricia*, meaning 'nourishing'. Records from ancient Egypt and Greece mention various nursing practices, including the giving of herbal remedies. The Roman armies employed male nurses to care for the wounded.

Nursing

People who are very ill, old or handicapped need nursing in their homes or in a HOSPITAL. Nursing can mean feeding, washing and giving treatment ordered by a doctor. It is hard work and requires special skills. Men and women train for several years before becoming nurses. Modern nursing owes much to the example set by Florence NIGHTINGALE.

Nut

Nuts are FRUITS with a hard, wooden shell. The seeds are called kernels. The kernels of many nuts are good to eat and rich in PROTEINS and FAT. Peanuts are crushed and made into peanut butter. Peanuts or groundnuts, walnuts and hazelnuts are all used to make cooking oil.

Nutrition

Nutrition is the process by which we take in and use food. We need food to keep our bodies running smoothly and to provide the energy for work and play. Malnutrition is a weakening of the body caused by eating too little food, or eating food that lacks enough of the nutrients that keep your body strong and healthy. Nutrients can be divided into six groups: proteins, carbohydrates, fats, vitamins, minerals and water. No one nutrient is more important than another. Each has its own work to do. A well-balanced diet contains all of them.

Hazelnut

Brazil nut

Walnut

Peanut

Sweet chestnut

Horse chestnut

▲ All these nuts can be eaten by humans, except the horse chestnut, or conker.

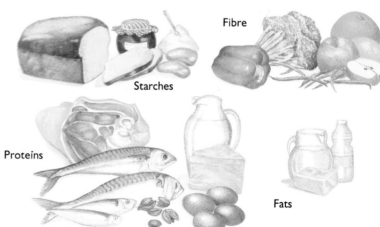

Fibre

Starches

Proteins

Fats

▶ A varied diet of fresh, natural foods is now known to be the best way to build a healthy body. When foods are processed they often lose some of their nutrients. A healthy diet should contain a good balance of starches, fibre, proteins and fats.

Oak

Oaks are trees with NUTS called acorns. Some oaks measure over 11 metres around the trunk. They grow slowly and may live for 900 years. There are about 275 kinds of oak. Most have leaves with deeply notched (wavy) edges. But evergreen oaks have tough, shiny, smooth-edged leaves.

Oak wood is hard and slow to rot. People used to build sailing ships from it. Tannin from oak bark is used in making LEATHER. CORK comes from cork oak bark.

Stalked acorns

Pendunculate oak

◄ *Most types of oak tree are deciduous; that is, they lose their leaves in autumn each year and grow new ones in spring. The fruit of an oak tree is called an acorn (above). Although squirrels eat them, humans cannot.*

Oasis

An oasis is a place where plants grow in a DESERT. It may be a small clump of palm trees, or much larger. Oases are found where there is water. This can come from rivers, wells or springs. These may be fed by rain that falls on nearby mountains and seeps through rocks beneath the surface of the desert. People can make oases by drilling wells and digging IRRIGATION ditches.

▼ *This oasis in the Sinai desert is the only source of water for miles around, and supports varied plant and animal life.*

Ocean

Oceans cover nearly three-quarters of the surface of the Earth. If you put all the world's water in 100 giant tanks, 97 of them would be full of water from the oceans. The oceans are always losing water as water vapour, drawn up into the air by the Sun's heat. But most returns as RAIN. Rain water running

OCEAN FACTS

Arctic Ocean
Surface area 14,350,000 sq km
Average depth 990 m
Greatest depth 4600 m

Indian Ocean
Surface area 73,500,000 sq km
Average depth 3890 m
Greatest depth 7450 m

Atlantic Ocean
Surface area 106,000,000 sq km
Average depth 1800 m
Greatest depth 9144 m

Pacific Ocean
Surface area 166,242,000 sq km
Average depth 4280 m
Greatest depth 11,022 m

WAVE, CURRENT AND TIDE FACTS

Highest storm wave: 34 m

Fastest waves: 500–800 km/h set off by earthquakes.

Largest ocean current: Antarctic Circumpolar Current. It carries 2200 times more water than the world's largest river pours into the sea.

Fastest ocean current: Nakwakto Rapids, off Western Canada: 30 km/h

Greatest range of tides on Earth: Bay of Fundy, Canada. A spring high tide here can be more than 16 m above a spring low tide.

▶ *Most life in the sea exists in the top levels where sunlight can penetrate. The exploration of the deepest levels, more than 10,000m down, was first carried out using special underwater vehicles called bathyscaphes.*

off the land takes salts and other MINERALS to the oceans. For instance, enough sea water to fill a square tank one kilometre long and one kilometre high would hold four million tonnes of magnesium. The oceans supply most of the magnesium we use.

There are four oceans. The largest and deepest is the PACIFIC OCEAN. The second largest is the ATLANTIC OCEAN. This is only half as large as the Pacific Ocean. The Indian Ocean is smaller but deeper than the Atlantic Ocean. The Arctic Ocean is the smallest and shallowest ocean of all.

The oceans are never still. Winds crinkle their surface into WAVES. The GULF STREAM and other currents (some warm, others cold) flow like rivers through the oceans. Every day the ocean surface

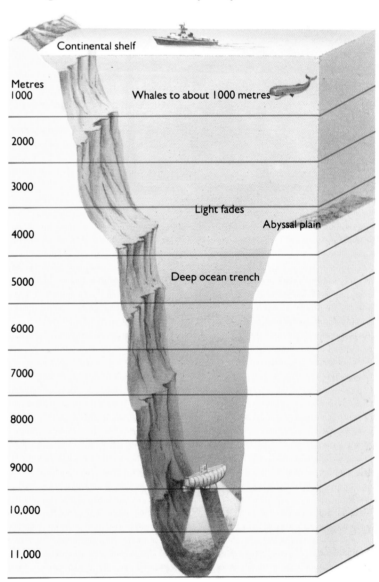

Continental shelf
Metres 1000
Whales to about 1000 metres
2000
3000
Light fades
Abyssal plain
4000
Deep ocean trench
5000
6000
7000
8000
9000
10,000
11,000

falls and rises with the TIDES. In winter, polar sea water freezes over. ICEBERGS from polar seas may drift hundreds of kilometres through the oceans.

Oceans are home to countless living things. The minerals in sea water help to nourish tiny plants drifting at the surface. The plants are food for tiny animals. These animals and plants are called PLANKTON. Fish and some whales eat the plankton. In turn, small fish are eaten by larger hunters.

Octopus

There are about 50 kinds of octopus. They are soft-bodied MOLLUSCS that live in the sea. Octopus means 'eight feet', but the eight tentacles of an octopus are usually called arms. The largest octopus has arms about 9 metres across, but most octopuses are no larger than a person's fist. Suckers on the tentacles grip crabs, shellfish or other prey. An octopus's tentacles pull its victim towards its mouth. This is hard and pointed, like the beak of a bird.

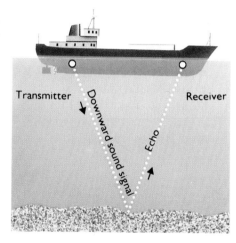

▲ *To work out the depth of the water they are sailing in, ships use sonar devices. They send sound waves to the bottom of the sea and measure the time it takes for the echo to return.*

▼ *In many countries, particularly those bordering the Mediterranean Sea, octopuses are eaten regularly.*

Each octopus hides in an underwater cave or crevice. It creeps about the seabed searching for food. Its two large eyes keep a watch for enemies. If danger threatens, the octopus may confuse its enemy by squirting an inky liquid. The ink hangs in the water like a cloud. An octopus can also dart forwards by squirting water backwards from a tube in its body.

> **The octopus is the most intelligent of the animals without backbones. It can be trained to find its way through a maze and to solve simple problems, such as removing the stopper from a sealed jar containing food.**

Most experts agree that it is likely that Homer could not read or write and that he recited his long poems to audiences. They think that the poems were written down long after Homer's death.

Odyssey

The *Odyssey* is a poem written by the ancient Greek poet HOMER. It tells the story of the Greek hero Odysseus (also called Ulysses) and his travels after the TROJAN WAR. On his way home, Odysseus battles with savages, monsters and angry gods. It takes the hero many years, but in the end he reaches his homeland and his faithful wife Penelope.

Oil

Oils are FATS and other greasy substances that do not dissolve in water. But when we say 'oil' we usually mean mineral oil. Mineral oil was formed millions of years ago from dead plants and animals. The oil was trapped under rocks. Engineers drill holes down through the surface rocks to reach the mineral oil beneath. It gushes up or can be pumped up to the surface.

Oil refineries separate the oil to make petrol, paraffin and lubricating oil. Mineral oil is also used in making artificial fertilizer, many kinds of medicine, paint, plastics and detergent. We may need to find new ways to make these things because the world's supplies of oil are running out. Scientists are working on new ways of extracting oil from shale, a kind of rock, and from tar sands.

The world's largest known oil deposits lie in the Middle East, in the countries of Saudi Arabia, Iran, Iraq and Kuwait.

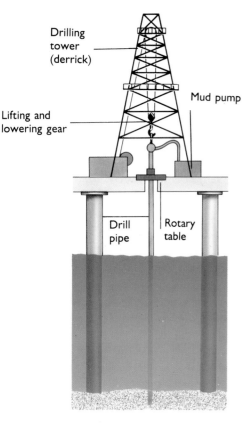

▲ The biggest part of an oil drilling platform is the derrick – the tall metal tower that houses the drilling equipment. The drill bit, at the end of the drill pipe, cuts through rock with sharp metal teeth. By examining the fragments of rock cut by the drill, scientists can tell when they are getting near an oil deposit.

▶ When petroleum oil is refined it is separated into many different chemicals. As well as producing petrol and paraffin, oil by-products can be used to make plastics, perfumes, soaps, paint and even animal feed.

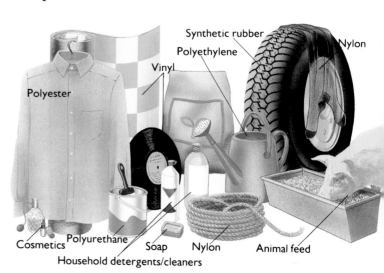

Olive

Olives grow on trees with slim, grey-green leaves and twisted trunks. Each FRUIT is shaped like a small plum. Farmers pick olives when they are green and unripe or, when the fruit is ripe, they hit the trees with sticks to knock the olives onto sheets spread on the ground. Olives taste slightly bitter and have a hard stone in the middle. People eat olives and cook food in olive oil made from crushed olives.

Most olives come from Italy, Spain and other countries by the Mediterranean Sea.

▲ *The oil we get from pressing olives is good for health. It can be used for cooking, in making medicine and soap, or as a salad dressing.*

Olympic Games

This athletics competition is the world's oldest. The first known Olympic Games took place at Olympia in Greece in 776 BC. The Greek Games ended in AD 394. The modern Olympic Games began in 1896.

They are held once every four years, each time in a different country. Athletes from different nations compete in races, jumping, gymnastics, football, yachting, and many more contests. The winners gain medals, but no prize money.

◄ *The opening ceremony of each Olympic Games features the lighting of the Olympic flame with a torch. Brought all the way from Greece, the torch is carried by athletes and sportspeople of all nationalities.*

OMAN

Government: Absolute monarchy
Capital: Muscat
Area: 212,417 sq km
Population: 1,587,000
Languages: Arabic, English, Urdu
Currency: Rial Omani

Oman

Oman is a country in south-east Arabia on the Persian Gulf. On the fertile coastal plain, dates, fruits and vegetables are grown. Oil is the main source of income. Many of Oman's people are nomads.

▲ *Papageno, the comic bird-catcher, from the 1816 Berlin production of Mozart's opera* The Magic Flute.

Onion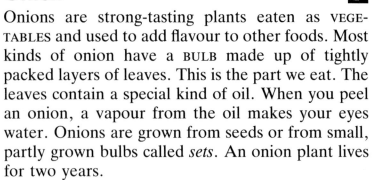

Onions are strong-tasting plants eaten as VEGE-TABLES and used to add flavour to other foods. Most kinds of onion have a BULB made up of tightly packed layers of leaves. This is the part we eat. The leaves contain a special kind of oil. When you peel an onion, a vapour from the oil makes your eyes water. Onions are grown from seeds or from small, partly grown bulbs called *sets*. An onion plant lives for two years.

Opera

An opera is a play with music. The 'actors' are singers who sing all or many of their words. An ORCHESTRA accompanies them.

The first opera was performed in Italy, nearly 400 years ago. Famous composers of serious opera include MOZART, Verdi, Puccini and WAGNER.

Light, short operas are called operettas. Operettas of the 1800s gave rise to the tuneful musical comedies of the 1900s.

Opinion Poll

Political parties and manufacturers want to know what people think of their party's policy or the goods they make. They employ a research firm to

---

SEE IT YOURSELF

You can take your own opinion poll. Decide on the question you want to ask, then pick your sample group. It can be everyone in your class, or, better still, everyone in your form. You do not have to record people's names, just their answers or whether they are undecided, and whether they are a boy or girl.

QUESTION: Do you prefer vanilla or chocolate ice cream?

TOTAL SAMPLE		ALL BOYS		ALL GIRLS	
Vanilla	40	Vanilla	18	Vanilla	22
Chocolate	50	Chocolate	28	Chocolate	22
Undecided	10	Undecided	4	Undecided	6
Total polled	100	Total polled	50	Total polled	50

FINDINGS: According to this poll, 50 per cent of the sample pupils prefer chocolate ice cream and 40 per cent prefer vanilla. However, 56 per cent of boys prefer chocolate and only 36 per cent vanilla. The girls are equally divided between the two. What do you think would happen if the whole school were polled and divided into two age groups – those below 12 and those above?

conduct an opinion poll – to ask questions and analyze the answers. It would be impossible to ask questions of everyone, everywhere, so a carefully selected group of people, called a *sample*, is chosen to represent a larger group. The sample may be only 1 per cent of the larger group, but it must contain the same sort of people. For example, if 20 per cent of the larger group are under 18 years of age, 20 per cent of the sample group must also be under 18.

The questions may be asked by a trained interviewer or they may be printed on a *questionnaire*. The answers are then analyzed and the results show the opinions of the larger group.

Some people say that opinion polls can be unfair. In election polls, for example, many people want to be on the winning side and therefore switch their votes to the candidate whom the polls show to be ahead. Careful studies have, however, failed to show that this 'bandwagon effect' exists.

Opossum

Opossums are MARSUPIALS found in North and South America. Some look like rats, others look like mice. The Virginia opossum is as big as a cat. This is North America's only marsupial. It climbs trees and can cling on with its tail. A female has up to 18 babies, each no larger than a honeybee at birth. If danger threatens, the Virginia opossum pretends to be dead. If someone pretends to be hurt, we say he or she is 'playing possum'.

▲ Like all marsupials, the American opossum gives birth to its babies when they are still in a very immature state. After about three months, they are able to ride around on their mother's back.

Orang-utan

This big, red-haired APE comes from the islands of Borneo and Sumatra in south-east Asia. Its name comes from Malay words meaning 'man of the woods'. A male is as heavy as a man, but not so tall. Orang-utans use their long arms to swing through the branches of trees as they hunt for fruit and leaves to eat. Each night they make a nest high up in the trees. A leafy roof helps to keep out rain.

Man is the orang-utan's main enemy. Hunters sometimes catch the babies and sell them to zoos. Orang-utans are already scarce. They could become extinct.

▶ Orang-utans live alone or in small family groups. Like many animals threatened with extinction, the orang-utans' habitat has been changed by the action of humans.

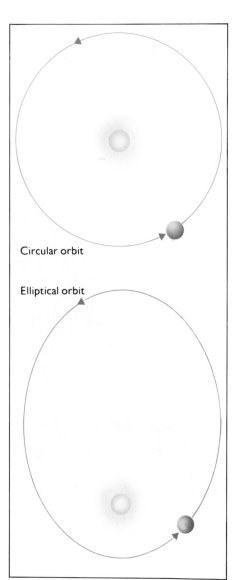

Circular orbit

Elliptical orbit

▲ *People used to think that planets moved in circular orbits (top), but actually the shape is more like a flattened circle, or ellipse (bottom).*

Orbit

An orbit is the curved path of something that spins around another object in space. Artificial SATELLITES and the MOON travel around the Earth in orbits. Each planet, including the Earth, has its own orbit around the SUN. Every orbit is a loop rather than a circle. An orbiting object tries to move in a straight line but is pulled by GRAVITY towards the object that it orbits.

Orchestra

An orchestra is a large group of musicians who play together. The word *orchestra* once meant 'dancing place'. In ancient Greek theatres, dancers and musicians performed on a space between the audience and the stage. When Italy invented OPERA, Italian theatres arranged their musicians in the same way. Soon, people used the word orchestra to describe the group of musicians, and not the place where they performed.

The modern orchestra owes much to the composer HAYDN. He arranged its MUSICAL INSTRUMENTS into four main groups: strings, woodwind, brass and percussion. Most orchestras have a conductor.

▶ *Soloists rehearse with an orchestra. The conductor has the job of coordinating all the musicians in the orchestra, which may number over a hundred.*

Orchid

There are more than 15,000 kinds of these lovely flowering plants. Most live in warm, rainy forests. Many grow on trees. Their roots draw nourishment from the damp air. Usually each kind of orchid is fertilized by one kind of insect. But some can be pollinated by snails or hummingbirds. A rare orchid can cost as much as a new car.

Organ

Pipe organs are musical instruments with many pipes of different lengths and widths. The largest organ has more than 30,000 pipes. Each pipe makes a special sound as air flows through it. An organist plays an organ by pressing keys arranged in rows called *manuals*. Each manual controls a different set of pipes. Levers or knobs called *stops* allow the organist to combine different groups of pipes. Electronic organs sound similar, but have no pipes.

▲ The common spotted orchid grows in damp or dry grassy places and in open woods. Its habitats are being threatened by modern farming methods.

◄ This organ, made nearly 200 years ago, had its pipes built into it and was elaborately decorated.

▼ The ostrich is one of the record-breaking birds for the number of eggs it lays – up to 15 at one time.

Ostrich

This is the largest living BIRD. An ostrich may weigh twice as much as a man and stand more than 2 metres high. Ostriches cannot fly. If an enemy attacks, an ostrich runs away. It can kick hard enough to rip a lion open. Frightened ostriches

▲ *The Parliament buildings, Ottawa. Although Ottawa is the capital of Canada, the capital of its province, Ontario, is Toronto.*

never hide their heads in sand, as people used to think.

Ostriches live in Africa. They roam in herds, led by a male. The females lay large, white eggs in a nest dug in the sand. Ostriches can live for 50 years or more.

Ottawa

Ottawa is the capital of CANADA, and its third largest city. With its suburbs, Ottawa holds about 900,000 people. Ottawa stands in the province of Ontario in south-east Canada. The Ottawa and Rideau rivers flow through the city.

Ottawa's best-known buildings are the Parliament buildings, which stand on a hill above the Ottawa River. They include the tall Peace Tower which contains 53 bells. Ottawa also has universities and museums.

British settlers began building Ottawa in 1826. They named it after the nearby Outawouais Indians. More than one citizen in three is French-speaking.

Otter

Otters are large relatives of the weasel. They have long, slender bodies and short legs. An otter is a bit heavier than a dachshund dog. It hunts in water for fish and frogs. Thick fur keeps its body dry. It can swim swiftly by waggling its tail and body like an eel, and using its webbed hind feet as paddles.

Otters are wanderers. By night they hunt up and down a river, or roam overland to find new fishing grounds. They love to play by sliding down a bank of snow or mud.

▼ *The number of otters in the wild is going down steadily, and they are now quite a rare sight. This could be due to pollution, but no one is sure.*

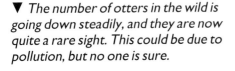

◀ *Barn owls are far less common now than they once were. This may be because there are fewer deserted buildings and hollow trees in the countryside for them to use as nesting places.*

Owl

These birds of prey hunt mainly by night. They have soft feathers that make no sound as they fly. Their large, staring eyes help them to see in the dimmest light. Owls also have keen ears. Some owls can catch mice in pitch darkness by listening to the sounds they make. An owl can turn its head right round to look backwards.

When an owl eats a mouse or bird, it swallows it complete with bones and fur or feathers. Later, the owl spits out the remains in a pellet. You can sometimes find owl pellets on the ground.

There are over 500 kinds of owl. Some of the largest and smallest owls live in North America. The great grey owl of the north is as long as a man's arm. The elf owl of the south is smaller than a sparrow.

▲ *The long-eared owl's tufted 'ears' are not ears at all, just feathers. But they help in the recognition of this bird, which is found in most of Europe, northern Asia and North America.*

▼ *Oxen are still used to pull heavy loads in many parts of the world.*

Ox

Oxen are a group of big, heavy animals that include domestic (farm) cattle, BISON, wild and tame BUFFALO, and the YAK. Oxen have split hooves and a pair of curved horns. They eat grass. The heaviest domestic cattle can weigh two tonnes.

For thousands of years, the ox has been a beast of burden, pulling carts or ploughs. People probably began domesticating cattle 9000 years ago in Greece.

SEE IT YOURSELF

Nothing can burn without oxygen. To find out roughly how much oxygen there is in the air, stand a candle in a bowl of water. Light the candle and cover it with a glass jar. Rest the jar on plasticine so that water can get under the rim. Mark the level of water in the jar. As the candle burns, oxygen is used up and water rises to take its place. Soon the candle goes out – all the oxygen has gone. You will find that the water has risen about one-fifth of the way up the jar. A fifth of the air is oxygen.

▲ An oyster makes a pearl when there is a foreign object, such as a grain of sand, inside its shell. To stop the irritation caused by the sand, the oyster deposits a substance called nacre around it, which gradually builds up to form a pearl.

Oxygen

Oxygen is a GAS. It is one of the most abundant ELEMENTS on Earth. It makes up one part in every five parts of AIR. Oxygen is found in water and many different rocks. Most of the weight of water, and half that of rocks, comes from the oxygen in them.

FIRE needs oxygen to burn. Almost all living things need oxygen for BREATHING and to give them the energy just to stay alive. Animals need extra oxygen to move about. PLANTS give out oxygen into the air.

Oyster

Oysters are MOLLUSCS with a soft body protected by a broad, hinged shell. This is rough on the outside. The inside of a pearl oyster's shell is smooth, shiny mother-of-pearl. Pearl oysters make pearls.

Several kinds of oyster are eaten as a food. People farm oysters in shallow coastal water. Oysters cling to empty shells, rocks or wooden posts on the seabed. When they have grown large enough they are harvested.

Ozone Layer

The ozone layer is a layer of gases that surrounds the Earth and shields it from harmful radiation from the Sun. The layer is found in the region between 10 and 50 km above the Earth's surface. Ozone is a form of the gas oxygen, and although the ozone layer contains only a very small quantity of ozone, it shields us from most of the Sun's dangerous ultra-violet rays. Without the protection of the ozone layer, animals and plants probably could not live on Earth.

Recently, scientists have been worried about a thinning of the ozone layer, especially over polar regions. They believe this may have been caused by the use of substances called *chlorofluorocarbons*, or CFCs, in aerosol dispensers, refrigerators and to make the bubbles in foam plastic. Most countries are now trying to stop the manufacture and use of these substances.

Pacific Ocean

This is the largest and deepest of all the OCEANS. Its waters cover more than one-third of the world. All the CONTINENTS would fit inside the Pacific Ocean with room to spare. Its deepest part is deep enough to drown the world's highest mountain.

The Pacific Ocean lies west of the Americas, and east of Australia and Asia. It stretches from the frozen Arctic to the frozen Antarctic. There are thousands of tiny islands in the Pacific. Most were formed when VOLCANOES grew up from the seabed. Sometimes earthquakes shake the seabed and send out huge tidal waves.

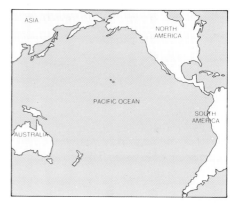

Pain

Pain is an unpleasant feeling. It is a warning that something is wrong somewhere in your body. You feel pain if something burns or presses hard on the ends of certain NERVES. Those parts of the body with the most nerve endings, such as your hands, feel pain most easily. The nerves carry the pain signals to the central nervous system.

Sometimes pain is useful. It teaches you to avoid what caused it. If you prick yourself with a pin you learn not to do it again. Toothaches tell you it is time to go to the dentist. Chemists have invented anaesthetic drugs, and other painkillers, to deaden pain caused by disease and injury.

▼ When this girl touches the hot iron, special nerves in her finger send a warning signal to her central nervous system. A message is sent back to the nerves that control the muscles of her arm, making her jerk her hand away.

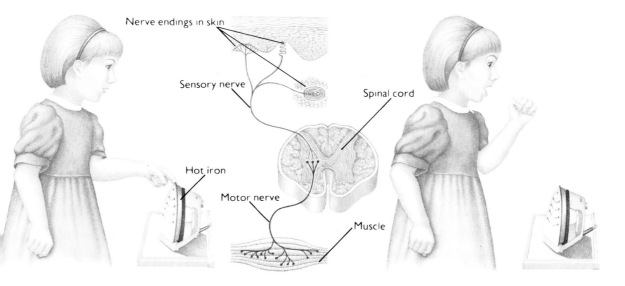

Nerve endings in skin

Sensory nerve

Spinal cord

Hot iron

Motor nerve

Muscle

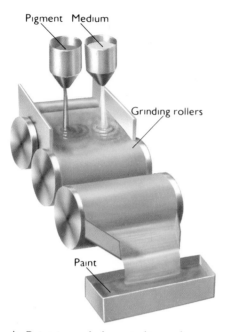

▲ *Paint is made by grinding colours called pigments, and a liquid medium (such as oil), between huge rollers.*

SEE IT YOURSELF

There are lots of fun ways to paint. Try this one: Put a spoonful of watery paint on a piece of white paper. Place one end of a drinking straw near the paint and blow gently through the other to spread out the paint. Using a clean spoon for each colour, put some other colours onto the paper and blow them around too.

▶ *The cleaning and restoration of dirty or damaged old paintings is a delicate and highly skilled craft.*

Paint

Paint is coloured powder mixed with a liquid. When it is spread over a solid surface it forms a thin coat. This decorates the surface and protects it from rotting. OIL-based paints are coloured powder in oil or resin. Emulsion paints are powder and drops of oil or resin in water.

Painting

Painting is a form of ART in which people use coloured PAINT to make pictures on canvas, plaster, wood or paper. Today most people paint for their own pleasure. But this was not always so.

STONE AGE hunters probably used painting as magic. They drew wounded wild beasts on their cave walls. They probably thought that such pictures would help them to kill real animals on their next hunt.

In the MIDDLE AGES most artists worked for the Church. Their paintings showed scenes from Bible stories. Such paintings helped people who could not read to understand the Bible.

By the 1400s Europe's rich princes and merchants were paying artists to paint pictures to decorate their homes. The pictures might be family portraits, still-life scenes of flowers and fruit, or landscapes showing their cities and country estates.

In the 1800s many artists began trying out new ideas. For example, some tried to give a feeling of the light and shade in a landscape. Others used bright, flat colours to bring out the patterns in still-lifes and landscapes. In the 1900s Pablo Picasso and other artists began to experiment with abstract paintings. These concentrate on the basic shapes, colours and patterns of the things painted.

Pakistan

Pakistan lies between India and Iran. There are more than 110 million Pakistanis. Most of them follow the religion of Islam.

Much of Pakistan is hot and dry, but crops such as wheat and cotton grow with the help of water from the Indus River. The Indus flows from the Hima-

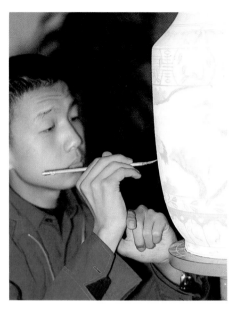

▲ *Once this boy has finished painting the design on the vase, it will be glazed and fired in a kiln to complete the finish.*

◀ *Street traders, selling all kinds of food, are a common sight in the city of Karachi in Pakistan.*

LAYAS to the Arabian Sea. Until 1947 Pakistan was part of British-ruled India. It then broke away to become an independent Muslim republic. In 1971 East Pakistan broke away and became Bangla-desh. In 1988 Benazir Bhutto was elected prime minister but she was defeated in the 1990 elections, only to be re-elected in 1993.

Palestine

Palestine is a land on the eastern shore of the Mediterranean Sea. Most of the stories in the Bible took place there. Palestine gets its name from the Philistines who once lived in part of it.

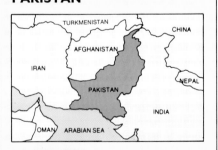

PAKISTAN

Government: Parliamentary democracy
Capital: Islamabad
Area: 796,095 sq km
Population: 122,666,000
Languages: Urdu and English
Currency: Rupee

> Historic Palestine covers an area of only 27,000 sq km, little more than a third the size of Scotland. People lived in Palestine at least 200,000 years ago, during the Old Stone Age.

By 1800 BC the HEBREWS had made Palestine their home. Later they ruled it as two nations, called Israel and Judah.

Today, most of what used to be called Palestine lies in the nation of ISRAEL. The rest is part of Jordan, Lebanon and Syria. There have been frequent clashes between Palestinians and Israelis, but in 1994 they signed a peace agreement.

Female coconut flower

Coconut

Dates

▲ The coconut palm can grow as high as 30 m. Its fruit contains a hollow space filled with coconut 'milk'. The white meat, or kernel, within the coconut is not only good to eat, but can be used in making soap, wax and oil. Dates are the fruits of the date palm. In the Middle East they are eaten raw, or split and filled with butter.

Palm

The most familiar palm tree has leaves that sprout straight out of the top of its trunk, rather like the fingers of an outspread hand. But there are more than 1000 kinds of palm and not all are trees. Some are shrubs and others are vines. Most palms grow in warm climates.

Palms are useful plants. People make mats and baskets from their leaves. We eat the fruits of some palms, such as coconuts.

Panama

Panama is a country about the size of Scotland. It occupies the narrow neck of land that joins Central and South America. Panama has a damp, tropical climate. Rice, sugar, bananas and pineapples are grown.

The Panama CANAL cuts the country in half. Much of Panama's wealth comes from the canal and it has made Panama City an international finance centre. Many ships are registered in Panama.

The world's shipping uses the Panama Canal as a short cut between the Atlantic and Pacific oceans.

◄ *Many huge cargo ships pass through the Panama Canal every day.*

PANAMA

Government: Democracy
Capital: Panama City
Area: 77,529 sq km
Population: 2,418,000
Languages: Spanish and English
Currency: Balboa

Sets of locks on the canal raise and lower ships as they cross the hilly countryside. In 1903, Panama granted the occupation and control of the canal to the United States. A new treaty in 1978 provided for the gradual takeover by Panama of the canal. The takeover will be completed in 1999.

Panda

There are two kinds of panda. Both live in the forests of east Asia. The giant panda looks like a black and white bear. It lives in bamboo forests in China. The red panda is not much larger than a cat. It has a bushy tail and reddish fur. Both kinds eat plants. Their nearest relatives are the raccoons of North and South America.

Paper

Paper gets its name from papyrus, a plant that grows in swamps in Egypt. The ancient Egyptians made a kind of paper from papyrus. But the Chinese

▼ *The steps in making paper from softwood pulp.*

The bark is removed from the logs at the paper mill

The logs are cut into small chips

The chips are 'cooked' with chemicals and the pulp produced is washed, bleached and beaten into finer fibres. It is mixed with resins and dyes depending on the type of paper required.

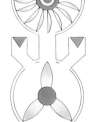

It is dried in steam-heated cylinders and polished in calender rollers

The pulp is passed through a series of rollers

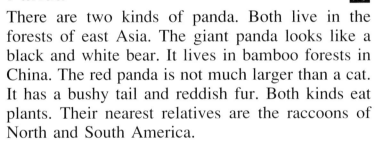

Reels of paper · Calender rollers · Steam heated cylinders · Felt rollers · Finished pulp

PAPUA NEW GUINEA

Government: Parliamentary
  democracy
Capital: Port Moresby
Area: 461,691 sq km
Population: 4,006,000
Language: English
Currency: Kina

invented paper as we know it. About 1900 years ago they learned to separate the fibres from mulberry bark. They soaked these, then dried them, making a flat, dry sheet that they could write on. Paper is still made of plant fibres. Some of the best paper is made from COTTON. Newspaper is made from wood.

Papua New Guinea

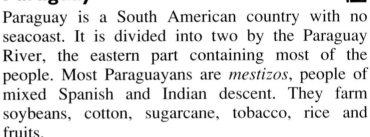

Papua New Guinea is a country that occupies the eastern half of the island of New Guinea, north of Australia. The western half of the island is Indonesian and is called Irian Jaya. Papua New Guinea is a hot, wet country. It gained its independence from Australia in 1975, and is a member of the Commonwealth. The chief crops are coffee, coconuts and cocoa.

Paraguay

Paraguay is a South American country with no seacoast. It is divided into two by the Paraguay River, the eastern part containing most of the people. Most Paraguayans are *mestizos*, people of mixed Spanish and Indian descent. They farm soybeans, cotton, sugarcane, tobacco, rice and fruits.

General Alfredo Stroessner became president in 1954 and ruled into the 1980s. In 1993, Paraguay's first civilian head of state was elected.

PARAGUAY

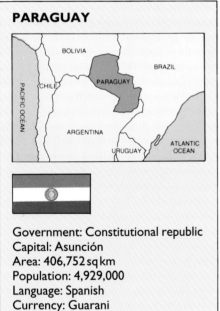

Government: Constitutional republic
Capital: Asunción
Area: 406,752 sq km
Population: 4,929,000
Language: Spanish
Currency: Guarani

▶ *Many of the people living in Paraguay are farmers, producing barely enough to feed themselves.*

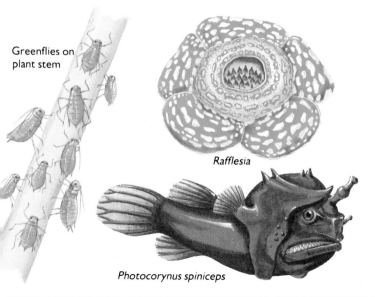

Greenflies on plant stem

Rafflesia

Photocorynus spiniceps

◀ *Greenflies suck the sap of plants such as roses, and can spread diseases among plants. Rafflesia is a parasitic plant that produces the largest flower in the world – up to a metre across. The tiny male deep-sea fish, Photocorynus spiniceps, lives by attaching itself to the much larger female and sucking her blood.*

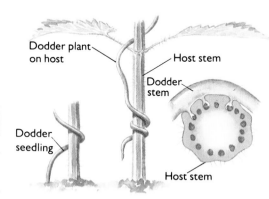

Dodder plant on host

Host stem

Dodder stem

Dodder seedling

Host stem

▲ *Dodder is a thread-like parasitic plant that twines around the host plant and 'sucks' nourishment from it. It is very difficult to get rid of once it is established.*

Parasite

Parasites are living things that live and feed on others larger than themselves.

Animal parasites include FLEAS, lice, ticks and mites. Different kinds live on different birds and mammals. Most suck blood, and some spread germs that cause disease. Certain kinds of WORM get inside the body and live in the intestine or burrow into muscles.

Greenfly and some other creatures live as parasites on plants. Plant parasites include many kinds of FUNGUS that cause disease in plants or animals. Mistletoe is a parasite. It feeds off the trees on which it grows.

▼ *Traffic skirts the Arc de Triomphe in Paris. built by Napoleon I, it is one of the city's most famous landmarks.*

Paris

Paris is the capital of FRANCE, and France's largest city. More than 2,000,000 people live there. The River Seine divides the city into the Left Bank and the Right Bank.

If you gaze down on Paris from the Eiffel Tower you will see many parks and gardens, fine squares and tree-lined avenues. Other famous landmarks are the cathedral of Notre Dame, the basilica of the Sacré Coeur, the Arc de Triomphe and the Louvre Palace, now a famous museum.

Paris is famous for its fashions, jewellery and perfume. Another important industry is car manufacturing.

▲ *Black Rod is an usher of the Lord Chamberlain's department. Each year when Parliament opens, he comes to the House of Commons as the Queen's representative and has to knock on the door to be let in. This is part of the ceremony that surrounds much of the activity in the Palace of Westminster.*

▶ *A Cuban parrot. Parrots climb more than they fly, using their strong, hooked beaks to pull themselves from branch to branch.*

The building of the Parthenon began in 447 BC. It was completed in 438 BC, when the great gold and ivory statue of Athena was dedicated. Work on the carvings and decoration of the temple went on until 432 BC.

Parliament

A parliament is a meeting of people held to make a nation's LAWS. One of the first parliaments was Iceland's *Althing*, which was founded more than a thousand years ago.

In Great Britain, the Houses of PARLIAMENT stand by the River Thames in London. Members of Parliament elected by the people sit in the House of Commons. Peers (nobles) and churchmen (who are not elected) sit in the House of Lords. The British Parliament was started in 1265. It grew gradually out of a meeting of nobles who advised the king. In the 1300s it was divided into the two Houses, and by the 1700s Parliament had become more powerful than the king.

Parrot

These tropical birds have brightly coloured feathers. They use their strong, curved beaks as 'hands' to help them climb about. Their beaks can also crack open nuts and bite off chunks of fruit.

There are hundreds of kinds of parrot. Cocka-toos, macaws and lovebirds all belong to the parrot family. Budgerigars can learn to 'talk', by imitating the sounds of speech and one African grey parrot could speak over 900 words.

Parthenon

The Parthenon is perhaps the world's most famous building. The ruins of this great white marble temple stand on the ACROPOLIS, a hill that overlooks the Greek capital of ATHENS.

The Athenians built the Parthenon around 440 BC in honour of Athena Parthenos, their patron goddess. Rows of columns like huge tree trunks held up its sloping roof. Everything was gracefully designed. Inside stood a huge statue of Athena.

The Parthenon has been damaged by an explosion and the effects of air POLLUTION, but its ruins still dominate Athens.

▲ The decoration on the Parthenon was as grand as the building itself. This frieze, showing a boy fastening his master's belt, was one of a number removed from Greece by Lord Elgin between 1803 and 1812.

◀ The Passover feast, or Seder, is a ritual that goes back many centuries. It is conducted by the head of the family on the first two nights of the eight days of Passover.

Passover

This Jewish festival celebrates the Israelites' escape from slavery in Egypt. The BIBLE tells how God punished the Egyptians ten times before they freed the Israelites. The tenth time an angel killed the eldest child in each Egyptian family, but *passed over* the Israelites' homes without harming them.

Pasteur, Louis

Louis Pasteur (1822–1895) was a great French scientist. He proved that BACTERIA and other germs cause diseases. Pasteur injected weakened germs into animals and people to stop them catching the diseases those germs usually caused. He invented *pasteurization*, a way of heating milk and cooling it quickly to stop it going bad. Pasteur also found out how tiny yeast cells turn sugar into alcohol.

▲ Pasteur developed vaccines against cholera, rabies, anthrax and other diseases.

In Rome and later in medieval Europe, peafowl were raised for the table. The emperor Charlemagne is said to have served thousands of the birds at a single state banquet.

▶ Only the male peafowl has the spectacular tail with its 'eyes'. The female is a duller bird with a short tail.

Peacock

Peacocks are male peafowl. Peafowl are big birds that live in Asia. Peacocks attract their mates by spreading out the long, blue-green feathers that grow just above the tail. Big spots on the feathers look like rows of eyes. As the peacock struts before the female it looks extremely proud, hence the term 'proud as a peacock'.

▼ In a pendulum clock, the movement of the pendulum is transmitted to the hands of the clock through the escapement, made up of an escape wheel and anchor, which also keeps the pendulum swinging.

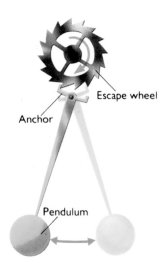

Escape wheel

Anchor

Pendulum

Pendulum

This is a hanging weight that is free to swing to and fro. When the weight is pulled to one side and then released, GRAVITY sets it swinging to and fro in a curved path called an *arc*. Each swing takes the same amount of time, no matter whether the swing is big or small. This makes pendulums useful for keeping time in CLOCKS. After a while a pendulum stops. But a pendulum clock keeps its pendulum swinging with a device called an escapement. This makes the 'tick-tock' sound.

Penguin

Penguins are swimming birds. They cannot fly, because their wings are shaped as flippers. Penguins use their wings to 'row' themselves through the sea. They swim and dive well. A penguin in the water can leap up nearly 2 metres to land on a rock or ice.

All penguins come from the southern part of the world. Emperor penguins live in the ANTARCTIC. In winter each female lays one egg on the ice. Her mate rolls the egg onto his feet and warms it for two months until it hatches.

▼ Four of the 18 different types of penguin.

Chinstrap penguin   Gentoo   Macaroni penguin

Emperor penguin

People of the World

All the people on Earth belong to the human race. But 'race' also means any group of people who look alike in certain ways. Nobody knows for sure when and how the different races came into being, but the three main ones in the world are the Mongoloid, the Caucasian and the Negroid.

The Mongoloid race is known for its straight dark hair, yellow-brown skin and almond-shaped eyes. The Caucasian race has hair colour ranging from blond and red to black, is fair- or dark-skinned and round-eyed. The Negroid race has dark, tightly curling hair and dark skin colour. In addition to these three main races, there are also a number of minor ones.

Thousands of years of migration, conquest and marriage between races have mixed all the races into a great variety of groups. For this reason it is not very sensible to speak of pure racial types.

▼ The main differences between the three major racial types are in the facial features, hair type and skin and hair colouring.

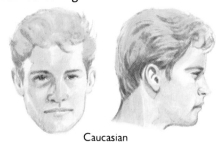

Caucasian

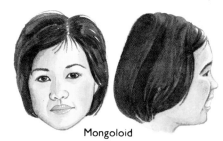

Mongoloid

Negroid

Pepys, Samuel

Samuel Pepys (1633–1703) was an English government official who wrote a famous diary. This gives us a lively idea of what life was like in London in the reign of CHARLES II. Pepys wrote about the fire that

▲ Samuel Pepys started his famous diary on January 1, 1660 and ended it on May 31, 1669, because he thought his eyesight was becoming weak.

burned down much of London in 1666. He set down gossip about the king, described family quarrels, and told of visits to the theatre.

Pepys became Secretary of the Admiralty. He doubled the size of England's navy, and helped make it very strong.

Perfume

Certain substances that produce a pleasant smell are called perfumes. People use perfumes on their bodies. Factories add perfumes to SOAP, DETERGENT and other products. Natural perfumes are oils squeezed from flowers, leaves or stems and mixed with special animal substances like musk. Factories make synthetic perfumes from substances including coal tar.

Peru

Peru is the third largest nation in SOUTH AMERICA. You could fit France, Great Britain, Spain, West Germany and Yugoslavia inside Peru with room to spare.

Peru touches five other countries. Western Peru is washed by the Pacific Ocean. The sharp, snowy peaks of the high Andes Mountains cross Peru from north to south like a giant backbone. Between the mountains and the ocean lies a thin strip of desert.

Rosemary | Rose | Bergamot | Lemon verbena | Mint | Delphinium

SEE IT YOURSELF

You can make a pot pourri to perfume your room. Rose petals, the most important ingredient, should, if possible, be taken from fully open roses the day before they would have dropped. Other good pot pourri flowers and herbs are rosemary, bergamot, delphinium, mint and lemon verbena. You can dry the plants by spreading them out in an airing cupboard before mixing them together in a bowl.

▶ Lake Titicaca is the highest navigated lake in the world. Situated between Peru and Bolivia, it is 3810m above sea level.

East of the mountains hot, steamy forests stretch around the AMAZON RIVER.

Peruvians grow sugarcane and coffee. The sheep and LLAMAS in the mountains produce wool. Peru mines copper, iron and silver. Its ocean fishing grounds usually hold plenty of fish.

People have been building towns in Peru for several thousand years. The most famous people were the INCAS who ran a mountain empire. In the 1530s the Spaniards seized Peru. Since the 1820s Peru has been an independent nation.

PERU

Government: Multi-party republic
Capital: Lima
Area: 1,285,216 sq km
Population: 22,767,000
Language: Spanish
Currency: Nuevo Sol

Pharaoh

We use the word *pharaoh* to mean 'king' when we talk of the kings of ancient EGYPT. (The ancient Egyptians gave their kings other titles as well.) 'Pharaoh' comes from *peraa*, which means 'great house'. This was the royal palace where the pharaoh lived.

Egyptians believed that each pharaoh was the same god in the shape of a different man. He lived in certain ways said to have been fixed by the gods. The pharaoh was said to look after all the needs of his people. He was supposed to rule everything and everyone in Egypt. He owned all the land. All of Egypt's nobles, priests and soldiers were supposed to obey him. But in fact the priests and nobles largely ran the country.

▼ *The funeral procession of a pharaoh. Four yoked oxen pull the sledge of the funeral boat, in which rests the coffin containing the mummy, the embalmed and wrapped body of the pharaoh.*

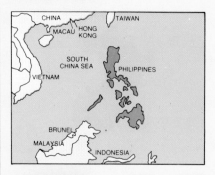

PHILIPPINES

Government: Republic
Capital: Manila
Area: 300,000 sq km
Population: 67,114,000
Languages: Filipino and English
Currency: Peso

Philippines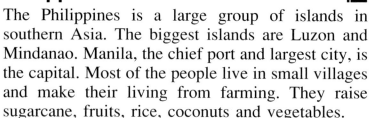

The Philippines is a large group of islands in southern Asia. The biggest islands are Luzon and Mindanao. Manila, the chief port and largest city, is the capital. Most of the people live in small villages and make their living from farming. They raise sugarcane, fruits, rice, coconuts and vegetables.

Spanish explorers named the islands after King Philip II of Spain. In 1898, after the Spanish-American War, the islands were turned over to the United States. They became independent in 1946, but the Philippines still has close links with the United States.

Ferdinand Marcos, who was elected president in 1965, restricted the activities of his opponents. In 1986 he was forced to flee the country. The government that followed faced economic problems and widespread poverty.

Philosophers will often ponder over the oddest questions. It is said that two famous 13th century philosophers, St Thomas Aquinas and Albert the Great, used to argue for hours about how many angels could sit on the point of a pin.

▼ From left, Socrates, Pythagoras, Plato and Aristotle laid down some of the first theories of life. Their work is still discussed and studied today.

Philosophy

The word *philosophy* comes from Greek words meaning 'love of wisdom'. Philosophers are thinkers who ask deep questions like these: How much can we really know about anything? If we argue that something is what we say it is, how can we be sure that our ideas are really right? When we say that God exists, what do we mean by 'God' and what do we mean by 'exists'? What is goodness? What is just? What is beauty?

The first great philosophers were Greeks, including Socrates, PLATO and ARISTOTLE.

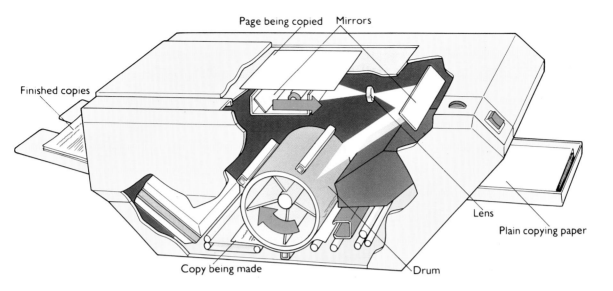

Page being copied   Mirrors

Finished copies

Lens

Plain copying paper

Copy being made

Drum

Photocopying

A photocopier is a machine that can copy a page of a book or a letter in a few seconds. When you press the button on a photocopier, a bright light comes on to light up the page. A lens inside the machine shines an image of the page onto a smooth metal drum. The drum is electrified all over. When the image shines on it, the light in the bright parts of the image destroys the electric charge. The dark parts of the drum are still electrified.

A black powder is dusted over the drum. This clings only to the parts of the drum's surface that are electrified. When a sheet of paper is pressed against the drum, the powder comes off onto the paper and there is a copy of the page. This process is called *xerography*.

▲ *Modern copiers can make an unlimited number of duplicates from an original, each as good as the first.*

Photography

The word *photography* comes from Greek words that mean 'drawing with light'. When you take a photograph, rays of LIGHT produce a picture on the film in your CAMERA.

What happens is this. First you look through a viewfinder at the subject you want to photograph. Then you press a button or lever that opens a shutter to let light from the subject enter the camera. The light passes a LENS that produces an image of your subject on a film in the camera. But

▲ *The first photographs were very different from today's snapshots. They were made by exposing large metal plates covered in tar-like chemicals to light. Exposures for photos such as the one above could take minutes, during which time the subjects had to hold very still.*

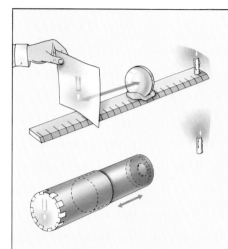

SEE IT YOURSELF

You can make a toy camera. Take the lens out of a magnifying glass. Fix the lens upright with plasticine on a ruler. Put a lighted candle in front of the lens. Hold a piece of white paper on the ruler behind the lens and move it backwards and forwards until you see a sharp image of the candle. Read off the distance between the lens and the paper. This is the focal length of that lens. Now take two cardboard tubes, one of which fits inside the other. Cover one end with tissue paper fixed with sticky tape. Cover the other end with card and make a hole about a centimetre across. Fix the lens here with plasticine or sticky tape. Focus the camera by sliding the tubes in or out until you get a clear image on the tissue paper. The image will be upside down.

the image shows up only when the film is developed (treated with chemicals). A developed film is called a *negative*. This shows black objects white, and white objects black. From negatives you can print *positives*, the final photos, either as paper prints or slides.

Physics

Physics is one of the sciences. Physicists are interested in *matter* – in solids, liquids and gases, and in the tiny atoms of which all matter is made up. They are interested in the different forms of *energy* – electric energy, light energy, sound energy, mechanical energy, chemical energy and nuclear energy. Some of the major fields of study in physics include mechanics (forces and motion; solids, liquids and gases); optics (light); acoustics (sound); electricity and magnetism; atomic, molecular and nuclear physics; and cryogenics (the study of extremely low temperatures and their effects, including superconductivity).

Physicists try to find things out by doing careful experiments. They record the results of their experiments so that other people can try the same experiments if they want to. Physics is a very big subject and no one physicist today understands all the different parts of the subject. For example, nuclear physicists who study the tiny atom and its

▶ *A hair-raising experience: the steel ball is a Van de Graaff generator that makes static electricity. When the girl puts her hand on it her hair springs to attention! The generator is on display at the Science Centre, Toronto, Canada.*

parts may know little about outer space and the movements of planets, stars and galaxies as studied by astrophysicists. But one subject they must all understand is mathematics.

Two of the greatest physicists who ever lived were Sir Isaac NEWTON and Albert EINSTEIN.

Piano

Piano is short for the Italian word *pianoforte*, meaning *soft* and *loud*. The piano was invented by Bartolomeo Cristofori in 1709. The name refers to its great range compared with the harpsichord that came before it. The piano has 88 keys. When a key is struck, a system of levers makes a felt-tipped hammer strike a stretched wire. At the same time a *damper*, which normally prevents the wire from vibrating, drops back from the wire and stays back until the key is released. The piano also has pedals to soften and extend the notes.

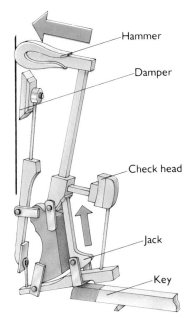

▲ The action of a piano is based on a lever movement by the key which is transmitted to a felt-covered hammer that strikes the piano string. A damper prevents the note from sounding after the key is released.

◀ This piano was given to the composer Beethoven by the piano maker Thomas Broadwood in 1818.

Picasso, Pablo

Pablo Picasso (1881–1973) was the most famous artist of this century. He was born in Spain but lived mostly in France.

People said Picasso could draw before he learned to talk. He disliked paintings that looked like

▲ Pablo Picasso was a very influential artist whose work changed the course of modern art.

► *One of Picasso's cubist paintings,*
The Three Musicians, *painted in 1921.*

It is said that Picasso could
draw before he could talk. At
the age of 14 he spent one day
on an art school test that most
people needed a month to
take. By 16 he had passed all
the tests that Spain's art
schools could offer.

photographs, and admired the curving shapes of
African sculpture. Picasso began painting people as
simple shapes such as cubes. He also produced
sculpture and pottery.

▲ *The wild boar is a tough, fierce
animal, unlike most of its domestic
relatives.*

Pig

These farmyard animals have a long, heavy body;
short legs ending in hoofed toes; a long snout; and a
short, curly tail. Males are called boars. Females are
called sows. The heaviest boars weigh over a tonne.

Pigs provide us with bacon, ham, pork and lard.
Different parts of a pig's body are used to make
brushes, glue, leather and soap.

Domestic pigs are descended from the wild boar
of Asian and European forests.

Pigeon and Dove

Pigeons and doves are birds that eat seeds or fruit.
Many make soft cooing sounds. Pigeons are larger
than doves. The crowned pigeon is bigger than a
chicken, but the diamond dove is almost as small as
a lark.

Tame pigeons all come from rock doves, which

Pigeons were the main source
of fresh meat for the people of
the Middle Ages.

Stock dove

Wood pigeon

Pallas's sandgrouse

Rock dove

Turtle dove

Collared dove

nest on cliffs. Pigeons and doves have become domesticated. Some are ornamental, others race. Homing pigeons will fly great distances to return home. A bird once flew 1300 km in one day.

▲ *Many members of the pigeon and dove family are seen all year round, in both town and country. Pallas's sandgrouse nests in central Asia, but migrates to Europe.*

Pine *See* Conifer

Pineapple

Pineapples earned their name because they look like large pine cones. Pineapples are big, juicy fruits from the tropics. They grow on top of short stems belonging to plants with long spiky leaves. Pineapple producers include Hawaii, Brazil, Mexico and the Philippines.

Plague

Since ancient times, terrible epidemics of plague have swept through Europe, Asia and Africa. Bubonic plague is one of the worst epidemic diseases. In the 1300s, a form of bubonic plague called the Black Death killed a quarter of the people in Europe. In London alone more than 150,000 people

▼ *The pineapple gets its name from the Spanish* piña, *meaning pine cone, because of the shape of the fruit.*

▲ *The nursery rhyme 'Ring o' roses' refers back to the time of the plague, when the first sign of infection was a rosy rash. Herbs and fragrant posies were thought to protect against the disease. Once the victims started to sneeze – 'Atishoo, atishoo' – they were almost certain to die – 'all fall down'.*

▼ *Despite their tiny size, plankton often have beautiful and complex structures. These diatoms have shells made up of silica.*

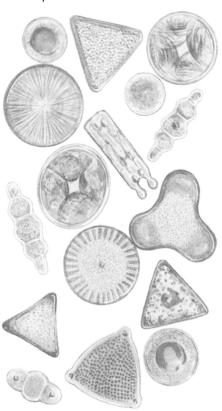

died from the plague during the first half of the 17th century.

Plague is given to people chiefly by fleas from infected rats.

Planet

The word planet comes from a Greek word meaning 'wanderer'. Long ago, skywatchers gave this name to 'stars' that appeared to move. We now know that planets are not STARS, but are heavenly bodies that travel around stars.

The EARTH and other planets of our SOLAR SYSTEM travel around the star we call the SUN. Each planet travels in its own ORBIT. But they all move in the same direction, and, except for Mercury and Pluto, they lie in the same plane (at about the same level).

Astronomers think the planets came from a band of gas and dust that once whirled around the Sun. They think that GRAVITY pulled parts of this band together as masses that became planets.

The nine planets in the solar system are MERCURY, VENUS, EARTH, MARS, JUPITER, SATURN, URANUS, NEPTUNE and PLUTO. Mercury is closest to the Sun, Pluto usually farthest away. The planets shine by reflected sunlight.

Plankton

Plankton is the mass of tiny plants and animals that drifts about in the sea and inland waters. Most plankton are so small they can be seen only with a microscope.

Planktonic plants are called *phytoplankton*. They live near the surface, where they find the light they need. Some tiny plants swim by lashing the water with little whip-like organs. Others have spiky shells that look like glass.

Planktonic animals are called *zooplankton*. Some live deep down and rise at night to feed. Zooplankton includes tiny one-celled creatures, and baby crabs and fish.

Plankton is the base for the ocean FOOD CHAIN. All sea creatures either depend directly on plankton for food or on animals that feed on plankton.

◀ Scientists think the Earth was born about four and a half thousand million years ago. The spare material around the Sun formed a ring, or 'doughnut', of gas and dust, whirling around the Sun at high speed. The planets may have formed out of the 'doughnut' rather like this.

1. To begin with, the doughnut was a spinning ring of gas and dust.

2. The solid particles began to strike each other and stick together, forming larger bodies. At first, these were mostly carbon and ice.

3. These particles rapidly grew to planetary size. As they grew larger they began to 'pull' against each other, which meant that if they passed too close to each other, they were pulled into a different orbit. Some of the very small carbon-ice bodies were pulled so violently by the larger ones that they were thrown right out towards the stars. Others found themselves pulled into very long orbits that carried them far beyond the planets and back again very near to the Sun. These are the comets.

4. Eventually there were just a few large bodies going around the Sun in orbits that did not meet each other, and so there were no more collisions or near misses – the nine major planets were formed.

5. With the passage of thousands of millions of years the planets continued to pull against each other, until their orbits have become almost level.

527

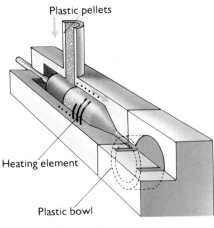

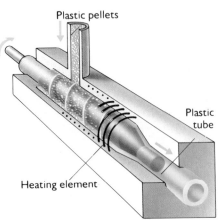

▲ Hot plastic can be squeezed, or extruded (above) into a long, thin tube shape by forcing it through a specially shaped hole. A bowl (top) is made by 'injection moulding'. Hot plastic is forced into a mould which is cooled to harden the plastic.

▶ Bakelite, an early kind of hard plastic, was invented in 1908 by Leo Baekeland. It was used for many household objects.

The word *Plato* was a nickname, meaning *broad-shouldered*. Plato's real name was Aristocles.

Plant

Most living things are either animals or plants. Plants differ from animals in several ways. For example, green plants can make food with the help of CHLOROPHYLL. Each plant CELL has a wall of cellulose. But unlike animals, most plants cannot move about.

There are more than 300,000 kinds of living plant on Earth (See pages 530–531.)

Plastic

Plastics are man-made substances and can be moulded into many different shapes. They are used to make anything from furniture and car seats to shoes and bags or cups and plates.

Most plastics are largely made from chemicals obtained from petroleum oil. Coal, limestone, salt and water are also used. Plastics can be hard, soft or runny. They can be made to look like glass, metal, wood or other substances.

Hard plastics are used in radio and camera cases. But fine threads of the hard plastic nylon make soft stockings.

Plastic bags and squeeze bottles are made of soft plastics like polyethylene. The first plastic was celluloid, discovered in the 1800s.

Plato

Plato (about 427–347 BC) was a great Greek thinker. His ideas were very important in the history of PHILOSOPHY. He believed that the things we see around us are only poor copies of the perfect things in an ideal world. He developed ideas like justice. In his book *The Republic*, Plato described his idea of a perfect nation.

Platypus

The platypus is an Australian MAMMAL that lays eggs. Its name means 'flat footed'. The platypus uses its webbed feet to swim in rivers and its duck-like beak to grub for worms and insects under water. It lives in a burrow in river banks. The female lays her soft-shelled eggs in a nest. They are as small as marbles.

The eyes, ears and nostrils of the platypus shut completely when the animal is under water. Although the platypus is blind and deaf in the water, its soft rubbery bill is so sensitive it has no difficulty in finding small creatures to eat.

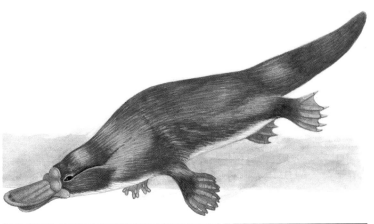

◀ The duck-billed platypus is just one of a number of very unusual animals found only in Australia and New Zealand. These land masses were cut off millions of years ago, when the continents drifted apart. The animals there evolved in isolation from those elsewhere.

Pluto

The PLANET Pluto is named after the Greek god who ruled the dreary world of the dead. Pluto must be bitterly cold, because it is farther away from the Sun than any of the other planets. It is almost 40 times farther from the Sun than the EARTH is.

Continued on page 532

PLUTO FACTS

Average distance from Sun: 5900 million km
Nearest distance from Earth: 5800 million km
Average temperature: −230°C
Diameter across the equator: 3000 km
Atmosphere: None?
Number of moons: 1 known
Length of day: 6 days 9 hours
Length of year: 247.7 Earth years

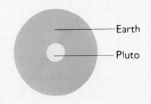

Earth

Pluto

◀ Pluto has one moon, Charon, which is about half as large as the planet it orbits. Many astronomers consider them a twin planet rather than a planet with a moon.

PLANTS

We could not live without plants. Only plants are able to use sunlight to build up living matter. They use the carbon dioxide gas (breathed out as waste by animals) and 'breathe out' life-giving oxygen. Without plants, there would be no animal life on Earth. Plants provide animals with food. People not only eat plants (and animals such as cattle that feed on plants), but also make use of plant products in all kinds of ways.

There are more than 300,000 different kinds of plant. Some trees may grow a hundred metres tall and live for hundreds of years. Other plants are so tiny they can be seen only through a microscope. Plants are found in the oceans, in deserts, on windswept mountains and cold tundra plains. When people first learned how to cultivate plants, civilization began. Today, many wild plants are endangered because their habitats are under threat. It is important to protect wild plants, and to save them for future generations.

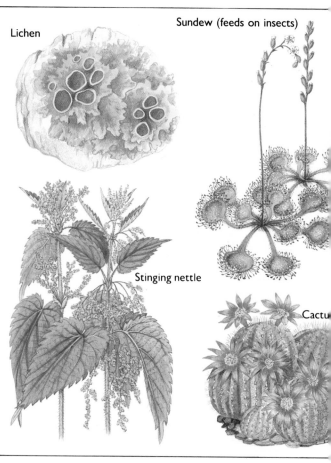

Lichen

Sundew (feeds on insects)

Stinging nettle

Cactus

THE PARTS OF A PLANT

Flower: concerned with reproduction. Most flowers have male and female parts.
Leaf: concerned with food-making.
Stem: supports the leaves and flowers. Tubes in the stem carry, and also store, food and water.
Roots: anchor the plant in the soil. They also take in water and minerals through delicate hairs.

Flower

Stem

Leaf

Roots

HOW PLANTS REPRODUCE

Flowering plants reproduce by pollination, transferring pollen grains from the male part of the flower to the female part. Plants have developed many amazing methods to make sure pollination takes place. Here are two common ones: pollination by insect and by wind.

When a bee collects nectar from a flower, pollen is brushed onto its body. When the bee visits another flower, the pollen is rubbed off.

Many trees and grasses are pollinated by wind. Vast amounts of pollen are produced to make sure that some will be caught by other flowers, but much pollen is wasted.

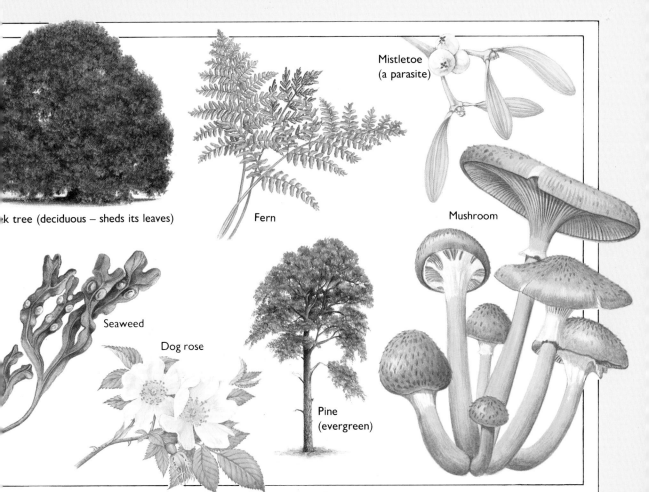

Mistletoe
(a parasite)

k tree (deciduous – sheds its leaves)

Fern

Mushroom

Seaweed

Dog rose

Pine
(evergreen)

HOW PLANTS FEED

ater
our
t

Carbon
dioxide
in

ve, the leaves of green plants
tain chlorophyll, a substance which
orbs light energy from the Sun and
it to make food for the plant.
ter from the plant's roots and
on dioxide gas taken in from the
by the leaves are combined to
e glucose (sugar) and oxygen. The
t takes in the sugar as food for its
. The oxygen is released into the
Plants are the only living things on
h which can do this.

ter (right) is taken in through the
ts and travels through tubes (the

xylem) to veins in the leaves. Some
water is given off as vapour (left), the
rest is used by the cells in
photosynthesis. The glucose made by
photosynthesis travels back around the
plant through other tubes (the
phloem) to feed the plant.

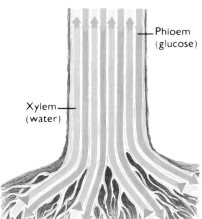

Phloem
(glucose)

Xylem
(water)

PLANT FAMILIES

Angiosperms: the most advanced
plants, ranging from common garden
flowers to trees such as the oak.
Gymnosperms: includes conifers
(firs and pines).
Pteridophytes: ferns, horsetails
and clubmosses. The simplest plants
with roots, stems and leaves.
Bryophytes: liverworts and
mosses. These are the simplest land
plants, without proper roots.
Fungi: mushrooms and toadstools
have no chlorophyll and so feed on
other living organisms or on dead
matter. Lichens are a kind of fungi.
Algae: includes seaweeds and tiny
single-celled plants called diatoms.
Bacteria and Blue-green Algae:
the smallest and most primitive of all
plants. Most have only one cell.

There are many articles on individual PLANTS in the encyclopedia. Use the Index to find them quickly. Useful information will also be
found in BOTANY; BULB; CHLOROPHYLL; CONIFER; FLOWER; FOREST; FRUIT; FUNGUS; LEAF; NUT; SEAWEED; SEED; and TREE.

▲ T.S. Eliot (1888–1965), whose poem 'The Wasteland' (1922) broke with 19th century poetic traditions and made him famous.

▼ Alfred, Lord Tennyson (below) wrote his poem 'The Charge of the Light Brigade' in 1854 after a tragic incident in the Crimean War when 247 men out of 637 were killed or wounded in a charge because of a misunderstood order (right).

Pluto spins and moves around the Sun much more slowly than the Earth. A day on Pluto may equal nearly a week on Earth. One year on Pluto lasts almost 248 of our years.

Pluto is only half as big as the Earth, and weighs one-sixth as much.

Poetry

Poetry is the oldest form of literature. Before people developed a system of writing, they found that the best way to remember a story was to sing it or put it in a rhyming pattern. In this way, poetry was born. Poets choose words carefully, for their sound as well as their meaning. Poetry is something like music because it creates beautiful sounds with words.

Much poetry is written in *rhyme*. This means that the words at the ends of lines sound alike. A simple rhyme is:

I wish I were an octopus, with arms on every corner;
I'd scare my granny half to death; I wouldn't even warn her!

Can you see that 'corner' and 'warn her' rhyme?

Rhyme is not necessary in poetry, however. Many poets use rhyme in some poems and not in others.

Poems are usually written in verses. The lines have a *rhythm* built up by strong and weak sounds. Can you see where the strong sounds occur in the lines above? You will find that there are 7 strong sounds in each line.

There are three main types of poetry. They are *narrative, lyric* and *dramatic*. Narrative poetry tells a story. Lyric poetry tells of the poet's own feelings. Dramatic poetry has characters who tell a story, just as a play does. SHAKESPEARE wrote nearly all his plays in verse.

▲ *An illustration for the poem 'Jabberwocky' by Lewis Carroll. This poem, from the book* Through the Looking Glass, *is a superb example of a nonsense rhyme.*

SOME POISONOUS SUBSTANCES

Many things around us – in our kitchens, our garages, or our garden sheds – can be poisonous if they are not used properly. These are just a few of them:

● Some **household substances** may be poisonous if swallowed. These include bleach, toilet cleaners, most detergents, furniture polish, petrol, lighter fuel, paraffin and household ammonia.

● Garden and farm **insecticides** and **weedkillers** can kill.

● **Carbon monoxide**, a gas given off by car exhausts, is poisonous, especially in badly ventilated areas. Car antifreeze is also a poison.

● Taken in excess, many **drugs and medicines** can be poisonous, including aspirin and sleeping pills.

● **Poisonous plants** include holly (berries), lily of the valley, hydrangea (leaves and buds) and deadly nightshade.

▼ *The symbol for poisonous substances is a skull and crossbones.*

Poison

Poisons are chemical substances that kill or damage living things. Some poisons get into the body through the skin. Some are swallowed. Poisonous gases are harmful if someone breathes them in with air.

Different poisons work in different ways. Strong ACIDS or alkalis 'burn'. NERVE poisons can stop the heart. Some other poisons can make the body bleed inside.

DRUGS called antidotes can cure people who are suffering from certain poisons.

POLAND

Government: Democratic state
Capital: Warsaw
Area: 312,677 sq km
Population: 38,385,000
Language: Polish
Currency: Zloty

Poland

Poland lies in eastern Europe, south of the Baltic Sea, and is the seventh largest country in EUROPE. Most of Poland is low farmland, although forests sprawl across the Carpathian Mountains in the south. Poland's largest river is the Vistula. It rises in the mountains and flows into the Baltic Sea. Rivers often freeze in Poland's cold, snowy winters.

There are more than 38 million Poles. Most of them speak Polish, and most are Roman Catholics.

In 1989 Poland had the first free elections in 40 years. The independent trade union Solidarity swept into power and Poland became the first non-communist country in the Eastern bloc. There are still problems with inflation and unemployment.

Police

Police work for a government to keep LAW and order in their country. Their main task is to see that everyone obeys their country's laws. Part of this job is protecting people's lives and property. Police also help to control crowds. They help people hurt in accidents, and take charge of lost children.

Police officers try to prevent crime, and track down and capture criminals. This can be dangerous and sometimes officers are killed.

In 1829, Sir Robert Peel organized a body of paid and trained policemen for day and night duty in London. The public called these first policemen 'peelers' or 'bobbies', after Sir Robert, and the name bobbies is still used today.

▶ Modern policing relies heavily on fast and efficient communication. This officer in the highway patrol has a radio car as well as a hand radio for instant contact away from the car.

Pollution

Pollution means the spoiling of air, soil, water or countryside by wastes. Before the INDUSTRIAL REVOLUTION most of the wastes produced by living things had been used by other living things. But today, people produce more wastes than nature can cope with.

Cars and factories pour smoke and fumes into the air. Chemical FERTILIZER and pesticides can kill off wild plants and animals. Poor sewage disposal and spilt oil make seas and rivers filthy.

▲ This plastic rubbish polluting a rocky shore in Wales must be cleared up by hand – it will not decompose naturally.

CLEAN POLLUTED

◄ Lichens that normally grow on trees in the countryside are sensitive to polluted air. As you get closer to towns, only certain types of lichen can survive. Where there are heavy concentrations of sulphur dioxide gas in the air only a thin film of algae will grow on trees and stones.

Polo, Marco

Marco Polo (1254–1324) was an Italian traveller. He is famous for the long journey he made to far-away China at a time when the people of Europe knew little about the East. His father and his uncle

▼ Marco Polo and his companions were kindly received by Kublai Khan, who was interested in other countries and their customs.

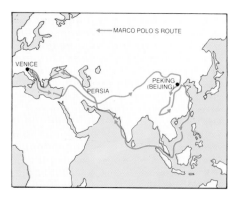

▲ *Even by modern standards, Marco Polo's journey was a long one, but in the 1200s it was a tremendous achievement.*

The Roman writer Pliny the Younger described what happened when Vesuvius destroyed Pompeii. Pliny saw the ground shake, the sea sucked back and then hurled forward and great tongues of flame spurt from the black cloud that boiled up from the volcano.

▼ *Archaeologists have uncovered almost half of the city of Pompeii (right). Bodies of Pompeiians trapped while fleeing (left) have been recreated by making plaster casts of their imprints in the volcanic ash.*

were merchants from Venice and they decided to take the young Marco with them when they set out for the East in 1271. They crossed Persia and the vast Gobi Desert. In 1275 they reached Peking (Beijing) and were welcomed by Kublai Khan, a great MONGOL conqueror. The Polos stayed for many years during which Marco travelled all over China in the service of the Khan. They left China in 1292 and arrived home in Venice in 1295. Later, Marco's stories of his travels were written down. The *Travels of Marco Polo* is one of the most exciting books ever written.

Pompeii

Two thousand years ago, Pompeii was a small Roman city in southern Italy. A sudden disaster killed many of its citizens and drove out the rest. But the same disaster preserved the streets and buildings. Today, visitors to Pompeii can learn a great deal about what life was like inside a Roman city.

In AD 79 the nearby volcano of VESUVIUS erupted and showered Pompeii with volcanic ash and cinders. Poisonous gases swirled through the streets. About one citizen in every ten was poisoned by fumes or burned to death by hot ash. The rest escaped. Ash and cinders soon covered up the buildings. In time people forgot that Pompeii had ever been there.

For centuries Pompeii's thick coat of ash protected it from the weather. At last, in the 1700s, people began to dig it out. The digging still goes on today. Archaeologists discovered buildings, streets, tools and statues. They even found hollows left in the ash by the decayed bodies of people and dogs killed by the eruption. The archaeologists poured plaster into these hollows. They let the plaster harden, then they cleared away the ash. They found that the plaster had formed life-size models of the dead bodies.

Pope

'Pope' is a title of the head of the ROMAN CATHOLIC CHURCH. (The word 'pope' comes from *papa*, which means 'father'.) The Pope is also the Bishop of Rome. He lives in the VATICAN CITY inside the city of Rome.

Roman Catholics believe that Jesus made St Peter the first Pope. Since then there have been hundreds of Popes. Each time one dies, church leaders choose another. The Pope makes church laws, chooses bishops and can declare people SAINTS.

Pop Music

'Pop music' is short for popular music. Modern pop music has strong, lively rhythms, and simple, often catchy, tunes. Most pop tunes are songs. A pop

▲ As Pope, John Paul II is recognized by Roman Catholics as the representative of Jesus Christ on earth. He is also head of the Vatican City State.

▼ Many people start pop groups when they are still at school, and a few have achieved success by being 'discovered' and given recording contracts. Take That, a group of singers from Manchester, have enjoyed enormous chart success.

▲ *Elvis Presley was one of the first rock and roll stars to become a cult hero.*

▼ *The bar chart shows how the populations of developed and developing countries have increased between 1750 and 1975, and estimates the population for the year 2000. The pie chart (inset) gives the percentage of the world's population in each of the largest countries.*

group usually has one or more singers with musicians who play such instruments as electronic guitars, synthesizers and electronic organs. Pop groups often need large vans to carry their equipment, as well as someone to set it up, take it down and repair it.

Famous pop groups and stars like the Beatles, the Rolling Stones and Madonna have attracted huge audiences to concerts. Millions of people around the world watched the 1985 Live Aid concert on television.

Population

All the people living in a place make up its *population*. That place may be a village, a city, a country or the world.

In the STONE AGE, the whole world held only a few million people. Their numbers were kept down by lack of food, injury and disease. As people have solved these problems, the population has increased.

Between AD 1 and 1650 the world's population doubled. It doubled again in only 150 years after 1650. Since then it has risen even faster. In 1930 the world had 2000 million people. By 1980 there were over twice that many. The world's population is now over 5 billion and is still growing too quickly.

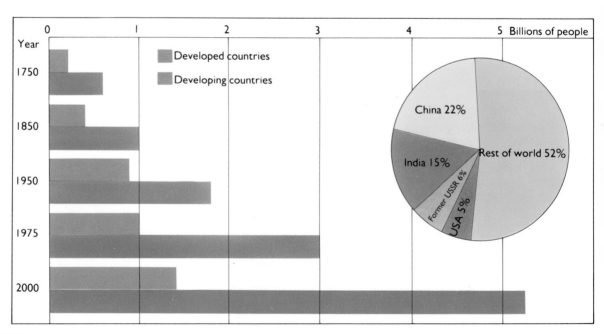

Porcupine

Porcupines are named from the Latin words for 'spiny pig'. A porcupine is really a RODENT with many hairs shaped as long, sharp spines or quills. If a porcupine is attacked it backs towards its enemy and lashes its tail. Some of the spines stick into its enemy and cause painful wounds or even death.

American porcupines are a different type from those of Asia, Africa and Europe.

Portugal

This is a long, narrow, country in south-west EUROPE. It is sandwiched between the Atlantic Ocean and Spain, a country four times the size of Portugal.

Much of Portugal is mountainous. Rivers flow from the mountains through valleys and across plains to the sea. Portugal's mild winters and warm summers help its people to grow olives, oranges and rice. Its grapes produce port, a wine named after the Portuguese city of Oporto. Portugal's woods yield more CORK than those of any other nation. Its fishermen catch sardines and other sea fish. Portugal also has mines and factories.

There are about 10 million Portuguese. They speak Portuguese, a language much like Spanish. Their capital is Lisbon.

Potato

Potatoes are valuable foods. They are rich in STARCHES and contain PROTEINS and different VITAMINS. Potatoes must be cooked to give nourishment that we can use.

Potato plants are related to tomatoes. Each plant is low and bushy with a soft stem. Each potato grows on a root as a kind of swelling called a tuber. When its tubers have grown, the plant dies. But new plants spring up from the tubers.

Potatoes were first grown by South American Indians. Spanish explorers brought potatoes back to Europe. After wheat, rice and maize they are the world's most important crop.

▲ The North American porcupine is not hurt by losing some of its quills. They are part of its defence system, and soon grow back.

PORTUGAL

Government: Parliamentary democracy
Capital: Lisbon
Area: 92,082 sq km
Population: 10,448,000
Language: Portuguese
Currency: Escudo

In 1845 and 1846 the Irish potato crop failed because of a plant disease. As a result, thousands of Irish died of starvation and many more emigrated to the United States.

POTTERY

▶ *Making a pot on a potter's wheel is much more difficult than it looks. The lump of clay must be positioned centrally on the platform. It is made to rotate either by the action of the potter's foot or by electricity. By pressing both thumbs on top of the clay, the inside can be hollowed out as the platform spins.*

▼ *A hollow pot can be made by pouring 'slip', or liquid clay, into a mould. Water seeps out of the slip into the mould and the clay next to the mould begins to thicken. When the required thickness of clay has hardened, the remaining slip can be poured away to leave a hollow shape.*

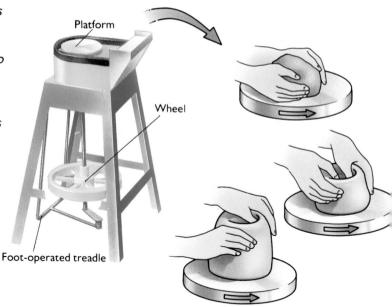

Platform

Wheel

Foot-operated treadle

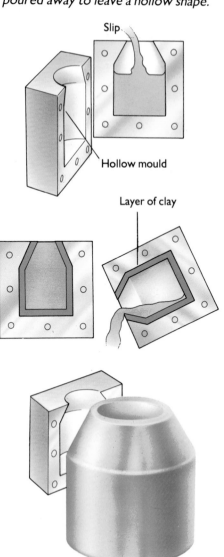

Slip

Hollow mould

Layer of clay

Pottery

All kinds of objects made of baked clay are called pottery. Many cups, saucers, plates, bowls, pots, vases and other tools and ornaments are made of this very useful substance.

People have been making pottery for thousands of years. Early pots were thick and gritty. They leaked, and they cracked if heated. In time people learned to make pottery that was more useful and more beautiful. Today the two main kinds of pottery are porcelain and stoneware. Porcelain is fine pottery made of white China clay. This porcelain lets the light show through. Stoneware is usually thicker than porcelain and it does not let the light show through.

To make a pot, a potter puts a lump of moist clay on a spinning disc called a *wheel*. He uses thumbs and fingers to shape the clay into a pot. He leaves this pot to dry. Next he may coat it with a wet mixture called a glaze. Then he fires (heats) the pot with others in an oven called a kiln. Firing makes the pots rock hard and turns their glaze into a smooth, hard, shiny coat. Different glazes produce different colours. Some glazes can even produce a metallic lustre on a pot.

Most pottery today is mass-produced in factories. It can be shaped, fired and decorated quickly and cheaply on an assembly line.

Poultry

All birds kept for meat or eggs are known as poultry. To most people, poultry means chickens, DUCKS, geese and turkeys. But guinea fowl, OSTRICHES, partridges, PEACOCKS, pheasants and PIGEONS can be kept as poultry too.

Chickens outnumber other kinds of poultry. There are probably more chickens than people, and they lay enough eggs to give everyone on Earth several hundred eggs each year. Chickens also produce meat more cheaply than sheep or cattle. This is because it costs less in food to produce a kilogram of chicken meat than it costs to make a kilogram of beef, lamb or mutton.

▲ *Partridges are small game birds, about 30 cm long, with brown and chestnut markings. They are often raised for their meat. In the wild they live on farmland and moorland.*

Power Station

Power stations are places where the ENERGY in heat or in flowing water is changed into electrical energy for use in homes and factories. Most power stations obtain their energy from a FUEL which makes steam that works a GENERATOR or a group of generators.

These produce electric CURRENT that often travels overland through wires slung between tall metal towers called pylons. First, the current passes

▼ *A coal-fired power station transforms the energy locked in coal into electricity. Bituminous, or soft coal is most commonly used as the fuel in power stations because it is cheaper and more plentiful than anthracite, or hard coal.*

The first public power station began operating in London on January 12, 1882. Because it produced direct electric current at a low voltage, the area it supplied with electricity was very small. In those days a single city was supplied by a dozen or more power stations.

▼ Homo habilis *was probably the first human being to make and use tools.*

▼ *The evolution of human beings, from the ape-like Ramapithecus to modern man.*

through a transformer. This raises the pressure (voltage) of the current and so reduces the amount that leaks away as the current flows. The voltage is reduced again before it reaches our homes.

Prehistoric Animals

Prehistoric animals are those that lived before history began, about 5000 years ago. We know about them from their FOSSILS found in rocks. Different kinds of creatures lived at different times. Each kind developed from earlier kinds, by EVOL-UTION. The first prehistoric animals probably looked like little blobs of jelly. (See pages 544–545).

Prehistoric People

Prehistoric people lived long ago before there were any written records of history. We know about them from the remains of their tools, weapons and bodies. Prehistory is divided into the STONE AGE, the BRONZE AGE and the Iron Age. The ages are named after the materials that people used to make their tools and weapons.

The Stone Age lasted for a long time. It began around 2½ to 3 million years ago when human-like creatures began to appear on the Earth. They were different from the ape-like animals that lived at the same time. They had larger brains, used stone tools and could walk upright.

Ramapithecus	*Australopithecus*	*Homo habilis*	*Homo erectus*	*Neanderthal man*	*Modern human*
15 million years ago. Africa, Asia	1 – 4 million years ago. Africa	1.5 – 2 million years ago. Africa	0.2 – 1.5 million years ago. Africa, Asia Europe	35,000–100,000 years ago. Europe	Since 35,000 years ago. Worldwide

◀ *About 20,000 years ago modern humans lived in caves or crude huts of wood or hides. They used tools of stone and bone for hunting and preparing food and for making clothing and shelters.*

Around 1½ million years ago, a more human-like creature appeared. Scientists call this kind of early man *Homo erectus*. This means 'upright man'. *Homo erectus* is probably the ancestor of more advanced types of man, called *Homo sapiens*. This means 'intelligent man'. One kind of *Homo sapiens* was Neanderthal man, who appeared about 100,000 years ago. Modern man, called *Homo sapiens sapiens*, first appeared in Europe and Asia around 35,000 years ago.

Towards the end of the Stone Age, prehistoric people began to use metals. The first metal they used was copper. They made copper tools about 10,000 years ago. About 5,000 years ago, people invented bronze. Bronze is a hard ALLOY of copper and tin. This was the start of the Bronze Age, when the earliest civilizations began. The Bronze Age ended about 3300 years ago in south-eastern Europe, when people learned how to make iron tools. Iron is much harder than bronze. With iron tools, people could develop farming and cities more quickly than ever before.

> It is difficult for us to imagine how few people there were in Stone Age times. It has been estimated that only a few thousand people lived in all of Africa and another few thousand in Asia. People moved around in small groups. During his or her whole lifetime, a Stone Age person might see only 25 to 50 other people.

Presbyterian

Presbyterians are PROTESTANTS whose churches are governed by ministers and elders, called *presbyters*.

A French religious thinker called John Calvin (1509–1564) led a reform movement in the Christian church, which gave rise to the Presbyterians. There are now about 50 million Presbyterians.

▲ *John Calvin set up a Protestant church in Geneva, Switzerland, and became governor there in 1536.*

Continued on page 546

PREHISTORIC ANIMALS

Animal life on Earth began in the oceans more than 570 million years ago. Simple crab-like animals and shellfish swarmed in the sea, but there was no life on dry land until much later – about 350 million years ago. Then air-breathing fish crawled out onto the land, and from them evolved amphibians and later reptiles. For many millions of years dinosaurs, some of them huge, roamed the Earth. They died out about 65 million years ago, and their places were taken by mammals. No one knows exactly why the dinosaurs became extinct. Today, only their fossilized bones remain.

◄ *Trilobites were crab-like sea animals with jointed legs and hard bodies. They lived on Earth for more than 340 million years.*

► Ichthyostega *was one of the first amphibians. It had a fin-like tail but walked on four legs.*

◄ *Giant dragonflies and other insects flew in the swamps and forests millions of years ago.*

▼ Triceratops *was an armoured dinosaur. Its bony frill and horns protected it from enemies.*

▲ *The first land reptiles, such as* Dimetrodon, *kept warm by using their huge 'sails' as solar panels to absorb the sunlight.*

▼ *The plesiosaurs were marine reptiles. They used their limbs as paddles for swimming.*

▼ *The largest dinosaurs, such as* Brontosaurus, *weighed over 150 tonnes. These vast creatures were harmless plant-eaters.*

◀ *Pterosaurs were flying reptiles, with bat-like wings. It is thought most pterosaurs fed on fish, gliding over seas and rivers.*

▼ *Archaeopteryx was a feathered animal, halfway between reptile and bird. It probably used its wings to glide short distances.*

Tyrannosaurus rex ing of the tyrant rds') was the fiercest sh-eater of all time. It od 6 metres high and asured 16 metres m jaws to tail.

▼ *The woolly mammoth was an Ice Age relative of the elephant. Its thick hairy coat kept it warm.*

We know little about e first mammals. They re small creatures that obably ate insects and orms.

▲ Toxodon *was a rhino-like plant-eater of the Pliocene epoch in South America.*

◀ *Humans and apes evolved from a common ancestor. This primitive man-like ape,* Dryopithecus, *lived 22 million years ago in Africa.*

The earliest mammals, tiny shrew-like animals, lived in the shadows of the great dinosaurs. After the dinosaurs died out, mammals developed and spread rapidly. From these early mammals (some of which were very curious-looking) developed the mammals of today. Some were much larger than their modern relatives. Animals that could not adapt to changing conditions (like the Ice Ages) died out. Others were hunted by human beings, the most powerful of all animals, whose primitive ancestors first appeared on Earth some 35 million years ago.

For more information turn to these articles: DINOSAUR, EVOLUTION, FOSSIL, ICE AGES and MAMMOTH. You will find lots of other useful references (such as Animal, Bird, Vertebrate) by looking in the Index.

President Andrew Jackson had a group of personal friends and advisers who were called the 'Kitchen Cabinet' because they were an unofficial, informal kind of cabinet.

Many of them live in France, Hungary, the Netherlands, Northern Ireland, Scotland, Switzerland and the United States.

President of the United States

The president of the UNITED STATES is the world's most powerful elected person. He is head of state, like the queen or king of Britain. He is also head of the government, like a PRIME MINISTER. The president is also the commander-in-chief of the army, navy and air force. The American people elect a president for a four-year term. A president may serve two terms. From 1789 to 1997 the USA had 42 presidents. The first was George WASHINGTON. Other famous presidents of the past include Thomas Jefferson and Abraham LINCOLN.

▲ Thomas Jefferson wrote the text of the American Declaration of Independence and became third president of the United States.

Prime Minister

A prime minister is a head of government. Britain and many other countries have a prime minister. The prime minister is usually the leader of the political party (or group of parties) with the greatest number of seats in PARLIAMENT. He or she chooses a

▲ Margaret Thatcher became the first woman to be elected Prime Minister of Great Britain in May 1979.

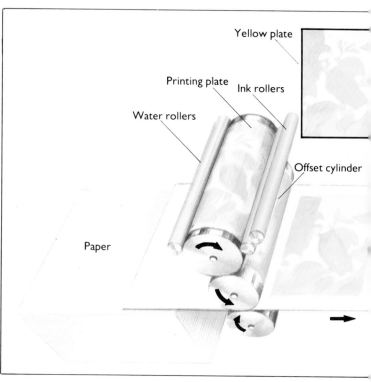

Yellow plate

Printing plate

Ink rollers

Water rollers

Offset cylinder

Paper

group of people to help run the government. These people are called *ministers*. The group is called a *cabinet*.

Printing

Printing is a way of copying words and pictures by mechanical means. It is used to produce books, newspapers, magazines and other items such as food can labels and printed carrier bags.

In *relief* printing, ink is put onto raised images, such as letters. The letters are then pressed against paper. The most common relief method is called *letterpress* printing. In *intaglio* or *gravure* printing, the image is not raised but cut away, or etched.

In other kinds of printing, the ink is put onto a flat surface. *Offset lithography* uses printing plates that are made photographically. The plates are treated with chemicals so that the greasy ink sticks only to the images to be printed.

The earliest printing, using wooden blocks, was done in China, probably as early as the AD 500s. Johannes GUTENBERG of Germany founded modern printing in the 1400s. He used movable type letters that could be used again and again.

Cabinet government began in Britain during the reign of George I. Sir Robert Walpole, First Lord of the Treasury, came to be known as the *prime (first) minister*, but the title did not become official until 1905. The prime minister still holds the title First Lord of the Treasury.

▼ *When a colour picture is printed, it is actually made up of tiny dots of the three primary colours – blue (cyan), yellow and red (magenta) – and black. Four different printing plates are prepared for the picture, one for each colour. In offset lithography, the flexible plates are rolled around cylinders and moistened by water rollers. The ink rollers spread colour over the image areas on the plate. This colour is transferred to the offset cylinder and from there to the paper passing beneath it. The paper moves from one colour to the next: the black is printed last.*

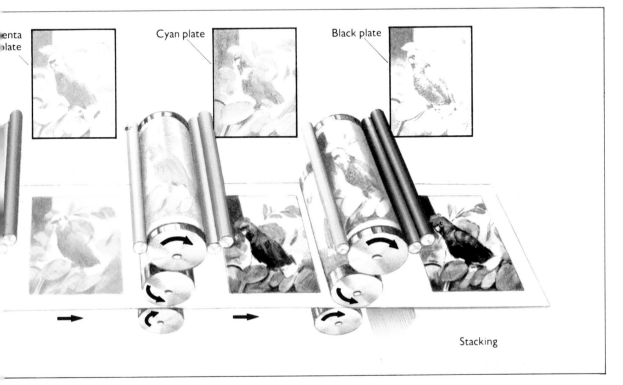

Magenta plate
Cyan plate
Black plate
Stacking

▲ *Meat, fish, eggs, cheese and nuts are all rich sources of protein.*

Protein

Proteins are substances in food which are vital to life. They contain CARBON, HYDROGEN, OXYGEN and nitrogen. They build up body tissue, especially muscle, and repair broken-down CELLS. They also give heat and energy, help us to grow, and help to protect us from disease. Our bodies do not store extra protein, so we must eat a regular supply.

Foods that come from animals provide most of our proteins. But some plant foods, such as groundnuts, peas and beans, are also rich in protein.

▲ *John Bunyan, who wrote* The Pilgrim's Progress, *joined a Nonconformist (a kind of Protestant) church in 1653. He was arrested in 1660 for preaching without a licence and spent almost 12 years in prison.*

Protestant

Protestants are Christians who do not belong to the Roman Catholic or the Eastern Orthodox churches. Protestants believe that the things written in the BIBLE are more important than any rules made by church leaders. There are some passages in the Bible that can be explained in different ways. Protestants believe that people should make up their own minds about what these mean.

Protestantism began with the REFORMATION, when Martin LUTHER led a movement to change the ROMAN CATHOLIC CHURCH. In 1529, the Roman Catholic Church in Germany tried to stop people from following Luther's ideas. Luther's followers protested against this and were then called Pro-

▶ *In France, the fight between Protestants and Catholics was very bitter. In 1572, on the eve of August 24th, St Bartholomew's Day, thousands of Protestants known as Huguenots were murdered by Catholics. This terrible event became known as the St Bartholomew's Day Massacre.*

testants. Early Protestant groups included the Lutherans, Calvinists (PRESBYTERIANS) and Anglicans. Later groups included the Baptists, Congregationalists, Methodists and QUAKERS.

Proverb

A proverb is a short sentence containing a piece of wisdom. The BIBLE contains a book called *Proverbs*. Proverbs are often easy to remember. One famous proverb is 'A stitch in time saves nine'. All peoples have proverbs. Many African languages are rich in them. Typical African proverbs are: 'He who takes his time does not fall' (Somalia); 'The dog you do not feed will not hear your call' (Zaire).

Pruning

Pruning is the cutting back of branches, shoots, buds or roots of mainly woody plants. Careful pruning helps the plant to bear more fruit or flowers, and to become stronger. Roses are often pruned in this way. Sometimes, gardeners prune plants so that they will grow to form special shapes.

Psychology

Psychology is the study of the behaviour of animals and people. Psychologists are interested in how the

> Proverbs are often international, and very old. 'A bird in the hand is worth two in the bush,' is first found in English in a manuscript of about 1470. It says 'Betyr ys a byrd in the hond than tweye in the wode'. The Spanish version is 'A sparrow in the hand is worth a vulture flying'; the German, 'A sparrow in the hand is better than a stork on the roof'.

▲ Shrubs and trees can be cut and trained to grow into special shapes. This art is called 'topiary'.

◄ Psychologists use tests to find out about people. You can test your short term memory by looking at these objects for 30 seconds. Cover them up and see how many you can remember. Short term memory becomes worse as you grow older.

PUERTO RICO

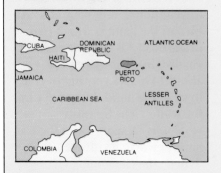

Government: Self-governing commonwealth of the USA
Area: 8897 sq km
Population: 3,316,000
Capital: San Juan
Highest peak: Cerro de Punta, 1338 m
Languages: English and Spanish

mind and senses work. They are able to measure some things, such as INTELLIGENCE, by using special tests.

There are several branches of psychology. For example, child psychology is the study of how children behave and what they can do at different ages. *Psychiatry* is a similar science. But psychiatrists are doctors who cure mental illness and abnormal kinds of behaviour such as drug addiction and depression.

Puerto Rico

Puerto Rico is an island in the WEST INDIES. It is a commonwealth that governs itself, but it has the military protection and some economic and political privileges of the United States. Puerto Ricans are US citizens, but they cannot vote in American elections. The island is densely populated and many people have emigrated to the United States. The tropical climate attracts many tourists.

Pulley

A pulley is a simple MACHINE. It consists of a wheel on a fixed axle. A rope or belt passed over the wheel is tied to a load. When the rope is pulled, the load is raised.

A *movable pulley* runs along a rope. One end of the rope is fixed to a support. The load hangs from

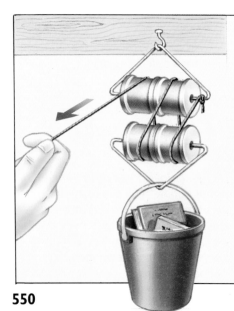

SEE IT YOURSELF

Try making your own pulley, like the one shown on the opposite page.
1. Bend about 20 cm of wire into a triangle shape and push the ends into a cotton reel. (Ask an adult to help you cut and bend the wire.)
2. Find a suitable place to hang your pulley. A hook in the shed or garage or the hook at the end of a plant hanger will do.
3. Tie one end of the string to the handle of the load.
4. Wind the string over the cotton reel and see how easy or difficult it is to lift the load.

Now try a double pulley . . .
1. Make two wire triangles. Use about 35 cm of wire for each one.
2. Attach two cotton reels to each triangle.
3. Thread string round the pulleys as shown in the diagram.
4. Attach the heavy load to the pulley as before.

The double pulley means you use only a quarter of the pull but you need four times the amount of string.

the pulley itself. When the other end of the rope is pulled, the pulley moves the load along the rope. Pulleys are used in machines such as cranes.

Pulsar

Sometimes a huge star, several times bigger than our Sun, becomes so hot that it explodes. For a few days it sends out as much energy as a whole galaxy of stars. It has become a *supernova*. After a supernova explosion, all that is left is a very hot ball of matter a few kilometres across. It spins at a tremendous rate and sends out a beam of light and radio waves like a revolving searchlight. The beam seems to 'pulse' on and off, so it is called a pulsar. Most pulsars are too faint to be seen except with a very large telescope, but they give out very powerful radio waves.

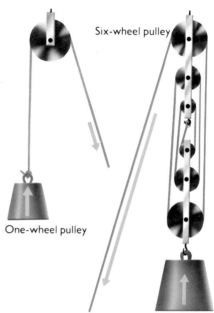

▲ *Pulleys make it easier to lift heavy loads. A six-wheel pulley (right) can lift a much heavier load than a one-wheel pulley (left). This is because the amount of force applied to the weight increases six times.*

 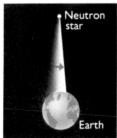 

▲ *As a pulsar, or neutron star, spins, its signal sweeps through space like the beam of light from a lighthouse. The signal reaches the Earth once in every rotation, and can be photographed or picked up by radio. Over millions of years, pulsars slow down.*

Pulse

The pulse is a beating or throbbing in the body's ARTERIES. These are BLOOD vessels that carry blood away from the HEART. A pulse beat occurs as the heart contracts and pumps blood into the arteries.

Doctors measure pulse rates to find out if the heart is beating normally. They usually feel the *radial artery* in the wrist. But the pulse can be felt wherever an artery passes over a bone. The normal pulse rate for men is 72 beats per minute. For women, it is 76 to 80 beats. But pulse rates between 50 and 85 are considered normal. Children have faster pulses.

SEE IT YOURSELF

Try taking your own pulse rate. Feel the inside of one of your wrists with the fingertips of the other hand. The best place is towards the edge of your wrist in line with the thumb. Use your watch to count the number of beats in one minute. Try measuring your pulse rate when you are doing various things that need different amounts of energy. Jot down the rates and compare them.

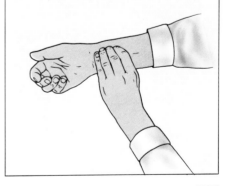

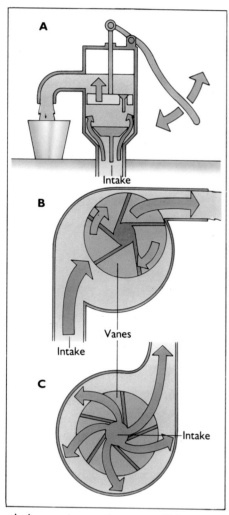

A

Intake

B

Vanes

Intake

C

Intake

▲ In a reciprocating pump (A), a piston forces liquid through an intake opening and out through a spout. A valve in the piston allows more liquid through as the piston is forced down. Rotary pumps (B) allow a steady flow of liquid, sucking the liquid in through the intake opening by means of a wheel instead of a piston. In a centrifugal pump (C) the liquid enters in the centre and is whipped round and out by the spinning blades.

Pump

Most pumps are used to move liquids, but some move gases or powders such as flour. There are several kinds of pumps. For example, a bicycle pump is a simple *reciprocating pump*. It has a piston which moves up and down inside a cylinder. A similar pump is the *lift pump*. This can raise water about 9 metres from the bottom of a well. It has an upright barrel with a close-fitting piston worked by a handle. *Force pumps* are used to raise water from greater depths.

Pyramid

Pyramids are huge, four-sided buildings. They have a square base. The sides are triangles that meet in a point at the top.

The Egyptians built pyramids as royal tombs. The first was built in about 2650 BC at Sakkara. It is 62 metres high. The three most famous pyramids are near Giza. The Great Pyramid, built in the 2600s BC by the PHARAOH Khufu, is 137 metres high. Khafre, who ruled soon after Khufu, built the second pyramid. It is 136 metres high. The third, built by Khafre's successor Menakaure, is 73 metres high. About 80 pyramids still stand in Egypt.

Central and South American Indians also built

▼ The huge pyramids built thousands of years ago in Egypt are great feats of engineering but it took countless numbers of slaves to move the great blocks of stone.

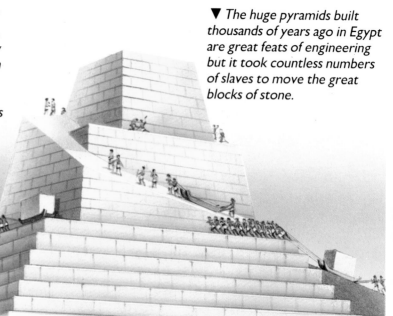

pyramids as temples during the first six centuries AD. One huge pyramid is at Cholula, south-east of Mexico City. It is about 54 metres high.

Pyrenees

The Pyrenees are a chain of MOUNTAINS that lie between France and Spain. They stretch about 435 km from the Bay of Biscay to the Mediterranean Sea. Throughout history they have formed a natural barrier between France and Spain, so that most trade between the two countries has been by sea. Iron, lead, silver and cobalt are mined in the mountains, and the beautiful scenery attracts many tourists.

The peaks of the Pyrenees rise to over 3000 metres, though most average about 1100 metres. The highest is Pico de Aneto at 3404 metres. On the southern slope of the eastern Pyrenees lies the tiny republic of ANDORRA.

▲ A view of the Pyrenees along a green valley in France.

Python

Pythons are large SNAKES. They live in Africa, south-eastern Asia and a few kinds are found in Australia. Some grow as long as 9 metres. They are *constrictors*. This means they squeeze their prey to death, before swallowing it whole.

► The reticulated python lives on the forest floor in South-east Asia. Its pattern and colouring are well matched to its surroundings.

▶ *A market in Doha, the capital of Qatar. The discovery of oil in this little emirate in the 1940s made it into one of the richest nations in the world.*

QATAR

[map showing IRAQ, KUWAIT, IRAN, THE ARABIAN GULF, BAHRAIN, QATAR, SAUDI ARABIA, UNITED ARAB EMIRATES, OMAN]

Government: Traditional monarchy
Capital: Doha
Area: 11,000 sq km
Population: 484,000
Language: Arabic
Currency: Riyal

Qatar

Qatar is an *emirate*, a nation ruled by an emir, in Arabia. It is on the Persian Gulf, next to the United Arab Emirates. Revenue from oil has helped to modernize and develop agriculture and industry in Qatar.

Quaker

The Quakers are also known as the Society of Friends. They are a PROTESTANT group that began in England during the 1650s.

They were called Quakers because some of them shook with emotion at their meetings. Early Quakers were often badly treated because of their belief that religion and government should not be mixed. Quakers have simple religious meetings and have elders not priests.

When you look at the light from a light bulb, it seems to be quite steady. Actually, light is not as steady as it seems. It is given off in a vast number of tiny packages of energy, like the bullets from a machine gun. Each package is a quantum.

Quantum

We think of light and other forms of energy such as radio waves and X-rays as travelling in waves. Light can also be thought of as a stream of tiny quanta (the plural of quantum) or *photons*. The energy of each photon depends on the wavelength and therefore the colour of the light. A photon of white light has more energy than a photon of red light. Scientists combine the two ways of thinking about light. They think of light streaming out in packets of waves, each packet being a quantum or photon. They also think that tiny particles of matter such as electrons behave like waves as well as behaving like solid particles.

> The world's largest quarry is **Bingham Canyon copper mine in Utah, USA.** It is about 770 metres deep.

Quarrying

Quarries are huge pits where rocks are cut or blasted out of the ground. As long ago as prehistoric times, people had quarries where they dug up flint to make into tools and weapons.

Today rock is quarried in enormous amounts. Explosives blast loose thousands of tonnes. This is scooped up by bulldozers and diggers, and taken to crushers. The rock is ground into stones for use in roads, railways, concrete and cement. Not all rock is removed in this way. Stone that is used in building and paving is cut out of the ground rather than blasted. Electric cutters, wire saws and drills are used to cut the rock.

▼ Rock is quarried for many uses: (1) In the quarry, workers prepare for blasting. (2) Dynamite or other explosives break up the rock, and diggers (3) load it into lorries for transporting (4) to the crushing plant (5). There the rock is broken down still further for use on railway lines (6), road beds (7) and as cement for concrete buildings (8).

QUARTZ

▶ *This thin disc of quartz will vibrate at a very regular frequency when exposed to an electric field. Such crystals are used as timers in watches and clocks because they are so accurate.*

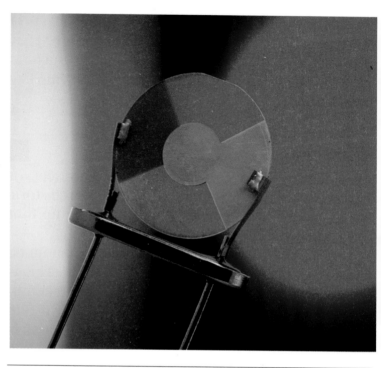

▼ *Pure quartz crystals are colourless, but when mixed with other substances they take on many different shades.*

▼ *Quasars are still a mystery to astronomers. They can only be detected by the most powerful radio telescopes. If we could get close enough to one, it might appear as a brilliant core of light surrounded by a spinning disc of shining material.*

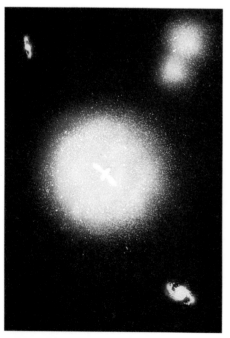

Quartz

Quartz is one of the most common MINERALS in the world. It is found everywhere. SAND is mostly made of quartz, and many ROCKS have quartz in them.

Quartz forms six-sided CRYSTALS. It is very hard, harder even than steel. In its pure form it has no colour and is as clear as glass. But most is smoky white or tinted with various colours. Many semi-precious GEMS, such as agate, amethyst, opal and onyx, are quartz.

Quartz is an important mineral. It is used in many things, including abrasives (such as sandpaper), lenses and electronics.

Quasar

Quasars are very distant, very powerful objects farther out in space than the most remote GALAXIES. They may be galaxies with some extra-powerful energy source at their centre. Quasars send out strong RADIO waves and X-RAYS. From Earth they look like very faint stars because they are so far away. All quasars are millions of light-years away, and so we see them now as they were that length of time ago. Quasars were not discovered by astronomers until the 1960s.

Rabbit

Rabbits originally came from Europe. Today they are found all over the world. They are small MAMMALS with a short tail and long pointed ears. Rabbits live in burrows in the ground. Each burrow is the home of a single family. A group of burrows is known as a warren.

Raccoon

In North America, raccoons are common creatures of the wild. They have long grey fur, a short pointed nose and a bushy tail ringed with black. They may grow to as much as 90 cm long.

Raccoons live in forests. They make their homes in tree holes and are good climbers. At night, they leave their hollows to hunt for food. They will eat almost anything: fruit and plants, eggs, insects, fish, birds and small mammals. But their main food comes from rivers, so their tree holes are usually found close by.

Wild rabbit

▶ *Raccoons are often thought of as pests in the United States, and are sometimes hunted. The frontiersman Davy Crockett's famous hat was made of raccoon fur, with the striped tail left hanging down at the back.*

Dwarf lop-eared rabbit

Himalayan rabbit

Radar

Radar is a device for tracking objects by RADIO beams. Because these beams work in the dark, in fog, and over distances well out of eyesight, radar is an enormously useful invention. It can detect objects thousands of kilometres away.

Radar works by sending out a narrow, high-powered beam about 500 times a second. It travels

▲ *All types of pet rabbit have been bred from wild rabbits. They now come in different sizes, colours and even shapes. The tiny dwarf lop-eared rabbit has ears that droop. The Himalayan rabbit is not really from the Himalayas. It just means a certain type of coat marking with darker face, ears, legs and tail.*

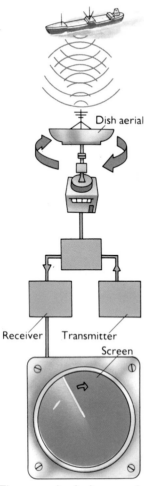

at a steady 300 metres every millionth of a second. When the beam strikes an object a faint echo bounces back. The echo is picked up and turned into a light 'blip' on a screen. A radar operator can tell by studying the blip how far away the object is, in what direction it is moving, and at what speed. Radar is used by air traffic controllers at airports, by the military to track missiles and planes, and by weather stations to find and follow the paths of storms. SATELLITES fitted with radar can map the ground.

Radio

The common household object we call a radio is only the receiving end of a great system of radio communications. Most of the system is never even seen.

A radio programme begins in a studio. There, voices and music are turned into electronic signals. These are made stronger (amplified), and then sent out from tall masts as radio waves. These are picked up by the radio in your home and changed back into

▲ *The name 'radar' comes from the phrase 'radio detecting and ranging'. The aerial that sends out the special radio signal usually acts as a receiver too, detecting the signal as it bounces back. To do this it has to change from one sort of operation to the other. This 'change-over' is controlled from inside the radar installation. When the signals are displayed on the screen, objects detected by the radar show up as bright spots. Experienced operators can tell the direction and distance of objects from the 'blips' on the screen, even though the 'blips' look nothing like the objects in real life.*

▶ *How a radio broadcast is carried to your radio. Inside the radio, the voice signals are separated from their carrier waves and turned back into sounds by the loudspeaker.*

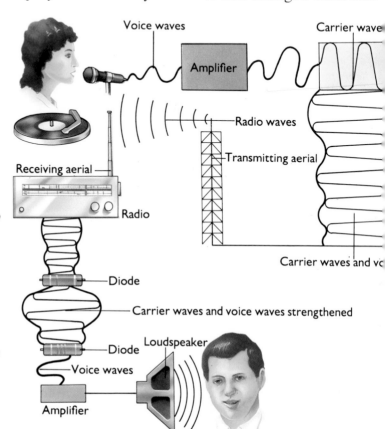

sounds you can hear. Radio waves travel at the speed of light. This is so fast that a signal can circle the world 7½ times in one second.

The first person to generate radio waves was Heinrich Hertz in 1887. But it was Guglielmo MARCONI who sent the first messages in 1894. His first signals travelled only a few metres. Seven years later he sent signals across the Atlantic.

Radioactivity

The atoms of some substances are always shooting off tiny particles and rays that we cannot see or feel. This is called radioactivity. These strange rays were discovered in 1896. It was soon found that nothing could be done to stop the rays shooting out. It was also found that in time these radioactive substances changed into other substances, and that they did this at a steady rate. If a piece of radioactive uranium was left for millions of years it would 'decay' and turn into a piece of lead. Scientists measure the rate of decay in radioactive carbon in animal and plant remains to find out how many thousands of years

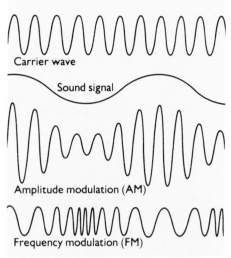

Carrier wave

Sound signal

Amplitude modulation (AM)

Frequency modulation (FM)

▲ *The station selector on your radio may have the initials AM and FM on it. These initials tell you how the carrier wave was joined with the signals at the transmitter. AM stands for 'amplitude modulation'. This means that the amplitude (height) of the carrier wave was altered to match the signals. FM – 'frequency modulation' – means that the frequency – the number of carrier waves passing each second – was changed to match the signal at the transmitter.*

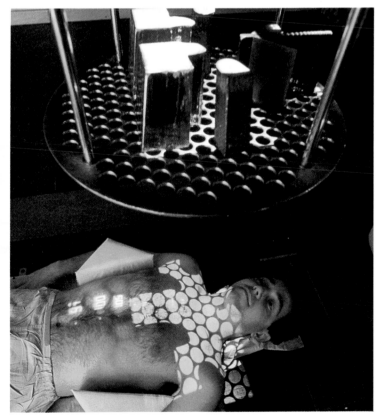

◀ *The power of radioactivity can be used to treat some types of illness, such as cancer. Radiotherapy can be used to destroy the cancer cells without harming the healthy cells. The illuminated discs over this patient's chest show the areas which are to receive radiation. The pattern can be altered by changing the position of the lead blocks (at the top of the picture) which shield the lungs from too much radiation.*

RADIO ASTRONOMY

▶ *There are three types of radiation: alpha particles, beta particles and gamma rays. Alpha particles are the least powerful. They cannot pass through paper. Beta particles can be stopped by a thin sheet of aluminium. But the power of gamma radiation can penetrate even thick blocks of iron.*

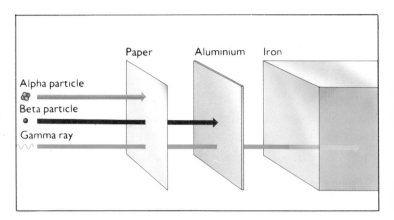

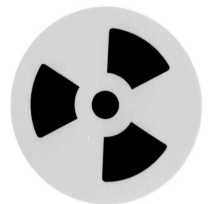

▲ *The international warning symbol used to label radioactive substances.*

▼ *The huge VLA (Very Large Array) radio telescope at Socorro, New Mexico, is made up of 27 dish aerials. Each of them is 25 metres in diameter, and they can be moved along a Y-shaped track to exactly the position the astronomers choose.*

ago the animals and plants lived. Radioactive materials can be dangerous. A nuclear explosion causes dangerous levels of radioactivity.

Radio Astronomy

A heavenly body, such as a STAR, does not only give off LIGHT waves. It sends out many kinds of radio waves too. Radio astronomers explore the UNIVERSE by 'listening' to the radio signals that reach Earth from outer space. These signals are not made by other forms of life. They come from natural events, such as exploding stars or heated clouds of gases. By studying these signals, radio astronomers can find out many things about different parts of the universe.

Radio telescopes have giant aerials – often dish-shaped. They pick up faint signals that have come from places much deeper in space than anything that can be seen by ordinary TELESCOPES. The first large radio telescopes were built after World War II. Today, the biggest in the world is at Arecibo in Puerto Rico. Its huge receiving dish has been built across an entire mountain valley. It is 305 metres wide.

Radium

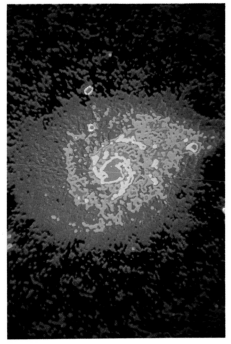

Radium is an ELEMENT. It is found only in URANIUM ore and was first discovered by Marie CURIE in 1898. She was examining some uranium and realized that it had much more RADIOACTIVITY than it should have had. Radium is very radioactive, and is dangerous to handle.

In its pure form, radium is a whitish metal. About five tonnes of uranium ore have to be mined to produce just one gram of radium. Each year, less than 75 grams are produced in the entire world. Most comes from Canada and Zaire.

Radium is used in medicine to treat cancer. COMPOUNDS of it are also used to make luminous dials that glow in the dark.

▲ *This image received by the Socorro radio telescope is of a galaxy 20 million light-years away from Earth. The colours are produced by computer, and show how much energy is coming from each part. Red is the highest energy level, and purple is the lowest.*

Railway

Railways have been in use since the 1500s. At first, rails were made of wood and wagons were pulled by horses. Steam railways were invented in the early 1800s. Railways are useful because heavy loads can be pulled along them very easily. (See pages 562–563.)

Rain and Snow

When rain pours down, it is only the sky returning the same water to Earth that originally evaporated from the land and sea.

Rain forms when water vapour in the air starts to cool. As the vapour cools it turns first of all into tiny droplets, which form wispy CLOUDS. The droplets grow and the clouds thicken and turn a dull grey. At

High mountains usually force rain out of any moist wind that strikes them. They force the air up to cooler heights, and as the moist air cools it makes rain. Most rain falls on the slopes that face the wind. The other side of the mountain receives little rain. Waialeale peak in Hawaii has the highest rainfall in the world – an average of 1200 cm a year. Yet only a few miles away, on the other side of the peak, the average rainfall is less than 50 cm.

Continued on page 564.

RAILWAYS

The railway age began when a Cornish engineer named Richard Trevithick drove a steam rail engine along a steel-plate track in South Wales. The year was 1804. The man who did more than any other to make the railways an important form of transport was another Englishman, George Stephenson. He built and equipped the first railways to carry passengers on trains pulled by steam locomotives.

Today, the age of steam is over, though you can still enjoy the thrill of riding on one of the many steam trains kept running by enthusiasts. Modern diesel and electric locomotives use less fuel and need less looking after. Railways are particularly useful for carrying heavy freight and for taking commuters to and from their jobs in city centres.

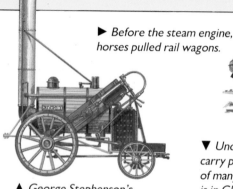

▶ Before the steam engine, horses pulled rail wagons.

▲ George Stephenson's Rocket *achieved the unheard-of speed of 58 km (36 miles) an hour at the 1829 Rainhill Trials. Its unrivalled power came from its multi-tube boiler.*

▼ Underground or subway tra~ carry passengers beneath the st~ of many of the world's cities. T~ is in Glasgow.

▼ A modern electric locomotive. ~ picks up electricity from overhead~ through the hinged pantograph on ~ roof.

▼ *A huge Union Pacific 'Big Boy' locomotive of the 1940s. It weighed 534 tonnes.*

▲ *Monorail trains run on a single rail. Some straddle the track, others are suspended beneath it.*

UNION PACIFIC 4021

▼ Japan's streamlined elec~ *'bullet trains' run at an aver~ speed of more than 160 km~ miles) an hour.*

▲ Mallard *set the world speed record for a steam locomotive in 1938 – 202 km (126 miles) an hour.*

▲ In some countries, steam locomotives can still be seen. This one is in daily use in Portugal.

RAILWAY HISTORY

◄765 Standard gauge (width of track) established at 4ft 8½in (1435mm).

◄804 Trevithick's first working locomotive.

◄814 Stephenson's *Blucher* locomotive begins working at a colliery.

◄825 Opening of Stockton and Darlington Railway, first regular steam railway.

◄829 Stephenson's *Rocket* wins Rainhill Trials.

◄830 Liverpool and Manchester Railway begins world's first passenger service using steam locos.

◄830 First US railroad, South Carolina.

◄859 First Pullman sleeping cars (USA).

◄863 First dining cars (USA).

◄863 World's first underground railway, in London.

◄869 Railroad across the USA is completed.

◄879 First electric railway (Germany).

◄885 Completion of Canadian Pacific line across Canada.

◄925 First diesel-electric locomotive (Canada).

THE RAILWAYS AT WORK

◄ *A busy marshalling yard, where freight wagons are sorted and made up into trains.*

▼ *Each section of track (known as a block) is controlled from a signal box. The signaller checks the track is clear, setting signals and points by flicking switches. The engine driver watches for a light signal to tell him it is safe to proceed. On busy lines, computers control the smooth flow of trains.*

For more information turn to these articles: DIESEL ENGINE; ELECTRICITY; MOTOR, ELECTRIC; STEAM ENGINE; UNDERGROUND RAILWAY.

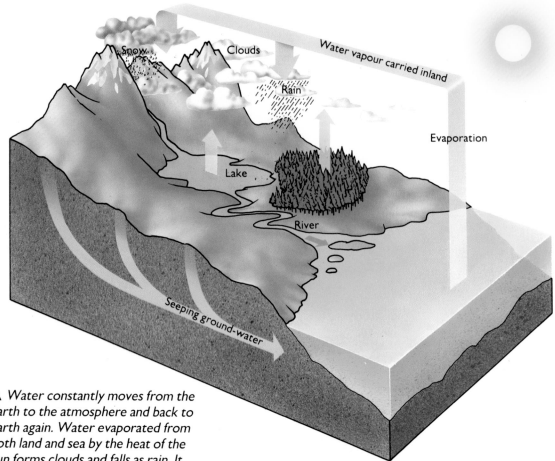

▲ *Water constantly moves from the Earth to the atmosphere and back to Earth again. Water evaporated from both land and sea by the heat of the Sun forms clouds and falls as rain. It flows into lakes and rivers and eventually into the sea, where it is turned into water vapour again, and so on. We call this movement of water the water cycle.*

last the drops become so heavy that they start to fall. If it is cold enough to freeze them, the drops hit the ground as either hail or snow.

The amount of rain that falls is widely different from place to place. In the Atacama Desert in Chile, less than 25 mm of rain falls in 20 years. But in eastern India, monsoon rains drop 1080 cm every year.

An old fairy story says that there is a crock of gold at the end of a rainbow. Nobody has ever found the treasure because a rainbow really has no end. It is a full circle. The bottom half of the circle lies below the horizon and out of sight.

Rainbow

The gorgeous colours of a rainbow are formed by sunlight shining on drops of rain. The best time for rainbows is right after a shower, when the clouds break up and sunlight streams through.

Rainbows can be seen only when the Sun is behind you and low over the horizon. When the Sun's rays strike the raindrops, each drop acts as a prism and splits the LIGHT into a SPECTRUM of colours ranging from red to violet. The lower the Sun, the higher the rainbow and the fuller its curved arch.

Raleigh, Walter

Sir Walter Raleigh (1552–1618) was an English knight at the court of ELIZABETH I. He was a soldier, explorer, historian and poet. He tried unsuccessfully to set up a colony in Virginia, in the newly discovered land of North America. He introduced potatoes and tobacco smoking to the English. He was imprisoned on an unfair charge of treason during the reign of James I. After 13 years he was freed from the Tower, and sailed to find gold in South America. On his return, penniless, he was executed.

▲ *Sir Walter Raleigh was a great favourite of Elizabeth I. But when he married, she sent him and his wife away from court.*

Rat

Rats are RODENTS. They are found all over the world in enormous numbers, and can live happily in towns and cities. They will eat almost anything. They are harmful to people because they spoil huge amounts of food and they spread diseases. Some rats carry a type of FLEA which can cause bubonic PLAGUE in human beings.

▼ *In the country, most rats live outside and do not represent much of a health risk. But rats in cities steal food intended for humans, and are a major health hazard. They breed quickly and are very difficult to get rid of.*

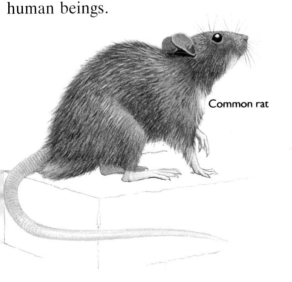

Common rat

Black rat

Recording

Sound can be recorded in a number of ways: on vinyl records, magnetic tape and tape cassettes, and compact discs (CDs).

A CD is a disc on which sound information is recorded using a laser beam. The digital signals are represented by a series of depressions on the surface

As many as 48 separate sound recordings can be made on one tape in parallel paths called 'tracks'. Any single track is a 'mono' recording. Two tracks are needed for stereophonic sound.

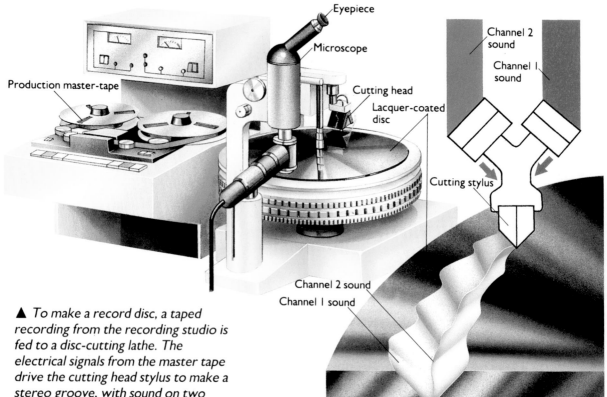

Eyepiece

Microscope

Channel 2 sound

Channel 1 sound

Cutting head

Production master-tape

Lacquer-coated disc

Cutting stylus

Channel 2 sound

Channel 1 sound

▲ To make a record disc, a taped recording from the recording studio is fed to a disc-cutting lathe. The electrical signals from the master tape drive the cutting head stylus to make a stereo groove, with sound on two channels, on a lacquer-coated aluminium disc. This becomes the 'master' disc, from which the records will be cut.

of the disc, which can then be played back using another laser. This technology is also being used to create video discs.

A TAPE RECORDER works by changing sound waves into magnetism. The sound is recorded as a magnetic pattern along the recording tape. When the tape is played, the magnetic pattern is turned back into sound.

You can record a television programme on a VIDEO cassette using a video recorder. The video cassette contains tape like a sound cassette. It records the electric signal coming from the television aerial. Sound recording was pioneered by Thomas EDISON.

Red Cross

Red Crescent

Magen David

▲ In other parts of the world, the Red Cross has different names and symbols. In some Muslim countries, for example, it is known as the Red Crescent, in Israel the symbol is the Magen David.

Red Cross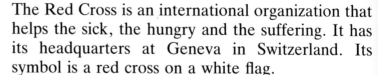

The Red Cross is an international organization that helps the sick, the hungry and the suffering. It has its headquarters at Geneva in Switzerland. Its symbol is a red cross on a white flag.

The Red Cross was founded by Henri Dunant in 1863 after he had seen the terrible suffering of wounded soldiers. The organization helps the wounded of all armies – it does not take sides. Today it is based in more than 70 countries and cares for soldiers and civilians all over the world.

Red Sea

The Red Sea is a narrow arm of the Indian Ocean. It stretches for 1900 km, dividing Arabia from north-east Africa. It has an area of about 440,300 sq km. At its northern end it is linked to the MEDITERRAN-EAN SEA by the SUEZ CANAL. Its southern end is guarded by the narrow straits of Bab el Mandeb.

The Red Sea is quite a shallow body of water. As there are no major currents which flow through it, it is also very warm and salty.

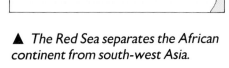

▲ The Red Sea separates the African continent from south-west Asia.

Reformation

The Reformation is the name given to the period of great religious upheaval that began in Europe in the 1500s.

At that time, a revolt occurred in the ROMAN CATHOLIC CHURCH. In protest at what they saw as bad practices and errors in the Church, groups of people broke away to set up their own churches. These people became known as PROTESTANTS.

▼ The Reformation reached England when King Henry VIII broke all ties with the Pope. He decided that all the monasteries should be closed, and their great wealth should go to the Crown. This act is often called the dissolution of the monasteries.

The Reformation saw the start of many long years of religious wars and persecution that have continued to this day. The Thirty Years' War was the result of rivalry between Catholics and Protestants. It began in Germany, but spread to involve most of the European countries. Most European countries now allow freedom of religion, but many people in the two sides still think the other's beliefs are mistaken.

What many Protestants wanted was a simpler, more basic form of CHRISTIANITY, and one that allowed them greater freedom to worship as they chose. As the Protestant movement grew, many kings and rulers saw the new movement as a chance to widen their power at the expense of the Church. They were happy to support the Protestant cause because in many ways the religious protest also helped them to gain more influence. The Reformation led to wars between Protestant and Catholic rulers.

Refrigerator

Refrigerators are used to keep food cold. The simplest ones are really just boxes, with an electric motor running a cooling system. They are made from insulating material that keeps the inside of the fridge cold for some time, even when the motor is not running. The average TEMPERATURE inside a fridge is 2 to 7°C.

The cooling system has a special gas in it. This gas is first compressed (squeezed) to turn it into a liquid. The liquid then flows through hollow tubes inside the fridge into an evaporator, which turns it back into gas. This gas is pumped on around the system. As it goes round the inside, it draws out any heat from within the refrigerator.

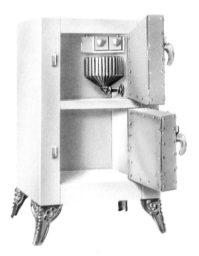

▲ Refrigerators first came into use in the 1860s, but this is the type you would have been able to buy in 1927.

▶ A modern refrigerator. In the evaporator the liquid absorbs heat as it is turned into a gas. The cold vapour that flows through the pipes goes to a condenser. There it gives out heat outside the refrigerator as it turns back into a liquid.

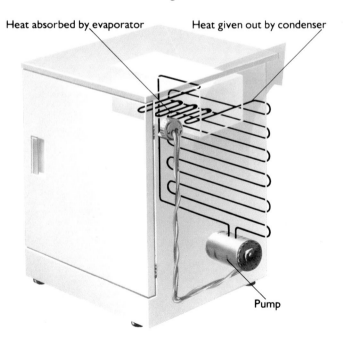

Heat absorbed by evaporator

Heat given out by condenser

Pump

When it is pumped outside the fridge the gas is compressed again. This turns it back into a liquid and it gives out the heat it picked up on the inside. The liquid is pumped round and round, turning from liquid to gas and back again. As this goes on, the air inside the fridge becomes colder and the heat is taken to the outside. The process works like a sort of heat sponge.

> We tend to think of the refrigerator as a comparatively recent invention. However, ice-making machines were slipped through the Union blockade of the South during the American Civil War in the 1860s.

Relativity

If you are travelling in a car at 60 km/h and you are overtaken by another car travelling at 80 km/h, the second car pulls away from you at 20 km/h. Its true speed relative to the ground is 80 km/h, but its speed *relative* to you is 20 km/h. This is the basic idea of relativity: assuming that you are not moving and working out the speed of something that is moving relative to you.

At the end of the last century scientists discovered that the speed of light is always the same, no matter how fast the source of the light is moving. In 1905, Albert EINSTEIN put forward his *special* theory of relativity to explain this strange fact. His theory concerns, among other things, the effect of motion on time, length and mass. For instance, the theory predicts that in a spaceship hurtling across the universe at nearly the speed of light, time would

▼ *Part of Einstein's theory of relativity was that gravity could make light rays bend. This means that, from the Earth, it would be easy to make a mistake about the real position of a distant star, because the rays of light coming from it could have been bent by the Sun's gravitational pull (below left). Another part of the theory of relativity says that time slows down for an object travelling at almost the speed of light. The example (below right) shows a rocket with a clock on board which takes off from Earth at 3 o'clock. As it nears the speed of light, its clock will be showing 5 o'clock. But time has slowed down on the rocket, and the clocks back on Earth will be showing 6 o'clock.*

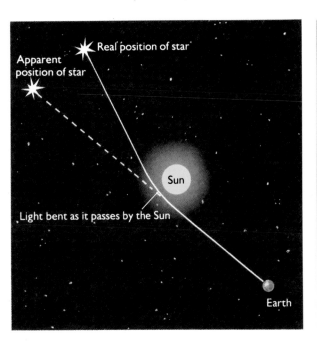

Real position of star

Apparent position of star

Sun

Light bent as it passes by the Sun

Earth

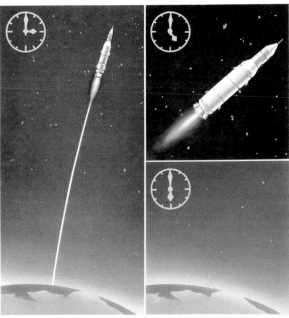

pass more slowly, the spaceship's length would become smaller and its mass would become greater than on a similar spaceship stationary on Earth.

Later, in 1915, Einstein produced his *general* theory of relativity. This theory has helped scientists understand more about space, gravity and the nature of the universe.

Religion

The greatest religions of today are Buddhism (based on the teachings of BUDDHA), CHRISTIANITY, HINDU-ISM (followed by Hindus), ISLAM (followed by Muslims) and JUDAISM (followed by Jews). All are very ancient. The most recent is Islam, which was founded about 1300 years ago. The largest, Christianity, has well over a billion followers.

There are also some people today who follow ancient religions based on the worship of many gods and spirits. Often these gods are part of nature. They may be rocks, trees or lakes.

Buildings devoted to religious worship include splendid churches and magnificent shrines and temples. Statues and works of art showing religious figures are common. Specially trained priests and holy people say prayers and lead religious ceremonies. They also study the laws and teachings of the religion. These are often written down in holy books. Examples are the BIBLE and the KORAN.

▲ All the world's religions have special symbols and signs. The dancing god is a Hindu image; the candlestick, called a menorah, is Jewish; the temple is a feature of Shinto, a Japanese religion; the cross is a Christian symbol; the crescent moon is Islamic; and the statue represents Buddha.

MAJOR RELIGIONS: ESTIMATED WORLD MEMBERSHIP	
	millions
Christians	1759
Roman Catholics	996
Orthodox	167
Protestants	363
Muslims	935
Hindus	705
Buddhists	303
Taoists	20
Jews	17
Confucians	6
Shintoists	3

▶ Jerusalem is a holy city to Jews, Christians and Muslims. The Dome of Rock is a Muslim shrine on the spot where Muhammad was said to have ascended into heaven.

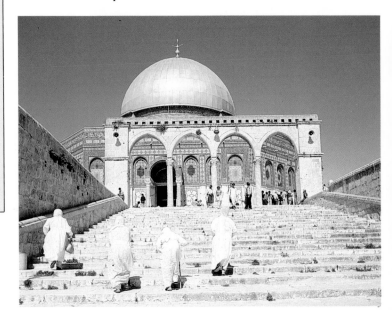

Rembrandt

Rembrandt Harmenszoon van Rijn (1606–1669) is one of the most famous of all Dutch painters. Helped by assistants, he produced hundreds of paintings and drawings.

Rembrandt is best known for his portraits of the wealthy townspeople of Holland. Unlike many painters, he became very successful while he was still alive. However, later in his career, many of the rich people no longer bought his pictures because they did not like the way his style of painting had changed. Although he became very poor, this was the time when he painted some of his best works.

Renaissance

The Renaissance is the name given to a period of about 200 years in the history of Europe. The word means 'rebirth' in French, and the Renaissance was

▲ *Rembrandt painted this portrait of himself late in his career.*

▼ *Goldsmiths working in Florence, Italy, during the Renaissance. Trading brought great wealth to the city.*

REPRODUCTION

▼ *A statue of Perseus holding the head of Medusa, by the Italian Renaissance sculptor Cellini.*

▶ *Florence cathedral is a supreme example of Renaissance architecture. The dome was designed by the artist Brunelleschi in 1420, but it was not completed until 15 years after his death, in 1461.*

▼ *An amoeba is one of the simplest forms of life – a single-celled animal. It can reproduce on its own. First the nucleus, in the middle of the cell, divides in two. Then the cell splits apart to become two identical amoebas.*

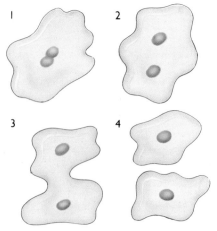

the time when people again became interested in every aspect of art, science, architecture and literature.

Since the times of the ancient Greeks and Romans there had been little interest in new ideas. Then, during the 1300s, Italian scholars began to take a fresh interest in the past. They also looked for new scientific explanations of the mysteries of the world and the universe. During the Renaissance a great number of painters, sculptors and architects were at work in Italy. The works of art of LEONARDO DA VINCI and MICHELANGELO are among the most famous products of this time. From Italy, the ideas of the Renaissance quickly spread to the rest of Europe.

At the same time as all these artistic and scientific ideas, there was a great growth in trade. Later, there were voyages to explore Africa and India, and in 1492 America was discovered by COLUMBUS.

Reproduction

Reproduction is the process by which plants and animals make new plants and animals like themselves. Some plants and animals can reproduce on their own. Some just split in two. Many plants reproduce *asexually* by producing buds that drop off and start a new life of their own. Other plants produce spores that may be carried away by wind or water until they land in a suitable place to grow into new plants.

◀ Part of the egg rope of a perch. Once a female fish has laid her eggs, and the male has fertilized them, the tiny fish embryos develop, one inside each egg. Once they have used up the food store in the egg it is time for them to hatch.

In *sexual* reproduction, a male cell, called a *sperm*, joins with, or fertilizes, a female cell, called an *ovum* or egg, to form a new fertilized cell. This cell divides over and over again until a whole new organism has been formed.

Most female FISH lay their eggs in the water. Then the male swims over the eggs and releases his sperm on them. After fertilization, the embryo (developing) fish grows while using the store of food in the egg.

In most higher animals, fertilization takes place inside the female's body. After fertilization the female BIRD OR REPTILE lays her eggs. The embryo then develops inside the egg until it is ready to hatch out. In MAMMALS, fertilization also takes place inside the female, but the embryo develops inside its mother until it is ready to be born. The embryo

SEE IT YOURSELF

Some seeds grow in an amazingly short time. Buy a packet of cress seeds. Put some potting compost or damp blotting paper in a shallow dish, and sow the seeds on top of it. It is fun to make the first letter of your name. After only a few days the seeds will start to grow, and in 12 to 15 days the cress will be ready to eat.

Take a leaf from an African violet or begonia and make cuts through some of the veins. Put the leaf on moist soil, and first roots and then a new plant will grow.

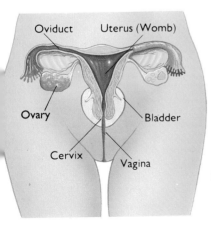

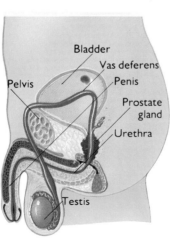

◀ The reproductive parts of the body are very different in men and women. The woman produces eggs in her ovaries. These travel down the oviducts and, if fertilized by sperm provided by a man during sexual intercourse, may develop into a baby in the woman's uterus, or womb. Men produce millions of sperm in their testicles. The sperm and the egg each contain half of what is needed to make another human being.

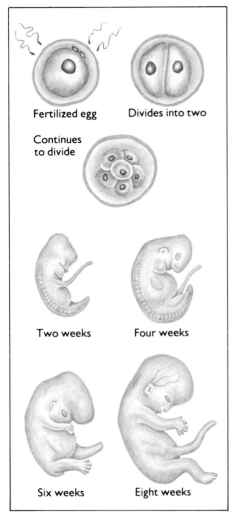

Once a human egg has been fertilized, it starts to divide to make countless new cells. At first the baby looks strange – it even has a tail – but after a few weeks it develops a human shape, with a face and tiny fingers and toes.

receives food from its mother's bloodstream. After it is born, the mother feeds it with her milk.

The number of offspring a mother gives birth to at one time depends on the number of eggs fertilized. In human mothers, only one egg is usually fertilized. If more than one is fertilized there may be twins, triplets or even more babies.

Reptile

Reptiles are the most advanced of all cold-blooded animals. They live on land and in the sea.

Reptiles live in all parts of the world except for the North and South Poles. Most, however, live in warm regions. This is because they are cold-blooded and must get their warmth from their surroundings.

When it is cold they become very sleepy and cannot move fast enough to catch food or escape from enemies. Most reptiles that live in cold places spend the winter in HIBERNATION.

Reptiles played a very important part in the EVOLUTION of the Earth. About 360 million years ago, the first reptiles appeared. They soon became the strongest form of life on Earth. They ruled the planet for close to 100 million years. One group of reptiles, the DINOSAURS, were the most spectacular creatures ever to walk the land. The biggest weighed more than 100 tonnes.

These primitive reptiles lived over 250 million years ago. They are called sail-backs because on their backs they had bony spines covered in skin. They used these to help control their body heat. If they turned sideways to the Sun, the sails could absorb heat. If they turned their backs to the Sun, the sails gave out heat and the creatures cooled down.

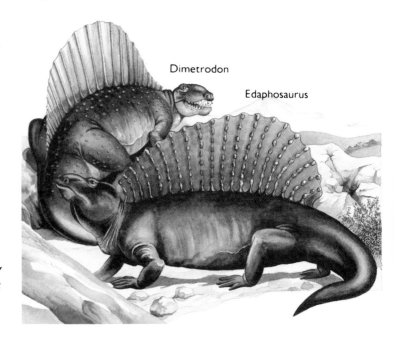

Dimetrodon

Edaphosaurus

Moorish gecko

Agama

Slow worm

Large Psammodromus

Three-toed skink

◀ *There are many different types of lizard, ranging in size from a few centimetres to three metres. Lizards are far more ancient reptiles than snakes. Lizard fossils have been found dating from 200 million years ago, but snakes appeared only about 100 million years ago. The slow worm is in fact a lizard, though its legs have disappeared.*

Galapagos giant tortoise

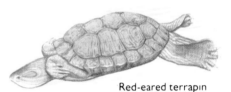

Red-eared terrapin

▲ *The Galapagos giant tortoise can have a shell over 1.5 metres long, and often weighs more than 200 kilograms. Red-eared terrapins are found in fresh water in North America.*

Today there are four main groups of reptiles: ALLIGATORS and CROCODILES, LIZARDS and SNAKES, TORTOISES and TURTLES, and the rare tuatara. The biggest reptiles are the alligators and crocodiles. The estuarine crocodile of South-east Asia grows to 6 metres in length, and is the biggest of them all.

There are over 5000 kinds of lizards and snakes. They live everywhere, from deserts to jungles and faraway ocean islands. Some have poisonous bites with which they kill their prey. Turtles and tortoises are well protected by their hard shells. The biggest are the lumbering giant tortoises of the Pacific and Indian Ocean islands.

Republic

A republic is a form of government by which the people are supposed to rule themselves. Usually they hold ELECTIONS to choose their leaders. Many republics have been formed to take over powers from kings who ruled unfairly.

The first republics were in ancient Greece and Rome, but many of the people in these countries were slaves. Today, some republics are run by people who have not been elected by the people. There are both COMMUNIST and DEMOCRATIC republics.

> Britain, Sweden, Norway and Denmark have monarchs and are therefore not republics. But the people of these countries are freer to choose the people who govern them than are those of many of the world's republics.

▲ At the time when the American Revolutionary War broke out, only a small fraction of America had been settled by people from Britain. The thirteen colonies were all situated along the eastern coast.

The Revolutionary War was a small war compared with modern ones. Large numbers of men were never involved. There were never more than 20,000 men in the American army at any one time. Britain sent about 60,000 men across the Atlantic during the entire six years of war.

▶ This picture shows a detail from the painting 'The Declaration of Independence', by John Trumbull. All the colonies agreed to the declaration.

Revolutionary War, American

The Revolutionary War was fought between Britain and her 13 American colonies from 1775 to 1783. The colonies won their independence from Britain and became a new nation, the United States of America.

For many years before the war Britain and the American colonies had disagreed about a number of things, chiefly over taxes. The British tried to force the colonies to pay taxes, but would not allow the colonies any representation in the British Parliament. The colonies insisted on 'no taxation without representation'.

The first shot in the war was fired at Lexington, Massachusetts, on April 19, 1775. In July, George WASHINGTON was made commander of the American forces. On July 4, 1776, the colonies declared their independence.

At first the war went poorly for the Americans. But in October 1777, the British were defeated at the Battle of Saratoga, in New York. This was the turning point. On October 19, 1781, a British army under Lord Cornwallis surrendered to Washington. The final peace treaty, the Treaty of Paris, was signed in 1783.

Rhinoceros

Sometimes described as a 'tank on legs', the rhinoceros is one of the largest and strongest of all land animals. A full grown male can weigh as much as 3.5 tonnes.

This massive beast has a tough leathery skin and sprouts one or two horns (actually made of hair) on its snout. These may grow as long as 127 cm.

The rhinoceros lives in Africa and in south-eastern Asia. There it feeds on leafy twigs, shrubs and grasses.

Although an adult rhino has no natural enemies, it is so widely hunted for its horns that it has become an endangered species. When ground into a powder, rhino horn is believed to be a powerful medicine. Some people claim it can be used to detect poisoned wine. None of these beliefs are true.

The rhino's ability to charge swiftly over short distances makes it a dangerous animal to hunt.

Rice

Rice is a member of the GRASS family. Its grains are one of the most important CEREAL crops in the world. It is the main food of most Asian people.

▲ Although their poor eyesight may make them an easier target for hunters, rhinos have a good sense of hearing and smell.

▼ Once rice is ready to be harvested, the stalks are cut and the seed heads are beaten on a hard surface to shake the rice grains out.

Young shoots of rice are planted in flooded fields called *paddies*. Here they grow in 5 to 10cm of water until they are ready to be harvested. Young rice has long narrow leaves and fine clusters of flowers that turn into the grains that we eat.

Richard (Kings)

Richard is the name of three English kings.

Richard I (1157–1199) spent only six months of his ten-year reign in England. He was crowned in Westminster in 1189 and set off at once to take part in the CRUSADES. In 1187 the armies of ISLAM, led by Saladin, had retaken Jerusalem. In 1189 a new crusade was called to drive them out.

Richard I, known as the Lion-Heart because of his courage and ferocity in battle, first sailed to Cyprus. After capturing the island he went on to the Holy Land where he and his allies, the French, took the city of Acre. In 1192 they tried to take Jerusalem but failed. On the return trip, Richard was taken prisoner and was freed only in 1194. The last years of his reign were spent mainly in France fighting his former allies, and he was killed there in 1199.

Richard II (1367–1400) became king when he was only ten years old. Because he was so young, the nobles thought they had a chance to gain more power. They fought among themselves and against the king. When Richard grew up he put to death

▲ *Richard II became unpopular towards the end of his reign, and was forced to leave the throne. It is thought that he was murdered at Pontefract Castle, where he was being held prisoner.*

▶ *Richard I spent much of his reign abroad, fighting. He died of an arrow wound during a siege when he went to war with his former ally, Philip of France.*

many of the rebellious nobles. But his enemies finally forced him to give up the throne.

Richard III (1452–1485) is said to have gained the throne by treachery. Richard was the brother of Edward IV. When Edward died, his young son was crowned Edward V, but Richard had himself declared king instead. Richard was accused of murdering his two young nephews in the Tower of London. His enemies, led by Henry Tudor, revolted against him, and Richard was killed at the Battle of Bosworth Field.

Riding

People have been riding HORSES for many hundreds of years. Horses were one of the earliest forms of transport, but today, most people ride purely for pleasure. It takes a great deal of skill to ride a horse well. Some people test their skill by riding in competitions, in jumping, cross-country events and various sports such as polo.

It takes a lot of patience and practice to ride well. One of the most important things a rider must learn is how to tell a horse what to do. There are two kinds of signals used for this. The first, known as natural aids, are given by hand, leg and voice commands. The second are artificial aids. These include using riding whips and spurs.

Command signals must be given smoothly and correctly, otherwise the horse will become confused

▲ *Clothes for riding do not have to be expensive, but they should be comfortable and practical.*

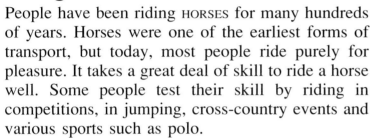

◀ *When you are learning to ride, it can be very useful to have lessons with an experienced rider. This class will ride in formation around the large indoor school. This helps them learn the basic skills of controlling the horse and telling it what to do.*

LONGEST RIVERS

	km
Nile *Africa*	6695
Amazon *South America*	6440
Chang Jiang (Yangtze) *China*	6380
Mississippi-Missouri *USA*	5970
Irtysh *Russia*	5410
Huang He (Yellow) *China*	4672
Zaire (Congo) *Africa*	4667
Amur *Asia*	4416
Lena *Russia*	4240
Mackenzie *Canada*	4240
Mekong *Asia*	4180
Niger *Africa*	4170

The longest river in the British Isles is the Shannon in Ireland at 386 km. The Severn is the longest river in Great Britain – 354 km in length. The Thames is 346 km long.

about what its rider wants it to do. A horse must be taught exactly what each signal means and it must learn to obey these signals promptly. There is no simple shortcut to learning how to control a horse, other than by hours of lessons.

River

Rivers are one of the most important geographical features in the world. They range in size from little more than swollen streams to mighty waterways that flow for thousands of kilometres.

The greatest rivers in the world are the AMAZON, the MISSISSIPPI and the NILE. They all drain huge areas of land. The basin of the Amazon, for example, stretches over an area larger than all of western Europe.

Some rivers serve as transport links that allow ocean-going ships to sail far inland. In tropical jungles they are often the only way to travel. Rivers with DAMS supply us with electric power. Water from rivers is also used to irrigate farmland in desert lands and other dry parts of the world.

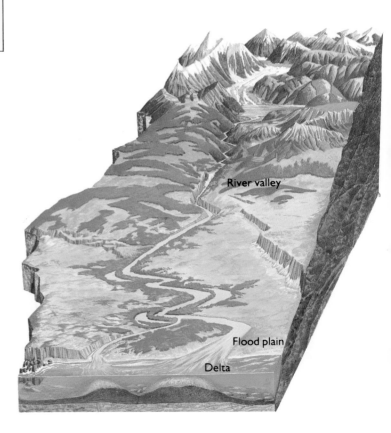

River valley

Flood plain

Delta

▶ *Over hundreds of years, rivers carve valleys out of the land as they flow towards the sea. From tiny mountain streams made from melted snow, they grow and swell, picking up mineral and other deposits as they flow through the landscape. These deposits sink to the bottom when the rivers slow down as they near the sea, forming great deltas.*

◀ Complex road systems have to be planned to cope with ever growing numbers of cars and other vehicles. In St. Louis, Missouri, USA, this huge interchange had to be built where two major highways cross the Mississippi River.

▼ Roman roads (below) were some of the first paved roads to be built in the world. They were built by the Roman army and had gutters built in for drainage. Modern roads (bottom) are made up of smooth layers of tar, or asphalt, over concrete or macadam.

Road

The Romans were the first great road builders. Some of their long, straight roads still survive. The Romans made roads of gravel and stones. The surface paving stones were arched so rain ran off into ditches.

Modern road building began during the INDUSTRIAL REVOLUTION. In the early 1800s a Scottish engineer, John McAdam, became the pioneer of modern road-making. But the stony surfaces of his roads were not good for vehicles with rubber tyres. Later, *macadamized* roads were built. They are covered with tar or asphalt to make them smooth. Many roads, especially motorways, are now made of concrete.

Robot

In films and books set in the future, robots often look like metal people and they can walk, talk and even think.

Real robots are very different. They are machines with arms that can move in several directions. Robots are *programmable* machines. This means they can be instructed to carry out different tasks. The instructions, or programs, are stored in the robot's computer brain.

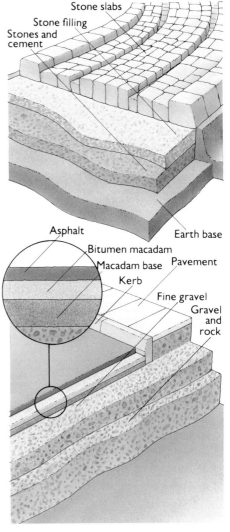

Stone slabs
Stone filling
Stones and cement

Asphalt
Earth base
Bitumen macadam
Macadam base
Pavement
Kerb
Fine gravel
Gravel and rock

Most robots work in industry and do jobs such as paint spraying, welding, and heavy lifting and loading. Some robots work in places that are dangerous for humans, such as nuclear power stations and outer space.

▼ *Unimate, made by the American firm Unimation, is one of the best-selling industrial robots. It can do a variety of jobs depending on how it is controlled. It can weld metal or move objects from place to place.*

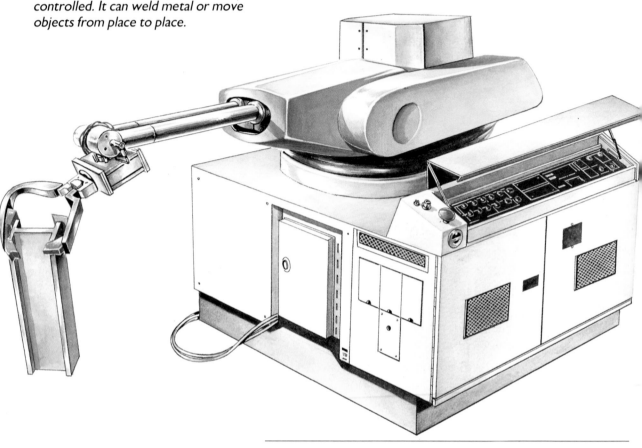

Rock

Rocks consist of grains of MINERALS. *Igneous rocks* form when magma (molten rock) hardens. Some harden on the surface to form rocks like basalt and obsidian. Some harden underground to form rocks like GRANITE. *Sedimentary rocks* are composed of sediments, like sand. For example, conglomerates are rocks made up of pebbles and sand. Many limestones are made of sediments formed mainly from the remains of dead plants and animals. *Metamorphic rocks* are igneous or sedimentary rocks that have been changed by great heat and pressure. For example, limestones may be *metamorphosed* (changed) into MARBLE.

Collecting rocks can be fun, and it will teach you

The whole Earth is covered by a crust of rock from 20 to 60 km thick. Most of this crust is covered by water or soil, but in many places the rocky crust is bare.

much about the Earth. It is easy to find rocks, even in a city. You can start by getting hold of a book that will tell you how to find and identify interesting rocks. Good hunting grounds for rocks are quarries, building sites and the base of ocean cliffs.

All gems except pearls come from rocks. We eat one kind of rock every day – halite or common salt.

Metamorphic rock
Marble

Igneous rock
Granite

Sedimentary rock
Limestone

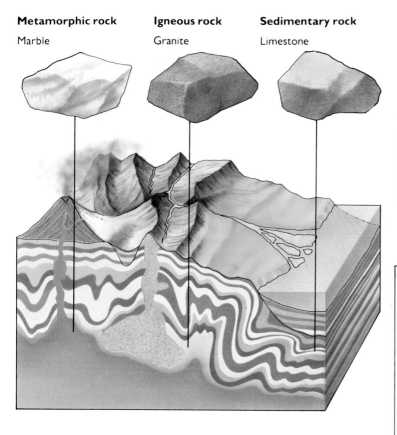

◀ *Granite is a rock that has hardened underground and limestone is made from layers of sediment made up of dead sea creatures. Heat and pressure on limestone inside the Earth forms marble, a metamorphic rock.*

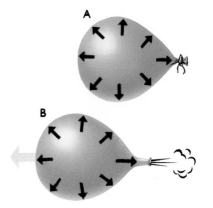

Rocket

A firework rocket and the rockets that took astronauts to the MOON work in much the same way. Both burn fuel to produce hot gases. The gases shoot out backwards. This creates a *reaction* force that thrusts the rocket forwards. Rockets do not need air for their engines, unlike jets. So they are ideal for moving in space (where there is no air).

The Chinese used rockets as weapons as early as the 1200s. Rockets used to launch SATELLITES and spacecraft were developed after World War II. They are *multistage* rockets, which means several rockets joined together. Each stage fires in turn.

Fuel for early rockets, such as Germany's V2 in World War II, was kerosene and oxygen. Today's rockets use liquid fuels. Not only do liquid fuels give

SEE IT YOURSELF

When air is let out of a balloon, it acts like a simple rocket. Fill a balloon with air. The balloon will stretch as you force a large amount of air into its small space. Once you close the mouth of the balloon (A), the air pushes equally in all directions. Now open the mouth (B). The balloon collapses as the air under pressure escapes. As this happens, the air pressure on the side opposite the mouth becomes greater than the pressure around the mouth, and the balloon flies in the direction of greater pressure. All rockets work on this principle.

► *Most engines run on fuel that burns in oxygen from the air, but out in space there is no air. If the rocket fuel is going to burn the rocket has to carry its own oxygen, in frozen liquid form. The rocket fuel is usually liquid hydrogen. Firework rockets burn gunpowder which pushes them up through the air. Chemicals in the tip of the rockets make the bangs and flashes.*

Today's space rockets use liquid fuels – usually a liquid called hydrazine or liquid hydrogen. In a liquid-fuel rocket, the fuel needs oxygen before it will burn. The fuel and the oxidizer are stored in separate tanks. When they are both pumped into a combustion chamber they burn explosively and produce the gases that rush out of a nozzle and give lift. Liquid hydrogen and liquid oxygen have to be refrigerated to stay liquid, so space rockets need complicated systems of refrigeration pipes.

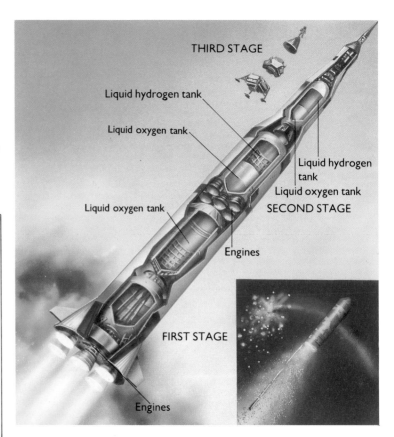

THIRD STAGE

Liquid hydrogen tank

Liquid oxygen tank

Liquid hydrogen tank

Liquid oxygen tank

SECOND STAGE

Liquid oxygen tank

Engines

FIRST STAGE

Engines

more energy, weight for weight, but they allow more control. The most powerful rocket in use today is the *Energia* rocket used in the Soviet shuttle.

▼ *A view of Mount Robson, the highest peak in the Canadian part of the Rocky Mountains.*

Rocky Mountains

The Rocky Mountains are a huge range of mountains in NORTH AMERICA. They stretch from Alaska through western Canada and the USA, as far south as New Mexico. The highest peak, Mt Elbert, is 4399 metres above sea level. The Rockies have several national parks, and many wild animals live there.

Rodent

Rodents are a group of gnawing animals. They have large, sharp front teeth that grow all the time. The animals wear down these teeth by gnawing their food. They also use their teeth to dig burrows in the ground for their homes and nests. BEAVERS even cut down good-sized trees with their gnawing teeth.

The 2000 or so rodents also include MICE, RATS, PORCUPINES and SQUIRRELS. The South American capybara is the largest rodent. It looks like a giant GUINEA PIG. It grows to a length of 1.25 metres and weighs over 45 kg. The smallest rodent is the European harvest mouse. It grows only about 7 centimetres long.

Rodeo

Rodeos are exciting shows where American COW-BOYS show off their skills. In bareback riding, a cowboy rides a bronco (a half wild or bad-tempered horse). In saddle-bronco riding, the cowboy rides one-handed, using one rein, a saddle and a halter. Bull riding and calf roping are other events. In steer wrestling, the cowboy chases a young bull, or steer, on horseback, grabs its head and pulls the steer down. A comic contest is catching a greased pig. The first recorded rodeo was held in 1869.

Roman Catholic Church

The Roman Catholic Church is the oldest and largest of all Christian churches. It has about 996 million members. The POPE is the head of the Church. He lives in VATICAN CITY in Italy.

Flying squirrel

Alpine marmot

Siberian chipmunk

▲ Three of the many species of rodent. The flying squirrel does not actually fly, but glides with the help of extra flaps of skin between its fore and hind legs. The marmot and chipmunk are both ground dwellers.

◄ In the Roman Catholic Church, great importance is given to celebrations and ceremonies. Special saints' days and festivals are commemorated by processions and masses. This confirmation procession winds its way along a Swiss valley.

ROMANIA

Government: Republic
Capital: Bucharest
Area: 237,500 sq km
Population: 23,278,000
Languages: Romanian, Hungarian,
   German
Currency: Leu

According to legend, Rome was founded by descendants of Aeneas, a Trojan who fled to Italy after the fall of Troy. Two of these descendants were Romulus and Remus. They were twin brothers who were abandoned at birth and suckled by a she-wolf. When they grew up, the brothers founded a town on one of Rome's seven hills and ruled it together. After a while they quarrelled and Romulus killed his brother to become the sole ruler of Rome. Tradition says that Rome was founded on April 21, 753 BC. The ancient Romans celebrated that day and it is still a national holiday.

▶ A view over Rome from the dome of St Peter's Basilica, looking over the colonnades in St Peter's Square. On important holy days, the square is packed with people from all over the world.

Roman Catholics follow the teachings of JESUS Christ. The Church also helps its followers by giving them rules for good living. The main church service is called the Mass. Some Roman Catholics become nuns, monks and brothers. They devote their lives to their faith in orders (societies) such as the Franciscans or Benedictines.

Roman Empire

The ancient Romans built up a vast empire around the Mediterranean Sea. ROME, in Italy, was the centre of the empire. (See pages 588–589.)

Romania

Romania is a small country in southeastern EUROPE. It has beautiful mountains and many forests. Most people are farmers, but there are also mines, and oil is produced too. In 1989, the people overthrew the corrupt communist government. They demanded democratic reforms and free elections.

Rome

Rome is the capital of ITALY. With a population of 2,816,000, it is also Italy's largest city. Rome stands on the river Tiber, about 27 km from the Mediterranean Sea. Many tourists visit Rome to see the

great ruins of ancient Rome, and the beautiful churches, fountains, palaces and art galleries.

Roses, Wars of the

The Wars of the Roses was the name given to a struggle between the houses of Lancaster and York for control of the English throne in the fifteenth century. The wars were named after the emblem of each house, that of Lancaster being a red rose, that of York a white rose.

For many years, especially under Edward IV, York was the winning side. Not until the Lancastrian Henry Tudor defeated Richard III at Bosworth Field (1485) and married Elizabeth of York did the two houses unite. The crown passed to the house of Tudor.

Rowing

There are two main ways of using oars to drive a boat: *sculling* and *rowing*. In sculling, each oarsman or woman uses a pair of lightweight oars. The boats are built to take one or two scullers.

In rowing, each person has a single oar. Boats are built to take eight, four or a pair of rowers. A boat for eight is always steered by a ninth crew member called the *coxswain* or *cox*. There are races for fours and pairs, with or without a cox.

▲ *Richard III (top), of the house of York, was not a popular king, and was eventually challenged by Henry Tudor (above) for the throne.*

◀ *Henry Tudor landed in Wales and with his following marched to do battle with Richard at Bosworth Field.*

ROMAN EMPIRE

The story of the Roman Empire began about 2700 years ago, in small villages on hills above the river Tiber in Italy. The people of these villages founded the mighty Roman Empire.

According to legend, Rome was founded by twin brothers called Romulus and Remus, who were reared by a wolf. About 590 BC the Romans set up a republic, and created a strong army. They began to conquer their neighbours.

The capital of this state was Rome, a city built on seven hills. Here was the Forum, or meeting place, and the Senate, or parliament. There were temples, markets, triumphal arches and villas (large houses). The language of Rome was Latin.

In 45 BC the soldier Julius Caesar made himself dictator of Rome. In 27 BC his nephew Octavian (Augustus) became the first Roman emperor. The Romans ruled most of Europe and the lands around the Mediterranean. They brought peace and firm government. Roman ideas spread everywhere. The Romans were skilful engineers and many remains of their roads, walls, forts and other buildings can still be seen.

In AD 364, the empire was divided: the western half was governed from Rome, the eastern half from Constantinople (Byzantium). For a thousand years, Eastern Roman, or Byzantine, emperors ruled from Constantinople.

Rome was now in decline. Its army struggled to fight off attacks from barbarian tribes. Around 476 Rome itself fell, and the empire in the west collapsed. The eastern empire lasted (in name) until 1453, when Constantinople was captured by the Turks.

▶ Two-wheeled Roman chariots were pulled by two, three or four horses in races at the circus.

▼ Roman engineers building an aqueduct, for carrying water. The crane was a Roman invention. The Pont du Gard in southern France was built in this way. It has three tiers, and stands 48 metres high.

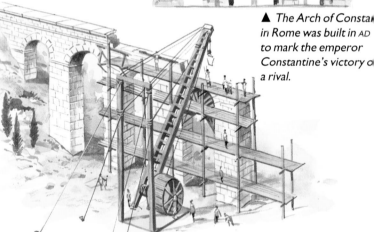

▲ The Arch of Constantine in Rome was built in AD to mark the emperor Constantine's victory over a rival.

HISTORY OF ROME	
753 BC	Founding of Rome (according to legend).
509 BC	Foreign kings driven from Rome and the republic set up.
264 BC	Punic Wars, against Carthage.
146 BC	Greece now controlled by Rome.
73 BC	Slaves revolt, led by Spartacus.
45 BC	Julius Caesar becomes dictator.
31 BC	Octavian (later called Augustus) defeats Mark Antony and Cleopatra.
AD 64	Emperor Nero blames Christians for setting fire to Rome.
AD 150	Peak of Roman power.
AD 330	Constantine, first Christian emperor, founds Constantinople.
AD 364	Division of the empire.
AD 378	Roman legions defeated at Adrianople by Goths.
AD 410	Alaric's Visigoths capture Rome.
AD 451	Attila the Hun attacks Rome.
AD 476	Fall of western empire.

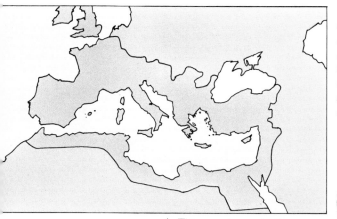

▲ This map shows the Roman Empire when it was at its greatest, in AD 117. At this time it was ruled by the emperor Trajan.

▶ This sign was found in the ruins of the Roman town of Pompeii, buried when the volcano Vesuvius erupted in AD 79. It says (in Latin): Beware of the Dog.

◀ A Roman coin.

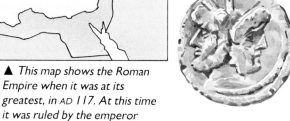

▶ A Roman senator. He is wearing the loose, flowing robe called a toga. The toga was made from an oval-shaped piece of material and had many folds. It was so difficult to drape that a special slave was sometimes employed to fix his master's toga. The colour of togas depended on the wearer's rank and age.

◀ The Roman army conquered a vast area. In the centre is a legate (a general); on the left is a cavalryman; and on the right is a legionary (an infantryman).

THE ROMAN ARMY

Rome controlled its huge empire by means of a powerful and well-disciplined army. The backbone of the Roman army was the *legion*. Each legion had up to 6000 foot-soldiers, divided into ten *cohorts*. The soldiers carried javelins, shields and short swords. Each man was a Roman citizen (a high honour) and was trained to march long distances. The Roman army also had cavalry, and siege artillery units equipped with giant crossbows and catapults.

For more information turn to these articles: CAESAR, JULIUS; COLOSSEUM; HANNIBAL; HOLY ROMAN EMPIRE; HUNS; POMPEII; ROAD.

Rubber was given its name by the scientist Joseph Priestley. He noticed that this strange material could rub out pencil marks. The French name for rubber is *caoutchouc*. This word comes from an American-Indian word meaning 'the wood that weeps'.

▶ *Steps in rubber production: (1) The rubber tree is tapped for latex. (2) Each tapping produces about a quarter of a litre of latex. (3) Formic acid is added to the latex to make the rubber particles stick together (coagulate). (4) The rubber is rolled into sheets, which are hung up to dry (5). The crude rubber sheets (6) are dyed and treated, and shaped by machines into various products.*

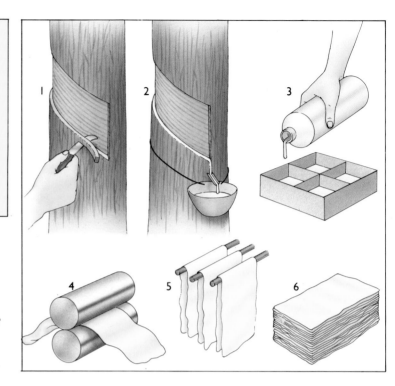

▼ *A rugby player has to run fast once he has the ball, to avoid being tackled by a member of the opposing team.*

Rubber

Rubber is an important material with many uses in industry and in the home. Most natural rubber comes from the rubber tree. When the BARK of the tree is cut, a white juice called *latex* oozes out. The juice is collected and made into rubber. Today most natural rubber comes from Malaysia and Indonesia.

Scientists found ways of making synthetic rubber during World War I. Synthetic rubber is made from oil and coal. About two-thirds of the rubber used today is synthetic rubber.

Rugby Football

Rugby football is a game played between two teams with an oval ball. The ball may be kicked or handled. To score a *try* in rugby, the ball must be taken over the other team's goal line and touched down on the ground. To score a goal, the ball must be kicked over the crossbar of the H-shaped goal.

In *rugby union*, each team has 15 players. *Rugby league* is a variation of the game, with some different rules. Rugby league teams have 13 players. The name rugby comes from Rugby School, where the game began in 1823.

Russia

Russia is by far the largest of the countries that formed from the former SOVIET UNION. It contains more people than the other states put together and has most of the great cities, including MOSCOW and St Petersburg. It is rich in mineral resources and is industrially powerful. Farming, including such crops as cereals, fodder and cattle, is also important.

Rust

Rust is a brownish-red crust that forms on ordinary IRON AND STEEL when they are left in damp air. As rust forms, the surface of the metal is eaten away. Grease, oil and paint protect the metal.

Rwanda

Rwanda is a small country in central Africa. Much of the country is mountainous, the climate is cool and pleasant. The people farm and raise cattle. Rwanda became independent in 1962. The country is one of the most densely populated in Africa. In 1994 it was torn apart by civil war.

RUSSIA

Government: Republic
Capital: Moscow
Area: 17,075,000 sq km
Population: 149,527,000
Language: Russian
Currency: Rouble

RWANDA

Government: Republic
Capital: Kigali
Area: 26,338 sq km
Population: 7,232,000
Languages: French, Kinyarwandu
Currency: Rwanda franc

◀ *Men fell trees in Rwanda, a country largely situated on a high plateau.*

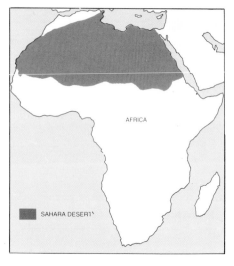

Sahara Desert

The Sahara is the world's largest hot DESERT. It covers about 9.1 million square km in North Africa. It extends from the Atlantic Ocean in the west to the Red Sea in the east. In the north, it stretches to the Mediterranean coast in Libya and in Egypt. Recently, the lands south of the Sahara have had very little rain. Because of this, the desert is slowly spreading southwards.

About a third of the Sahara is covered by sand. Other parts are covered by gravel and stones, or by bare rock. The Sahara is the hottest place on earth. The world's highest air temperature in the shade, 57.7°C, was recorded there.

Sailing

At one time nearly all types of SHIPS used sails. But by the mid-1800s, sailing ships had been largely replaced by steamships. Today, sailing is done mostly for pleasure.

Sailing boats vary in size from small dinghies to large yachts. The *hull*, or body, of the boat may be made of wood, fibreglass or moulded plywood. Poles called *spars* support the sails. The sails are made of canvas or man-made materials. They can be moved to catch the wind by pulling on ropes, called *rigging*. Sailing boats can sail in any direction, except straight into the wind.

▼ *The caravel (below) was used by the Portuguese to explore the African coast in the 1400s. The* Victory, *Nelson's flagship at the Battle of Trafalgar (1805), had 100 guns.*

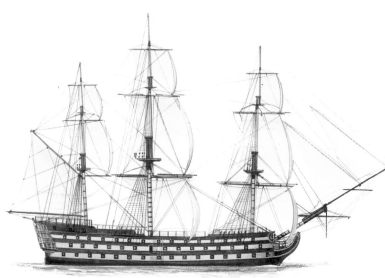

The modern sport of sailing yachts began in Holland in the 1600s. Today, one of the most famous races is for the America's Cup, which began in 1870. Olympic sailing events were started in 1908.

Saint

Saints are holy people. Christian saints are people who have been *canonized* (named as saints) by the ROMAN CATHOLIC CHURCH or the Eastern Orthodox churches. When someone is being made a saint, the Church looks at the person's life to see if he or she was very good. The saint must also have taken part in a miracle.

▲ *This 12-metre yacht has many features of modern sailing design.*

◄ *St Francis of Assisi (1182–1226) believed that to do God's work he should give up everything he owned and lead a simple life of prayer and hard work. He formed an order of friars, called the Franciscans, that still exists today.*

ST KITTS AND NEVIS

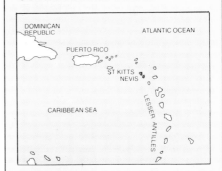

Government: Monarchy
Capital: Basseterre
Area: 261 sq km
Population: 44,000
Language: English
Currency: East Caribbean dollar

St Kitts and Nevis

These two tiny islands are in the Lesser Antilles in the Caribbean. They were settled by the British in 1623 and governed as a colony until they became fully independent in 1983. Sugar is the principal industry.

ST LUCIA

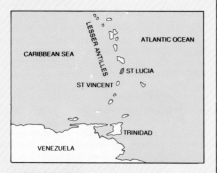

Government: Parliamentary
    democracy
Capital: Castries
Area: 616 sq km
Population: 153,000
Languages: English, French, Patois
Currency: East Caribbean dollar

ST VINCENT AND
THE GRENADINES

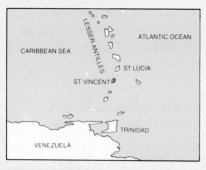

Government: Constitutional
    monarchy
Capital: Kingstown
Area: 388 sq km
Population: 116,000
Language: English
Currency: East Caribbean dollar

▶ *Salmon hatch from eggs laid in
rivers. Newly hatched* alevins *live on
the yolk attached to them. Young fish,
called* parr, *become* smolts, *which
migrate to the sea. Mature salmon
return to the rivers to breed.*

St Lucia

St Lucia in the Lesser Antilles is one of the
Windward Islands. The people are farmers, the
main crops being bananas, cocoa, coconuts and
citrus fruit. St Lucia was given to Britain by France
in 1814 and gained its independence in 1979.

St Vincent and the Grenadines

These are islands in the Lesser Antilles in the
Caribbean. St Vincent is a forested volcanic island.
The chief crops are bananas, arrowroot and
coconuts. Tourism is important. Columbus landed
on St Vincent in 1498. The islands were granted
independence by Britain in 1979.

Salamander *See* Amphibian

Salmon

Salmon are fish which breed in shallow rivers. After
the eggs hatch, the young fish swim down the river
to the sea. They spend their adult life (about one to
three years) in the sea. Then they return to their
birthplace to breed. This may mean a journey of
hundreds of kilometres. Most salmon die after
laying their eggs.

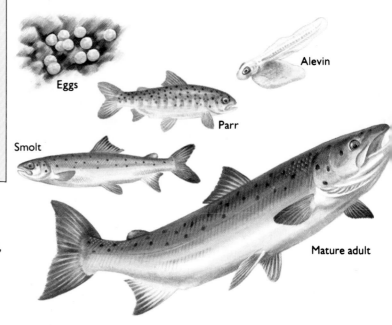

Eggs

Alevin

Parr

Smolt

Mature adult

◄ *Salt made from sea water, evaporated by the heat of the Sun, contains other minerals such as iodine.*

Salt

The chemical name for the salt we eat is sodium chloride. We need some salt to stay healthy, but not too much. Salt is also used to preserve foods and it is important in many industries. Much of our salt comes from sea water, but some is mined from deposits in the ground.

Sand

Sand is made up of small grains of rock. The grains are smaller than those in gravel, but larger than those in silt or mud. Sand piles up on coasts. Inland, in dry places, it forms hills called dunes. The main mineral in sand is *quartz*. Layers of sand may be pressed together in the ground to form a hard rock called sandstone.

San Marino

San Marino, in Italy, is the oldest and smallest republic in the world. It has made most of its money by frequent issues of its postage stamps. The people are ruled by two 'captains regent' who are elected every six months. San Marino has had a treaty of friendship with Italy since 1862.

São Tomé and Príncipe

These tiny volcanic islands are in the Gulf of Guinea off the coast of west Africa. They were discovered

SAN MARINO

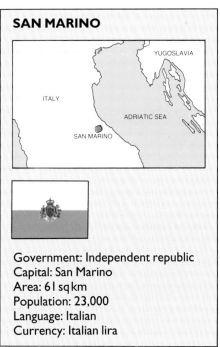

Government: Independent republic
Capital: San Marino
Area: 61 sq km
Population: 23,000
Language: Italian
Currency: Italian lira

SÃO TOMÉ AND PRÍNCIPE

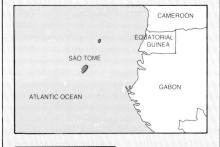

Government: Republic
Capital: São Tomé
Area: 965 sq km
Population: 132,000
Language: Portuguese
Currency: Dobra

Cocoa accounts for 90 per cent of São Tomé's exports. Many of the people of São Tomé were brought from Angola and Mozambique to work on the island's plantations.

by the Portuguese in 1471 and slave trading became the main activity until coffee and cocoa growing were introduced in the 1800s. The islands became independent of Portugal in 1975.

Satellite

A body that moves in orbit around another body is called a satellite. The EARTH and the other planets are satellites of the SUN. The MOON is the Earth's satellite, but the Earth has many more satellites. These are the artificial satellites launched by rockets into fixed orbits. Weather satellites have cameras

▶ The first satellite in space was the Soviet *Sputnik 1*, launched in 1957.

▼ A cutaway view of an Intelsat news satellite. Its small rocket motor is used to position the satellite exactly after launching from Earth. Electrical power is provided by solar panels.

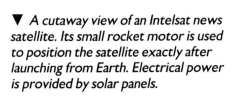

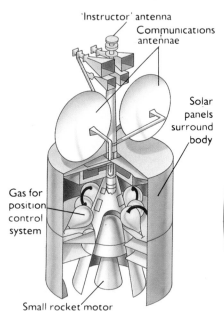

'Instructor' antenna
Communications antennae
Solar panels surround body
Gas for position control system
Small rocket motor

▶ There are many Intelsat communications satellites positioned over different parts of the world. The satellites relay signals between each other as well as to hundreds of ground stations.

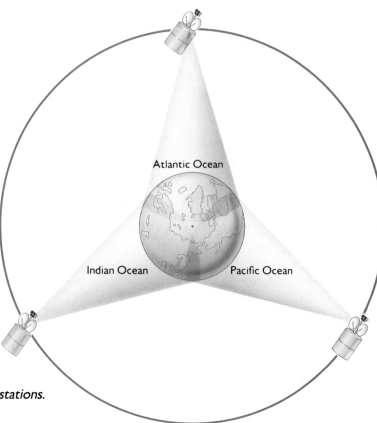

Atlantic Ocean

Indian Ocean

Pacific Ocean

that send back pictures of cloud and storm formations. Communications satellites relay television and telephone signals around the world. They have radio and other equipment powered by batteries charged by the Sun's rays. The satellites receive a signal from the transmitting station on Earth, amplify it, and beam it down to another Earth station, which may be thousands of kilometres away.

The first artificial satellite was *Sputnik 1*, launched by the Soviet Union in 1957.

Saturn

Saturn is the second largest PLANET in the SOLAR SYSTEM after JUPITER. It is about 120,000 km across. Saturn is famous for the rings that circle it. These rings are made of billions of icy particles. The rings are more than 272,000 km across, but they are very thin. The particles in the rings may be the remains of a moon that drifted too close to Saturn and broke up.

To the naked eye, Saturn looks like a bright star. The planet is actually mostly made up of light gases, and it is less dense than water, but scientists think

The most useful satellites are the communications and weather satellites, most of which are launched into *geostationary* orbit. This means that they are placed in a fixed orbit 36,000 km high where they orbit the Earth in exactly 24 hours. Because of this they appear to remain stationary in the sky, always over the same spot on Earth.

SATURN FACTS

Average distance from Sun: 1427 million km
Nearest distance from Earth: 1280 million km
Average temperature (clouds): −190 degrees
Diameter across equator: 120,200 km
Diameter of ring system: 272,000 km
Atmosphere: Hydrogen, helium
Number of moons: 24 known
Length of day: 10 hours 14 minutes
Length of years: 29.5 Earth years

Earth

Saturn

◀ Saturn's rings are made up of pieces of ice, rock and dust. They form a band that, measured across, is more than 20 times the diameter of the Earth.

SAUDI ARABIA

Government: Monarchy
Capital: Riyadh
Area: 2,149,690 sq km
Population: 16,900,000
Language: Arabic
Currency: Riyal

Schoolchildren may be surprised to learn that the word 'school' comes from the Greek word *schole*, meaning leisure. The ancient Greeks thought learning was something to be done in one's spare time.

▶ *In developing countries, schools such as this one in Lesotho have very little equipment. The pupils often have to walk many kilometres there and back.*

that it may have a solid core. Saturn has 24 satellites. The largest is Titan. It measures about 5,200 km across – larger than MERCURY. Titan is the only known moon to have an atmosphere – a layer of gases surrounding it.

Saudi Arabia

Saudi Arabia is a large country that occupies most of the Arabian peninsula in south-west Asia. It is named after the Saudi family which has ruled the country since it was founded in 1932. In 1933, oil was discovered along the Persian Gulf coast of Saudi Arabia, bringing vast wealth to the country. It is estimated that the country has about one quarter of the world's oil reserves. It has used its money to modernize. During the Gulf War, Saudi Arabia was the base for the Allied forces' liberation of Kuwait.

School

Nearly all countries try to provide enough schools to give their children some education. In many countries laws are passed by which children have to go to school between certain ages, such as between 5 and 16. But some poor countries do not have enough schools or teachers. They try to make sure that children go to school for long enough to learn to read, write and use numbers. However, nearly a third of the world's people over 15 cannot read or write.

‘The Orrery’ by Joseph Wright. Orreries – working models of the planets in the solar system – were very popular in the 1700s and 1800s.

Science

The main divisions of science are ASTRONOMY, BIOLOGY, CHEMISTRY, GEOLOGY, MATHEMATICS, MEDICINE, and PHYSICS, which deals with types of ENERGY.

Modern scientists use the *scientific method*. First they *observe*, or look at, something carefully to find out everything they can about it. Then they make a *theory* which explains what the thing is made of, or how it works. Then they test the theory with *experiments*. If the experiments agree with the theory, it becomes a *law* of science. Sometimes a law is changed when scientists discover new facts about something. Science is always changing.

Scientific studies began in early times. Great

▲ Democritus was a Greek scientist and philosopher who lived about 2300 years ago. He taught that all things were made of atoms.

SEE IT YOURSELF

Density measures how heavy a substance is compared to its size or volume. You can find out how dense some things are by carrying out the following scientific experiment. You will need some water, syrup, cooking oil, a tall glass jar and a jug. Pour the liquids carefully into the glass jar, one after the other. Use a spoon so they do not mix. You will see that they separate into three layers. The syrup is more dense (or heavier) than the other two, and the oil is the least dense. Try floating some other objects on the different layers. What happens?

SCIENCE FICTION

▶ *Scientific research is often aimed at making life easier and safer for people. This walking robot is for use in the nuclear industry. It can be controlled remotely.*

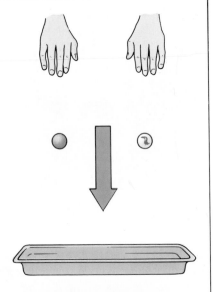

SEE IT YOURSELF

The famous scientist Galileo found out that objects always gather speed as they fall to the ground. Try dropping two objects onto a tray at the same time. Use objects which have the same shape but different weights. Do they land together? Galileo proposed that objects of the same size and shape fall at the same speed no matter what they weigh.

advances were made during the first civilizations, especially in ancient Greece and China. Science nearly died out in Europe in the MIDDLE AGES, but during the RENAISSANCE scientists began making discoveries that changed the way people thought and lived. This process speeded up during the INDUSTRIAL REVOLUTION, and scientific research has been increasing ever since.

Science Fiction

Imaginative stories which are set in the future or on other planets are called science fiction. The writers often use new scientific discoveries in their stories.

▶ *This is one artist's idea of how an alien spacecraft heading towards Earth might look. Many science fiction stories are set in outer space.*

They imagine how these discoveries might change the world in the future. Many of the stories are about space travel and time travel, and meetings between creatures from different planets. Some writers describe life in the future to show how many things they think are wrong in the world today.

Jules Verne (1828–1905) and H.G. Wells (1866–1946) were two of the first great science fiction writers. Recent writers include Isaac Asimov, Ray Bradbury and Arthur C. Clarke.

Science fiction is not new. In the AD 100s, the Greek writer Lucian of Samosata described journeys to the Moon and the strange creatures to be met there. Johannes Kepler, the famous astronomer who lived in the 16th century, wrote a book entitled *Somnium* in which he also described a trip to the Moon and the serpent-like creatures met by the hero.

Scorpion

Scorpions are animals related to spiders, with poisonous stings in their tails. Most live in warm, dry places and grow to 15 cm long. They have four pairs of legs, and a pair of large claws. Scorpions use their sting to stun or kill their prey. The poison can also make people ill, but it very seldom kills them.

▲ *When scorpions are frightened, they curl their tails up over their heads and may sometimes sting.*

Scotland

Scotland is part of the United Kingdom of Great Britain and Northern Ireland. Most Scots live in a narrow belt in the south where most industry is. In this belt are Glasgow, Scotland's largest city, and Edinburgh, the capital. The Highlands of Scotland have very few people and many beautiful mountains and lochs. The highest mountain in Britain is Ben Nevis, 1343 metres high. There are many islands off the Scottish coast. These include the Hebrides, Orkneys and Shetlands.

Scotland joined with England and Wales in 1707, but the Scots have kept many of their own traditions. Some Scots want their own government.

SCOTLAND

Area: 78,772 sq km
Population: 5,094,000
Agriculture: About 75% of land in use
Chief products: Barley, cattle, oats, sheep, wheat
Fishing: Crabs, herring, lobsters and white fish.
Chief industries: Iron and steel, motor vehicles, textiles, industrial machinery, chemicals, whisky and shipbuilding.

Scott, Robert Falcon

Captain Robert Falcon Scott (1868–1912) was an English naval officer and an explorer of the ANTARCTIC. His first expedition was in 1901–1904. With four companions, he began a march to the SOUTH POLE in 1911. After suffering great hardships, he reached the Pole on January 17, 1912. But he was disappointed to find that Roald AMUNDSEN, of Norway

▲ *Sir Walter Scott grew up on his grandfather's farm in the border country between England and Scotland. This area later became the location for many of his novels.*

▲ *Robert Baden-Powell was a soldier who served in both India and Africa. He wrote and illustrated many books.*

▶ *The scouting movement has spread to many countries and there are now organizations to suit a wide range of age groups. Here, some Girl Scouts from the United States are doing origami together.*

had been there just a month earlier. Scott and his companions died in a snow storm on the journey back. They died only a short distance from a supply base where they would have been safe.

Scott, Walter

Sir Walter Scott (1771–1832) was one of the most popular of all story writers. He was born in Edinburgh, Scotland. He became a lawyer, but was more interested in Scottish history and folklore. He wrote several poems and many novels of historical adventures, including *Rob Roy* and *Ivanhoe*.

Scouting

Scouting is an international movement for boys and girls. It was founded in England in 1907 by Robert Baden-Powell for boys only. Three years later a similar organization called the *Girl Guides* was founded for girls. The movement spread rapidly to other countries.

Young children from the age of 6 or 7 to 11 belong to the Cub or Brownie units. Young people from 14 to 16 upwards become Venture Scouts or Ranger Guides.

One aim of scouting is to build character and self-reliance in young people. Another is to teach helpfulness to others.

Screw

A screw is a simple machine. There are many kinds of screws, but those we know best are the metal ones used to join things together. The spiral part of a screw is called the *thread*. When a screw is turned round in a piece of wood, the thread pulls the screw into the wood.

When things are joined together by a screw, the squeezing force is very great. For example, if a spanner 30 cm long is turned with a force of 1.5 kg on an average screw nut and bolt, the nut and bolt are drawn together with a force of half a tonne after one complete turn.

Sculpture

Sculpture is a way of making attractive models, statues and objects as works of ART. They may be carved from stone or wood, or they may be made by *casting*. In making a cast, the sculptor first makes a

▼ *Sculpture is a very ancient art, as some of the earliest examples show.*

Female figure dating from about 5750 BC, found in Anatolia.

Bronze head of an ancient Akkadian king, who ruled in Mesopotamia.

A Phoenician ivory carving dating from about the 800s BC.

An ivory carving of a Byzantine empress from the AD 700s.

Neapolitan Fisherboy, a marble sculpture by Carpeaux (1800s).

A famous modern sculpture by Brancusi, called *The Kiss* (1908).

▲ *The 19th century French artist Edgar Degas made a large number of paintings and sculptures inspired by ballet dancers.*

▶ *The angles and shapes in this modern sculpture by Jean Dubuffet are in sharp contrast to the flat New York skyscrapers that surround it.*

▼ *Sea anemones attach themselves to rocks by a suckerlike disc. The upper end of the column expands into the mouth opening.*

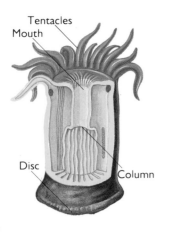

model in clay or wax. He or she uses this model to make a mould. Hot molten metal, such as bronze, is then poured into the mould. When the metal has cooled and hardened, it is taken out of the mould. The metal 'cast' is a perfect copy of the original model.

Early Greek statues were models for RENAISSANCE sculptors such as MICHELANGELO, who was possibly the finest sculptor ever.

Modern sculptors have moved away from lifelike figures. Great artists such as Henry Moore have made *abstract* figures and groups.

Sea Anemone

Sea anemones are soft-bodied, tube-like animals. They are closely related to CORALS, but they do not build a hard cup around themselves as corals do.

Sea anemones cling to rocks. Many live on or near the seashore. They look like flowers because they have one or more rings of petal-like tentacles around their mouths. The tentacles have stinging CELLS, and trap small fish and other tiny animals that float by. The sea anemone then pulls the food into its stomach through its mouth, and digests it.

Sea Horse

Sea horses are strange fish with delicate, bony bodies. They are called sea horses because of their horse-shaped heads. Most are between 15 and 25 cm long.

Sea horses swim by waving their back fin. They often cling to seaweed with their tail. The males look after the eggs. They keep them in a pouch on their belly until they hatch. Sea horses are found in tropical and warm seas.

Seal and Sea Lion

Seals and sea lions are large sea mammals. Many of them live in icy waters. They spend most of their time in the sea, but sometimes come ashore to lie in the sun. They also have their young, called pups, on land. Seals have streamlined bodies and legs shaped like flippers for swimming. They also have a thick layer of fat, or blubber, under their skin to protect them from the cold. Seals and sea lions eat fish and other sea creatures.

Sea lions have small ears outside their heads and have fur all over their bodies. The males often have a shaggy mane. The Californian sea lion is the smallest. It is often seen in circuses and zoos.

▲ Sea horses swim upright. If they want to feed, they hold onto seaweed with their tails and pick food out of the water as it floats past.

▼ Seals and sea lions are wonderful swimmers, but on land they move slowly. They spend most of their time at sea, but they come ashore to breed.

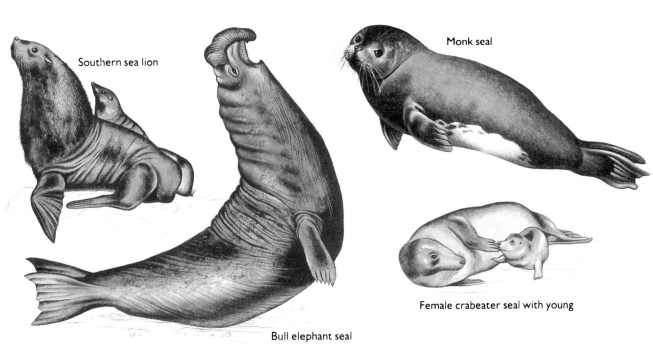

Southern sea lion

Monk seal

Bull elephant seal

Female crabeater seal with young

Seashore

The shores surrounding Earth's seas and oceans are shaped by water. Along some shores, fierce waves hammer at rocks and carry away loads of stones and earth. Along others, the waves and tides bring in pebbles and sand and dump them. All over the world, the edge of the land is being changed by restless waves and by the constant rise and fall of TIDES.

There are several kinds of seashore. They can be rock, sand, mud, pebble or a mixture. All shores are home for many living things.

Limpets, winkles, whelks, barnacles, SEA ANEMONES and SPONGES are some of the creatures found on rocky shores. All these animals cling to rocks and eat tiny pieces of food that float by in the water. Others, such as cockles, razor shells, mussels

▼ *Some of the many creatures found along the seashore: (1) Blackheaded gull (2) Starfish (3) Jellyfish (4) Curlew (5) Starfish (6) Lugworm (7) Razor shell (8) Tellin (9) Masked crab (10) Common cockle.*

Apart from the birds and the jellyfish, most of these animals like sandy and muddy beaches where they can bury themselves at low tide to keep from drying out.

and CRABS, like sandy and muddy beaches.

Seashores have their own plants. Many of these plants are SEAWEEDS. But other plants have learnt to grow in these wet, salty places. Most shore plants and animals are able to live in and out of water. When the tide is in, they are often underwater, but when the tide is out, they are left on land.

Many birds live along the seashore. Some shore birds use their long beaks to dig for worms and insects in the mud. Others catch fish in the sea.

▲ These sand dunes along the west coast of England are constantly on the move. Fences and marram grass are used to control the movement of the sand. The lime-rich sands are also home to two rare creatures, the sand lizard and the natterjack toad.

Season

The year is divided into four seasons. They are spring, summer, autumn and winter. Each season has its own kind of weather.

In spring, for example, the days become warmer; plants begin to grow again after the winter cold and most animals have their young. In autumn, the days are cooler; leaves fall from the trees and many birds fly to warmer places for the winter.

Seasons happen because the EARTH is tilted on its *axis* (a line through the centre of the planet between the North and South Poles). As the Earth travels around the SUN, first one pole, then the other, leans towards the Sun. When the North Pole tips towards the Sun it is summer in the northern half of the world and winter in the southern half. Six months later, it is the South Pole's turn to lean sunward, making it summer in southern lands and winter in northern ones. Spring and autumn, the halfway

One of the factors affecting seasonal temperatures is how far a place is from the ocean. Somewhere on the coast or on a small island has seasons that are much less marked than places that are far inland. This is because water is slow to heat up and cool down. The sea therefore helps to keep a fairly even temperature at places near it. In the centre of vast continents, it can be very hot in summer and very cold in winter.

▶ *The Earth's axis always tilts in the same direction. In June, the northern half, or hemisphere, of the planet is in summer because it is leaning towards the Sun. It receives more direct rays and therefore more heat, and the days are longer. At the same time the southern hemisphere is in midwinter. Six months later in December, the Earth has gone halfway around the Sun, and the seasons are reversed. In March and September both hemispheres have an equal share of day and night.*

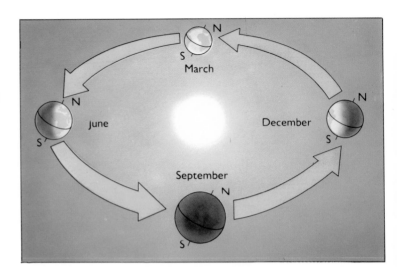

▼ *Seaweeds all belong to the class of simple plants we call algae. They live in shallow water where they give out oxygen and feed and shelter many creatures.*

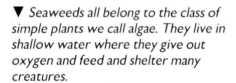

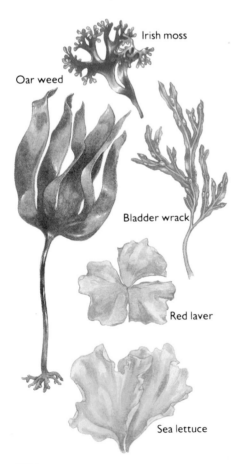

Irish moss

Oar weed

Bladder wrack

Red laver

Sea lettuce

seasons between summer and winter, happen when the Earth is between its summer and winter positions.

At the poles, there are only two seasons: summer and winter. During the polar winter the sun never rises and days are dark. In the summers the sun shines all the time and there are no real nights.

Farthest from the poles, at the EQUATOR, the Earth's tilt has no effect. There are no clear differences between the seasons.

Seaweed

Seaweeds are a group of plants that live in the sea. They grow on rocks or on the seabed. Like most plants, seaweeds need sunlight to make food. Because the Sun's rays do not reach very far down into the sea, there are no seaweeds in deep water.

In some countries people eat different types of seaweeds as vegetables.

Seed

Seeds are the most important part of a PLANT; they are the beginnings of new plants. A seed is formed when pollen reaches the female part of a FLOWER. The new seed grows inside a FRUIT, which protects it. In a grape, for example, the fleshy part is the fruit and the pips are the seeds.

Seeds have to be scattered to find new ground to grow on. Some fruits have wings and are carried by

Pea

Dandelion

Maple

Blackberry

Acorn

Burdock

◄ *Seeds are scattered in many different ways. Some, such as the pea, are in pods that burst open when ripe. Others, such as the dandelion, are carried by the wind. Acorns and blackberries are stored or eaten by animals, while the burdock has tiny hooks that cling to animals' fur.*

the wind. Others are prickly and stick to the fur of passing animals. Many seeds contain the baby plant and a little supply of food. When the seed begins to grow, the baby plant takes in this food until it has roots and leaves and can make its own food.

Semiconductor

Some materials allow ELECTRICITY to pass through them easily – they are good *conductors*. Most of these materials are metals. Other materials do not allow electricity to pass–they are *insulators*. Semiconductors are materials such as silicon, germanium and gallium arsenide, which are neither conductors nor insulators. When small amounts of other elements are added to semiconductors, important electronic devices can be made. These devices – such as the 'chip' – can be made to pass low or high

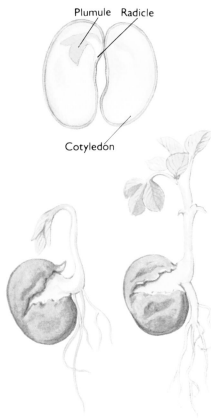

Plumule   Radicle

Cotyledon

▲ *A bean seed (top, split open), has large fleshy cotyledons (seed leaves) and a radicle and plumule. The radicle grows downwards into the soil, then the plumule appears, growing upwards (above left). To protect the young shoot, it remains bent over until it reaches the surface (above right).*

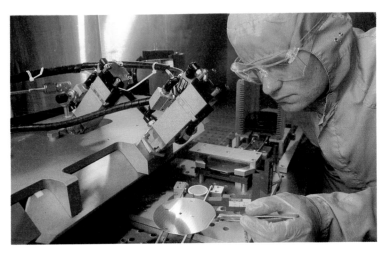

◄ *Wafer-thin slices of the semiconductor silicon are prepared for cutting into microchips.*

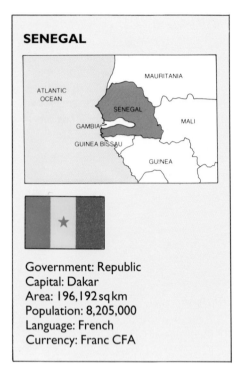

SENEGAL

MAURITANIA

ATLANTIC
OCEAN

SENEGAL

GAMBIA

MALI

GUINEA BISSAU

GUINEA

Government: Republic
Capital: Dakar
Area: 196,192 sq km
Population: 8,205,000
Language: French
Currency: Franc CFA

amounts of electric current, to block it completely, or to allow it to pass in one direction only. Transistors are made from semiconductors.

Senegal

The country of Senegal lies on the far westernmost coast of Africa. Neighbouring Gambia is surrounded on three sides by Senegal. Peanuts are the country's chief crop and export. Millet and rice are also grown. Fishing is important.

Senegal was the first French colony in Africa. Full independence came in 1960. From 1982–9, Senegal and Gambia were joined together in a defence and monetary confederation called Senegambia.

Senses *See* Ear, Eye, Hearing, Smell, Taste, Touch

Seven Wonders of the World

The Seven Wonders of the World were seven outstanding man-made objects that were built in ancient times and were so called because people marvelled at them. Only one of these wonders, the PYRAMIDS, exists today. The others have all been destroyed. They were:

The Hanging Gardens of Babylon were probably built high up on the walls of temples. They were probably a gift from King Nebuchadnezzar II to one of his wives.

The Temple of Artemis at Ephesus (now in Turkey). This temple was one of the largest in the ancient world. Some of its marble columns are in the British Museum in London.

The Statue of Zeus at Olympia, Greece, which showed the king of the gods on his throne. It was made of gold and ivory.

The tomb at Halicarnassus (now in Turkey), which was a massive tomb built for Mausolus, a ruler in Persia. It became so famous that all large tombs are now called *mausoleums*.

The Colossus of Rhodes in Greece, which was a huge, bronze statue of the sun god, Helios. It stood

**SEVEN NATURAL WONDERS
OF THE WORLD**

1 Mount Everest on the Nepalese-Tibetan border.
2 Victoria Falls on the Zimbabwean-Zambian border.
3 Grand Canyon of the Colorado River in Arizona.
4 Great Barrier Reef of Australia, the largest coral reef in the world.
5 Mauna Loa, the world's largest active volcano, in Hawaii.
6 Rainbow Natural Bridge in Utah, the largest in the world.
7 Yellowstone National Park, the world's largest geyser area.

◀ *The Seven Wonders of the Ancient World – only the Egyptian pyramids remain.*

It has been estimated that to build the Great Pyramid today would require at least 400 men using modern equipment to work for more than five years at a cost of about £600 million!

SEVEN WONDERS OF THE WORLD

1 The Pyramids of Egypt. 2 The Lighthouse of Pharos at Alexandria. 3 The Colossus of Rhodes. 4 The Statue of Zeus at Olympia. 5 The Hanging Gardens of Babylon. 6 The Temple of Artemis. 7 The Mausoleum at Halicarnassus.

towering high over the harbour entrance.

The Pharos of Alexandria in Egypt, which was the first modern lighthouse. It was built in 270 BC on the island of Pharos outside Alexandria harbour. It had a wood fire burning on top.

Sex *See* Reproduction

Seychelles

The islands of the Seychelles make up a small country about 1600 km off the east coast of Africa in the Indian Ocean. The country has volcanic mountains, sandy beaches and coconut palm plantations.

SEYCHELLES

Government: Single party republic
Capital: Victoria
Area: 280 sq km
Population: 70,000
Languages: English, French
Currency: Rupee

▲ *William Shakespeare is probably the most famous name in English literature, but very few facts are known about his life.*

▼ *These sharks are all hunters. They have sharp teeth that grow in rows. As one set wears out, the row behind takes over (inset).*

Tourism is an important business. The islands were ruled by Britain, but gained their independence in 1976. The inhabitants are of mixed African and European ancestry.

Shakespeare, William

William Shakespeare (1564–1616) is thought by most people to be England's greatest writer. He is most famous for his plays—about 40 altogether—which include *A Midsummer Night's Dream*, *Hamlet*, *Macbeth*, and *Romeo and Juliet*.

Very little is known about Shakespeare's life. He was born in Stratford-upon-Avon and was the son of a glovemaker. When he was 18, he married Anne Hathaway, a farmer's daughter, and had three children. Then, at the age of 20, he left Stratford and went to London where he became an actor and playwright. At the end of his life he returned to Stratford. Shakespeare's plays are acted and studied all over the world. Many of the words and phrases we use today were first used by Shakespeare.

Shark

The shark family includes the world's largest and fiercest fish. Many sharks have a wedge-shaped head, a long body and a triangular back fin that often sticks out of the water. Their skeletons are

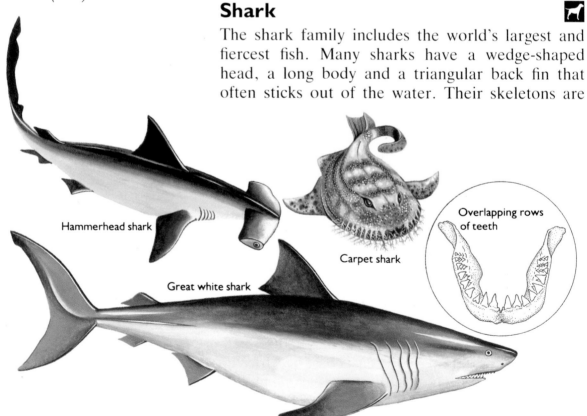

Hammerhead shark

Carpet shark

Great white shark

Overlapping rows of teeth

made of rubbery gristle, not bone. Most sharks live in warm seas. They vary greatly in size. The dogfish, one of the smallest sharks, is only 60 cm long. The largest fish in the oceans, the whale shark, measures over 15 metres—as long as two buses.

The whale shark and the basking shark are harmless to people and other animals because they live on plankton. But many sharks are cruel killers with rows of razor-sharp teeth. Several will attack humans. The greediest monster, the great white shark, swallows its prey whole. The remains of big animals, such as horses, seals and other sharks, have been found in its stomach.

Other dangerous sharks are the blue shark, the tiger shark and the leopard shark, which has leopard-like spots. The smell of blood in water can cause sharks to attack anything nearby, even other sharks.

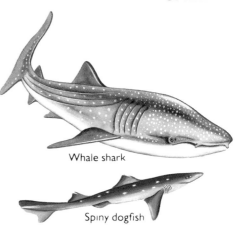

Whale shark

Spiny dogfish

▲ The smallest and the largest members of the shark family. The dogfish is about 60 centimetres long, while the whale shark is more than 15 metres long.

Sheep

Sheep have been kept as domestic animals for thousands of years. At first, sheep were kept for their milk and skins. Milk could be made into cheese and the skins were used for clothing. Then people discovered that the animals' thick coats could be *sheared* (shaved off) and the wool woven into cloth. Today sheep are kept mostly for wool and for meat (*mutton* or *lamb*).

Merino

Ile-de-France

Dorset horn

Suffolk

▲ The mouflon is a truly wild sheep that lives in mountainous areas in mainland Europe and in open country on Mediterranean islands.

◄ Modern sheep have been specially bred to give the best combination of wool and meat.

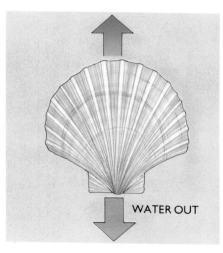

▲ *Scallops swim by opening their shells then shutting them quickly. The jet of water they force out pushes them along.*

WATER OUT

▶ *Many different types of mollusc shell can be found on the seashore.*

▼ *The tellin buries itself in the sand then sucks tiny pieces of food from the water through a tube it extends above the surface.*

Shells and Shellfish

Many animals live inside shells. This is because they have soft bodies that need protection. Shells are usually hard and are all sizes and colours. The shells of some sea snails are no bigger than a grain of sand, but the giant clam of the Pacific Ocean has a shell 120 cm across.

Some land animals such as SNAILS have shells, but most creatures with shells belong in the sea. Shelled sea animals include MOLLUSCS and CRUSTACEANS. Some of these, such as OYSTERS, scallops, and LOBSTERS, can be eaten. These are often called shellfish although they are not really fish at all. Shellfish have been an important food for thousands of years. In some places, kitchen refuse of prehistoric people has been found that consists entirely of enormous mounds of shells, as high as a two-storey house.

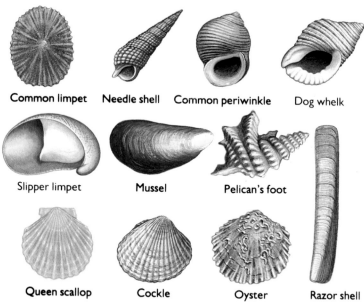

Common limpet   Needle shell   Common periwinkle   Dog whelk

Slipper limpet   Mussel   Pelican's foot

Queen scallop   Cockle   Oyster   Razor shell

Shinto

Shinto is a Japanese religion. The word 'Shinto' means 'the way of the gods'. Unlike other religions, Shinto does not teach that there is one supreme being. It says that there is an eternal truth called *kami*. Kami is to be found in every form of nature and in rivers, mountains and lakes. All over Japan there are shrines, large and small, dedicated to different kami.

Ship

Today most ships are cargo vessels. They are usually built to carry a certain type of cargo. *Tankers* carry liquids such as oil or wine. Some oil tankers are so long that the crew can ride bicycles around the deck. *Bulk carriers* take dry cargoes like coal and wheat

▲ *This super-tanker is 380 metres long – over a third of a kilometre. It is 62 metres wide, with a cruising speed of 16 knots (29.6km/h). Yet it has a crew of only 35 to 50. Compare the size of this ship with the famous ocean liners shown below.*

that can be loaded loose. *Container ships* carry all kinds of goods packed in large boxes called containers. *Refrigerator ships* are for carrying fresh food such as fruit and meat.

Planes have replaced most passenger ships, but there are still many ferries that take people and

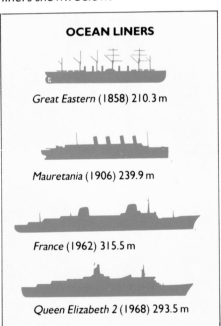

OCEAN LINERS

Great Eastern (1858) 210.3 m

Mauretania (1906) 239.9 m

France (1962) 315.5 m

Queen Elizabeth 2 (1968) 293.5 m

◀ *Roll-on roll-off ferries can take cars, lorries and their passengers.*

▶ *Aircraft carriers must have enough room on deck for planes and helicopters to take off and land.*

Bicoloured white-toothed shrew

Alpine shrew

vehicles across smaller stretches of water. There are also luxury cruise liners. Various kinds of warship are used by the navy.

Shrew

Shrews are furry creatures about the size of a mouse. They have a pointed snout and are seldom seen because they only come out at night. Shrews are very active animals and have to eat almost continually to live. They eat insects and worms.

Siberia

Siberia is a vast region that covers most of Russian Asia, east of the Ural Mountains. It is a very cold land. Along Siberia's northern coast lies the *tundra*,

▲ *Shrews often fall prey to larger night hunters, such as owls, cats or even badgers.*

▶ *The huge area covered by Siberia is largely undeveloped and many animals enjoy the unspoilt habitat. Lake Baikal, right, is home to many species of animal not found anywhere else in the world, including the world's only freshwater seal.*

a cold semi-desert. Forests cover about a third of Siberia's 15 million square kilometres. Towards the Mongolian border lies Lake Baikal, the largest fresh-water lake in Asia or Europe.

For the last few years the former Soviet government had been encouraging young people to settle in Siberia to develop the region.

Sierra Leone

SIERRA LEONE

Sierra Leone is a country on the west coast of Africa. It is about the size of Scotland. The climate is hot and damp. Around Freetown, the capital, about 380 cm of rain fall each year. Most people are farmers, producing rice, palm kernels, ginger, coffee and cocoa. Iron ore, bauxite and diamonds are mined.

Sierra Leone was a British colony. It became an independent state in 1961 and a republic in 1971, but there have been several revolutions.

Government: Republic
Capital: Freetown
Area: 71,740 sq km
Population: 4,456,000
Language: English
Currency: Leone

Sikhs

Sikhs are people who live in the Punjab in northern India. The Sikh religion was started by a pious man called Nanak (1469–1539). He was the first Sikh *guru* (teacher). The teachings of the *gurus* were written in the Sikh sacred book, the *Granth*. This was kept at Amritsar in the Golden Temple.

The Sikhs were a warlike people. They fought

Many devout Sikhs in their own land carry a short dagger or *kirpan*. They may also wear a bangle, a comb and short trousers.

◄ *The Golden Temple of Amritsar, in the Punjab, is sacred to Sikhs. It was built in 1579 on land granted by the Mogul emperor Akbar.*

▲ This silicon chip, the tiny square in the centre of the panel, is smaller than any of the cherries around it. Yet its circuits are capable of running a small computer.

against the Muslim rulers of India and against the British.

Sikh men do not shave or cut their hair, and they wear a turban. There are about 14 million Sikhs.

Silicon Chip

Silicon chips are tiny pieces of the ELEMENT silicon. (Silicon is a SEMICONDUCTOR.) They can be made to carry very small electrical circuits, called microcircuits. These are used in transistor radios, digital watches, calculators and computers. Because the chips are so small, the electronic devices in which they are used can be small too.

Silk

Silk is a natural fibre made from the cocoon of one kind of moth. Silkworms, which are really caterpillars, are kept in special containers and fed on mulberry leaves for about four weeks. At the end of this time they spin their cocoons and start to turn into moths. Then they are killed and each cocoon is unwound as a long thread between 600 and 900 metres long.

Silk was first used in Asia centuries ago, especially in China and Japan. Silk WEAVING in Europe began in the 1400s. Silk makes a very fine, soft material. It was used for stockings before nylon was invented. Silk can be made into other fabrics such as satin and chiffon, and can be dyed in beautiful colours.

▼ Once the silkworms have eaten enough mulberry leaves they start to spin their cocoons. They produce a liquid through a hole in their lower lip which hardens in the air, and makes the fine silk thread. The cocoons are put into hot water to loosen the threads for winding. The threads from several cocoons are wound together to make a stronger thread.

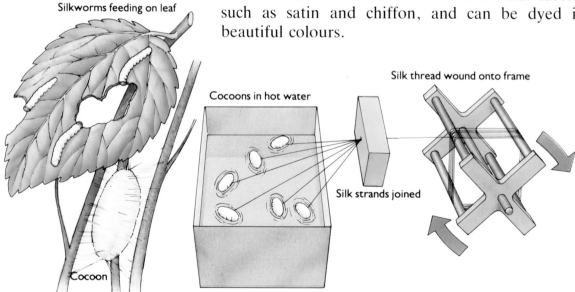

Silkworms feeding on leaf

Cocoon

Cocoons in hot water

Silk strands joined

Silk thread wound onto frame

◀ *This set of silverware consists of a mug, napkin ring, knife, spoon and fork, all made in 1903.*

Silver

Silver is a precious metal. It has been used by people all over the world for thousands of years. Although many countries have silver deposits, the mining process is very expensive.

Silver bends very easily, and can be beaten into many shapes and patterns. Like gold, it can be hammered out into thin sheets. It is used to make useful and decorative things such as spoons and forks, bowls, and jewellery. Sometimes it is used as a coating on cheaper metals such as copper or nickel, to make them look like silver. It can also be mixed with another metal (usually copper), and then it is called *sterling* silver.

Silver used to be made into coins, but most of today's 'silver' coins are really made of a mixture of copper and nickel.

Silver carries electricity well and is used for this in industry. Some chemicals made from silver react to light and are used in photography. Another chemical, silver nitrate, is painted on the back of glass to make mirrors.

> The chemical symbol for silver is Ag, from the Latin *argentum*, meaning 'white and shining'. It melts at 960.8°C and boils at 2210°C. A tiny gram of the metal can be drawn into a wire nearly 2 km long. The main silver-producing countries are the United States and Mexico.

Singapore

Singapore is a small country in SOUTH-EAST ASIA, off the southern end of the Malay peninsula. Three-quarters of the population are Chinese, but people from all over the world live there.

The capital city is also called Singapore. It has

SINGAPORE

Government: Republic
Capital: Singapore
Area: 581 sq km
Population: 2,792,000
Languages: Chinese, Malay, Tamil, English
Currency: Singapore dollar

▲ British skaters Jayne Torvill and Christopher Dean were ice dancing champions in the 1980s.

▲ Lobsters have an exoskeleton, that is, their skeleton is in the form of hard plates on the outside of their body.

▶ Examples of animals with internal skeletons. The shape of their skeleton is perfectly adapted to the way they move.

one of the busiest ports in the world and trades with many countries. For a short time Singapore was part of Malaysia, but now it has its own government. It is a member of the Commonwealth.

Skating

Roller skating and ice skating are both popular sports. Roller skates have four wheels made of steel and rubber. Ice skates have a thin steel blade.

There are two main kinds of ice skating. Figure skating and ice-dancing to music are Olympic sports. Speed skaters race against each other.

The first ice skates had runners, or blades, of bone. Today, figure skates have jagged teeth at the front to help grip the ice when starting and stopping. Speed skates have longer blades.

Ice hockey players also wear skates.

Skeleton

Our skeleton is made up of BONES. If we did not have a skeleton, our bodies would be shapeless blobs. The skeleton protects our vital organs, such as the heart, liver and lungs. It is also an anchor for our MUSCLES.

In humans and other animals with backbones (VERTEBRATES), the skeleton is inside the body, covered by the flesh and skin. In other animals, such as INSECTS and SPIDERS, the skeleton is like a hard crust on the outside of the body. It is called an *exoskeleton*. Some animals, such as the jellyfish and octopus, do not have a skeleton. Their bodies are supported by the water they live in.

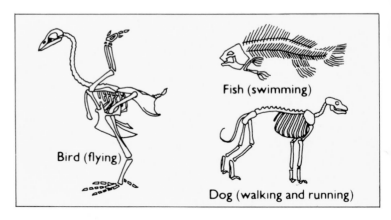

Bird (flying)

Fish (swimming)

Dog (walking and running)

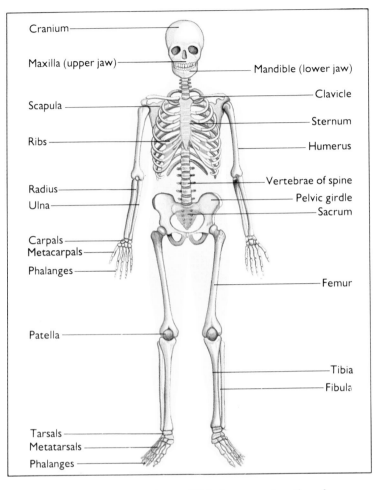

Cranium
Maxilla (upper jaw)
Mandible (lower jaw)
Scapula
Clavicle
Sternum
Ribs
Humerus
Radius
Vertebrae of spine
Ulna
Pelvic girdle
Sacrum
Carpals
Metacarpals
Phalanges
Femur
Patella
Tibia
Fibula
Tarsals
Metatarsals
Phalanges

◄ *The skeleton provides a framework for your body, holding it together and supporting its weight. Bones also protect important organs.*

Babies are born with about 350 bones. But as a child grows, some of these bones join together and an adult ends up with about 206. The number varies because some people have more bones in their hands and feet than others. The largest bone in your body is the *femur*, or thigh bone. The smallest is the *stapes*, or stirrup bone, in your middle ear. It is only about 2.6 to 3.4 mm long.

There are more than 200 bones in the human skeleton. These include the bones of the spine, skull (which protects the brain), ribs, pelvis, breastbone and limbs. Joints are places where bones meet. Some joints (like those in the skull) do not move. Others, like those in the shoulders and hips, help us to move about. Muscles across the joints tighten, or *contract*, to move the bones.

A human skeleton develops before the baby is born, and grows along with the body.

Skiing

Skiing is a way of moving across snow on long runners, or skis. It probably started around 3000 BC. The oldest skis ever found date back to 2500 BC. and we know that the VIKINGS used skis. Today, skiing is a popular sport and is part of the Winter OLYMPIC GAMES.

There are four main kinds of skiing: cross-

▼ *Great skill and split-second timing are needed to tackle slalom races in skiing.*

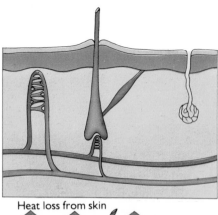

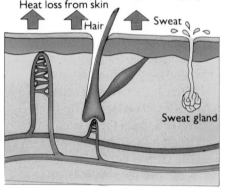

▲ *The skin goes through changes to make you warmer or cooler. When you are cold, erector muscles make the tiny hairs on the skin stand upright to trap a layer of warm air (top). When you are hot, the hairs lie flat to let the air circulate, and sweat evaporates from the skin to cool you (above).*

▶ *The skin is a waterproof, elastic covering for the body. It helps to keep germs and dirt out, and can even repair itself. Sebaceous glands give off oil that keeps the skin from becoming too dry.*

The common skunk grows to a length of about 28 to 36 cm, with a 43-cm tail. When attacked, it can spray its foul-smelling liquid accurately as far as 3.5 metres. Before it sprays, the animal gives warning by stamping its front feet and hissing.

country, slalom (obstacle course), downhill and ski jumping. Downhill skiing is especially popular. There are special ski resorts in the mountains of Europe, North America and Australia, where people can spend skiing holidays.

Skin

Skin is the covering on the outside of our bodies. It protects our bodies and is sensitive to heat, cold and pain. Human skin can be quite thick and hard on places that get a lot of wear, such as the soles of the feet. It can also be very thin on other places, such as the eyelids.

Human skin is made up of two layers. The outer layer, the *epidermis*, has a chemical called melanin which gives skin its colour. The inner layer, the *dermis*, contains nerves, blood vessels, sweat glands and the roots of hairs. The skin of an adult human covers about 1.7 square metres.

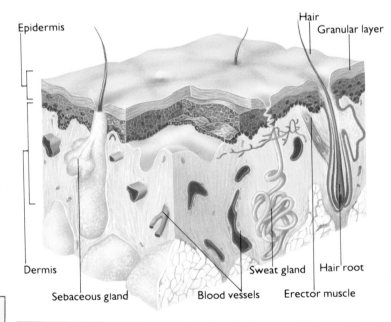

Epidermis — Hair — Granular layer — Dermis — Sebaceous gland — Blood vessels — Sweat gland — Hair root — Erector muscle

Skunk

Skunks are MAMMALS, members of the same family as weasels and BADGERS. There are three kinds: the hog-nosed, the spotted and the striped skunk. They all live in North America. The best known is the striped skunk, which is black with white markings on its back. All skunks are able to drive away

enemies by squirting a stinking liquid from a gland under their tails. If another animal is hit by this liquid, the smell will cling to its fur for days.

Skunks eat most kinds of food, including insects, rats, mice, birds, eggs and plants. They feed at night and sleep in burrows during the day.

Skydiving

Skydiving is a form of parachute jumping. It started in the 1940s, and now it is a popular sport. Skydivers jump from an aircraft and fall a long way before they open their parachutes. They have to steer their parachutes to land on a target marked on the ground.

Skyscraper

'Skyscraper' is a name for a very tall building. The first one was built in 1884 in Chicago in the United States. It was designed by William Le Baron Jenney, and it had an iron frame.

All the early skyscrapers were built in NEW YORK and Chicago. Now they are built all over the world. For many years the tallest skyscraper was the Empire State Building in New York—102 storeys high. Now there are two taller—the Sears Tower in Chicago and the World Trade Center in New York, both 110 storeys. The Sears Tower is the higher at 443 metres.

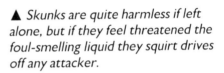

▲ Skunks are quite harmless if left alone, but if they feel threatened the foul-smelling liquid they squirt drives off any attacker.

▼ The skyline of Vancouver, in Canada, includes many impressive skyscrapers.

▲ *The abolition of the slave trade was largely due to William Wilberforce (1759–1833). He was a Church of England priest who became a politician and campaigned for more than 20 years to have slavery banned.*

▶ *The conditions suffered by the people who were kidnapped and made slaves were appalling. Many died on the ships carrying them from Africa to the Americas.*

Most people need less sleep as they grow older. Someone who slept 8 hours a day when he or she was 30 years old may need only 7 hours of sleep at the age of 60. Young babies sleep most of the time; 4-year-olds average from 10 to 14 hours sleep a day; 10-year-olds from 9 to 12 hours.

Slavery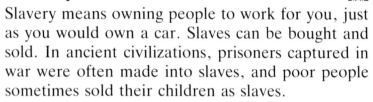

Slavery means owning people to work for you, just as you would own a car. Slaves can be bought and sold. In ancient civilizations, prisoners captured in war were often made into slaves, and poor people sometimes sold their children as slaves.

From the 1500s, the Spanish took people from Africa as slaves for their colonies in America. By the 1770s, British ships were carrying slaves to America. Hundreds were packed tightly into ships. Conditions were terrible, and many slaves died on the way. Britain abolished the slave trade in 1808. Slavery was ended in the USA in 1865, after the CIVIL WAR. But racial discrimination continued even after CIVIL RIGHTS laws were passed to guarantee equal rights for black people.

Sleep and Dreams

Sleep is a time when we are unconscious and resting. People and some animals need sleep to stay healthy. Without it, people become short-tempered and after a long time they may start having *hallucinations*—seeing things that are not there.

There are four different stages of sleep. At each stage the electrical waves given off by the BRAIN change. When we are deeply asleep, these waves are slow and large. When we are only lightly asleep the waves are faster. This is the time when we—and all MAMMALS—dream.

Sloth

Sloths are a group of MAMMALS that live in South America. They move very slowly, usually at night. Sloths spend most of their lives hanging upside down in trees. They eat leaves, buds and twigs. Their fur is often covered with masses of tiny green creatures called algae. There are two main kinds of sloth—the two-toed and the three-toed.

Slovakia

A country in eastern Europe that was once part of the country known as CZECHOSLOVAKIA. The territory was ruled for many centuries by the Hungarians, but in 1918 the Slovak and Czech regions were joined into Czechoslovakia. The country came under Communist rule in 1948.

A democratic government took over after the Communists fell in 1989. However, the Slovak people began to feel that they were not being treated fairly by the government and called for independence. The country split into Slovakia and the Czech Republic in 1993.

SLOVAKIA

Government: Republic
Capital: Bratislava
Area: 49,035 sq km
Population: 5,268,935
Languages: Slovak, Hungarian
Currency: new Koruna

Slovenia

Slovenia was the most westerly republic of what was formerly YUGOSLAVIA. It declared its independence in 1991. Until 1918, Slovenia was ruled by AUSTRIA. It is the most westernized of the former Yugoslav republics and its people are mainly Roman Catholic. Ljubljana, the capital of Slovenia, is also an important industrial centre. In the north of Slovenia are the ALPS.

Smell

Smell is an important sense, like sight and hearing. Humans and other MAMMALS smell through the nose. We sniff the air, and the scents given off by the things around us are picked up by special cells in the nose. These cells send messages to the BRAIN.

Our sense of smell is useful when we are eating. It helps us to TASTE things. It can also let us know

SLOVENIA

Government: Republic
Capital: Ljubljana
Area: 19,991 sq km
Population: 11,974,000
Language: Slovenian
Currency: Tolar

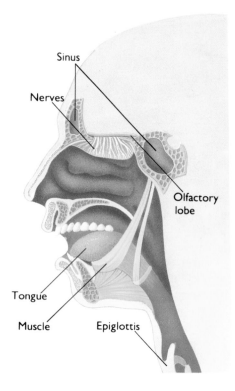

▼ *Our sense of smell is closely linked to our sense of taste. When we have a cold and lose our sense of smell, it makes our food taste less interesting.*

Sinus

Nerves

Olfactory lobe

Tongue

Muscle

Epiglottis

when food is bad. Most other animals have a much better sense of smell than humans. Dogs can use their sense of smell to track down and follow prey. Moths do not have noses, but they can still smell things. Some male moths can smell a female moth many kilometres away.

Smog

There are two kinds of smog. One is a very thick, smelly mixture of smoke and fog. It used to be very common in London. In the winter of 1952, there was a very bad smog and about 4000 people died of chest diseases. Since then, laws have been made to make sure there is less smoke in London and no more smog.

The other kind of smog is caused by air pollution from car exhausts and other fumes. These are changed by sunlight into a white mist that hangs over cities. Smog of this sort can be dangerous to the people who live in cities. It can hold chemicals that are harmful.

► *Air pollution in the form of smog blankets the city of Santiago in Chile.*

▲ *All snails are molluscs; those shown here eat living or dead plant matter. Snails often seal up their shells with slime which hardens into a parchment-like cap.*

Snail

Snails are MOLLUSCS with a coiled shell on their back. There are more than 80,000 kinds in the world. Some live on land, some in fresh water and some in the sea.

Most snails are less than 3 cm long. But one of the largest, the giant land snail, is about 20 cm long.

Snake

Snakes are REPTILES. They are long and thin and have no arms or legs. They move along by wriggling their bodies.

Snakes have a dry, smooth skin. Most live in warm places. Those that live in colder climates spend the winter in *hibernation*.

A few snakes have poison glands. They inject this poison into animals that they bite. The rattlesnake and the cobra are both poisonous snakes.

Most snakes hatch from eggs. A female snake can lay up to ten eggs at a time. Others give birth to live young. The largest snakes are pythons and anacondas. These can grow to 10 metres long.

▲ *Pythons can grow to as long as 10 metres. They can unhinge their jaws to swallow quite large prey.*

▼ *The viperine snake and the cat snake are both European snakes. The cat snake has venomous fangs but is not dangerous to humans.*

Snooker and Billiards

Snooker and billiards are popular games played with a wooden cue on a billiards table. Billiards is by far the older, snooker having been played only since the beginning of this century.

Billiards is played with three balls, one red and two white. Points can be scored in three ways – by 'cannons', 'pots' and 'in-offs'.

In snooker there are 22 balls: the player's white ball, 15 reds scored as 1 each, and the 'colours', valued as yellow (2), green (3), brown (4), blue (5), pink (6) and black (7). The player starts by potting a red, then any colour, then another red, and so on. Each time a red is potted it stays in the pocket, but the colours are replaced on their respective spots on the table. After all the red balls have been potted, the player then tries to pot the colours in their correct order, starting with the yellow. When the black is potted, the game, or 'frame', is over. If a

Viperine snake

Cat snake

▶ *A snooker table with its markings. The size of the table and the positions of the spots are specified by the Billiards and Snooker Control Council.*

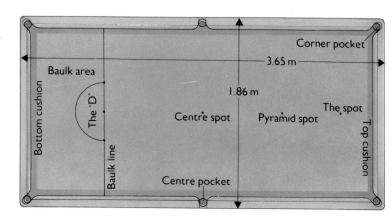

Corner pocket
Baulk area
3.65 m
Bottom cushion
1.86 m
The 'D'
Centre spot
Pyramid spot
The spot
Top cushion
Baulk line
Centre pocket

player fails to score, his opponent comes to the table. To 'snooker' one's opponent is to make a stroke so that the ball the opponent has to strike is obstructed by another ball. If the opponent fails to hit the correct ball, he or she suffers a penalty.

Snow *See* Rain and Snow

Soap

Soap is used for cleaning things. It is made by mixing FAT or vegetable oil with a chemical such as caustic soda. It loosens dirt in clothes and carries it away. Today chemical cleaners called DETERGENTS are often used instead. Detergents clean better than soap in hard water, but they do not by themselves make suds. Suds are not necessary for cleaning, but substances that make suds are added to detergents.

Soil

Soil is a layer of small MINERAL particles on the surface of the EARTH. It covers the rocks the Earth is made of and is sometimes quite thick. Soil may be sand or clay, and may contain the rotted remains of plants, called *humus*.

If soil particles are very fine, it is called clay. If they are coarser, it is silt, and if they are very coarse, it is called sand. Good soil is a mixture of all of these, with plenty of humus. People often add animal manure or chemical FERTILIZERS to poor soil. This makes the soil richer in extra minerals, which some plants need.

Floating humus
Clay
Silt
Fine sand
Coarse sand

SEE IT YOURSELF

To show that soil is made up of different particles, put a sample of soil in a jar of water and shake. When you stop shaking, the heavier particles sink to the bottom and the soil separates into its different layers (shown above). You should be able to calculate (roughly) how much sand, clay and silt there was in your original soil sample.

Solar Energy

Solar energy is energy from the Sun. It reaches the Earth as light and heat. Without these things there could be no life on Earth.

Only about 15 per cent of the Sun's energy that reaches the Earth is absorbed by the Earth's surface. Much of it bounces off the Earth and back into space. Solar energy can be collected by special panels and mirrors and used to make electricity.

Solar System

The solar system is made up of the Sun and the planets travelling around it. Mercury is the planet nearest the Sun. Next comes Venus, Earth, Mars, Jupiter, Saturn, Uranus, Neptune and Pluto.

Until the 1500s, most people thought that the

▲ Solar panels can be used to collect energy from the Sun. The energy can be made into electricity or just used to help heat a house.

◀ Seen in comparison with the Sun and the four 'giant' planets, the Earth looks very small. The nine planets in our solar system are:
1 Mercury
2 Venus
3 Earth
4 Mars
5 Jupiter
6 Saturn
7 Uranus
8 Neptune
9 Pluto

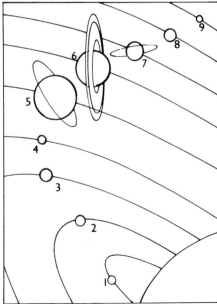

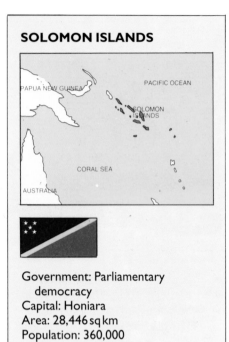

SOLOMON ISLANDS

Government: Parliamentary
   democracy
Capital: Honiara
Area: 28,446 sq km
Population: 360,000
Language: English
Currency: Solomon Islands dollar

SOMALIA

Government: Republic
Capital: Mogadishu
Area: 637,657 sq km
Population: 7,235,000
Languages: Somali, Arabic
Currency: Somali shilling

▶ Sonar stands for 'sound navigation and ranging' and can be used to map the bottom of the sea. Sonic pulses are produced by an echo sounder fixed beneath a ship. These are reflected back and recorded as a trace on a screen.

Earth was the centre of the universe, and that the Sun and planets travelled around it. In 1543 a Polish astronomer, Nicolaus COPERNICUS, discovered that, in fact, the Earth moved around the Sun.

Solomon Islands

The Solomon Islands lie in the Pacific Ocean about 1600 km from Australia. They are an independent state within the Commonwealth. The long chain of islands stretches for about 1400 km, but the total area of the Solomons is less than that of Scotland. The chief crops are coconuts, rice and bananas. There is a fish canning industry.

Somalia

Somalia is a country in an area called the 'Horn of Africa' – the easternmost part of Africa, jutting out into the Indian Ocean. It is a poor country, most of the people being nomads. Low rainfall means that agriculture is possible only around the Shebelle and Juba rivers. The chief crops are sugar, bananas, sorghum and incense. In recent years the country has suffered war, drought and famine.

Sonar

Sonar is used in ships to find the depth of anything beneath them. It can measure the depth of the sea bed as well as locate shoals of fish and submarines.

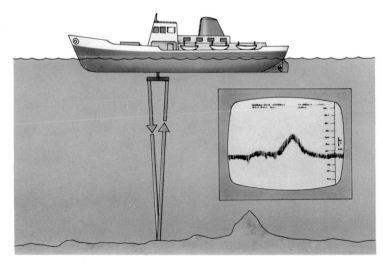

It works like RADAR, except that sonar uses SOUND signals instead of radio signals.

The sonar device on the ship turns electric signals into pulses of sound. These travel down through the water. Any object in the water struck by the sound pulses sends back an ECHO. The sonar equipment turns the echoes back into electric signals and measures the time delay. This indicates how deep the object in the water is. The depth is shown on a screen.

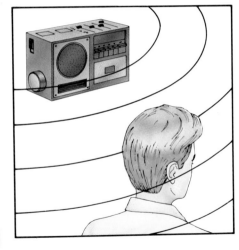

▲ Sound waves travel outwards from the source of the sound like ripples on a pond. They make vibrations in the air and, when they reach your ear they make your ear drum vibrate too, so you can hear the sound.

Sound

Sound is made by vibrating objects that send sound waves through the air. When these vibrations reach our EARS, we hear them as sounds.

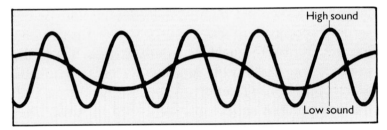

◄ The frequency of sound waves makes sounds high or low. High sounds make waves that are close together. The waves of low sounds are farther apart.

Sound travels through air at about 334 metres a second. This is slow enough for us to see a far-off explosion, for example, before we hear it. The sound takes time to reach us.

The speed of the vibrations makes a difference to the kind of sound we hear. If the vibrations are very fast, they are said to be 'high frequency' and the

SEE IT YOURSELF

You can produce sound by tapping milk bottles containing water. Arrange four milk bottles in a row. Leave the first one nearly empty and pour different amounts of water into the other three. Tap all four bottles with a spoon, one after the other. This makes the air inside each of the bottles vibrate, producing a sound. Because there is a different amount of air left in each of the bottles, each of them will make a different sound.

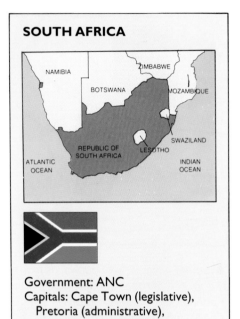

SOUTH AFRICA

Government: ANC
Capitals: Cape Town (legislative),
    Pretoria (administrative),
    Bloemfontein (judicial)
Area: 472,360sq.miles (1,223,412sq.km)
Population: 41,700,000
Languages: Afrikaans, English
Currency: Rand

sound we hear is high-pitched. If they are slow, the sound is said to be 'low frequency' and the sound we hear is low-pitched.

South Africa

South Africa is a country in southern AFRICA. Most of the country is tableland, a high region of flat-topped hills. Around the coast is a narrow plain. The climate is warm and dry.

South Africa is a rich country. Factories make a wide range of goods. Mines produce gold, diamonds, uranium, copper, iron and other minerals. Farms grow big crops of maize, wheat and fruit.

Over 41 million people live in South Africa. Almost three-quarters of them are black Africans. There are fewer than 5 million whites. The whites, who are descended mainly from Dutch and British settlers, controlled the country's government and money. Since the 1940s, South Africa has had a policy of APARTHEID or 'apartness'. This meant that whites and non-whites lived separately. But in 1991 the government ended apartheid, and in April 1994, free elections throughout South Africa gave the black African National Congress (ANC) a resounding victory. NELSON MANDELA, the ANC leader, became president of South Africa.

South America

South America is the world's fourth largest continent. Lying between the Atlantic and Pacific oceans, it stretches from the EQUATOR in the north to the ANTARCTIC in the south, from the ANDES Mountains in the west to the wide AMAZON delta in the east.

The Andes are the longest mountain range in the world. They run along the Pacific coast for 8000km. They are also the starting point of one of the world's greatest rivers, the Amazon. This huge waterway travels nearly 6450km across South America and empties 118 million litres of water into the ocean every second. The huge area drained by the Amazon includes thick tropical rain forest.

Two other great rivers are the Orinoco in the

▼ *South America is a huge continent. It stretches from the Antarctic right up to north of the equator.*

SOUTH AMERICA

Barranquilla
Caracas
Maracaibo
Orinoco
Georgetown
Medellin
Paramaribo
VENEZUELA
Cayenne
Llanos
Bogotá
GUYANA
SURINAM
FRENCH
GUIANA
ATLANTIC OCEAN
Cali
COLOMBIA
Quito
ECUADOR
GALAPAGOS IS.
Manáus
Belém
Guayaquil
Amazon
PERU
Fortaleza
Selvas
Chiclayo
BRAZIL
Trujillo
Recife
Callão
Salvador
Lima
Cuzco
BOLIVIA
La Paz
Brasília
ANDES
Oruro
Cochabamba
Brazilian Highlands
Sucre
PACIFIC OCEAN
Paraná
PARAGUAY
MOUNTAINS
Rio de Janeiro
Gran Chaco
São Paulo
Asunción
Córdoba
Pôrto Alegre
ATACAMA DESERT
Mt Aconcagua
URUGUAY
Valparaiso
Rosario
Santiago
Buenos Aires
Montevideo
ARGENTINA
La Plata
PAMPAS
Bahia Blanca
ATLANTIC OCEAN
CHILE
Colorado

■ Capital Cities

```
0        500        1000 miles
0     500    1000   1500 kilometres
```

Chubut

Patagonia

FALKLAND IS.

Tierra
del Fuego
Cape Horn

633

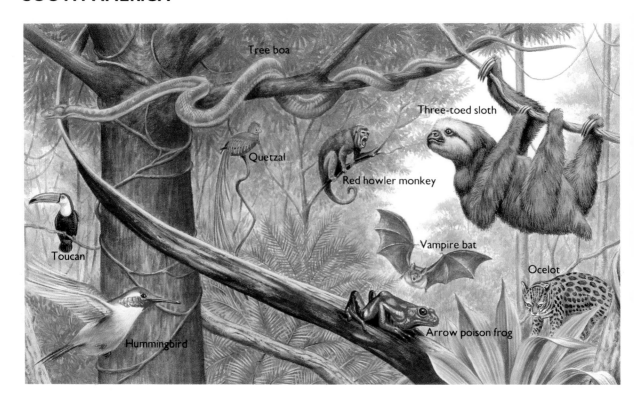

Tree boa

Quetzal

Three-toed sloth

Red howler monkey

Vampire bat

Ocelot

Toucan

Hummingbird

Arrow poison frog

▲ *Many of the creatures of the South American rain forest live high above the forest floor. These and the forests themselves are under threat as thousands of hectares of rain forest are felled for valuable hardwoods or to create farmland.*

SOUTH AMERICA
Area: 17,000,000 sq km
Population: 298,200,000
Highest mountain: Mount Aconcagua in Argentina, 6960 m
Lowest point: Valdes Peninsula, Argentina, 40 m below sea level
Principal rivers: Amazon (6440 km), Madeira, Magdalena, Orinoco, Plate-Paraguay-Parana system, Purus, Sao Francisco, Uruguay
Principal lakes: Maracaibo, Mirim, Poopo, Titicaca
Largest city: São Paulo, 16,832,000
Highest waterfall: Angel Falls, 979 m, highest in the world

north and the Plate in the south. The land south of the Amazon jungle has swamps, lakes, grasslands and, near the continent's tip, the Patagonian desert.

There are 13 countries in South America. The largest, BRAZIL, takes up half the continent. Most South Americans speak Spanish. But in Brazil they speak Portuguese, in Guyana they speak English, in French Guiana, French, and in Surinam, Dutch. These different languages are the leftovers of history. South America was explored by the Spanish and Portuguese in the 1500s. Then Spain, Portugal and other European countries set up colonies. In the 1800s, most of these colonies won their independence.

The first people of South America were Indians. Most of them, including the INCAS, were killed by foreign conquerors. Later the Europeans brought in African slaves. Today most South Americans come from European and African ancestors. There are still some Indians in the Andes and Amazonia.

South America has rich natural resources. The rocks of the Andes are full of minerals. There is silver in PERU, tin in BOLIVIA and copper in CHILE. There are also huge amounts of oil in VENEZUELA in the north. The open grasslands of ARGENTINA,

URUGUAY, and PARAGUAY provide food for millions of sheep and cattle. Brazil's farmers produce a third of the coffee in the world. So far all this wealth has not been used properly. Most South Americans are poor. Bad government and poor management of the land have held back South America's progress.

South-east Asia

South-east Asia is a large spread-out area that lies to the south of CHINA and to the east of INDIA. It is not one country, but many. Joined to the Asian mainland are BURMA (Myanmar), THAILAND, MALAYSIA, SINGAPORE, CAMBODIA, VIETNAM and LAOS. Farther south there is a chain of islands forming the countries of INDONESIA, BRUNEI, PAPUA NEW GUINEA and the PHILIPPINES.

South-east Asia is mainly mountainous. It has a tropical climate, with heavy rainfall in the wet season. Most of the people are farmers. They grow rice, maize, rubber, sugarcane and tea. Mineral resources include oil, tin and bauxite (aluminium ore). Although many South-east Asian people live in small villages, there are also big cities such

▲ An Indian of the Amazon region ferries his son in a dugout canoe. The lives of many of the Indians of the South American rain forests are changing as the forests diminish.

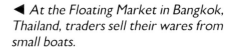

◄ At the Floating Market in Bangkok, Thailand, traders sell their wares from small boats.

From the 900s to the 1400s, much of South-east Asia was ruled by people called Khmers, who built up a powerful empire. The Khmer built hundreds of beautiful stone temples, canals, reservoirs and roads. The temple of Angkor Wat in Kampuchea is their greatest architectural achievement. The enormous temple is 1550 metres long by 1400 metres wide, with an entrance hall of more than a hundred square columns.

The South Pole reached by Amundsen in 1911 lies on a great field of ice nearly 3000 metres thick. The thickness of ice under Amundsen's feet was more than twice the height of Ben Nevis.

as Bangkok in Thailand, Kuala Lumpur in Malaysia, Ho Chi Minh City in Vietnam, and Singapore, one of the world's greatest ports.

A great many different peoples live in the region. They are made up of different races, speak different languages and follow different ways of life.

South Pole

The South Pole is not an object. It is the point on the map that marks the southern end of the EARTH's axis. The NORTH POLE marks the northern end. The South Pole lies among high, frozen mountains in the middle of ANTARCTICA. The first person to journey to the pole was the Norwegian explorer, Roald AMUNDSEN, in December 1911. The British explorer Captain SCOTT reached the pole one month later.

In 1956, the USA set up a scientific base at the South Pole and called it the Amundsen-Scott Station.

▼ Transport is a major problem in Antarctica. Heavily laden sledges have to be dragged by tractors such as this one, used by the British Antarctic Survey.

Soviet Union (former)

The vast area that was the Soviet Union in 1990 is now a complex of independent states, each trying to come to terms with its freedom from Kremlin control. Latvia, Lithuania and Estonia, the three BALTIC STATES, declared their independence from the Soviet Union at the end of 1991.

By 1992, eleven of the republics that had formerly made up the USSR had become members of the Commonwealth of Independent States (CIS). They were: ARMENIA, AZERBAIJAN, BELARUS, KAZAKHSTAN, KYRGYZSTAN, MOLDOVA, RUSSIA, TAJIKISTAN, TURKMENISTAN, UKRAINE, and UZBEKISTAN. GEORGIA, the fifteenth former Soviet republic, refused to join. However, each country is now fully independent, with its own government, military and economic system. The CIS has been dominated economically and militarily by the power of Russia under the leadership of Boris YELTSIN. In 1991 the Communist Party was disbanded. The economic situation worsened and food shortages became widespread.

Before 1917, the Soviet Union was called Russia. It was ruled by *tsars*, or emperors. In 1917, there was a revolution. A COMMUNIST government took over, led by Vladimir LENIN. Between 1918 and 1920 Russia was nearly destroyed by a civil war be-

▲ *A rural scene in Siberia, Russia. Siberia covers almost three quarters of Russia, although very few people live there due to the freezing weather conditions. This bleak and deserted land can often reach −50°C in winter.*

During the reign of the Tsars, the Soviet Union was an isolated and backward country. The Tsars were uncaring and often cruel. Ivan the Terrible terrorised the country with a secret police force. The last ruler, Nicholas II lived in luxury while his country starved.

◀ *The republics of the former Soviet Union and their boundaries.*

▲ *St. Basil's Cathedral in Red Square, Moscow, dating back to 1560. This dazzling building is famous for its brilliant domes. Originally built as a tribute to Ivan the Terrible's success in battle, it is now a national museum.*

tween the communists and their enemies. The communists won, and began to turn Russia into a great industrial nation.

The landscape of the former Soviet Union is varied. Large parts of it are cold or dry and have few people. More than 70 per cent of the people live in the European part of the country, west of the Ural Mountains.

Farmers grow a variety of crops, including wheat, rye and barley. They also grow vegetables, fruit, tea and cotton.

The former Soviet states are rich in MINERALS. They have great deposits of coal, oil and natural gas, iron, chromium, lead and manganese. Fishing and forestry are also important.

At the beginning of the 1900s Russia was a country of farmers. There were few factories. Today it is a leading industrial country, but much of the country's machinery is becoming old-fashioned.

During World War II Germany invaded the Soviet Union, but after fierce fighting the Soviet Army drove the Germans back. The Soviets occupied Hungary, Bulgaria, Romania, Czechoslovakia, Poland and part of Germany itself. After the war, communist governments closely tied to the Soviet Union were set up in these countries.

The United States and the Soviet Union grew to distrust each other and what was called the Cold War

▶ *Sheep farming in the foothills of the Caucasus mountains in Georgia.*

developed. Under its last leader, Mikhail Gorbachev, the Soviet Union entered a period of change and unrest. US and Soviet leaders signed agreements to reduce the numbers of nuclear and conventional weapons. The United States and countries of the European Community have been helping the former Soviet states with economic and food aid.

Soya Bean

The soya bean is one of our oldest crops. It comes from China, where it has been grown for over 5000 years. During the 1900s, the soya bean spread to other places. It is now an important crop in many countries, especially the USA, Russia and Brazil.

Most soya beans are grown for oil and meal (a type of flour). The oil is used for salads, cooking and to make MARGARINE. Soya meal is full of PROTEIN and is a nourishing food for animals and people. Both oil and meal are also used to make paint, ink and SOAP.

Spacecraft

The first spacecraft were launched in the late 1950s. There were two types: SATELLITES and probes. Satellites go into ORBIT round the Earth. Probes zoom away from Earth to explore other planets. These first spacecraft had no crew. Probes and most

▲ In the south lies the republic of Uzbekistan, which is part of Asia, and has many Asian traditions. This Uzbek trader is selling pumpkins at a bazaar in the city of Tashkent.

▼ The soya plant grows up to two metres high. The pods grow in clusters on the stem and there can be up to four beans in each pod. The pod and beans are shown enlarged inside the circle.

SPACECRAFT

▼ *To escape the pull of the Earth's gravity, a spacecraft needs a huge amount of thrust, provided by fuel contained in the different sections, or stages, of the rocket. Many satellites and spacecraft have been sent into space in this way, including the manned Soviet Vostok, the three-man American Apollo, and the huge Soviet space station Mir.*

satellites are still unmanned, but there are now some manned spacecraft.

All spacecraft leave Earth in the same way. They are thrust into space by huge, powerful ROCKETS. These rockets are in three parts or stages. As one stage runs out of fuel, it falls away and the next

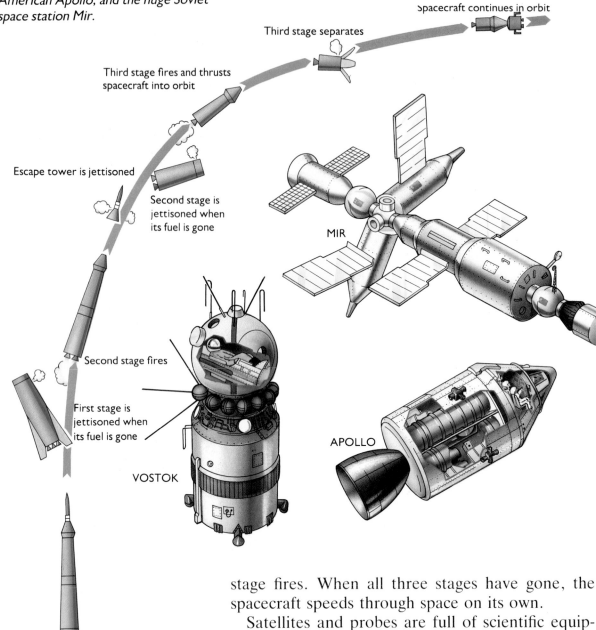

Spacecraft continues in orbit

Third stage separates

Third stage fires and thrusts spacecraft into orbit

Escape tower is jettisoned

Second stage is jettisoned when its fuel is gone

MIR

Second stage fires

First stage is jettisoned when its fuel is gone

VOSTOK

APOLLO

Lift-off: first stage fires

stage fires. When all three stages have gone, the spacecraft speeds through space on its own.

Satellites and probes are full of scientific equipment such as measuring instruments, cameras, tape recorders and radio transmitters. This equipment runs on electricity made from sunlight. The information collected is radioed back to Earth, where scientists study it.

Manned spacecraft are far more complicated. As well as scientific equipment, they carry other special equipment to keep their astronauts alive and well.

Space Exploration

People have always gazed in wonder at the Sun, Moon and the stars. Yet for thousands of years, they had no means of studying the heavens above. Then, in the 1600s, TELESCOPES were invented and people were able to take a closer look at the universe. More recently, scientists have been able to discover a lot more about space. We are living in the Space Age. (See pages 642–643.)

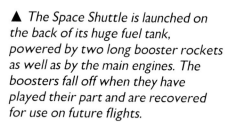

▲ The Space Shuttle is launched on the back of its huge fuel tank, powered by two long booster rockets as well as by the main engines. The boosters fall off when they have played their part and are recovered for use on future flights.

Spain

Spain lies in south-west EUROPE, beyond the PYR-ENEES. Most of the country is covered by high plains and mountains, with a low plain around the coast. The highlands have hot summers, cold winters and little rain. The coast is milder and wetter, especially in the north.

Half the people work on farms, growing potatoes, wheat, grapes, olives and fruits. Wine, olive oil and oranges are exported. Many Spaniards who live on the coast are fishermen. They catch sardines and anchovies. Others work in the tourist trade. Each year, millions of tourists visit Spain to enjoy its sunny beaches. The two main industrial areas are around Bilbao in the north and Barcelona in the north-east.

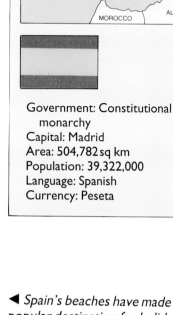

SPAIN

Government: Constitutional monarchy
Capital: Madrid
Area: 504,782 sq km
Population: 39,322,000
Language: Spanish
Currency: Peseta

◀ Spain's beaches have made it a popular destination for holiday-makers. This beach near Tarragona is on the Costa Dorada, or Golden Coast, in eastern Spain.

SPACE EXPLORATION

The Space Age began in 1957, when the Soviets launched the first artificial satellite. In 1961 came the first manned flight, and only eight years later astronauts were exploring the surface of the Moon.

People had long dreamed of escaping the Earth's gravity and flying in space. It was the multi-stage rocket, developed in Germany during World War II, that made space flight possible. The Soviets and Americans dominated the early years of space exploration. But Europe has its own space rocket, and other countries such as China and India have also launched satellites.

The Americans call their space travellers 'astronauts', while the Soviets call theirs 'cosmonauts'. The Americans were the first to build a reusable Space Shuttle, but the Soviets have made much longer flights in their orbital space stations. These flights will show if human travellers can ever voyage to Mars (which would take three years). Unmanned spacecraft have already landed on Mars and sent TV pictures and signals back from other planets.

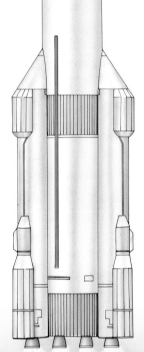

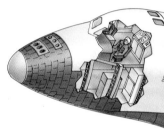

▲ The first artificial satellite, Soviet Sputnik 1 (1957). It weighed just over 83 kg and carried a radio transmitter.

◄ The Soviet rocket Energia is the most powerful space rocket in the world.

SPACE PIONEERS

Konstantin Tsiolkovsky: Russian who predicted use of rockets for space travel in the early 1900s.

Robert H. Goddard: American who tested small rockets in the 1930s.

Wernher von Braun: German who helped to design V2 war rocket and later the US Saturn Moon rocket.

Sergei Korolyev: Designed first Soviet space rockets.

Yuri Gagarin: Soviet who was the first person to fly in space (1961).

John Glenn: First American astronaut to orbit the Earth (1962).

Valentina Tereshkova: Soviet cosmonaut, first woman to make a spaceflight (1963).

Neil Armstrong: American who was the first person to set foot on the Moon (1969).

▲ Yuri Gagarin was the first person to fly in space. He made one orbit of the Earth on April 12, 1961. Tragically, Gagarin was killed in a plane crash in 1968.

▲ The two-man American Gemini spacecraft weighed 3.5 tonnes. It was flown in Earth orbit to practise techniques later used on the Apollo Moon flights.

SPACE FIRSTS

1942	First flight of German V2 rocket
1957	First Earth satellite: *Sputnik 1*
	First animal in space, a dog called Laika
1959	First man-made object hits the Moon (Luna 2)
1961	First manned spaceflight: by Yuri Gagarin
1965	First space 'walk': by Alexei Leonov
1968	First manned flight around the Moon: by Apollo 8
1969	First men on the Moon: Armstrong and Aldrin
1971	First space station: Salyut 1
1975	First close-up photos of Venus: by Venera probes
1976	First landing on Mars: by Viking probes
1981	First flight of Space Shuttle
1986	First close look at Uranus (Voyager 2)
1988	Soviets launch first space shuttle (*Buran*)
1989	First close look at Neptune (Voyager 2)

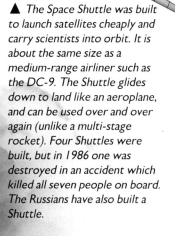

▲ The Space Shuttle was built to launch satellites cheaply and carry scientists into orbit. It is about the same size as a medium-range airliner such as the DC-9. The Shuttle glides down to land like an aeroplane, and can be used over and over again (unlike a multi-stage rocket). Four Shuttles were built, but in 1986 one was destroyed in an accident which killed all seven people on board. The Russians have also built a Shuttle.

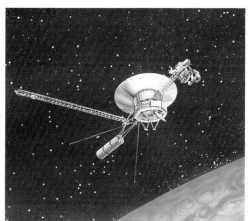

▲ Skylab was a manned scientific workshop that was launched into orbit by the USA in 1973. It was used by three crews to study the Earth, Sun, Moon, space and the influence of space on living things. It broke up and fell to Earth in 1979.

◄ The Voyager 2 space probe was launched in 1977 to visit Saturn and Jupiter, Uranus and Neptune. It passed Neptune in August 1989 and went on into outer space.

For more information, turn to these articles: ASTRONOMY; GAGARIN, YURI; GRAVITY; JUPITER; MARS; MOON; ORBIT; PLANET; ROCKET; SATELLITE; SATURN; SPACECRAFT; URANUS.

SPECTRUM

▶ *We can see only a very limited range of the electromagnetic spectrum – visible light – but unseen waves are around us all the time. Different wavelengths of the electromagnetic spectrum are used for different things, and have many different effects. The infrared photo shows the heat given out by an office block. White areas are the hottest, red are warm, green cool and blue cold.*

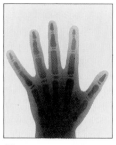
X-rays

Radar

Television

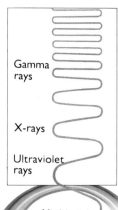
Gamma rays

X-rays

Ultraviolet rays

Visible light

Infrared rays

Microwaves

Radio waves

Ultraviolet rays

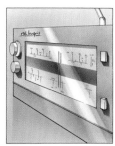
Infrared rays

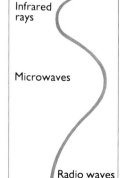

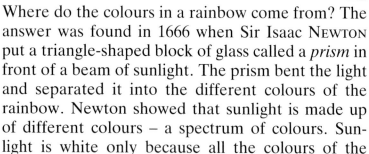
Radio

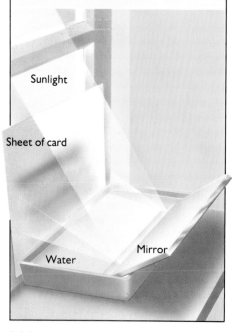

Sunlight

Sheet of card

Water

Mirror

Spectrum

Where do the colours in a rainbow come from? The answer was found in 1666 when Sir Isaac NEWTON put a triangle-shaped block of glass called a *prism* in front of a beam of sunlight. The prism bent the light and separated it into the different colours of the rainbow. Newton showed that sunlight is made up of different colours – a spectrum of colours. Sunlight is white only because all the colours of the rainbow are mixed together in it.

The spectrum of light is only one small part of the whole *electromagnetic spectrum*. The electromagnetic spectrum is arranged according to the *wavelength* (distance between waves) and *frequency* (number of waves per second) of the waves. Radio waves have the lowest frequency and the longest wavelength. Gamma rays have the highest frequency and shortest wavelength. In between these come ultraviolet rays, X-rays and other rays.

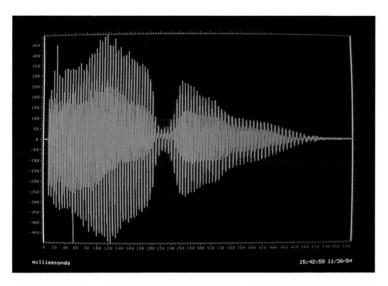

milliseconds

◀ *This computer graphic image shows the wave pattern made by the word 'baby'. The word was produced in a female voice by a computerized speech synthesizer that copies real human speech.*

▼ *Your tongue, teeth and lips work together to make sounds. The lips here (top) are pushed forwards to make the sound 'oo'. In the lower picture, the sound 'th' is formed by the tongue, teeth and lips combined.*

Speech

Once, the only sounds people could make were grunts, yells and other simple sounds. Then, over tens of thousands of years, they learned to form words. Languages slowly developed.

Speech sounds are made by air from our lungs passing around two membranes called vocal cords. We change the pitch of the sound by altering the tension of the vocal cords, just as we can alter the pitch of a guitar by tightening or slackening the strings. By changing the shape of the passages in our throat, mouth and nose, and by using our tongue, we can alter the sounds produced. We can make the words of speech.

Women usually have higher-pitched voices than men because their vocal cords are shorter.

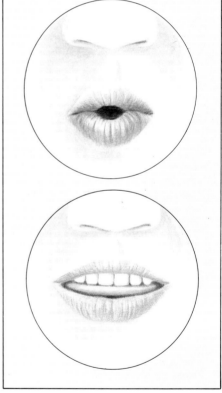

Spice

Spices have a strong taste and smell and are used to flavour foods and drinks. They are made from the

◀ *Some common spices. Cloves are the dried flower buds of a plant native to South-east Asia (left). Nutmeg is the dried kernel of a fruit that looks rather like an apricot (centre). Cinnamon is the dried bark of an evergreen plant (far left).*

In the Middle Ages the value of spices was often greater than that of gold or jewels. Most spices were brought to Europe from India or the Moluccas – the Spice Islands. The route was from India to the Persian Gulf, then across the Arabian Sea by ship. The spices were then taken by caravan across the Middle East to the Mediterranean or the Black Sea, and from there to the countries of Europe. No wonder spices were very costly.

dried parts of plants, usually ground into a powder. Most spice plants grow in hot places such as Africa, India, and Indonesia. Pepper, ginger, cloves, cinnamon and nutmeg are common spices.

Spider

Spiders are small animals. Although they look like insects, they are not. Insects have six legs; spiders have eight. Insects have feelers and wings; spiders do not. Insect bodies have three parts; spiders' bodies have two.

All spiders spin silk threads. Many of them use the threads to make a sticky web for catching insects. Not all spiders trap their food in webs. Some are hunters and chase their prey; others lie in wait, then pounce. When a spider catches something, it stuns or kills it with a poisonous bite. All spiders have poison, but in most cases it does not hurt people.

There are about 30,000 kinds of spider. They are all sizes. The comb-footed spider is no bigger than a pinhead, but some bird-eating spiders can be 25 cm across. They have different life stories. Some live for only a year, others for 20 years. Some mate in winter, others in spring. Tiny spiders lay a few eggs, perhaps just one, but the largest lay up to 2,000.

▲ The name tarantula has been given to many different types of spider – usually larger ones. The tarantula of southern Europe was once thought to have a sting deadly to humans, but it causes serious harm only to the small insects it eats.

▶ Spiders use their silk in different ways. The orb web spider builds a complex web to snare insects. The Australian Dinopis spider throws its silk net over an insect below. The trapdoor spider hides in its burrow and springs out if an insect touches one of its silk trip-wires. The European purse-net spider spins itself a pouch. If an insect steps on the pouch, the spider 'stabs' it through the silk wall and drags it inside.

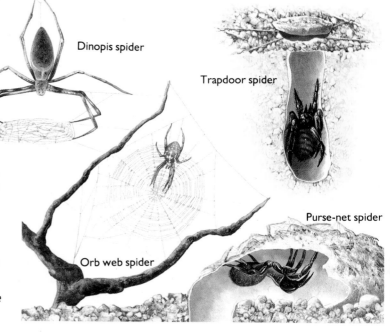

Dinopis spider

Trapdoor spider

Purse-net spider

Orb web spider

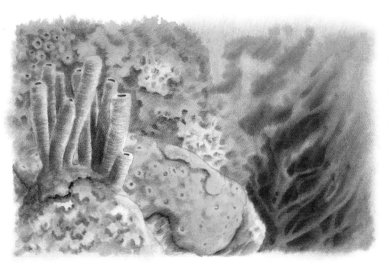

◀ *Despite their elaborate shapes, sponges are very simple forms of life. There were sponges living in the seas on Earth 600 million years ago when dry land was still a barren, lifeless place.*

Sponge

A sponge is a simple water animal. Most sponges belong to warm seas and oceans, but some live in cold seas. A few are freshwater creatures. A sponge's body is a mass of jelly-like flesh full of tiny canals, which end in holes in the body's surface. Water, carrying oxygen and food pieces, goes in through the holes and travels along the canals. This is how the animal breathes and feeds. Wastes are taken away through other canals.

When a sponge dies, the flesh rots and the SKELETON is left. Some skeletons are soft. These are used in homes as bath sponges. Most sponges come from the Gulf of Mexico and the Mediterranean. Today, most bath 'sponges' are not real. They are rubber or plastic.

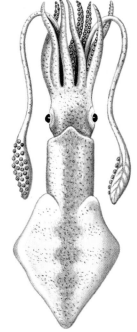

▲ *Each of the squid's ten arms has rows of sucking discs. It uses these to seize and hold on to its prey. Squids can propel themselves backwards by squirting water through a narrow funnel pointing forwards.*

Squid

Squid are MOLLUSCS related to the octopus. Many live deep in the sea by day but rise to feed at night. A squid uses its 10 tentacles to catch fish and feed them into its beaklike mouth. Some squid are no bigger than a thumb. But the giant squid can grow to 12 metres in length.

Squirrel

Most people think of squirrels as a kind of RODENT that is good at climbing trees. Tree squirrels are exactly that. They have sharp claws for climbing and

The giant squid can attain a length of 12 metres and a weight of nearly 500 kg. An old sailing ship sailor has described a battle between a giant squid and a sperm whale. The squid's great tentacles were wound around the whale's body and the whale had the hind part of the squid in its mouth. The squid's great black eyes were at least 30 cm in diameter.

▲ Prairie dogs are ground squirrels that live in large groups in huge burrow systems. Members of the group take it in turn to do jobs that benefit the whole group, such as standing guard at the entrances to the burrow.

▼ The red squirrel is the only native tree squirrel in Europe. It lives mostly in coniferous woodland, where it eats cones and shoots.

a long, bushy tail that helps them to steer and keep their balance. Tree squirrels can leap 3 metres to reach one tree from another.

Flying squirrels jump 10 times farther than that. These little creatures have flaps of skin between their front and back legs. The flaps form a parachute when a flying squirrel jumps and spreads its limbs. Tree squirrels and flying squirrels feed on leaves, twigs or seeds.

Ground squirrels live in burrows under the ground. They include the chipmunks, prairie dogs and woodchucks.

The most common squirrel in Britain is the grey squirrel. There are more than 300 different kinds of squirrel.

Sri Lanka

Sri Lanka is an island country off the southern tip of INDIA. Sri Lanka used to be called Ceylon. The island is near the equator, and so the climate is tropical. Most of the tropical trees and shrubs have been cleared away to make room for crops, but there are still bamboo and palm trees. Animals such as elephants, leopards, monkeys, snakes and colourful birds live in the wilder areas. Sri Lanka's crops include tea, rubber and coconuts.

There is continuing unrest between the ruling Sinhalese, who are mainly Buddhist, and the Tamils, who are mainly Hindu.

Stalin, Joseph

Joseph Stalin (1879–1953) ruled the USSR from 1929 to 1953. After LENIN died, Stalin made the Soviet Union one of the two most powerful nations in the world. He killed or imprisoned millions who disliked him or disagreed with his kind of COMMUNISM. The name Stalin is Russian for 'man of steel'.

Stamp

A stamp can be a special mark, or a piece of printed paper with a sticky back. A passport and many other kinds of documents must bear the correct government stamp. Postage stamps are stuck on letters and parcels to be carried by the post office. Each nation has its own postage stamps. Millions of people collect postage stamps. Some kinds are scarce and valuable. A very rare stamp can cost more than a house.

Star

The stars we can see from earth are just a few of the many billions scattered through space. Stars look small because they are so far away. But most are

SRI LANKA

Government: Republic
Capital: Colombo
Area: 65,610 sq km
Population: 17,631,000
Languages: Sinhala, Tamil
Currency: Rupee

▼ An artist's impression of the life of a star, first formed by a cloud of gas that condenses and solidifies. Over thousands of millions of years, the star grows larger. Suddenly, it expands into a red giant, then begins to shrink and fade. The arrow shows where our Sun is in this process.

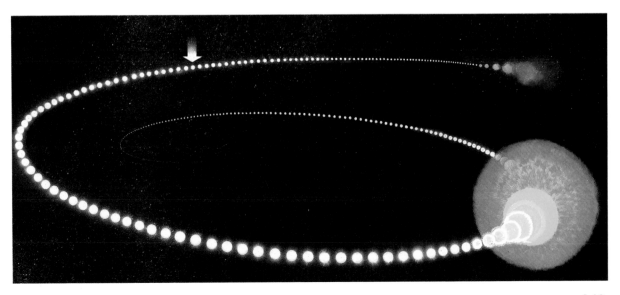

► *This diagram shows how stars can be grouped according to how bright they are. The brilliant 'lighthouse' stars are blue giants – large and very hot. The dim 'matchstick' stars are small red dwarfs. Our Sun is a yellowish 'table-lamp' star. If a blue giant were placed in the middle of our solar system instead, it would melt the Earth and boil away the ice on the farthest planets.*

Bright	20,000°C Blue-white	10,000°C White	6,000°C Yellow	4,500°C Orange	3,000°C Red
🗼	○				
💡		○			
💡			○		
🔦				○	
Dim					○

▼ *Stars appear to us to twinkle because their light bends as it travels through the Earth's atmosphere.*

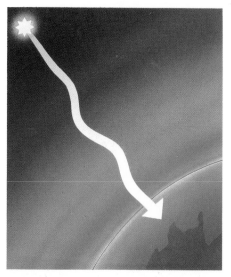

huge, fiery balls of gas like our SUN.

Stars begin as clouds of gas. GRAVITY pulls the gas particles in towards the middle of each cloud. There the particles collide and grow hot, and other particles press in.

HYDROGEN atoms change into helium atoms by a process called nuclear fusion. That process gives off NUCLEAR ENERGY. This is what makes stars glow so brightly.

Stars swell as they use their hydrogen. Astronomers call such stars *red giants*. Red giants later shrink into tiny white-hot stars called *white dwarfs*. In time, these cool and fade into the darkness of space.

Starch

Starch is a substance found in plants. Cereals such as wheat, rice and maize are particularly rich in starch. Other plants that contain it are peas, beans and potatoes. Starch is a *carbohydrate*, which means that it is made up of carbon, oxygen and hydrogen, the same ingredients found in sugar. It is important to have starch in our diet because it gives energy.

Pure starch is a white powder that is used in the making of many food products. It is also used to glaze paper and for stiffening cottons, linens and other materials.

> **Starch makes up about four-fifths of rice and three-quarters of wheat, rye and maize. About 80 per cent of all commercial starch is made from maize and is called corn starch.**

Starfish

Starfish are creatures that live on the seabed. Most have five arms that stick out like the spokes of a wheel. Starfish do not have backbones. But they have a SKELETON made up of bony plates. They creep about on tiny tube feet arranged along the underside of their arms.

A starfish can open and eat a cockle. It uses its tube feet to grip both halves of the cockle's shell. Then it pulls the shell open. The starfish pushes part of its stomach out of its mouth, which is under the middle of its body. The stomach slips inside the cockle shell and digests the cockle's soft body.

Starfish larva

▲ *The larva of the starfish looks nothing like the adult. It floats in the sea with other plankton (tiny animals and plants).*

Steam Engine

Boiling water turns into steam. Steam will fill 1700 times more space than the water that it came from. So if you squash steam into a small container it presses hard against the sides. If one side is free to move, the steam pressure will push it outwards.

In the 1700s British inventors began to use this fact to build engines powered by steam. Early steam engines worked with a simple to-and-fro motion. In Thomas Newcomen's engine, a furnace heated water in a boiler. The water gave off steam that pushed a piston up inside a cylinder. When the steam cooled and turned back to water, air pressed the piston down again. Newcomen's engine was used to pump water from flooded mines.

James Watt built a more powerful engine where steam pushed the piston first one way and then the

▼ *Inside a steam engine, steam is produced by heating water to boiling point. The pressure of the expanding steam is used to push a piston to and fro in a hollow tube called a cylinder. The piston fits tightly inside the cylinder so the steam cannot seep around the sides of the piston head. The piston is attached to the piston rod. As the piston rod goes in and out, it drives another rod called the driving rod. The driving rod turns a wheel called the flywheel, which turns steadily even when the piston is at the end of its stroke and is not pushing. In a steam locomotive, the driving rod is attached to a driving wheel.*

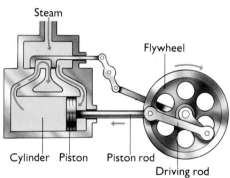

Steam

Flywheel

Cylinder   Piston   Piston rod

Driving rod

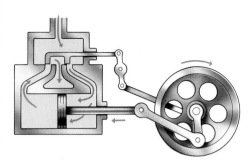

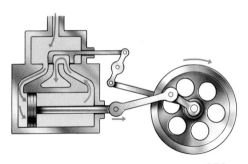

Steam turbines are more efficient than ordinary steam engines. They run more smoothly and are more powerful. In a steam turbine, high-pressure steam is made to strike cupped vanes or propeller-like blades attached to a shaft. The shaft turns at a very high speed. About 80 per cent of all our electricity is produced by steam turbines.

other. Rods from the piston spun a wheel. By the early 1800s, such engines were moving heavy loads faster than men or horses could. Yet, unlike men and horses, steam engines never tired.

Steam engines powered factory machines that made the INDUSTRIAL REVOLUTION possible. They also powered locomotives and steamships. For the first time, people travelled faster than horses.

The INTERNAL COMBUSTION ENGINE has largely taken the place of steam engines. But many ships' propellers, and power station GENERATORS are worked by steam which spins wheels called TURBINES.

▶ Some early cars were driven by steam. This picture shows the Scotte Steam Wagonette, made in 1892.

▲ Robert Louis Stevenson settled with his family on the island of Samoa, in the South Seas, where he died in 1894.

Stevenson, Robert Louis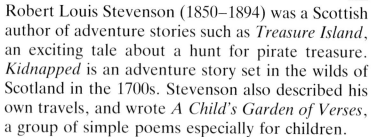

Robert Louis Stevenson (1850–1894) was a Scottish author of adventure stories such as *Treasure Island*, an exciting tale about a hunt for pirate treasure. *Kidnapped* is an adventure story set in the wilds of Scotland in the 1700s. Stevenson also described his own travels, and wrote *A Child's Garden of Verses*, a group of simple poems especially for children.

Stock Exchange

A stock exchange is a place where people called stockbrokers buy and sell *stocks* and *shares*. These are pieces of paper that show that someone owns a share in a business company. A company's stock tends to cost more if the company does well, and

◄ There are a number of important stock exchanges in business centres throughout the world. The pace of buying and selling stocks and shares can be very fast, and computers are now widely used to provide information quickly.

Most people's stomachs are in the upper left side of the abdomen, but the position can vary. Tall, thin persons usually have long, narrow stomachs. Short persons usually have short, wide stomachs. The stomach of a newborn baby is about the size of a small hen's egg. Adult stomachs can hold about a litre.

gets cheaper if it does badly. People buy stock hoping to sell it at a higher price later. Meanwhile they expect to get *dividends* – shares of the money the company makes.

As business grew after the MIDDLE AGES, people needed a market place for buying and selling stock. In 1531 Antwerp opened Europe's first stock exchange. Now, many cities have stock exchanges. Millions of stocks change hands each day in the exchanges of London, New York and Tokyo.

Stomach

Your stomach is a muscular bag, open at both ends and shaped like a fat letter J. It plays an important part in the DIGESTION of food.

When you eat a meal, food travels down your throat to your stomach. The stomach can store a large meal. Juices produced in the stomach kill germs in food. They also moisten and start digesting the food. Stomach muscles churn the mixture, then force it into the small intestine.

Stone Age

The Stone Age was the great span of time before people learned how to make metal tools. Stone Age people used stone, wood, and bone instead of metal. The Stone Age probably began more than

▼ Early stone tools were very simple. They could be held easily and had different edges for cutting or scraping. They may have been used to prepare animal flesh for eating and for scraping skins clean.

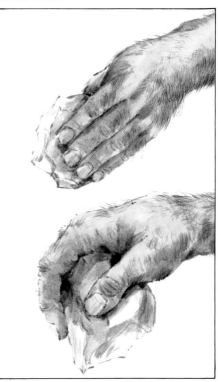

The words 'Stone Age' do not mean a fixed period of time that began and ended on certain dates. When the people of Britain were still in the Stone Age, the ancient Egyptians were living in cities and using metals. On the other hand, there are some people today in remote regions who are living as the people of Britain did in their Stone Age.

three million years ago. It ended in Iraq and Egypt when the Bronze Age began there about 5000 years ago.

The Stone Age had three parts: Old, Middle and New. The Old Stone Age lasted until 10,000 years ago in the Middle East. When it began, hunters could scarcely chip a stone well enough to sharpen it. When the Old Stone Age ended, people had learned to chip flint into delicate spearheads, knives and scrapers.

In the Middle Stone Age, hunters used tiny flakes of flint in arrows and harpoons.

The New Stone Age began in the Middle East about 9000 years ago. New Stone Age people made smooth axe heads of ground stone. Farming replaced hunting in the New Stone Age.

Stonehenge

Stonehenge is a huge prehistoric temple on Salisbury Plain in southern England. The main part is a great circle of standing stones. Each is more than twice as tall as a man and weighs nearly 30 tonnes. Flat stones were laid across the tops of the standing stones to form a ring. Inside the ring stood smaller stones, and a great block that may have been an altar. The big stones were raised 3500 years ago. Other parts are older.

▼ *Archaeologists can tell that some of the huge stones that form Stonehenge were dragged from a site over 400 kilometres away. This task must have taken our prehistoric ancestors years to complete.*

Stork

These big birds have long beaks and legs. They can wade in swamps and capture fish and frogs. But some kinds prefer feeding on dead animals. More than a dozen kinds of stork live in warm parts of the world.

The white stork is the best-known kind. In summer, white storks nest in Europe and central Asia. In autumn, they fly south. Flapping their wings soon makes storks tired. They prefer to soar and glide.

▲ White storks often nest on rooftops in towns in Europe, Asia and North Africa. Black storks breed in northern Germany and in Eastern Europe.

Stuarts

The House of Stuart was a royal family that ruled Scotland from 1371 to 1603 and England and Scotland from 1603 until 1714.

In the 1000s the family lived in France. But by the middle of the 1100s a member of the family had become the king of Scotland's steward (the man who ran the royal household). From then on, the family always provided the Scottish king with a steward. Because of this, the family name became Stewart, which later changed to Stuart.

As royal rulers, the Stuarts were unlucky. Out of 14 who were crowned, 6 were killed, and 7 became king or queen before they were old enough to rule

▼ The Stuart kings and queens of England began with James I, who ruled as James I of England and as James VI of Scotland.

THE STUARTS

JAMES I
1603–1625

CHARLES I
1625–1649

JAMES II
1685–1688

CHARLES II
1660–1685

ANNE
1702–1714

WILLIAM III
1689–1702

MARY II
1689–1694

The Stuart family came from Brittany in France and were originally *stewards* to the Scottish kings. The first spelling was Stewart, the old Scots version. During the 16th century, French influence led to the adoption of the spellings Steuart and Stuart. This was because the French have no letter 'w' in their alphabet.

▲ *One of the earliest submarines, the* Turtle *was powered by a hand propeller and had room for just one person. In 1776 it was used for the first submarine attack on a warship.*

▼ *This cutaway view of a nuclear submarine shows how much of its interior is taken up with the nuclear reactor and turbines that drive it. The crew's quarters and operating area occupy relatively little space.*

for themselves. The first Stuart was Robert II.

MARY, QUEEN OF SCOTS was put to death by ELIZABETH I, who feared that Mary might replace her as the Queen of England. Mary's grandfather had been married to the daughter of an English king. So when Elizabeth died without leaving a child to inherit her throne, the crown went to Mary's son James. He ruled as JAMES I of England and as James VI of Scotland.

The Stuart kings of England claimed so much power that they became unpopular. CHARLES I was executed in the English CIVIL WAR, and CHARLES II's brother JAMES II was forced to leave the country. The throne went to his eldest daughter Mary and her husband William of Orange, then to James's sister ANNE. Under Anne, England and Scotland were united as Great Britain. Anne was the last Stuart ruler. She died in 1714.

Stuart supporters called Jacobites led two revolts to win back the throne for James's descendants. In 1715 they fought for his son, James Edward. In 1745 they fought for Charles Edward, James Edward's son 'Bonnie Prince Charlie'. Both revolts failed.

Submarine

Submarines are boats that can travel under water. To dive, the crew of a submarine make it heavier than the amount of water needed to fill the space taken up by the submarine. To rise, the crew make the submarine lighter than that amount of water. When water and submarine both weigh the same, the boat stays at the same level under the surface.

In 1620 someone rowed a wood and leather submarine down the river Thames. But the first submarine that worked well was not built until the

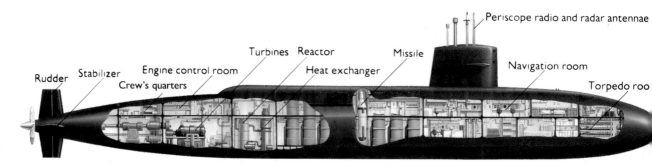

Rudder Stabilizer Engine control room Turbines Reactor Heat exchanger Missile Navigation room Periscope radio and radar antennae Torpedo roo

Crew's quarters

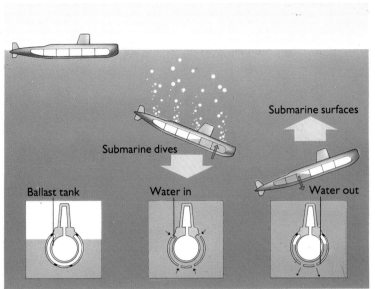

Submarine surfaces

Submarine dives

Ballast tank | Water in | Water out

◀ *A submarine can float when its ballast tanks are kept full of air. If water is pumped into the tanks and the air is pumped out, the submarine begins to sink. To come back to the surface, compressed air is pumped back into the ballast tanks, forcing the water out.*

▼ *Deepstar IV, one of the smaller deep-diving submarines, can operate at depths of more than 1200 metres.*

1770s. Both these early submarines were worked by hand. They were slow and under-powered.

In the 1870s an English clergyman invented a submarine powered by a steam engine. But each time it dived the crew had to pull down its chimney and put out the fire that heated water to produce steam.

By 1900 the American inventor John P. Holland had produced a much better underwater boat. Petrol engines drove it on the surface. But petrol needs air to burn. Under water the boat ran on battery-driven motors that did not need air.

In 1955 came the first nuclear-powered submarine. Such boats can travel around the world without having to come to the surface. In 1958 the nuclear submarine *Nautilus* of the United States Navy made the first submerged crossing under the North Pole. These submarines are armed with nuclear missiles that can strike at enemy targets thousands of kilometres away.

Sudan

This is the largest nation in AFRICA. It is nearly four times the size of France.

Sudan is a hot country in north-east Africa. Desert sprawls across the north. There are flat grasslands in the middle. The south has forests and a huge swamp.

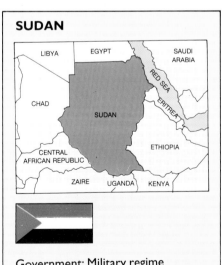

SUDAN

LIBYA | EGYPT | SAUDI ARABIA
CHAD | | RED SEA
| SUDAN | ERITREA
CENTRAL AFRICAN REPUBLIC | | ETHIOPIA
| ZAIRE | UGANDA | KENYA

Government: Military regime
Capital: Khartoum
Area: 2,505,813 sq km
Population: 28,311,000
Language: Arabic
Currency: Sudanese pound

▶ *Dinka tribespeople at a cattle market at Wafu in the Sudan. The traditional way of life of many tribes is being threatened by drought and civil war, both in the Sudan and in other parts of Africa.*

▲ *The Suez Canal crosses the narrow isthmus between the Mediterranean and the long, thin Gulf of Suez, at the northern end of the Red Sea.*

The average sugar beet weighs about a kilogram and stores about 14 teaspoons of sugar in its fat root. For many years sugar was an expensive luxury. Elizabeth I had sugar at her table, but at that time its main use was in medicine.

Saccharin is a white powder made from coal tar. It is 400 times sweeter than sugar, but it has no food value. It is used in reducing and diabetic diets.

Sudanese people include Arabs and blacks. Most live near the NILE, which flows north across the country. Khartoum is the capital city. The north and south of the country have been at war since 1988.

Suez Canal

The Suez Canal crosses Egypt between Port Said on the Mediterranean Sea and Suez on the Red Sea. It is the world's longest canal that can be used by big ships. It measures 160 km from end to end and 60 metres across its bed. Ships use it as a shortcut on voyages between Europe and Asia. This saves them from sailing 9000 km around southern Africa.

The canal was begun in 1859 by a French company run by the engineer Ferdinand de Lesseps. More than 8000 men and hundreds of camels worked on it for 10 years. France and the United Kingdom operated the canal until Egypt took it over in 1956. Sunken ships blocked the canal for eight years after Egypt's war with Israel in 1967. But dredging has now made it much wider and deeper than it was a century ago.

Sugar

Sugar is a sweet-tasting food. We eat it as an ingredient in ice cream, sweets and soft drinks. We use sugar crystals to sweeten cereals, coffee and tea.

Sugar gives our body energy more quickly than

any other food. But eating too many sugary things can cause your teeth to decay.

All sugar contains carbon, hydrogen and oxygen. Different groupings of these ATOMS produce different kinds of sugars. The kind we eat most of is known as *sucrose*.

Every green PLANT produces sugar. But most of the sugar that we eat comes from two plants. One is sugarcane, a type of giant grass. The other is sugar beet, a plant with a thick root rich in sugar.

Sulphur

Sulphur is an ELEMENT often found as yellow CRYSTALS lying at the mouth of volcanoes and hot springs. Cabbages, eggs and other foods contain some sulphur. Plants and animals need a little sulphur in order to grow well.

People use sulphur to make drugs, gunpowder, fertilizer, and other useful chemicals.

Sun

The Sun is just one of many millions of STARS in the MILKY WAY. But it is also the centre of the SOLAR SYSTEM. The PLANETS and their moons all whirl around it. The heat and light given out by the Sun make it possible for plants and animals to live here on the planet that we call the EARTH.

The Sun seems small because it is so far away. A

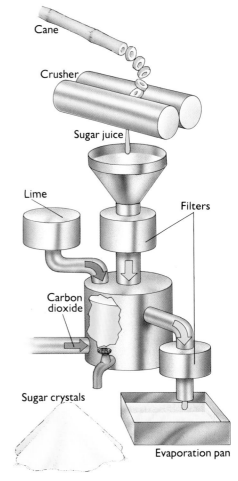

▲ Sugarcane is processed by extracting the juice and then filtering it and heating it to make crystals of sugar. Carbon dioxide and lime are used in the purification process.

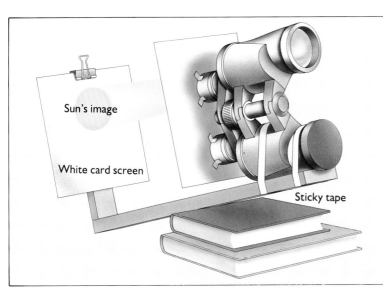

SEE IT YOURSELF
This is a safe way to study the Sun. Clip a sheet of white card onto an L-shaped wooden frame. Place a pair of binoculars onto the frame so that the eyepieces are about 30 cm away from the card. Move the binoculars around until images of the Sun appear on the card. Focus the binoculars to get a sharp image. Now stick another sheet of card over the eyepieces, cutting a round hole for one of them in the card. Tape the binoculars onto the wooden frame. Cover one of the lenses. You should get a single, sharp, steady image of the Sun on the card.

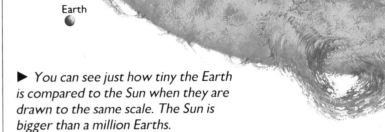

Core of helium

Hydrogen layer

Photosphere

Earth

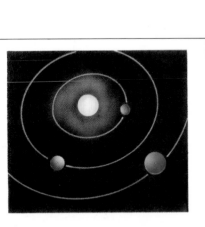

▲ *The Sun has been a yellowish star for about 4600 million years – as long as the Earth has existed.*

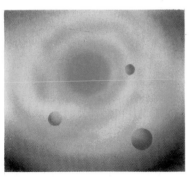

▲ *In some 5000 million years, the Sun will become a hot, red giant.*

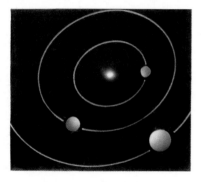

▲ *In another 5000 million years, it will fade to become small and dim.*

▶ *You can see just how tiny the Earth is compared to the Sun when they are drawn to the same scale. The Sun is bigger than a million Earths.*

spacecraft that took an hour to zoom around the Earth would need five months to reach the Sun. In fact, the Sun is so big that you could fit a million Earths inside it with room to spare. A bucketful of the Sun's substance would weigh far less than a bucketful of rock from the Earth. But the whole Sun would weigh over 750 times more than all the planets put together.

The Sun is a great glowing ball of gases. In the middle of the Sun a process called nuclear fusion turns HYDROGEN gas into helium gas. The change releases huge amounts of NUCLEAR ENERGY. The Sun beams out its energy in all directions as *electromagnetic waves*. Some of these waves give us HEAT and LIGHT. But there are also radio waves, ultraviolet rays, X-rays and others.

The Sun was formed from a mass of gas and dust five billion years ago. It contains enough fuel to keep it glowing for another five billion years.

Superconductivity

Some materials allow electricity to flow through them more easily than other materials. Good conductors such as copper and silver have little resistance to an electric current – but they do have some. Electricity struggling to pass through them makes them warm. However, in 1911 it was discovered that the metal mercury loses all its electrical resistance when it is cooled to about minus 270°C – very, very cold indeed. It became a superconductor – but it was very expensive and difficult to produce such a low temperature.

Then, in 1987, scientists began to experiment with new materials. They found that certain ceramic (clay-based) mixtures could be made to superconduct at higher temperatures – as high as about minus 170°C – still very cold, but easier to achieve. Now the race is on to find materials that are superconductors at room temperature. If this is achieved, the whole electronics industry will be changed. Computers will become smaller and faster, and machines such as medical scanners will be much cheaper to produce and run.

> **If scientists succeed in making substances superconductive at ordinary air temperatures, it will be possible to produce electromagnets that generate large magnetic fields without losing any energy. These could be used for high-speed trains supported above the track by powerful magnets. But perhaps the most important use for superconductive materials will be in super-efficient power generation plants.**

Supersonic Flight

'Supersonic' flight means flying faster than sound travels through the air. This speed is about 1225 km/h at sea level. Higher up, sound travels at a slower speed.

When a plane flies slower than the speed of sound, the air ahead has time to divide smoothly and flow around the plane. But with supersonic flight the air ahead has no time to prepare for the coming of the plane. Instead, the air is disturbed so much it forms a shock wave that makes a loud bang and may badly buffet the plane.

▼ *A plane flying slower than the speed of sound (left) creates disturbances in the air pressure, which travel at the speed of sound and so move along ahead of the plane. A plane moving at the speed of sound (centre) is moving as fast as the disturbances it causes. These pile up in front of the plane and form a shock wave. A plane travelling faster than the speed of sound (right) breaks through the sound 'barrier', but creates a shock wave which, when it reaches the ground, is heard as a sonic boom.*

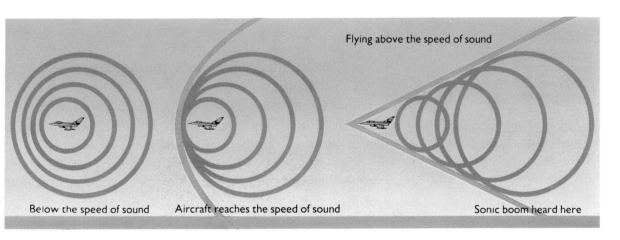

Flying above the speed of sound

Below the speed of sound   Aircraft reaches the speed of sound   Sonic boom heard here

When an aircraft is flying at the speed of sound it is said to be flying at Mach 1. Mach 2 means twice the speed of sound, and so on. At a height of 40,000 feet (12,000 metres) the speed of sound is only about 1000 km/h, instead of 1225 km/h at ground level.

Aircraft builders prevented buffeting by building planes such as *Concorde* with long, sharp noses and thin, swept-back wings. A supersonic plane has flown six times as fast as sound.

Surgery

Surgery involves making an incision in a person's body to remove or mend a damaged part of the body. Surgery is performed in a hospital by a specially trained doctor called a surgeon. He or she works in a specially equipped room. X-RAY and other tests may help to show the surgeon how best

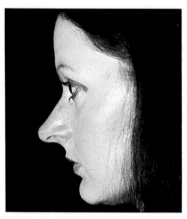

to operate. Before an operation, a patient is given an anaesthetic so that he or she feels no pain.

The surgeon cuts the patient open with a sharp knife called a scalpel. Other tools help the surgeon prevent bleeding and hold back flaps of skin. After operating, the surgeon closes the wound by sewing its edges together or with a special tape.

▶ Plastic surgery is usually performed to repair the surface of the body after serious burns or accidents. It may also be performed for purely cosmetic reasons, to improve a person's appearance. These photographs show the same woman's profile before and after cosmetic surgery to reduce the size of her nose.

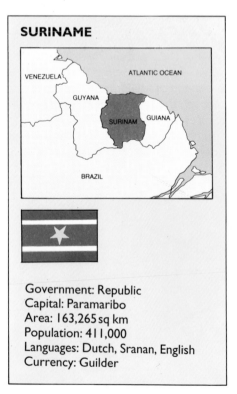

SURINAME

VENEZUELA
ATLANTIC OCEAN
GUYANA
SURINAM
GUIANA
BRAZIL

Government: Republic
Capital: Paramaribo
Area: 163,265 sq km
Population: 411,000
Languages: Dutch, Sranan, English
Currency: Guilder

Suriname

Suriname is a small country on the north-central coast of South America. People of many races live there and grow rice, bananas, cocoa, sugar and fruits along the coastal lowlands. The most important product of Suriname is bauxite, from which aluminium is made.

Suriname became a Dutch possession in 1667 when Britain handed it over in exchange for the Dutch colony of New Amsterdam (now New York). Suriname became independent in 1975.

◀ *This surveyor is taking measurements so that a new road can be built exactly along the route planned for it.*

Surveying

Surveying means using measuring instruments and working out certain sums to find out the exact positions of places on the Earth's surface. This kind of information makes it possible for people to make maps and charts and to build bridges, roads and buildings.

The ancient Egyptians used surveying methods as early as 1400 BC to position boundary marks that were covered each year by the Nile's flood waters. They must also have used surveying to build the pyramids as accurately as they did. The Babylonians, about 3500 BC, made maps to an accurate scale.

Swan

These big, graceful waterbirds are among the heaviest birds able to fly. To take off, they need a long, clear stretch of water.

Swans swim with webbed feet, lowering their necks to feed on underwater plants. They build bulky nests by pools or rivers. Their young are known as cygnets.

Some kinds of swan fly south in spring and autumn. They fly in V-shaped flocks.

▼ *Although swans are heavy birds, their long, broad wings and powerful breast muscles allow them to fly. But they need a good long 'runway', on land or water, for take-off.*

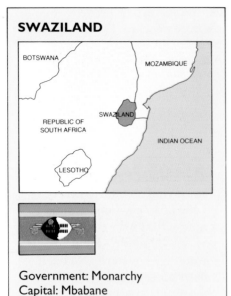

SWAZILAND

Government: Monarchy
Capital: Mbabane
Area: 17,363 sq km
Population: 913,000
Languages: Siswati, English
Currency: Lilangeni

▶ *Fishing boats and huts at the port of Kyrkesund, near Göteborg, on the western coast of Sweden. Fishing is an important part of the Swedish economy.*

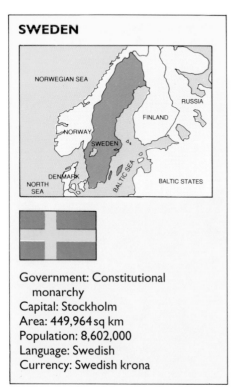

SWEDEN

Government: Constitutional
  monarchy
Capital: Stockholm
Area: 449,964 sq km
Population: 8,602,000
Language: Swedish
Currency: Swedish krona

Swaziland

The kingdom of Swaziland in south-east Africa is almost completely surrounded by South Africa. Most of the people live by raising cattle and growing maize. Large forests yield wood products. Swaziland is dependent on South Africa for most of its trade. It is a former British protectorate that became independent in 1968, and is a member of the Commonwealth. The king is Mswati III.

Sweden

Sweden is the fourth largest nation in EUROPE. The country lies in the north between Norway and the Baltic Sea. Mountains cover most of the west, and forests take up more than half of the land. Their CONIFER trees yield much of the world's softwood. Most of Sweden's electricity comes from rivers flowing down the mountains. Farmers produce milk, meat, grains and sugar beets on farmlands near the coast. The north is too cold for farming, but it has rich iron mines.

Most of the eight million Swedes live in the south. The capital, Stockholm, is there.

Swift, Jonathan

Jonathan Swift (1667–1745) was an English writer, famous for books that poked fun at the silly, cruel behaviour of people and governments. Most children enjoy stories from *Gulliver's Travels*. This tells of voyages to very strange lands. On his first voyage, Gulliver reaches the land of Lilliput, where the people are only two centimetres tall. Then he travels to a land of giants.

Swimming

Swimming is the skill or sport of staying afloat and moving through water. Swimming is healthy exercise, and being able to swim may save your life if you fall into water by accident. Many animals know how to swim from birth. But people have to learn, usually with help from a trained instructor.

Learners often start in a pool or at the edge of the sea. First they should float or glide. Then they can try kicking. Arm movements come last. Beginners must learn to fit in breathing with arm movements. Swimmers usually use one or more of five main strokes. These are called the breaststroke, butterfly stroke, backstroke, sidestroke, and crawl.

▲ *Apart from* Gulliver's Travels, *Jonathan Swift published all his work anonymously and without being paid.*

▼ *These pictures show how the arm and leg movements are co-ordinated in four of the main swimming strokes: crawl, backstroke, butterfly and breaststroke.*

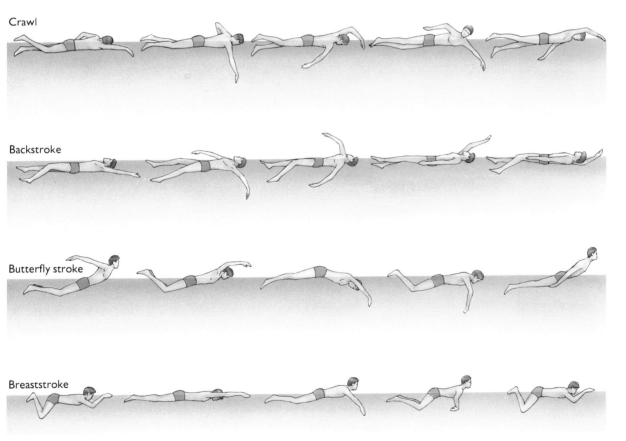

Crawl

Backstroke

Butterfly stroke

Breaststroke

SWITZERLAND

Government: Federal state
Capital: Bern
Area: 41,288 sq km
Population: 6,828,000
Languages: German, French, Italian
Currency: Swiss franc

Switzerland

This small, mountainous country lies in the south-central part of EUROPE. The sharp, snowy peaks of the Alps and their steep-sided valleys fill most of southern Switzerland. In summer, tourists pick wild flowers and watch dairy cattle grazing on the mountain meadows. Winter visitors to the many resorts ski down the snowy alpine slopes.

Most of the country's crops are grown where the mountains meet the lower land of the Swiss Plateau. Here, too, stand most of Switzerland's cities, including Bern, the capital. Swiss factories make chemicals, machinery, watches and chocolates.

Most of the six and a half million Swiss speak German, French or Italian. The Swiss people are among the most prosperous in the world.

Sydney

Sydney is the largest city in AUSTRALIA, and the capital of New South Wales. More than three million people live in Sydney. It stands on a fine natural harbour (Port Jackson) crossed by a famous steel-arch bridge. Sydney makes chemicals, machinery and ships and is an important port. It was founded in 1788 as a settlement for convicts sent out from England.

Syria

This Arab country lies just east of the Mediterranean Sea. Much of Syria is covered by dry plains that are hot in summer and chilly in winter. There are over 12 million people. Nomads drive flocks of sheep and goats over the dry lands. Farmers grow grains, grapes and apricots in areas where rivers or rain provide water.

Most Syrian towns grew up on the roads used long ago to bring goods from the East. In 1516, Syria was conquered by the Turks, and was ruled by Turkey for 400 years. After World War I, the French ruled the country on behalf of the League of Nations. Syria gained its independence in 1943 and has close ties with Libya.

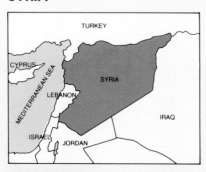

SYRIA

Government: Republic
Capital: Damascus
Area: 185,180 sq km
Population: 12,113,000
Language: Arabic
Currency: Syrian pound

Taiwan

Taiwan is an island country 140 km off the coast of China. Also called Formosa, its official name is the Republic of China. Rice is the main crop. Most Taiwanese are Chinese whose ancestors emigrated to the island in the 1700s. Others are Chinese who fled from the mainland after the Communist take-over of China in 1949. Taiwan held the Chinese seat in the United Nations until 1971, when Communist China was admitted and Taiwan expelled. Taiwan's economy is one of the strongest in the world.

Tajikistan

Tajikistan is a mountainous country in central Asia. The people are mostly Moslem. Tajikistan was a republic of the former Soviet Union until 1991.

Taj Mahal

This is the world's most beautiful tomb. It stands on the Jumna River at Agra in northern India. The emperor Shah Jahan built it for his favourite wife, Mumtaz Mahal, who died in 1631.

▼ *The Taj Mahal, in Agra, India.*

TAIWAN

Government: Democracy
Capital: Taipei
Area: 36,000 sq km
Population: 20,878,000
Languages: Chinese, Taiwan, Hakka
Currency: Taiwan dollar

TAJIKISTAN

Government: Parliamentary republic
Capital: Dushanbe
Area: 143,000 sq km
Population: 5,680,000
Languages: Tadzhik, Russian
Currency: Ruble

TANZANIA

Government: Republic
Capital: Dodoma
Area: 945,087 sq km
Population: 27,791,000
Languages: Swahili, English
Currency: Tanzanian shilling

▶ In a tape recorder, the record and replay heads are made up of coils wound around an iron core. When a cassette is placed in a tape recorder, the tape drive motor moves the tape smoothly over the record/replay heads. When sounds are recorded they pass through the recording head as signals. They make a magnetic pattern which is stored on the tape. Meters on the tape recorder show how loud the recording level is. To play back something that has been recorded, the head reads the patterns, turns them back into signals and passes them on to the amplifier.

Tanzania

Tanzania consists of two parts: Tanganyika on the east African mainland and the islands of Zanzibar and Pemba off the coast. They joined to form one country in 1964. The country contains part of Africa's largest lake, Lake Victoria, and Africa's highest mountain, Mount Kilimanjaro (5895 m). Tanzania has much wildlife and beautiful scenery. Diamonds are the country's most valuable mineral. Gold is also mined. Tanzania's former capital and largest city is Dar es Salaam.

Tape Recorder

A tape recorder turns sound waves into a magnetic pattern on tape. When played, the pattern changes back into sound.

A microphone inside or connected to the recorder changes sound into an electrical signal. This is

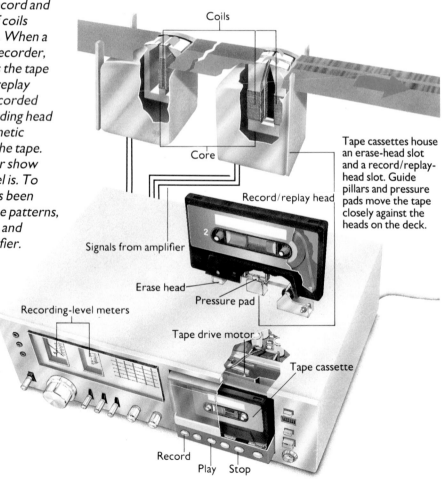

Coils

Core

Tape cassettes house an erase-head slot and a record/replay-head slot. Guide pillars and pressure pads move the tape closely against the heads on the deck.

Record/replay head

Signals from amplifier

Erase head

Pressure pad

Recording-level meters

Tape drive motor

Tape cassette

Record

Play   Stop

amplified (made stronger) and fed to the recording head. The head produces a magnetic field which magnetizes the tape as it passes the head.

When playing the tape back, the magnetic field produces an electrical signal which goes to an amplifier and loudspeaker.

Tapestry

Tapestries are designs or pictures woven in cloth. Making tapestries is a very old craft. The Egyptians made tapestries about 1700 years ago.

Tapestries are made by WEAVING coloured silk thread across rows of strong linen or wool threads held in a frame.

The tapestry design is drawn onto the linen threads with ink. The weaver works from the back of the tapestry.

▲ Tapestries such as this 15th century Flemish work give us a clear idea of how people dressed and behaved at the time.

Taste

We can taste food because we have taste buds on our TONGUES. Your tongue is covered in tiny bumps. The taste buds are buried in the sides of these bumps. There are clusters of buds on the back, tip and sides of the tongue. NERVES running from the buds to the brain tell you whether the food you are eating is sweet, sour, bitter or salty.

Flavour is a mixture of the taste and the SMELL of food. If you have a bad cold and your nose is blocked, food hardly tastes of anything. The most comfortable way to take bad-tasting medicine is to hold your nose while you swallow.

Bitter

Sour

Sweet

Salt

▲ Each patch of taste buds on the tongue picks up one kind of taste.

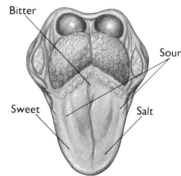

SEE IT YOURSELF
This simple experiment will show you where your different taste buds are. Place some sugar, lemon juice, salt and vanilla essence on a plate. Make sure they do not mix. Using a clean paintbrush, put a little of each substance on different parts of your tongue. Can you taste the sugar and salt on the sides of your tongue? Where do you taste the other substances?

Many different ways of taxing people have been used in the past. There are many old houses around England with some of their windows bricked up. This happened because a window tax was introduced in 1696 and stayed in force until 1851. People had to pay a tax on every window over ten that they had in their house, so many people bricked up windows that were not really necessary.

Tax

The government of a country must have money to carry on its work. It gets most of this money by taxing people. *Direct* taxes are those people pay directly to the government on their income – income tax. How much income tax a person pays depends on several things. The higher a person's income, the more he or she pays in tax. A married person pays less than a single person with the same income.

Indirect taxes are those charged on some goods bought in the shops or elsewhere. Every time a motorist buys petrol, a part of the cost is tax which goes to the government.

In addition to government taxes, many people pay taxes to their local council.

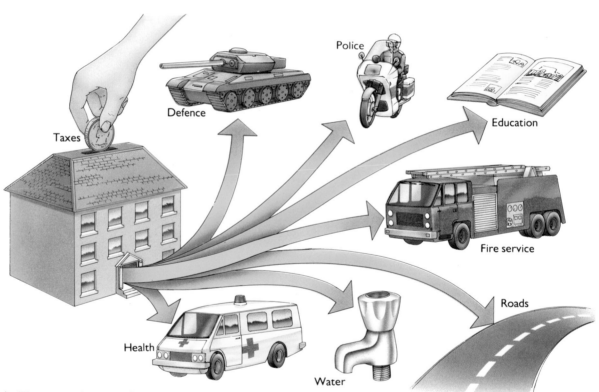

▲ The taxes that people pay are used to keep essential services running so that they are available to everyone. Some of the things paid for by taxes are shown in this picture, but there are many more, too.

Tchaikovsky, Peter Ilyich

Peter Tchaikovsky (1840–1893) was one of the most famous and popular musical composers. He was born at Votkinsk in Russia and studied music at the conservatory in St Petersburg. He lived in great poverty until a wealthy lady, Nadezhda von Meck,

▲ *Tchaikovsky wrote beautiful ballet music and* Sleeping Beauty *(left) is one of the most popular ballets. But though his works of music were successful, the composer suffered from deep depression.*

offered to make him a yearly allowance of money to support himself. Tchaikovsky never met Madame von Meck, but they wrote many letters to each other.

Tchaikovsky was an unhappy man, but his music was full of warmth. He made several tours abroad, but he preferred to be at home in the countryside. Among his best-known works are the ballet *Swan Lake*, his first *Piano Concerto*, the *Violin Concerto in D Major*, the ballets *Nutcracker* and *Sleeping Beauty*, and his *Symphony No.6*, the 'Pathétique'.

▼ *If a tea plant were allowed to grow to its full height, it could reach 10 metres. Instead, it is kept small and bushy by pruning so that all its energy goes into making new leaves.*

Tea

Tea is a refreshing drink that is made by pouring boiling water over the dried, chopped leaves of the tea plant.

Tea was first grown in China. It was brought to Europe by the Dutch in the 1660s. Today most tea is grown in northern India, China and Sri Lanka.

Teeth

Teeth are made to cut, tear or crush food so that it can be swallowed. Cutting teeth are called incisors; tearing teeth are called canines; and crushing teeth are called molars. Meat-eating animals have large

▶ *Your first set of teeth are called milk teeth. There are 10 on top and 10 on the bottom. As you grow, these teeth become loose and fall out. They are replaced by a permanent set of teeth, 32 in all.*

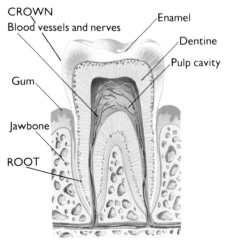

CROWN
Blood vessels and nerves
Enamel
Dentine
Pulp cavity
Gum
Jawbone
ROOT

Incisors
Molars
Canines
CHILD'S MILK TEETH
ADULT'S (PERMANENT) TEETH

▲ *There are three layers in a tooth. At the centre is a space full of nerves and blood vessels; around that is a bony wall of dentine. On top is a layer of hard, shiny enamel.*

canines for tearing flesh. Plant-eaters have sharp incisors and large molars for snapping off and grinding stringy stalks. Humans have all three kinds of teeth because we eat all kinds of food.

There are two parts to a tooth. The root, which has one, two, or three prongs, is fixed in the jawbone. The crown is the part you can see. Tooth decay happens when bacteria mix with sugar. This dissolves tooth enamel, making holes that let infection get inside the tooth.

Telecommunications

The Greek word *tele* means 'far off'. Telecommunications refers to long-distance communication by RADIO, telegraph, TELEPHONE and TELEVISION. Most of today's long-distance communication is electronic.

Telecommunications are very fast because the sound and picture signals travel as electric currents along wires, radio waves through the air and space, or light waves along glass fibres. Radio waves and light waves travel at 300,000 km a second. Electric signals travel almost as fast. Telephone and radio networks use communications satellites orbiting in space high above the Earth.

Telex and facsimile (fax) machines play a big part

Telephone systems and cable television have until recently used metal wires to carry their electric signals. These services are now beginning to use cables containing optical fibres – long, thin, glass fibres. These fibres carry signals in the form of light rays fired along each fibre by a laser. Each fine glass fibre can carry more channels than a much heavier and bulkier copper wire.

◀ *A facsimile machine looks similar to a photocopier, but it is equipped with a telephone. When sending a message, the scanner inside the fax machine reads the page and converts it into electronic signals that can be sent down the phone line. The machine at the receiving end then translates the signals back and prints out a copy.*

in today's communications. Messages are typed or fed as documents into these machines and are reproduced in seconds at the receiving terminal.

Telephone

Telephones let you speak to someone far away. When you pick up a telephone receiver, a weak electric current is switched on. When you speak into the mouthpiece, you speak into a microphone.

Waves of SOUND from your voice hit a metal disc inside the microphone and make it vibrate. These vibrations travel along the telephone wires as electrical waves. When they reach the other end, they hit another metal disc in the earpiece. This changes the vibrations back into sound waves, which the person you are calling hears as your voice.

The first electric telephone, made by Alexander BELL in 1876, produced only a very weak sound over long distances. Today, telephone networks use a worldwide system of cables and communications SATELLITES.

▶ *Speaking into a telephone mouthpiece makes a diaphragm vibrate and compresses carbon granules, to make an electric current vary. The current flows along wires to another telephone and enters the earpiece, where an electromagnet makes a diaphragm vibrate to produce the sound of your voice.*

▲ *A refracting telescope uses two lenses to focus rays of light from distant stars and planets.*

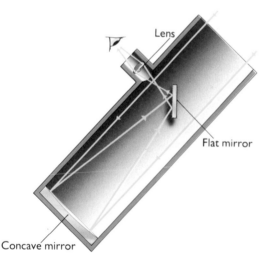

▲ *Reflecting telescopes use a large concave mirror to reflect light onto a smaller mirror that directs it through a lens to the eye.*

▶ *The 4.2-metre William Herschel telescope in its dome at the La Palma Observatory in the Canary Islands. It is the third largest single-mirror telescope in the world. It is at a high altitude – 2400 metres above sea level – where the sky is clear.*

Telescope

Telescopes make things that are far away look nearer. They work by gathering the LIGHT from an object and bending it to make a tiny picture called an image. The image is then made larger so we can see it.

There are two kinds of telescope. The LENS or refractor telescope uses two lenses fixed in a tube to keep out unwanted light. A large lens at one end of the tube collects the light. It is called the object lens. A smaller lens called the eyepiece makes the image larger.

The image you see through this kind of telescope is upside down. If you want to turn the image the right way around, a third lens is needed. Binoculars are two lens telescopes fixed together.

The other kind of telescope is called a reflecting telescope. Instead of a lens it has a curved mirror to collect light. The mirror is shaped so that the light rays bouncing off it are directed at a second mirror which reflects the ray towards the eyepiece. Since 1900, most of the big astronomical telescopes built have been reflectors.

The idea of the lens telescope was discovered by accident in 1608 by Hans Lippershey, a Dutch eyeglass maker. While holding up two lenses he noticed that the church weathervane looked much closer through them.

Television

Television is a way of sending sounds and pictures through the air. Scientists have been interested in the idea of television since the 1880s. Although John Logie Baird was the first to show how television worked, his success was based on work by many other scientists from all over the world. Baird showed his set in 1926. The first television service opened in 1936 in Britain. Colour television began in the United States in 1956.

At first, all television was black and white. Few people owned television sets because they were very expensive. Now nearly every home has one.

Television works by changing LIGHT waves into electric signals. This happens inside the TV camera. A picture of what is happening in front of the camera forms on a special screen behind the LENS. Behind the screen is an electron gun. This *scans* the screen. It moves from left to right to cover each part of the picture. Each part is turned into an electric signal which is made stronger, then sent to the transmitter. All the signals are broadcast by the transmitter as RADIO waves. They are picked up by

John Logie Baird's first television set was made of old cans, bicycle parts, lenses, sealing wax and string.

▼ *The main part of a television set is the cathode ray tube. The big end is the screen. The narrow end contains three electron guns that fire electrons through the shadow mask onto the phosphor dots on the screen. All the colours you see on a colour television screen are made up from three colours – red, blue and green – and each of the colours is supplied by one of the guns. To receive the signals that provide the programmes, you need an aerial. The aerial may be attached to the set, as here, or installed high up on the roof of a building, so it can receive the radio waves broadcast by the transmitter as clearly as possible.*

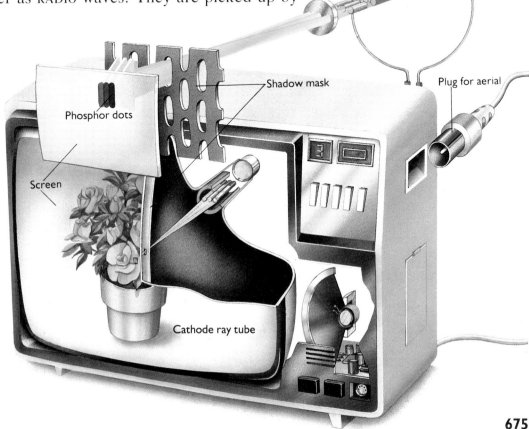

Three electron guns

Shadow mask

Plug for aerial

Phosphor dots

Screen

Cathode ray tube

Rotating disc

▲ *John Logie Baird demonstrated the first TV in 1925. Light from the doll's head passed through holes in a rotating disc. This was turned into electrical signals and back into a beam of light that was projected onto a screen.*

home TV aerials and changed back into electric signals. These pass into the TV set.

Inside the set is a large glass tube called the *cathode ray tube*. The screen that you look at is the front of this tube. The screen is covered with tiny chemical dots. In a colour set, these are arranged in groups of three: one red, one blue, one green. At the back of the tube are three electron guns. These fire beams of electrons to scan the screen just as the camera gun does. As each electron hits the screen, it lights up a dot. These tiny flashes of colour build up the picture on your screen. You do not see lines of coloured flashing lights, because the electron gun moves too fast for the eye to follow. What you see is a picture of what is happening in the television studio.

Live television programmes show you what is happening as it happens. Most programmes are recorded on film or *videotape* and sent out later.

TEMPERATURE CONVERSION TABLE

	Celsius (Centigrade)	Fahrenheit
Freezing Point	**0**	**32**
	10	50
	20	68
	30	86
	40	104
	50	122
	60	140
	70	158
	80	176
	90	194
Boiling Point	**100**	**212**
	110	230
	120	248
	130	266
	140	284
	150	302
	200	392
	250	482
	300	572

To convert Fahrenheit to Celsius, subtract 32, multiply by 5, and divide by 9. To convert Celsius to Fahrenheit, multiply by 9, divide by 5, and add 32.

Temperature

Temperature is the measurement of heat. It is measured on a scale marked on a THERMOMETER. Most people in the world today use the Celsius scale. The Fahrenheit scale is most often used in the United States.

Some animals, including mammals such as humans, are warm-blooded. Their temperature stays much the same. Humans can stand quite a wide range of body temperatures. A healthy person's normal body temperature is 37°C. When he or she is ill, their temperature might go up to 41°C or more, and they could still survive.

Other animals, such as snakes, lizards and frogs, are cold-blooded. Their body temperature goes up and down with the temperature of their surroundings. Many cold-blooded animals can survive until their body temperature drops almost to freezing point.

Tennis

Tennis is a game for two or four people played on a specially marked court, which is divided in half by a net 3 feet (91 cm) high. If two people play it is called a singles match. If four people play it is called a doubles match.

Tennis balls must be about 2½ inches (63 mm) in diameter and weigh about 2 ounces (56.7 grams). A tennis racket can be any size.

A tennis match is divided into sets. Usually women play the best of three sets and men the best of five. Each set has at least six games. To win a game, a player, or pair of players, must score at least four points. Modern tennis is a version of an old French game called real tennis or royal tennis.

Teresa, Mother

Agnes Gonxha Bojaxhiu was born in 1910 in Skopje, which is now in Macedonia. She gave up her life in a Catholic convent in India to devote herself to helping the poor in the slums of Calcutta.

In 1948 she founded a new order of nuns called the Missionaries of Charity. The woman who had come to be known as Mother Teresa of Calcutta was awarded the Nobel Peace Prize in 1979.

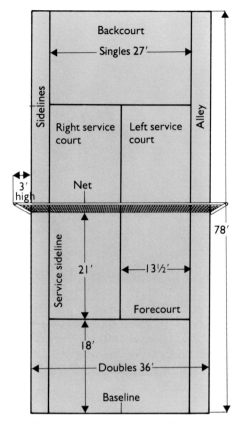

▲ The court markings used for the modern game of tennis.

Termite

Termites are insects that eat wood. They have soft pale bodies and thick waists, and live in the warmer parts of the world. Some termites burrow underground or tunnel into house timbers, causing a lot of

In some species of termite the queen grows to an enormous size, sometimes as much as 20,000 times the size of an ordinary worker termite. She becomes so distended with eggs that she is unable to move about. Some queen termites can lay as many as 30,000 eggs a day.

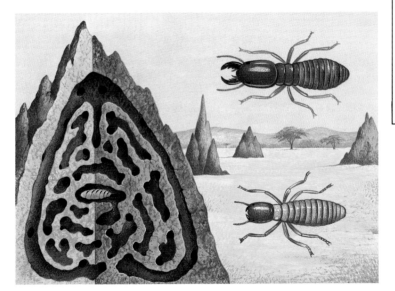

◀ Many termites build their nests inside huge mounds of earth. Inside the nest is a maze of tunnels and chambers where the workers (left, below) look after the young. The queen is at the centre of the nest. Soldier termites (left, above) defend the nest against attack.

▲ *Rigid security checks are carried out on visitors to the Olympic Games in Seoul, Korea in 1988. Terrorists often select major international events as targets for attack.*

damage. Others live in huge mounds of earth.

All termites live in large groups called colonies. Each colony has a queen, her king, soldiers and workers. Most termites are workers. They are small, blind and wingless. They dig the tunnels or build the mound and find food for the rest of the colony.

Soldier termites have large strong heads, and are also blind and wingless. They defend the colony from attack. The queen is many times larger than the other termites and does nothing but lay eggs. She is kept in a chamber in the middle of the colony, with her king. The workers feed her and look after the eggs until they hatch.

Terrorism

Terrorism is the use of violence and terror to achieve political ends. There has been a marked increase in terrorism throughout the world since the end of World War II. Terrorists murder by bombing and shooting, they hijack aircraft, they kidnap people and hold them as hostages, they rob banks and often take part in drug trafficking.

Terrorism is a worldwide problem and countries are banding together more and more to try and get rid of this evil.

Textile

A textile is any cloth made by WEAVING. Before the INDUSTRIAL REVOLUTION, all cloth was made by hand from natural fibres of wool, silk, cotton or linen. Since then, scientists have developed many kinds of man-made fibre. Rayon is made from

▼ *Different patterns of cloth are made by different kinds of weaving. These include (left to right): looped weft threads; weft threads woven in and out of warp threads; plaited weave; a third thread added to a plain (criss-cross) weave.*

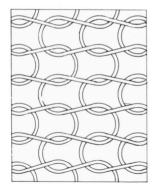
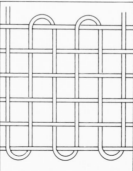
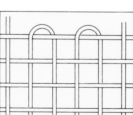
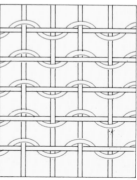

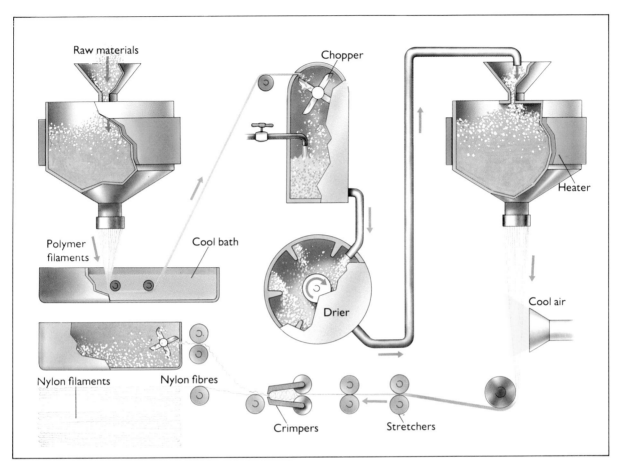

Raw materials

Chopper

Polymer filaments

Cool bath

Heater

Drier

Cool air

Nylon filaments

Nylon fibres

Crimpers

Stretchers

wood. Nylon comes from oil. There are even some fibres made from glass. Man-made fibres are cheaper and often easier to wash and take care of. Sometimes they are mixed with natural fibres to get the best of both materials. Some fabrics are treated to keep them from creasing or fading.

▲ *Stages in the production of nylon fibre. A chemical called caprolactam is heated under pressure to make long polymer filaments. These are cooled, chopped and dried before being melted again. The molten polymer is forced through tiny holes to make fine threads which harden in the air. They can then be twisted together to make nylon yarn.*

Thailand

Thailand is a country in SOUTH-EAST ASIA. It is surrounded by BURMA (Myanmar), LAOS and CAMBODIA. The south coast opens onto the Gulf of Thailand, which is part of the South China Sea.

Most of the people live in the central part of the country. Many rivers flow through this area, making it very fertile. Most people are farmers. Rice is the main crop. They also grow cotton, tobacco, corn, coconuts and bananas. In the north there are large forests of teak, which is a major export. The peninsula in the south-west is very rich in minerals, especially tin.

> Many young men in Thailand become monks for a short time. They put on the monk's saffron-yellow robe, carry a begging bowl and ask for food. This was once the only way to get an education, but nowadays most children go to school between the ages of 7 and 14.

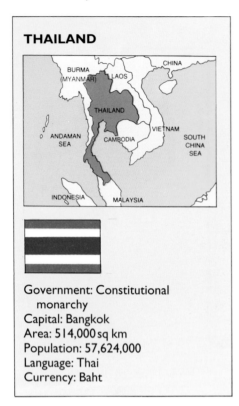

THAILAND

Government: Constitutional
  monarchy
Capital: Bangkok
Area: 514,000 sq km
Population: 57,624,000
Language: Thai
Currency: Baht

Thailand was called Siam before 1939. Thai means 'free', so Thailand means the land of the free. There is a king, but the country is ruled by an elected government.

Thames, River

The river Thames is the longest and most important river in ENGLAND. It begins in the Cotswold Hills and flows eastward, growing wider and wider, until it reaches the North Sea. The Thames flows through the middle of London, which was once the most important port in Europe. Now the docks that once stretched 56km along the riverside are closed, and ships stop lower down the river.

Not very long ago, the Thames around London was one of the dirtiest rivers in the world, full of sewage and chemical waste. Now it has been cleaned so thoroughly that fish are coming back to live in it.

Thatcher, Baroness

Margaret Thatcher (born 1925) became the first woman to head the government of a Western nation. The daughter of a grocer, she went to Oxford University, where she studied chemistry. In 1959 she was elected to parliament. During the Conservative government of 1970 to 1974 she held the post of Secretary of State for Education and Science. In

▼ The river Thames has frozen hard on several occasions in the past. This old print shows the fair held on the frozen river in February 1814.

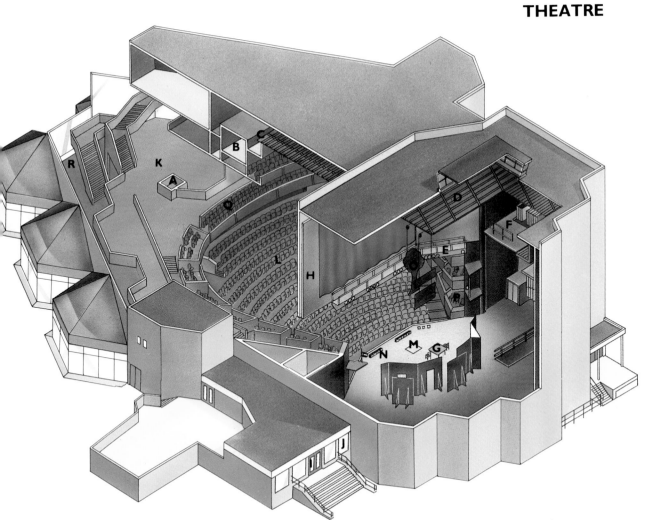

1975 she took over the leadership of the Conservative Party from Edward Heath, and in the 1979 election became PRIME MINISTER. She led the Conservatives to a second term in office in 1983, and again in 1987. In 1990 she resigned as prime minister and was succeeded by John Major.

Margaret Thatcher's policy was to give Britain a sound economic base from which it could compete internationally. Her determination earned her the nickname of 'The Iron Lady'. In 1992 she became Baroness Thatcher OM, PC and joined the House of Lords.

▲ A cutaway view of a modern theatre, showing:

A Lift
B Projection room
C Lighting gallery
D Gridiron
E Lighting bridge
F Fly floor
G Prop
H Safety curtain
I Stage door
J Stage manager's office
K Circle foyer
J Stalls
M Trap door
N Footlights
O Scenery
P Boxes
Q Circle
R Stalls foyer

Theatre

A theatre is a place where plays are performed by actors and watched by an audience. The theatre may be just a patch of ground or a large, expensive building.

The earliest theatres we know about were in Greece. They were simply flattened patches of

▲ *The theatre at Delphi in Greece was built in the 300s BC. It was so skilfully built that even people sitting right at the back could hear every word the actors spoke.*

ground on a hillside. The audience sat in rows on the hill above so that they could all see the 'stage'. When the Greeks built theatres, they cut a half-moon shape in the hillside and lined it with rows of stone seats that looked down on a round, flat stage.

The Romans copied the Greek pattern, but they built most of their theatres on flat ground. The rows of seats were held up by a wall. The Romans built a theatre in nearly every large town in the Roman Empire.

In Britain, there were no theatre buildings before the 1500s. Troupes of actors travelled around using their carts as stages. Later, they performed in rich people's houses and in the courtyards of inns. The first theatres to be built were made of wood and looked very much like inns. The stage jutted out into a large yard. Galleries of seats ran all round the sides. There were even seats on the stage, but only for rich people. These theatres had no roofs. When it rained, the *groundlings*, people who stood in the yard around the edge of the stage, got wet. SHAKES-PEARE'S plays were performed in theatres like this.

Later on, theatres had proper roofs. The stage was moved back and the audience sat in rows in front of it.

Thermometer

A thermometer is an instrument that measures TEMPERATURE. It is usually a glass tube marked with a scale. Inside is another, thinner glass tube, which

▶ *Maximum and minimum thermometers are used to indicate the highest and lowest temperatures recorded. In a maximum thermometer, mercury flows through a narrow neck in the tube. As the thermometer cools, a small amount of mercury stays above the neck, showing the highest temperature to which the thermometer has been exposed. A minimum thermometer is usually an alcohol thermometer which stays at the lowest point reached. Oven thermometers (below) make use of the difference in expansion of different metals. As the temperature rises, the bimetallic strip bends as one metal expands, moving a pointer on a dial.*

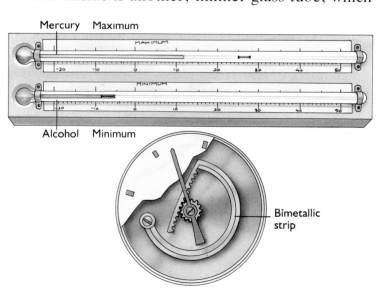

Mercury Maximum

MAXIMUM

-20 -10 0 10 20 30 40 50

MINIMUM

-20 -10 0 10 20 30 40 50

Alcohol Minimum

Bimetallic strip

ends in a bulb containing mercury or alcohol. When the temperature goes up, the mercury or the alcohol gets warm and expands (grows bigger). It rises up the tube. When it stops, you can read the temperature on the marked scale. When it gets cold, the mercury contracts (grows smaller) and sinks down the tube. If alcohol is used in a thermometer it is usually coloured red. Most thermometers measure temperatures between the boiling and freezing points of water. This is between 0° and 100° on the Celsius scale. Most countries use the Celsius scale, but some, such as the United States, also use Fahrenheit, in which the freezing and boiling points of water are 32° and 212°.

Medical thermometers, which are small enough to go in your mouth, measure your blood heat. Household thermometers tell you how warm or cold the air is inside or outside your house.

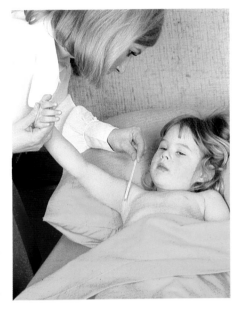

▲ *A medical thermometer placed under this feverish girl's arm will indicate how high above normal (37°C) her body temperature is. It is safer to take a very young child's temperature in this way than to risk putting a glass thermometer into his or her mouth.*

Thermostat

A thermostat is an instrument which keeps a TEMPERATURE steady. It is usually part of a central heating system. It switches the boiler on or off when the temperature gets too low or high. Thermostats are also fitted in kettles, cars, spacecraft, ovens, hot water heaters, and other machinery.

Until recently, thermostats were made with metal strips inside. When the strips got hot, they expanded (grew bigger). They had to bend to fit into their space. When they bent, they broke electrical

> **The name Centigrade is sometimes used for the Celsius scale, but this is not correct in the international system of units.**

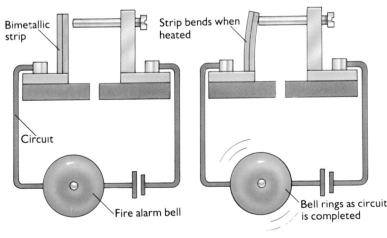

Bimetallic strip

Strip bends when heated

Circuit

Fire alarm bell

Bell rings as circuit is completed

◄ *This electrical circuit is in a fire alarm system. It consists of a loud bell, an electric circuit and a bimetallic strip – a strip of two metals bonded together. When the temperature rises, one of the metals expands faster than the other, making the strip bend. This completes the electric circuit, and the bell rings.*

▲ *The terrible conditions that many people suffer in these slums in Rio de Janeiro, Brazil, are typical of those in many Third World countries.*

▶ *The number of infant deaths per thousand people in a country is one indication of that country's wealth and standard of living. In poorer countries, lower standards of health and education usually result in a greater number of infant deaths.*

Thunderstorms are most frequent in the tropics. In some areas they may occur on as many as 200 days a year. In the British Isles they may happen on more than 15 days a year, but along western coasts thunder is seldom heard on more than 5 days a year.

contacts. This switched the boiler or heater off. Modern thermostats are electronic. They can work in temperatures that would melt most metals.

Third World

The Third World is a polite way of describing the poorer nations in our world. The first two 'worlds' are the rich and powerful nations of the East, including the communist countries led by the former SOVIET UNION; and the western countries, of which the most powerful is the UNITED STATES.

The Third World countries are in ASIA, AFRICA and SOUTH AMERICA. Many of them supply the rest of the world with cheap food, minerals, timber and fibres, as well as cheap labour. This pattern of wealth in one part of the world and poverty in

INFANT MORTALITY IN VARIOUS NATIONS

Third World	Per 1000	Other	Per 1000
China	50	Australia	9
Bangladesh	140	Canada	8
Bolivia	123	Denmark	7
Brazil	70	Finland	6
Burma	96	France	8
Cameroon	113	Greece	13
Chile	22	Italy	12
Congo	110	New Zealand	10
Gabon	162	Poland	18
Gambia	217	Portugal	18
Ghana	98	Sweden	3
India	101	United Kingdom	10
Liberia	127	United States	10

another is very difficult to change. The rest of the countries in the world do not want to give up the wealth and power they have been used to for so long. This means that many countries in the Third World go on getting poorer while the rich countries go on getting richer.

Thunderstorm

Thunderstorms are caused by ELECTRICITY in the air. Different electrical charges build up inside big rain clouds. When the charges are strong enough, a spark leaps from one charged part of the cloud to another. Sometimes the spark jumps from the cloud

◀ Lightning will jump from a cloud to the tallest conductor available on the ground, such as a skyscraper. For protection, a tall building has a lightning rod on the roof which harmlessly earths the lightning down a wire to the ground.

to the ground. We see the spark as LIGHTNING. Lightning heats up the air. The air expands (gets bigger) so quickly that it explodes, making the crashing noise we call thunder.

Since sound travels much slower than LIGHT, you always hear thunder after you see lightning. It takes the noise of thunder about three seconds to travel one kilometre. To find out how many kilometres away the storm is, count the seconds between seeing the lightning and hearing the thunder, and divide the number by three.

Tibet

Tibet is a country in central ASIA. It is the highest country in the world. The flat part of Tibet, which is in the middle, is as high as the peaks of the ALPS. Enormous mountain ranges surround this high plain. In the south lie the HIMALAYAS, the home of Mount EVEREST.

Tibet used to be ruled by Buddhist monks called *lamas*. In 1959, the country was taken over by China.

TIBET

Government: Communist
Capital: Lhasa
Area: 1,217,300 sq km
Population: 2,100,000

By Tibetan custom, a woman cannot choose a husband, and if she marries the eldest brother in a family, the younger brothers also become her husbands.

◀ This isolated Buddhist monastery in the mountains of Tibet lies at a height of 4000 metres above sea level.

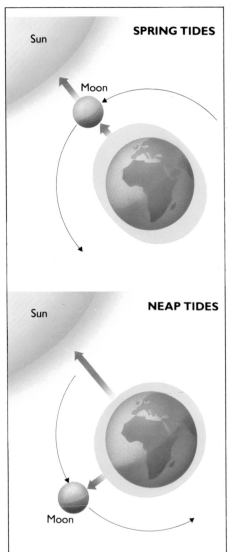

SPRING TIDES

Sun

Moon

NEAP TIDES

Sun

Moon

▲ When the Sun's gravity and the Moon's gravity pull in the same direction, their combined force causes a very high, or spring, tide. When the Sun and Moon pull against each other at right angles, a very low, or neap, tide occurs. Spring tides occur when there is a full or new moon. The red arrows show the pull of gravity.

Tide

Tides are regular movements of the OCEANS. They are mainly caused by the MOON. The Moon is like a giant magnet. It tugs the oceans towards it as it loops around the Earth. The Earth is spinning at the same time, so most places get two high tides and two low tides about every 24 hours.

High tide happens when the water flows as far inland as it can. Low tide happens when it flows out as far as it can.

Tiger

Tigers are the biggest members of the cat family. They live in the forests of Asia and Indonesia, and hunt deer or large cattle. Tigers usually lie still during the day, and hunt alone by night. They are very strong. One tiger can pull a dead buffalo that is so heavy a group of people would find it difficult to move.

Until the 1800s, thousands of tigers roamed through the forests of Asia. Then men began to shoot them, and as a result they are now very rare.

▶ Tigers are rarely seen out in the open. They prefer the cool shade of forests. Their markings make them more suited to areas of dappled shade, where they are well camouflaged.

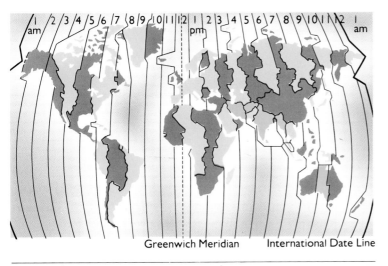

Greenwich Meridian   International Date Line

◀ *Because of the rotation of the Earth, sunrise in, for example, the eastern United States occurs three hours earlier than in the western part. For this reason, the world has been divided into 24 time zones. At the International Date Line the date changes.*

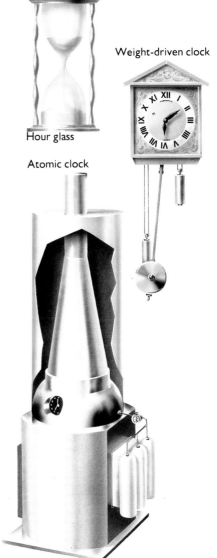

Weight-driven clock

Hour glass

Atomic clock

Time

Nobody has ever really explained what time is. But people have invented many ways of measuring it. First, they divided up the years and months by natural things that happened regularly, such as the SEASONS and the size and shape of the Moon. The position of the SUN in the sky told them the time of day.

The very first clock was probably invented by the Egyptians. It was a sundial. As the Sun moved across the sky, an upright rod in the middle of the dial cast a shadow onto a scale of hours drawn around it.

But this was no good at night time. Other ways of telling the time, without the Sun's help, were invented. One was the hour glass. This was two glass bulbs joined together. Sand in one bulb took exactly one hour to trickle through a hole into the other bulb.

Mechanical CLOCKS were not made until the 1200s. These were driven by weights. Clocks which worked by springs were made in the 1500s. In the early 1600s, the PENDULUM was being used to make clocks more accurate. Modern clocks are very accurate. They work by ELECTRONICS. Scientists need ever more accurate timekeeping. They use atomic clocks that are accurate to 10 millionths of a second.

We think of time as being something that is always the same in all situations, but this is not necessarily so. Albert Einstein showed that the rate

▲ *Hour glasses were one of the earliest ways of measuring time. Pendulum clocks came into use in the 1600s. More precise methods of time-keeping have been developed over the years. An atomic caesium clock is so accurate that it should lose only one second in 1000 years.*

Packaging

Tin plate

Pewter

▲ *Tin is useful for packaging because it does not rust. It can also be used for plating other metals to give a bright shiny surface. Mixed with antimony and copper it makes pewter, a soft alloy once used for most tableware.*

at which time passes varies according to the speed at which we are travelling. On a supersonic jet, clocks and watches move just very slightly slower than they do on the ground. The difference would only be noticeable, however, in a spacecraft travelling at close to the speed of light.

Tin

Tin is one of the oldest metals known to us. People were mining tin before IRON was discovered. Tin was mixed with COPPER to make bronze.

Tin was mined in Cornwall long before the birth of Christ. An ancient people called the Phoenicians sailed from the Mediterranean to trade cloth and precious stones for it.

Tin cans are made from sheets of steel that have been coated with tin. Tin does not rust.

Tin is not a common metal. The main tin mines are in Bolivia, south-eastern Asia, and western Africa.

Tobacco

Tobacco is made from the dried leaves of the plant *Nicotiana*, which belongs to the same family as potatoes. It was first found in America, but is now grown all over the world. The Spanish traveller Francisco Hernandez brought it to Europe in 1599.

Tobacco leaves can be rolled together to make cigars, or shredded up to be smoked in pipes or cigarettes. Smoking is very bad for your health. It is particularly harmful to the lungs and heart.

▼ *Tobacco leaves are picked, then dried and packaged to be sent abroad for processing to make cigarettes, cigars, loose tobacco or snuff, a powder that can be sniffed. Cheap tobacco is dried in the sun. More expensive types are dried by hot air or over fires in sheds.*

Picking   Drying   Bales for shipping

Togo

The Republic of Togo is a thin strip of land in West Africa. The climate is hot and damp, especially near the coast. The country has little industry apart from mining large deposits of phosphates for fertilizers. Germany ruled the territory until World War I. After Germany's defeat, Togo was governed by France. The country gained independence in 1960.

Tokyo

Tokyo is the capital of JAPAN. It is one of the biggest cities in the world. Tokyo is on the south-east coast of Honshu, the main island of Japan.

Almost every kind of work goes on in this enormous city. There are factories which make paper, electronic and electrical goods, cars and

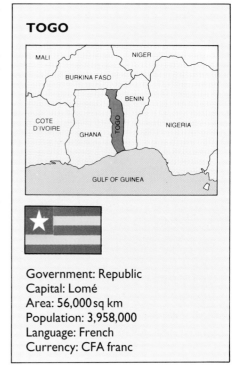

TOGO

Government: Republic
Capital: Lomé
Area: 56,000 sq km
Population: 3,958,000
Language: French
Currency: CFA franc

◀ One of the religions in Japan is called Shinto. Followers worship many gods, nature and their ancestors. This picture is of a Shinto shrine.

motorbikes. There are also huge shipyards and oil refineries on the coast. So many people work in Tokyo that most of them have to live on the outside edge of the city. Some people have to spend four hours a day going to and from their work. Tokyo has some of the worst traffic jams in the world.

Much of the city was destroyed by an EARTHQUAKE in 1923. What was left was badly bombed in WORLD WAR II. Since then the city has been almost entirely rebuilt, but a number of beautiful old buildings remain. The Imperial Palace is an old *shogun* castle, and there are many ancient temples and shrines.

Tokyo has had an unusual population history. In 1787 it had a population of 1,400,000, making it the world's largest city at that time. Then Tokyo's population became smaller and smaller until by 1868 it was only half that size. When the city was almost completely destroyed by an earthquake in 1923, the population had again risen to 2,200,000.

▲ Leo Tolstoy inherited land from his family, but had very advanced ideas for his time. He made sure the people who worked for him had proper homes and education.

Tolstoy, Leo

Leo Tolstoy (1828–1910) was a Russian author who wrote two of the world's greatest novels, *War and Peace* and *Anna Karenina*. He was born into a noble family and fought in the Crimean War. Tolstoy hated the greed and selfishness he found on his travels. He turned away from the Russian Orthodox Church and started a new kind of Christianity. At the age of 82, Tolstoy left home, but he soon became ill and died in a small railway station hotel. He was refused burial by the Church, but the people thronged to his funeral, seeing him as a man who had done his best to improve their lot.

Tomato

Tomatoes are round, red, fleshy fruits. They contain a very good supply of some of the VITAMINS we need, especially vitamins A and C.

Tomatoes were first grown in South America. They were being grown in the Andes mountains thousands of years ago. In 1596 the Spanish brought them to Europe. But at first, no one there would eat them. People thought they were poisonous. Tomatoes were kept as ornamental plants. For a long time, they were called 'love apples', or 'golden apples'.

Although tomatoes are really fruit, they are almost always eaten as vegetables. In the 1900s they started to become a popular food. Now they are grown all over the world.

TONGA

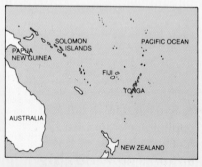

Government: Constitutional monarchy
Capital: Nuku'alofa
Area: 699 sq km
Population: 102,000
Languages: Tongan, English
Currency: Pa'anga

Tonga

Tonga is an island kingdom in the Pacific. It is also known as the Friendly Islands. There are three main groups of small islands, which have a warm, pleasant climate. The main crops are copra and bananas.

The kingdom was taken under the protection of Great Britain in 1900, and gained its independence in 1970. From 1918 to 1965 the islands' ruler was Queen Salote Tupou, who was known throughout the world as the Queen of Tonga. Tonga is the only remaining kingdom in Polynesia.

Tongue

The tongue is a muscular, flexible flap fixed inside the mouth. Only VERTEBRATES have tongues. Our own tongues help us to TASTE and eat food, and to talk. The letters T and D for instance, cannot be said without using the tongue in a special way.

In toads, the tongue is fixed to the front of the mouth. Snakes have forked or split tongues which can 'smell' the air. Cats' tongues are covered in tiny hooks of flesh. Cats can use their tongues like combs to clean their fur.

Tonsils

Tonsils are two small lumps at the back of the throat. There is one on each side. They help to protect the body from germs coming in through the mouth.

Children have very large tonsils. These gradually shrink as they grow older. Sometimes, tonsils can become infected. They swell up and are very painful. This illness is called tonsillitis. The tonsils may have to be taken out by doctors in a hospital. Having our tonsils taken out does not seem to harm our bodies in any way.

Cup-shaped papillae —carry taste buds

Hook-shaped papillae—carry no taste buds

▲ *The cat's tongue is long and flexible. The little hooks that make it rough are called* papillae. *They help the cat lap up liquids and keep its fur clean.*

▼ *At the centre of a tornado, winds can reach speeds of almost 650 kilometres per hour. Tornadoes cause great damage where they touch the ground.*

Tornado

Tornadoes are violent, whirling windstorms. Most of them happen in America, but they can occur anywhere in the world.

The most violent tornadoes happen in the centre of the United States. They travel at about 50 kilometres an hour with a roaring sound that can be heard 40 kilometres away. Many farmhouses have special cellars where people can shelter from tornadoes.

Hurricanes are strong winds that build up over the sea. Tornadoes build up over land. They happen when large masses of cloud meet. The clouds begin to whirl around each other. Gradually, these whirling clouds join together to make a gigantic, twisting funnel. When this touches the ground, it sucks up anything in its path – trees, houses or people.

Tortoise

Giant tortoises live in the Galapagos Islands and islands in the Indian Ocean. They can weigh up to 225 kg and be 1.8 metres long. Some large tortoises live for over 150 years.

Tortoises are slow-moving REPTILES. They can walk only about 5 metres in a minute. When frightened, they pull their heads and legs inside their domed shells. The 40 or so kinds of tortoise live on land, mostly in warm parts of the world. They are similar to TURTLES and terrapins, but these reptiles live in water.

▲ The Hermann's tortoise is a European type. The shell has three layers: a thin layer of living skin is sandwiched between horny plates on the outside and bony plates on the inside.

Touch

There are different nerve cells in your skin called receptors that respond to five main kinds of sensation. These are light touch, heavy touch (pressure), pain, heat and cold. Receptors pass sensations along NERVES to the brain.

Pain receptors are the most numerous; cold receptors the least numerous. Some parts of the

▶ The size of the area of the brain that deals with touch signals from the various parts of the body corresponds to how sensitive that part is. For example, the part that deals with signals from the mouth is very large, because there are so many nerves in the mouth. This chart shows how sensitive each part of the body is.

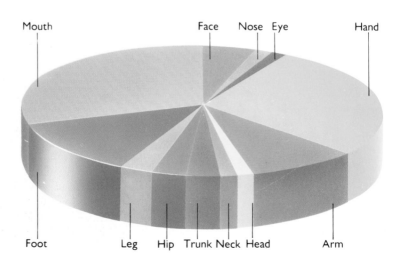

body, such as the tongue and fingertips, have more receptors than others.

We also have receptors inside the body. Usually we do not realize that these are working, except when they produce sensations such as hunger or tiredness.

Trade

The buying and selling of goods and services is called trade. Trade also includes *barter*, which is the exchange of one type of goods for goods of a different kind. Domestic trade is trade that takes place within one country.

Companies that buy goods in large quantities and then sell them to shopkeepers, are called *wholesalers*. Companies that sell the goods to us are called *retailers*.

International trade is trade between countries. *Imports* are things that a country buys. *Exports* are things that a country sells. Some imports and exports are said to be *visible*. These include raw materials, such as iron ore, and farm products, such as wheat. They also include factory-made goods, ranging from pencils to jet aircraft. Other imports and exports are *invisible*. These include banking and insurance, transport services and money spent by tourists.

The chief trading nations are those with the most industries. But nearly every country now depends on trade.

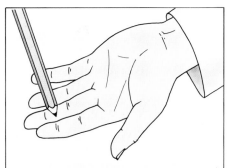

SEE IT YOURSELF
Some parts of your body are more responsive to light touch than others. Try this experiment with a friend. Blindfold yourself and ask your friend to press either one or two pencil points lightly on your fingertip. You will probably be able to tell how many pencil points your friend is using each time. Try doing this on your back, shoulders and on other parts of your body. Can you tell how many pencil points are being used each time? Which areas are receptive to light touch?

The total trade of the European Union nations in the 1980s was almost three times that of the United States, but this included trade among the European Union members as well as their trade with other countries.

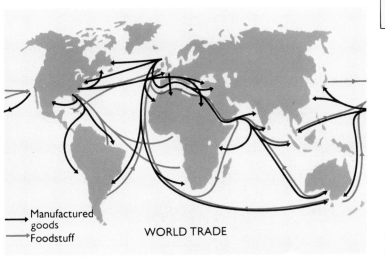

Manufactured goods
Foodstuff

WORLD TRADE

◀ *This map shows the general flow of world trade: foodstuffs and raw materials from the developing nations; manufactured goods from the industrialized nations.*

Trade Union

Trade unions are groups formed by workers. Their main aim is to get better wages for their members. They also ask for shorter hours and better working conditions, and some form of job security. Some unions look after their members and their families in times of trouble. If a trade union has a serious disagreement with an employer, it may ask its members to stop working. This is called a *strike*.

Modern trade unions were formed in the early days of the INDUSTRIAL REVOLUTION. They were first made legal in Britain in the 1870s. Since then, unions have gradually increased their power. Today, trade unions play an important part in the affairs of many countries.

▲ *John L. Lewis was a powerful American trade union leader and was president of the United Mine Workers of America for 40 years.*

▼ *The Battle of Trafalgar was Britain's most famous naval victory, and a turning point in the long struggle against Napoleon's attempts at building an empire.*

Trafalgar, Battle of

The Battle of Trafalgar was a famous sea battle that took place on October 21, 1805 off Cape Trafalgar, not far from the Straits of Gibraltar. In it, Admiral NELSON with 27 ships defeated a combined French and Spanish fleet of 33 ships. As a result of this battle, NAPOLEON was forced to concentrate his attention on winning victories on land.

It was before the Battle of Trafalgar that Nelson gave his famous signal: 'England expects that every man will do his duty'. But in spite of the greatness of the victory, Nelson's death in the battle cast a gloom over the British nation.

Transistor

Transistors are small ELECTRONIC devices. They are usually made to amplify (strengthen) electric currents in electronic equipment such as radios, televisions, computers and satellites. They can also switch electric currents on and off. Transistors have largely replaced other devices, called valves, which were once used for the same purpose.

The first research into transistors was done, not with silicon, but with the hard greyish-white metal germanium. William Shockley, the American scientist, used germanium to make the first transistor in 1948.

Transistor

Electric current

◄ A transistor in a circuit (left), and shown in section (right). The transistor shown here is made of a sandwich of three differently treated pieces of silicon. This type of transistor amplifies a signal and has the same effect as the more old-fashioned triode valve. The flow of electrons is shown by the blue arrows.

Today complicated circuits containing thousands of transistors can be put into SILICON CHIPS that are only a centimetre square. The first practical transistors were developed in the 1940s by the American scientists Walter Brattain, John Bardeen and William Shockley. The invention of transistors completely revolutionized electronics and millions of these devices are now made every year.

▼ The monkey puzzle tree has sharp spiny leaves that cover its branches. It bears cones and can grow as high as 30 metres.

Tree

Trees are the largest of all PLANTS. They are woody plants with a thick stem, or trunk. Most trees grow to more than 7 metres high. The biggest tree is a type of sequoia. These giants can grow to over 100 metres high, and can measure 25 metres around the trunk. Trees can also live a very long time. (See pages 696–697.)

TREE

Trees are beautiful to look at and also very useful plants. Some trees give us fruits and nuts. Many trees, especially the conifers, are grown for timber. Wood is not only a valuable building material. It is also used to make paper and in some countries it is burned for fuel. Trees are vital to the environment, for they enrich the atmosphere with oxygen and help protect the soil from erosion by wind and rain.

Trees are the largest and oldest living things. The biggest tree is a type of sequoia. These giants can grow to more than 100 metres high. A bristle-cone pine tree in Nevada, USA, is at least 4900 years old.

There are two main kinds of trees. Conifers, such as pines, firs and spruces, have needle-like leaves. They produce seeds in cones, not flowers. Most conifers are evergreens (they do not shed their leaves in the autumn). Their timber is known as softwood.

The other kind of tree is the broad-leaved flowering tree. Many, such as the oak, are *deciduous* (they shed their leaves in the autumn). However, some broad-leaved trees are evergreen: an example is the holly. Many tropical trees, too, are evergreen. Broad-leaved trees have flowers which develop into fruits. Their timber is called hardwood.

COMMON LEAF SHAPES	
Needle Pine, Fir, Spruce, Larch, Yew, Cedar, Cypress	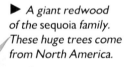
Narrow Willow, Sweet chestnut, Almond, Peach	
Lobed Oak, Hawthorn, Holly	
Forked Maple, Sycamore, London plane, Horse chestnut	
Oval Elm, Apple, Cherry, Weeping willow, Alder, Beech	
Pinnate (Feathery) Rowan, Elder, Ash, Walnut	

▶ *A giant redwood of the sequoia family. These huge trees come from North America.*

▼ *A tree trunk sawn through reveals the life history of the tree. The darker heartwood is surrounded by the lighter sapwood. A fresh growth ring is added every year. By counting the rings, you can tell the age of the tree.*

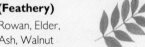

TREE SPOTTING

Catkin

Alder

Sallow

Cones

Scots pine

Norway spruce

mond

its

d cherry

Winged seed

Sycamore

Acorn (English oak)

Nuts

Walnut

Bark

London plane

Silver birch

◄ *A massive English oak. Oaks are common forest trees in north-west Europe.*

For more information, turn to these articles: BARK, CONIFER, CORK, FOREST, FRUIT, LEAF, NUT, PALM, SEED, WOOD.

TRINIDAD AND TOBAGO

LESSER
ANTILLES

CARIBBEAN SEA

ATLANTIC
OCEAN

TOBAGO

TRINIDAD

VENEZUELA

GUYANA

Government: Parliamentary
  democracy
Capital: Port of Spain
Area: 5,130 sq km
Population: 1,321,000
Language: English
Currency: Trinidad dollar

▼ *According to Homer's poem, the hero Odysseus and other men from the Greek army were hidden inside the wooden horse.*

Trinidad and Tobago

Trinidad and Tobago is a country made up of two islands in the West Indies. The islands lie near the coast of Venezuela. The climate is warm and damp and the main occupation is farming. Trinidad is a large producer of oil and this brings most of the island's wealth. Its annual carnival attracts many tourists, who come to hear the steel bands and calypsos for which Trinidad is famous.

Trojan War

The Trojan War was fought in about 1200 BC between the Trojans of Troy, a city in what is now Turkey, and the Greeks. It lasted for 10 years. The poet HOMER, in his poem the *Iliad*, tells the story of only a few days of the war. We know the story of the rest of the war from other writings.

Paris was a prince of Troy. He fell in love with Helen, the wife of King Menelaus of Sparta in Greece. Paris took Helen to Troy, and Menelaus with other Greek kings and soldiers went to get her back. They besieged Troy for years. In the end they won by tricking the Trojans with a huge wooden horse filled with Greek soldiers, which they left standing outside the city. The Trojans, thinking that the horse was a gift, took it inside the city walls. The hidden soldiers then opened the gates and Troy was destroyed. No one knows if the story is true.

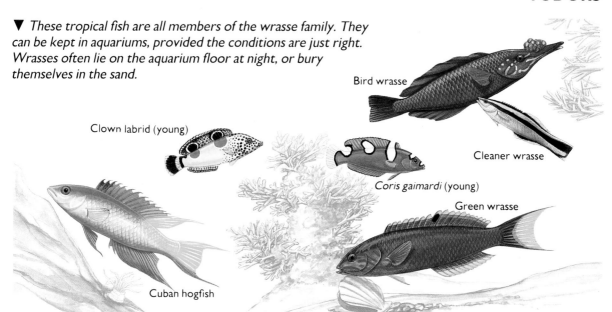

▼ These tropical fish are all members of the wrasse family. They can be kept in aquariums, provided the conditions are just right. Wrasses often lie on the aquarium floor at night, or bury themselves in the sand.

Bird wrasse

Clown labrid (young)

Cleaner wrasse

Coris gaimardi (young)

Green wrasse

Cuban hogfish

Tropical Fish

Tropical fish are among the prettiest fish in the world. They live in the warm seas of tropical regions, often along the edges of CORAL reefs.

Many small, brightly coloured freshwater tropical fish are popular aquarium pets. Marine fish can also be kept, but they are more expensive and difficult to look after. They have to have salt water containing just the right amount of salt to live in.

Tropical fish live in warm water. Most tanks have a heater to keep the water at around 24°C. A cover on the tank holds the heat in and stops the water from evaporating (drying up). Electric light bulbs in the cover light the tank and also heat the water. Most aquariums have air pumps that add OXYGEN to the water and filter it to keep it clear. Water plants also provide oxygen. Special food for tropical fish can be bought at pet shops.

The most common tropical freshwater fish is the guppy. Other common tropical fish are angelfish, barbs and neon tetras.

▼ The porcupine fish inflates itself like a balloon and erects sharp spines if it senses danger nearby.

Tudors

The House of Tudor was an English royal family that ruled from 1485 to 1603. The first Tudor king was HENRY VII. He was a grandson of a Welsh squire, Owen Tudor, who had married Henry V's

Tudor times saw a new style of architecture in England. The old fortress castles gave way to brick and stone manor houses and palaces. The windows of the new houses overlooked spacious lawns, gardens and parks. Hampton Court is such a palace.

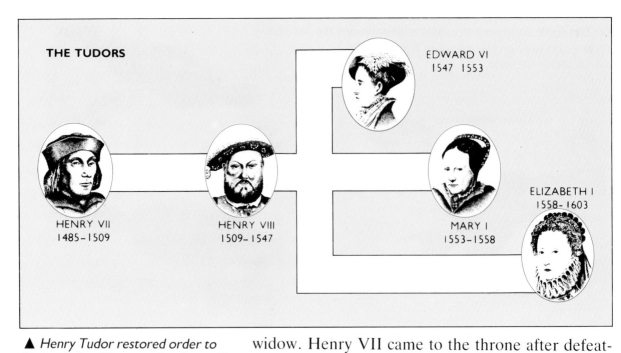

THE TUDORS

EDWARD VI
1547 1553

HENRY VII
1485–1509

HENRY VIII
1509–1547

MARY I
1553–1558

ELIZABETH I
1558–1603

▲ Henry Tudor restored order to England after 30 years of civil war. He and most of the Tudor monarchs who followed put England on the road to becoming a major world power.

▼ Tuna fishermen show off their catch as it is unloaded at the port of Yaizu, in Japan. The Japanese catch more tuna each year than any other nation.

widow. Henry VII came to the throne after defeating RICHARD III at the Battle of Bosworth. This ended the WARS OF THE ROSES (1455–1485) between the houses of Lancaster and York. To join the houses, Henry VII, who belonged to a branch of Lancaster, married Elizabeth of York.

Henry VII was succeeded by his son, HENRY VIII. During the reign of Henry VIII the arts flourished in England. The King used PARLIAMENT to pass laws which broke all ties between England and the Roman Catholic Church.

Henry VIII was succeeded first by his son, EDWARD VI, then by his daughters, MARY I and ELIZABETH I. When Elizabeth died in 1603, the crown went to King JAMES VI of Scotland, the first of the Stuart kings.

The Tudors were strong rulers. During their time, England became richer and more powerful, especially at sea. The voyages of England's daring seamen led to more trade and new colonies. William SHAKESPEARE wrote his plays during the reign of Elizabeth I.

Tuna

The tuna, also called tunny, is a large fish, whose firm flesh is rich in PROTEINS and VITAMINS. Most tuna live in warm seas, but they may swim into northern waters in summer. Different kinds of tuna include the blue fin, which may be 3 metres long, and the albacore. Tuna are the only fish whose body temperature is higher than that of the water around them.

Tunisia

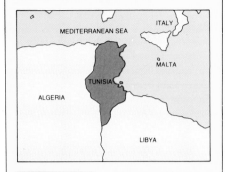

TUNISIA

Tunisia is a sunny country in North AFRICA. Its beaches attract many tourists from Europe. The north is rugged. It has the most rain. The south is part of the dry SAHARA. Farming is the main industry in this small nation, but oil and phosphates are important exports.

There are about 8,000,000 people, most of whom are Muslims. Near the capital, also called Tunis, are the ruins of Carthage. Carthage was a great Mediterranean Sea power until it was destroyed by the ROMAN EMPIRE in 146 BC.

Government: Republic
Capital: Tunis
Area: 163,610 sq km
Population: 8,445,000
Languages: Arabic, French
Currency: Tunisian dinar

Tunnel

Tunnelling is important in mining, transport and water supply. The Romans built tunnels to carry water. And today, a tunnel that brings water to New York City is the world's longest. It is 169 km long.

A Channel tunnel between France and England was first suggested to Napoleon in 1802 by the French engineer, Albert Mathieu. He decided that the tunnel should come to the surface on an island half-way across the Channel. This was so that men and horses could have a breath of fresh air.

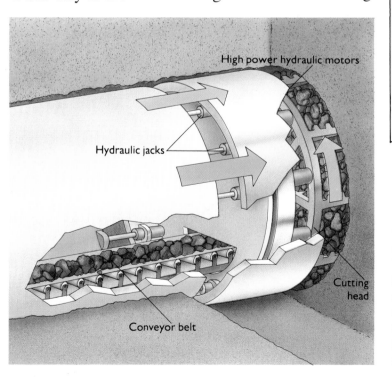

High power hydraulic motors

Hydraulic jacks

Cutting head

Conveyor belt

◀ The automatic tunnel digging machines used today are called moles. They have rotating cutters at the front and the soil or rock they dig out is carried away by a conveyor belt. Hydraulic jacks act like springs to force the mole forward. The mole is powered by electricity and hydraulic motors.

LONGEST TUNNELS		
	Km	**Opened**
Railway		
Seikan (Japan)	53.9	1988
Channel Tunnel		
(England/France)	44.94	*
Oshimizu (Japan)	22.2	1982
Simplon		
(Switz./Italy)	19.8	1922
Road		
St Gotthard		
(Switzerland)	16.32	1980
Arlberg (Austria)	14.0	1978
Mont Blanc		
(France/Italy)	11.6	1965
*Due to open 1993/4		

Different methods are used to build tunnels. In hard rock, the tunnel is blasted out with explosives. Cutting machines, like those used to drill oil wells, are used in softer rock. In the softest rocks, *tunnel shields* are used. These are giant steel tubes, the same size as the intended tunnel. The front edge of the shield is sharp and is pushed into the earth. The earth is dug out, and the tunnel behind the shield is lined to stop it from caving in.

Some tunnels under rivers are built by lowering sections of tunnel into the river. Divers join them together. When the tunnel is complete, the water is pumped out. Underground railway tunnels can be built in deep trenches. When they are finished the tunnel is covered over. The biggest tunnelling operation of recent years has been digging the Channel Tunnel between England and France.

Turbine

A turbine is a machine, in which a wheel, drum or SCREW is turned around by fast flowing water, or by steam or gas. Water wheels and WINDMILLS are simple turbines.

Water turbines are used at hydroelectric POWER STATIONS. These stations are next to DAMS or WATER-FALLS. The force of falling water carried through a pipe from a dam turns the turbine. The turbine does

Small turbines driven by compressed air are used for dentists' drills. These turbines drive the drill at more than 250,000 revolutions per minute, so the drilling of a tooth is quickly done. There is also less vibration than with an electric drill.

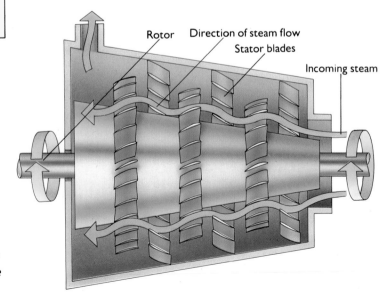

Rotor Direction of steam flow
Stator blades
Incoming steam

▶ *In a steam turbine, high pressure steam is directed through fixed, or stator, blades to strike a series of blades on a central shaft. The steam expands as it passes through each set of blades, driving the shaft round. The fixed blades direct the steam onto the turbine blades at the correct angle.*

not produce electricity. But as the turbine spins it drives a GENERATOR, which produces the electricity. Some turbines are wheels or drums, with blades or cup-shaped buckets round their edges. Others are shaped like screws or propellers.

Steam turbines are operated by jets of steam. They have many uses. They are used to produce electricity, to propel ships and to operate PUMPS. Gas turbines are turned by fast-moving jets of gas. The gases are produced by burning fuels such as oil. Gas turbines are used to turn the propellers of aircraft.

Turkey

Turkey is a country that is partly in EUROPE and partly in ASIA. The small European part covers three per cent of the land. It lies west of the waterway which links the Black Sea to the Mediterranean Sea. This part includes the largest city, Istanbul, which was once called CONSTANTINOPLE. The Asian part, which is sometimes called Anatolia or Asia Minor, includes the capital, Ankara.

Most of Turkey's people follow the religion of ISLAM. Much of the land is mountainous and large areas are covered by dry plateaus (tablelands). But the coastal plains are fertile and farming is the main industry. Turkey also produces chromium.

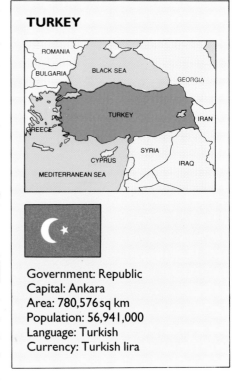

TURKEY

Government: Republic
Capital: Ankara
Area: 780,576 sq km
Population: 56,941,000
Language: Turkish
Currency: Turkish lira

▼ There are many beautiful mosques in Istanbul. Hagia Sophia was originally built as a Christian cathedral by the Emperor Justinian I between 532 and 536. After 1453, when the Turks conquered the area, it became a mosque. Since 1935 it has been in use as a museum.

TURKMENISTAN

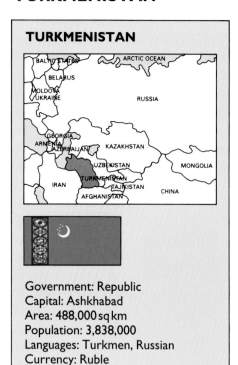

TURKMENISTAN

Government: Republic
Capital: Ashkhabad
Area: 488,000 sq km
Population: 3,838,000
Languages: Turkmen, Russian
Currency: Ruble

Turkey was once part of the Byzantine empire, which was the eastern part of the ROMAN EMPIRE. But after Constantinople fell in 1453, the Muslim Ottoman conquerors built up a huge empire. At its height, it stretched from southern Russia to Morocco, and from the Danube River to the Persian Gulf. But it slowly declined after 1600 and collapsed in World War I. After that war, Turkey's president, Kemal Atatürk (1881–1938) modernized the nation. Atatürk means 'Father of the Nation'.

Turkmenistan

Turkmenistan was a republic in the former Soviet Union until 1991. Eight per cent of the country is desert. Grapes, cotton and grapes are grown in the fertile areas, and there are coal and salt mines.

Turtle and Terrapin

Some people give the name 'turtle' to all shelled REPTILES, including TORTOISES. But generally, the name is just used for those that live in water. The shells of turtles are similar to those of tortoises. These are both made of bony 'plates' which are covered by large horny scales. Small turtles that live in fresh water are called terrapins.

Marine, or sea, turtles spend most of their lives in warm seas. They swim great distances to find food, and many of them have webbed toes, or flipper-like legs to help them swim well.

▼ Snapping turtles are not very good swimmers. They usually walk over the bottom of the rivers and lakes where they live. They are found in central and eastern parts of the United States and in some parts of Central America.

Turtles go ashore to lay their eggs. They usually bury their eggs in sand, or hide them among weeds. The baby turtles hatch out on their own. When they have hatched, they dig themselves out of their nest and head for the sea.

There are several kinds of marine turtle. The largest kind is called the leatherback turtle. It can weigh over 725 kg and be up to 1.8 metres long. The green turtle is used for turtle soup and its eggs are eaten in Asian countries.

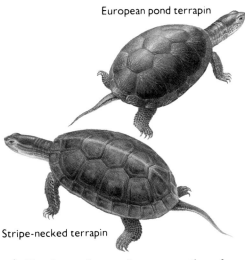

European pond terrapin

Stripe-necked terrapin

▲ *Turtles and terrapins are reptiles of a type that have existed on Earth for over 200 million years. They have a horny beak instead of teeth.*

Tutankhamun

Tutankhamun was a PHARAOH of ancient EGYPT. His tomb was discovered in 1922 by a British archaeologist, Howard Carter (1873–1939). Carter, with the Earl of Carnarvon, was digging in the Valley of the Kings, in Egypt. The discovery was an exciting one, because Carter had found the only tomb of a pharaoh that had not already been robbed of its treasures. In the tomb were a golden throne, caskets, statues, precious stones and furniture. There were four gold shrines, one inside another, in the burial chamber. The *sarcophagus* (coffin) contained the mummified body of the pharaoh. These treasures can now be seen in a museum in Cairo.

Tutankhamun became pharaoh when he was about 11 years old. He probably became ruler because, as a child, he had married the daughter of

▼ *This detail from one of Tutankhamun's burial caskets shows the pharaoh in a war chariot attacking the Syrians.*

Pharaoh Akhenaton. Akhenaton had made everyone worship the Sun god Aton and had set up a new capital at Amarna. Tutankhamun brought back the old religion and moved the capital back to Thebes. He died in 1352 BC, having ruled for about eight years.

Tuvalu

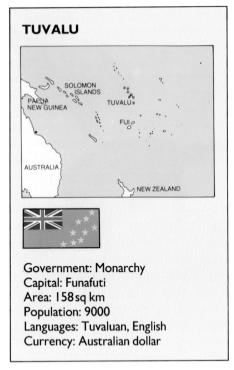

TUVALU

Government: Monarchy
Capital: Funafuti
Area: 158 sq km
Population: 9000
Languages: Tuvaluan, English
Currency: Australian dollar

Tuvalu is a country consisting of a group of tiny islands in the Pacific Ocean. The islands are coral reefs and little grows on the poor soil. The people of Tuvalu are Polynesians whose chief occupation is fishing. From 1888, Tuvalu, along with the Gilbert Islands, was a British colony. It became independent in 1978.

Twain, Mark

Before he became a well-known writer Mark Twain had various jobs, including steamboat worker on the Mississippi River. The steamboat expression 'mark twain' means 'two fathoms'. A fathom is a nautical measure equal to 6 feet (1.8 m).

Born Samuel Langhorne Clemens in 1835, he grew up in Hannibal, Missouri, on the Mississippi. Twain lectured all round the world, and wrote about his travels and life on the Mississippi. His most famous books are *The Adventures of Tom Sawyer* and *The Adventures of Huckleberry Finn*. He died in 1910.

▲ *Mark Twain, the great American humourist and author of* Tom Sawyer *and* Huckleberry Finn.

Expert typists can operate at incredible speeds. In international typing competitions speeds of over 500 characters per minute are achieved. This means that the typist is making more than 8 keystrokes every second!

Typewriter

Typewriters are hand-operated writing machines. They produce letters and figures, which look like lines of type in a book. When you strike a key on the keyboard, it moves a metal bar. A raised letter on the end of this bar is pressed against an inked ribbon. This marks an image of the letter onto a sheet of paper which is held in a roller.

The first practical typewriter was invented in 1867 by an American, Christopher Latham Sholes (1819–1890). Most of today's typewriters work electronically.

▼ *Coffee beans are sorted and bagged before being sent by rail to the coast. Coffee is one of Uganda's main exports.*

Uganda

Uganda is a small republic in East AFRICA. It was ruled by Britain until 1962, when it became independent. General Idi Amin seized power in 1971, but in 1979 Ugandan and Tanzanian troops took over Uganda and Amin fled. Most of the people are farmers. They grow coffee, tea and cotton.

Ukraine

Ukraine is a country in the European part of the former Soviet Union. The countryside ranges from fertile plains to forested mountains. Ukraine has a great mineral wealth and its industries include steel, chemicals and cement.

Ultraviolet Light

If LIGHT from the Sun shines through a prism it splits up into a rainbow of colours, called a SPECTRUM. Red is at one end of the spectrum and violet at the

▼ *Ultraviolet (UV) light is useful to scientists. In this photograph, taken through a high powered microscope, antibodies used in cell research have been stained with a green dye which fluoresces (shines) when exposed to ultraviolet light to make them visible.*

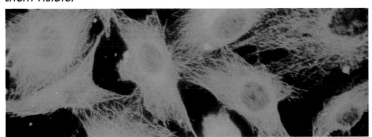

UGANDA

Government: Republic
Capital: Kampala
Area: 236,036 sq km
Population: 19,386,000
Languages: Luganda, Swahili, English
Currency: Ugandan shilling

UKRAINE

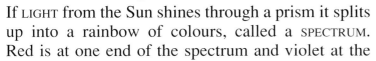

Government: Republic
Capital: Kiev
Area: 604,000 sq km
Population: 51,994,000
Languages: Ukrainian
Currency: Karbovanet

Ultraviolet light has many uses. It is a powerful germ-killer and can be used to sterilize foodstuffs and medical equipment. Pictures can be taken in the dark by turning ultraviolet light on an object. Forged documents can be detected by shining ultraviolet light on them. The different kinds of ink on the document can be spotted by the glow they give off.

In Homer's *Odyssey*, the gods were always interfering in human affairs. Ulysses' chief enemy was Poseidon, god of the sea. This is why the hero was always being driven off his course at sea or being shipwrecked.

other. Ultraviolet light lies just beyond the violet end of the spectrum. We cannot see it, but it will blacken photographic film and make some chemicals glow. Most ultraviolet light from the Sun is lost in the atmosphere. But enough rays reach Earth to give us suntans. If more ultraviolet rays reached us, they would be very harmful.

Ulysses

Ulysses is the Roman name for a brave and cunning Greek hero, called Odysseus. His famous adventures are told in HOMER's poem the ODYSSEY. It tells how Ulysses took ten years to return home after the TROJAN WAR.

On his journey he was captured by the Cyclops, a one-eyed, man-eating giant. A witch called Circe changed his men into pigs. And sirens (sea maidens) lured his men to their deaths. When he finally reached home, his wife, Penelope, was surrounded by suitors. She had agreed to marry any man who could shoot an arrow from Ulysses' bow through 12 rings. Ulysses, in disguise, was the only man to do this. He then killed all the suitors.

▼ *Ulysses had to trick the Cyclops by giving him very strong wine to make him drunk. This gave the Greeks time to escape from the island where they were being held prisoner, and continue on their journey.*

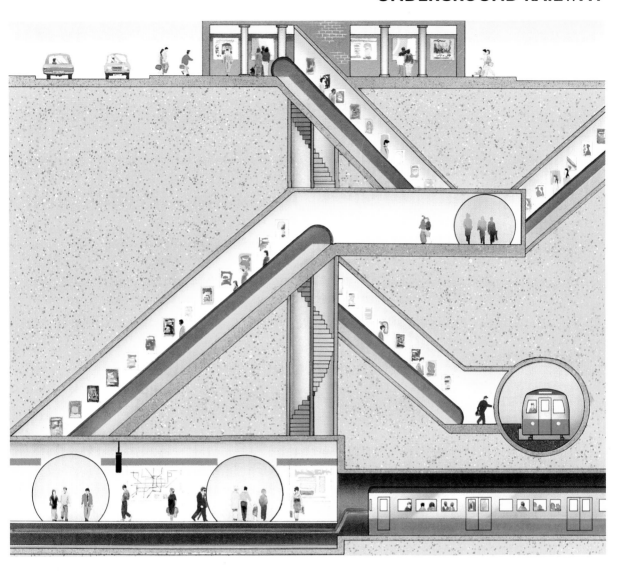

Underground Railway

Each day millions of people use underground RAIL-WAYS. Underground electric trains can carry passengers across cities much faster than buses, driving slowly through the busy streets above. Most underground railways run through TUNNELS driven through the rock beneath a city. Lifts and escalators carry passengers from the surface to the station deep underground.

The first underground railway opened in London in 1863. Today the world has over 60 underground systems. Some of these are vast. London's system employs enough workers to people a town. Its 480 trains run on 400 km of track. New York City's track is almost as long. This is the busiest underground of

▲ *Underground train stations have a maze of tunnels and stairways so that passengers can move from one train line to another and to the surface. Most people use escalators but there are always emergency staircases leading to the surface, in case of breakdowns.*

London Underground's tunnel lines are equipped with automatic signals. The trains themselves operate the signals so that red lights always show in sections behind a train.

709

UNITED ARAB EMIRATES

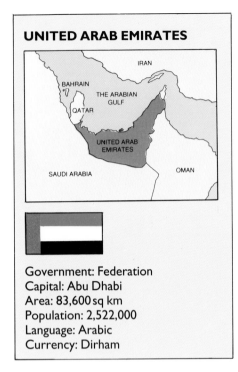

Government: Federation
Capital: Abu Dhabi
Area: 83,600 sq km
Population: 2,522,000
Language: Arabic
Currency: Dirham

UNITED KINGDOM

Government: Constitutional
  monarchy
Capital: London
Area: 244,100 sq km
Population: 58,489,975
Languages: English, Welsh, Gaelic
Currency: Sterling pound

▶ *Eilean Donan Castle in Scotland is the sort of picturesque location that many tourists like to visit when they come to the United Kingdom.*

all. About 1000 million people travel on it every year.

New York has almost 500 underground stations. But the largest underground stations are in Moscow. Their huge platforms were also built to serve as giant air raid shelters.

United Arab Emirates

The United Arab Emirates is made up of seven small states – Abu Dhabi, Dubai, Fujairah, Sharjah, Umm al-Qaiwain, Ajman and Ras al-Khaimah. Most of the country is hot, dry desert, but oil in Abu Dhabi and Dubai make the area one of the richest in the world. The sheikhs (rulers) of the emirates sit on a governing council.

United Kingdom

The United Kingdom of Great Britain and Northern IRELAND is the eleventh largest nation in Europe. ENGLAND, WALES and SCOTLAND make up the island of Great Britain, which takes up most of the BRITISH ISLES. Northern Ireland, Scotland and Wales are mountainous. The highest mountain is Ben Nevis in Scotland. Plains and valleys cover much of England. The longest river is the SEVERN, which flows through parts of England and Wales. The British climate is mild.

About 58 million people live in the United

Kingdom. Few other countries are so crowded. Four out of five people live in cities such as Belfast, Glasgow, and LONDON. London is the capital. Great Britain grows half of the food it needs. Its industries help to pay for the food that is bought from abroad. The United Kingdom manufactures a wide range of goods. Service industries, such as tourism, that provide services rather than producing goods, are increasing. Traditional industries, such as coal mining, are declining.

United Nations

Most of the world's countries belong to the United Nations. This is an association that works to keep peace and help people everywhere.

Each member country sends delegates to regular meetings of the United Nations' General Assembly in New York City. The General Assembly suggests how countries should behave. It cannot make them take its advice. But the United Nations' Security Council can ask member countries for troops to help stop nations from fighting.

The United Nations works largely through 14 agencies. The Food and Agriculture Organization helps countries to grow more food. The World Health Organization fights disease. The International Monetary Fund lends countries money.

The United Nations has managed to prevent some wars and has helped millions of people.

England

Northern Ireland

Scotland

Wales

▲ The flags of the countries that make up the United Kingdom: England, Northern Ireland, Scotland and Wales.

SOME UNITED NATIONS AGENCIES

FAO Food and Agriculture Organization
IBRD International Bank for Reconstruction and Development (World Bank)
ICAO International Civil Aviation Organization
ICJ International Court of Justice
IFC International Finance Corporation
ILO International Labour Organization
IMF International Monetary Fund

UNCTAD United Nations Conference on Trade and Development
UNESCO United Nations Educational, Scientific and Cultural Organization
UNICEF United Nations Children's Emergency Fund
UNIDO United Nations Industrial Development Organization
UNRWA United Nations Relief and Works Agency
WHO World Health Organization

▼ The flag of the United Nations. It shows a map of the world surrounded by an olive wreath. The olive branch is a symbol of peace.

UNITED STATES OF AMERICA

Government: Federal republic
Capital: Washington, D.C. (635,185)
Area: 9,373,614 sq km
Population: 256,561,000
Largest city (population): New York, 7,346,000
Highest point: Mount McKinley, Alaska, 6194 m
Agriculture: Nearly 50% of land in use
Chief crops: Soya beans, cotton, fruits, maize
Chief industries: Coal, oil, steel, textiles, tobacco
Language: English
Currency: US dollar

▲ *The bald eagle is a symbol of the United States.*

▶ *The modern skyline of Boston, Massachusetts, one of America's oldest cities.*

United States of America

The United States of America is the world's fourth largest nation. Russia, Canada and China are bigger in area, and more people live in China, India and Russia. There are 50 states in the United States. Forty-eight are in the same part of NORTH AMERICA. The other two are Alaska in the north, and the Pacific islands of Hawaii.

The mainland United States stretches from the Pacific to the Atlantic. Long mountain ranges run down the Pacific coast. Inland are flat-topped mountains and basins. In this region is Death Valley, the lowest place in the Americas. Here, too, is the GRAND CANYON, a huge gorge cut by the Colorado River. Farther east lie the tall peaks of the ROCKY MOUNTAINS that run from Canada to Mexico. Beyond these stretch the Great Plains where the mighty MISSISSIPPI RIVER flows. Another mountain range, the Appalachians, runs down the eastern side of the United States.

The United States is a young country. In 1976 it was just 200 years old. The original 13 colonies declared their independence from Britain in 1776. George WASHINGTON was elected first president in 1789. By the mid 1800s the United States had grown to much the same size as it is today. Explorers had added new land to the original colonies, and the country stretched as far west as the Pacific. From 1861 to 1865 a CIVIL WAR was fought between the

◄ *Scotts Bluff, Nebraska, is a tall, rocky landmark that once guided westward-bound travellers along the Oregon Trail.*

South, which believed in SLAVERY, and the North, which wanted every man to be free. The northern states won and slavery was abolished. Between 1870 and 1900 thousands of Europeans came and settled in the United States. They were seeking land and a new life. By 1900 the country's population had doubled.

The 250 million citizens of the United States include Eskimos, Indians, and people whose ancestors came from Europe or Africa. Seventy in every 100 Americans live in cities. WASHINGTON, D.C. is the capital but NEW YORK is the largest city. LOS ANGELES and Chicago each have over three million inhabitants.

The United States is one of the world's richest countries. Its farms produce huge wheat crops, and more oranges, meat, eggs and cheese than any other country. American miners mine more coal, copper, lead and uranium. The United States is the world's largest manufacturer of cars and chemicals.

Until recently the United States produced enough coal, oil and gas of its own to run its farms, factories and homes. But now it has to buy oil from abroad.

(See pages 714–715.)

Universe

The universe is made up of all the STARS, PLANETS, MOONS and other bodies scattered through the emptiness of space. The EARTH is just a tiny part of the SOLAR SYSTEM, in a great group of stars known as

Continued on page 716.

THE PRESIDENTS OF THE UNITED STATES	
President	Served
1. George Washington	1789–1797
2. John Adams	1797–1801
3. Thomas Jefferson	1801–1809
4. James Madison	1809–1817
5. James Monroe	1817–1825
6. John Quincy Adams	1825–1829
7. Andrew Jackson	1829–1837
8. Martin Van Buren	1837–1841
9. William H. Harrison	1841
10. John Tyler	1841–1845
11. James K. Polk	1845–1849
12. Zachary Taylor	1849–1850
13. Millard Fillmore	1850–1853
14. Franklin Pierce	1853–1857
15. James Buchanan	1857–1861
16. Abraham Lincoln	1861–1865
17. Andrew Johnson	1865–1869
18. Ulysses S. Grant	1869–1877
19. Rutherford B. Hayes	1877–1881
20. James A. Garfield	1881
21. Chester A. Arthur	1881–1885
22. Grover Cleveland	1885–1889
23. Benjamin Harrison	1889–1893
24. Grover Cleveland	1893–1897
25. William McKinley	1897–1901
26. Theodore Roosevelt	1901–1909
27. William H. Taft	1909–1913
28. Woodrow Wilson	1913–1921
29. Warren G. Harding	1921–1923
30. Calvin Coolidge	1923–1929
31. Herbert C. Hoover	1929–1933
32. Franklin D. Roosevelt	1933–1945
33. Harry S. Truman	1945–1953
34. Dwight D. Eisenhower	1953–1961
35. John F. Kennedy	1961–1963
36. Lyndon B. Johnson	1963–1969
37. Richard M. Nixon	1969–1974
38. Gerald R. Ford	1974–1977
39. James E. Carter	1977–1981
40. Ronald W. Reagan	1981–1989
41. George H.W. Bush	1989–1993
42. William Clinton	1993–

UNITED STATES

IMPORTANT DATES IN AMERICAN HISTORY

1492 Columbus sights the Bahama islands
1607 First English settlement, Virginia
1620 Voyage of the *Mayflower*
1754 French and Indian War: Britain gains control of North America
1776 Declaration of Independence
1783 End of Revolutionary War: USA is a new nation
1789 George Washington is first US president
1804 Lewis and Clark explore the West
1812 War with Britain (ends 1815)
1841 First wagon trains set out for California

1848 USA defeats Mexico and gains new territory
1848 Gold rush in California
1861 Start of Civil War between Northern and Southern States (ends 1865)
1867 Alaska sold to USA by Russia
1898 War with Spain
1917 USA enters World War I
1920 Women get the vote
1927 Charles Lindbergh flies the Atlantic
1929 Stock market crash and Great Depression begins
1941 Pearl Harbor attacked; USA enters World War II

1950 US involved in Korean War
1958 First American space satellite, Explorer I
1962 John Glenn is first US astronaut in orbit
1963 Assassination of President John F. Kennedy
1969 Apollo astronauts land on the Moon
1974 Nixon is first President to resign, over the Watergate scandal
1975 Vietnam War ends in defeat for Americans
1991 Gulf War; Cold War draws to close

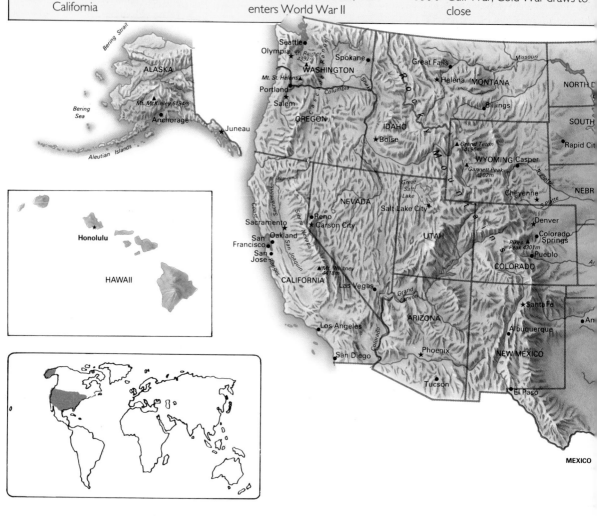

▲ Monument Valley in north-east Arizona is part of the Navajo Indian reservation lands.

N.H. = NEW HAMPSHIRE
MASS. = MASSACHUSETTS
CONN. = CONNECTICUT

▲ Historic Williamsburg was the colonial capital of Virginia.

MAINE
Bangor
Augusta
Portland
Montpelier ★ N.H.
VT. ★ Concord
Boston
Cape Cod
MASS.
Syracuse Albany
Buffalo NEW YORK CONN. ★ Providence RHODE ISLAND
★ Hartford
Long Island
Newark New York City
PENN-SYLVANIA Philadelphia
Pittsburgh Trenton NEW JERSEY
Cleveland Baltimore ★ Dover
OHIO Washington D.C. DELAWARE
Columbus Annapolis
Indianapolis Cincinnati WEST VIRGINIA MARYLAND
Springfield Richmond
Charleston VIRGINIA Norfolk
Louisville ★ Frankfort
Evansville
KENTUCKY NORTH CAROLINA
★ Raleigh
Nashville CAROLINA Charlotte
TENNESSEE Columbia
Memphis SOUTH CAROLINA
Atlanta Charleston ATLANTIC OCEAN
Birmingham
Columbus Savannah
ALABAMA GEORGIA
Montgomery
Jackson Jacksonville
★ Tallahassee
LOUISIANA FLORIDA Cape Canaveral
Baton Rouge New Orleans
Tampa Orlando
Fort Lauderdale
Miami
GULF OF MEXICO

Lake Superior
SOTA
WISCONSIN MICHIGAN
Minneapolis St. Paul
Lake Michigan Lake Huron
Grand Rapids
Milwaukee Lansing Detroit Lake Erie
Madison Chicago Toledo
City Davenport
Des Moines INDIANA
IOWA ILLINOIS
Springfield
Kansas City St. Louis
Jefferson City
MISSOURI
Springfield
ulsa
City Fort Smith
ARKANSAS
Little Rock
MISSISSIPPI
Monroe
llas
ouston
onio
rpus Christi

▲ A husky waits patiently outside a trapper's hut in Alaska, the northernmost state.

▲ The island of Maui is the second largest island in Hawaii; the island of Hawaii is largest.

For more information turn to these articles: AMERICAN INDIANS; CIVIL WAR, AMERICAN; FRANKLIN, BENJAMIN; JEFFERSON, THOMAS; KING, MARTIN LUTHER JR.; LINCOLN, ABRAHAM; REVOLUTIONARY WAR, AMERICAN; SLAVERY; WASHINGTON, GEORGE; WRIGHT BROTHERS.

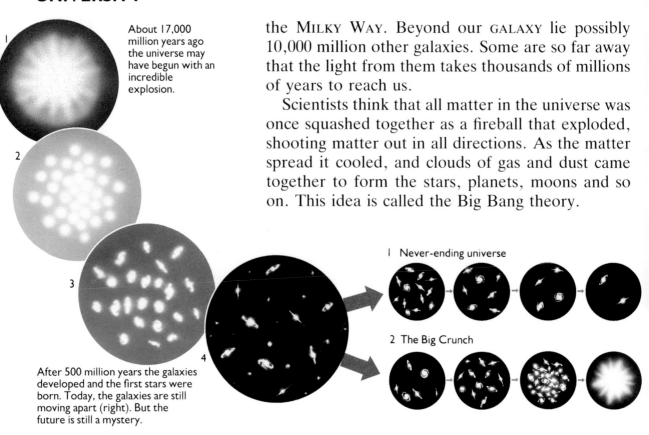

About 17,000 million years ago the universe may have begun with an incredible explosion.

After 500 million years the galaxies developed and the first stars were born. Today, the galaxies are still moving apart (right). But the future is still a mystery.

1 Never-ending universe

2 The Big Crunch

▲ *This diagram shows two ways in which the universe might continue. In the 'never-ending universe' theory, the galaxies will continue to fly apart until space is almost all black emptiness. In the 'big crunch' theory, the galaxies stop moving apart. Their gravity will then pull them inwards again until they collide and explode.*

the MILKY WAY. Beyond our GALAXY lie possibly 10,000 million other galaxies. Some are so far away that the light from them takes thousands of millions of years to reach us.

Scientists think that all matter in the universe was once squashed together as a fireball that exploded, shooting matter out in all directions. As the matter spread it cooled, and clouds of gas and dust came together to form the stars, planets, moons and so on. This idea is called the Big Bang theory.

University

Some people who leave school at 18 go on to university. At school people are taught a little about several subjects. But at university a student often learns about just one or two subjects. He or she goes to talks called *lectures*, and smaller study groups known as *tutorials* or *seminars*. The student has to write essays and maybe carry out experiments in a laboratory. University students use libraries to find out much of what they need to know from books.

After three years or so students take their final examinations. If they pass they are given a degree, usually a Bachelor of Arts or a Bachelor of Science. If they continue their studies they can earn higher degrees.

Arab peoples had universities more than 1000 years ago. Europe's first university was founded in the 1000s at Bologna in Italy. Soon after, universities were founded at Paris in France, Salamanca in Spain and Oxford in England. Today most countries have universities.

Uranium

This metal is one of the heaviest of all known ELEMENTS. It was named after the planet Uranus. Uranium gives off RADIOACTIVITY. As it loses atomic particles it decays, and ends up, after millions of years, as LEAD. People working with uranium often need protective clothing to shield their bodies from radiation damage.

Uranium is the fuel used to make NUCLEAR ENERGY in atomic bombs and nuclear power stations. It is mined in many countries. Most of the western world's uranium comes from the United States and Canada.

Uranium was discovered in 1789 by the German chemist Martin Heinrich Klaproth. He named it after the planet Uranus.

One tonne of uranium can produce as much energy as 30,000 tonnes of coal.

◄ *The American space probe, Voyager 2, passed Uranus in June 1986. The pictures it sent back showed that the planet has rings, and is tilted on its axis. This tilt is shown by the red lines.*

Uranus

The PLANET Uranus is 19 times farther away from the Sun than the Earth is. We cannot see Uranus just with our eyes. It was the first planet discovered with the help of a TELESCOPE. It looks like a greenish-yellow disc.

Uranus is unlike our Earth in many ways. For one thing, it is much larger. You could fit 52 planets the size of the Earth inside Uranus. The distance through the middle of Uranus is nearly four times the distance through the middle of the Earth.

URANUS FACTS

Average distance from Sun: 2870 million km
Nearest distance from Earth: 2650 million km
Average temperature (clouds): −200 degrees C
Diameter across equator: 51,000 km
Atmosphere: Hydrogen, helium
Number of moons: 15 known
Length of day: 17.24 hours
Length of year: 84 Earth years

Earth
Uranus

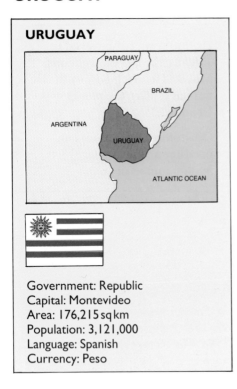

URUGUAY

Government: Republic
Capital: Montevideo
Area: 176,215 sq km
Population: 3,121,000
Language: Spanish
Currency: Peso

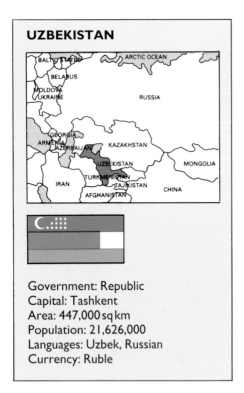

UZBEKISTAN

Government: Republic
Capital: Tashkent
Area: 447,000 sq km
Population: 21,626,000
Languages: Uzbek, Russian
Currency: Ruble

▶ *Gauchos in Uruguay round up a herd of cattle. Uruguay's mild climate and vast pasturelands make cattle raising one of its chief industries.*

Unlike our planet, Uranus is mainly made up of gases. It spins at a speed that makes one of its days about the length of 17 Earth hours. But one of its years lasts 84 of Earth years.

In 1986, *Voyager 2* flew close to Uranus and took pictures that told scientists a great deal about the planet. It has at least 15 moons, one of which – Miranda – has mountains 26 km high.

Uruguay

Uruguay is one of the smallest countries in SOUTH AMERICA. It lies in the south-east, between the Atlantic Ocean and its two big neighbours, Argentina and Brazil. Uruguay was formerly a province of Brazil. It became independent in 1825.

Low, grassy hills and lowlands cover most of Uruguay. Many rivers flow into the big Uruguay River or into the river mouth called the River Plate. Uruguay has mild winters and warm summers.

Most of Uruguay's inhabitants are descended from Spanish or Italian settlers. More than one in three of them live in the capital, Montevideo. Its factories make clothing, furniture and other goods. But most Uruguayans work in meat-packing plants, wool warehouses, or on country ranches. Millions of sheep and cattle graze on these ranches.

Uzbekistan

Uzbekistan was a republic of the former Soviet Union from 1925–91. It is a country of plains and desert in central Asia. Most of the people are Moslems.

Vacuum

A vacuum is a space with nothing in it. It gets its name from *vacuus*, the Latin word for 'empty'. In fact there are no complete vacuums. When you try to empty a container by pumping out the air, a small amount of air always stays behind. This partly empty space is called a partial vacuum. New air always rushes in to fill the space. This is how your LUNGS work. When you breathe out, you make a partial vacuum in your lungs. Air rushes to fill the space, making you breathe in.

SEE IT YOURSELF

A partial vacuum can be used to inflate a balloon. Try it yourself. Stand a bottle in a bowl of warm water for a few minutes. As heat makes the air inside the bottle expand, the pressure inside the bottle increases. Now fit a balloon over the neck of the bottle and put it in a bowl of cold water. What happens? The cold water cools the air inside the bottle and the pressure drops. Because the pressure of the air outside the bottle is greater, it pushes the balloon into the bottle and inflates it.

You can see partial vacuums at work in many ways. The space does not always fill up with air. When you suck air from a straw dipped in lemonade, it is the lemonade that rushes to fill the vacuum and so reaches your mouth. It is a partial vacuum that helps to keep aircraft in the air. As an aeroplane flies along, its wings are so shaped that they make a partial vacuum just above them. Air underneath the wings pushes them up to fill the space.

Van Gogh, Vincent

Vincent Van Gogh (1853–1890) was a Dutch painter who worked mostly in the south of France. Van Gogh lived a troubled life. Only his brother Theo believed in his genius while he was alive. Now Van

During his short life as an artist, Van Gogh produced some 750 paintings and 1600 drawings. We know a great deal about his life because of 700 letters he wrote to his brother Theo and others.

▲ Italian Woman *(1887)*, a painting by Van Gogh.

VANUATU

Government: Republic
Capital: Port Vila
Area: 14,763 sq km
Population: 174,000
Languages: Bislama, French, English
Currency: Vatu

Gogh's paintings are famous all over the world.

Van Gogh failed in every career he attempted. He turned to art to express his strong religious feelings, but it was not until 1880 that he decided to become a painter. In 1886 he went to Paris to visit his brother and was immediately attracted to the Impressionist work he saw there. In 1888 Van Gogh moved to Arles in the south of France, where he did most of his most famous paintings. During his last years he suffered from terrible fits of depression. He committed suicide in 1890.

Vanuatu

Vanuatu is a country made up of volcanic islands in the south-west Pacific Ocean. The soil is good and the main products are copra, cocoa, coffee and livestock. The islands were discovered in 1606 by a Portuguese navigator, but they were not charted until Captain COOK explored the area in 1774. From 1906 to 1980 the islands were ruled jointly by Britain and France. Independence came in 1980.

Vatican City

Vatican City is the POPE's home and headquarters of the ROMAN CATHOLIC CHURCH. It stands on Vatican Hill in north-west Rome, and is the world's smallest

► *A Swiss Guard sits at the entrance to the Vatican. The guards' uniforms are believed to have been designed by Michelangelo in the 1500s.*

independent country. It is only the size of a small farm and about 750 people live in it. Yet it has its own flag, radio station and railway. It also issues its own stamps.

Vatican City is surrounded by walls and contains many famous buildings. These include the Vatican Palace, which has more than 1000 rooms; the Sistine Chapel, decorated by MICHELANGELO; and St Peter's Basilica.

Vegetable

Vegetables are plants with parts that we can eat. They taste less sweet than the plant foods we call FRUIT. Vegetables such as lettuce and spinach are eaten for their leaves. Other vegetables are eaten for their roots or stems. Carrots and parsnips are roots. Celery and asparagus are stems. Peas, beans, and sweet corn are seeds. Tomatoes and squash are fruits.

Peas and beans supply body-building PROTEINS. Leafy and root vegetables provide VITAMINS, minerals and fibres to help keep our DIGESTION working properly. Potatoes contain *starches*, which the body can burn up to make energy.

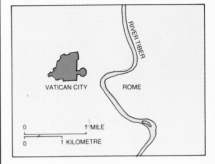

VATICAN CITY

Capital: Vatican City
Area: 0.44 sq km
Population: about 1,000
Languages: Italian, Latin
Currency: Italian lira

Many people are vegetarians – they do not eat the flesh of animals, including red meat, poultry and fish. The vegetarian diet consists mostly of vegetables, cereals, nuts, seeds and fruits. Soya beans are a popular source of protein. People who eat a well-balanced vegetarian diet generally have lower blood pressure and less excess fat than those who eat meat. Vegetarians must take care, however, to consume enough proteins and vitamins.

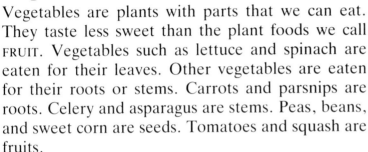

Plantain

Okra

Yam

Kohlrabi

Fennel

Curly kale

Mange tout

◀ Here are seven very different kinds of vegetables. Curly kale is rich in vitamins A, B and C. Plantains and yams can be boiled, fried or roasted. Okra is sometimes called 'ladies' fingers'. Kohlrabi is related to the cabbage, and fennel adds an aromatic flavour to various dishes. Mange tout means 'eat all' in French. This is because both the peas and pods are eaten.

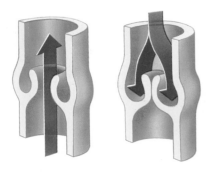

▲ *De-oxygenated blood flows back to the heart through the veins. Blood flowing in the right direction (left) forces valves in the vein open. Blood flowing the wrong way (right) forces the valves shut. The valves make sure that blood always flows towards the heart.*

Vein

Veins are narrow tubes that carry used BLOOD from all parts of your body back to the HEART. Blood flowing through the ARTERIES is pushed along by the pumping of the heart. Blood in the veins has nothing to push it along. So many veins have flaps, or *valves*, inside them which close the tube if the blood begins to flow backwards.

Venezuela

Venezuela is a large country on the north coast of SOUTH AMERICA. Most of southern Venezuela is covered by flat-topped mountains. Here stand the Angel Falls, the highest waterfall in the world. A grassy plain stretches across the middle of the country on either side of the Orinoco river.

Venezuela grows coffee, cotton and cocoa. But its minerals, especially oil, make it the richest country in the continent.

VENEZUELA

(map showing: CARIBBEAN SEA, LESSER ANTILLES, ATLANTIC OCEAN, TRINIDAD, VENEZUELA, GUYANA, SURINAM, COLOMBIA, BRAZIL)

Government: Federal republic
Capital: Caracas
Area: 912,050 sq km
Population: 20,695,000
Languages: Spanish, Indian
Currency: Bolívar

Venice

Venice is a beautiful city in ITALY, on the Adriatic Sea. It is built on a cluster of low, mud islands. There are more than 100 of them. The houses are built on wooden posts driven into the mud. Instead of roads, Venice has CANALS.

For hundreds of years, Venice was the most

▶ *An 18th century painting of the Grand Canal in Venice, by the artist Canaletto. The elegant black gondolas are still a common sight on the canal.*

important centre for trade between Europe and the empires of the East. The city became very rich and is full of palaces and fine houses built by merchants.

▲ *From the Earth, we have an almost edge-on view of the orbit of Venus. As it travels around the Sun, we see different amounts of its sunlit surface. These are known as its 'phases'. The planet looks larger in its crescent phase, when it is closest to Earth.*

Venus (planet)

The PLANET Venus is named after the Roman goddess of beauty and love. Venus is the brightest planet in the SOLAR SYSTEM. We see it as the morning star or the evening star, depending on where it is on its journey around the Sun. If you look at Venus through binoculars, you may see it looking like a small Moon, showing just the part that is lit by the Sun.

Venus takes only 225 days to go around the Sun. So more than three years pass on Venus for every two on Earth. But Venus itself spins so slowly that one day on Venus lasts for 117 days on Earth. It is the only planet to spin in the opposite way to the direction of its ORBIT.

Venus is about the same size as Earth, but weighs a little less. It is also much hotter, because it is much closer to the Sun. The surface of Venus is hidden under a dazzling white cloak of cloud. This may be made up of tiny drops of sulphuric acid. The atmosphere on Venus consists mainly of the gas *carbon dioxide*. This acts rather like a greenhouse roof, trapping the Sun's heat. The rocks on Venus are hotter than boiling water. Above the hot rocks are fierce winds blowing at more than 320 km/h.

VENUS FACTS

Average distance from Sun: 108 million km
Nearest distance from Earth: 40 million km
Average temperature: 455 degrees C
Diameter across equator: 12,104 km
Atmosphere: Mainly carbon dioxide
Number of moons: 0
Length of day: 117 Earth days
Length of year: 225 Earth days

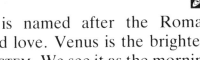

— Earth
— Venus

VERB ENDINGS		
Tense	**Singular**	**Plural**
Present		
1st person	I sing	We sing
2nd person	You sing	You sing
3rd person	He, she or it sings	They sing
Past		
1st person	I sang	We sang
2nd person	You sang	You sang
3rd person	He, she or it sang	They sang
Future		
1st person	I shall sing	We shall sing
2nd person	You will sing	You will sing
3rd person	He, she or it will sing	They will sing

Verb

Verbs are 'doing' or 'being' words, such as *go, hit, choose, have, be*. Verbs tell you what people or things are doing, or what is happening to them.

Here are three examples of verbs in sentences: 'It *is* a cold night. Tom *ate* the hamburger. Jill *was drinking* a milkshake.' In the first two examples, the verb is just one word. In the third example it is two words.

In the first sentence, the verb is describing something happening in the present. We call this the use of the present *tense*. If the action happened in the past, the verb changes: 'It *was* a cold night'. Similarly, if the action is to happen in the future: 'It *will be* a cold night'.

Verbs can also be *active* or *passive*. In the sentence 'Tom ate the hamburger', the verb *ate* is active. If we said 'The hamburger *was eaten* by Tom', the verb *was eaten* is passive.

Versailles

Versailles is a famous palace in France. It stands in a town, also called Versailles, just outside Paris.

The palace at Versailles was begun by LOUIS XIV in 1661, as a kind of 'holiday home' for the king and his court. It was built on the site of a hunting lodge. The most famous architects, sculptors and gardeners of the time worked on the palace and its magnificent park.

◀ *Architects show Louis XIV their ideas for his palace at Versailles. Louis wanted it to be the most splendid palace in France.*

◀ *A view of the beautiful palace of Versailles today. Louis XIV spent over £58,000,000 on the palace, an enormous sum for the time.*

The palace is built of pink and cream stone. It is more than 800 metres long. Inside are hundreds of beautiful rooms. The most famous is the Hall of Mirrors. It is lined with 483 enormous mirrors, and is full of paintings.

Louis XIV spent enormous sums of money on the palace. The great expense and luxury of the palace at Versailles was to be one of the causes of the FRENCH REVOLUTION a century later.

Vertebrate

Vertebrates are animals with a backbone or spine. The backbone is made up of short bones called *vertebrae*. This name comes from a Latin word that means 'to turn'. Most vertebrates can bend and straighten their backbones by turning their vertebrae slightly.

Many things make vertebrates different from other animals. Most have a bony case to protect their BRAIN, ribs to protect their HEART, LUNGS and other delicate parts, and one or two pairs of limbs. And most vertebrates have a SKELETON made of BONE.

There are seven main groups of vertebrates. The simplest group includes the lampreys. Lampreys are eel-like fish with no jaw. They have a spine but no skeleton. Next come SHARKS and skates, which have a skeleton of cartilage. All other vertebrates have bones. They are the bony FISH, AMPHIBIANS, REPTILES, BIRDS and MAMMALS.

▼ *The forelimbs of these vertebrates show that the animals may have evolved from the same ancestor. Each animal has the same special bones, though the shapes and sizes differ. This is because the bones gradually changed, over many millions of years, to suit the particular animal's environment.*

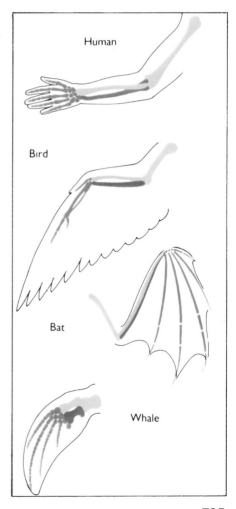

Human

Bird

Bat

Whale

VESUVIUS

▶ A group of tourists gazes at Vesuvius' crater from the high ridge called Mt Somma that surrounds it. Vesuvius is the only active volcano on the mainland of Europe.

It is difficult to imagine what the eruption of Vesuvius must have been like in AD 79. We think of volcanoes pouring out molten lava, but Vesuvius went off like an atomic bomb, shooting out ash, pumice stone and pebbles of lava over a great area. Even the city of Naples, 11 km from the volcano, was covered in a thick layer of ash. Pompeii, 8.5 km away, was buried under nearly 4 metres of ash and stones.

Vesuvius

Vesuvius is one of the world's most famous VOL-CANOES. The mountain rises over the Bay of Naples in southern Italy. It is about 1200 metres high, but gets shorter every time it erupts.

The first eruption we know about happened in AD 79. Nobody realized that it was an active volcano and so people had built towns close by and farmed the slopes of the mountain. For three days Vesuvius threw out ash and lava that buried the Roman cities of POMPEII and Herculaneum. Part of the wall of the old crater is still there. There have been nine bad eruptions in the last 200 years. The worst eruption in recent years happened in 1944 during World War II. The village of San Sebastiano was destroyed and Allied troops helped people to escape from the flowing lava.

Victoria, Queen

Queen Victoria (1819–1901) ruled Great Britain for 64 years, longer than any other British monarch. During her reign, the nation grew richer and its empire larger than ever before. She was the queen of many countries, including Australia, New Zealand, Canada and South Africa, and she was the empress of India.

Victoria was the daughter of Edward, Duke of Kent. GEORGE III was her grandfather. She was just

▲ A portrait of Queen Victoria by Bertha Muller. During Victoria's reign Great Britain reached the height of its power.

18 when she inherited the throne from her uncle, William IV. Two years later she married her German cousin, Prince Albert. They had four sons and five daughters. Prince Albert died of typhoid fever in 1861. His death left the Queen deeply unhappy. For many years she wore only black clothes to show her grief. She also stopped going to public ceremonies.

Victoria was very popular with her people. In 1887, she had been queen for 50 years. All over the British Empire there were huge parades and parties to celebrate this Golden Jubilee. In 1897, there were more celebrations for her Diamond Jubilee. Her reign is known as the Victorian age.

> Prince Albert had a great influence on Queen Victoria. He was her closest adviser and often restrained the impulsive queen. He was a patron of the arts and sciences, and helped to organize the Great Exhibition of 1851. He probably did more to set the tone of Victorian England than the queen herself.

Video

A video is a recording of moving pictures and sound. It is usually made on a videotape, but there are also videodiscs, which are like large versions of compact discs.

▶ *A video cassette recorder has three 'heads'. The erase head wipes off previous recordings; the video head records picture signals received from the TV aerial; and the audio head records sound signals on the edge of the tape. Rollers guide the videotape from one reel to the other. The section of videotape inside the circle shows the patterns the signals make on the videotape. The picture signals are recorded in a diagonal pattern across the tape, in strips close together. If the signals were recorded straight across the video head, it would take 33 km of tape to make a one-hour recording!*

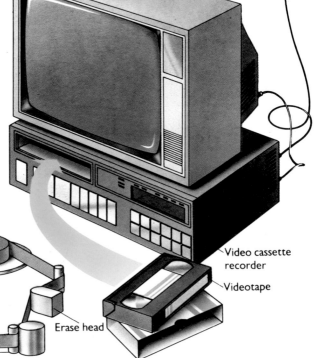

VIDEOTAPE
Sound track
Video track
Control track

Aerial

Video cassette recorder

Videotape

Audio head

Video head

Guiding rollers

Erase head

Video recording is not a new idea. In the late 1920s, John Logie Baird used an ordinary '78' record to store still pictures for showing on his newly invented television set. The video system used today by the broadcasting industry gives a better picture than that used in home recorders. Broadcast tapes are 5 cm wide and the head-to-tape speed is very fast – about 3810 cm per second.

You play a videotape in a video recorder that is connected to a television set. You see the video on the television screen. A video recorder can record television programmes on tape. Old programmes can be erased and new ones recorded on the same tape. You can also make your own videos if you have a videocamera. Electric signals from the camera or from a television programme are recorded on magnetic tape. The main difference from a music cassette recorder is that the record and replay heads in a video recorder spin round as the tape passes. This allows the head to move over the surface of the tape at high speed, giving the high recording speed needed to record picture signals.

Most of the programmes you see on television are video recordings.

Vienna

Vienna is the capital city of AUSTRIA. More than one and a half million people live there. Until the end of WORLD WAR I it was the home of the powerful HAPSBURG family.

Vienna stands on the Danube River. It is a very ancient site. CELTS settled there more than 2000 years ago. Then the Romans built a city called

▼ A view of Vienna and the Schönbrunn Castle. When the French occupied Vienna in 1805 and 1809, Napoleon lived in this castle for a while.

Vindobona. Many buildings from the MIDDLE AGES still stand in Vienna. The most famous is St Stephen's Cathedral.

Vienna has always been popular with artists and musicians. BEETHOVEN and MOZART lived there.

Vietnam

VIETNAM

Government: Communist
Capital: Hanoi
Area: 329,556 sq km
Population: 68,964,000
Languages: Vietnamese, French,
   English
Currency: Dong

Vietnam is a country in SOUTH-EAST ASIA. It is a little smaller than England and only 55 km wide in some parts. Vietnam is a hot, damp country.

Vietnam was once ruled by France as part of Indochina. After World War II, it was divided into two countries, North Vietnam and South Vietnam. Hanoi was the main city in the north and Saigon (now called Ho Chi Minh City) the capital of the south. From the 1950s until 1975, the two countries were at war. South Vietnam was supported by the United States. North Vietnam was communist. Now the whole country is communist.

Vikings

The Vikings were a fierce people who lived in Norway, Sweden and Denmark. Between 800 and 1100, a great number of Vikings left their homes to raid villages and build settlements in northern Europe. They settled in England, Ireland and France. Vikings also travelled to Russia, and even to CONSTANTINOPLE (See pages 730–731.)

Violin

The violin is a MUSICAL INSTRUMENT. It belongs to the string family. It is usually the smallest string instrument in an ORCHESTRA.

A violin is a curved wooden box, shaped rather like a figure eight. A long neck is fixed to one end of the box. Four strings, made of gut or nylon, are stretched from the top of the neck to the bottom end of the box.

The violin is played with a bow that has a flat ribbon, made up of about 150 horsehairs. When this is drawn across the strings they vibrate to make sounds. The strings can also be plucked.

▼ The wooden body of a violin amplifies (makes louder) the sound, which comes through two curved soundholes called f-holes. The shape of the violin has changed very little since the 1500s.

THE VIKINGS

The age of the Vikings lasted from about AD 800 to AD 1100. The Vikings came from Scandinavia (Norway, Denmark and Sweden). They were originally farmers, but to find new lands to settle they crossed the seas in swift sailing ships with carved dragon prows.

The Vikings earned a reputation for being bloodthirsty warriors, and were feared throughout western Europe. Vikings raided the coasts of England from the year 789 and eventually controlled the eastern part of the country.

However, the Vikings were not only raiders and pirates. They were superb seamen, braving the Atlantic Ocean to explore Greenland and even North America. They traded as far to the east as Russia and Constantinople. They had their own laws and a parliament. They were also skilled artists and they especially loved to recite poems and to tell tales of adventures involving heroes, gods and monsters.

HELLULAND
(Baffin Island)

GR

MARKLAND
(Labrador)

L'Anse A
Meadow

VINLAND
(Newfoundland

Western voya
ocean trade ro

Overland trade

▲ *The map shows how widely the Vikings travell*
They explored across oceans and land in search of
settlements and trade. At left is a Viking warrior.

<table>
<tr><td colspan="3">VIKING HISTORY</td></tr>
<tr><td>AD</td><td>789</td><td>First Viking attacks on England</td></tr>
<tr><td></td><td>800</td><td>Beginning of the Viking Age</td></tr>
<tr><td></td><td>830s</td><td>Vikings found the city of Dublin</td></tr>
<tr><td></td><td>850</td><td>Swedes begin to settle in East Baltic and Russia</td></tr>
<tr><td></td><td>860</td><td>Discovery of Iceland
Harald Fairhair becomes the first king of all Norway, and many Norwegians settle in Britain</td></tr>
<tr><td></td><td>874</td><td>First settlers in Iceland</td></tr>
<tr><td></td><td>876</td><td>Norwegian Healfdene rules Northumbria</td></tr>
<tr><td></td><td>886</td><td>King Alfred defeats Guthrum
Danes allowed to settle in the Danelaw in eastern England</td></tr>
<tr><td></td><td>911</td><td>Scandinavians settle in Normandy</td></tr>
<tr><td></td><td>930</td><td>The first meeting of the Althing, the national assembly in Iceland</td></tr>
<tr><td></td><td>982</td><td>Eric the Red discovers Greenland</td></tr>
<tr><td></td><td>986</td><td>Coast of North America sighted by Bjarni Herjolfsson</td></tr>
<tr><td></td><td>1000</td><td>Iceland becomes a Christian land</td></tr>
<tr><td></td><td>1003</td><td>Leif Ericsson lands in North America</td></tr>
<tr><td></td><td>1030</td><td>King Olaf of Norway killed at Battle of Stiklastad.</td></tr>
<tr><td></td><td>1047</td><td>Harald Hardrada becomes king of Norway</td></tr>
<tr><td></td><td>1066</td><td>Harald Hardrada killed at Battle of Stamford Bridge in England, by King Harold of England. Duke William of Normandy defeats Harold to become king of England</td></tr>
<tr><td></td><td>1100</td><td>End of Viking Age</td></tr>
</table>

▶ *The head of a Viking warrior (far right) is carved from a piece of elk horn and forms the handle of a stick. The god Thor is often shown in Viking art. This silver amulet (top right) is made in the shape of the god's hammer, decorated with a face with large, staring eyes. The Viking spear is richly decorated with engraving.*

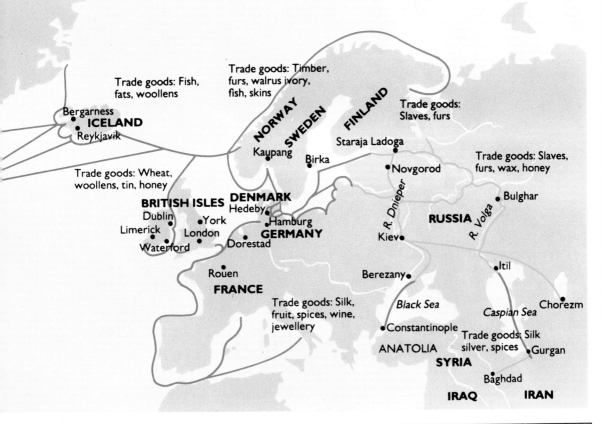

Trade goods: Fish, fats, woollens

Trade goods: Timber, furs, walrus ivory, fish, skins

ICELAND
Bergarness
Reykjavik

NORWAY
SWEDEN
Kaupang
Birka

FINLAND
Staraja Ladoga

Trade goods: Slaves, furs

Trade goods: Wheat, woollens, tin, honey

Novgorod

Trade goods: Slaves, furs, wax, honey

BRITISH ISLES
Dublin
Limerick
Waterford
York
London

DENMARK
Hedeby
Hamburg
GERMANY
Dorestad

Bulghar
RUSSIA
R. Dnieper
R. Volga
Kiev

Itil

Rouen
FRANCE

Berezany

Chorezm

Trade goods: Silk, fruit, spices, wine, jewellery

Black Sea

Caspian Sea

Constantinople
ANATOLIA

Trade goods: Silk, silver, spices
Gurgan

SYRIA

Baghdad

IRAQ   **IRAN**

The Oseberg ship is a Viking ship dug up on a farm in Norway in 1904. It is 21.5 ...tres long and had been buried as part of the funeral ceremony for a Viking ...een.

YGGDRASIL'S ASH TREE

The Vikings had a myth about a huge world tree called Yggdrasil's Ash. Its branches held up the sky. Beneath the tree was Asgarth, the home of the gods. Long roots spread out from the base of the trunk. One covered Midgarth, the world of men. Another root covered the realm of the terrible Frost Giants. A third root covered Hel, the world of the dead. Also among the roots were two wells. A drink of water from the well of the wise god Mimir gave knowledge. Beside the other well, the Well of Fate, lived the three Norns. They were called Past, Present and Future. They wove a cloth. Every thread represented the life of a person. When they cut a thread, that person died.

For more information turn to these articles: ALFRED THE GREAT, ANGLO-SAXONS, ENGLISH LANGUAGE, MYTHOLOGY, SHIP.

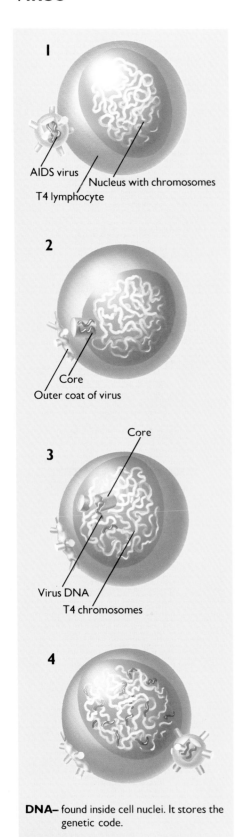

1

AIDS virus
T4 lymphocyte
Nucleus with chromosomes

2

Core
Outer coat of virus

Core

3

Virus DNA
T4 chromosomes

4

DNA– found inside cell nuclei. It stores the genetic code.

◄ *White blood cells (T4 lymphocytes) defend the body by attacking viruses. The AIDS virus prevents the cells from doing this. AIDS can be transmitted in several ways, but once it enters the bloodstream (1) it attaches itself to a white blood cell. Then the core of the virus (2) slowly moves into the white blood cell. Once inside (3) the core breaks open and releases its genetic material (DNA). The virus makes its DNA match that of the white blood cell. The AIDS DNA may stay hidden inside the cell for years before it is activated. Then, the white blood cell begins to make copies of the virus and dies (4).*

Virus

Viruses are very small living things that cause diseases in plants and animals. They are smaller than BACTERIA and can be seen only with a very powerful electron MICROSCOPE.

You can be infected with viruses by swallowing them or breathing them in. Some insects carry viruses, which they pass on when they bite you. Once inside the body, a virus travels around in the bloodstream. It gets inside a living CELL where it produces more viruses. Sometimes the cell is entirely destroyed by the viruses.

Diseases caused by viruses include measles, chicken pox, mumps, AIDS, influenza, and colds. Viruses are very hard to kill. INOCULATION helps to prevent some of these diseases.

When a virus enters the body, the blood produces substances called *antibodies*. After a while there are usually enough antibodies to kill all the viruses and the patient recovers.

Vitamins and Minerals

Vitamins are chemicals that our bodies need to stay healthy. They are found in different kinds of FOOD. Scientists call the six kinds of vitamins A, B, C, D, E and K. Vitamin B is really a group of vitamins.

The first people to realize that certain kinds of food were important to health were sailors. On long voyages they got a disease called *scurvy* if they could not eat fresh fruit and vegetables. These contain vitamin C. From the 1700s, English sailors were given limes to eat to prevent scurvy. This is why they were nicknamed 'limeys' by the Americans.

SOURCES AND USES OF VITAMINS

Vitamin	Found in	Needed for
A	Milk, butter, eggs, green vegetables, fish oil, liver, carrots	Fighting disease and seeing in the dark
B_1 (thiamine)	Yeast and wheatgerm (whole wheat bread)	All 'B' vitamins needed for healthy appetite, energy production and healthy nerves and skin
B_2 9 other 'B' vitamins	Yeast Milk, meat and green vegetables	
C	Oranges, lemons, tomatoes and fresh vegetables	Healthy blood and gums, healing, protection against colds
D	Cod-liver oil, cream, egg yolks (and with sunlight, fat below the skin forms vit. D)	Strong bones and teeth
E	Whole wheat bread, brown rice and butter	Not fully understood
K	Green vegetables, liver	Clotting blood

MINERAL SALTS

Calcium and **phosphorus** are found in milk and cheese. They help to build healthy bones and teeth.

Iron, found in meat, liver and spinach, is needed by the red blood cells.

Sodium and **potassium** are needed by the nerves, in body fluids and in nearly all cells. We can get sodium from sodium chloride – table salt.

Iodine is found in fish. It is needed for growth and helps the thyroid gland function properly.

Fluoride helps to prevent tooth decay.

Copper, cobalt and **manganese** are also required in very small quantities.

All these minerals are contained in a normal balanced diet.

No one food has all the vitamins we need. That is why it is important to eat a mixture of things. Some people take their vitamins in pills. No one really needs pills if they eat well. Very old people, young babies and women expecting babies all need more vitamins than usual. But too much of some kinds of vitamins, such as vitamin A, can be bad for you.

We also need minerals in small amounts. Calcium is an important part of BONES and TEETH. We get it from milk and cheese. Iron is needed for haemoglobin, the part of red blood cells that carries oxygen from your lungs to tissues. Other minerals needed are iodine, phosphorus, sodium, and potassium.

> Four vitamins – A, D, E and K – can be stored in the body's fat. These vitamins, therefore, do not have to be consumed every day. The other vitamins – the B vitamins and vitamin C – cannot be stored in the body in this way, so we should have some of them every day.

Voice *See* Speech

Volcano

A volcano is an opening in the surface of the Earth. Burning gas, boiling rocks and ash escape from this opening. Sometimes they trickle out, sometimes they explode. An explosion is called an *eruption*.

Some volcanoes are gently sloping mountains with cracks, or fissures, in them. Hot liquid rock called *lava* flows out through the fissures. Other

VOLCANO FACTS

Active volcanoes: There are about 535 of these, 80 below the sea.

Largest known eruption: Tambora, Indonesia, in 1815. The volcano threw out about 150 cubic km of matter and lost 1250 m in height.

Greatest disaster: 36,000 people were drowned by a giant wave unleashed when Krakatoa, Indonesia, exploded in 1883.

Greatest volcanic explosion: About 1470 BC, Santorini in the Aegean Sea exploded with 130 times the force of a hydrogen bomb.

volcanoes are steep-sided mountains with a large hole at the top. These are called cone volcanoes. They are the kind that explode.

Erupting volcanoes can do a lot of damage. The city of POMPEII was destroyed by VESUVIUS in AD 79. In 1883 Krakatoa, a volcano in Indonesia, erupted, causing a tidal wave that killed 36,000 people. Volcanoes can also make new land. An island called Surtsey, south of Iceland, was made by a volcano erupting under the sea in 1963.

If you look at where volcanoes are found around the world, they make a pattern of long chains. These chains mark the edges of the huge 'plates' that form the Earth's surface. They are the weakest part of the Earth's crust. One chain, called 'the ring of fire', goes right round the Pacific Ocean. Earthquakes, geysers and hot springs are all found in the same area as volcanoes.

▼ *A simple section through a volcanic region. Magma from the underground chamber (1) rises up the central vent (2) or side vent (3). During eruptions, ash (4) may shoot into the air and lava (5) flows out of the vent. Many volcanoes are made up of hardened layers of ash and lava (6). Magma which hardens underground creates formations called dykes (7) and sills (8). Laccoliths (9), push up the overlying rocks to form domes.*

Volume

The volume of an object is the amount of space it takes up. You can find out the volume of a rectangular solid by measuring its height, width and depth and multiplying the figures together. So a block with equal sides, each 10 cm long, has a volume of 1000 cubic cm (1000 cc): that is, $10 \text{ cm} \times 10 \text{ cm} \times 10 \text{ cm}$.

It is easy to find out the volume of boxes or bricks or anything with straight edges. Measuring the volume of something with an irregular shape is more difficult. A very simple method was discovered by ARCHIMEDES, the Greek scientist. A story told about him says that he was getting into his bath, which was full to the brim, and water spilled over the side. He suddenly realized that the volume of water that had spilled over must be exactly the same as the volume of his body. This means that any irregular object can be measured by plunging it into water and measuring the rise in the water level.

SEE IT YOURSELF

You can use Archimedes' principle to find the volume of an egg. Put some water into a measuring jug and note the level. Using a spoon, gently lower an egg into the jug. What level does the water rise to? The difference between the two water levels will give you the volume of the egg. Try doing this with other irregular objects and recording their volumes.

Vowel

Vowels are the letters A, E, I, O and U. Sometimes the letters Y and W are used as vowels. Vowels are

The pronunciation of vowel sounds changes over the years. Chaucer, who lived in the 1300s, pronounced 'do' with the vowel sound we use for 'go'. He pronounced 'bee' with the vowel sound we use for 'bay'; 'by' the way we say 'bee'; and 'cow' as we pronounce 'coo'.

pronounced with the mouth open. What they sound like depends on the position of your TONGUE in your mouth. The shape your lips make is also important. If they are pushed forward, as if you are whistling, you make an *oo* sound. If they are pulled right back, you make an *ee* sound.

Because the tongue and the lips can shape themselves in hundreds of different ways, there are hundreds of different vowel sounds. Sometimes two or three vowel sounds are run together to make a new sound. The vowel sounds in one LANGUAGE are often very difficult for speakers of another language to say.

▼ These vultures are usually found around mountains, although the Egyptian vulture visits rubbish dumps in villages. The lammergeyer has an unusual habit of dropping bones onto rocks to break them open so it can eat the marrow inside.

Vulture

Vultures are large birds of prey. They live in the hot, dry parts of the world. The largest land bird in North America is a type of vulture. This is the California condor. When its wings are spread out, they measure up to 3 metres from tip to tip.

Vultures do not hunt for their food. They live on carrion, the rotting bodies of dead animals. Sometimes vultures have to wait for their dinner until a large hunter such as a lion has made a kill. When the lion has eaten its fill, wild dogs and hyenas gorge on the remains. Then it is the vulture's turn.

Most vultures have bald heads and necks. This stops their feathers getting messy when they plunge their heads into large carcases. They have very good eyesight and can spot dead or dying animals from far away. They also have a keen sense of smell.

Griffon vulture

Egyptian vulture

Black vulture

Lammergeyer

◄ *The god Wotan bids farewell to his daughter, Brünnhilde, in a scene from Wagner's opera* The Valkyrie, *one of the four great works in* The Ring of the Nibelung.

Wagner, Richard

Richard Wagner (1813–1883) was a German composer whose music brought about great changes in the art of opera. He believed that the music and the plot of an opera should be closely bound together, in the same way that the words and the plot of a play are. Wagner wrote his own *librettos* (scripts) for his operas.

In 1848, Wagner took part in a political revolution in Germany and he had to escape to Switzerland. There he began his greatest work, *The Ring of the Nibelung*. This long work consists of four music dramas based on old German legends. They tell the story of a magic ring and the adventures of the hero, Siegfried, and the beautiful Brünnhilde. When Wagner returned to Germany he designed at Bayreuth a festival theatre especially for his operas. Today, people from all countries still go to Bayreuth to hear them.

Among Wagner's other operas are *The Flying Dutchman*, *Tannhäuser*, *Lohengrin*, *The Mastersingers of Nuremberg*, *Tristan and Isolde* and *Parsifal*.

▲ *Richard Wagner spent the latter part of his life in debt. He died a year after his opera* Parsifal *was performed.*

Wales

Wales is part of the UNITED KINGDOM of Great Britain and Northern Ireland. It lies to the west of England and is a country of low mountains and

> The title 'Prince of Wales' is given only to the eldest son of an English sovereign. Prince Charles is the 21st Prince of Wales. The first was Edward, son of Edward I, who was given the title in 1301.

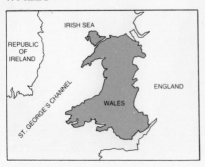

WALES

Area: 20,768 sq km
Population: 2,857,000
Capital: Cardiff
Languages: Welsh, English
Highest point: Snowdon, 1085 m
    above sea level
Chief products: Coal, steel, wool,
    paper, textiles
Agricultural products: Barley, hay,
    oats, potatoes, turnips

The rock wallaby is about 70 cm high. It is the acrobat of the wallaby family. Not only is it extremely agile, leaping from rock to rock, it can scale trees at top speed, making huge leaps to reach the branches. It has been seen to leap across chasms 4 metres wide.

▶ *The red-necked wallaby lives in Australia and Tasmania. The female carries her young in a pouch for nine months after it is born. The red-necked wallaby can grow up to 70 cm high.*

green valleys. The highest mountain is Snowdon and Cardiff is the capital city.

The Welsh are descended from the CELTS. English is their main language today, but about a quarter of the people still speak Welsh. Many Welsh people are striving passionately to keep their language alive.

South Wales is a traditional coal-mining region but there are now few mines left. Most of the people live in industrial towns like Swansea and Cardiff. Steel is another important industry. In the mountains of north and mid-Wales many people are sheep farmers. Wool is one of Wales' main exports.

Wallaby

Wallabies are small members of the KANGAROO family. They live in Australia, New Zealand and parts of New Guinea. There are many different kinds of wallaby. Most are about the size of hares, though the biggest is roughly a metre long with a 60-cm tail.

Wallabies feed mostly on grass. They also make good food for other animals. Two of their natural enemies are the dingo, the Australian wild dog, and the eagle. Some breeds are hunted for their valuable fur. Too much hunting has made some of them very scarce. The aborigines of Australia and New Guinea have always hunted wallabies for food, especially the hare wallaby.

◀ The walrus swims in shallow Arctic seas. It has flippers but no tail. Clumsy on land, the walrus can swim at speeds of about 24 km/h.

Walrus

The walrus belongs to the SEAL family. Its enormous canine teeth look like two tusks. These tusks can be up to a metre long. The walrus uses them to scrape up the clams and shellfish it eats. It also uses its tusks to fight, and even polar bears keep away from fully grown walruses.

The Atlantic and the Pacific walrus both live in the cold ARCTIC. They are big animals. The male Atlantic walrus measures up to 4 metres and weighs as much as 1800 kg.

In the 1930s walruses almost disappeared through being hunted for their tusks and skins. Now there are laws against hunting them and their numbers are slowly increasing.

▲ A view of the east side of the Capitol building in Washington, D.C. This is where the American Congress meets.

Washington, D.C.

Washington, D.C. is the capital of the UNITED STATES. It is named after the first president, George WASHINGTON, who chose its site on the Potomac River between Maryland and Virginia. It stands on a piece of land called the District of Columbia, which is why it is always called Washington, D.C. It is not the biggest city in America but it is the most important. It has all the government buildings, the White House, and the headquarters of the United States armed forces. A third of Washington's workers are employed by the government. The city also has the embassies and legations of some 140 nations.

Washington, D.C. has a larger proportion of black residents than any other large city in the United States. In 1950, 35 per cent of Washington's population was black. Today, that figure has risen to more than 70 per cent.

▲ In 1781, after a six-year war, the British finally surrendered to the American army at Yorktown, Virginia. George Washington, who had been commander-in-chief, went home to Mt. Vernon. But he soon returned to public life and became first president of the new nation in 1789.

▲ George Washington began his career as a surveyor and mapmaker.

Washington, George

George Washington (1732–1799) was the first PRESIDENT of the United States of America. He commanded the victorious colonial troops in the REVOLUTIONARY WAR against the British. One of his officers said this about him in a speech to Congress: 'He was first in war, first in peace, and first in the hearts of his countrymen.'

George Washington was born on a farm in Westmoreland County, Virginia. In 1752, he inherited an estate called Mount Vernon. In 1760, just married, he went to live there. For a while he farmed his land. Then, in 1775, the Revolutionary War broke out. Washington was chosen to be commander-in-chief of the American troops. Despite many problems, the American colonies won their independence from Britain.

He tried to return to farming, but in 1787 he was asked to help in drawing up the Constitution. In the first election, he became president. Altogether, he held office from 1789–1797. When he finally withdrew from public life, Washington retired to his beloved Mount Vernon, where he died two years later.

Water

Water is the most common substance on Earth. Seven-tenths of the world's surface is covered by water. Water is also the most important substance on Earth. Without it life would be impossible. Life first started in water, and the bodies of all living things are mostly water.

There is no such thing as 'pure water'. Water contains MINERALS, which it has picked up from the surrounding earth and rocks.

Water exists in three forms. At 0°C it freezes into solid ice. At 100°C it boils into steam. Normal air takes up water easily, and CLOUDS are huge collections of water particles. At any time, clouds contain millions of tonnes of water, which falls back to Earth as RAIN. Some of this water stays in the soil or underground for years, but most of it returns to the oceans.

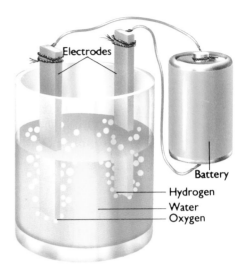

▲ The chemical formula for water is H_2O. This means that each molecule of water is made up of two atoms of hydrogen and one atom of oxygen. By using two electrodes to pass electricity through water (shown above), it can be separated into hydrogen and oxygen gas. This process is known as electrolysis.

Waterfall

Any sudden drop, or fall, in a river is a waterfall. These are made by the water slowly wearing away the rock of the river bed it flows over. Some sorts of rock are softer than others, and so get worn away faster. The soft rock is worn away, leaving a cliff of hard rock, over which the river's water pours.

The most famous waterfalls are NIAGARA, between the USA and Canada, and the Victoria Falls

MAJOR WATERFALLS	
Highest	Metres
Angel Falls (Venezuela)	979
Yosemite Falls (California)	739
Tugela Falls (South Africa)	614
Greatest volume	m³/sec
Boyoma (Zaire)	17,000
Niagara (N. America)	6000

◀ The Iguassu Falls lie on the boundary of Argentina and Brazil. The falls plunge over 82-metre high cliffs in separate cascades totalling over 3 km in width.

The great Victoria Falls on the Zambezi River are more than 107 m high and about 1.6 km wide. Nearly 100 million litres of water plunge over this drop every minute. If all this power could be used, there would be enough energy to supply all the electricity for a city of 5 million people.

in the Zambezi River, Africa. The highest waterfall in the world is Angel Falls in Venezuela. It is 979 metres high.

Waterloo, Battle of

The Battle of Waterloo was fought on June 18, 1815. It was fought between the French on one side, and the allied armies on the other – one from Prussia (north Germany) and the other a mixture of British, Germans, Dutch and Belgians. The French lost.

It was an important battle because NAPOLEON BONA-PARTE led the French army. He had escaped from his prison island to become Emperor of France again. Other European countries were very worried by Napoleon's return. They thought he would destroy their plans for Europe. So they decided to fight him.

The battle was fought near a village in Belgium called Waterloo. One of the allied armies was led by the British Duke of WELLINGTON. Wellington kept in contact with the Prussian army leader, Blücher. He hoped the Prussians could join the battle and help against the French.

▼ A scene from the Battle of Waterloo. At the end of the battle, about 45,000 men lay dead or wounded.

The ground was thick with mud, and heavy guns are very hard to move in mud. Napoleon waited to attack until the sun had dried the mud a bit. That gave Blücher more time to get his army into position to help Wellington.

At first the French did very well. But after the Prussian army arrived the French were outnumbered. In the end, late that night, Napoleon realized his army had lost.

Napoleon's defeat at the Battle of Waterloo was so crushing that today, when someone who has been successful for a time is at last defeated, we say he has 'met his Waterloo'.

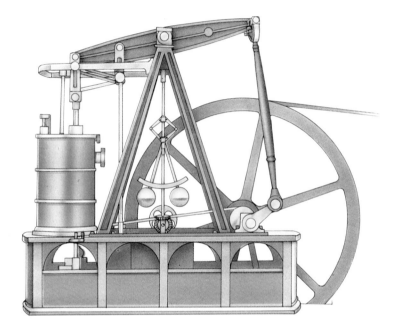

◄ *James Watt's steam engine was more efficient than other steam engines of his time. This model was made towards the end of his career. One of the improvements Watt made was to add a steam governor, using two heavy balls mounted on swinging arms. This steadied the speed of the engine by regulating the amount of steam admitted from the boiler.*

Watt, James

James Watt (1736–1819) was a Scottish engineer who spent most of his life developing STEAM ENGINES. In early steam engines, steam was heated and cooled inside a cylinder. Watt designed a model in which steam cooled outside the cylinder. This made the engine much more powerful.

Watt made many other improvements to steam engines so that they could work all kinds of machinery.

Wave

When the wind blows over the sea it disturbs the water's surface. A light breeze causes gentle ripples, but a storm gale can whip up waves higher than a house.

▲ *Apart from the steam engine, James Watt invented other equipment such as the screw-propeller for use in ships and a hydrometer, used to measure the density of liquids.*

▶ *Wave energy can be used to make electricity. One experimental machine for harnessing wave energy is called the 'nodding boom' or 'duck'. The 'ducks' have small generators inside them. As waves make the 'beak' of each 'duck' move up and down (inset), electricity is produced by the generators.*

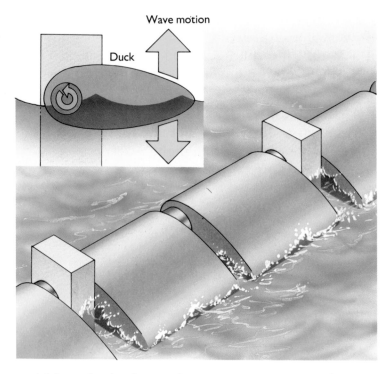

Wave motion

Duck

▼ *These five instruments are used to measure weather conditions. Anemometers measure wind speeds and vanes show wind direction. The psychrometer, a kind of hygrometer, measures humidity. Thermometers record air temperatures and barographs record changing air pressure on a rotating drum.*

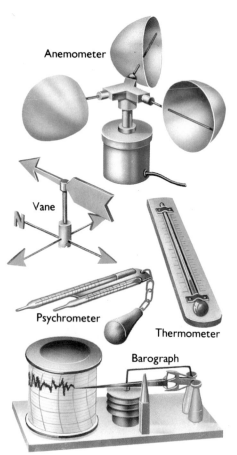

Anemometer

Vane

Psychrometer

Thermometer

Barograph

Although ripples and waves move across the sea, the water itself does not travel with them. Instead, each passing wave just lifts the water up and down. This explains why floating objects like seabirds and bottles bob up and down on waves but do not travel with them.

Most sea waves are caused by the wind. But the most dangerous waves are set off by underwater earthquakes and volcanoes. These giant waves, called tsunamis or tidal waves, sometimes flood coasts and drown many people.

Sea waves carry energy, usually energy from the wind. Some other forms of energy travel in waves. LIGHT, SOUND and RADIO, for example, all move from one place to another in waves. Just as sea waves travel without taking the water with them, so a sound wave crosses a room without actually moving the air along.

Weather

The weather – sunshine, fog, RAIN, CLOUDS, WIND, heat, cold – is always changing in most parts of the world. These changes are caused by what happens in the atmosphere, the layer of air above the Earth.

The atmosphere is always moving, driven by the

Sun's heat. Near the EQUATOR the Sun's strong rays heat the air. At the North and South poles the Sun's rays are weaker and the air is colder. This uneven heating means the atmosphere is never still. Huge masses of warm and cold air flow round and round between the tropics and the polar regions. As these wandering air masses meet, rise and fall, heat and cool, they cause weather.

When cold and warm masses meet, the air whirls inward in a giant spiral called a *depression*. Depressions bring clouds, wind, rain and summer thunderstorms. They can also cause violent TORNADOES and HURRICANES.

The meeting line between two air masses is called a *front*. When cold air pushes up behind warm air, it forms a *cold front*; when a warm air mass catches up

▼ *This chart is a summary of the weather conditions in Europe at a particular time. The lines are called isobars; they show air pressure. Weathermen use symbols on their charts to represent various things. The meanings of the symbols on this chart are shown beside it.*

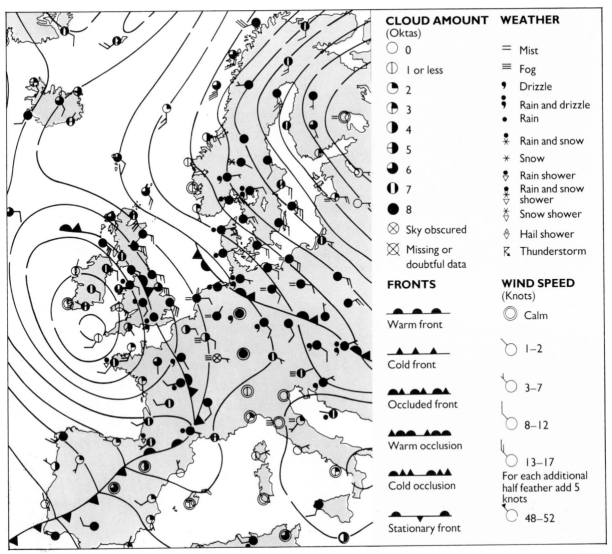

CLOUD AMOUNT (Oktas)

- ◯ 0
- ◍ 1 or less
- ◕ 2
- ◕ 3
- ◑ 4
- ◑ 5
- ◑ 6
- ◕ 7
- ● 8
- ⊗ Sky obscured
- ⊠ Missing or doubtful data

WEATHER

- = Mist
- ≡ Fog
- ❜ Drizzle
- ❟ Rain and drizzle
- • Rain
- ⁎ Rain and snow
- ＊ Snow
- ⩟ Rain shower
- ⩟ Rain and snow shower
- ⩟ Snow shower
- ⩟ Hail shower
- ⏃ Thunderstorm

FRONTS

Warm front

Cold front

Occluded front

Warm occlusion

Cold occlusion

Stationary front

WIND SPEED (Knots)

- ◎ Calm
- 1–2
- 3–7
- 8–12
- 13–17

For each additional half feather add 5 knots

- 48–52

▲ *Warm air is lighter than cold air. The edge of a moving mass of cold air is called a cold front and that of warm air is called a warm front. Warm air rises up from the ground and can form rain clouds.*

with a cold mass, it creates a *warm front*. An *occluded front* is formed when a cold front overtakes a warm front. Weathermen expect rain and snow ahead of a warm front. Showers usually form along a cold front.

Weaving

Curtains and sheets, shirts and carpets, towels and suits are just some of the many useful articles made by weaving. In weaving, threads are joined together in a criss-cross pattern to make cloth.

People have been weaving cloth to make clothes since the STONE AGE. The oldest fabric we know of was woven nearly 8000 years ago in what is now Turkey. These first weavers learned to make linen from *flax*. By 2000 BC the Chinese were weaving cloth from SILK. In India, people learned to use fibres from the COTTON plant. Meanwhile *nomads* (travellers) from the deserts and mountains of Asia discovered how to weave WOOL.

For thousands of years, making cloth was slow work. First, the fibres were drawn out and twisted into a long thread. This process is known as spinning. Then, rows of threads were stretched

One man can easily operate 20 of today's fully automatic looms. If a thread breaks, the power is cut off automatically and the machine stops. Some machines use compressed air to blow the weft through the warp.

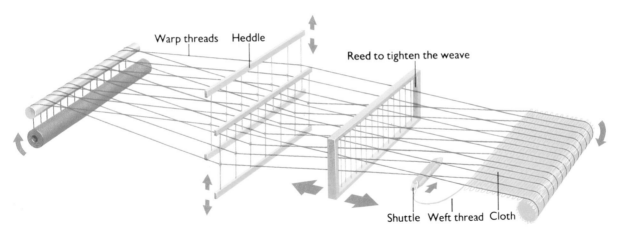

Warp threads · Heddle · Reed to tighten the weave · Shuttle · Weft thread · Cloth

lengthwise, side by side, on a frame called a *loom*. These threads made up the *warp*. A crosswise thread, the *weft*, was then passed through from one side of the loom to the other, going over and under the warp threads. A *shuttle*, like a large needle, was used to feed the weft through the warp.

Spinning wheels and looms were worked by hand until the 1700s. Then, machines were invented for spinning and weaving. These machines worked far faster than hand looms, and cloth became cheap and plentiful. Today most woven fabrics are made by machine.

▲ Cloth is made by weaving two different types of thread together on a loom. During weaving, the heddle creates a gap by raising and lowering different warp threads. Then the shuttle moves the weft thread through the gaps, going over some of the warp threads and under others, to make the cloth.

◄ Workers in a textile mill bring large spools of thread to the loom. Fully automatic looms are common today in many countries, though hand looms are still used for very special woollen or silk fabrics.

Greater plantain
Purple loosestrife
Dandelion
Black bindweed
Common chickweed

▲ These weeds grow in a variety of places: black bindweed grows on cultivated land; the dandelion grows in fields and meadows; greater plantain grows on paths and purple loosestrife grows in damp places. Young plants of the common chickweed can be eaten in salads and sandwiches.

Weed

A weed is any PLANT that grows where it is not wanted. On farms and in gardens, weeds damage crops and flowers by taking a large share of water, minerals and sunlight. In places where weeds grow thickly, cultivated plants do not develop properly; they may produce only a few flowers, small seeds, unhealthy leaves or weak roots.

There are several ways of controlling weeds. In gardens, people break up the soil with a hoe. This disturbs the weed roots and stops growth. They also pull the weeds out of the ground: this is called weeding. On farms, the soil is broken up by ploughing and harrowing. Farmers also spray their fields with weedkiller. Weedkillers are chemicals that destroy weeds. Most of them are *selective*. This means the chemicals only affect certain plants: they destroy weeds without harming crops.

Weeds are only a nuisance when they interfere with cultivated plants. In woods and fields, away from gardens and farms, weeds are useful plants. Weeds are food for many animals.

Weightlessness

GRAVITY is the force that pulls everything on Earth downwards. It keeps objects on the Earth's surface and stops them floating away. This force of gravity

▶ Astronaut Kathryn D. Sullivan floats in the mid-deck area during a Space Shuttle flight in 1984. Weightlessness affects every aspect of life on board the Shuttle. Even the simple act of drinking liquid through a straw is different. The straw must have a clip for pinching off the flow of liquid between mouthfuls.

gives objects, including our bodies, *weight*.

The pull of gravity becomes weaker with distance. Out in space, Earth's gravity has very little effect. Also, the pull of gravity from other planets is very weak because they, too, are far away. This means objects in space weigh nothing, for weight is caused by gravity. They are *weightless*.

Weightlessness makes life difficult for an astronaut in a spacecraft. If he tries to take a step his feet leave the cabin floor and he floats about. If he pours a drink into a glass, the liquid bounces out and drifts around. It he lets go of a tool in mid-air, it hangs there instead of falling. Also, weeks of weightlessness can affect the way in which his body works. Special gadgets help astronauts live in weightless surroundings.

> **In the zero gravity of space, astronauts need no furniture because they never have to sit down. There is plenty of floor space in the cabin because the walls and ceiling are 'floors' too. To sleep, the astronauts simply tuck themselves into sleeping bags and attach the bags to a wall.**

Weight-lifting

Weight-lifting is one of the sports included in the OLYMPIC GAMES. In a weight-lifting contest, the competitors lift very heavy weights from the floor to above their heads. Weight-lifters, like boxers, are divided into classes according to their own body weight. Champion weight-lifters can lift over 250 kg.

Many other sportsmen, such as swimmers and footballers, do weight-lifting as an exercise to strengthen their muscles and at the same time improve their breathing.

WEIGHT-LIFTING CLASSES	
Flyweight	52 kg limit
Bantam	56 kg
Feather	60 kg
Welter	67.5 kg
Middle	75 kg
Light-heavy	82.5 kg
Middle-heavy	90 kg
1st heavy	100 kg
2nd heavy	110 kg
Super-heavy	Over 110 kg

◄ *Weight-lifting is an Olympic sport. There are two kinds of lift — the snatch and the clean and jerk. In the snatch, the bar is lifted straight from the floor to above the head. In the clean and jerk, the bar is raised to the chest and then overhead, the legs being used to give extra power.*

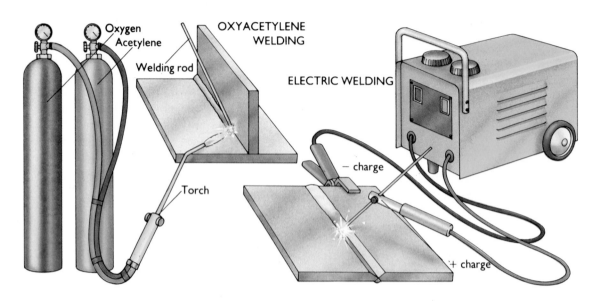

OXYACETYLENE
WELDING

Oxygen
Acetylene

Welding rod

ELECTRIC WELDING

Torch

– charge

+ charge

▲ *In oxyacetylene welding, acetylene gas is burnt to produce a very hot flame in the torch. Oxygen is added to make the flame even hotter. Electric welders use a powerful electric current to melt two pieces of metal at the point of contact and make a join. The welders must protect their eyes from the heat and bright light by wearing dark goggles or masks.*

Weights and Measures

Weights and measures are used to work out the size of things. The two main kinds of measurement are weight and length. They answer the questions 'How heavy?' and 'How long?'. Length is also used to find area and VOLUME. There are several systems of weights and measures. The most common is the METRIC SYSTEM. (See pages 752–753.)

Welding

Welding is a way of joining metals by heating. The edges of two pieces of metal are heated until they melt together. When they cool they form just one piece of metal. A join made by welding is extremely strong.

Welders work with gas or electricity. In gas welding a very hot flame from a gas torch melts the metal. In electric welding, an electric CURRENT jumps from an electric welding rod to the metals and melts them.

Although Wellington was a great general, he was never loved by his soldiers as Napoleon was loved by his. This is not too surprising as Wellington described his men as 'the mere scum of the earth'.

Wellington, Duke of

Arthur Wellesley, the Duke of Wellington (1769–1852), was a famous British soldier and statesman. In 1803 he led the troops whose victories put India firmly under British rule. In 1808 he began to drive NAPOLEON's French troops out of Portugal and

Spain. In 1815 his British troops helped to defeat Napoleon at the great Battle of WATERLOO in Belgium.

Wellington later held important jobs in the British government. He was made commander in chief of the army in 1827. From 1828 to 1830 he served as Prime Minister.

Western Samoa

Western Samoa is a small COMMONWEALTH country, part of the Samoan chain of islands. It is made up of two volcanic islands, Savaii and Upolu, and some smaller islands. The islanders grow coconuts, bananas and timber. Western Samoa became independent in 1962.

West Indies

This chain of tropical islands stretches from Florida in the United States to Venezuela in South America. On one side lies the Caribbean Sea, on the other stretches the Atlantic Ocean. The islands are really the tops of a drowned range of mountains. Palm trees and tropical grasses grow here, where it is almost always warm. But fierce autumn hurricanes often destroy trees and houses.

The thousands of islands are divided into more than 20 countries. CUBA, JAMAICA, HAITI, and the

Continued on page 754

WESTERN SAMOA

Government: Parliamentary democracy
Capital: Apia
Area: 2842 sq km
Population: 190,000
Languages: Samoan, English
Currency: Tala

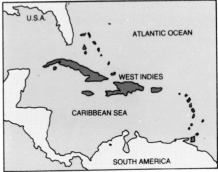

◀ *The city of San Juan is the capital of Puerto Rico, an island in the Greater Antilles, one of the three main island groups in the West Indies. Puerto Rico is an overseas commonwealth of the USA, which also owns some of the Virgin Islands.*

WEIGHTS AND MEASURES

'How many?' 'How far?' 'How big?' are all questions to do with weights and measures. People first needed units of measurement when they began to build towns and to trade goods. The ancient Egyptians, for example, based their measurements on the proportions of the body. Our word 'mile' comes from the Roman *mille* which meant '1000 paces'.

Most countries now use the metric system for measuring lengths, distances and so on. The metric system is a decimal system (based on 10) and was first used in France in the late 1700s. Another system was used for a long time in Britain and the United States, and is known as the imperial system. The table gives some common units of measurement in both systems, and some useful conversion factors.

▼ *In the ancient Egyptian system of measurement, based on the human body, 4 digits = 1 palm. Seven palms, or two spans (little finger to thumb tip) = 1 cubit, the distance from a person's fingertips to the elbow.*

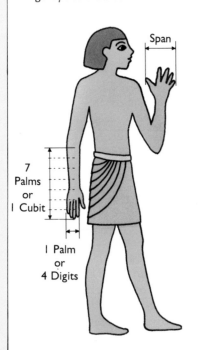

Span

7 Palms or 1 Cubit

1 Palm or 4 Digits

WEIGHTS AND MEASURES

Length
Metric units
millimetre (mm)
10 mm = 1 centimetre (cm)
100 cm = 1 metre (m)
1000 m = 1 kilometre (km)

Imperial units
inch (in)
12 in = 1 foot (ft)
3 ft = 1 yard (yd)
1760 yd = 1 mile = 5280 ft

Area
Metric units
square millimetre (mm^2)
100 mm^2 = 1 square centimetre (cm^2)
10,000 cm^2 = 1 square metre (m^2)
100 m^2 = 1 are (a) = 1 square decametre
100 a = 1 hectare (ha)
100 ha = 1 square kilometre (km^2)

Imperial units
square inch (in^2)
144 in^2 = 1 square foot (ft^2)
9 ft^2 = 1 square yard (yd^2)
4840 yd^2 = 1 acre
640 acres = 1 square mile ($mile^2$)

Volume
Metric units
cubic millimetre (mm^3)
1000 mm^3 = 1 cubic centimetre (cm^3)
1000 cm^3 = 1 cubic decimetre (dm^3) = 1 litre
1000 dm^3 = 1 cubic metre (m^3)

Imperial units
cubic inch (in^3)
1728 in^3 = 1 cubic foot (ft^3)
27 ft^3 = 1 cubic yard (yd^3)

Capacity
Metric units
millilitre (ml)
1000 ml = 1 litre (l)
100 l = 1 hectolitre (hl)

Imperial units
gill
4 gills = 1 pint
2 pints = 1 quart
4 quarts = 1 gallon = 277.274 in^3

Apothecaries' fluid
minim (min)
60 min = fluid drachm (fl dr)
8 fl dr = 1 fluid ounce (fl oz)
5 fl oz = 1 gill
20 fl oz = 1 pint

▲ *This ancient Egyptian painting shows the god Anubis weighing souls, using weighing machine known as an equal arm balance. This kind of weighing machine has been around for 6000 years.*

Measuring time is just as important as measuring distance. The Egyptians
[...]d the sundial: they stuck a stick into the ground and marked out the path of
[...]shadow. By checking the shadow's position, they could tell the time of day.

[...] units

[...]S gallon (liquid) = 0.8327 gallon
[...]mp)
[...]S gallon (dry) = 0.9689 gallon
[...]mp)
[...]uid oz (US) = 1.0408 fl oz (apoth)
[...]l oz (US) = 1 US pint

[We]ight

[Me]tric units

[...] gram (mg)
[...]0 mg = 1 gram (g)
[...]0 g = 1 kilogram (kg)
[...] kg = 1 quintal (q)
[...]0 kg = 1 metric ton, or
[t]onne (t)

[Imp]erial units (Avoirdupois)
[oun]ce (oz)
[...]oz = 1 lb
[...]b = 1 stone
[...] lb = 1 hundredweight (cwt)
[...]cwt = 1 (long) ton = 2240 lb
[...]0 lb = 1 short ton (US)

[Na]utical Measurement

[fa]thom = 6 ft
[n]autical mile
[(i]nternational) = 1.151 statute
[m]ile (= 1852 metres)
[...] nautical miles = 1 degree
[kn]ot = 1 nautical mile per hour

SOME USEFUL CONVERSION FACTORS

1 acre = 0.4047 hectares
1 centimetre = 0.3937 inch
1 cubic centimetre = 0.0610 cubic inch
1 foot = 0.3048 metre = 30.48 centimetres
1 gallon (imperial) = 4.5461 litres
1 gram = 0.0353 ounce
1 hectare = 2.4710 acres
1 inch = 2.54 centimetres
1 kilogram = 2.2046 pounds
1 kilometre = 0.6214 mile
1 litre = 0.220 gallon (imperial) = 0.2642 gallon (US) = 1.7598 pints (imperial)
1 metre = 39.3701 in = 3.2808 ft = 1.0936 yd
1 metric ton (tonne) = 0.9842 long ton = 1.1023 short ton
1 mile (statute) = 1.6093 kilometres
1 mile (nautical) = 1.852 kilometres
1 millimetre = 0.03937 inch
1 ounce = 28.350 grams
1 pint (imperial) = 0.5683 litre
1 pound = 0.4536 kilogram
1 ton (long) = 1.0160 metric tons (tonnes)
1 ton (short) = 0.9072 metric ton (tonne)
1 yard = 0.9144 metre

▲ This jug can measure liquids in fluid ounces and centilitres (cl). Most wine bottles hold 70 or 75 cl.

A cube (below) is a solid shape. It takes up space, and the amount of
[spa]ce it takes up is called volume (measured in cubic units). The face of a
[cub]e is a square; it has length and width only: it is two-dimensional and its
[...] (the amount of surface it has) is called area. On the faces of a cuboid
[are] rectangles. Other solid shapes (right) have on their faces two-
[dim]ensional shapes such as circles and triangles.

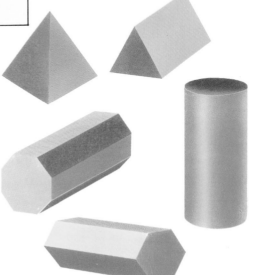

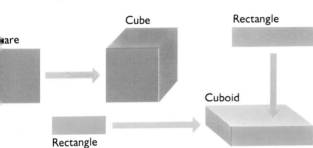

Cube

Rectangle

Cuboid

[Squ]are

Rectangle

For more information turn to these articles: CALCULATOR; CLOCK; COMPUTER; FRACTION; GEOMETRY; MATHEMATICS; METRIC SYSTEM; THERMOMETER.

WESTMINSTER ABBEY

▶ *During the 1700s, pirates working from bases in the West Indies attacked many Spanish ships sailing through the Caribbean Sea. These ships often carried treasures collected from Spanish colonies in Central and South America.*

When Columbus discovered the West Indies he claimed all the islands for Spain. But, as Spanish power weakened in the 1600s, pirates of many countries began to sail the Caribbean. The English government employed the fierce buccaneer Henry Morgan to attack the Spaniards, and in 1674 he was knighted for his services.

▼ *The towers of Westminster Abbey are 68.5 m high. They are believed to have been designed by Sir Christopher Wren but were built by Nicholas Hawksmoor. The towers were the last major part of the Abbey to be built.*

DOMINICAN REPUBLIC are among the largest. The Bahamas are a scattering of islands near Florida. Their capital is Nassau. Barbados is the most easterly island in the West Indies. Its capital is Bridgetown and it became an independent member of the Commonwealth in 1966. Most West Indians are dark skinned. Many are at least partly descended from Negro slaves who were taken there long ago from Africa. Other West Indians have ancestors who lived in India or Europe. Most West Indians speak English, Spanish or French.

People grow bananas, cotton, sugarcane and other tropical crops. Some work in hotels beside the warm blue sea. Tourists from many lands come here to swim and sunbathe.

The West Indies were discovered in 1492 by Christopher COLUMBUS.

Westminster Abbey

Westminster Abbey is a famous church in England. It stands in London, near the Houses of Parliament. Almost all English monarchs were crowned here. Kings, great leaders and poets lie buried in it.

A church has stood here for more than 900 years. Building the present abbey began in 1245. The abbey is laid out like a giant cross. It is called an abbey because it was once a church belonging to a monastery.

Whale

Whales are big sea MAMMALS well built for living in the water. A thick layer of fat called blubber keeps out the cold. A whale's body is shaped for easy swimming. Its front limbs are shaped as flippers. It also has a broad tail flattened from top to bottom, not from side to side like a fish tail.

Unlike fishes, whales must swim to the surface to breathe. Before breathing in, they blow out stale air through a *blowhole*, or two slits on top of the head. Baby whales are born in water. As soon as they are born they swim up to take a breath.

There are two groups of whales. Toothed whales like the DOLPHIN mostly catch fish. But killer whales are toothed whales that attack seals, penguins and other whales.

Baleen whales are the other main group of whales. Baleen whales include the gigantic blue whale. Each baleen whale catches tiny shrimplike

The blubber under the skin of large whales can be up to half a metre thick. For hundreds of years, whales have been killed for this blubber. Oil was taken from it and used to make soap and margarine.

▼ *The blue whale is the largest mammal in the world. It can grow as long as 30 m. The killer whale is a carnivore. It feeds on other whales, seals, penguins and fish. Bottle-nosed whales have beaks like some dolphins. They move around in schools of up to fifty. Humpback whales feed on fish, krill and plankton.*

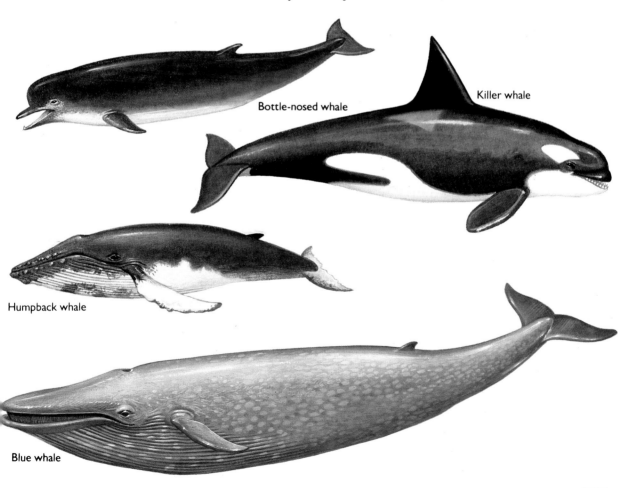

Bottle-nosed whale

Killer whale

Humpback whale

Blue whale

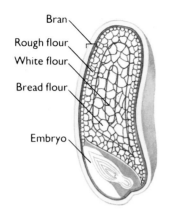

Bran
Rough flour
White flour
Bread flour
Embryo

SOFT WHEAT   HARD WHEAT

▲ A grain of wheat (top), has been cut to show its different sections. Wheat can be grouped into hard wheat and soft wheat. The flour from hard wheat makes very good bread and soft wheat makes very good pastry.

Although we think of China as a rice-eating country, it produces more wheat than any other country in the world, followed by Russia and the United States.

creatures with a special sieve. This is made of a horny substance called baleen or whalebone. When the whale opens its mouth, long baleen plates hang from its upper jaw like the teeth of a giant comb. A large whale can swallow over a tonne of these tiny *krill* at one time. Hunting by man has made the biggest whales very scarce.

Wheat

Wheat is a valuable food crop. Grains of wheat are seeds produced by a certain kind of grass. Mills grind the seeds into flour for making bread, breakfast cereals, cakes, pies, noodles and spaghetti. Most wheat foods are good for us because each grain of wheat is largely made of energy-giving STARCHES. It also contains plenty of body-building PROTEIN, as well as FATS, MINERALS and bran.

Wheat grows best in dry, mild climates. Farmers sow the seed in winter or spring. They harvest it when the grain is dry and hard. Most wheat comes from Russia, the United States, China and India. The world grows more wheat than any other kind of grain.

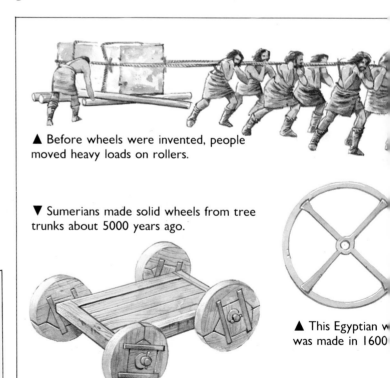

▲ Before wheels were invented, people moved heavy loads on rollers.

▼ Sumerians made solid wheels from tree trunks about 5000 years ago.

▲ This Egyptian w was made in 1600

Wheel

Wheels are one of man's most useful inventions. This is because a wheel turning on an axle is a very good way to move loads. It is easier to move a heavy load with wheels than it is to lift the load or drag it on the ground.

STONE AGE people may have learned to roll loads along on logs. But BRONZE AGE people first invented the wheel about 5000 years ago. The oldest known wheels looked like slices cut across a log. But each solid disc was made of three parts.

At first, the wheels were fixed on the axle, and it was the axle that turned in holes in the cart frame. Later, the axle was fixed and the wheels revolved on its ends.

Then people learned that a wheel with spokes was just as strong as a solid wheel, but much lighter. Today the wheels of cars and planes have hollow rubber tyres filled with air to make them springy.

Ball bearings keep wheel hubs turning easily on their axles. Wheels with notched edges turn one another in the GEARS that help to work all kinds of machinery.

> Although the wheel was being used throughout a large part of the East by 1500 BC, it seems strange that the wheel was unknown anywhere on the American continent until it was introduced by Europeans in the AD 1500s.

▼ Modern wheels are different from the wheels invented 5000 years ago. This illustration shows some of the wheels that have been used throughout history.

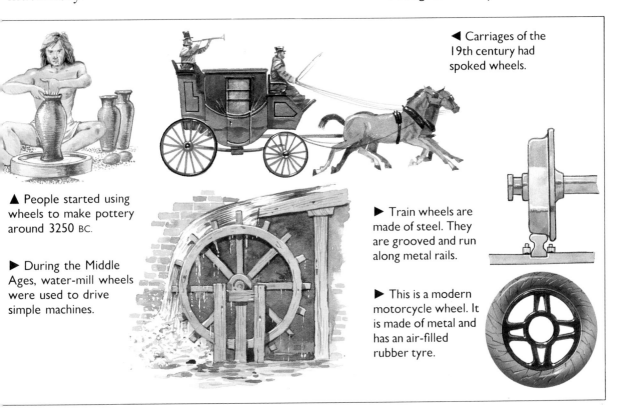

◄ Carriages of the 19th century had spoked wheels.

▲ People started using wheels to make pottery around 3250 BC.

► During the Middle Ages, water-mill wheels were used to drive simple machines.

► Train wheels are made of steel. They are grooved and run along metal rails.

► This is a modern motorcycle wheel. It is made of metal and has an air-filled rubber tyre.

▲ *William of Orange was the grandson of Charles I. He suffered from an asthmatic cough all his life.*

William of Orange

William of Orange (1650–1702) was a PROTESTANT ruler of the Netherlands, who became King William III of England, Scotland and Ireland.

William of Orange was born in the Netherlands. His parents were the Prince of Orange and Mary, the daughter of Charles I of England. In 1677 William of Orange married his Protestant cousin Mary. In 1688 the English invited William and Mary to rule them in place of Mary's father, James II, who was a Roman Catholic. James fled to France when William landed in England with an army of 14,000 men. The event became known as the 'Glorious Revolution'. William and Mary became joint rulers of England in 1689. William defeated James II in the Battle of the Boyne in Ireland the following year, and James fled to France.

▼ *The Normans built many fine castles in their newly-conquered land. Though Bodiam Castle, shown here, was built much later, in the 1300s, it reflects the Norman style, with thick walls and perfectly rounded towers.*

William the Conqueror

William the Conqueror is another name for William I of England. He was England's first Norman king. He was born in France, where his father Robert was the Duke of Normandy. He inherited his father's

title when he was just eight years old. William was a strong ruler. During his youth there were many rebellions which he defeated, with the help of the King of France, Henry I. (Normandy was named after the Normans or Northmen, also called VIKINGS.)

When William visited England in 1050, his relative EDWARD the Confessor may have promised him the throne of England. In 1064 William forced Edward's brother-in-law HAROLD to agree to help to make William king. But when Edward died in 1066, Harold had himself crowned king of England.

William quickly set about invading England to seize it for himself. His Norman army sailed across the English Channel from France in open boats. There were about 7000 troops, including knights who brought their war horses. William defeated Harold's ANGLO-SAXON army at the Battle of HASTINGS, which was fought in Sussex near where the town of Battle stands today. He was crowned King William I of England in Westminster Abbey on Christmas Day in 1066.

People in many parts of England rebelled against William's rule. He built strong castles from which his knights rode out to defeat their Anglo-Saxon enemies. He also ordered a massive survey of all the land and people in his new kingdom, which was known as the DOMESDAY BOOK.

By 1069, the Normans had conquered a third of England, and William the Conqueror had become the most powerful king in western Europe. He claimed all the land in England as his, but he lent some to his Norman nobles. In return, the nobles supplied soldiers for William's army. This was known as the feudal system. William's descendants ruled England for many years.

When William the Conqueror conquered England in 1066, he and his nobles brought over their own language – Norman French. For many years the words that the common people used were still old English, while the words of the wealthy and ruling classes were largely French. The common people tended 'sheep'. When the sheep was cooked and put on the ruling class table it became the French 'mutton'. In the same way, old English 'cow' became the French 'beef', 'hog' became 'pork' and so on. Modern English contains these and many other words that came from Norman French.

William II

William II (about 1056–1100) became king of England when his father WILLIAM THE CONQUEROR died in 1087. William II was called William Rufus because of his red complexion (Rufus means red).

William II was a very harsh and cruel king. He was hated by many of his subjects. In 1088 he defeated a group of nobles who had rebelled against

▲ William II spent his life hunting and going to war. He never married and had no children.

> **William II was so disliked that the clergy refused to give him a Christian burial. When he was killed by an arrow while out hunting, his body was left lying where it fell. After a while, some peasants took it in a farm cart to Winchester and buried it under the cathedral tower.**

him. He won control in Normandy and Scotland, but quarrelled with the Roman Catholic Church.

William was hunting when a nobleman's arrow killed him. It was probably murder.

Wind

Wind is moving air. Slow winds are gentle breezes. Fast winds are gales. You can see the speed of the wind by its effect on trees and buildings.

Wind blows because some air masses become warmer than others. In warm air, the tiny particles of air spread out. So a mass of warm air is lighter than a mass of cold air that fills the same amount of space. Because warm air is light it rises. As warm air rises, cool air flows in to take its place. This causes the steady trade winds that blow over tropical oceans. CLIMATE and WEATHER largely depend on the wind.

A scale of wind speeds was worked out in 1805 by Admiral Sir Francis Beaufort. It is called the Beaufort Scale. In it the force of the wind is shown by numbers from 0 to 12. The number 0 shows that

▼ *The Beaufort Scale from 0 to 12 indicates the strength of the wind. It is based on the effect of wind on such things as trees and houses.*

Force: 0 **Strength:** Calm
Speed: Under 4 km/h
Effect: Smoke goes straight up.

Force: 1–3
Strength: Light breeze
Speed: 4–24 km/h
Effect: Small branches move.

Force: 4–5
Strength: Moderate wind
Speed: 25–46 km/h
Effect: Small trees sway a little.

Force: 6–7
Strength: Strong wind
Speed: 47–74 km/h
Effect: Big trees sway a little.

Force: 8–9
Strength: Gale
Speed: 75–110 km/h
Effect: Slates fall off.

Force: 10–11
Strength: Storm
Speed: 111–150 km/h
Effect: Widespread damage.

Force: 12
Strength: Hurricane
Speed: Above 150 km/h
Effect: Disaster.

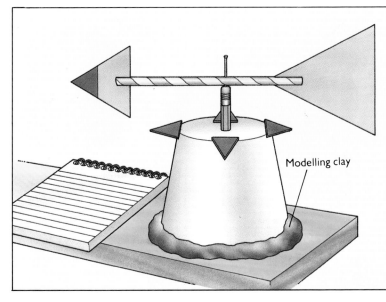

SEE IT YOURSELF

Wind vanes measure the direction of wind. Try making one at home. Turn a yoghurt carton upside down and push a pencil through the middle. Use a pencil that has an eraser at one end. Fix the carton onto a board with modelling clay. Now cut out two small triangles from some thin card. Make slits at each end of a straw and glue one triangle to each end. Push a pin through the middle of the straw into the eraser as shown. Take your wind vane outside and use a compass to mark north, south, east and west on your carton. You can use the information from your wind vane to make a chart showing from which direction the wind is blowing each day.

there is a calm in which smoke rises straight up. At 1 smoke drifts slowly. By the time we get to 4 we have a breeze in which small branches are moving and flags flap. At force 7 whole trees are moving and it is difficult to walk against the wind. Force 12 is something few of us will ever see. It is a full hurricane, with terrible damage to ships at sea and houses on land.

Windmill

Windmills are machines that make the wind's energy perform useful work. They were used in Asia as early as the AD 600s and came to Europe in the 1100s.

In early windmills a wheel with long sails was fixed to a tower. The whole tower could often turn to face the wind. As the wind turned the sails, the turning wheel moved machinery inside the mill. This machinery was used to do useful work such as turning heavy stone wheels to grind corn or pumping water from wells.

Nowadays, people are trying to make better windmills as a way of generating electricity. These windmills, often called wind turbines, are usually on a tower made of steel girders. Some have blades like aeroplane propellers which turn at a high speed when the wind blows. The propellers turn a generator which makes electricity.

▼ *This traditional windmill was used to grind corn. As the wind blew, the axle turned the millstones that ground the corn.*

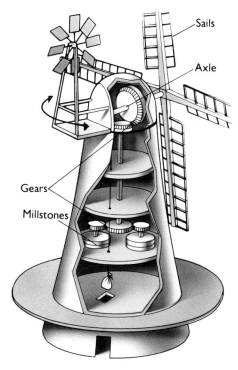

Sails

Axle

Gears

Millstones

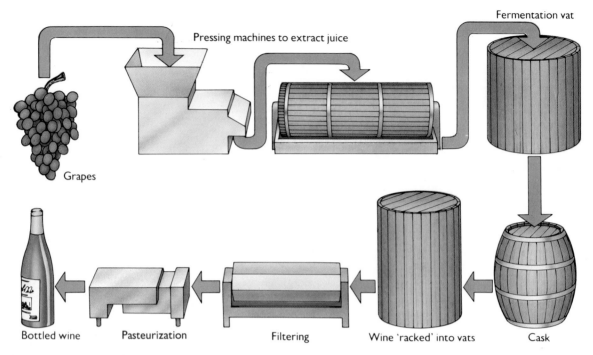

Pressing machines to extract juice

Fermentation vat

Grapes

Cask

Wine 'racked' into vats

Filtering

Pasteurization

Bottled wine

▲ *Grapes go through many processes before they reach your home as bottled wine. After fermentation, some wines are stored in cellars to 'mature' into fine wines. Cheaper wines are not allowed to mature. They are filtered, pasteurized and then bottled as soon as they are taken out of the casks.*

Wine

Wine is a drink made from plant juice, containing alcohol produced by FERMENTATION.

Most wine is made from grapes. But you can make wine from other fruits as well. First the fruit is crushed. Then the juice is fermented in containers called vats. The wine is stored in casks until it is ready to drink. Sweet wines are rich in sugar. In dry wines most sugar has become alcohol.

Wire

Wire is metal that has been drawn out into a long thin rod that is easy to bend. Wire has many uses. Barbed-wire fences keep sheep and cows in fields. Wires twisted together form cables strong enough to hold up some of the world's largest bridges. Wires also carry electric CURRENT. Flex, and telephone and telegraph lines also use wires.

Metals used for making wire include copper, iron, aluminium and silver. Heavy blocks of metal are heated, and then passed through rollers that squeeze the part-melted metal into long narrow holes to make still longer and thinner strips. Then the wire is wound onto a turning drum. Lastly, the wire is heated in a furnace to make it less brittle.

For centuries, wire was pulled by hand. The piece of metal to be drawn was beaten to a point and pushed through a small hole in a fixed metal block. The wiredrawer grasped it and pulled it through the hole to make wire. The fineness of the wire was limited by the strength of the wiredrawer.

Witch

Many people once believed in witches as people with magic powers. Most witches were said to worship the devil. They cast spells that 'bewitched' people, sometimes causing death or disease. Witches supposedly rode through the air at night on broomsticks. They met at secret meetings called sabbaths.

Unlike these 'black' witches, 'white' witches worshipped an ancient goddess and worked to help and protect people.

Long ago, many harmless women were burnt to death as witches. Few of us believe in witches now. But some would-be witches try to practise good or evil magic.

▲ *An early woodcut of two witches adding various live ingredients to their cauldron. This image of witches as ugly old women casting evil spells is still with us today.*

Wolf

These CARNIVORES include the red wolf of South America, and the grey wolf of the world's northern forests. Grey wolves have thick fur, long legs, and powerful jaws. A pack of wolves can chase and kill a sick or injured deer much larger than themselves. When grey wolves are hunting, they howl to signal to each other where they are. Each spring a she-wolf has four to six pups.

> Throughout history there have been stories of wolves raising human children from infancy. The most famous story is that of Romulus and Remus, the twin brothers who founded Rome. More recently, there is a story from India of a child raised by a wolf until she was about nine years old.

◀ *Wolves belong to the same family as the domestic dog. This wolf lives in remote northern forests and feeds on deer, reindeer and elk.*

763

▲ *Emmeline Pankhurst fought for the British woman's right to vote. She died in 1928, the year that women finally won equal voting rights.*

Women's Rights

'Women's rights' means the right of women to be full citizens, equal to men in every way. Until this century, women did not have these rights. In some countries today they still have very few rights.

At the beginning of the 20th century, women did not have a vote, so they were powerless to get changes through parliament. In 1903, Mrs Emmeline Pankhurst and her daughter Christabel started the Women's Social and Political Union, fighting for women's right to vote. These suffragettes addressed crowds, chained themselves to railings, broke windows and set fire to pillar boxes. Again and again they were put in prison, but they kept on protesting. It was not until 1928 that the voting law for women became the same as that for men in Britain.

Today, most people accept that women should be judged as individuals, just as men are. More women than ever are working outside the family. Many have professional careers in business, but in some fields women's struggle for equality is not yet complete.

▼ *Women in London campaign for the vote, or* suffrage. *Because of this they were dubbed 'suffragettes'.*

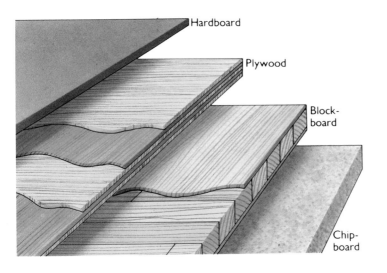

 Wood and wood products are made into sheets for building. Plywood is made up of thin sheets of timber glued together. Most modern furniture is made from plywood. Blockboard is used for making doors. Although it looks like plywood, it has blocks of softwood within it. Hardboard and chipboard, used in building and furniture-making, are made from wood chips. The chips are heated and rolled out into sheets.

Wood

Wood is one of the most valuable materials that people use. It can be sawn, carved and worked into almost any shape.

Thick timber is used for buildings and boats, while roughly cut logs and boughs are used as fuel for fires. Planks are made into furniture, barrels and boxes. Seasoned pieces can be shaped into musical instruments and delicate ornaments.

The wood we use is the tough inner material of trees and shrubs. It is protected by a thin layer of BARK. It is very strong, and can support many times its own weight. The wood of a TREE is made up of thick fibres that give it strength.

Softwood, from pines and firs, is used mostly as pulp to make paper. Some is used for building. Hardwood, such as oak and mahogany, is used to make furniture.

 The great spotted woodpecker is found in woods, forests, parks and gardens. The male bird has a red patch on the back of its head.

Woodpecker

There are about 200 kinds of woodpecker. They are found in many parts of the world, but most live in America and Asia.

Woodpeckers have sharp, powerful bills with which they drill holes through the bark of trees. They reach in with their long tongues to fish out insects. Some also nest in holes in trees.

Most woodpeckers have bright colours and markings, especially on their heads.

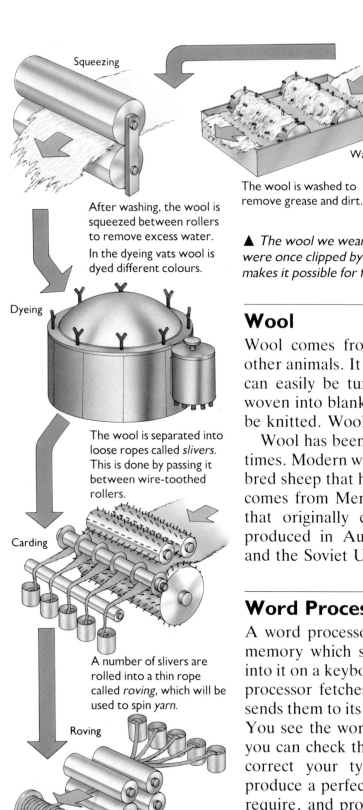

Squeezing

Washing

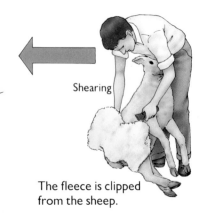

Shearing

The wool is washed to remove grease and dirt.

The fleece is clipped from the sheep.

After washing, the wool is squeezed between rollers to remove excess water.

In the dyeing vats wool is dyed different colours.

Dyeing

The wool is separated into loose ropes called *slivers*. This is done by passing it between wire-toothed rollers.

Carding

A number of slivers are rolled into a thin rope called *roving*, which will be used to spin *yarn*.

Roving

▲ *The wool we wear comes from the fleece of sheep. Sheep were once clipped by hand, but the invention of electric shears makes it possible for farmers to clip over 200 sheep a day.*

Wool

Wool comes from the fleece of SHEEP and some other animals. It is a long and thick kind of hair that can easily be turned into yarn. The yarn may be woven into blankets, carpets and clothing, or it can be knitted. Woollen cloth is heavy and warm.

Wool has been spun and woven since STONE AGE times. Modern wool, however, comes from specially bred sheep that have good fine wool. The best wool comes from Merino sheep. These are white sheep that originally came from Spain. Most wool is produced in Australia, New Zealand, Argentina and the Soviet Union.

Word Processor

A word processor is a kind of COMPUTER. It has a memory which stores all the words that you type into it on a keyboard. Then, whenever required, the processor fetches the words from its memory and sends them to its typing unit to be typed onto paper. You see the words you have typed on a screen, so you can check that there are no mistakes. You can correct your type and the processor will then produce a perfect letter or whatever document you require, and produce as many copies as you want. Some word processing programs can also check your spelling.

Wordsworth, William

William Wordsworth (1770–1850) was a British poet who wrote about nature and the English countryside. He led a movement to restore simplicity and truth to POETRY. Wordsworth joined forces with another poet, Samuel Taylor Coleridge (1772–1834), to publish a volume called *Lyrical Ballads*. Most of the poems in this book were by Wordsworth, including the well known poem 'Lines Composed a Few Miles Above Tintern Abbey'. Among his other best-loved poems were 'Daffodils' and 'The Prelude', a long poem based on events in his own life.

▲ *William Wordsworth wrote many of his best poems while living in the Lake District of England.*

World War I

Between 1914 and 1918 Europe, the United States and much of the Middle East were locked in the first struggle that could be called a world war. On one side were Germany, Austria-Hungary and Turkey. On the other were France, the British Empire, the United States, Italy and Russia.

The battle soon became a stalemate in the west. The two sides spent four years in trenches in

German soldier

British soldier

US soldier

▲ *Uniforms of American, British and German infantrymen during World War I. The opposing sides were often in trenches only a few hundred metres apart.*

◀ *Canadian troops fight off an attack at the second battle of Ypres in 1915. Hundreds of thousands of men were killed in such battles in World War I, but the front line hardly ever shifted.*

▶ *World War I saw the first use of two new machines of war: the aeroplane and the tank. Flying 'aces' such as Germany's Baron von Richthofen and Britain's Albert Ball fought daring battles in the sky. The first tank was driven into battle in 1916.*

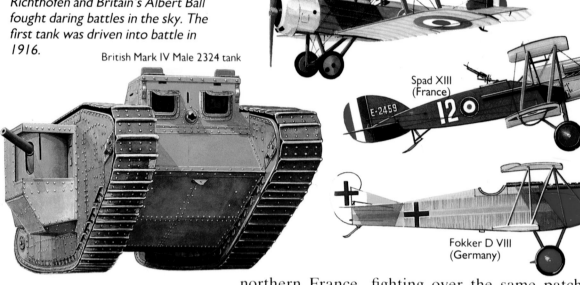

Sopwith 1½ Strutter (Great Britain)

Spad XIII (France)

E-2459

Fokker D VIII (Germany)

British Mark IV Male 2324 tank

northern France, fighting over the same patch of ground. But in the east, Germany had better luck. The Germans attacked Russia so strongly that by 1917 Russia withdrew from the war.

After the United States joined the war in 1917, the Allied armies slowly pushed the Germans back. In November 1918 peace was declared.

World War II

With the invasion of Poland in the autumn of 1939, Germany, Italy and then Japan entered into a six-year war with most of the major nations of Europe, Asia, Africa and America. The battles raged from the Pacific Ocean, China and South-east Asia to Africa, Europe and the North Atlantic.

Germany's early attacks were hugely successful. Her armies swept through Europe and on into Russia and North Africa. However, the tide turned after 1941 when the United States entered the war. (See pages 770–771.)

Worm

There are hundreds of different animals with soft flat bodies that are commonly called worms. Some are very simple creatures, such as roundworms or flatworms. Others, such as earthworms, leeches and the larvae of some INSECTS, are more complicated animals. Their bodies are divided into several segments.

Most of the simple worms are small. They usually live as PARASITES inside the bodies of animals or plants. Liver flukes and tapeworms are two such creatures.

Wren, Christopher

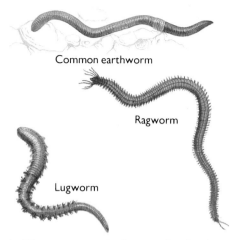

Sir Christopher Wren (1632–1723) was one of the most brilliant of all English architects. He was responsible for many famous and beautiful buildings, perhaps the most celebrated being St Paul's Cathedral in London. Wren also built more than fifty other churches.

Among Wren's other works were the Royal Exchange, Kensington Palace, Marlborough House and an addition to Hampton Court.

Common earthworm

Ragworm

Lugworm

▲ The common earthworm has both male and female organs. Ragworms and lugworms live in muddy and sandy shores.

▼ In 1666, the Great Fire of London destroyed the old St Paul's Cathedral. Sir Christopher Wren designed its replacement, which still stands today.

WORLD WAR II

World War II cost between 35 and 60 million lives. The German dictator, Adolf Hitler, murdered millions of Jews and dreamed of world domination. Germany was supported by Italy. In Asia, Japan also had ambitions to control its neighbours. The so-called Axis powers (Germany, Italy and Japan) were opposed by the Allies (Britain, France, Soviet Union, the United States and other nations). Important war leaders were Winston Churchill (Britain), Franklin D. Roosevelt (USA) and Joseph Stalin (Soviet Union).

The war was fought on land, on sea and in the air. Civilians suffered as much as soldiers, especially from bombing of towns and cities. On land, there were huge tank battles in the USSR and North Africa, while at sea submarines sank many merchant ships. In great naval battles fought in the Pacific, aircraft carriers proved to be more effective than battleships. It was a scientific war, with new inventions such as radar and the V2 rocket.

When the Allied armies invaded Germany, ending the war in Europe, people were shocked by the horrors of the Nazi concentration camps in which millions of prisoners had been killed. The war in Europe ended in May 1945. In the East, Japan fought until August 1945, when the Americans dropped the first atomic bombs on the Japanese cities of Hiroshima and Nagasaki. Only then did Japan finally surrender, bringing World War II to an end.

▲ Battleships were engulfed in smoke and flames during the Japanese attack on Pearl Harbor, Hawaii in December 1941.

▲ German infantry scout in advance of tanks on the Eastern Front during the winter of 1941–42.

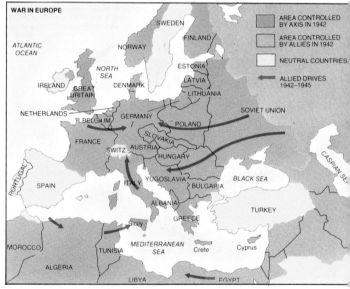

WAR IN EUROPE

AREA CONTROLLED BY AXIS IN 1942
AREA CONTROLLED BY ALLIES IN 1942
NEUTRAL COUNTRIES
ALLIED DRIVES 1942–1945

ATLANTIC OCEAN · SWEDEN · NORWAY · FINLAND · ESTONIA · LATVIA · LITHUANIA · NORTH SEA · IRELAND · GREAT BRITAIN · DENMARK · NETHERLANDS · BELGIUM · GERMANY · POLAND · SOVIET UNION · FRANCE · SWITZ · AUSTRIA · SLOVAKIA · HUNGARY · PORTUGAL · SPAIN · ITALY · YUGOSLAVIA · BULGARIA · BLACK SEA · CASPIAN SEA · ALBANIA · GREECE · TURKEY · Sicily · MOROCCO · TUNISIA · MEDITERRANEAN SEA · Crete · Cyprus · ALGERIA · LIBYA · EGYPT

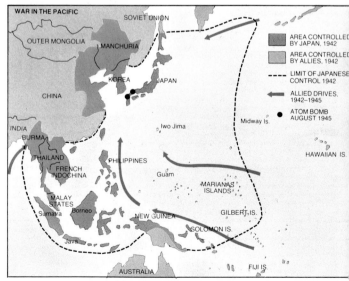

WAR IN THE PACIFIC

AREA CONTROLLED BY JAPAN, 1942
AREA CONTROLLED BY ALLIES, 1942
LIMIT OF JAPANESE CONTROL 1942
ALLIED DRIVES 1942–1945
ATOM BOMB AUGUST 1945

SOVIET UNION · OUTER MONGOLIA · MANCHURIA · KOREA · JAPAN · CHINA · INDIA · BURMA · THAILAND · FRENCH INDOCHINA · PHILIPPINES · Guam · MARIANAS ISLANDS · MALAY STATES · Sumatra · Borneo · NEW GUINEA · SOLOMON IS. · Java · GILBERT IS. · Iwo Jima · Midway Is. · HAWAIIAN IS. · FIJI IS · AUSTRALIA

IMPORTANT EVENTS OF THE WAR

1939 Sept. Germany invades Poland. Britain and France declare war on Germany.

1940 April–June German forces capture Norway, and much of western Europe, including France.

May Churchill becomes Britain's prime minister.

June Italy joins war on Germany's side.

Oct. End of Battle of Britain. Bombing raids on Britain.

1941 June Germany invades USSR.

Dec. Japanese attack Pearl Harbor; USA enters war.

1942 Feb. Japanese capture Singapore.

May Battle of the Coral Sea: US Navy defeats Japanese.

June Battle of Midway: another US naval victory. Allies invade Morocco and Algeria.

Oct. Allies defeat Germans and Italians at El Alamein (North Africa).

Nov. Soviets defeat Germans at Stalingrad.

1943 July Sept. Allies land in Sicily, southern Italy. Italy surrenders.

1944 June Allies invade western Europe, in Normandy.

July Plot to kill Hitler fails.

Oct. Battle of Leyte Gulf (biggest naval battle of war): US fleet defeats Japanese.

1945 Jan. Soviets invade Germany from east.

March Allies cross the Rhine River.

April In the East, US troops recapture Philippines.

May Hitler commits suicide in Berlin.

Aug. US forces face bitter fighting as Japanese retreat.
End of fighting in Europe.
Americans drop atomic bombs on Hiroshima and Nagasaki; Japan surrenders to end the war.

After more than two years' preparation, Allied soldiers under the command of the American General Eisenhower landed on the Normandy beaches on D-Day, June 6, 1944.

Spitfire

P-51 Mustang

Messerschmitt

The British Spitfire and the German Messerschmitt were both involved in the Battle of Britain in 1940. The American P-51 Mustang was a long-range fighter and one of the most successful warplanes ever.

For more information turn to these articles: AIR FORCE; ARMY; CHURCHILL, WINSTON; DE GAULLE, CHARLES; HITLER, ADOLF; MUSSOLINI, BENITO; STALIN, JOSEPH; SUBMARINE.

▲ *Orville Wright pilots the Wright Flyer on the sands of Kitty Hawk, North Carolina. The aircraft stayed in the air for 12 seconds on its first flight.*

▼ *Chinese writing has changed over the centuries. This table compares an ancient script with modern characters.*

Ancient Chinese	Modern Chinese	Meaning
𐤐	牛	Ox
𐅃	羊	Sheep Goat
𐌗	木	Tree
田	田	Field
禱	祝	Praying
𝒟	月	Moon
𝛀	土	Earth

Wright Brothers

Wilbur and Orville Wright were two American bicycle engineers who built and flew the first powered AIRCRAFT. Their successful machine was made after years of testing models and gliders.

The first actual flight took place at Kitty Hawk, North Carolina, in December 1903. Their simple petrol-engined craft flew for 12 seconds. Five years later they flew an improved machine for 75 minutes.

The original Wright *Flyer 1* is in the National Air and Space Museum in Washington, D.C.

Writing

The earliest forms of writing were simple picture messages, or notches on sticks that were used for counting. Gradually, pictures that were used again and again became simplified. These symbols meant certain objects, like 'man' or 'house'. Egyptian HIEROGLYPHICS were used in this way.

In time, the symbols came to stand for sounds and could be combined to form words. Later still, ALPHABETS of these sounds came into being. VOWELS appeared in the languages spoken by the ancient Greeks and Romans. From their alphabets came the one we use today.

X-ray

X-rays are waves of energy like RADIO or LIGHT waves. They can pass through or into most living things. They can also leave an image on a photographic plate, making a picture of whatever they have passed through. Doctors can use them to take 'photographs' of the insides of people. This helps the doctor to find out if anything is wrong with the patient.

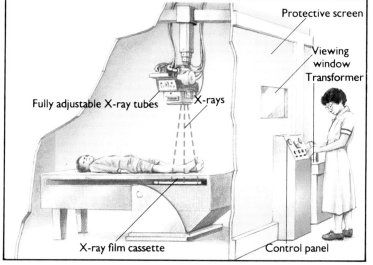

Protective screen

Viewing window

Transformer

Fully adjustable X-ray tubes

X-rays

X-ray film cassette

Control panel

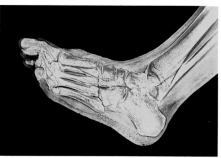

◀ *A radiographer takes an X-ray of a child's foot. The resulting 'photograph' (above) has been coloured to show the foot and ankle bones more clearly.*

X-rays are produced inside a glass tube that has no air or other gases in it. Inside the tube, at opposite ends, are a *cathode* that gives off electrons and an *anode*, or target. When the cathode is heated, electrons fly off and strike the anode, producing X-rays.

Wilhelm Roentgen, a German scientist, discovered X-rays by accident in 1895 while he was passing electricity through a gas.

▼ *The xylophone is used in orchestras and bands. Resonators, metal tubes below each bar, help to amplify the sound.*

Xylophone

The xylophone is an odd-looking MUSICAL INSTRUMENT that produces a crisp, bell-like sound when played.

A xylophone has rows of solid wooden or metal bars fixed to a frame. Each bar is a different length and produces a different sound when struck. An electric version of the xylophone, called a *vibraphone*, is sometimes used.

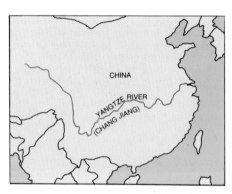

▶ A junk sails on the Yangtze River, the third longest river in the world. The river has always been an important trade route, and the port of Shanghai, China's largest city, lies at its mouth.

The first people to measure the length of a year were the ancient Egyptians. They noticed that when the brightest star in the sky – Sirius the dog-star – rose just before sunrise, the Nile always overflowed its banks. They counted the days that went by before this happened again and found that it came to 365 days – a year.

Yak

The yak is a large, shaggy kind of ox with a pair of long, thick horns. Yaks live in Tibet, China and northern Asia. Wild yaks may be as tall as a man, but tame yaks are about the size of a European cow.

Yangtze River (Chang Jiang)

The Yangtze is the longest, most important river in CHINA. From its beginnings, high in the mountains of Tibet, it flows 6380 km across the centre of China, pouring into the Yellow Sea near Shanghai.

The river takes its name from the ancient kingdom of Yang, which grew up along its banks 3000 years ago. Today, the Yangtze is still one of the main trade routes in China. Big ships can sail up it as far as Hankow, nearly 1125 km inland. Smaller boats can reach I-Ch'ang, which is 1600 km from the sea.

Millions of people live and work on the Yangtze. Some live on the river itself in wooden sailing boats called *junks*.

Year

A year is the amount of time it takes for the Earth to travel once around the SUN. It takes $365\frac{1}{4}$ days. A calendar year is only 365 days long. Every four years, the extra quarter days are lumped together to make a year of 366 days. These longer years are called leap years.

Yeast

Yeast is a plant which is also a kind of FUNGUS. The whole plant consists of just one CELL. It is so tiny that you cannot see it without a microscope. It is very useful because it turns sugar into alcohol and carbon dioxide gas. This process is called FERMENTATION. Yeast plants do this because they do not produce their own food. They live on sugar instead. Today yeast is grown in huge vats. It is then pressed into cakes or small pellets, ready to be sold.

In wine- and beer-making, yeast turns the sugar in grapes or malted barley into alcohol, while most of the gas produced bubbles away. In bread-making, the carbon dioxide gas forms bubbles, which makes the bread dough rise.

Yeltsin, Boris

Boris Yeltsin was elected President of the Russian Republic in 1991 (then part of the SOVIET UNION), and became the first leader of RUSSIA to be chosen in a popular vote. He pressed for democratic and economic reforms faster than Mikhail GORBACHEV.

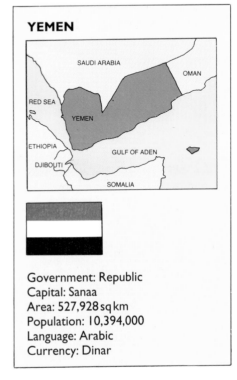

▲ *Boris Yeltsin resigned from the Communist party in 1990, later becoming the first democratically elected leader in Russian history. He has suffered recurring health problems.*

Yemen

The republic of Yemen is a country on the coasts of the Red Sea and the Gulf of Aden. The republic was formed when North and South Yemen united in 1990, after years of political upheaval. North Yemen became independent in 1918 after years of Ottoman–Turkish rule. Its land is the most fertile in the whole of the Arabian Peninsula, thanks to the monsoon rains which fall on the mountains each April. South Yemen was made up of the former British colony of Aden and the former British protectorate of South Arabia. It became independent in 1967.

Many Yemenis are farmers, growing cotton, wheat, coffee, millet and fruit. The port of Aden, on the south coast, has been a trading post between East and West for 2000 years. In 1994, civil war broke out between the former North and South Yemin, but the country remained united.

YEMEN

SAUDI ARABIA
OMAN
RED SEA
YEMEN
ETHIOPIA
GULF OF ADEN
DJIBOUTI
SOMALIA

Government: Republic
Capital: Sanaa
Area: 527,928 sq km
Population: 10,394,000
Language: Arabic
Currency: Dinar

YUGOSLAVIA

(Serbia and Montenegro)
Government: Federal republic
Capital: Belgrade
Area: 102,168 sq km
Population: 10,000,000

Yugoslavia

Yugoslavia is a country in south-east EUROPE. Most of it lies in the BALKANS. It is a rugged, mountainous country. In the west, the mountains sweep down to the Adriatic Sea. Inland, the country is mostly scrubby and poor. Around the river Danube in the north, the land is fertile. Most of the country's farming goes on around here. Farmers grow wheat, barley, maize, plums, olives and grapes, and keep cattle and sheep.

Until 1991, Yugoslavia was a federation of six republics: Bosnia-Herzegovina, Croatia, Macedonia, Montenegro, Serbia and Slovenia. Its 24 million (estimated) people spoke many different languages and followed different religions—Roman Catholic, Muslim and Greek Orthodox—and included Serbs, Croats, Slovenes, Albanians and Macedonians as well as other minority groups.

In 1991, growing tensions between the republics led to CROATIA and SLOVENIA declaring their independence from Yugoslavia. BOSNIA and HERZEGOVINA also declared independence in 1992. Fierce fighting followed these declarations, first of all, briefly, between Serbia and Slovenia, then between Serbia and Croatia and Serbia and Bosnia and Herzegovina.

By 1994, the Federal Republic of Yugoslavia was made up only of Serbia and Montenegro. Macedonia became an independent member of the UN in 1993, under the name 'The Former Yugoslav Republic of Macedonia'. Serbia was still trying to regain control of Bosnia and Herzegovina. A peace agreement was signed in 1995 between the Serbians and the Croatians and Bosnians.

Two very different scenes from Sarajevo, the capital of Bosnia and Herzegovina. Before the break up of former Yugoslavia, views from the rooftops of the city (top) show the beautiful architecture and scenery. This child running through the streets in 1993 (right) shows how the town has been ravaged by war.

◀ *Fishing nets hang out to dry in a village along the Zaire River. The river is an important 'highway' for people and goods through the country.*

Zaire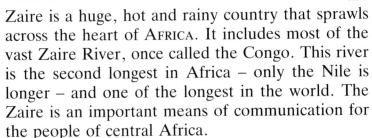

Zaire is a huge, hot and rainy country that sprawls across the heart of AFRICA. It includes most of the vast Zaire River, once called the Congo. This river is the second longest in Africa – only the Nile is longer – and one of the longest in the world. The Zaire is an important means of communication for the people of central Africa.

Much of Zaire is covered with thick jungle. There are lakes and highlands in the east and south. Copper, cobalt, and diamonds are mined here. But most of Zaire's 34 million inhabitants are farmers. They grow tea, coffee, cocoa, and cotton.

Zambia

Zambia is a country in southern AFRICA. It is entirely surrounded by land. Zaire, Tanzania, Malawi, Mozambique, Botswana, Zimbabwe, Namibia and Angola all share borders with Zambia.

The name Zambia comes from the Zambezi River. This runs across the western part of the country along the border with ZIMBABWE. Zambia was the British protectorate of Northern Rhodesia until it became an independent republic in 1964.

Much of the country is rolling, highland plains. The majority of Zambians are farmers. But most of

ZAIRE

Government: Republic
Capital: Kinshasa
Area: 2,345,409 sq km
Population: 34,138,000
Languages: Bantu, French
Currency: Zaire

Until 1953, Zambia was called **Northern Rhodesia**. From 1953 to 1963 it joined the countries that are now Malawi and Zimbabwe in the **Federation of Rhodesia and Nyasaland.**

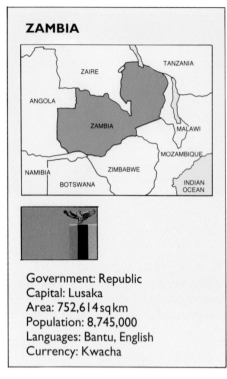

ZAMBIA

Government: Republic
Capital: Lusaka
Area: 752,614 sq km
Population: 8,745,000
Languages: Bantu, English
Currency: Kwacha

▶ Burchell's zebra is the most common type of zebra found in East Africa. It has wide black or brownish-black stripes.

▼ This statue of Zeus comes from Heraklion. The Romans worshipped a similar god whom they called Jupiter.

the country's wealth comes from its copper mines. In the 1980s severe drought caused famine, and in 1990 Zambia suffered its worst violence since 1964.

Zebra

Zebras belong to the HORSE family. They live in the open grasslands of Africa to the south of the Sahara Desert. Zebras have creamy white coats covered with black or dark brown stripes. Each animal has its own special pattern of stripes.

Zebras live in herds. They feed on grass and are often found roaming the grasslands with herds of antelope. Although zebras can run very fast, they are often hunted by lions, leopards and hyenas. People also used to hunt them for their attractive skins and tasty meat.

Zeus

According to the MYTHS and legends of the ancient Greeks, Zeus was the ruler of all the gods. He lived on Mount Olympus and was married to Hera. He was the father of the gods Apollo, Dionysus and Athena.

Zeus was the son of the ancient god Kronos. The stories say that Zeus and his brothers, Poseidon and Hades, killed Kronos and took over his throne and powers. Poseidon took the seas, Hades took the underworld and Zeus took the world and the sky. Zeus ruled over the Sun, the Moon, all the other stars and planets, and the weather. When he was angry he would hurl thunderbolts.

◀ A wealthy empire grew up in the area we now know as Zimbabwe from about the AD 900s through the Middle Ages. The Great Zimbabwe stone ruins are an impressive reminder of this early civilization. The site later became a ceremonial centre. It became known to the western world in 1868 when it was discovered by accident by a hunter.

Zimbabwe

Zimbabwe is a small country in southern AFRICA. It lies inland, about 240km from the Indian Ocean. About 97 out of every 100 people are black Africans; the others are mostly white.

Zimbabwe is bordered by the Zambezi River in the north. The Zambezi is famous for the Victoria Falls and the Kariba Dam. The Kariba Dam is part of a great hydroelectric operation that supplies power to both Zimbabwe and its neighbour ZAMBIA.

Until 1965, Zimbabwe was the British colony of Southern Rhodesia. In that year, it declared itself the independent country of Rhodesia. Britain, however, did not recognize the new nation's existence. During the next 15 years, growing unrest and guerrilla warfare caused many problems. In 1980 the country became independent, under a black-majority government, as Zimbabwe.

ZIMBABWE

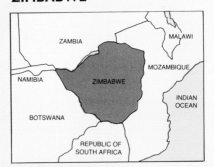

Government: Parliamentary democracy
Capital: Harare
Area: 390,580 sq km
Population: 11,033,000
Languages: English, Shona, Sindebele
Currency: Zimbabwe dollar

Zinc

Zinc is a hard, blue-white metal ELEMENT. It has been mined since ancient times and has been used in making brass for over 2000 years. Brass is an ALLOY of zinc and copper.

A large share of the world's zinc comes from Canada, Australia and the United States. Zinc mines usually contain other metals such as copper, gold, lead and silver as well.

We need a tiny quantity of zinc in our diet. People who do not get any zinc are anaemic (they do not have enough red blood cells) and their growth is retarded. Any normal diet gives us all the zinc we need.

▲ *A piece of zinc, a metal that is mined chiefly in the USA, Canada, Australia and Mexico. Zinc is never found in the pure state, but always combined with other substances.*

Most zinc is used to *galvanize* steel. Galvanizing is putting a thin coat of zinc on steel to protect it. Zinc is also used to make cells in electric BATTERIES. As well as brass, zinc forms part of many other alloys including nickel and bronze.

Zinc

Zoos are places where wild animals are kept. They are cared for, bred, studied and sometimes saved from dying out. There are now more than 330 zoos in the world.

The first zoos were in ancient Egypt. Queen Hatshepsut kept a zoo in 1500 BC. More than 3000 years ago, the emperors of China kept animals, birds and fish in natural gardens where they would feel at home. In the MIDDLE AGES in Europe, kings gave each other presents of apes, peacocks and lions. Private collections of animals were called *menageries*. Travelling menageries used to tour through the towns of Europe in the 1800s.

Since the 1700s, scientists have been interested in the study of animals. They began to sort animals into groups and give them Latin names so that the same animal would be known by the same name all over the world. Their work led directly to the building of the first public zoos. These were first called zoological gardens, then shortened to zoo. One of the first was London Zoo, built in 1829.

The world's zoos range in size from small, privately owned collections to large public zoos. Berlin Zoo houses more than 2000 different species of animals, more than any other zoo in the world.

▶ *This painting of the Broad Walk with elephants at Regent's Park Zoo in London was done at the turn of the century. The zoo was founded in the 1820s by the Zoological Society of London, though today it is more generally known as the London Zoo.*

About Your Index

No encyclopedia can have entries on every subject, so there is a vast amount of information that can only be found by looking in the Index. There is no encyclopedia entry for Istanbul, for example, but if you look in the Index you will find lots of information and pictures under **Architecture, Byzantine Empire, Constantinople** and **Turkey.**

Page numbers in **boldface type** (heavy and dark) indicate where the main reference to the subject can be found. Page numbers in *italic type* (slanting) refer to pages on which illustrations will be found.

Take the entry on Roald Amundsen for example:
Amundsen, Roald 29, *33*, 490
The main entry on the explorer is on page 29. On page 33, under the entry on **Antarctic**, there is a map showing his route to the South Pole. The **North-west Passage** entry on page 490 tells us that Amundsen was first to sail through the passage.

After the main index you will find a **Subject Index**. In this, all the entries in the encyclopedia are divided up by subject. The entries are in alphabetical order within each subject.

Dd

Jj

Kk

Ll

Mm

Acknowledgements

The publishers would like to thank the following for kindly supplying photographs for this book:

Facing page 1 The Hutchison Library; page 3 ARDEA; 5 Heather Angel; 6 Picturepoint; 7 ZEFA; 12 ZEFA; 20 Derby Museum & Galleries; 22 Sonia Halliday; 24 ZEFA; 36 ZEFA; 38 ZEFA; 41 ZEFA; 43 The Hutchison Library; 46 SCALA (top right), Bridgeman Art Library (top left), ZEFA (middle), Michael Holford (bottom); 47 Michael Holford (top right), Bridgeman Art Library (top left), Tate Gallery (middle), Bridgeman Art Library (bottom); 50 ZEFA; 52 Istanbul University; 53 ZEFA; 57 ZEFA (top), Mary Evans Picture Library (middle), Frank Spooner (bottom); 61 Science Photo Library; 64 Zoe Dominic (top), Frank Spooner (bottom); 71 Michael Holford; 79 ZEFA; 80 Sonia Halliday; 90 Denis Gilbert/Grisewood & Dempsey Ltd; 92 British Library (Harley MS2897, folio 188b); 95 ZEFA; 97 ZEFA; 101 Dennis Gilbert/Grisewood & Dempsey Ltd; 106 ZEFA; 107 ZEFA; 110 M. Kroenlein; 111 ZEFA; 114 ZEFA; 117 Columbia/Kobal Collection; 119 ZEFA; 122 ZEFA; 126 ZEFA; 127 ZEFA; 128 Dennis Gilbert/Grisewood & Dempsey Ltd; 129 Kobal Collection; 130 Giraudon; 131 Mansell Collection; 132 Science Photo Library; 137 ZEFA; 138 Mary Evans Picture Library; 140 Popperfoto; 141 Kobal Collection; 142 Lucas Film/Kobal Collection (top), UPI/Bettmann Newsphotos (bottom); 144 Hulton Picture Company; 145 ZEFA; 150 Frank Spooner; 152 Grisewood & Dempsey Ltd; 153 ZEFA; 155 Science Photo Library; 156 Illustrated London News; 161 ENIAC; 164 ZEFA; 170 ZEFA; 173 ZEFA; 175 Peter Newark's Western Americana; 176 ZEFA; 178 Crown Copyright/Reproduced with the permission of the Controller of Her Majesty's Stationery Office; 182 ZEFA; 187 Picturepoint; 189 Mansell Collection; 194 ZEFA; 196 Popperfoto; 197 ZEFA; 198 ZEFA; 201 Geological Museum (top), Mansell Collection (bottom); 202 ZEFA; 207 ZEFA (top), Walt Disney Productions (bottom); 210 Bridgeman Art Library; 211 ZEFA (top), Crown Copyright/Public Record Office (bottom); 213 National Gallery; 219 Frank Lane Picture Agency; 220 NASA; 224 ZEFA (top), A. Sington (bottom); 225 Popperfoto; 228 ZEFA; 230 Science Photo Library; 234 Picturepoint (top), ZEFA (bottom); 238 Dennis Gilbert/Grisewood & Dempsey Ltd; 239 The Hutchison Library; 243 ZEFA; 246 Michael Holford (top), Mansell Collection (bottom); 249 The Hutchison Library; 251 ZEFA; 253 Mary Evans Picture Library; 255 ZEFA; 256 Frank Spooner; 257 Metropolitan Police (top), ZEFA (bottom); 260 Greenpeace; 264 Hulton Picture Company; 265 ZEFA; 269 Allsport; 270 ZEFA; 274 Allsport; 275 Mansell Collection; 279 ZEFA; 286 Popperfoto; 287 ZEFA (top), Bridgeman Art Library (bottom); 289 Jane Burton/Bruce Coleman; 294 Picturepoint; 295 The Hutchison Library; 299 ZEFA; 300 Courtesy, Royal Brierley Crystal; 301 Courtesy, Pilkington; 302 ZEFA (top), Frank Spooner (bottom); 304 ZEFA; 305 ZEFA; 307 ZEFA; 308 ZEFA; 310 ZEFA; 311 ZEFA; 318 ZEFA; 321 Michael Holford; 324 ZEFA; 327 Simon Bruty/Allsport; 329 Mary Evans Picture Library; 330 National Portrait Gallery (top), British Museum (bottom); 333 ZEFA; 334 ZEFA; 335 SCALA; 338 Rex Features; 339 Popperfoto; 340 Bergstrom & Boyle; 342 ZEFA; 343 Allsport; 346 Robert Harding (top), ZEFA (bottom); 347 ZEFA; 348 ZEFA; 349 ZEFA; 355 ZEFA; 357 Science Photo Library; 360 Steve Powell/Allsport (top), ZEFA (bottom); 362 Bridgeman Art Library; 363 ZEFA; 366 Science Photo Library (left), Frank Spooner (right); 368 Heather Angel; 369 Heather Angel; 373 ZEFA; 376 ZEFA; 377 ZEFA (top), Jean Vertut (bottom); 378 N.H.P.A.; 379 ZEFA; 381 National Gallery; 383 ZEFA; 386 ZEFA; 387 Mary Evans Picture Library; 390 Allsport; 391 ZEFA; 392 ZEFA; 393 Science Photo Library; 397 ZEFA; 399 Bridgeman Art Library (left), SCALA (right); 401 ZEFA; 404 ZEFA (top), Mary Evans Picture Library (bottom); 409 ZEFA; 410 ZEFA; 411 Mary Evans Picture Library; 415 Mary Evans Picture Library; 417 ZEFA; 418 ZEFA; 421 Rex Features; 422 Michael Holford; 424 The Hutchison Library, ZEFA (right); 427 Popperfoto; 430 ZEFA; 431 Sonia Halliday; 433 Sonia Halliday; 435 Science Photo Library; 437 Science Photo Library; 438 ZEFA; 439 Science Photo Library; 440 N.H.P.A.; 446 ARDEA; 447 Science Photo Library; 448 Sonia Halliday; 454 ZEFA; 455 Michael Holford; 456 Science Photo Library; 457 Science Photo Library; 458 ZEFA; 463 Courtesy, Suzuki; 472 National Gallery of Art, Washington DC; 473 Military Archive & Research Services; 474 National Portrait Gallery; 477 Hutchison Library; 479 ZEFA; 480 ZEFA; 481 ZEFA; 488 ZEFA (top), Science Photo Library (bottom); 482 Spectrum; 489 Shell Photographic Library; 490 Shell Photographic Library; 495 The Hutchison Library; 499 Pascal Rondeau/Allsport; 500 Westermann Foto; 502 Courtesy, English Chamber Orchestra; 504 ZEFA; 505 South American Pictures; 506 Promotion Australia; 508 ZEFA; 509 ZEFA (right), The Hutchison Library (left); 511 ZEFA; 512 South American Pictures; 513 ZEFA; 514 Courtesy, House of Commons; 515 Michael Holford (left), ZEFA (right); 518 South American Pictures; 521 Hulton Picture Company; 522 Ontario Science Centre, Toronto; 524 Visual Arts Library; 531 ZEFA; 532 The Mansell Collection (left), Bridgeman Art Library (right); 533 Mary Evans Picture Library; 534 ZEFA; 535 N.H.P.A.; 536 ZEFA; 537 The Hutchison Library (top), Rex Features (bottom); 546 The Hutchison Library; 548 Mary Evans Picture Library; 549 ARDEA; 552 N.H.P.A.; 554 The Hutchison Library; 556 Science Photo Library; 559 Science Photo Library; 560 Science Photo Library; 561 The Hutchison Library; ZEFA (top), Spectrum (bottom); 570 ZEFA; 571 Michael Holford; 572 Michael Holford (right), SCALA (left); 573 Heather Angel; 576 Peter Newark's Western Americana; 577 ZEFA; 579 Mike Grey; 581 Picturepoint; 584 ZEFA; 585 ZEFA; 586 Picturepoint; 591 Science Photo Library (top), The Hutchison Library (bottom); 593 Michael Holford (left), Allsport (right); 595 ZEFA; 598 ZEFA (right); 599 Derby Museum & Galleries; 600 Science Photo Library; 602 Mary Evans Picture Library (top), Courtesy, World Bureau of Girl Guides & Girl Scouts (bottom); 604 Picturepoint (right), Tate Gallery Publications (left); 607 Dennis Gilbert/Grisewood & Dempsey Ltd; 609 Science Photo Library; 612 National Portrait Gallery; 615 Courtesy, Sally Ferries; 616 The Hutchison Library; 617 ZEFA; 618 Courtesy, Ferranti; 619 Bridgeman Art Library; 620 Allsport; 621 Allsport; 623 ZEFA; 624 Peter Newark's Western Americana; 625 The Hutchison Library (top), ZEFA (bottom); 626 ZEFA; 629 Picturepoint; 636 Science Photo Library; 637 Robert Harding; 638 ZEFA (top), The Hutchison Library (bottom); 639 The Hutchison Library; 641 ZEFA; 643 Novosti; 644 Science Photo Library; 645 Science Photo Library; 653 ZEFA; 654 Michael Holford; 658 The Hutchison Library; 662 Science Photo Library; 663 ZEFA; 664 ZEFA; 667 ZEFA; 669 Michael Holford; 671 The Dance Library; 673 ZEFA; 674 Science Photo Library; 678 David Cannon/Allsport; 680 The Mansell Collection; 682 ZEFA; 683 Picturepoint; 684 The Hutchison Library; 685 ZEFA; 689 ZEFA; 694 Peter Newark's Western Americana; 697 Heather Angel (top), N.H.P.A. (bottom); 700 ZEFA; 703 ZEFA; 705 Peter Clayton; 707 The Hutchison Library (top), Science Photo Library (bottom); 710 ZEFA; 712 ZEFA; 713 ZEFA; 714 ZEFA; 715 ZEFA; 718 South American Pictures; 720 Visual Arts Library (top), The Hutchison Library (bottom); 722 Visual Arts Library; 725 ZEFA; 726 G.S.F. Picture Library (top), National Portrait Gallery (bottom); 728 ZEFA; 731 Spectrum; 737 Mary Evans Picture Library; 739 ZEFA; 741 ZEFA; 747 ZEFA; 748 Science Photo Library; 749 Billy Stickland/Allsport; 751 ZEFA; 752 Michael Holford; 759 ZEFA (top), The Mansell Collection (bottom); 763 Ancient Art & Architecture Collection; 764 Mary Evans Picture Library; 767 National Army Museum; 770 Military Archive & Research Services; 773 Science Photo Library; 774 The Hutchison Library; 775 Rex Features; 776 ZEFA (top), Camera Press (bottom); 777 The Hutchison Library; 778 Visual Arts Library; 779 The Hutchison Library; 780 Science Photo Library (top), Mary Evans Picture Library (bottom).

Charles II
Churchill, Winston
Civil War
Civil War (American)
Cleopatra
Clothing
Cook, James
Copernicus, Nicolaus
Cortés, Hernando
Crimean War
Cromwell, Oliver
Crusades
Curie, Marie and Pierre
Dark Ages
D-day
De Gaulle Charles
Domesday Book
Drake, Francis
Edward (Kings)
Egypt, Ancient
Elizabeth I
Elizabeth II
Fawkes, Guy
Franklin, Benjamin
French Revolution
Gandhi
Garibaldi, Giuseppe
Genghis Khan
George (Kings)
Gladiator
Great Wall of China
Greece, Ancient
Hannibal
Hapsburgs
Harold, King
Hastings, Battle of
Henry (Kings)
Heraldry
History
Hitler, Adolf
Holy Roman Empire
Hundred Years' War
Huns
Incas
Industrial Revolution
Ivan The Terrible
James (Kings)
Joan of Arc
John, King
Knight
Kublai Khan
Lenin, Vladimir
Lincoln, Abraham
Louis (French Kings)
Magna Carta
Marie Antoinette
Mary I, Queen
Mary, Queen of Scots
Middle Ages
Mussolini, Benito
Napoleon Bonaparte
Nelson, Horatio
Nightingale, Florence
Pharaoh
Polo, Marco
Pompeii
Raleigh, Walter
Reformation
Renaissance
Revolutionary War,
   American
Richard (Kings)
Roman Empire
Roses, Wars of the
Scott, Robert Falcon
Seven Wonders of
   the World
Slavery
Stalin, Joseph
Stone Age
Stuarts
Trafalgar, Battle of
Tudors
Tutankhamun
Victoria, Queen
Vikings
Washington, George
Waterloo, Battle of
Wellington, Duke of
William of Orange
William the Conqueror
William II
World War I

World War II
Wright Brothers

Our Earth

Acid Rain
Air
Alps
Amazon, River
Andes
Antarctic
Arctic
Atlantic Ocean
Atmosphere
Ayers Rock
Balkans
Cave
Chalk
Clay
Climate
Cloud
Coal
Conservation
Continental Shelf
Continent
Coral
Crystal
Day and Night
Deep-sea Life
Delta
Desert
Diamond
Earth, The
Earthquake
Ecology
Equator
Everest, Mount
Fiord
Flint
Flood
Fog
Fossil
Frost
Ganges, River
Gem
Geography
Geology
Geyser
Glacier
Grand Canyon
Granite
Great Barrier Reef
Gulf Stream
Himalayas
Hurricane
Ice Ages
Iceberg
Indian Ocean
Island
Lake
Latitude and Longitude
Lightning
Marble
Mediterranean Sea
Mining
Mississippi River
Monsoon
Mountain
Natural Gas
Nile
North Pole
Ocean
Ozone Layer
Pacific Ocean
Pollution
Pyrenees
Quartz
Rain and Snow
River
Rock
Rocky Mountains
Sahara Desert
Sand
Seashore
Season
Silver
Smog
Soil
Thames, River
Thunderstorm
Tide
Tornado
Vesuvius

Volcano
Water
Waterfall
Waves
Weather
Wind
Yangtze River

Religion, Philosophy and Myth

Apostles
Aristotle
Astrology
Bible
Buddha
Christianity
Christmas
Confucius
Dragon
Easter
Francis of Assisi
Greek Mythology
Helen of Troy
Hercules
Hinduism
Homer
Islam
Jesus
Judaism
Koran
Legend
Luther, Martin
Magic
Mars (God)
Mercury (God)
Mermaid
Monastery
Mormon
Muhammad
Myth
Norse Myth
Odyssey
Passover
Philosophy
Plato
Pope
Presbyterian
Protestant
Quaker
Religion
Roman Catholic
   Church
Saint
Shinto
Sikhs
Teresa, Mother
Trojan War
Ulysses
Witch
Zeus

Science

Acceleration
Acid
Acoustics
Addition
Adhesive
Aerosol
Alchemy
Alcohol
Algebra
Alloy
Aluminium
Angle
Antibiotics
Archimedes
Atom
Bacon, Roger
Bacteria
Battery
Binary System
Biochemistry
Biology
Carbon
Cell
Colour
Compound
Copper
Cube

Current, Electric
Dam
Darwin, Charles
Detergent
Distillation
Drug
Dye
Echo
Edison, Thomas
Egg
Einstein, Albert
Elasticity
Electricity
Electronics
Element
Energy
Evolution
Explosive
Faraday, Michael
Fermentation
Fermi, Enrico
Fertilizer
Fibre Optics
Fire
Flame
Fleming, Alexander
Fraction
Freud, Sigmund
Friction
Fuel
Fuel Cell
Galileo
Gas
Geometry
Glass
Gold
Gravity
Heat
Holography
Humidity
Hydrogen
Infrared rays
Invention
Laser
Lead
Lens
Light
Liquid
Loudspeaker
Magnetism
Marconi, Guglielmo
Mathematics
Matter
Medicine
Mendel, Gregor
Mercury (Metal)
Metal
Metric System
Mirror
Newton, Isaac
Nobel Prize
Nuclear Energy
Number
Oil
Oxygen
Paint
Pasteur, Louis
Pendulum
Perfume
Photocopying
Photography
Physics
Plastic
Poison
Radioactivity
Radio Astronomy
Radium
Rainbow
Relativity
Rust
Science
Semiconductor
Silver
Soap
Solar Energy
Sound
Spectrum
Sulphur
Superconductivity
Surveying
Telecommunications
Temperature
Thermometer

Time
Tin
Ultraviolet Light
Uranium
Vacuum
Volume
Watt, James
Weightlessness
Weights and Measures
X-rays
Zinc

Astronomy and Space

Apollo Space
   Programme
Asteroid
Astronomy
Black Hole
Constellation
Eclipse
Gagarin, Yuri
Galaxy
Halley, Edmond
Jupiter
Mars (Planet)
Mercury (Planet)
Meteor
Milky Way
Moon
Neptune (Planet)
Orbit
Planet
Pluto
Pulsar
Quasar
Satellite
Saturn
Solar System
Spacecraft
Space Exploration
Star
Sun
Universe
Uranus
Venus (Planet)
Year

Sport and Pastimes

Archery
Athletics
Baseball
Basketball
Boomerang
Bowling
Boxing
Cricket
Doll
Fencing
Fireworks
Football
Golf
Gymnastics
Hobby
Hunting
Ice Hockey
Marathon Race
Martial Arts
Models
Olympic Games
Riding
Rowing
Rugby Football
Sailing
Scouting
Skating
Skiing
Skydiving
Snooker and Billiards
Swimming
Tennis
Weight-lifting

Language and Literature

Abbreviation
Adjective
Aesop
Alphabet
Andersen, Hans Christian
Book
Brontë Sisters
Carroll, Lewis
Chaucer, Geoffrey
Dickens, Charles
Dictionary
English Language
Fable
Grammar
Gutenberg, Johannes
Hieroglyphics
Johnson, Samuel
Kipling, Rudyard
Newspaper
Noun
Novel
Paper
Poetry
Printing
Proverb
Science Fiction
Scott, Walter
Shakespeare, William
Speech
Stevenson, Robert Louis
Swift, Jonathan
Tolstoy, Leo
Twain, Mark
University
Verb
Vowel
Wordsworth, William
Writing

Peoples and Government

Aborigine
Accounting
Advertising
Air Force
American Indians
Apartheid
Arabs
Army
Aztecs
Bank
Cave Dweller
Celts
Census
Civil Rights
Clans
Clothing
Coin
Commonwealth
Communication
Communism
Congress
Cowboy
Crown Jewels
Democracy
Dictator
Discrimination
Economics
Election
Eskimo
European Community
Famine Relief
Fascism
Flag
Gandhi, Indira
Government
Guerrilla Warfare
Gypsy
Hebrews
Inflation
Insurance
King, Martin Luther
Language
Law
Maoris
Mao Tse-tung
Marx, Karl
Maya

Money
Mongols
NATO (North Atlantic
   Treaty Organization)
Nomad
Opinion Poll
Parliament
People of the World
Police
Population
Prehistoric People
President of the United
   States
Prime Minister
Red Cross
Republic
School
Stamp
Stock Exchange
Tax
Terrorism
Thatcher, Margaret
Third World
Trade
Trade Union
United Nations
Women's Rights

The Arts

Art
Bach, Johann Sebastian
Ballet
Beethoven, Ludwig
   Van
Bernhardt, Sarah
Cartoon
Chaplin, Charles
Cinema
Circus
Commercial Art
Dance,
Disney, Walt
Drawing
Drum
Embroidery
Handel, George Frideric
Harp
Harpsichord
Haydn, Franz Joseph
Impressionism
Jazz
Jewellery
Leonardo da Vinci
Michelangelo
Mime
Moore, Henry
Mozart, Wolfgang
   Amadeus
Music
Musical Instrument
Opera
Orchestra
Organ
Painting
Pepys, Samuel
Pop Music
Pottery
Rembrandt
Rodeo
Sculpture
Tapestry
Tchaikovsky, Peter Ilyich
Theatre
Van Gogh, Vincent
Violin
Wagner, Richard
Wren, Christopher
Xylophone

Plants and Food

Bamboo
Bark
Bean
Botany
Bread
Bud
Bulb
Cactus
Cereal
Cheese
Chlorophyll

Chocolate
Coffee
Conifer
Cork
Cotton
Farming
Fat
Fern
Fishing
Flower
Food
Food Chain
Forest
Fruit
Fungus
Garden
Grass
Herb
Leaf
Lichen
Margarine
Milk
Moss
Mould
Mushroom and Toadstool
Nut
Nutrition
Oak
Oasis
Olive
Onion
Orchid
Palm Tree
Pineapple
Plankton
Plant
Potato
Protein
Pruning
Rice
Rubber
Seaweed
Seed
Soya Bean
Spice
Starch
Sugar
Tea
Tobacco
Tomato
Tree
Vegetable
Vitamins and Minerals
Weeds
Wheat
Wine
Wood
Yeast

Machines and Mechanisms

Abacus
Arkwright, Richard
Babbage, Charles
Barometer
Bell, Alexander Graham
Calculator
Camera
Clock
Compass
Computer
Crane
Diesel Engine
Engine
Engineering
Fuse
Gear
Generator
Guided Missile
Gun
Gyroscope
Hydroelectric Power
Internal Combustion
   Engine
Iron and Steel
Irrigation
Jet Engine
Knot
Lock and Key
Loudspeaker
Machine (Simple)
Microphone

Microscope
Morse Code
Motor, Electric
Motor Car
Motorcycle
Power Station
Pulley
Pump
Radar
Radio
Recording
Refrigerator
Robot
Rocket
Screw
Silicon Chip
Sonar
Steam Engine
Tape Recorder
Telephone
   Telescope
Television
Textile
Tunnel
Turbine
Typewriter
Video
Weaving
Welding
Wheel
Windmill
Wire
Word Processor

Buildings

Abbey
Architecture
Building
Castle
Cathedral
Church
Colosseum
Concrete
Dome
Furniture
House
Parthenon
Pyramid
Quarrying
Skyscraper
Stonehenge
Taj Mahal
Westminster Abbey

Human Body

Acupuncture
Adolescence
Ageing
Artery
Birth Control
Black Death
Blood
Bone
Brain
Breathing
Common Cold
Cosmetics
Deafness
Digestion
Disease
Dream
Exercise
Eye
Fingerprint
Genetics
Gland
Harvey, William
Health
Hearing
Heart
Hormone
Hospital
Human Body
Immunity
Inoculation
Insulin
Jenner, Edward
Kidney
Lister, Joseph
Liver
Lung

Malaria
Nerve
Nursing
Pain
Plague
Psychology
Pulse
Salt
Skeleton
Skin
Sleep and Dreams
Smell
Stomach
Surgery
Taste
Tongue
Tonsils
Touch
Vein
Virus

Travel and Transport

Aircraft
Airport
Balloons and Airships
Bicycle
Blériot, Louis
Boat
Bridge
Canal
Explorer
Ford, Henry
Gama, Vasco da
Gliding
Helicopter
Hotel
Hovercraft
Hydrofoil
Lindbergh, Charles
Livingstone, David
Magellan, Ferdinand
Map and Chart
Navigation
Railway
Road
Ship
Submarine
Supersonic Flight
Underground Railway

Special Features

Aircraft
Australia
Battles
China
Communication
Dance
Earth
Farming
Fish
Glass
House
Insects
Middle Ages
Moon
Plants
Prehistoric Animals
Railways
Roman Empire
Space Exploration
Tree
United States
Vikings
Weights and Measures
World War II